Neurobiology of Learning and Memory

Neurobiology of Learning and Memory

Edited by
Gary Lynch
James L. McGaugh
Norman M. Weinberger
University of California, Irvine

THE GUILFORD PRESS
New York • London

A Division of Guilford Publications, Inc.
200 Park Avenue South, New York, N.Y. 10003

Printed in the United States of America

LIBRARY OF CONGRESS CATALOGING IN PUBLICATION DATA

Main entry under title:

Neurobiology of learning and memory.

Includes indexes.

1. Learning—Physiological aspects. 2. Memory—Physiological aspects. 3. Neurobiology. I. Lynch, Gary. II. McGaugh, James L. III. Weinberger, Norman M.

QP408.N49 1984 153.1 84-19775

ISBN 0-89862-645-5

Contributors

W. C. Abraham, Department of Psychology, University of Otago, Dunedin, New Zealand

Bernard W. Agranoff, Neuroscience Laboratory, University of Michigan, Ann Arbor, Michigan

Jocelyne Bachevalier, Laboratory of Neuropsychology, National Institute of Mental Health, Bethesda, Maryland

Carol A. Barnes, Department of Psychology, University of Colorado, Boulder, Colorado

Michel Baudry, Center for the Neurobiology of Learning and Memory, University of California, Irvine, California

Cathy Bennett, Center for the Neurobiology of Learning and Memory and Department of Psychobiology, University of California, Irvine, California

Edward L. Bennett, Melvin Calvin Laboratory, Lawrence Berkeley Laboratory, Berkeley, California

T. V. P. Bliss, Division of Neurophysiology and Neuropharmacology, National Institute for Medical Research, London NW7, England

Vincent Bloch, Department of Psychophysiology, University of Paris XI and C.N.R.S., Gif-sur-Yvette, France

Gregory A. Clark, Center for Neurobiology and Behavior, College of Physicians and Surgeons, Columbia University, New York, New York

Neal J. Cohen, Department of Psychology, The Johns Hopkins University, Baltimore, Maryland

J. Anthony Deutsch, Department of Psychology, University of California, San Diego, La Jolla, California

David de Wied, Rudolph Magnus Institute for Pharmacology, Medical Faculty, University of Utrecht, Utrecht, The Netherlands

David M. Diamond, Center for the Neurobiology of Learning and Memory and Department of Psychobiology, University of California, Irvine, California

John F. Disterhoft, Department of Cell Biology and Anatomy, Northwestern University Medical School, Chicago, Illinois

A. C. Dolphin, Department of Pharmacology, St. George's Hospital Medical School, London SW17, England

Nelson H. Donegan, Department of Psychology, Stanford University, Stanford, California

Adrian J. Dunn, Department of Neuroscience, University of Florida, Gainesville, Florida

Walter J. Freeman, Department of Physiology–Anatomy, University of California, Berkeley, California

Michela Gallagher, Department of Psychology, University of North Carolina, Chapel Hill, North Carolina

Michael S. Gazzaniga, Division of Cognitive Neuroscience, Department of Neurology, Cornell University Medical College, New York, New York

G. V. Goddard, Department of Psychology, University of Otago, Dunedin, New Zealand

Paul E. Gold, Department of Psychology, University of Virginia, Charlottesville, Virginia

William T. Greenough, Departments of Psychology and Anatomical Sciences, and Neural and Behavioral Biology Program, University of Illinois, Urbana–Champaign, Champaign, Illinois

Robert D. Hawkins, Center for Neurobiology and Behavior, College of Physicians and Surgeons, Columbia University, and The New York State Psychiatric Institute, New York, New York

Leslie L. Iversen, Neuroscience Research Centre, Merck Sharp & Dohme Ltd., Herts, England

Ivan Izquierdo, Department of Biochemistry, Institute of Biosciences, UFRGS (Central), Pôrto Alegre, RS, Brazil

Eric R. Kandel, Center for Neurobiology and Behavior, College of Physicians and Surgeons, Columbia University, and The New York State Psychiatric Institute, New York, New York

Raymond P. Kesner, Department of Psychology, University of Utah, Salt Lake City, Utah

Franklin B. Krasne, Department of Psychology and Brain Research Institute, University of California, Los Angeles, California

Serge Laroche, Department of Psychophysiology, University of Paris XI and C.N.R.S., Gif-sur-Yvette, France

David G. Lavond, Department of Psychology, Stanford University, Stanford, California

K. C. Liang, Department of Psychology, National Taiwan University, Taipei, Taiwan, Republic of China

Benjamin Libet, Department of Physiology, School of Medicine, University of California, San Francisco, California

Jann S. Lincoln, Department of Psychology, Stanford University, Stanford, California

Gary Lynch, Center for the Neurobiology of Learning and Memory, University of California, Irvine, California

John Madden IV, Departments of Physiology and of Psychiatry and Behavioral Sciences, Stanford University Medical School, Stanford, California

Barbara Malamut, Laboratory of Neuropsychology, National Institute of Mental Health, Bethesda, Maryland; present address: Department of Psychology, City College, New York, New York

Laura A. Mamounas, Department of Psychology, Stanford University, Stanford, California

Michael D. Mauk, Department of Psychology, Stanford University, Stanford, California

David A. McCormick, Department of Neurology, Stanford University Medical School, Stanford, California

James L. McGaugh, Center for the Neurobiology of Learning and Memory and Department of Psychobiology, University of California, Irvine, California

Thomas M. McKenna, Center for the Neurobiology of Learning and Memory and Department of Psychobiology, University of California, Irvine, California

Bruce L. McNaughton, Department of Psychology, University of Colorado, Boulder, Colorado

Mortimer Mishkin, Laboratory of Neuropsychology, National Institute of Mental Health, Bethesda, Maryland

Richard G. M. Morris, Psychological Laboratory, University of St. Andrews, St. Andrews, Fife, Scotland

Lynn Nadel, Program in Cognitive Science, School of Social Science, University of California, Irvine, California

Michael I. Posner, Department of Psychology, University of Oregon, Eugene, Oregon; Cognitive Neuropsychology Laboratory, Department of Neurology, Good Samaritan Hospital and Medical Center, Portland, Oregon

G. Rao, Department of Psychology, University of Colorado, Boulder, Colorado

Mark R. Rosenzweig, Department of Psychology, University of California, Berkeley, California

Martin N. Rossor, MRC Neurochemical Pharmacology Unit, Medical Research Council Centre, Medical School, Cambridge, England; present address: Department of Neurology, Kings College Hospital, London SE5, England

Aryeh Routtenberg, Departments of Psychology and Neurobiology/Physiology, Northwestern University, Evanston, Illinois

Larry R. Squire, Department of Psychiatry, Veterans Administration Medical Center, San Diego, California; Department of Psychiatry, University of California, San Diego School of Medicine, La Jolla, California

Debra B. Sternberg, Center for the Neurobiology of Learning and Memory and Department of Psychobiology, University of California, Irvine, California

Judith K. Thompson, Department of Psychology, Stanford University, Stanford, California

Richard F. Thompson, Department of Psychology, Stanford University, Stanford, California

Nakaakira Tsukahara, Department of Biophysical Engineering, Faculty of Engineering Science, Osaka University, Toyonaka, Osaka, Japan; National Institute for Physiological Sciences, Okazaki, Japan

Forrest F. Weight, Laboratory of Preclinical Studies, National Institute on Alcohol Abuse and Alcoholism, Rockville, Maryland

Norman M. Weinberger, Center for the Neurobiology of Learning and Memory and Department of Psychobiology, University of California, Irvine, California

Kenneth Wexler, Program in Cognitive Science, School of Social Science, University of California, Irvine, California

Charles D. Woody, Brain Research Institute, Mental Retardation Research Center, Departments of Anatomy and Psychiatry, University of California, Los Angeles Medical Center, Los Angeles, California

Preface

Investigations into the biology of memory began with the first stirrings of what was to become behavioral neuroscience; the events that followed make for an exciting and complex history. Today, fueled by discoveries from both new approaches and determined work in older areas, the field is marked by enthusiasm and optimism. This book, which grew out of a conference held to inaugurate the Center for the Neurobiology of Learning and Memory at the University of California, Irvine, is intended to describe a number of these findings and to provide a sense of the excitement they have engendered. It is divided somewhat arbitrarily into four sections. The first is concerned with the nature of memory and contains much discussion of the hypothesis that different types of memory with distinct anatomical substrates are found in mammals. Here we find that the differences between the neurology of memory in humans and in animals have to some extent been resolved. This is followed by reviews of work attempting to locate the sites in brains at which the changes responsible for memory actually occur. We suspect that the reader will be surprised that so much progress has occurred in what once seemed an insurmountable problem. The third section of the book deals with the pharmacology and what might be called the endocrinology of memory. As will be seen, learning, like so many other brain functions, does not occur in isolation from actions of the pituitary–adrenal axis and the adrenal medulla. The volume closes with chapters on possible biochemical mechanisms responsible for memory storage. The diversity of approaches and postulated cellular processes being advanced as candidate substrates is well represented, as is the extent to which behavioral and physiological discoveries are now informing molecular investigations of memory.

Each of these sections is followed by a series of brief comments and critiques. We hope that these, and the reviews they are directed at, will allow the reader to appreciate one critical step in the evolution of contemporary memory research—namely, the degree to which ideas and, in some cases, hypotheses transcend the levels of analysis that produced them. The emergence of a common ground for interchange among a diversity of specialists is perhaps as much responsible for the excitement felt by those studying the biology of memory as are the recent discoveries that have occurred in the field. If a sense of this is conveyed to the reader, then we will consider this book to be as successful as the conference that produced it.

A number of people and organizations participated in the several stages involved in the preparation of this volume. The conference was generously funded by the University of California, Irvine, the Office of Naval Research, the Air Force Office of Scientific Research, Monsanto Company, and Beckman

Instruments. Special thanks are due to Lynn Brown and Nan Collett for coordinating all aspects of the conference and this book. We should also like to acknowledge the support and remarkable patience of Seymour Weingarten, who not only provided financial support to help in the preparation of the book but, as well, the persistent nudging needed to bring it into existence.

Gary Lynch
James L. McGaugh
Norman M. Weinberger

Contents

IV. MODELS AND CELLULAR MECHANISMS OF LEARNING AND MEMORY

SECTION ONE

Neurobiology of Human Learning and Memory

CHAPTER ONE

Human Memory and Amnesia

LARRY R. SQUIRE / NEAL J. COHEN

INTRODUCTION

Analysis of behavioral plasticity and the neurobiological principles that account for its expression has long been a major goal of research in neuroscience. The study of behavioral plasticity, that is, of learning and memory, introduces a field whose breadth and excitement can be glimpsed by noting the wide range of contributions to the present volume: from analysis of cellular events to analysis of neuropsychological disorders, from neurobiological models to psychological theories. This broad approach is based on the conviction that a complete account of learning and memory should include both (1) a description of the neural changes—neuroanatomical, neurophysiological, and neurochemical—that underlie learning and memory; and also (2) a description of the learning processes and memory systems whose neurobiological mechanisms we wish to understand, plus information about how they are organized and where they are localized in the brain.

This chapter is a review of the progress that has been made toward providing the second type of description. The focus of this review, accordingly, is on issues of acquisition of memory, recall of recent and remote events, and distinctions among various kinds of knowledge. Because these issues must be related ultimately to brain function, wherever possible our conclusions will be related to current thinking about the specific brain regions involved and the particular roles they play.

As in other investigations of brain and behavior where disordered function has been studied to illuminate principles of normal function, these issues are considered here through an analysis of memory pathology. In some cases of brain injury, memory impairment can occur as a relatively circumscribed disorder in the absence of other cognitive impairment—the amnesic syndrome. Analysis of this syndrome has guided our inquiries into the structure and organization of normal memory (for other recent reviews, see Stern, 1981; Hirst, 1982; Squire, 1982b; Baddeley, 1982b; Weiskrantz, 1982; Cermak, 1982).

Larry R. Squire. Department of Psychiatry, Veterans Administration Medical Center, San Diego, California; Department of Psychiatry, University of California, San Diego School of Medicine, La Jolla, California.

Neal J. Cohen. Department of Psychology, The Johns Hopkins University, Baltimore, Maryland.

In the present chapter we consider several major aspects of amnesia. The first section presents a description and detailed analysis of anterograde amnesia, that is, the deficit in learning and memory that is the hallmark of the amnesic syndrome. The second section identifies and characterizes a domain of preserved learning capacity in amnesia. The third section deals with issues of retrograde amnesia, that is, memory impairment for events that occurred prior to the onset of amnesia, and provides a framework for understanding this phenomenon. The final section summarizes the recent success in establishing animal models of human amnesia in the monkey. Because we believe that analysis of memory pathology holds considerable promise for understanding the structure of normal memory, for each of these topics we discuss the specific theoretical issues that have emerged from the experimental work. In this way we hope to arrive, in the end, at some understanding of the general principles governing the organization of memory and its neurological substrate.

ANTEROGRADE AMNESIA

Amnesia Is a Nonunitary Disorder

Amnesia has traditionally been considered to reflect a unitary disorder that occurs following trauma, vascular accident, tumor, or other injury to one or several of a group of critical brain structures. Thus, for example, amnesia is reported to occur after damage to the medial temporal lobe region following surgical resection, as in the noted case H. M. (Scoville & Milner, 1957); following encephalitis (e.g., Rose & Symonds, 1960; Drachman & Adams, 1962); following a vascular accident, as in patients with posterior cerebral artery occlusion (Benson, Marsden, & Meadows, 1974); and after hypoxic ischemia (Volpe & Hirst, 1983). Amnesia also can result from damage to the region surrounding the third ventricle, which includes the dorsomedial nucleus of the thalamus and the mammillary bodies, in patients with Korsakoff syndrome (e.g., Talland, 1965; Victor, Adams, & Collins, 1971; Butters & Cermak, 1980), and in some patients with third ventricle tumors (e.g., Williams & Pennybacker, 1954). What seems to tie these amnesias together is that they all reflect damage to limbic system structures (Papez, 1937). However, the anatomical relatedness of these two types of amnesia (medial temporal and diencephalic) has recently been questioned on a number of grounds (e.g., Squire, 1980a, 1982b). This issue is of much interest because, to the extent that amnesia can result from damage to distinct anatomical systems, the different etiologies of amnesia might be expected to produce different amnesic syndromes.

Because the study of amnesia in any one laboratory has usually been limited to one patient type (i.e., to a single etiology), the possibility of distinct amnesic syndromes is only now beginning to be addressed in a comprehensive way. Nevertheless, available comparisons of etiologically distinct amnesias suggest that the amnesic syndrome is a nonunitary disorder. There are two different senses in which this is true: (1) Some etiologies of amnesia, but not others, occur together with cognitive deficits that have no obligatory relationship to the memory disorder; yet these deficits can profoundly influence how the disorder is expressed; and (2) the fundamental disorder in amnesia can itself take different forms, depending on the etiology.

Before considering the evidence on these two points, it is worth noting that much of what we know about the amnesic syndrome, and about similarities and differences among examples of the syndrome, derives from the study of three particular kinds of patients. By far the most frequently studied example has been Korsakoff syndrome (Korsakoff, 1887). This syndrome has been the subject of intensive investigation during the past one hundred years (e.g., Talland, 1965; Victor *et al.*, 1971; Butters & Cermak, 1980). The syndrome typically develops after many years of alcohol abuse, and it is characterized by symmetrical lesions along the walls of the third and fourth ventricles, as well as in cerebellum and cerebral cortex (Figure 1-1A). Although the critical brain lesions responsible for the amnesia have not yet been conclusively identified, lesions of the mammillary bodies and the dorsomedial thalamic nucleus are best correlated with the memory disorder (Brierley, 1977; Victor *et al.*, 1971; but see Mair, Warrington, & Weiskrantz, 1979; Brion & Mikol, 1978).

A second example has been the rare individual case where amnesia occurs as a strikingly circumscribed entity. In a few of these cases, circumstances have permitted careful, repeated assessments over a period of many years. The best-known and most thoroughly studied of these is case H. M. (Scoville & Milner, 1957) who in 1953 sustained bilateral resection of the medial temporal lobe region in an attempt to relieve severe and otherwise intractable epilepsy. The resection included the anterior two-thirds of the hippocampal formation, hippocampal gyrus, amygdala, and uncus (Figure 1-1B). As a result of the surgery, H. M. exhibited a severe, chronic amnesia that has persisted to the present day. A second, well-studied patient is case N. A. (Teuber, Milner, & Vaughan, 1968; Kaushall, Zetin, & Squire, 1981), who became amnesic in 1960 as a result of a penetrating brain injury with a miniature fencing foil. Recent CT scans have identified a lesion in the region of the left dorsomedial thalamic nucleus (Squire & Moore, 1979; Figure 1-1C). N. A.'s amnesia is primarily for verbal material (Teuber *et al.*, 1968; Squire & Slater, 1978), consistent with the left-hemisphere localization of his lesion. In both of these patients, amnesia occurs against a background of above-average intelligence and without other demonstrable neuropsychological deficits.

The third major example is the amnesia associated with bilateral electroconvulsive therapy (ECT) (e.g., Squire, 1982a), sometimes prescribed for the treatment of depressive illness. Because ECT is a scheduled event, it permits before-and-after studies, whereby each patient can be used as his own control. Treatments are typically scheduled every other day, three times per week, for a series of 6 to 12 treatments. The amnesia associated with ECT recovers to some extent after each treatment in a series and cumulates across treatments. Following a postictal confusional period of some 30–45 minutes, amnesia appears after treatment as a relatively circumscribed deficit in the absence of disorientation or changes in intellectual status.

The amnesic patient, as reflected by the three kinds of patient just described, is characterized by a profound deficit in the ability to acquire most new information or to remember day-to-day events, despite an intact immediate memory (e.g., digit span) and normal intellectual capacity. In addition, patients can have, to varying extents, difficulty in remembering information acquired prior to the onset of amnesia. Memory for overlearned information acquired early in life, such as general world knowledge and social and language skills, seems to be normal.

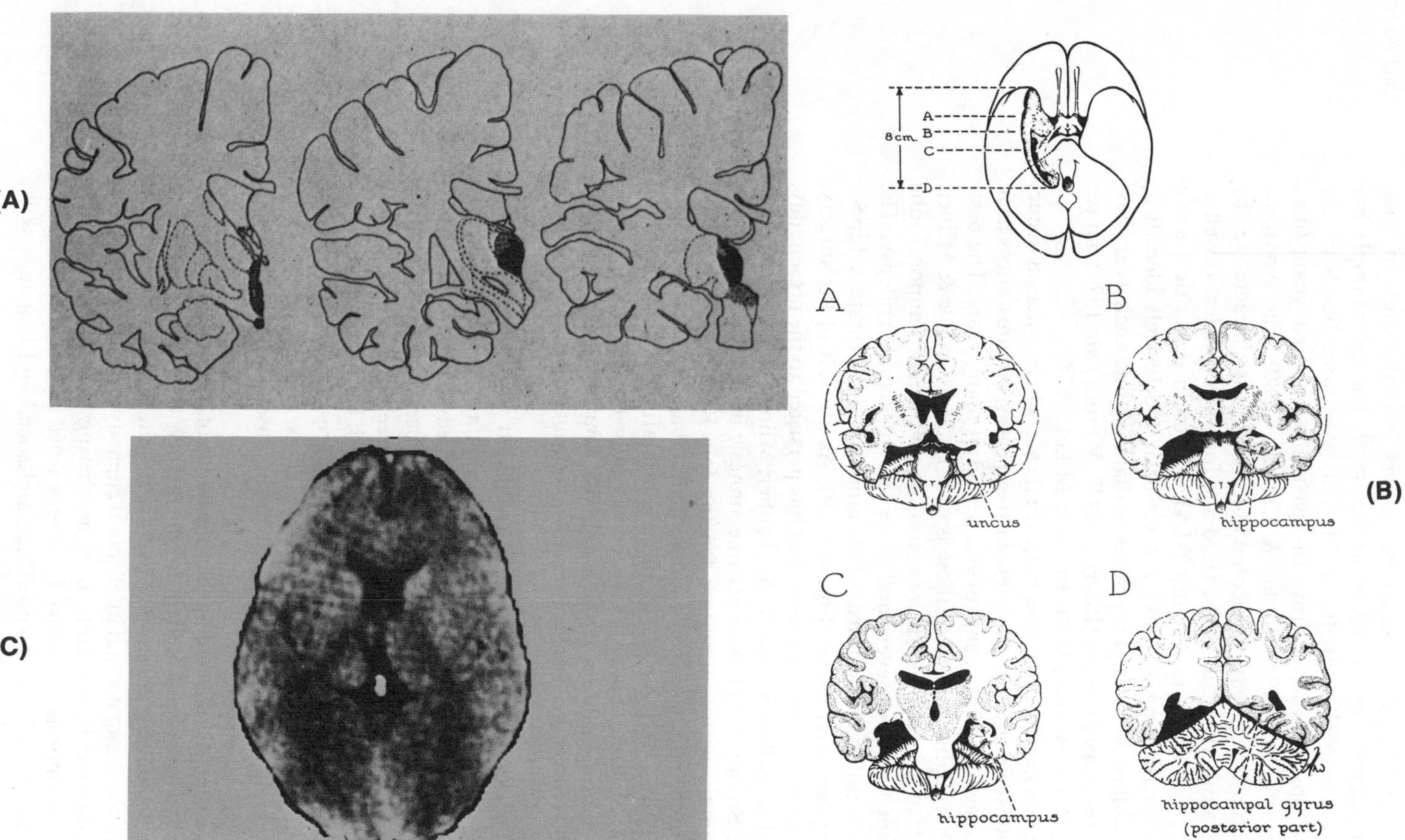

Figure 1-1. Anatomical information about three instances of amnesia. (A) Pathological findings in a representative case of Korsakoff syndrome. The diencephalic localization of the lesions is shown in diagrams of three coronal sections: from left to right, at the level of the mammillary bodies, midthalamus, and pulvinar. (From Victor, Adams, & Collins, 1971.) (B) Drawings in cross-section showing the estimated extent of removal in case H. M. Surgery was a bilateral, single-stage procedure, but one side is shown intact here for illustrative purposes. (From Milner, 1959.) (C) Computerized tomography (CT) scan of case N. A., who sustained a stab wound to the brain with a miniature fencing foil. The only positive finding in three separate scans was a lucency in the left dorsal thalamus, corresponding to the position of the dorsomedial thalamic nucleus. The CT scan, of course, can identify only the minimal extent of the lesion. (From Squire & Moore, 1979.)

The first experimental demonstration of a behavioral distinction between different amnesic etiologies seems to have come from a direct comparison between patients with Korsakoff syndrome and postencephalitic patients (Lhermitte & Signoret, 1972, 1976). It was found that although both groups fared poorly in learning a set of nine unrelated items, the patients with Korsakoff syndrome were impaired with respect to the postencephalitic patients when the same number of items were related by a simple rule; that is, unlike the postencephalitic patients, the patients with Korsakoff syndrome were unable to derive benefit from the organized structure of the stimulus material. Other work (Talland, 1965; Oscar-Berman, 1973) has confirmed that patients with Korsakoff syndrome have a diminished capacity in tests of problem solving and concept formation. These findings are consistent with Talland's (1965) conclusion that the memory disorder in patients with Korsakoff syndrome "does not present simply a derangement in memory" (p. 108), and Zangwill's (1966) contention that "other and more extensive psychological dysfunction must co-exist with amnesia for the classic picture of Korsakoff's syndrome to emerge" (p. 113).

More recently, the analysis of certain features of memory impairment in Korsakoff syndrome has suggested the presence of frontal lobe dysfunction. This point is well illustrated by studies of release from proactive interference (PI). Based on the paradigm used by Wickens (1970), these studies asked subjects to learn successive groups of words, all belonging to the same category (e.g., animal names). Recall was tested shortly after presentation of each word group. Performance of normal subjects and Korsakoff patients declined with each new group of words, because of buildup of PI. Normal subjects, but not patients with Korsakoff syndrome, exhibited an improvement in recall due to release from PI after shifting to words that belonged to a new category (e.g., vegetable names) (Cermak, Butters, & Moreines, 1974).

The failure to release from PI when a new category of words is introduced turns out not to be linked to amnesia in any obligatory way. First, a severely amnesic postencephalitic patient, who performed even more poorly on standard verbal memory tasks (e.g., paired-associate learning and word-list recall) than did patients with Korsakoff syndrome, exhibited normal release from PI (Cermak, 1976). Second, case N. A. and patients receiving ECT also exhibited normal release from PI (Squire, 1982c). Failure to release from PI appears to be related to frontal lobe pathology and not to memory dysfunction (Moscovitch, 1982). In contrast to the results reported for Korsakoff syndrome, patients who had sustained left or right temporal lobectomy, and who had material-specific memory disorders (see Milner, 1968) exhibited normal release from PI. But patients who had sustained surgical removals of portions of the frontal lobe, and who were not amnesic, resembled patients with Korsakoff syndrome in that they failed to release from PI.

The conclusion that patients with Korsakoff syndrome exhibit deficits indicative of frontal lobe dysfunction, which are not found in other examples of amnesia, also rests on a study of memory for temporal order (Squire, Nadel, & Slater, 1981; Squire, 1982c). Subjects read 12 unrelated sentences, waited 3 minutes, and then read another 12 sentences. Later, they were tested both for their ability to recognize the sentences they had read and for their ability to remember on which of the two lists each sentence had appeared. Case N. A. and patients receiving ECT exhibited impaired recognition memory as well as a deficit in temporal order information. Control subjects, who were tested at a retention interval sufficiently long to match their recognition performance to that of the amnesics were found to score the same as amnesic patients on the temporal order test. In contrast to case N. A. and patients receiving ECT, patients with Korsakoff syndrome exhibited a disproportionately large deficit in temporal order information, which could not be explained by their level of recognition performance: The Korsakoff patients performed the same as case N. A. and patients receiving ECT on the recognition test, but performed significantly worse on the temporal order test (Figure 1-2).

There are two reasons for linking this finding to frontal lobe dysfunction. First, Milner (1974) showed that patients with surgical removals of left or right frontal lobes were impaired on a similar task. Second, for Korsakoff patients, the severity of the deficit in temporal order information as well as the failure to release from PI correlated significantly with performance on cognitive tests sensitive to frontal lobe dysfunction (Squire, 1982c). Although the pathology in patients with Korsakoff syndrome has been reported in two cases to be restricted to two subcortical regions (Mair *et al.*, 1979), it seems clear that these patients usually have more widespread damage (Victor *et al.*, 1971) including involvement of the frontal lobe. There is also considerable evidence for cortical

Figure 1-2. Recognition memory and judgments of temporal order in amnesic patients. Top: Recognition memory (d') for two lists of 12 sentences presented 3 minutes apart. Bottom: Temporal-order judgments as to which of the two lists each sentence belonged. N.A. = case N.A.; ECT = patients receiving bilateral electroconvulsive therapy. (From Squire, 1982c.)

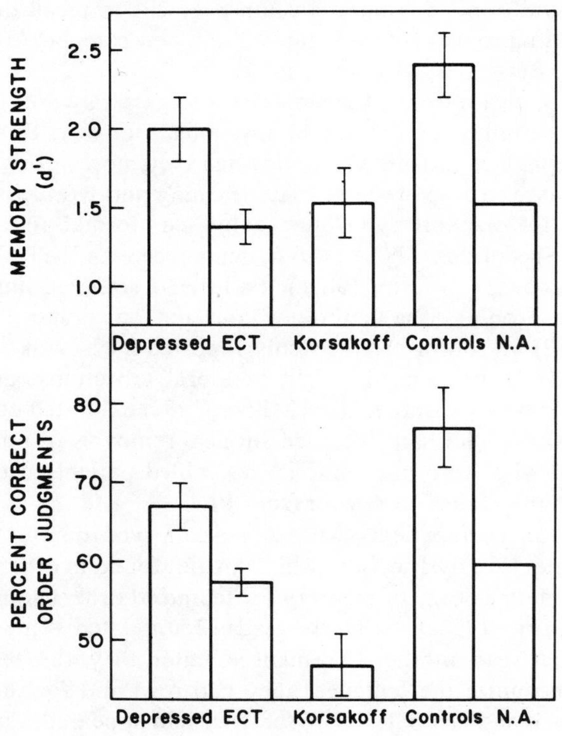

atrophy and frontal lobe pathology in chronic alcoholics (see review by Wilkinson & Carlin, 1981). This widespread damage and, in particular, the specific involvement of the frontal lobe may be responsible for superimposing on the memory disorder of Korsakoff syndrome certain cognitive deficits that are not found in other examples of amnesia.

A similar example of how certain features of amnesia can be determined by frontal lobe dysfunction comes from a study of patients who became amnesic following a ruptured aneurysm of the anterior communicating artery (Cohen & Corkin, 1982). A subset of these patients exhibited deficits in recency judgments and failed to release from PI. This subset of patients also differed from the rest of the group by exhibiting an impairment on tests of verbal fluency and on the Wisconsin card-sorting test, sensitive indicators of frontal lobe dysfunction (Milner, 1963), and by showing evidence on CT scan of frontal lobe atrophy and enlarged anterior horns of the lateral ventricles.

It might be supposed that frontal lobe damage, in addition to determining some features of the memory disorder, might also be essential for the full expression of the memory disorder itself. By this view, the deficit in learning and memory exhibited by patients with Korsakoff syndrome or by patients with anterior communicating artery aneurysm requires damage to the frontal lobes. However, this idea is discounted by the evidence. First, case N. A.'s lesion is diencephalic, and his amnesia occurs in the absence of frontal lobe signs. Yet his anterograde amnesia for verbal material is as severe as that of Korsakoff patients (Cohen & Squire, 1981). Second, patients with anterior communicating artery aneurysm, who have many of the same frontal lobe signs exhibited by Korsakoff patients, have a memory impairment for verbal material less severe than that of N. A. (Cohen & Corkin, 1982). Third, patients with frontal lobe lesions are not amnesic (Milner, 1974). Thus, some of the unique features of Korsakoff syndrome and other kinds of amnesia may be determined by damage to regions of the brain that are not ordinarily damaged in amnesia.

Amnesia Takes Fundamentally Different Forms

When some new material is presented to an amnesic patient and retention of that material is tested after a short delay, a marked impairment is commonly observed. This tendency to forget what has been previously encountered (whether due to actual loss of stored information or to its inaccessibility) is one of the constant features of amnesia, even a defining feature. In the casual bedside examination, abnormal forgetting appears to be the cardinal disorder, common to all etiologies of amnesia. According to studies of normal subjects (Slamecka & McElree, 1983), the rate of forgetting following presentation of to-be-remembered material is an unchanging property of the memory system, not affected by wide variation in experimental conditions. Thus, in normal subjects the rate of forgetting might be viewed as a fundamental property of how memory operates.

These considerations for normal subjects raise an interesting question about the deficit in amnesia. Do amnesic patients have a deficit that increases the rate of forgetting, as casual examination might suggest? Or do amnesic patients have a normal rate of forgetting, in which case their amnesia must be explained by other deficits in information processing? For example, they might have difficulty in acquiring information initially, and then forget this information at a normal rate.

The evidence now suggests that both normal and abnormally rapid rates of forgetting can be observed in amnesia, and that different etiologies of amnesia can be systematically characterized according to whether their forgetting rates are normal or abnormal. This evidence distinguishes between diencephalic and medial temporal amnesia (Huppert & Piercy, 1978, 1979; Squire, 1981), confirming the original suggestion by Lhermitte and Signoret (1972, 1976) that these two kinds of amnesia are distinct entities.

This work employed a procedure designed to minimize the problem of comparing forgetting rates in groups who already differ in the levels of initial learning (Huppert & Piercy, 1978). By allowing amnesic patients more time than control subjects to view the to-be-learned material, performance of the two groups could be equated at a short learning-retention interval, and forgetting rates could then be compared over longer retention intervals. During the learning phase, subjects saw 120 colored slides and were then tested for retention by a yes–no recognition procedure at various times after learning. While control subjects viewed the slides for 1 second each, patients with Korsakoff syndrome viewed them for either 4 or 8 seconds, and case H. M. for 15 seconds, in order to equate performance at the 10-minute retention interval. The results were that patients with Korsakoff syndrome exhibited a normal rate of forgetting for this material over the retention interval studied (Huppert & Piercy, 1978), whereas H. M.'s forgetting rate was reported to be abnormally rapid (Huppert & Piercy, 1979; Figure 1-3).

Unfortunately, H. M.'s data were ambiguous. First, H. M.'s performance reached chance at the longest retention interval (see Figure 1-3), so that a convincing difference between his performance and the performance of control subjects, if present, could not have been expressed. Second, H. M., required a longer exposure time to learn the material during the learning phase than did patients with Korsakoff syndrome. The fact that he then apparently forgot the material more rapidly might cause one to worry that the severity of the amnesic deficit, rather than its etiology, was the major determinant of forgetting rates.

More convincing evidence that amnesic groups can differ in their forgetting rates is now available (Squire, 1981, in press). Patients receiving bilateral ECT and patients with Korsakoff syndrome viewed stimulus materials for 8 seconds (vs. 1 second for the control subjects) and achieved comparable retention scores at 10 minutes after learning. Over the next 32 hours, patients with Korsakoff syndrome exhibited a normal rate of forgetting, but patients receiving bilateral ECT exhibited an abnormally rapid rate of forgetting (Figure 1-4). Case N. A. also exhibited a normal rate of forgetting when tested with verbal material (Figure 1-4). Thus, patients with Korsakoff syndrome and case N. A., both with diencephalic amnesia, have normal forgetting rates. Conversely, patients receiving bilateral ECT have an abnormally rapid forgetting rate. Although little is known about the anatomy of amnesia in the case of bilateral ECT, indirect evidence (e.g., the special seizure sensitivity of the hippocampal region) tentatively links ECT amnesia to temporal lobe dysfunction (Inglis, 1970). These data, taken together, show conclusively that some forms of amnesia are characterized by normal forgetting and some by abnormal forgetting, even when the severity of the amnesias are similar. However, these data do not permit strong conclusions about the anatomical basis of the differences between amnesias.

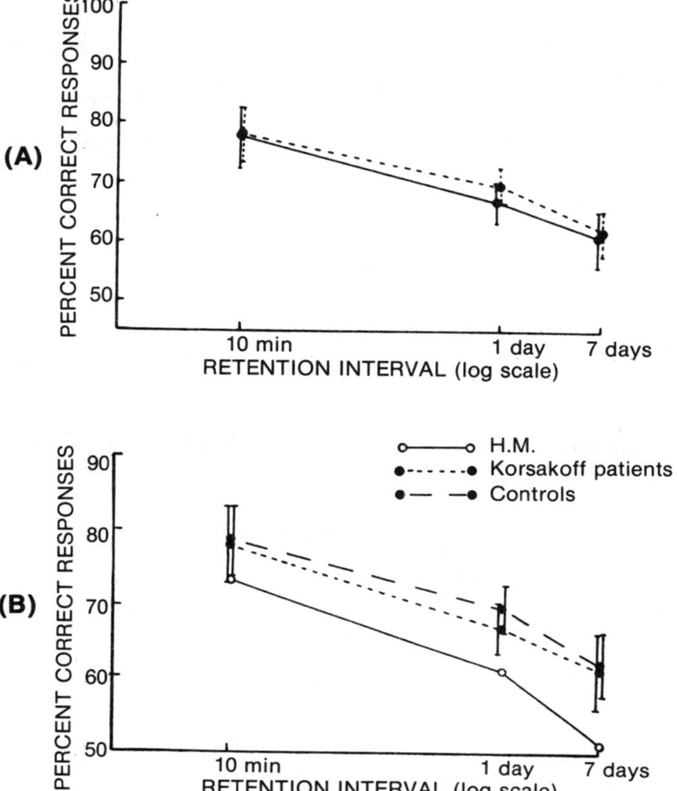

Figure 1-3. Patients with Korsakoff syndrome (A) and case H. M. (B) were given extra exposure to pictorial material in order to equate their recognition memory to that of control subjects at 10 minutes after learning. Forgetting was then assessed across an interval of 7 days. (From Huppert & Piercy, 1978, 1979.)

More direct evidence for the view that amnesia can be usefully classified according to the locus of the underlying neuropathology comes from a study of forgetting rates in operated monkeys (Zola-Morgan & Squire, 1982). Monkeys with conjoint hippocampus–amygdala (H-A) lesions and monkeys with lesions of the dorsomedial thalamic nucleus (DM) were given a test of delayed retention (delayed non-matching-to-sample using junk objects as test stimuli) that tests memory in monkeys in much the same way that it can be tested in human amnesic patients. Normal monkeys saw the sample stimulus once; the operated monkeys were given repeated exposures to the sample stimulus (H-A = 12 exposures, DM = 10 exposures). Ten minutes, 2 hours, or 24 hours later, all monkeys were given a choice between the sample stimulus and a novel stimulus. The monkeys were always rewarded for choosing the novel stimulus. For the 10-minute test, repetition of the sample stimulus was sufficient to elevate the choice performance of operated monkeys to the same level as that of normal monkeys, who had seen the sample only once. On choice tests scheduled 2 hours or 24 hours after the sample presentation, the monkeys with diencephalic DM lesions performed normally; that is, they forgot at a normal rate. Monkeys with

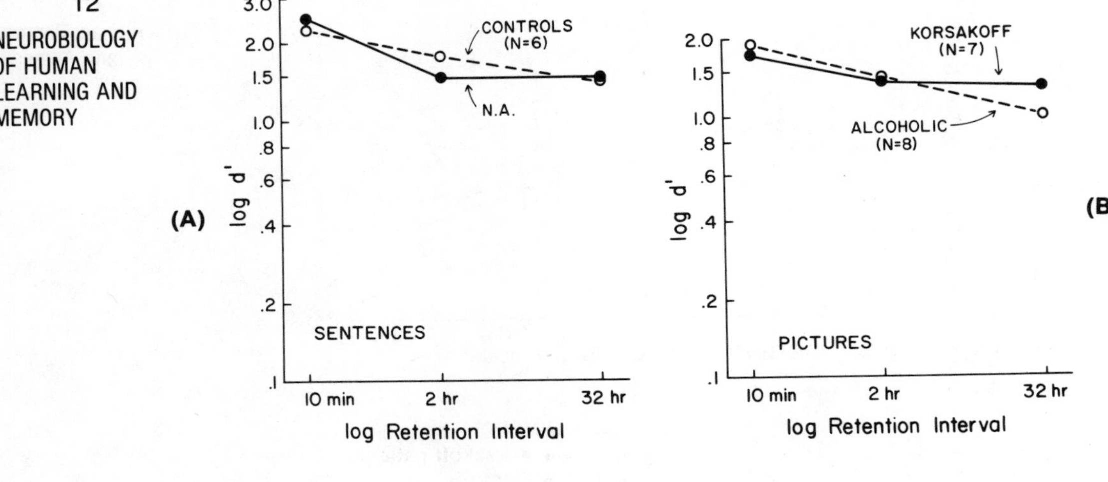

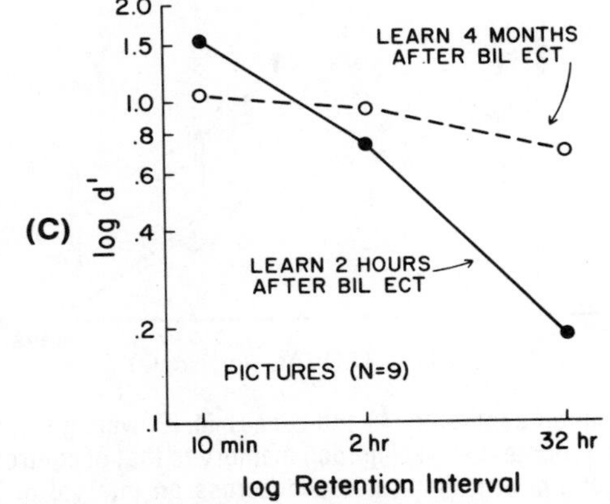

Figure 1-4. Forgetting across an interval of 32 hours by case N. A. (A), patients with Korsakoff syndrome (B), and patients receiving bilateral ECT (C). Case N. A. was tested with verbal material, and the other patients were tested with pictorial material. All patients viewed the material for 8 seconds. Control subjects viewed the material for 1 second in the case of pictures, and 2½ seconds in the case of sentences. (From Squire, 1981.)

medial temporal H-A lesions performed poorly; that is, they forgot abnormally quickly. It will be important to repeat these studies with operated groups that are equivalently amnesic and whose performance can therefore be matched at the 10-minute retention interval following equal numbers of exposures to the sample stimulus. It would also be useful to show that, under some conditions, monkeys with medial temporal lesions exhibit more rapid forgetting than monkeys with diencephalic lesions, even when the diencephalic lesions produce more severe amnesia.

Taken together, these findings provide evidence that diencephalic and medial temporal amnesia are distinct entities. They therefore provide support for a nonunitary view of the amnesic syndrome, a view reflected in Piercy's (1977) claim, which preceded these demonstrations, that "the unitary character of the organic amnesic syndrome was always a rather dubious assumption and it is now seriously in question" (p. 45).

The implications of these recent findings is that it is no longer possible to speak about amnesia in a general way when one's data base is limited to just one kind of patient. The superimposition of cognitive deficits on certain forms of amnesia reminds us that the observation of any particular deficit in a given amnesic patient (or group of patients) does not guarantee that the deficit always reflects the memory disorder itself, nor can it imply that the same deficit will be present in other examples of amnesia. Moreover, the fact that the memory disorder itself can be fundamentally different complicates attempts to specify the nature of the amnesic disorder, since different explanatory concepts may need to be formulated to account for different amnesic syndromes. This is the subject to which we now turn our attention.

Analysis of the Nature of the Disorder

Dating back to the very earliest reports of the amnesic syndrome, a major focus of interest has concerned which processes of memory or aspects of information processing are impaired. For example, the fact that amnesic patients exhibit relatively preserved intellectual functions, language and social skills, and very remote memories (e.g., memories of childhood; see section on Retrograde Amnesia and Remote Memory Impairment) has always been taken to mean that amnesia does not simply reflect the destruction of brain areas storing the records (or traces) of all past experience. Accordingly, the disorder in amnesia has seemed to lie in mechanisms that ordinarily influence the way in which memory traces are formed, maintained, or retrieved, and analytic approaches to the disorder have focused on the following possible loci for the impairment: (1) the analysis or encoding of information, or the ability to attend to information delivery—that is, processes that operate at the time of training; (2) the maintenance or elaboration of stored information—that is, processes that operate during the retention interval; (3) the retrieval of stored information—that is, processes that operate at the time of testing.

Encouraged by the analytic power of the information-processing metaphor in experimental psychology, most contemporary researchers have attempted to localize the fundamental disorder in one of these particular stages of information processing. It should be kept in mind that these attempts to account for amnesia as a deficit in a particular processing stage or a particular mechanism has often led to emphasis on certain "critical" features of the disorder (cf. Rozin, 1976). Thus, theories that view amnesia as an encoding disorder have stressed effects on memory of changes in stimulus exposure duration or type of encoding strategy employed. Theories that view amnesia as a storage disorder have stressed the effects on memory of changes in the retention interval between training and testing. Theories that view amnesia as a retrieval disorder have stressed the effects on memory of changes in type of retention test administered. Due in part to this tendency to focus on particular features of amnesia in attempting to characterize the amnesic disorder, many disagreements still exist among the proponents of different theories. Disagreement can also be attributed to certain theoretical and methodological issues that will be considered prior to examining the experimental work.

1. First, the nonunitary nature of amnesia has considerable bearing on efforts to describe the underlying impairment. The evidence for distinct amnesic syndromes suggests that more than one kind of deficit can occur; that is, there is more than one critical locus (neuroanatomical and psychological) whose disruption can cause memory dysfunction.

2. Second, the fact that deficits found in certain etiologies of amnesia are not inextricably tied to the basic memory disorder in amnesia complicates the analysis of the amnesic syndrome, as indicated earlier; yet it helps to clarify the task—that is, those deficits observed in amnesic patients that turn out to be unrelated to the memory disorder do not need to be accounted for by a theory of amnesia. Attributing a critical role to such deficits would be profoundly misguided.

3. A third issue is the tendency of theories to treat amnesia in absolute terms. For example, consider a verbal learning task in which retention is tested first by free (unaided) recall and then by a cueing procedure (e.g., two-choice recognition). It has sometimes been supposed that theories taking amnesia as a storage deficit should predict that amnesic patients would not benefit at all from the cueing procedure, whereas theories taking amnesia as a retrieval deficit should predict that in the presence of retrieval cues amnesic patients would equal the performance of control subjects. Not surprisingly perhaps, the results for amnesic patients in such paradigms almost always favor an intermediate position. Amnesic patients do indeed benefit from cueing procedures, but so too do control subjects, who continue to maintain an advantage in performance over that of the amnesic patients (see Figure 1-5, section on Amnesia as a Retrieval Deficit). This altogether typical result is not decisive for either a storage or a retrieval view of amnesia. The partial improvement exhibited in the presence of cues could be interpreted either as evidence for a reduction of a problem in information retrieval or as evidence for a problem in the storage of information whose "strength" provides an insufficient basis for unaided recall but a sufficient basis to be expressed by recognition. All we can conclude from such a finding, then, is that experiments that would clearly distinguish between these views of amnesia are not easily formulated. This issue will reappear in various guises in the present review.

4. A fourth issue, related closely to the one just discussed, is that terms like storage and retrieval are prone to a certain degree of semantic confusion (e.g., Squire, 1980b). For example, it should be clear that any deficit in the initial encoding or storage of information will necessarily result in a deficit in its retrievability. Moreover, any retrieval explanation of amnesia that "localizes" the disorder to the time of training—that is, one that hypothesizes a failure to establish effective retrieval cues at the time of information input—would be particularly difficult to distinguish from explanations based on deficient encoding processes that operate at that time. It is known that the nature of the encoding operations employed at the time of training determines in large measure the efficacy of subsequent retrieval; indeed, encoding operations help to specify the kind of retrieval cues that will be effective (e.g., Tulving & Thomson, 1973; Jacoby & Craik, 1979). Tulving and Thomson (1973) argued that "specific encoding operations performed on what is perceived determine what is stored, and what is stored determines what retrieval cues are effective in providing access to what is stored" (p. 369), a view that has come to be known as the encoding specificity principle. In short, these two possibilities about amnesia cannot be distinguished behaviorally; any evidence for a deficit in processes that operate at the time of training would favor either view. Consequently, in the sections that follow, our discussion of retrieval theories of amnesia will consider only disorders hypothesized to occur at the time of retention testing.

5. A fifth issue is that when a deficit is demonstrated in some particular area of memory function, the deficit has sometimes been taken as evidence that amnesia reflects a selective or qualitatively specific disorder. However, such an observation can always be interpreted two different ways. One possibility is that the deficit indeed reflects a selective disorder and thereby identifies a specific process that is affected in amnesia. The other possibility is that the deficit occurs for an aspect of memory that is weak or fragile in all subjects, normal controls and amnesic patients alike. This issue has been stated clearly by Mayes, Meudell, and Som (1981):

> [One must consider] the possibility that differences [between amnesic and control subjects] reflect consequences and not causes of amnesia. If a difference reflects a consequence then it should also be found when the memories of normal subjects tested at long retention intervals are compared with those of controls tested immediately. Failure to find such a difference strengthens the case that the amnesic pattern of memory performance reveals a specific cause of memory problems. When normal subjects with attenuated memory show the amnesic pattern of performance, the case is weakened. (p. 655)

The point is that a discriminating method is available for evaluating the pattern of memory deficits in amnesia. One can therefore test for the possibility that some aspects of memory seem more impaired than others simply because this is the natural pattern of dysfunction that occurs whenever memory fails. According to this method, normal subjects are tested at a long retention interval in order to match their performance to some measure of amnesic performance (e.g., recognition memory). Then at the same retention interval, it can be determined whether another measure of interest reveals a disproportionate impairment. This logic has been employed successfully by a number of investigators in testing cued recall (Squire, Wetzel, & Slater, 1978; Woods & Piercy, 1974; Mayes & Meudell, 1981; Wetzel & Squire, 1982), and recognition of faces and shapes (Mayes, Meudell, & Neary, 1980). In all cases, the pattern of performance exhibited by amnesic patients was recapitulated by control subjects during the course of natural forgetting. For these amnesic patients, no support was obtained for the existence of selective deficits in these areas of memory; hence, the results suggest nothing more than the idea that certain forms of amnesia can result in a representation in memory that is qualitatively similar to that seen in normal control subjects tested long after learning.

There are two instances, however, where apparently qualitative deficits have been demonstrated (Squire, 1982c; Hirst & Volpe, 1982). In one case (Squire, 1982c); patients with Korsakoff syndrome exhibited a disproportionate deficit in temporal order memory. Because this deficit was correlated with frontal lobe signs, it was taken to reflect a superimposed cognitive deficit unrelated to amnesia (see section on Superimposition of Cognitive Deficits on

Amnesia). In the other case (Hirst & Volpe, 1982), a mixed group of six patients exhibited a disproportionate deficit in placing remote events in correct temporal order. A better understanding of the underlying neuropathology in these cases is needed, together with information about the possible involvement of brain systems that could contribute deficits other than memory problems. In particular, it would be important to test for the presence of frontal lobe signs.

6. A final issue is the relation of these questions about the nature of amnesia to a more fundamental neurobiological question. Is material permanently stored in memory so that normal forgetting reflects only a failure in its retrievability, or is forgetting accompanied by an actual loss of information from the brain? Impressed with (1) the ability of all people to retrieve spontaneously details about events that seemed to have been already forgotten (consider what happens when you hear a song that was a favorite many years ago—for many people, the song can evoke vivid memories from that period of their lives), and (2) popular ideas about the ability of hypnosis and psychoanalysis to provide access to forgotten or repressed memories, most people seem to believe that most or all memories are stored permanently in the brain (Loftus & Loftus, 1980). This popular view seems to agree with Freud's contention that "in mental life nothing which has once been formed can perish" (Freud, 1930, p. 69) and that forgetting is motivated in part by repression. What view one takes of this historic question seems likely to color one's view of amnesia. For example, the idea that the brain stores memory permanently and that normal forgetting is simply a temporary inaccessibility of memory—that is, a retrieval failure—suggests that the abnormal forgetting seen in amnesia might also reflect retrieval failure.

However, Loftus and Loftus (1980) have argued convincingly against this popular view of normal forgetting, claiming that none of the behavioral data require us to postulate a permanent memory store. Thus, the fact that certain circumstances (e.g., the presence of contextual cues or other retrieval aids) promote the expression of memories that could not otherwise be recalled proves only that there are memories represented in the brain that are not always readily accessible; it does not indicate that all past experiences are permanently represented. Freud, too, recognized this point of view:

> Perhaps we have gone too far in this. Perhaps we ought to content ourselves with asserting that what is past in mental life *may* be preserved and is not *necessarily* destroyed. It is always possible that even in the mind some of what is old is effaced or absorbed—whether in the normal course of things or as an exception—to such an extent that it cannot be restored or revivified by any means or that preservation in general is dependent on ceratin favorable conditions. It is possible, but we know nothing about it. We can only hold fast to the fact that it is rather the rule than the exception for the past to be preserved in mental life. (1930, p. 73)

It seems unlikely that behavioral data alone can further resolve this issue. Disagreement about whether the representation of memory is maintained permanently in the brain or whether it dissipates with time is likely to persist until some direct neurobiological evidence about the neural substrate of memory can be obtained. For example, in favorable invertebrate preparations like *Aplysia* it is now possible to study simple forms of behavioral memory at the cellular and synaptic level. The available evidence is that behavioral forgetting is accompanied by a gradual disappearance of the relevant neural changes over a period of days and weeks (Kandel, 1976). The neural basis for more long-lasting forms of memory, that is, of the kind that could endure for months or years, cannot yet be studied at this level. These comments notwithstanding, the popular bias toward conceiving of forgetting as a retrieval problem seems to have led quite naturally to viewing amnesia also as a retrieval deficit. Accordingly, retrieval theories of amnesia will be considered first.

Amnesia as a Retrieval Deficit (Disorder of Processes Operating at the Time of Retention Testing)

The view that amnesia might reflect a deficit in retrieval of information that had been adequately stored is based primarily on two important facts about amnesia: (1) Manipulation of testing procedures can affect dramatically the memory performance of amnesic patients; in particular, use of certain cueing and prompting techniques can elicit from amnesic patients information that otherwise seemed entirely absent from memory; and (2) all amnesic patients exhibit some form of retrograde amnesia, that is, apparent loss of memory from the period prior to the onset of amnesia. Information acquired during this period must have been encoded and stored in a normal way. These two facts should be considered complementary in the way they appear to favor a retrieval view of amnesia, and evaluation of the adequacy of such a view of amnesia must address both points. The first indicates that some amount of information must have been adequately encoded and stored in order for it to be revealed when appropriate testing procedures are employed. The second indicates that some information that must at some time have been adequately encoded and stored cannot later be expressed. The discussion that follows will consider both of these points.

1. Manipulation of testing methods can affect dramatically the memory performance of amnesic patients. For example, it has been amply documented that the use of retrieval cues facilitates the expression of memories that could not be recalled on demand. Techniques such as semantic prompting, cued recall, and recognition procedures can all benefit the performance of amnesic patients. However, just as the demonstration of improved performance by normal control subjects who are given retrieval cues cannot prove that memory storage is permanent and that forgetting is therefore due to a retrieval problem, so too improved performance by amnesic patients given retrieval cues does not prove that amnesia is due to a retrieval problem. The critical question is not whether amnesic performance can be improved at all by such techniques. The question is whether such techniques disproportionately enhance the performance of amnesic patients, or whether they simply benefit the performance of all subjects, amnesic patients and normal controls alike.

A number of experiments have addressed this question. One good example comes from a study by Mayes, Meudell, and Neary (1978). In this study of word-list learning in patients with Korsakoff syndrome, retention was tested after a 30-second retention interval, first by free (unaided) recall and then by either semantic cueing or cueing with the initial three letters of the to-be-remembered word. Performance of the amnesic patients was greatly aided by the cues. The control subjects exhibited a similar pattern of improvement and maintained a substantial advantage over the amnesic patients. A similar finding has been obtained for a study involving Korsakoff patients, patients receiving bilateral ECT, and patients with amnesia due to hypoxic ischemia (Graf, Squire, & Mandler, 1984; Figure 1-5). In another study, a comparison of free recall and recognition memory for past public events (Squire & Slater, 1977) showed that case N. A., like control subjects, performed better on the recognition test but was still impaired. Finally, patients receiving bilateral ECT were impaired with respect to control subjects on a test of word-list learning, whether the method of retention testing was multiple-choice recognition, yes–no recognition, or cued recall (Squire *et al.*, 1978).

These findings, taken together, demonstrate that performance on cued recall or recognition tests is superior to performance on free recall tests for control subjects as well as for amnesic patients. This view is consistent with Talland's (1965) conclusion that "like other men and women [amnesics] too are more likely to succeed in recognition than in unaided recall, but in all tests of memory their capacity and reliability are abnormally small" (p. 23).

Unlike recognition and cued recall methods, which explicitly require subjects to retrieve information that has been acquired previously, there is another testing method that assesses whether performance can be influenced by previously presented material without asking subjects to retrieve from memory. The first studies using this method involved the presentation of a series of fragmented drawings (Warrington & Weiskrantz, 1968; Milner, Corkin, & Teuber, 1968) or words (Warrington & Weiskrantz, 1968, 1970; Weiskrantz & Warrington, 1970) of various degrees of completeness. Subjects were first shown the most fragmented version of the test materials and then progressively more complete versions of the test materials, with the instruction simply to try to identify each drawing or word. Then the test was readministered in the same manner after a delay, again with the instruction to try simply to identify the material. The experimental question was whether amnesic patients could identify the materials more readily, that is, in a more fragmented form, on the second test occasion as compared to the first, regardless of whether they were able to recognize the materials as having been presented previously. The consistent finding was that prior presentation of the test materials did facilitate subsequent identification, although patients could not remember having previously participated in the study.

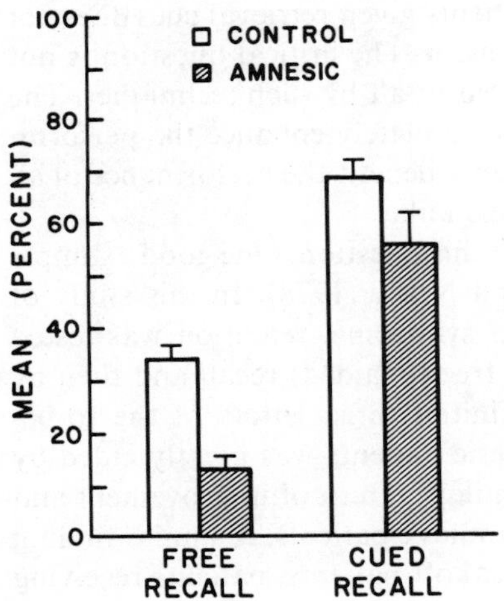

Figure 1-5. Seventeen amnesic patients, representing three different etiologies of amnesia, and 26 control subjects saw lists of words. Retention was tested by free (unaided) recall and then by cued recall. In cued recall, subjects saw the first three letters of previously presented words and were asked to use these word stems as cues to help them to recall the words. (From Graf, Squire, & Mandler, 1984.)

A variation on this testing method has involved presenting a list of words and then later presenting three-letter word fragments with the instruction to complete these word fragments to form whole words. The experimental question was whether the formation of words from three-letter fragments was biased by the prior presentation of key words. For example, after presentation of a word list including the word *motel*, one asks whether a subject's tendency to complete the fragment *mot–* to form *motel* is greater than would be expected if that word had not been on the list. A number of studies using this method have reported that the bias on word-completion performance produced by previously presented words was normal in amnesic patients, despite impaired recognition memory (Warrington & Weiskrantz, 1970, 1974, 1978; Graf *et al.*, 1984). However, other studies have not found amnesic patients to perform normally on this task (Squire *et al.*, 1978; Wetzel & Squire, 1982; Mayes *et al.*, 1978). It is now clear that the test instructions are critical in determining whether the performance of amnesic patients is normal or impaired (Graf *et al.*, 1984; see section on Preserved Capacity for Learning and Memory in Amnesia for an extended treatment of this point). In brief, performance is normal only when the instructions require subjects simply to complete the word fragments to form the first word that comes to mind, without asking subjects to use the fragments as cues to search memory for presented words that match these cues. This completion technique seems to make the same requirements of the subject as the studies discussed above involving repeated presentations of fragmented drawings or words.

The finding that performance can be normal on this test (and on tests of skill learning to be described in the section on Preserved Capacity for Learning and Memory in Amnesia) seems to suggest that information based on previous experience is stored normally in amnesia and can be retrieved under appropriate test conditions. By this account, amnesia might be construed as a retrieval deficit. Note that this view rests on the assumption that memory is a unitary entity and that any evidence for the influence of prior experience on subsequent behavior necessarily reflects the integrity of the representation of that experience. However, there is another account of these data that considers memory to reflect the operation of more than one memory system. By this account, performance on a particular test may require the integrity of only one memory system, and successful performance would carry no implications about the status of other memory systems. Evidence in support of this latter view will be developed fully in the following section. A central theme of the argument will be that all the tasks that yield normal performance in amnesia differ in a principled way from the tasks that yield impaired performance in that they assess fundamentally different kinds of knowledge.

An entirely different example of the way in which manipulation of testing methods produces a marked effect on the memory performance of amnesic patients comes from the study of reversal learning, a body of work that has often been offered in support of a retrieval explanation of amnesia. In one type of experiment (Warrington & Weiskrantz, 1974, 1978), subjects learned in turn two different word lists constructed so that each word on one list began with the same three letters as some word on the second list. Subjects were given a single trial to study list 1 and then multiple trials with list 2. After each trial, retention was assessed by presenting initial-letter cues. The cues would, of course, be identical for the two lists. Thus, the prompt *mot* might be used to cue the word *motel* from list 1 and then, after presentation of list 2, the same prompt would be used again to cue the word *mother*. For normal control subjects, performance on the first trial of list 2 was markedly inferior to performance on list 1. Repeated trials on list 2 produced increasingly accurate performance. Most errors in this paradigm were intrusion errors—that is, responding inappropriately with words from the previous list. Amnesic patients performed rather well on list 1 and, like the control subjects, experienced considerable interference of list 1 learning on list 2 responses. However, the amnesic patients, in addition, demonstrated very poor acquisition of list 2 words during the ensuing learning trials, and continued to exhibit a high incidence of intrusion errors from list 1. The inability of amnesic patients to restrict list 1 intrusions, which suggests heightened susceptibility to interference as well as clear storage of some list 1 information, has been interpreted as favoring a retrieval theory of amnesia in which response competition at the time of retrieval interferes excessively with performance (Warrington & Weiskrantz, 1974).

Further study of reversal learning has identified several weaknesses in this retrieval interpretation. Warrington and Weiskrantz (1978) themselves have pointed out two problems: First, the deleterious effects of interference did not automatically appear at the first opportunity to express itself (i.e., test scores and intrusion errors on the first reversal learning trial were no worse for amnesic patients than for control subjects); and second, performance of amnesic patients was not enhanced by reducing the number of response alternatives at retention testing. This second point was established in the reversal learning paradigm by carefully selecting word lists so that each pair of words beginning with the same three letters—one word from list 1 and one word from list 2—were the only common words in the English language with those initial letters. This manipulation had no effect on the amnesic patients' performance, and it prompted Warrington and Weiskrantz (1978) to view as inadequate a retrieval view of amnesia that stresses an inability to constrain competing responses at the time of retention testing.

Although one might suppose that other, more suitable retrieval explanations could be formulated, the studies just reviewed provide little empirical basis for emphasizing retrieval over other aspects of information processing (such as encoding and storage). Indeed, recent work has led to an alternative way of viewing some of these data that places retrieval explanations in a broader context. Using a method similar in many respects to the reversal learning task just described. Kinsbourne and Winocur (1980) tested the ability of patients with Korsakoff syndrome to accomplish paired-associate learning. The patients learned in turn two lists of semantically related word pairs, constructed so that the first word of each pair appeared on both lists but was associated with a different word (e.g., if the pair "army–battle" was on list 1, then the pair "army–soldier" appeared on list 2). This task resulted in a considerable number of list 1 response intrusions during list 2 learning for all subjects. Amnesic patients exhibited a particularly large number of intrusions and very poor list 2 acquisition. Most important, through the use of cueing manipulations it was possible to vary the number of list 1 intrusions independently of the level of list 2 performance—that is, the number of response intrusions was dissociated from the level of list 2 performance (Table 1-1).

Clearly, response competition during retrieval is not the critical factor in amnesia. It was suggested that these results could be understood instead as a

Table 1-1. Comparison of errors made by five patients with Korsakoff syndrome during learning of two successive lists of paired associates, where the first word of each pair appeared on both lists but associated with different words (e.g., army-battle; army-soldier)

	List 1 errors	List 2 errors			
		TE	SE	RI	OE
Winocur and Kinsbourne					
Standard transfer	3.4	70.7	66.0 (93.3)	45.2 (63.9)	2.3 (3.3)
Contextual shift	3.0	38.7	33.8 (87.3)	20.7 (53.4)	3.9 (10.1)
Kinsbourne and Winocur					
Contextual shift	3.8	70.0	62.2 (88.9)	26.6 (38.0)	3.5 (5.0)
Contextual shift/recognition	3.0	47.6	36.2 (76.1)	19.4 (40.8)	11.4 (23.9)

Note. TE = total errors during nine trials with list 2; SE = semantic errors; RI = response intrusions from list 1; OE = omission errors. Numbers in parentheses are percentages of total errors. Rows 1 and 3 show that a shift in experimental context at retention reduced the number of response intrusions without changing error scores. Rows 3 and 4 show that error scores can change without a change in intrusion errors. Adapted from Winocur and Kinsbourne (1978); Kinsbourne and Winocur (1980).

failure to learn the second set of paired associates at least in part because of an abnormal tendency during both encoding and retrieval to be influenced by persisting mental sets (Kinsbourne & Winocur, 1980). Recent studies of Korsakoff syndrome have also been interpreted as revealing deficits that operate at both the input and output stages (e.g., McDowall, 1979; Cermak, 1982; Winocur, Kinsbourne, & Moscovitch, 1981). McDowall (1979) and Cermak (1982) argued that neither a deficit in encoding nor a deficiency in retrieval is sufficient by itself to account for the impaired memory performance of patients with Korsakoff syndrome. Winocur and associates (1981) extended this idea by suggesting that a single cognitive deficit that operated both at the time of training and at the time of retention testing could account for the impaired performance of these patients. Work with normal subjects emphasizes the similarity in processes operating at the time of encoding and at the time of retrieval and makes plausible the idea that a single deficit could exert its effects at both these times (see also Jacoby, 1983).

It should be emphasized that these experiments on interference and response intrusions are based on studies of Korsakoff syndrome. For this patient group, the findings are consistent with the idea that the deficit includes an impairment operating at the time of retention testing. But this idea is not meant to imply that the disorder operates solely at the time of retention testing. Nor is it meant to imply that similar studies of other kinds of amnesia would lead to the same conclusion.

2. Amnesic patients exhibit retrograde amnesia. That amnesia is also associated with apparent loss of memory for some events that occurred prior to the onset of amnesia indicates the unavailability of information that must have originally been encoded and stored in a normal manner. In this sense, the phenomenon of retrograde amnesia can be considered to support a retrieval explanation of amnesia. However, it is important to note that a retrieval view of amnesia of the type under consideration here would predict temporally unlimited memory loss, affecting all past time periods. To the extent that remote memory loss can be characterized in this way, the view that amnesia at least in part affects retrieval mechanisms would be supported. Extensive remote memory impairment has in fact been amply documented in Korsakoff syndrome; hence, for this patient group, a deficit in processes operating at retrieval would appear to be part of the disorder. Yet in other examples of amnesia, retrograde amnesia is temporally limited, affecting only the several months or years immediately preceding the onset of amnesia. This finding will be discussed fully in the sections on Amnesia as a Storage Deficit, Retrograde Amnesia and Remote Memory Impairment, where the evidence suggests a deficit operating at a different stage of information processing.

Amnesia as an Encoding Deficit (Disorder of Processes Operating at the Time of Training)

Another body of work has suggested that amnesia might reflect a deficit that occurs at the time of training, so that information is not organized or encoded in the normal way. This view seems to be based on two principal findings: (1) Patients with Korsakoff syndrome appear to have difficulty engaging in deeper, more elaborative levels of information processing; and (2) if patients are given extra time to accomplish encoding, then some kinds of amnesic patients exhibit an entirely normal rate of forgetting across at least seven days. These two findings and their relevance to encoding explanations of amnesia will now be considered.

1. Extensive study of Korsakoff syndrome has suggested that these patients have difficulty engaging in deeper, more elaborative levels of information processing, at least one result of which is that they manage only an impoverished stimulus analysis (Butters & Cermak, 1980). For example, patients with Korsakoff syndrome are impaired at distinguishing among unfamiliar faces, apparently limiting their analysis to the most superficial features. Thus, on the Diamond–Carey facial recognition task (Diamond & Carey, 1977), they often considered photographs of different people to be identical if they showed the same facial expression or wore the same hat (Dricker, Butters, Berman, Samuels, & Carey, 1978). Similarly, it has been suggested that their performance on verbal tests indicates a limited processing of verbal material as well (e.g., Cermak, 1979).

Two studies that have been taken to illustrate this deficit in analysis of verbal material will now be considered. One of them (Cermak *et al.*, 1974) was based on the release from PI paradigm, discussed above (section on Superimposition of Cognitive Deficits on Amnesia). The relevance of release from PI to the present issue rests on Wickens's (1970) suggestion that when a shift of stimulus dimension improves a subject's performance, the subject must have been encoding the stimuli along the shifted dimension. Failure to release from PI after one kind of stimulus shift, but not after some other type of shift, might therefore be interpreted as a failure to encode the former stimulus dimension. Patients with Korsakoff syndrome exhibited normal release from PI in an alphanumeric-shift condition (e.g., a shift from letters to numbers), but they failed to release from PI in a category-shift condition (e.g., a shift from animal names to vegetable names). Thus, patients with Korsakoff syndrome appeared not to encode effectively along a semantic dimension.

The second study (Cermak & Reale, 1978) suggested that patients with Korsakoff syndrome might have difficulty with semantic encoding even when explicitly directed to attend to that stimulus dimension. Orienting questions were used to control the type of encoding operations employed during learning (see Craik & Tulving, 1975). Specifically, attention was directed during learning to different stimulus features of the to-be-remembered words: to the superficial appearance of the word, to its sound, or to the semantic category to which it belonged. On such a task, normal subjects are known to exhibit superior retention of words that initially had been encoded semantically. Patients with Korsakoff syndrome were impaired on this task and failed to exhibit the normal pattern of superior retention for semantically encoded words.

These two findings were taken to reflect a reluctance or inability of patients with Korsakoff syndrome to accomplish semantic encoding (Cermak, 1979). However, each of the two findings has difficulty supporting this particular formulation. In the case of the PI paradigm, the deficit reported for Korsakoff syndrome does not occur in other groups. Failure to release from PI does not extend to case N. A., patients receiving bilateral ECT, postencephalitic patients, and patients who have sustained unilateral temporal lobectomy (Cermak, 1976; Squire, 1982c; Moscovitch, 1982). In addition, some patients with Korsakoff syndrome can exhibit release from PI after a shift in semantic category, if they are provided with repeated exposure to the new category members (Kinsbourne & Wood, 1975), or if they are presented with either associated contextual cues or given forewarning of the impending shift (Winocur *et al.*, 1981; Figure 1-6). Finally, this deficit is associated with frontal lobe dysfunction, has no obligatory relationship to amnesia, and therefore cannot explain the nature of the memory deficit in Korsakoff syndrome. The second finding, the failure of patients with Korsakoff syndrome to show superior performance for semantically encoded words in the Craik–Tulving orienting task (Cermak & Reale, 1978), also did not extend to other types of amnesia, as mentioned above (Wetzel & Squire, 1980). Indeed, this particular deficit was not even observed in another population of Korsakoff patients (Squire, 1982c).

Other studies, involving similar test paradigms, have questioned the general description of the disorder in Korsakoff syndrome as an inability or reluctance to engage in semantic encoding. For example, some studies have demonstrated that, contrary to earlier reports, patients with Korsakoff syndrome do not always resort to superficial, nonsemantic stimulus analysis when left to their own devices (Mayes *et al.*, 1978; McDowall, 1979). In each of these studies, patients learned a list of words under conditions that either directed attention to graphic or semantic attributes (graphic and semantic conditions) or that left them free to learn the words in any way they chose (free condition). When retention was tested by free recall, the patients exhibited no better retention of words learned in the free condition than of words learned in the graphic condition. For control subjects, performance in the free condition was similar to performance in the semantic condition. This result seemed to indicate that the patients with Korsakoff syndrome, but not the control subjects, encoded the words along the superficial, graphic dimension. However, when semantic cues were given at retention testing, the patients' recall of words learned in the free condition improved considerably more than their recall of words learned in the graphic condition. In McDowall's (1979) study, cued recall performance was as good for words learned in the free condition as for words learned in the semantic condition. This result suggests that patients with Korsakoff syndrome, even when left to their own encoding devices, can accomplish considerable semantic encoding. Accordingly, it seems clear that the deficit in Korsakoff syndrome, and certainly in amnesia in general, cannot be formulated so as to depend critically on a deficiency in this particular ability. A similar view has been taken recently by others (Mayes *et al.*, 1980; Winocur *et al.*, 1981).

In summary, the view that amnesia in Korsakoff syndrome results from the failure of patients to engage spontaneously in semantic encoding of information appears to describe the deficit too narrowly. This conclusion follows from studies of encoding, as just described, and also from observations that patients with Korsakoff syndrome are impaired in nonverbal tasks, even when the to-be-remembered information involves extremely simple stimulus material that would not require much semantic analysis (Warrington & Baddeley, 1974; DeLuca, Cermak, & Butters, 1975; Riege, 1977). Moreover, qualitatively normal encoding of semantic information can be demonstrated under many circumstances, as just described.

A somewhat more convincing case for the view that an encoding deficit plays a role in Korsakoff syndrome could be made by supposing that patients

Figure 1-6. Two groups of patients with Korsakoff syndrome learned and recalled consecutively presented lists of words. In the practice condition, patients exhibited no release from proactive interference (PI) when all the words came from the same category on trials 1–8 and from a new category on trial 9. However, in the instruction condition, release from PI did occur when a new category was introduced on trial 5, if patients were forewarned that the category shift would occur. (From Winocur, Kinsbourne, & Moscovitch, 1981.)

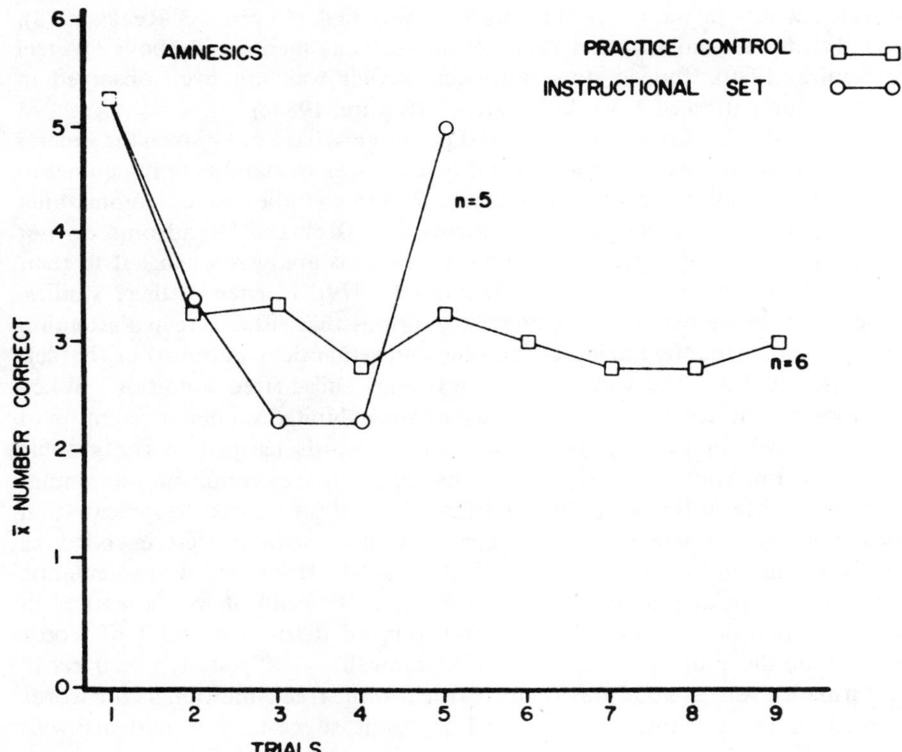

with Korsakoff syndrome engage in a generally impoverished level of analysis for all material. Such patients do tend to rely on superficial stimulus features (e.g., Dricker *et al.*, 1978) and do seem to focus on certain problem-solving strategies or classification principles to the exclusion of others (e.g., Oscar-Berman, 1973). Talland (1965) argued that the amnesia exhibited by patients with Korsakoff syndrome reflected a "premature closure of activation" that hampered the active processing required for encoding and for retrieval. Thus, one might suppose that patients are deficient at encoding time in actively establishing a rich network of associations and deficient at retrieval time in searching actively through memory. Several authors (Kinsbourne & Winocur, 1980; Winocur *et al.*, 1981; Jacoby, 1983) have proposed the presence of a cognitive deficit that could impair both encoding and retrieval. These proposals are not strictly encoding theories but are instead broader explanations in which encoding deficiencies play a role. Thus, deficiencies in deeper, more elaborative kinds of active processing might constitute one prominent feature of a more general deficit. Such a formulation attempts to explain why patients with Korsakoff syndrome engage in such an impoverished analysis and why such patients might sometimes fail to engage spontaneously in semantic encoding.

One formulation of an encoding deficit, which does not include a related retrieval deficit, postulates a selective deficit in the acquisition of information about the context (i.e., spatial, temporal, or both) in which events occur (Huppert & Piercy, 1976; O'Keefe & Nadel, 1978; Stern, 1981; Winocur, 1982; Hirst & Volpe, 1982; Hirst, 1982). For diencephalic amnesia, such as Korsakoff syndrome, a theory based on impaired acquisition of contextual information provides a well-reasoned account of the encoding deficit (see Stern, 1981; Hirst, 1982). However, a deficit in the processing of spatial and temporal context should have no additional impact on processes that operate at the time of retention testing beyond what would be expected to follow from the deficit that already occurred at the time of encoding. Therefore, this account of amnesia is distinct from and does not accommodate the view that amnesia reflects a deficit in a process that operates at both encoding and retrieval. Moreover, an additional deficit must be postulated to account for such findings as the remote memory impairment associated with Korsakoff syndrome. A deficit in acquiring contextual information may be a salient feature of diencephalic amnesia, but it appears together with a deficit in acquiring or processing other kinds of information as well. Finally, for medial temporal amnesia, we argue in the next section (Amnesia as a Storage Deficit) that the deficit is not in encoding at all, but in postencoding processes that operate during the period after learning.

2. Some forms of amnesia are associated with an entirely normal rate of forgetting. When certain amnesic patients were given extra stimulus exposure time (four to eight times longer than that given to control subjects) to equate their recognition memory performance to that of control subjects at a few minutes after learning, their subsequent rate of forgetting of that material was normal for at least 7 days. A normal forgetting rate has been demonstrated in this manner for two examples of diencephalic amnesia—Korsakoff syndrome (Huppert & Piercy, 1978; Squire, 1981; Figures 1-3 and 1-4) and case N. A. (Squire, 1981; Figure 1-4). As described in a previous section (Amnesia Takes Fundamentally Different Forms), a normal forgetting rate seems to be characteristic of diencephalic amnesia and appears to differentiate it from at least two other examples of amnesia: patients receiving bilateral ECT and perhaps case H. M. When, through stimulus manipulations at the time of training, information can be acquired and then forgotten at a normal rate after that point, the effects of such manipulations would appear to operate at an early stage of information processing. This finding seems to rule out a storage interpretation of the deficit, and on the surface seems to support the view that diencephalic amnesia reflects an encoding disorder that results in an inadequate record of experience.

A retrieval view of the forgetting rate findings can also be entertained, however. By this account, allowing the amnesic patients increased exposure time during acquisition can mitigate the effects of a retrieval deficit by establishing a representation in memory that is stronger than the representation established in normal subjects. In light of the view emphasized here that encoding and retrieval processes are closely linked, it is not surprising that much data should be consistent with either an encoding or a retrieval interpretation.

It is also worth emphasizing that theories of amnesia that attribute the memory disorder to an encoding disorder can shed no light on the phenomenon of retrograde amnesia—that is, if some forms of amnesia do reflect a disorder of processes operating at the time of initial training, then some additional disordered process is required to account for memory loss for the period prior to the onset of amnesia. This issue will be taken up again in the section on Retrograde Amnesia and Remote Memory Impairment.

Amnesia as a Storage Deficit (Disorder of Processes Operating during the Retention Interval)

Theories that view amnesia as a storage deficit emphasize a disorder in postencoding processes such that memory is poorly maintained or elaborated with the passage of time. This interpretation is supported by two principal findings: (1) Some forms of amnesia are associated with an abnormally rapid rate of forgetting; and (2) the same forms of amnesia are associated with a temporally limited retrograde amnesia, affecting only the several months or years immediately preceding the onset of amnesia.

1. Some forms of amnesia are associated with an abnormally rapid rate of forgetting. After equating the memory performance of amnesic patients with that of normal control subjects at a few minutes after learning, certain patients exhibit an abnormally rapid forgetting rate for this material. This result has been reported for case H. M. (Huppert & Piercy, 1979; Figure 1-3), for patients receiving bilateral ECT (Squire, 1981; Figure 1-4), and for monkeys with medial temporal lesions (Zola-Morgan & Squire, 1982). Accordingly, it has been supposed that this phenomenon is a characteristic feature of medial temporal amnesia. For this kind of amnesia, the findings suggest a disorder of postencoding processes involved in the maintenance or elaboration of memory, which would ordinarily strengthen those memories not forgotten with the passage of time (Squire, Cohen, & Nadel, 1984). The interruption of processes that ordinarily operate on stored information for a time after learning would seem to lead quite naturally to a progressively larger impairment in memory performance as the learning–retention interval is increased. One hypothetical postencoding process is consolidation, usually considered to be the process that mediates the transition of memory from a labile short-term store to a more stable long-term store. A deficit in this process has been suggested by several investigators (Milner, 1962, 1966; Drachman & Arbit, 1966) to underlie medial temporal amnesia. We have developed a somewhat different formulation of consolidation, based on the facts of retrograde amnesia and on developments in cognitive psychology (Squire, Cohen, & Nadel, 1984), and it will be considered later (section on Temporally Limited Retrograde Amnesia). This view postulates the existence of a postencoding process (consolidation) that operates in long-term memory for as long as years after learning.

2. Some forms of the amnesic syndrome are associated with a temporally limited retrograde amnesia. It should be clear that if postencoding processes indeed play an important role in maintaining and elaborating memory for a time after learning, then any brain injury that interfered with such processes would result in both a deficit in the formation of new memory (i.e., anterograde amnesia) as well as a deficit in the availability of information that still required these processes when the injury occurred (i.e., temporally limited retrograde amnesia). This idea, and the evidence that temporally limited retrograde amnesia is a characteristic feature of medial temporal amnesia, will be developed more fully later in this review (section on Temporally Limited Retrograde Amnesia). Of the theories of anterograde amnesia discussed so far, only these storage theories provide an account of temporally limited retrograde amnesia. Thus, at least some forms of amnesia—in particular, medial temporal amnesia, such as that exhibited by case H. M.—are considered to reflect a disorder of post-encoding processes that ordinarily operate during the time after learning to maintain and elaborate memory.

PRESERVED CAPACITY FOR LEARNING AND MEMORY IN AMNESIA

In keeping with other discussions of the amnesic syndrome, we have focused here on the severe and pervasive disorder of learning and memory demonstrated by amnesic patients: a disorder that affects both verbal and nonverbal material irrespective of the modality of stimulus presentation. Nonetheless, it is known that in some circumstances patients reliably exhibit good memory performance across long retention intervals. Indeed, amnesic patients can sometimes acquire information at a normal rate and can maintain normal performance across a delay. These findings have raised fundamental questions about the nature of the amnesic syndrome, about differences among kinds of memory, and about the way memory is organized in the brain. This section reviews the evidence for preserved learning capacity in amnesia and describes a framework for understanding the experimental findings.

The evidence comes from two classes of findings: (1) the ability to acquire and retain normally a variety of motor, perceptual–motor, and cognitive skills, despite poor memory for the learning episodes and despite impaired memory test performance for the facts that are normally accumulated in using the skills; and (2) the facilitation of certain aspects of test performance based on prior exposure to or "priming" of stimulus materials, despite impaired recall or recognition memory for the same materials. Each class of findings will be discussed in turn. In considering the data, we will emphasize comparisons between amnesic patients and control subjects and, in particular, evidence for normal or intact performance by amnesic patients. Ideas about spared learning and retention in amnesia have too often been influenced by anecdotal reports and informal observations, which can seldom be interpreted unambiguously.

One often-cited anecdotal account that illustrates this point comes from Claparède (1911). Upon shaking hands with a patient with Korsakoff syndrome, Claparède pricked her finger with a pin hidden in his hand. Subsequently, whenever he again attempted to shake her hand, she promptly withdrew it. When he questioned her about her actions, she replied, "Isn't it allowed to withdraw one's hand?" and "Perhaps there is a pin hidden in your hand," and, finally, "Sometimes pins are hidden in hands." Thus, the patient learned from previous experience, but she never seemed to attribute her behavior to personal memory of some previously experienced event. What is of interest here is the finding that the patient's behavior was altered by experience and that this altered behavior outlasted the patient's memory of the experience itself. One might be tempted to conclude that the acquired avoidance response provides evidence for some spared learning capacity in amnesia. However, though this amnesic patient showed a long-lasting avoidance behavior, one cannot be sure that the patient's learned response would last as long as the avoidance behavior of a normal control subject. Indeed, Barbizet (1970) reported that the response to bring pricked with a pin can be quite short-lived for an amnesic patient:

> If the examiner pricks his hand with a needle while shaking hands with him, he withdraws it with a cry; twenty seconds later he will offer his hand again without distrust, and the same performance may be repeated several times. Only after fifteen days of conditioning does he begin to show a certain reticence over offering his hand to the examiner several times in close succession, but he will always offer it at the first meeting of the day with complete confidence. (p. 38)

Such considerations give us pause in accepting anecdotal reports as evidence for preserved learning by amnesic patients. Without data from control subjects against which to measure amnesic performance, no firm conclusions can be drawn.

Acquisition of Skills

The earliest and most clearly documented demonstration of good learning in the amnesic syndrome comes from studies of perceptual–motor skills. Milner (1962) and Corkin (1965, 1968) showed that the patient H. M. could exhibit considerable learning and retention of such skills despite his profound global amnesia. For example, H. M. steadily learned a mirror-tracing task across 3 days of testing, reducing his error score and the time required for completion (Milner, 1962). This occurred without any indication in his verbal reports of his accumulating experience with the task. In addition, despite H. M.'s inability to learn the correct sequence of turns through a 10-choice tactual maze over 80 trials, he nevertheless gradually reduced the time required to complete each trial (Corkin, 1965). H. M. also demonstrated dramatic learning on two tracking tasks—rotary pursuit and bimanual tracking. In each case, H. M. increased his time on target across 7 days of testing. When retested 1 week later on the rotary pursuit task (bimanual tracking was not retested), H. M.'s performance was at the level of performance attained 1 week earlier (Corkin, 1968; Figure 1-7A).

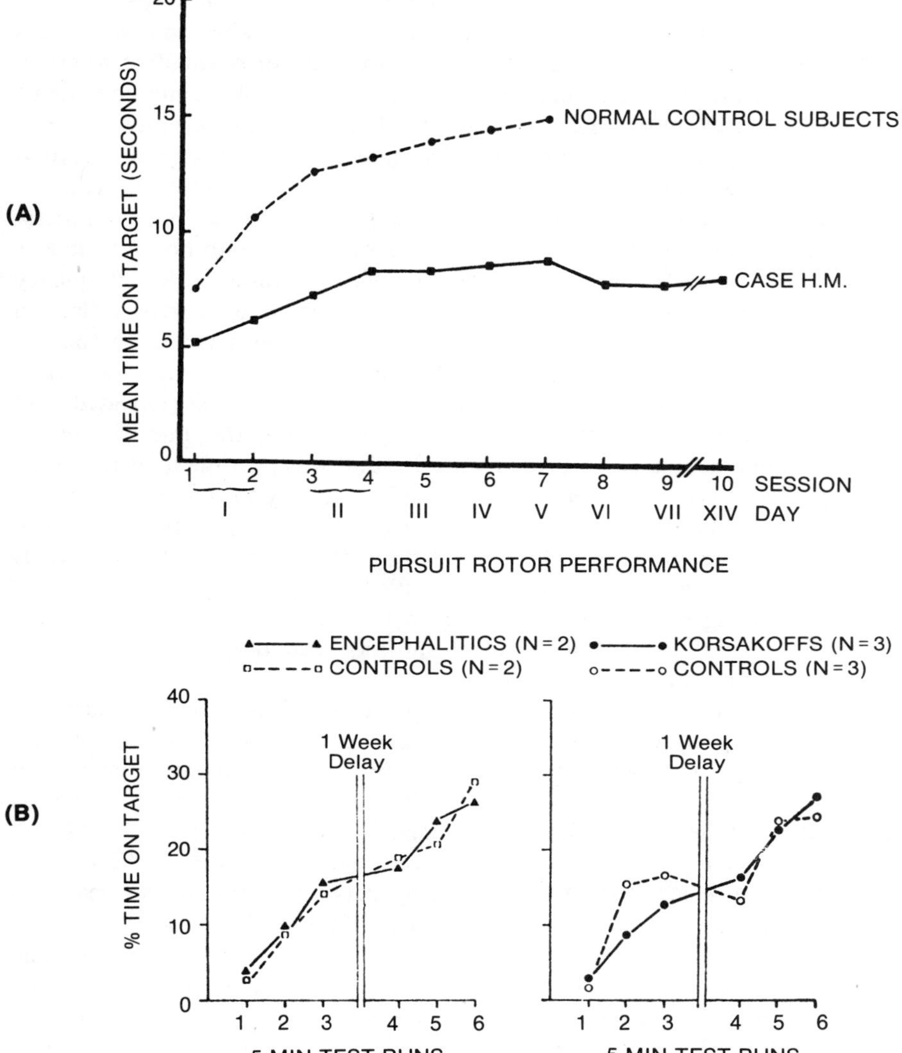

Figure 1-7. (A) Performance of case H. M. and normal controls on a motor-learning task (rotary pursuit). Although he was slower than controls in a variety of timed tasks, H. M. Improved his performance on rotary pursuit from session to session and maintained that performance across sessions. (From Corkin, 1968.) (B) Normal performance by postencephalitic and Korsakoff patients on the pursuit rotor task and normal retention across a 1-week interval. (From Brooks & Baddeley, 1976.)

Further investigations of rotary pursuit have corroborated that learning and retention of this perceptual–motor skill can occur in a variety of amnesic patients (Figure 1-7): in patients with Korsakoff syndrome (Cermak, Lewis, Butters, & Goodglass, 1973; Brooks & Baddeley, 1976; Cohen, 1981), post-encephalitic patients (Brooks & Baddeley, 1976), patients receiving bilateral ECT (Cohen, 1981), and patient N. A. (Cohen, 1981). In most of these studies, the performance of amnesic patients was equivalent to that of normal control subjects. A final example of perceptual–motor learning in amnesic patients was reported by Brooks and Baddeley (1976), who found a reliable reduction across trials in the time needed to complete both the adult version of the Porteus visual maze and a 12-piece jig-saw puzzle. For each of these tasks, amnesic patients exhibited good retention when retested 1 week after initial learning.

The capacity for preserved skill learning in amnesia extends beyond perceptual–motor tasks to tasks in the perceptual and cognitive domains. A particularly clear example comes from a study of mirror reading in amnesia (Cohen & Squire, 1980), based on similar tasks studied with normal subjects (Kolers, 1976, 1979). Subjects saw triads of eight- to ten-letter, low-frequency words (e.g., bedraggle–capricious–grandiose) presented by mirror reflection in a tachistoscope. Subjects read five blocks of 10 word triads on each of 3 consecutive days and also on a fourth day approximately 13 weeks later. For each block of ten word triads, half were common to all blocks (repeated) and half were unique (nonrepeated). By analyzing separately the time required to read each nonrepeated and repeated word triad, it was possible to evaluate the ability to acquire the operations or procedures necessary for mirror reading, as well as the ability to benefit from frequent repetition of specific words. The results are shown in Figure 1-8. Results for the nonrepeated word triads indicate that patient N. A., five patients with Korsakoff syndrome, and three patients receiving bilateral ECT all learned the mirror-reading skill at a rate equivalent to that of matched control subjects, and they retained the skill normally over an interval of 3 months.

Figure 1-8 also shows results for the repeated word triads and measures the facilitatory effect on reading speed of previous experience with particular words. Faster reading speed was observed for both amnesic patients and control subjects, but this facilitatory effect on reading speed of repeating specific words was smaller for the patients than for the controls, particularly on the first block of each new testing day. This can be appreciated most clearly in Figure 1-9, which provides a measure of the forgetting between testing days (mean difference in reading time between the last block of ten trials on each testing day and the first block on the following testing day). For performance on the nonrepeated word triads, which depends solely on learning the operations or procedures required for mirror reading, there was no forgetting between testing days by either the amnesic patients or the normal control subjects. However, for performance on the repeated word triads, which depends in addition on memory for (or record of) the specific word triads that were repeated from block to block, there was marked forgetting by the amnesic patients. This dissociation between the intact ability of amnesic patients to acquire the mirror-reading skill and their inability to benefit as much as normal subjects from the repetition of specific items was reflected also in verbal reports. Whereas none of the amnesic patients reported upon questioning that word triads had been repeated during the task, all of the control subjects reported spontaneously that some word triads were repeated frequently. Amnesic patients who were asked to explain why they read some word triads so rapidly invariably claimed that those triads were "easier" than the others.

A final indication that amnesia was associated with a deficit in specific-item memory despite completely intact acquisition and retention of the mirror-reading skill came from a recognition memory test administered after the third day of testing. The amnesic patients exhibited markedly impaired recognition

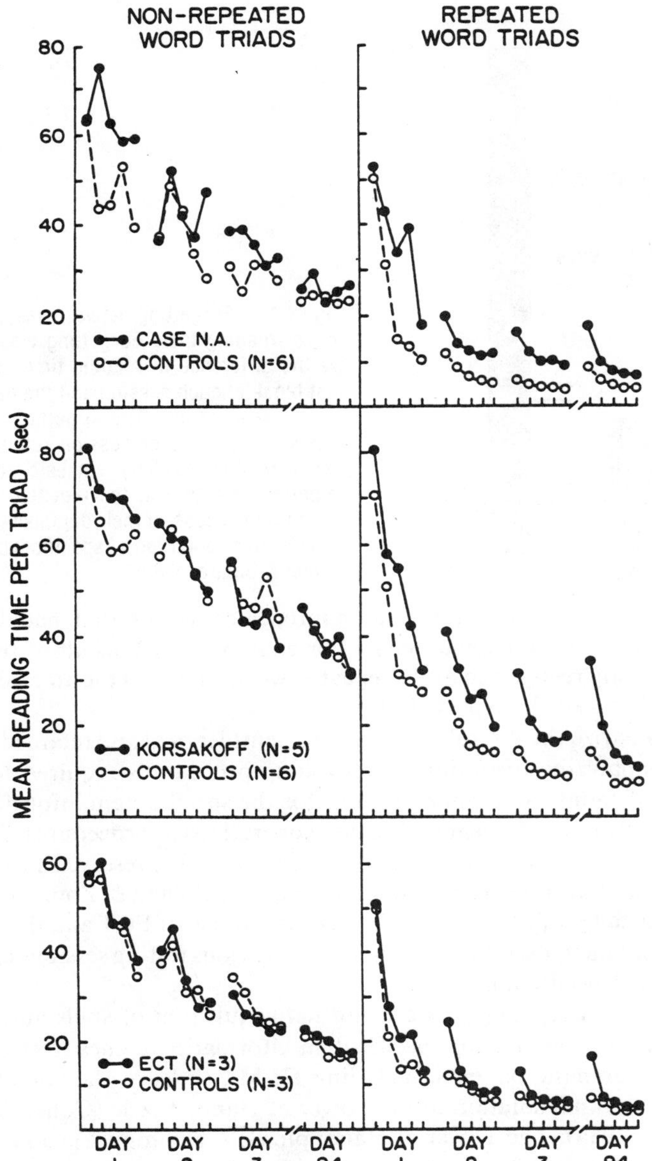

Figure 1-8. Acquisition of a mirror-reading skill during three daily sessions and retention 3 months later. The ability to mirror-read unique (nonrepeated) words was acquired at a normal rate by amnesic patients. The ability of amnesic patients to mirror-read repeated words was inferior to that of controls because amnesic patients, unlike control subjects, were unable to remember the specific words that they had read. (From Cohen & Squire, 1980.)

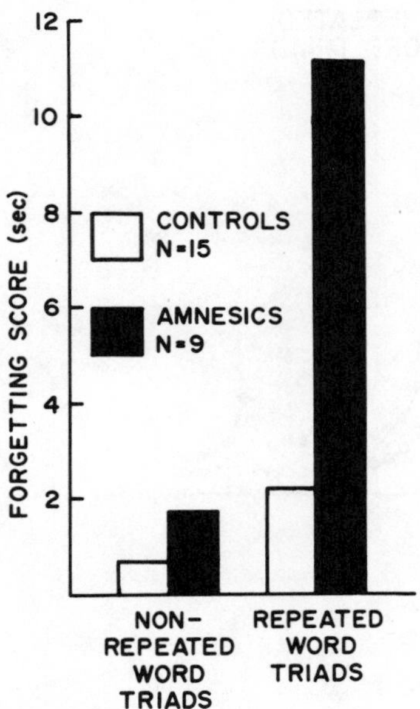

Figure 1-9. Forgetting between sessions for the mirror-reading task. Forgetting was measured by the difference in reading time between the last block of each session and the first block of the subsequent one. The forgetting score illustrates intact between-session retention of the mirror-reading skill by amnesic patients but impaired retention in the repeated word-triad condition because of their diminished ability to benefit from repetition of specific words. (From Cohen & Squire, 1980.)

memory for both the repeated and nonrepeated words that had been read during the course of the experiment. For example, whereas all of the control subjects correctly recognized all 15 repeated words, none of the amnesic patients could identify all of the repeated words.

To summarize these results, amnesic patients learned and retained normally the pattern-analyzing operations or encoding procedures required for mirror reading but demonstrated poor memory for the specific-item information that would normally result from applying these operations or procedures. Recently it has been shown that the same mirror-reading skill is preserved in retrograde amnesia, as well as anterograde amnesia (Squire, Cohen, & Zouzounis, 1984). The skill was taught just prior to a prescribed course of ECT and then survived the treatment intact, despite amnesia for the previous testing sessions and for the words that had been read.

A similar discrepancy between normal acquisition of skills and impaired memory test performance for specific-item information comes from a study of the ability of amnesic patients, including H. M., to learn the cognitive skills required for optimal solution to the Tower of Hanoi puzzle (Cohen & Corkin, 1981; Cohen, 1984). The Tower of Hanoi puzzle is a complex problem-solving task, involving at least 31 steps; (Figure 1-10); it has been studied extensively in normal subjects (Simon, 1975; Anzai & Simon, 1979; Karat, 1982). Patients learned the solution to this task at a normal rate across 4 days of testing. Case H. M. also exhibited impressive savings when retested 1 year later. The normal acquisition of the cognitive skills required to solve the puzzle occurred despite little or no recollection of having worked at the task previously and despite poor insight into what was being learned. This point was illustrated in a second experiment, in which the puzzle was prepared beforehand to portray various stages of completion. Some of the presentations (Figure 1-10, middle), but not others (Figure 1-10, bottom), portrayed stages of completion that subjects would have passed through when they solved the puzzle in an optimal way. The patients were markedly impaired in their ability to distinguish configurations that led directly to solution, and that they would have encountered previously, from configurations that were not on the solution path and that might never have been encountered previously. Nonetheless, they were as good as normal subjects at completing the puzzle from all stages of completion that were presented to them. These and other findings indicated that the patients had learned to solve the puzzle in a rule-governed manner and not by memorizing specific steps.

There are other, less formal, reports of impressive learning by amnesic patients that illustrate further the preserved capacity for learning and memory in amnesia. One report (Kinsbourne & Wood, 1975; Wood, Ebert, & Kinsbourne, 1982) demonstrated the ability of patients with Korsakoff syndrome to learn a rule that enabled them to predict each successive number in different examples of a Fibonacci number series. Retention of the rule was observed 17 weeks after training, at a time when none of the patients could recall their previous experience with the task. More recently, a study of two amnesic patients demonstrated acquisition and 24-hour retention of avoidance (eyelid) conditioning, though the patients could not recall the learning episode just minutes after testing when still seated in front of the conditioning apparatus (Weiskrantz & Warrington, 1979). Although both of these findings were reported without data from comparably tested control subjects, which thus prevents a determination of whether acquisition and retention by the amnesic patients was indeed normal, the results are nevertheless consistent with the more formal experimental demonstrations of skill learning in amnesic patients who have an otherwise global disorder of learning and memory. All of the findings taken together support the view of a preserved learning capacity in amnesia.

Figure 1-10. The Tower of Hanoi puzzle used to test cognitive skill learning in patient H. M. and other amnesic patients. To solve the puzzle, subjects must move the five blocks shown in the top panel to the rightmost peg. Only one block can be moved at a time, and a large block can never be placed on a smaller one. The optimal solution to the puzzle requires 31 moves. The other two panels show an arrangement of blocks that leads directly to the optimal solution (middle) or an arrangement that does not lead directly to solution because it is not on the optimal solution path (bottom).

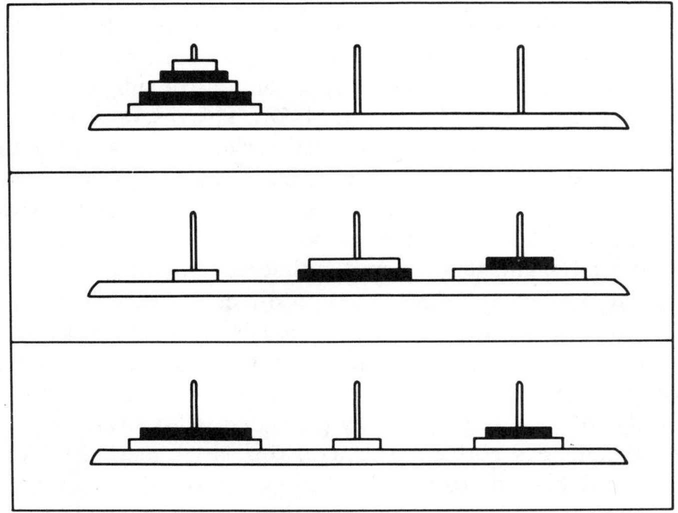

Priming

A second class of findings that support the claim of a preserved learning capacity in amnesia comes from studies of priming. There is a growing literature that documents the facilitation of certain aspects of test performance in both amnesic patients and normal control subjects, based on prior exposure to—that is, priming of—the stimulus materials. In amnesic patients as well as in normal control subjects, these (repetition) priming effects occur independently of recognition memory for the same previously presented material.

Perhaps the best illustration of the facilitation of test performance in amnesia due to priming comes from the many studies that employed fragmented verbal or nonverbal material (see section on Amnesia as a Retrieval Deficit). As discussed earlier, the ability of amnesic patients to identify fragmented drawings or words presented in varying degrees of completion was markedly facilitated when retested with the same material, although the patients could not remember being previously exposed to the material (Warrington & Weiskrantz, 1968, 1970; Milner *et al.*, 1968). That this facilitation of performance was due to priming by the previously presented drawings or words rather than due to a more general learning of how to complete fragmented materials is indicated by the report that facilitation did not occur for presentation of a set of fragmented materials different from that presented during initial training (Weiskrantz, 1978; Baddeley, 1982b).

Similar findings have been obtained by several investigators in a somewhat different paradigm, which tested the influence of previously presented whole words on the formation of words from three-letter stems (Warrington & Weiskrantz, 1970, 1974; Graf *et al.*, 1984), as discussed above (section on Amnesia as a Retrieval Deficit). The word-completion performance of amnesic patients was biased toward producing words that had been presented previously to the same extent as was the performance of normal control subjects. The normal priming effect on word completion occurred in amnesic patients despite markedly impaired recall and recognition of the previously presented words themselves.

It is important to remember that other studies using a superficially identical method found that the performance of amnesic patients, though again consistently biased toward producing words that had been presented previously was nonetheless consistently inferior to that of control subjects (Squire *et al.*, 1978; Wetzel & Squire, 1982; Mayes *et al.*, 1978). This discrepancy in results can be explained by the nature of the test instructions; its exposition here should help to clarify the nature of the intact priming effects in amnesia (see Graf *et al.*, 1984). In the reports finding normal performance by amnesic patients, the patients were asked simply to "identify" the word fragments (Weiskrantz, 1982) or were told to "complete each [fragment] to form the first word that came to mind" (Graf *et al.*, 1984), an instruction that seems to direct the subject away from an intentional retrieval of memory for the previously presented words (Graf *et al.*, 1984; Baddeley, 1982b; Jacoby, 1983). By contrast, in the reports finding the performance of amnesic patients to be poorer than normal, the patients were asked explicitly to recall the previously presented words using the word fragments as cues. Whereas performance with this latter method of cued recall would appear to depend on explicit, intentional retrieval of episodic memory, performance with the former method would appear to depend on some more incidental or automatic process (Baddeley, 1982b; Jacoby, 1983) whereby performance is automatically influenced by the level of activation produced by prior stimulus presentation (Mandler, 1980). Other accounts call this process perceptual fluency (Jacoby & Dallas, 1981; Jacoby & Witherspoon, 1982) or the hot-tubes effect (Rozin, 1976). Such a process is presumed to be intact in amnesia.

Consistent with this account are a number of other findings. In one study (Jacoby & Witherspoon, 1982), five patients with Korsakoff syndrome were asked orienting questions designed to prime the lower-frequency meanings of several homonyms: for example, "What is an example of a reed instrument?" Later, the patients were asked to spell a set of words that included the homonyms (i.e., reed–read). The patients tended to respond with the spelling that corresponded to the low-frequency meaning that had been biased by the orienting questions. This priming effect was as large for the amnesic patients as it was for normal control subjects, even though the patients were impaired with respect to the controls in recognizing which words they had previously heard. Other evidence for such priming effects can be inferred from informal reports that amnesic patients can achieve perception-in-depth of random-dot stereograms more rapidly as a function of previous experience with the stimulus materials and can demonstrate retention of the McCullough color-after-effect (Weiskrantz, 1978), and that amnesic patients improve their performance in detecting anomalous features of repeatedly presented line drawings from the McGill picture anomalies test (Warrington & Weiskrantz, 1973; Baddeley, 1982b).

What is so striking about all of these examples is that prior exposure to stimuli can influence the performance of amnesic patients in a normal manner, even though the patients cannot recall or recognize those same stimuli. Yet in normal control subjects, too, the facilitatory effects of prior experience on subsequent performance with the same materials can be independent of recognition memory (Scarborough, Gerard, & Cortese, 1979; Jacoby & Dallas, 1981; Jacoby & Witherspoon, 1982; Tulving, Schacter, & Stark, 1982). Thus, prior study of a word list can facilitate later perceptual identification of the same words presented very briefly (Jacoby & Dallas, 1981) or can facilitate completion of the same words when they are presented in fragmented form (Tulving *et al.*, 1982), regardless of whether or not the subjects successfully recognize the previous occurrence of those words.

On the face of it, such findings would seem easily explained by assuming that recognition is simply a less sensitive index of memory than a performance-bound measure such as word completion. Nelson (1978) has elegantly demonstrated that performance measures of retention based on savings can reveal evidence for memory in normal control subjects at a time after learning when recognition memory is at chance. Applying this account to amnesia, one need only imagine that the memory of amnesic patients is so weak (due to inadequate encoding or faulty storage) or retrieval so inefficient that only the most sensitive tests will provide evidence of memory for prior experience. The key to this account is the idea that various tests are differentially sensitive to an underlying unitary memory trace. Such an argument has been advanced by Meudell and Mayes (1981), who were able to reproduce in normal control subjects, tested long after learning, the same dissociation between facilitated performance and impaired recognition that is exhibited by amnesic patients soon after learning. In this study, amnesic patients showed facilitation of search for hidden objects in cartoons upon re-presentation of the same cartoons 7 weeks later, at a time when recognition memory was at chance; normal control subjects, retested after 17 months, also demonstrated facilitation of search for cartoons that they could not recognize. The authors concluded from this study that the facilitatory influence of previous exposure on subsequent performance that occurs in the absence of recognition memory is not limited to amnesic patients but is instead a general feature of attenuated memory—that is, the facilitation of performance by previous exposure, together with poor recognition memory, is related to the differential sensitivity of two measures of memory; and it can be observed whenever memory is sufficiently weak, whether in amnesic patients or in control subjects tested long after learning.

This interpretation of preserved capacity in amnesic patients is refuted by the evidence. First, a number of studies have demonstrated the independence of recognition memory and priming effects in normal control subjects (Scarborough *et al.*, 1979; Jacoby & Dallas, 1981; Jacoby & Witherspoon, 1982; Tulving *et al.*, 1982), as discussed above. Independence of recognition memory and priming effects can be demonstrated when recognition memory performance is very good. Indeed, the finding of independence means that priming effects are not in any way related to the level of recognition memory performance. Accordingly, the results in amnesic patients cannot be explained by supposing that priming simply measures memory in a more sensitive way than recognition memory techniques.

The second point turns on the claim that patterns of amnesic performance simply mimic the patterns of performance that appear in normal subjects during the course of forgetting. Yet priming effects for words are as large in amnesic patients as in normal subjects, and they can disappear at an entirely normal rate after word presentation (Graf *et al.*, 1984). This finding means that the priming effect is normal in amnesic patients, not that priming effects are a little less fragile than other aspects of memory.

Such considerations suggest a fundamental difference between the kind of information or processing that underlies priming effects and the kind of information or processing that supports recognition memory. Our proposed account of this difference, to be developed in the next section, comprises part of a more general characterization of preserved learning capacity in amnesia. The central claim of the proposal is that the dissociation in amnesia between the tasks on which learning is preserved and tasks on which learning is impaired reflects the operation of two fundamentally different kinds of knowledge mediated by different memory systems, each with a different neurologic basis.

Characterization of Preserved Learning in Amnesia

It has been argued that the sheer number and variety of the above examples of good, and often intact, learning by amnesic patients make it unlikely that a dimension or category could be found to embrace all of them (Weiskrantz, 1978; Weiskrantz & Warrington, 1979). Recently, however, a formulation that synthesizes these findings has been developed (Cohen, 1981, 1984). This view will be considered along with a number of other current accounts (O'Keefe & Nadel, 1978; Olton, Becker, & Handelmann, 1979; Wickelgren, 1979; Warrington & Weiskrantz, 1982; Weiskrantz, 1982; Baddeley, 1982b; Moscovitch, 1982; Kinsbourne & Wood, 1975).

The present formulation begins with consideration of some related ideas from the psychological and philosophical literatures. Ryle (1949) was impressed by the apparent difference between the knowledge required to perform motor skills and the knowledge of words or facts about the world: "knowing how" as opposed to "knowing that." He argued that access to these two kinds of knowledge was fundamentally different in that remembering facts and other specific information (i.e., knowledge that) required the conscious directing of attention to the act of recall, whereas the performance of a skilled action (i.e., knowledge how), which just as surely reflects past experience, does not involve active attention or conscious recall.

A rather similar view was expressed by Jerome Bruner (1969), who distinguished between "memory with record" and "memory without record." As he defined it, memory with record refers to the facts we acquire and events we experience in daily life, which are stored away for later use: the words, names, faces, routes, and so forth, that are the substance of most memory tests. By contrast, memory without record reflects the way in which "encounters are converted into some process that changes the nature of an organism, changes his skills, or changes the rules by which he operates, but are virtually inaccessible in memory as specific encounters" (p. 254). Thus, the processing rules or operating procedures are themselves modified. Skills like playing golf or tennis improve despite poor access to the "specific instances that led to the perfection of the [skill]" (p. 254). Memory without record does not require a concomitant memory with record of specific instances.

The notion that memory without record is fundamentally different from memory with record was originally intended to account for the way in which perceptual–motor learning is distinct from other types of learning. It seems reasonable, however, that a class of memory without record capable of supporting the learning of perceptual–motor skills should extend beyond that limited domain to include any skill. Thus, for any skill, memory without record would involve a modification of operations or procedures, regardless of the degree of perceptual–motor involvement in that skill. In recent years, experimental support for such a view has been obtained (e.g., Kolers, 1975, 1976, 1979). Examining the ability of normal subjects to read geometrically inverted or otherwise transformed text, Kolers distinguished the acquisition of pattern-analyzing operations or encoding procedures ("that are directed at the surface lexical features of the text" [Kolers, 1979, p. 374]) from specific memory for the results or outcomes of these operations ("the semantic or other grammatical content of text that is the subject of most contemporary studies" [Kolers, 1979, p. 374]). It was suggested that skilled reading, like other perceptual identification processes, involves the application of analytic operations or procedures that analyze the information at the level of visual patterns to produce a resultant semantic outcome. These operations and procedures are modified by experience; the outcomes are stored separately.

Another, somewhat similar distinction has been discussed in the artificial intelligence literature (Winograd, 1975; Winston, 1977; Anderson, 1980), using the terms procedural versus declarative knowledge. The distinction between procedural and declarative knowledge is a statement of the contrast between, on the one hand, information that is represented implicitly in the cognitive processes, operations, or procedures that specify its use and that can be accessed only by "running off" particular routines; and, on the other hand, information that is represented explicitly as a set of facts or data structures in a declarative data base and that can be accessed directly on demand. For an example of the difference between these two kinds of representations, consider the ways in which one could program a device to supply answers to multiplication problems. In a declarative system of representation, answers can be generated by consulting a prestored data base of multiplication tables and simply locating the appropriate entries. Adults undoubtedly use this method for accomplishing multiplication of two single-digit numbers. In a procedural system of representation, answers can be generated by actually implementing the multiplication operations: namely, by iteratively adding x to itself n times, just as children do before they learn the multiplication tables. Thus, in a declarative system, there is explicit access to the data base from which the answers will be selected, whereas in a procedural system answers are derived through the application of particular algorithms.

What these accounts share in common is the claim for a distinction between different kinds of knowledge or different types of memory. We have been guided by these ideas in formulating our account of preserved learning in amnesia (Cohen & Squire, 1980; Cohen, 1981, 1984), an account that supports the claim of a fundamental distinction between two different kinds of knowledge (and the memory systems that support them). We argue that this distinction is honored by the nervous system, as reflected by the differential susceptibility of these systems to amnesia. The acquisition of skills and the phenomenon of priming, both of which can occur in the absence of memory for the stimulus materials presented previously or for the previous learning experience itself, represent a particular class of knowledge dependent on the integrity of a particular kind of memory system. This knowledge—knowing how—is acquired and expressed by virtue of a memory system that, like Bruner's memory without record, does not permit explicit access to the contents of the knowledge base and does not support the ability to reflect in verbal reports a patient's accumulating experience with the tasks. Knowledge-how is tied to and expressible only through activation of the particular processing structures or procedures engaged by the learning tasks; and it is acquired and retained by virtue of the plasticity inherent in these processing structures or procedures. Thus, experience serves to influence the organization of processes that guide performance, without providing access to the knowledge that underlies the performance.

By contrast, a different kind of knowledge—knowing that—is represented in a system of the kind Bruner called memory with record that is quite compatible with the traditional memory metaphor of experimental psychology, in which information is said to be first processed or encoded, then stored in some explicitly accessible form for later use, and then ultimately retrieved on demand. This type of memory constitutes the subject of most experimental investigations of memory and is markedly impaired in amnesic patients who have damage to medial temporal or diencephalic brain structures. This memory system acquires and maintains a representation of the specific outcomes or results of the operations performed by those processing structures or procedures activated by the learning tasks. Thus, whereas knowing how involves the reorganization or modification of existing processing structures or procedures, knowing that is claimed to involve the creation of new data structures that represent explicitly the outcomes of engaging these processes or procedures.

This theory begins with a modular view of the brain as composed of distinct processing and action systems. These systems handle different kinds of information as determined by the pattern of connectivity among systems, and they handle information in different ways as determined by the intrinsic organization of the systems. Performing a task engages procedures within the appropriate processing–action systems. Because of the plasticity inherent in these systems, their operation produces temporary activation and potentially longer-term modifications—that is, the operation of the processes or procedures within any of these systems is accompanied by direct on-line changes that tune or otherwise increase the efficiency of the relevant processes and procedures. It is such changes that provide the basis for priming effects (through temporary activation) and that underlie the acquisition of skills (through longer-term modification).

Because of the differences among systems in the information being processed and in the nature of the processing itself, the possibilities for communication among different systems would seem to be very limited. Indeed, the format or code of the knowledge represented by modification of particular processes and procedures could be so closely tied to the nature of the processes and procedures that are used by any particular brain system that this knowledge would be functionally inaccessible to other brain systems. As a means of supporting communication among the different systems, it is suggested that a code fundamentally different from what is used by the processing and action systems is available for storage of the outcomes or results of having engaged their systems. This common code represents explicitly the new data structures derived from the operation of any available process or procedure. The storage of these data structures in the form of a common code affords the ability to compare and contrast information from different processes or processing systems, and it affords the ability to make inferences from and generalizations across facts derived from different processing sources. Such a common code thereby supports knowing that; hence, it provides the basis for access to facts acquired during the course of experience and for conscious recollection of the learning experiences themselves. This memory system depends on the medial temporal and diencephalic brain structures damaged in amnesia.

It follows from these considerations that the interruption of such a system would produce a selective impairment of learning and memory, sparing the ability to benefit from previous experience in the form of skill acquisition and priming effects but affecting dramatically the storage of or access to memory ordinarily acquired during the learning experience. This dissociation between the ability of amnesic patients to benefit from experience without being able to reflect the experience in their verbal reports was noted repeatedly in our discussion of the data above; its importance for understanding the phenomenon of preserved learning has been stressed by a number of authors (Weiskrantz, 1978; Baddeley, 1982b; Moscovitch, 1982; Jacoby & Witherspoon, 1982). This dissociation follows naturally from the present formulation of amnesia as a deficit selective to the particular knowledge-representation system that supports memory with record, without having to postulate a specific deficit in "monitoring" (Weiskrantz, 1978), "evaluative memory" (Baddeley, 1982a, 1982b), or "attribution" (Jacoby, 1983) processes. A further treatment of these issues and their cognitive implications is provided elsewhere (Cohen, 1984).

To consider how these ideas are related to brain mechanisms of learning and memory, it is instructive to look at forms of learning that have been analyzed with some success in neurophysiological terms. In *Aplysia*, for example, habituation of the gill-withdrawal response involves synaptic changes in the same system responsible for the response (Kandel, 1976). Here, the mechanisms involved in executing the gill-withdrawal response are themselves modified by experience. Habituation does not seem to require an explicit representation of having experienced a particular pattern of stimulation in a specific place at a specific time. The tuning of visual cortical cells in cats through selective early experience illustrates the same point. Restricting the animal's early experience to horizontal contours modifies the properties of individual cells in visual cortex, resulting in special sensitivity to horizontally oriented lines (Hirsch & Spinelli, 1970; Blakemore, 1974). But there is no sense in which such changes depend on a memory with record of having undergone a particular experience, or even knowledge of the fact that the world is composed primarily of horizontally oriented lines. Such changes appear to reflect the gradual modification of neuronal structures that are themselves involved in the analysis of information and the expression of behavior. This kind of modification of neuronal elements seems to provide a clear example of what we have termed knowing how. It occurs gradually, it changes the rules by which an organism operates, and it does not require a memory with record of the specific instances that comprised the learning experience. Storage of the specific instances would seem to require additional brain mechanisms, and we suggest that it is these mechanisms that are damaged in amnesia.

There have been other formulations of amnesia that also are founded on a proposed distinction between memory systems. For example, it has been argued (Kinsbourne & Wood, 1975; Kinsbourne, 1982; Wood, Ebert, & Kinsbourne, 1982; Schacter & Tulving, 1982a, 1982b; Parkin, 1982) that the pattern of deficits and sparing seen in the amnesic syndrome supports Tulving's (1972) proposed distinction between episodic and semantic memory. Episodic memory is autobiographical memory for specific, temporally dated and spatially located events (e.g., a memory of watching the space shuttle *Columbia* touch down at Edwards Air Force Base), whereas semantic memory is context-free knowledge of language, concepts, facts, and rules (e.g., the fact that the space shuttle is a reusable space vehicle built and operated by the United States). The fact that amnesic patients have, on the one hand, preserved general intelligence as well as intact language, perceptual skills, and social skills, yet on the other hand, have profoundly impaired memory for day-to-day events and are often confused as to time and place, has been offered in support of the idea that amnesia reflects a selective impairment in episodic memory. Unfortunately, this comparison between episodic and semantic memory is confounded with premorbid and postmorbid memory. Information that would support performance on intelligence tests and that would mediate language, perceptual skills, and social skills is acquired early in life during the premorbid period, long before the onset of amnesia. By contrast, memory for day-to-day events and appreciation of current context obviously depends on recent postmorbid memory. The point is that to evaluate fairly the distinction between semantic and episodic memory in amnesia, one must compare either new learning (postmorbid memory) of both semantic and episodic information or remote (premorbid) memory for both semantic and episodic information. Now that this has been done, it is clear that the deficit in new learning as well as whatever deficit is present in remote memory affects both episodic and semantic information. For example, in the domain of new learning, case H. M. is not only profoundly impaired in learning new word lists, but he also exhibits a profound impairment in learning the meanings of eight new vocabulary words: He showed virtually no learning over 10 days of testing with 115 repetitions per day of either the definitions of the words, synonyms of the words, or sentence frames that used the words (Gabrieli, Cohen, & Corkin, 1983). In the domain of remote memory, case N. A., patients with Korsakoff syndrome, and patients receiving bilateral ECT all exhibited some loss of premorbid memory, and their deficit extended to information about both public (largely semantic) and personal (episodic) events (Zola-Morgan, Cohen, & Squire, 1983). Moreover, from very remote memory all of these patient groups were able to recall personal (episodic) events; see section on Retrograde Amnesia and Remote Memory Impairment).

Another argument for relating the semantic–episodic distinction to amnesia has been that the examples of preserved learning in amnesia described here might all be considered to reflect intact semantic memory (Kinsbourne & Wood, 1975; Wood, Ebert, & Kinsbourne, 1982). Yet it seems to us that much of semantic memory belongs to the category of knowing that, and that preserved learning of motor and cognitive skills reflects the operation of a separate procedural system. Schacter and Tulving (1982) have also argued that the semantic–episodic distinction, as originally formulated, dealt only with propositional knowledge and that the acquisition and modification of knowing how follow fundamentally different rules. These considerations suggest that, regardless of the usefulness of the semantic–episodic distinction in work with normal human memory, there is as yet no compelling evidence for the view that these two domains of memory are differentially susceptible to amnesia.

Another proposed distinction among memory systems is the distinction between reference memory and working memory (Olton *et al.*, 1979), which was developed from studies with experimental animals. Reference memory refers to a system involved in learning those aspects of a task that are constant from trial to trial, and it requires no updating or modification across trials. This type of memory has been claimed to be spared in experimental animals with lesions of the hippocampal system. Working memory is a limited-capacity system for short-term storage of the aspects of a task that change from trial to trial and that must be remembered in order to achieve success on a given trial. According to the reference-memory–working-memory formulation, this type of memory is selectively affected by hippocampal damage. However, work with amnesic patients indicates that the constant features of a task are not automatically protected. Thus, simple repetition of specific information (knowing that) is not sufficient to ensure learning (Drachman & Arbit, 1966; Corsi, 1972; Cohen, 1981). For example, H. M. was unable to recall a string of digits that was one digit in excess of his immediate memory span despite 25 consecutive repetitions of the same string (Drachman & Arbit, 1966); and he was unable to learn the meanings of eight new vocabulary words despite 60 repetitions of their appropriate definitions and 60 repetitions of their appropriate synonyms (Gabrieli *et al.*, 1983). Moreover, intact acquisition of mirror-reading skill by amnesic patients (Cohen & Squire, 1980; Cohen, 1981) was not based on simple repetition of the skill. Acquisition was normal in amnesic patients from the beginning of training; it did not become normal as the result of repetition. Thus, the preserved learning of knowing how is postulated to occur because of the nature of the information, not because of the number of times that the information is repeated. Hence, we find in the facts of human amnesia no support for the proposed distinction between reference memory and working memory (see Squire & Cohen, 1979a).

Despite the problems just outlined with these two attempts to understand amnesia as a dissociation among kinds of memory, they share with the formulation presented here a conviction that memory is *not* a unitary, monolithic entity that is likely to be affected in a uniform way by brain injury. Neuropsychological evidence and evidence from the cognitive sciences are converging on the view that the capacity for learning and memory is based on several systems that can be dissociated under certain circumstances. The facts of amnesia, reviewed here, suggest that a distinction between knowing how and knowing that is honored by the nervous system.

RETROGRADE AMNESIA AND REMOTE MEMORY IMPAIRMENT

Two Forms of Impairment

In a previous section (Anterograde Amnesia), it was concluded that anterograde amnesia differs according to the etiology of amnesia. In this section, it is argued that the same is true for retrograde amnesia. Objective tests of remote memory administered to etiologically distinct amnesic groups have distinguished between a relatively brief, that is, temporally limited, retrograde amnesia covering a few years and an extensive remote memory impairment covering several decades. This difference between kinds of retrograde amnesia cannot be explained by differences in the severity of anterograde amnesia (see Cohen & Squire, 1981). Here we consider separately these two forms of memory impairment and discuss their implications for understanding the neuropsychology of memory. The finding that retrograde amnesia can sometimes be temporally limited will be taken as support for a storage explanation of amnesia, involving a disorder of postencoding processes that normally operate to maintain and elaborate memory for a time after learning. The finding of an extensive remote memory impairment will be taken to mean that the amnesia associated with Korsakoff syndrome, and possibly other examples of diencephalic amnesia, includes a deficit that operates at the time of retrieval.

Temporally Limited Retrograde Amnesia

Clinical assessment of memory loss in patients with medial temporal lobe resections, including case H. M. (Scoville & Milner, 1957; Penfield & Milner, 1958), and in patients who have sustained severe head trauma (Russell & Nathan, 1946), has revealed brief or temporally limited retrograde amnesias that can extend from several months to a few years prior to the onset of amnesia. For example, since 1953, H. M. has exhibited a profound and persistent anterograde amnesia that has impaired dramatically his learning and memory of new material; yet his ability to recall premorbid events (i.e., events that occurred prior to the onset of his amnesia in 1953) appeared by clinical interview to be affected for only the 1 to 3 years immediately preceding his surgery. His memory for more remote time periods seemed largely unaffected (Milner *et al.*, 1968). Recent attempts to assess H. M.'s remote memory using formal tests suggest that his impairment, though still temporally limited, may, for some kinds of material, date back to the time of onset of generalized convulsions in 1942 (Corkin, Cohen, & Sagar, 1983).

In any case, formal testing has confirmed that premorbid memory is less affected than postmorbid memory. H. M.'s remote memory for the 1920s through the 1960s was assessed with a test of famous faces (Marslen-Wilson & Teuber, 1975). H. M. performed as well as did control subjects for faces from his premorbid period, 1920s–1940s, but he was markedly impaired for his postmorbid period (since the onset of his anterograde amnesia), identifying fewer than 20% of the faces from the 1950s and 1960s (Figure 1-11).

Studies of patients receiving bilateral ECT have established that temporally limited retrograde amnesia is a robust phenomenon that can be demonstrated by formal testing. In these studies, patients were tested prior to the first treatment of their series and then again an hour or more after the fifth treatment, at a time when patients can perform normally on standard tests of jects. After ECT, memory was selectively affected for events that occurred up to a few years before ECT but was intact for events that occurred prior to that time (Squire, Slater, & Chace, 1975; Squire, Chace, & Slater, 1976; Squire & Cohen, 1979b; Cohen & Squire, 1981). For example, in one test involving recall of details about former television programs (Squire & Fox,

Figure 1-11. Identification of faces of famous persons who had come into prominence in specific decades (1920–1969). Case H. M. performed as well as control subjects in recognizing faces from the premorbid period prior to his surgery in 1953 but was poor at recognizing faces that became known after that time. (From Marslen-Wilson & Teuber, 1975.)

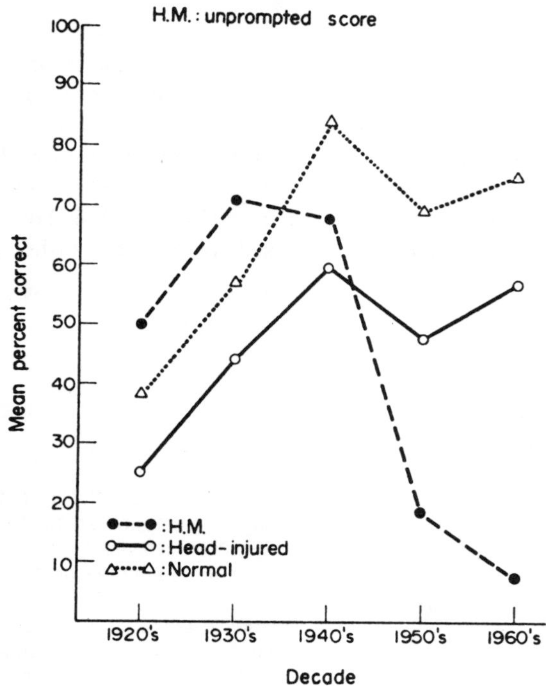

1980), amnesia was observed for programs that broadcast 1–2 years prior to ECT, but not for programs that broadcast 3–8 years prior to ECT (Squire & Cohen, 1979b; Figure 1-12). In another study, temporally limited retrograde amnesia was also elicited in a test that sampled recall of details about past public events (Cohen & Squire, 1981). These retrograde amnesias have been shown to resolve gradually during the months following treatment (Squire, Slater, & Miller, 1981).

The finding that premorbid memory can be less affected than postmorbid memory, and that retrograde amnesia can be restricted to a few years in at least some amnesic groups, has several important implications for the neuropsychology of memory. First, the relative preservation of premorbid memory confirms that the affected brain regions of these patients are not the permanent sites of memory storage. Second, the finding that memory for events of the recent past can be lost or rendered inaccessible without affecting memory for more remote events indicates that retrograde amnesia, like anterograde amnesia, need not affect all memories equally. It is not the case that memory storage is a uniform entity whose integrity can be disrupted in an all-or-none fashion by damage to medial temporal and diencephalic structures.

The latter point can be taken as confirmation of Ribot's Law (1882) that, in the dissolution of memory, "the new perishes before the old" (p. 127).

> We thus see that the progressive destruction of memory follows a logical order—a law. It advances progressively from the unstable to the stable. It begins with the most recent recollections, which, lightly impressed upon the nervous elements, rarely repeated and consequently having no permanent associations, represent organization in its feeblest form. It ends with the sensorial, instinctive memory, which, becoming a permanent and integral part of the organism, represents organization in its most highly developed stage. From the first term of the series to the last, the movement of amnesia is governed by natural forces. (p. 121)

Temporally limited retrograde amnesia suggests the existence of a normal process by which memory becomes gradually more resistant to disruption with the passage of time. We have used the term consolidation to describe this process (Squire, Cohen, & Nadel, 1984), in much the same sense that this term has been used to describe memory storage processes in experimental animals that change gradually with time after learning (McGaugh & Herz, 1972). The concept of consolidation has often been used to refer to a rather short-lasting

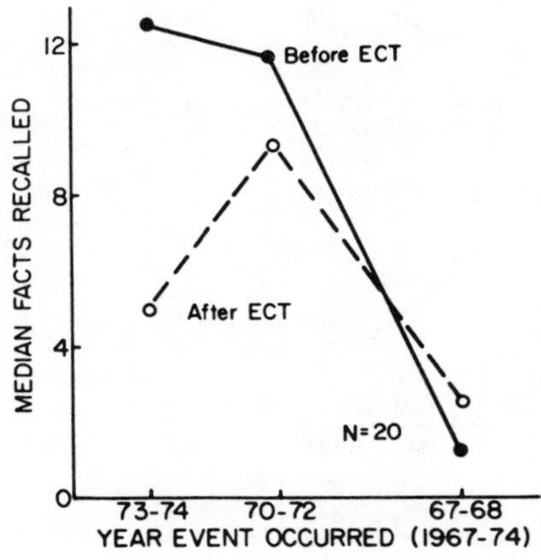

Figure 1-12. Psychiatric patients recalled everything they could remember about former, one-season television programs that began during the autumn season (1967–1974). Testing occurred during 1976. After ECT, recall was markedly impaired for programs that broadcast 1 to 2 years before treatment and not affected for programs that broadcast prior to that time. (From Squire & Cohen, 1979b.)

process during which memories become fixed in long-term memory. However, the data from experimental animals indicate only that memory changes after learning, gradually becoming less susceptible to disruption; the data do not permit an estimate of the maximal time required for this process (McGaugh & Gold, 1976). In our view, consolidation is not a process with a fixed lifetime but one that can vary over a broad time scale. A recent study of mice showed that memory could continue to change up to a period of 1 to 3 weeks after learning, and this finding appears to establish continuity with the findings from humans (Squire & Spanis, 1984).

In the case of memory for former one-season TV programs, which are remembered for years, consolidation can apparently continue for a few years after initial learning. In the case of memory for events that are forgotten much more quickly, consolidation presumably is a more rapid process. Modifications of memory that result from consolidation may occur in concert with the processes responsible for the normal forgetting of information, thereby relating the time course of consolidation to the time course of normal forgetting. The fate and time course of these processes are influenced by a number of factors during the time after learning, including rehearsal, retrieval episodes, and the learning of related materials. These considerations suggest that there develops gradually after learning a representation of the original experience that has lost detail through forgetting but the organization of which has become more abstract, schematized, and more resistant to disruption. Thus, consolidation could provide the basis for gradual reorganization and restructuring of memory (Norman & Rumelhart, 1975) and for the appearance of schemata (Bartlett, 1932; Rumelhart, 1982) that have been suggested to develop in long-term memory over time.

H. M.'s temporally limited retrograde amnesia connects these ideas about memory consolidation to the medial temporal region of the brain, as developed in detail elsewhere (Squire, Cohen, & Nadel, 1984). The medial temporal region is viewed as permitting storage and retrieval of new memories until consolidation is completed. The medial temporal region establishes a relationship with distributed memory storage sites in neocortex and perhaps elsewhere; it then maintains the coherence of these ensembles until, as a result of consolidation, they can be maintained and can support retrieval on their own. By this view, newly established memories cannot be maintained and consolidated without the participation of the medial temporal region. This region either specifies the storage sites that will become coherent as the result of consolidation or actually causes consolidation to occur through retrieval episodes or by other kinds of periodic interaction with the storage sites. These ideas and the facts of temporally limited retrograde amnesia thus make a case for the view that the amnesic deficit is due to impaired consolidation. The brain structures affected appear to constitute an essential neuroanatomic system responsible for the formation of new memories, for the maintenance and elaboration of memories for a few years after learning, and for their retrieval during the consolidation period. By considering temporally limited retrograde amnesia in this way, as resulting from the interruption of a postencoding (consolidation) process normally responsible for developing and maintaining stable memory representations, we find support for a storage interpretation of medial temporal amnesia.

Impairment of such a process leads predictably to both anterograde amnesia (rapid forgetting) and to temporally limited retrograde amnesia. In support of this idea are studies of experimental amnesia in animals (e.g., McGaugh & Herz, 1972) as well as reports of traumatic amnesia in man (Russell & Nathan, 1946) that have stressed the link between anterograde amnesia and brief retrograde amnesia. In the case of human traumatic amnesia, more severe anterograde amnesia appears to be correlated with more prolonged retrograde amnesia (Russell & Nathan, 1946; Table 1-2). Many will also recall a favorite dictum of the late Professor Teuber: "no RA [retrograde amnesia] without PTA [posttraumatic amnesia]." More recent accounts of amnesia (Wickelgren, 1979; Squire, Cohen, & Nadel, 1984) have made explicit the suggestion that the two deficits involve a common mechanism.

It is sometimes supposed that a consolidation view of any kind of amnesia is weakened or refuted by the finding that certain kinds of learning and memory are spared. However, once it is established that amnesia is a relatively selective impairment affecting only a particular kind of learning and memory (see section on Preserved Capacity for Learning and Memory in Amnesia), it should be clear that the consolidation view is meant to apply to and to provide an explanation of the impairment for only the domain of learning and memory that is impaired. Further, the consolidation view is applicable only to medial temporal amnesia. Rapid forgetting and temporally limited retrograde amnesia, the two cardinal features of medial temporal amnesia, are considered to be related deficits that appear when consolidation is affected. Diencephalic amnesia (e.g., Korsakoff syndrome) does not have these features and is not considered to reflect a deficit in consolidation.

The consolidation view has been presented here as a storage interpretation of medial temporal amnesia, that is, an interpretation of amnesia as an actual loss of some of the synaptic changes that would ordinarily subserve infor-

Table 1-2. Relationship between anterograde or posttraumatic amnesia (PTA) and retrograde amnesia (RA) in the amnesia associated with head trauma

	Duration of PTA						
Duration of RA	Nil	> 1 hr	1–24 hr	1–7 days	> 7 days	No record	Total
Nil	99	23	9	2	0	0	133
Under 30 min	—	178	274	174	80	1	707
Over 30 min	—	3	16	41	73	0	133
No record	—	4	14	14	15	9	56
Total	99	208	313	231	168	10	1029
Nil		9	1	1	—		11
1 min		34	35	15	12		96
1–30 min		6	13	21	18		58
½–12 hr		1	1	9	6		17
½–2 days		—	—	3	7		10
2–10 days		—	—	1	6		7
Over 10 days		—	—	—	1		1
Total		50	50	50	50		200

Note. The top panel shows durations of PTA and RA for 1029 cases of head injury. The bottom panel shows the same comparisons in a more detailed way, using 50 consecutive cases from each PTA group. In both comparisons, the duration of RA is positively correlated with the duration of PTA. Adapted from Russell and Nathan (1946).

mation storage. Although it is not possible to prove that a storage interpretation (as opposed to a retrieval interpretation) of medial temporal amnesia is absolutely required by the data, the kinds of retrieval explanation that have most often been applied to amnesia can be discounted by the available data. First, one might suppose that the medial temporal region is necessary in a general way for memory retrieval to succeed. However, the fact of temporally limited retrograde amnesia by itself rules out this idea. According to a general retrieval deficit view, H. M. should have difficulty in recalling all past memories, not just those that occurred since his surgery and up to a few years before his surgery.

Second, one might suppose that the medial temporal region is necessary for memory retrieval but only for retrieval of newly established memories. By this view, memory storage processes, including consolidation, proceed quite normally in the absence of the medial temporal region, but retrieval during the consolidation period depends on this region. Moreover, once consolidation is completed, memory retrieval is normal in the absence of the medial temporal region. However, if the medial temporal region were needed only to retrieve memories until they are consolidated, then H. M., who after surgery could not retrieve memories from the previous few years, should eventually have been able to do so. As time passed, and these memories became 5, 10, or 15 years old, retrieval should have become possible. To explain why these memories do not eventually become available to recall, it is necessary to postulate that many years after learning, when the medial temporal region is no longer needed for recall, these memories have become different in some way from normal memories. Presumably, some kind of interaction between memory storage sites and the medial temporal region is needed during consolidation, or else memories become unavailable. The need to postulate a difference in the status of these memories, one which develops during the retention interval, signifies the need for a storage interpretation of amnesia.

Storage and retrieval interpretations of both normal memory phenomena and amnesia have been a major topic of discussion for many years. This discussion seems appropriate because of the fundamentally different ideas about memory and the brain that follow from the various interpretations. In the end, direct neurobiological evidence concerning what neural events and synaptic changes do and do not occur at the time of learning and during consolidation may be the only kind of evidence that can settle these important issues satisfactorily.

The foregoing discussion has documented that retrograde amnesia can be temporally limited and has considered the importance of this phenomenon to issues of memory and amnesia. There is a second form of retrograde amnesia—in particular, as seen in Korsakoff syndrome—that is strikingly severe and extensive. This form of impairment is the subject of the next section.

Extensive Remote-Memory Impairment

Patients with Korsakoff syndrome exhibit a severe and extensive impairment of remote memory that affects the majority of their adult lives. This impairment has been demonstrated in several Korsakoff populations with different memory tests (Sanders & Warrington, 1971; Seltzer & Benson, 1974; Marslen-Wilson & Teuber, 1975; Albert, Butters, & Levin, 1979; Meudell, Northern, Snowden,

& Neary, 1980; Cohen & Squire, 1981). The impairment typically is temporally graded, affecting recent time periods to a greater extent than more remote time periods. For example, in one series of seven remote-memory tests (Cohen & Squire, 1981), patients with Korsakoff syndrome demonstrated on six tests a more pronounced impairment for recent time periods than for more remote time periods. Moreover, on each test the impairment extended to and included the most remote time period sampled. Figure 1-13 illustrates a typical finding, in a case where the same test of memory for famous faces was given to Korsakoff populations in both Boston (Albert *et al.*, 1980) and San Diego (Cohen & Squire, 1981).

In order to interpret the extensive remote-memory impairment observed in patients with Korsakoff syndrome, it is essential to consider its relationship to the accompanying anterograde amnesia. A simple view of memory dysfunction might suppose that the brain lesions causing the most severe impairment of new learning also cause the most severe or most extensive impairment of remote memory. Indeed, in the case of closed head injury, more severe anterograde amnesia correlates with more prolonged retrograde amnesia (Russell & Nathan, 1946). However, the evidence indicates that the remote-memory impairment observed in Korsakoff syndrome is distinct from brief retrograde amnesia and dissociable, at least in part, from anterograde amnesia. Consider patient H. M., for example, who has a profound anterograde amnesia for events that have occurred since his surgery in 1953. In a study comparing H. M. and patients with Korsakoff syndrome on remote memory for famous faces (Marslen-Wilson & Teuber, 1975), H. M.'s score for the 1960s was worse than that

Figure 1-13. Performance on the same remote-memory test for famous faces (Albert, Butters, & Levin, 1979) by patients with Korsakoff syndrome in Boston (A) and San Diego (B). The absolute level of performance is difficult to compare, as the cueing procedure used was somewhat different in each case. For A, cueing was by phonetic and circumstantial prompts. For B, cueing was by yes–no recognition and multiple choice. In both cases, the remote-memory impairment exhibited by patients with Korsakoff syndrome was extensive and graded. (From Albert, Butters, & Levin, 1980; Cohen & Squire, 1981.)

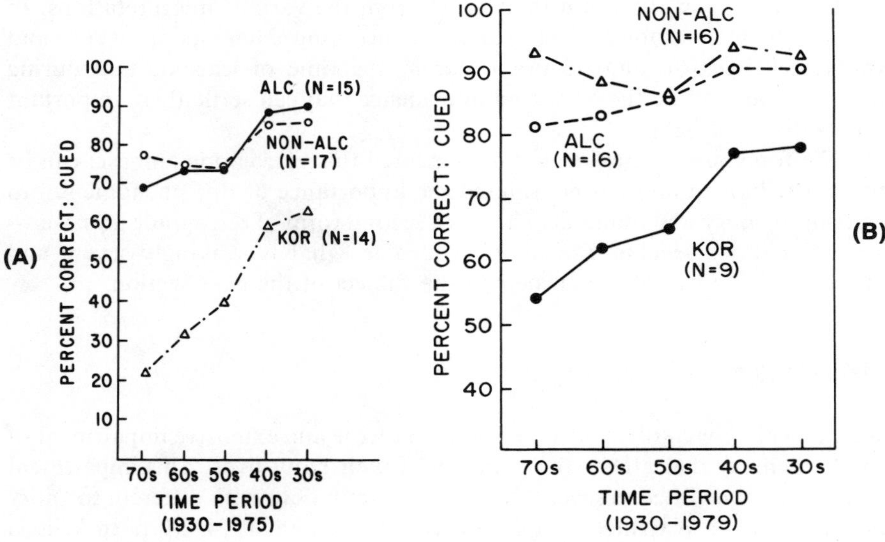

exhibited by patients with Korsakoff syndrome, yet his score for the 1930s and 1940s was markedly better. That is, although H. M. showed a greater deficit than patients with Korsakoff syndrome for material that was learned subsequent to his surgery (during his period of anterograde amnesia), he was considerably less affected than patients with Korsakoff syndrome for material that was learned prior to his surgery (i.e., during the retrograde period). This comparison indicates that anterograde amnesia and remote-memory impairment are not linked in amnesia. However, considering what is now known about differences between kinds of amnesia, one could accept these data but suppose that the link between anterograde amnesia and remote-memory impairment holds true within diencephalic amnesia.

Our work with case N. A. and patients with Korsakoff syndrome addresses this possibility. Whereas N. A. and the patients with Korsakoff syndrome scored comparably on four tests of new-learning capacity, the patients with Korsakoff syndrome demonstrated a more extensive impairment than N. A. on seven different tests of remote memory (Cohen & Squire, 1981). Recently, we have also shown that even within the Korsakoff population, the severity of anterograde amnesia cannot account for the severity of the remote-memory impairment (Shimamura & Squire, 1984). Hence, the severity of anterograde amnesia can provide no explanation for examples of amnesia, like Korsakoff syndrome, in which remote memory is grossly affected. Accordingly, the extensive remote-memory impairment of Korsakoff syndrome appears not to be coupled inextricably to anterograde amnesia; in this respect Korsakoff syndrome differs from the other examples of amnesia that have been considered here.

Although the severity of anterograde amnesia cannot explain the extensiveness of the remote-memory impairment in Korsakoff syndrome, anterograde amnesia can explain the pattern of remote-memory impairment, that is, the temporally graded deficit. The presence in chronic alcoholics of information-processing deficits (Parker & Nobel, 1977; Ryan, Butters, & Montgomery, 1980), together with an impairment on only the more recent time periods of remote-memory tests (Butters & Albert, 1982; Cohen & Squire, 1981; e.g., Figure 1-13), suggests that with continued drinking chronic alcoholics gradually lose ground to nonalcoholic control subjects with respect to their ability to recall recent public events. Accordingly, after years of alcohol abuse, the patient with Korsakoff syndrome (who develops a more severe impairment of new-learning capacity than does the alcoholic) would be expected to demonstrate an amnesia for public events that is more severe for recent events than for more remote events. By this view, that portion of the remote-memory impairment that is temporally graded could well be due to progressive anterograde amnesia that develops over a period of decades.

The fact that only a portion of the remote-memory performance of the Korsakoff patients is temporally graded (1950–1979; see Figure 1-13) suggests that anterograde amnesia is not the basis for the entire remote-memory impairment. The same point follows from the observation that for many patients the remote-memory impairment extends to a time in their lives before they began to drink. This idea has now been directly confirmed by careful study of a single Korsakoff patient who had written an autobiography only a few years prior to testing (N. Butters, personal communication). The patient's family reported that the onset of severe memory problems occurred after writing the autobiography. Formal testing confirmed that this patient in many instances claimed no knowledge of persons and events that (1) had been included in the autobiography and (2) had been familiar to the patient during his career. These important observations make clear that remote-memory impairment in Korsakoff syndrome can include a true retrograde amnesia, that is, an effect on memories that had been acquired previously.

These considerations lead to questions about the neurologic basis of retrograde amnesia in this patient group. Is the extensive remote-memory impairment exhibited by Korsakoff patients due to the diencephalic lesions that have been associated with their amnesia? Or does extensive remote-memory impairment require additional deficits and additional brain damage beyond diencephalic lesions? One way to address these questions is to assess remote memory in patients with amnesia due to circumscribed diencephalic lesions. Case N. A., who has a lesion in the region of the left dorsomedial thalamus has been evaluated repeatedly with tests of remote memory. His amnesia for verbal material is as severe as that of the San Diego Korsakoff population (Cohen & Squire, 1981), but his remote-memory impairment is considerably less severe. Similarly, two recent cases of diencephalic amnesia due to vascular injury revealed only mild retrograde amnesia (Speedie & Heilman, 1982; Michel, Laurent, Foyatier, Blanc, & Portafaix, 1982). These results suggest that at least a part of the severe and extensive remote-memory impairment associated with Korsakoff syndrome is due to deficits not present in other available examples of diencephalic amnesia. Although the possible contribution of such deficits to remote-memory impairment has not been explored experimentally, they could contribute uniformly to a remote-memory impairment across time periods.

This view leads to the expectation that for the amnesic patients in whom remote-memory dysfunction can be demonstrated, additional deficits would be detectable by careful neuropsychological examination. Some support for this view can be found in a study of brain stimulation (Fedio & Van Buren, 1974). Stimulation of left anterior temporal lobe electrode placements in human beings undergoing neurosurgery tended to produce amnesia for material that was learned during the stimulation (i.e., anterograde amnesia), without producing much difficulty in naming (anomia) or in recalling material that was learned prior to stimulation (i.e., retrograde amnesia), whereas stimulation of more posterior temporal–parietal electrode placements produced anomia and errors for previously learned material, without producing much anterograde amnesia. Although these findings reflected relative rather than absolute differences, they nonetheless raise the possibility that some forms of remote-memory loss might be tied to disturbances of language and not to anterograde amnesia.

Although language disturbances are not obvious in Korsakoff syndrome and cannot account for the extensive remote-memory impairment, the possible relationship between remote-memory capacity and other cognitive capacities is only beginning to be explored. For example, postencephalitic patients, who have anterograde amnesia as a result of damage to the temporal lobe (Drachman & Adams, 1962), often have additional damage to other brain regions such as cingulate gyrus and posterior orbital frontal cortex (e.g., Brierley, 1977); they exhibit remote-memory impairment that can be relatively brief (Cohen & Corkin, unpublished observations; Rose & Symonds, 1960) or can be very extensive (Albert *et al.*, 1980; Rose & Symonds, 1960). In one study (Albert *et al.*, 1980), three postencephalitic patients with anomia exhibited an extensive remote-memory impairment that, like the impairment seen in patients with

Korsakoff syndrome, covered the majority of their adult lives. The link between language disturbances and remote-memory impairment must be considered as only tentative. It nonetheless supports the possibility of a relationship between remote-memory impairment and cognitive deficits.

If the severe remote-memory impairment associated with Korsakoff syndrome is due in part to additional deficits that do not always occur in amnesia, what can be said about retrograde amnesia or remote-memory impairment in case N. A. and in other more circumscribed cases of diencephalic amnesia? On six of eight remote-memory tests given to N. A., he performed normally for the premorbid period (Cohen & Squire, 1981; Zola-Morgan, Cohen, & Squire, 1983). On clinical examination, he appeared to have some retrograde amnesia covering a period of perhaps 6 months prior to his accident in 1960. This originally gave us the impression that N. A. had a relatively limited retrograde amnesia (Squire & Cohen, 1982; Cohen & Squire, 1981). But on two tests, both asking for detailed recall about events prior to 1960, N.A. produced less material across all time periods tested than control subjects (Cohen & Squire, 1981; Zola-Morgan, Cohen, & Squire, 1983). For two other diencephalic amnesic patients, retrograde amnesia was considered to have been absent or mild (Speedie & Heilman, 1982; Michel *et al.,* 1982). But these patients were not assessed with test instruments such as those that revealed a deficit in case N. A.

Accordingly, it is possible that diencephalic amnesia is associated with a mild but extensive remote-memory impairment. This conclusion cannot be considered a strong one, however, until patients who have become amnesic only recently are assessed with sensitive remote-memory tests. The problem is that N. A. became amnesic in 1960 at the age of 22. It is possible that his prolonged anterograde amnesia has prevented him from adding to or reorganizing memories about events that occurred before 1960. To the extent that normal subjects add to, rehearse, or otherwise reorganize old memories, and thereby strengthen them over the years, N. A. might become progressively disadvantaged in comparison to normal subjects. If this were true, then his deficit on the two most sensitive tests of remote memory would reflect his anterograde amnesia and not retrograde amnesia at all.

On the other hand, the presence of some degree of remote-memory impairment in diencephalic amnesia is consistent with the notions about this form of amnesia developed earlier in this review (section on Amnesia as an Encoding Deficit). By this view, diencephalic amnesia reflects a deficit at both encoding and at retrieval. Note that this view predicts that memory should be measurably better, though not normal, for events that occurred before the onset of amnesia than for events that occurred after the onset of amnesia. Memory acquired before the onset of amnesia was encoded normally, and now the only problem would be in retrieving it. For memories acquired after the onset of amnesia, there would be a problem in both encoding and retrieval.

To summarize these points, the extent and graded pattern of remote memory impairment in Korsakoff syndrome suggests a role for two factors: (1) progressive anterograde amnesia, which exerts a greater effect on memory for recent events than on memory for remote events, and could explain that portion of the impairment that is temporally graded; and (2) additional deficits that affect in a uniform way across time periods the ability to reconstruct past memories and that could explain the extensiveness of remote-memory impairment. Patients with more circumscribed diencephalic amnesia, such as case N. A., have less severe remote-memory impairment than patients with Korsakoff syndrome, but it remains unclear whether they have no retrograde impairment at all or a mild impairment affecting most of remote memory.

A Pluralistic View of Amnesia

Taken together, the available data suggest that temporally limited retrograde amnesia and extensive remote-memory impairment appear as distinct entities. Brief retrograde amnesia has been demonstrated most clearly in the amnesia associated with bilateral ECT, but it seems reasonable to conclude that it is present as well in case H. M. and in some postencephalitic cases. Extensive remote-memory impairment has been clearly and repeatedly demonstrated in Korsakoff syndrome. Presumably, a severe and extensive remote-memory impairment is related to the involvement of brain regions outside the areas affected in cases H. M. and N. A., who do not exhibit this particular deficit. Thus, for medial temporal amnesia, remote-memory impairment would imply damage to areas beyond the medial temporal region. The postencephalitic patients who do exhibit remote-memory impairment are presumably examples of this circumstance. For diencephalic amnesia, remote-memory impairment would imply damage to areas beyond the dorsal thalamus. The patients with Korsakoff syndrome are an example of this circumstance. Whereas temporally limited retrograde amnesia suggests a deficit in postencoding processes that normally operate during the time after learning, extensive remote-memory impairment suggests a deficit in memory retrieval mechanisms operating at the time of retention testing.

Finally, the fact that temporally limited retrograde amnesia, but not extensive remote-memory impairment, has been correlated to the severity of anterograde amnesia has important implications for theories of amnesia. That is, the link in some forms of the amnesic syndrome between the extent of (temporally limited) retrograde amnesia and severity of anterograde amnesia has provided support for storage explanations of the memory disorder in these patients, in that both kinds of memory deficit in such cases can be explained by a hypothesized disorder of postencoding processes that normally operate on stored information for a time after learning (see section on Amnesia as a Storage Deficit). Conversely, in other forms of amnesia, the link between the extent of (temporally unlimited) remote-memory impairment and the severity of anterograde amnesia is less clear. In patients of this type, a disorder of retrieval mechanisms that normally operate at the time of retention testing is implicated by the extensive impairment of remote memory; but until a relationship between extensive remote-memory impairment and anterograde amnesia can be clearly demonstrated, such a retrieval disorder cannot be assumed to account for the anterograde memory deficit. If there were no relationship, patients who exhibit extensive remote-memory impairment must have separate deficits in more than one stage of information processing: in both retrieval processes and either encoding processes (e.g., patients with Korsakoff syndrome) or storage processes (e.g., some postencephalitic patients). In view of the importance of these issues for theories of amnesia, the precise relationship between remote-memory impairment and anterograde amnesia deserves further study.

Information about which brain structures must be damaged to produce amnesia is as important as understanding the nature of the syndrome. Identifying which brain structures are involved provides a link between structure and function and sets the stage for more detailed neurobiological study.

Until recently, most of what was known about the specific brain structures damaged in amnesia came from human neuropathological cases and from surgical reports or radiographic evidence for patients who continue to be tested. Yet it has also been recognized that the surest and most direct way to obtain this information would be to establish a model of the human amnesic syndrome in the monkey. In the last few years, suitable tasks for testing memory in the monkey have been identified, and impairments following lesions have been described that resemble human amnesia in important ways.

Several tasks are now available that appear to test memory just as it can be tested in human patients. The best studied of these is trial unique, delayed non-matching to sample (Gaffan, 1974; Mishkin & Delacour, 1975). The monkey first sees a novel object, which he displaces to obtain food. Then, seconds, minutes, or even hours later, the monkey sees two objects side by side—the original one and a new one. The food is always under the new object. Normal monkeys can demonstrate retention on this task across long intervals. Another useful paradigm is the concurrent learning test (Correll & Scoville, 1965; Moss, Mahut, & Zola-Morgan, 1981), in which the monkey is given several pairs of objects a few times each day (e.g., eight pairs five times each, for 40 trials per day). One member of the pair is always correct, and the monkey learns over several days to choose the correct member of each pair. In trial-unique association learning (Gaffan, 1974), the monkey sees two objects in succession, only one of which is rewarded. Then after a delay, the monkey sees the same two objects side by side and must choose the object that was previously associated with reward.

Using tasks like these, considerable headway has been made toward identifying which brain regions must be damaged to produce amnesia (for reviews, see Mishkin, 1982; Squire & Zola-Morgan, 1983; Figure 1-14). In the case of medial temporal amnesia, Mishkin (1978) suggested that conjoint hippocampus–amygdala damage may be required to produce amnesia. Although the hippocampus and the amygdala were removed in the famous case H. M., it had been widely assumed for a number of reasons that damage to hippocampus was solely responsible for the amnesia in his case. Using the delayed non-matching-to-sample task, Mishkin reported, however, that monkeys with separate hippocampal or amygdala damage were only mildly and equivalently impaired. Only monkeys with combined removal of both structures exhibited a severe impairment. An impairment following combined lesions also appeared in the tactile modality, suggesting that the impairment is modality-general in the monkey, just as it is in human beings (Murray & Mishkin, 1981).

There are other reports, however, indicating that hippocampal lesions alone can produce a decided impairment in memory as measured by concurrent learning (Moss *et al.*, 1981), retention of simple object discriminations (Mahut, Moss, & Zola-Morgan, 1981), and even delayed non-matching-to-sample (Mahut, Zola-Morgan, & Moss, 1982). In the only recent study other than Mishkin's (1978) report that compared monkeys with combined lesions of hippocampus

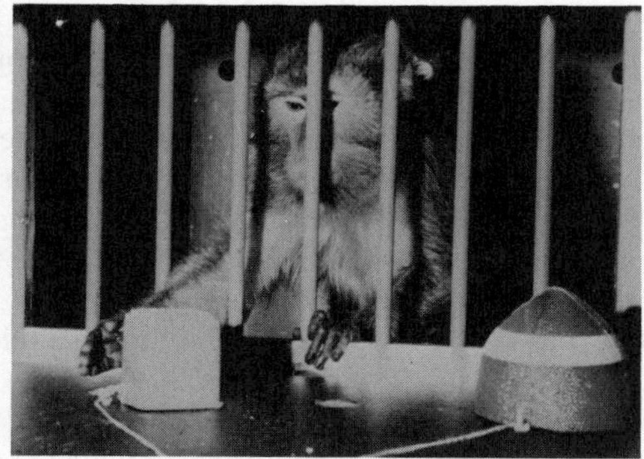

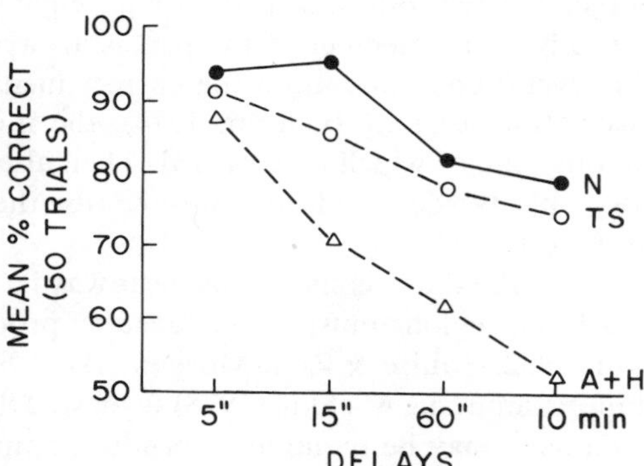

Figure 1-14. The delayed non-matching-to-sample task, which tests memory in monkeys just as it can be tested in human amnesic patients. Top: The monkey displaces a single object, presented alone, to obtain a raisin reward. Middle: After a delay, which can vary from seconds to hours, the monkey sees the original object and a novel one. The monkey must displace the novel object to find a raisin reward. A different pair of objects is used on every trial. Bottom: Performance on delayed non-matching-to-sample by normal monkeys (N), monkeys with conjoint amygdala-hippocampal lesions (A+H), and monkeys with lesions of temporal stem (TS). The A+H group was severely impaired. The TS group did not differ from normal. (From Zola-Morgan, Squire, & Mishkin, 1982.)

and amygdala to monkeys with hippocampal lesions, the two groups were equivalently and severely impaired (Mahut *et al.*, 1981). Further studies of this important issue are needed across several tasks, and with histological verification of lesions to ensure that the lesions are both circumscribed and complete.

One idea about medial temporal amnesia that can now be ruled out is the suggestion that the temporal stem, and not the hippocampus or the amygdala, is the critical brain region that must be damaged to produce amnesia (Horel, 1978). The temporal stem is a band of white matter overlying the hippocampus, said to have been damaged inadvertently in case H. M. and in similar cases. Work with monkeys has discounted this idea by showing that (1) temporal stem lesions do not cause amnesia (Zola-Morgan, Squire, & Mishkin, 1982); (2) conjoint hippocampal–amygdala lesions that do not include temporal stem nevertheless do cause amnesia (Zola-Morgan *et al.*, 1982; Figure 1-14); and (3) separate hippocampal lesions that do not include temporal stem can cause amnesia (Moss *et al.*, 1981). Current evidence also minimizes the role in memory of the fornix, a major efferent tract of the hippocampal formation (Zola-Morgan, Dabrowska, Moss, & Mahut, 1983; Moss *et al.*, 1981; Mahut *et al.*, 1982). Fornix sections in the monkey can cause deficits in memory (Gaffan, 1974), but where they have been compared to hippocampal lesions, the effects of fornix section on memory have been considerably less than the effects of hippocampal lesions (for reviews see Squire & Zola-Morgan, 1983; Mahut *et al.*, 1982).

Diencephalic amnesia has not yet been addressed comprehensively in monkey studies. Lesions of dorsomedial nucleus do cause memory deficits on delayed non-matching-to-sample tasks (Aggleton & Mishkin, 1983; Zola-Morgan & Squire, 1982). It is not yet clear how lesions of mammillary bodies, another structure prominent in the human neuropathological literature, affect performance on this task. The experimental approach now available for monkeys should permit the present uncertainty about the role of dorsomedial nucleus and mammillary bodies, and about the possible role of other diencephalic structures, to be resolved in the next few years.

The finding that the domain of the memory impairment in human amnesia is more limited than was once believed (section on Preserved Capacity for Learning and Memory in Amnesia) makes it easier to understand why the development of an animal model has been difficult. It is only recently that tasks suitable for the detection of amnesia in the monkey have been constructed. At the same time, other tasks that might originally have seemed to test memory in an appropriate way now appear to depend substantially on skill learning and thus cannot be expected to be sensitive to amnesia. One example of such a task is visual-pattern-discrimination learning, which can require hundreds of trials and many daily sessions to learn. Though this task requires retaining information from day to day and might seem to involve the kind of memory capacity that is impaired in human amnesia, monkeys with hippocampal–amygdala lesions can acquire this task at an almost normal rate. Iversen (1976) first suggested that this task shared certain similarities with motor learning in man and should not be expected to be impaired in monkeys with medial temporal lesions.

Recently, it was suggested that pattern-discrimination learning involves a substantial skill-like component, that is, the gradual tuning in and identification of the correct stimulus dimension; this component was argued to be spared after medial temporal lesions (Zola-Morgan & Squire, 1984). The remaining component, that is, remembering which stimulus is the correct one, is impaired by medial temporal lesions. Two pieces of evidence were consistent with this point of view. First, human pattern-discrimination learning and retention, which is not incremental and which is acquired as a simple fact (i.e., which stimulus is correct) and not as a skill, is impaired in human amnesia (Squire & Zola-Morgan, unpublished observations). Second, when the monkey discrimination task was simplified by making the two stimuli so distinctive that they were readily discriminated, as in human discrimination learning, monkeys with medial temporal lesions exhibited a severe impairment (Zola-Morgan & Squire, 1984).

These findings suggest that a rapprochement between the facts of human amnesia and the results of studies with operated monkeys may be close at hand. Tasks appropriate for experimental animals have been identified that are sensitive to human amnesia and that reveal a deficit in operated monkeys. Other tasks that are substantially skill-like, which depend either on perceptual–motor skills or on perceptual skills (Zola-Morgan & Squire, 1984), can be performed well by the same monkeys. With this approach it should be possible to identify precisely those brain regions that must be damaged to produce amnesia.

COMMENT

We began with the intention of describing the learning processes and memory systems, the neurobiological substrates of which are the subject of this volume. Consideration of the amnesic syndrome has permitted us to address some fundamental questions about the nature of memory, its organization, and its localization in the brain. What clearly emerges from this inquiry—what is perhaps the major contribution of the study of amnesia to our understanding of learning and memory—is the view that memory is not a monolithic entity but a more complex function dependent on multiple brain structures and a set of processes that under favorable circumstances can be identified, dissociated, and analyzed.

Memory pathology occurs in various forms that affect different memory processes. One form of amnesia (medial temporal amnesia) is associated with an abnormally rapid rate of forgetting and a temporally limited retrograde amnesia. This form is proposed to reflect a disorder of storage or postencoding processes that ordinarily operate during the time after learning to maintain and elaborate memory. Another form of amnesia (diencephalic amnesia) is associated with impoverished stimulus analysis (but a normal rate of forgetting) and extensive remote-memory impairment. This form is proposed to reflect disorders of both encoding and retrieval processes that ordinarily operate at the time of learning and at the time of retention. Since the severity of remote-memory impairment cannot be explained by the severity of anterograde amnesia, these disorders appear to be separate and unrelated, at least to some extent.

The nature of memory pathology indicates that the information stored in memory is not all of the same type, but belongs to different categories. For example, rather than preventing all new learning, both medial temporal and diencephalic amnesia selectively impairs the acquisition of what has been termed "knowing that." What has been termed "knowing how" can be acquired normally in those forms of amnesia that have been studied. Similarly, retrograde amnesia need not extend to all past memories but can affect memory for recent events without affecting memory for more remote events.

The facts of temporally limited retrograde amnesia indicate that, after initial learning, memory continues to change over a time span as long as 1 to 3 years so as to become gradually more resistant to disruption. The brain regions damaged in amnesia appear to be essential to memory during the time when these changes are occurring. Memory must eventually acquire a different form or be incorporated into cognitive structures that do not require the support of these brain regions.

The facts of temporally limited retrograde amnesia also indicate that memory is not actually stored in the regions of the brain where damage causes amnesia. Instead, these brain regions appear to be specialized for the formation of new memories and for their maintenance and elaboration after learning, in a way that permits successful retrieval. The sites of permanent memory storage are elsewhere in the brain.

Impaired memory performance can result not only from damage to brain systems specialized for learning and memory functions but also from damage to other cognitive systems that ordinarily interact with these brain systems. Patients with Korsakoff syndrome, for example, often have damage to areas of the brain in addition to damage in the regions critical for amnesia, and such damage (e.g., to the frontal lobes) seems to superimpose on amnesia cognitive deficits that affect performance on some tests of learning and memory.

Studies of memory in nonhuman primates, with surgical lesions of those brain regions implicated in human amnesia, suggest that a rapprochement between the findings for monkey and man is close at hand. Tasks are now available for the monkeys that also reveal a deficit in human amnesic patients, and monkeys with medial temporal or diencephalic lesions are impaired on these same tasks.

Study of the amnesic syndrome has led to new understanding of the organization of memory and its biological foundations, particularly insofar as brain structures specialized for memory functions have been identified, different kinds of memory have been dissociated, and the processes that operate on these memories have been analyzed. This kind of scientific inquiry should continue to instruct us about how the brain accomplishes learning and memory.

ACKNOWLEDGMENTS

This work was supported by the Medical Research Service of the Veterans Administration and by NIMH Grant MH24600. We thank Drs. Stuart Zola-Morgan, Lynn Nadel, and Mary Jo Nissen for critical discussions of the issues considered here, and Elizabeth Leonard for manuscript preparation.

REFERENCES

Aggleton, J. P., & Mishkin, M. Visual recognition impairment following medial thalamic lesions in monkeys. *Neuropsychologia*, 1983, *21*, 189–197.

Albert, M. S., Butters, N., & Levin, J. Temporal gradients in the retrograde amnesia of patients with alcoholic Korsakoff's disease. *Archives of Neurology*, 1979, *36*, 211–216.

Albert, M. S., Butters, N., & Levin, J. Memory for remote events in chronic alcoholics and alcoholic Korsakoff patients. In H. Begleiter (Ed.), *Advances in experimental medicine and biology: Biological effects of alcohol* (Vol. 126). New York: Plenum Press, 1980.

Anderson, J. R. *Cognitive psychology and its implications.* San Francisco: Freeman, 1980.

Anzai, V., & Simon, H. A. The theory of learning by doing. *Psychological Review*, 1979, *86*, 124–140.

Baddeley, A. Amnesia: a minimal model and an interpretation. In L. Cermak (Ed.), *Human memory and amnesia.* Hillsdale, N.J.: Erlbaum, 1982. (a)

Baddeley, A. Implications of neuropsychological evidence for theories of normal memory. In D. E. Broadbent & L. Weiskrantz (Eds.), *Philosophical transactions of the Royal Society of London* (Vol. 298). London: The Royal Society, 1982. (b)

Barbizet, J. *Human memory and its pathology.* San Francisco: Freeman, 1970.

Bartlett, F. C. *Remembering.* Cambridge: Cambridge University, 1932.

Benson, D. F., Marsden, C. D., & Meadows, J. C. The amnesic syndrome of posterior cerebral artery occlusion. *Acta Neurologica Scandinavia*, 1974, *50*, 133–145.

Blakemore, C. Developmental factors in the formation of feature extracting neurons. In F. O. Schmitt & F. G. Worden (Eds.), *The neurosciences: Third study program.* Cambridge, Mass.: MIT Press, 1974.

Brierley, J. B. Neuropathology of amnesic states. In C. W. M. Whitty & O. L. Zangwill (Eds.), *Amnesia* (2nd ed.). London: Butterworths, 1977.

Brion, S., & Mikol, J. Atteinte du noyau latéral dorsal du thalamus et syndrome de Korsakoff alcoolique. *Journal of the Neurological Sciences,* 1978, *38*, 249–261.

Brooks, D. N., & Baddeley, A. What can amnesic patients learn? *Neuropsychologia*, 1976, *14*, 111–122.

Bruner, J. S. Modalities of memory. In G. A. Talland & N. C. Waugh (Eds.), *The pathology of memory.* New York: Academic Press, 1969.

Butters, M., & Albert, M. S. Processes underlying failures to recall remote events. In L. Cermak (Ed.), *Human memory and amnesia.* Hillsdale, N.J.: Erlbaum, 1982.

Butters, N., & Cermak, L. S. Some analyses of amnesic syndromes in brain-damaged patients. In R. L. Isaacson & K. H. Pribram (Eds.), *The hippocampus.* New York: Plenum Press, 1975.

Butters, N., & Cermak, L. S. *Alcoholic Korsakoff's syndrome: An information processing approach to amnesia.* New York: Academic Press, 1980.

Cermak, L. S. The encoding capacity of patients with amnesia due to encephalitis. *Neuropsychologia*, 1976, *14*, 311–326.

Cermak, L. S. Amnesic patients' level of processing. In L. S. Cermak & F. I. M. Craik (Eds.), *Levels of processing in human memory.* Hillsdale, N.J.: Erlbaum, 1979.

Cermak, L. S. (Ed.). *Human memory and amnesia.* Hillsdale, N.J.: Erlbaum, 1982.

Cermak, L. S., Butters, N., & Moreines, J. Some analyses of the verbal encoding deficit of alcoholic Korsakoff patients. *Brain and Language*, 1974, *1*, 141–150.

Cermak, L. S., Lewis, R., Butters, N., & Goodglass, H. Role of verbal mediation in performance of motor tasks by Korsakoff patients. *Perceptual and Motor Skills*, 1973, *37*, 259–262.

Cermak, L. S., & Reale, L. Depth of processing and retention of words by alcoholic Korsakoff patients. *Journal of Experimental Psychology: Human Learning and Memory*, 1978, *4*, 165–174.

Claparède, E. Récognition et moiité. *Archives of Psychology* (Geneva), 1911, *11*, 79–90.

Cohen, N. J. *Neuropsychological evidence for a distinction between procedural and declarative knowledge in human memory and amnesia.* PhD thesis, University of California at San Diego, 1981.

Cohen, N. J. Preserved learning capacity in amnesia: Evidence for multiple memory systems. In L. R. Squire & N. Butters (Eds.),*Neuropsychology of memory.* New York: Guilford Press, 1984.

Cohen, N. J., & Corkin. S. The amnesic patient, H. M.: Learning and retention of a cognitive skill. *Society for Neuroscience Abstracts*, 1981, *7*, 235.

Cohen, N. J., & Corkin, S. Chronic global amnesia after ruptured aneurysms of the anterior communicating artery. *Society for Neuroscience Abstracts,* 1982, *8*, 25.

Cohen, N. J., & Squire, L. R. Preserved learning and retention of pattern analyzing skill in amnesia: Dissociation of knowing how and knowing that. *Science*, 1980, *210*, 207–209.

Cohen, N. J., & Squire, L. R. Retrograde amnesia and remote memory impairment. *Neuropsychologia*, 1981, *19*, 337–356.

Corkin, S. Tactually-guided maze-learning in man: Effects of unilateral cortical excisions and bilateral hippocampal lesions. *Neuropsychologia*, 1965, *3*, 339–351.

Corkin, S. Acquisition of motor skill after bilateral medial temporal lobe excision. *Neuropsychologia*, 1968, *6*, 255–265.

Corkin, S., Cohen, N. J., & Sagar, H. J. Memory for remote personal and public events after bilateral medial temporal lobectomy. *Society for Neuroscience Abstracts*, 1983, *9*, 28.

Correll, R. E., & Scoville, W. B. Effects of medial temporal lesions on visual discrimination performance. *Journal of Comparative and Physiological Psychology*, 1965, *60*, 175–181.

Corsi, P. M. *Human memory and the medial temporal region of the brain*. Unpublished PhD dissertation, McGill University, 1972.

Craik, F. I. M., & Tulving, E. Depth of processing and the retention of words in episodic memory. *Journal of Experimental Psychology: General*, 1975, *104*, 268–294.

DeLuca, D., Cermak, L. S., & Butters, N. An analysis of Korsakoff patients' recall following varying types of distractor activity. *Neuropsychologia*, 1975, *13*, 271–279.

Diamond, R., & Carey, S. Developmental changes in the representation of faces. *Journal of Experimental Child Psychology*, 1977, *23*, 1–22.

Drachman, D. A., & Adams, R. D. Herpes simplex and acute-inclusion body encephalitis. *Archives of Neurology*, 1962, *7*, 45–63.

Drachman, D. A., & Arbit, J. Memory and the hippocampal complex. *Archives of Neurology*, 1966, *15*, 52–61.

Dricker, J., Butters, N., Berman, G., Samuels, I., & Carey, S. The recognition and encoding of faces by alcoholic Korsakoff and right hemisphere patients. *Neuropsychologia*, 1978, *16*, 683–695.

Fedio, P., & Van Buren, J. M. Memory deficits during electrical stimulation in the speech cortex of conscious man. *Brain and Language*, 1974, *1*, 29–42.

Freud, S. S. *Civilization and its discontents* (*Standard Edition*, Vol. 21). London: Hogarth Press, 1930.

Gabrieli, J. D. E., Cohen, N. J., & Corkin, S. Acquisition of semantic and lexical knowledge in amnesia. *Society for Neuroscience Abstracts*, 1983, *9*, 28.

Gaffan, D. Recognition impaired and association intact in the memory of monkeys after transection of the fornix. *Journal of Comparative and Physiological Psychology*, 1974, *86*, 1100–1109.

Graf, P., Squire, L. R., & Mandler, G. The information that amnesic patients do not forget. *Journal of Experimental Psychology: Learning, Memory, and Cognition*, 1984, *10*, 164–178.

Hirsch, H. V. B., & Spinelli, D. N. Visual experience modifies distribution of horizontally and vertically oriented receptive fields in cats. *Science*, 1970, *168*, 869–871.

Hirst, W. The amnesic syndrome: Descriptions and explanations. *Psychological Bulletin*, 1982, *91*, 435–462.

Hirst, W., & Volpe, B. T. Temporal order judgments with amnesia. *Brain and Cognition*, 1982, *1*, 294–306.

Horel, J. A. The neuroanatomy of amnesia: A critique of the hippocampal memory hypothesis. *Brain*, 1978, *101*, 403–445.

Huppert, F. A., & Piercy, M. Recognition memory in amnesic patients: Effect of temporal context and familiarity of material. *Cortex*, 1976, *12*, 3–20.

Huppert, F. A., & Piercy, M. Dissociation between learning and remembering in organic amnesia. *Nature*, 1978, *275*, 317–318.

Huppert, F. A., & Piercy, M. Normal and abnormal forgetting in organic amnesia: Effect of locus of lesion. *Cortex*, 1979, *15*, 385–390.

Inglis, J. Shock, surgery, and cerebral symmetry. *British Journal of Psychiatry*, 1970, *117*, 143–148.

Iversen, S. D. Do hippocampal lesions produce amnesia in animals? *International Review of Neurobiology*, 1976, *19*, 1–49.

Jacoby, L. L. Perceptual enhancement: Persistent effects of an experience. *Journal of Experimental Psychology: Learning, Memory, and Cognition*, 1983, *9*, 21–38.

Jacoby, L. L., & Craik, F. I. M. Effects of elaboration of processing at encoding and retrieval: Trace distinctiveness and recovery of initial context. In L. S. Cermak & F. I M. Craik (Eds.), *Levels of processing in human memory*. Hillsdale, N.J.: Erlbaum, 1979.

Jacoby, L. L., & Dallas, M. On the relationship between autobiographical memory and perceptual learning. *Journal of Experimental Psychology: General*, 1981, *3*, 306–340.

Jacoby, L. L., & Witherspoon, D. Remembering without awareness. *Canadian Journal of Psychology*, 1982, *32*, 300–324.

Kandel, E. R. *Cellular basis of behavior*. New York: Freeman, 1976.

Karat, J. A model of problem solving with incomplete constraint knowledge. *Cognitive Psychology*, 1982, *14*, 538–559.

Kaushall, P. J., Zetin, M., & Squire, L. R. Amnesia: Detailed report of a noted case. *Journal of Nervous and Mental Disease*, 1981, *169*, 383–389.

Kinsbourne, M. Episodic–semantic distinction. In L. Cermak (Ed.), *Human memory and amnesia*. Hillsdale, N.J.: Erlbaum, 1982.

Kinsbourne, M., & Winocur, G. Response competition and interference effects in paired-associate learning by Korsakoff amnesics. *Neuropsychologia*, 1980, *18*, 541–548.

Kinsbourne, M., & Wood, F. Short-term memory processes and the amnesic syndrome. In D. Deutsch & J. A. Deutsch (Eds.), *Short-term memory*. New York: Academic Press, 1975.

Kolers, P. A. Specificity of operations in sentence recognition. *Cognitive Psychology*, 1975, *1*, 289–306.

Kolers, P. A. Pattern-analyzing memory. *Science*, 1976, *191*, 1280–1281.

Kolers, P. A. A pattern-analyzing basis of recognition. In L. S. Cermak & F. I. M. Craik (Eds.), *Levels of processing in human memory*. Hillsdale, N.J.: Erlbaum, 1979.

Korsakoff, S. S. Disturbance of psychic function in alcoholic paralysis and its relation to the disturbance of the psychic sphere in multiple neuritis of non-alcoholic origin. *Vestnik Psichiatrii*, Vol. IV, fascicle 2, 1887.

Lhermitte, F., & Signoret, J.-L. Analyse neuropsychologique et différenciation des syndromes amnésiques. *Revue Neurologique* (Paris), 1972, *126*, 161–178.

Lhermitte, F., & Signoret, J.-L. The amnesic syndromes and the hippocampal–mammillary system. In M. R. Rosenzweig & E. L. Bennett (Eds.), *Neural mechanisms of learning and memory*. Cambridge, Mass.: MIT Press, 1976.

Loftus, E. F., & Loftus, G. R. On the permanence of stored information in the human brain. *American Psychology*, 1980, *35*, 409–420.

Mahut, H., Moss, M., & Zola-Morgan, S. Retention deficits after combined amygdala–hippocampal and selective hippocampal resections in the monkey. *Neuropsychologia*, 1981, *19*, 201–225.

Mahut, M., Zola-Morgan, S., & Moss, M. Hippocampal resections impair associative learning and recognition memory in the monkey. *Journal of Neuroscience*, 1983, *2*, 1214–1229.

Mair, W. G. P., Warrington, E. K., & Weiskrantz, L. Memory disorder in Korsakoff's psychosis: A neuropathological and neuropsychological investigation of two cases. *Brain*, 1979, *102*, 749–783.

Mandler, G. Recognizing: The judgment of previous occurrence. *Psychological Review*, 1980, *87*, 252–271.

Marslen-Wilson, W. D., & Teuber, H.-L. Memory for remote events in anterograde amnesia: Recognition of public figures from newsphotographs. *Neuropsychologia*, 1975, *13*, 353–364.

Mayes, A., & Meudell, P. How similar is immediate memory in amnesic patients to delayed memory in normal subjects? A replication, extension and reassessment of the amnesic cueing effect. *Neuropsychologia*, 1981, *19*, 647–654.

Mayes, A. R., Meudell, P. R., & Neary, D. Must amnesia be caused by either encoding or retrieval disorders? In M. M. Bruneberg, P. E. Morris, & R. N. Sykes (Eds.), *Practical aspects of memory*. London: Academic Press, 1978.

Mayes, A. R., Meudell, P. R., & Neary, D. Do amnesics adopt inefficient encoding strategies with faces and random shapes? *Neuropsychologia*, 1980, *18*, 527–540.

Mayes, A., Meudell, P., & Som, S. Further similarities between amnesia in normal attenuated memory: Effects of paired-associate learning and contextual shifts. *Neuropsyrhologia*, 1981, *18*, 655–664.

McDowall, J. Effects of encoding instructions and retrieval cuing on recall in Korsakoff patients. *Memory and Cognition*, 1979, *7*, 232–239.

McGaugh, J. L., & Gold, P. E. Modulation of memory by electrical stimulation of the brain. In M. R. Rosenzweig & E. L. Bennett (Eds.), *Neural mechanisms of learning and memory*. Cambridge, Mass.: MIT Press, 1976.

McGaugh, J. L., & Herz, M. J. *Memory consolidation*. San Francisco, 1972.

Meudell, P., & Mayes, A. The Claparède phenomenon: A further example in amnesics, a demonstration of a similar effect in normal people with attenuated memory, and a reinterpretation. *Current Psychological Research*, 1981, *1*, 75–88.

Meudell, P. R., Northern, B., Snowden, J. S., & Neary, D. Long-term memory for famous voices in amnesic and normal subjects. *Neuropsychologia*, 1980, *18*, 133–139.

Michel, D., Laurent, B., Foyatier, N., Blanc, A., & Portafaix, M. Infarctus thalamique paramedian gauche. *Revue Neurologique*, 1982, *138*, 533–550.

Milner, B. The memory defect in bilateral hippocampal lesions. *Psychiatric Research Reports*, 1959, *11*, 43–52.

Milner, B. Les troubles de la mémoire accompagnant des lésions hippocampiques bilatérales. In P. Passouant (Ed.), *Physiologie de l'hippocampe*. Paris: Centre National de la Recherche Scientifique, 1962.

Milner, B. Effects of different brain lesions on card sorting. *Archives of Neurology*, 1963, *9*, 100–110.

Milner, B. Amnesia following operation on the temporal lobes. In C. W. M. Whitty & O. L. Zangwill (Eds.), *Amnesia*. London: Butterworths, 1966.

Milner, B. Disorders of memory after brain lesions in man. Preface: Material-specific and generalized memory loss. *Neuropsychologia*, 1968, *6*, 175–179.

Milner, B. Hemispheric specialization: scope and limits. In F. O. Schmitt & F. G. Worden (Eds.), *The neurosciences: Third study program*. Cambridge, Mass.: MIT Press, 1974.

Milner, B., Corkin, S., & Teuber, H.-L. Further analysis of the hippocampal amnesic syndrome: 14-year follow-up study of H. M. *Neuropsychologia*, 1968, *6*, 215–234.

Mishkin, M. Memory in monkeys severely impaired by combined but not by separate removal of amygdala and hippocampus. *Nature*, 1978, *273*, 297–298.

Mishkin, M. A memory system in the monkey. In D. E. Broadbent & L. Weiskrantz (Eds.), *Philosophical transactions of the Royal Society of London* (Vol. 298). London: The Royal Society, 1982.

Mishkin, M., & Delacour, J. An analysis of short-term visual memory in the monkey. *Journal of Experimental Psychology*, 1975, *1*, 326–334.

Moscovitch, M. Multiple dissociations of function in amnesia. In L. Cermak (Ed.), *Human memory and amnesia*. Hillsdale, N.J.: Erlbaum, 1982.

Moss, M., Mahut, H., & Zola-Morgan, S. Concurrent discrimination learning of monkeys after hippocampal, entorhinal, or fornix lesions. *Journal of Neuroscience*, 1981, *1*, 227–240.

Murray, E., & Mishkin, M. The role of the amygdala and the hippocampus and tactual memory. *Society for Neuroscience Abstracts*, 1981, *7*, 237.

Nelson, T. O. Detecting small amounts of information in memory: Savings for nonrecognized items. *Journal of Experimental Psychology: Human Learning and Memory*, 1978, *4*, 453–468.

Norman, D. A., & Rumelhart, D. E. *Explorations in cognition*. San Francisco: Freeman, 1975.

O'Keefe, J., & Nadel, L. *The hippocampus as a cognitive map*. London: Oxford University Press, 1978.

Olton, D. S., Becker, J. T., & Handelmann, G. E. Hippocampus, space, and memory. *Behavioral Brain Science*, 1979, *2*, 313–365.

Oscar-Berman, M. Hypothesis testing and focusing behavior during concept formation by amnesic Korsakoff patients. *Neuropsychologia*, 1973, *11*, 191–198.

Papez, J. W. A proposed mechanism of emotion. *Archives of Neurology and Psychiatry*, 1937, *38*, 725–743.

Parker, E. S., & Nobel, E. Alcoholic consumption and cognitive functioning in social drinkers. *Journal of Studies in Alcohol*, 1977, *38*, 1224–1232.

Parkin, A. J. Residual learning capability in organic amnesia. *Cortex*, 1982, *18*, 417–440.

Penfield, W., & Milner, B. Memory deficit produced by bilateral lesions in the hippocampal zone. *Archives of Neurology and Psychiatry*, 1958, *79*, 475–497.

Piercy, M. F. Experimental studies of the organic amnesic syndrome. In C. W. M. Whitty & O. L. Zangwill (Eds.), *Amnesia* (2nd ed.). London: Butterworths, 1977.

Ribot, T. *Diseases of memory*. New York: Appleton, 1882.

Riege, W. Inconstant non-verbal recognition memory in Korsakoff patients and controls. *Neuropsychologia*, 1977, *15*, 269–276.

Rose, F. C., & Symonds, C. P. Persistent memory defect following encephalitis. *Brain*, 1960, *83*, 195–212.

Rozin, P. The psychobiological approach to human memory. In M. R. Rosenzweig & E. L. Bennett (Eds.), *Neural mechanisms of learning and memory*. Cambridge, Mass.: MIT Press, 1976.

Rumelhart, D. E. Schemata: The building blocks of cognition. In R. Spiro, B. Bruce & W. Brewer (Eds.), *Theoretical issues in reading comprehension*. Hillsdale, N.J.: Erlbaum, 1982.

Russell, W. R., & Nathan, P. W. Traumatic amnesia. *Brain*, 1946, *69*, 290–300.

Ryan, C., Butters, N., & Montgomery, L. Memory deficits in chronic alcoholics: Continuities between the intact alcoholic and the alcoholic Korsakoff patient. In H. Begleiter (Ed.), *Advances in experimental medicine and biology: Biological effects of alcohol* (Vol. 126). New York: Plenum Press, 1980.

Ryle, G. *The concept of mind*. San Francisco: Hutchinson, 1949.

Sanders, H. I., & Warrington, E. K. Memory for remote events in amnesic patients. *Brain*, 1971, *94*, 661–668.

Scarborough, D. L., Gerard, D., & Cortese, C. Accessing lexical memory: The transfer of word repetition effects across task and modality. *Memory and Cognition*, 1979, *7*, 3–12.

Schacter, D. L., & Tulving, E. Amnesia and memory research. In L. S. Cermak (Ed.), *Human memory and amnesia*. Hillsdale, N.J.: Erlbaum, 1982a.

Schacter, D. L., & Tulving, E. Memory, amnesia, and the episodic/semantic distinction. In R. L. Isaacson & N. E. Spear (Eds.), *Expression of knowledge*. New York: Plenum Press, 1982b.

Scoville, W. B., & Milner, B. Loss of recent memory after bilateral hippocampal lesions. *Journal of Neurology, Neurosurgery, and Psychiatry*, 1957, *20*, 11–21.

Seltzer, B., & Benson, D. F. The temporal pattern of retrograde amnesia in Korsakoff's disease. *Neurology*, 1974, *24*, 527–530.

Shimamura, A., & Squire, L. R., *Korsakoff syndrome: Remote memory impairment and anterograde amnesia as separate disorders*. Manuscript submitted for publication, 1984.

Simon, H. A. The functional equivalence of problem solving skills. *Cognitive Psychology*, 1975, *7*, 268–288.

Slamecka, N. J., & McElree, B. Normal forgetting of verbal lists as a function of their degree of learning. *Journal of Experimental Psychology: Learning, Memory, and Cognition*, 1983, *9*, 384–397.

Speedie, L. J., & Heilman, K. M. Amnestic disturbance following infarction of the left dorsomedial nucleus of the thalamus. *Neuropsychologia*, 1982, *20*, 597–604.

Squire, L. R. The anatomy of amnesia. *Trends in Neuroscience*, 1980a, *3*, 52–54.

Squire, L. R. Specifying the defect in human amnesia: Storage, retrieval, and semantics. *Neuropsychologia*, 1980b, *18*, 368–372.

Squire, L. R. Two forms of human amnesia: An analysis of forgetting. *Journal of Neuroscience*, 1981, *1*, 635–640.

Squire, L. R. Neuropsychological effects of ECT. In W. B. Essman & R. Abrams (Eds.), *Electroconvulsive therapies: Biological foundations and clinical applications*. New York: Spectrum, 1982a.

Squire, L. R. The neuropsychology of human memory. *Annual Review of Neuroscience*, 1982b, *5*, 241–273.

Squire, L. R. Comparisons between forms of amnesia: Some deficits are unique to Korsakoff syndrome. *Journal of Experimental Psychology: Learning, Memory, and Cognition*, 1982c, *8*, 560–571.

Squire, L. R. Memory and the brain. In S. Friedman, K. Klivington, & R. Peterson (Eds.), *Brain, cognition, and education*. New York: Academic Press, in press.

Squire, L. R., Chace, P. M., & Slater, P. C. Retrograde amnesia following electroconvulsive therapy. *Nature*, 1976, *260*, 775–777.

Squire, L. R., & Cohen, N. J. Hippocampal lesions: Reconciling the findings in rodents and man. *Behavioral Brain Science*, 1979a, *2*, 345–346.

Squire, L. R., & Cohen, N. J. Memory and amnesia: Resistance to disruption develops for years after learning. *Behavioral Neurology and Biology*, 1979b, *25*, 115–125.

Squire, L. R., & Cohen, N. J. Remote memory, retrograde amnesia, and the neuropsychology of memory. In L. Cermak (Ed.), *Human memory and amnesia*. Hillsdale, N.J.: Erlbaum, 1982.

Squire, L. R., Cohen, N., & Nadel, L. The medial temporal region and memory consolidation: A new hypothesis. In H. Weingartner & E. Parker (Eds.), *Memory consolidation*. Hillsdale, N.J.: Erlbaum, 1984.

Squire, L. R., Cohen, N. J., & Zouzounis, J. A. Preserved memory in retrograde amnesia: Sparing of a recently acquired skill. *Neuropsychologia*, 1984, *22*, 145–152.

Squire, L. R., & Fox, M. M. Assessment of remote memory: Validation of the television test by repeated testing during a seven-day period. *Behavioral Research Methods and Instrumentation*, 1980, *12*, 583–586.

Squire, L. R., & Moore, R. Y. Dorsal thalamic lesion in a noted case of chronic memory dysfunction. *Annals of Neurology*, 1979, *6*, 503–506.

Squire, L. R., Nadel, L., & Slater, P. C. Anterograde amnesia and memory for temporal order. *Neuropsychologia*, 1981, *19*, 141–145.

Squire, L. R., & Slater, P. C. Forgetting in very long-term memory as assessed by an improved questionnaire technique. *Journal of Experimental Psychology: Human Learning and Memory*, 1975, *1104*, 50–54.

Squire, L. R., & Slater, P. C. Remote memory in chronic anterograde amnesia. *Behavioral Biology*, 1977, *20*, 398–403.

Squire, L. R., & Slater, P. C. Anterograde and retrograde memory impairment in chronic amnesia. *Neuropsychologia*, 1978, *16*, 313–322.

Squire, L. R., Slater, P. C., & Chace, P. M. Retrograde amnesia: Temporal gradient in very long-term memory following electroconvulsive therapy. *Science*, 1975, *187*, 77–79.

Squire, L. R., Slater, P. C., & Chace, P. M. Anterograde amnesia following electroconvulsive therapy: No evidence for state-dependent learning. *Behavioral Biology*, 1976, *17*, 31–41.

Squire, L. R., Slater, P. C., & Miller, P. L. Retrograde amnesia following ECT: Long-term follow-up studies. *Archives of General Psychiatry*, 1981, *38*, 89–95.

Squire, L. R., & Spanis, C. W. Long gradient of retrograde amnesia in mice: Continuity with the findings in humans. *Behavioral Neuroscience*, 1984, *98*, 345–348.

Squire, L. R. Wetzel, C. D., & Slater, P. C. Anterograde amnesia following ECT: An analysis of the beneficial effect of partial information. *Neuropsychologia*, 1978, *16*, 339–347.

Squire, L. R., & Zola-Morgan, S. The neurology of memory: The case for correspondence between the findings for human and nonhuman primates. In J. A. Deutsch (Ed.), *The physiological basis of memory* (2nd ed.). New York: Academic, 1983.

Stern, L. D. A review of theories of human amnesia. *Memory and Cognition*, 1981, *9*, 247–262.

Talland, G. A. *Deranged memory*. New York: Academic Press, 1965.

Teuber, H.-L., Milner, B., & Vaughan, H. G. Persistent anterograde amnesia after stab wound of the basal brain. *Neuropsychologia*, 1968, *6*, 267–282.

Tulving, E. Episodic and semantic memory. In E. Tulving & W. Donaldson (Eds.), *Organization of memory*. New York: Academic Press, 1972.

Tulving, E., & Thompson, D. M. Encoding specificity and processes in episodic memory. *Psychological Review*, 1973, *80*, 352–373.

Tulving, E., Schacter, D. L., & Stark, H. A. Priming effects in word-fragment completion are independent of recognition memory. *Journal of Experimental Psychology: Learning, Memory, and Cognition*, 1982, *8*, 352–373.

Victor, M., Adams, R. D., & Collins, G. H. *The Wernicke–Korsakoff syndrome*. Philadelphia: F. A. Davis, 1971.

Volpe, B. T., & Hirst, W. The characterization of an amnesic syndrome following hypoxic ischemic injury. *Archives of Neurology*, 1983, *40*, 436–440.

Warrington, E. K., & Baddeley, A. D. Amnesia and memory for visual location. *Neuropsychologia*, 1974, *12*, 257–263.

Warrington, E. K., & Weiskrantz, L. A new method of testing long-term retention with special reference to amnesic patients. *Nature*, 1968, *217*, 972–974.

Warrington, E. K., & Weiskrantz, L. The amnesic syndrome: Consolidation or retrieval? *Nature*, 1970, *228*, 628–630.

Warrington, E. K., & Weiskrantz, L. An analysis of short-term and long-term memory defects in man. In J. A. Deutsch (Ed.), *The physiological basis of memory*. New York: Academic Press, 1973.

Warrington, E. K., & Weiskrantz, L. The effect of prior learning on subsequent retention in amnesic patients. *Neuropsychologia*, 1974, *12*, 419–428.

Warrington, E. K., & Weiskrantz, L. Further analysis of the prior learning effect in amnesic patients. *Neuropsychologia*, 1978, *16*, 169–177.

Weiskrantz, L. A comparison of hippocampal pathology in man and other animals. In *Functions of the septo-hippocampal system* (CIBA Foundation Symposium 58). Oxford: Elsevier, 1978.

Weiskrantz, L. Comparative aspects of studies of amnesia. In D. E. Broadbent & L. Weiskrantz (Eds.), *Philosophical transactions of the Royal Society of London* (Vol. 298). London: The Royal Society, 1982.

Weiskrantz, L., & Warrington, E. K. Verbal learning and retention by amnesic patients using partial information. *Psychonomic Society*, 1970, *20*, 210–211.

Weiskrantz, L., & Warrington, E. K. Conditioning in amnesic patients. *Neuropsychologia*, 1979, *17*, 187–194.

Wetzel, C. D., & Squire, L. R. Encoding in anterograde amnesia. *Neuropsychologia*, 1980, *18*, 177–184.

Wetzel, C. D., & Squire, L. R. Cued recall in anterograde amnesia. *Brain and Language*, 1982, *15*, 70–81.

Wickens, D. D. Encoding categories of words: An empirical approach to meaning. *Psychological Review*, 1970, *77*, 1–15.

Wicklegren, W. A. Chunking consolidation: A theoretical synthesis of semantic networks, configuring in conditioning, S-R v. cognitive learning, normal forgetting, the amnesic syndrome and the hippocampal arousal system. *Psychological Review*, 1979, *86*, 44–60.

Wilkinson, D. A., & Carlin, P. Chronic organic brain syndrome associated with alcoholism: Neuropsychological and other aspects. In Y. Israel (Ed.), *Research advances in alcohol and drug problems* (Vol. 6). Toronto: Addiction Research Foundation, 1981.

Williams, M., & Pennybacker, J. Memory disturbances in third ventricle tumours. *Journal of Neurology, Neurosurgery, and Psychiatry*, 1954, *17*, 115–123.

Winocur, G. The amnesic syndrome: A deficit in cue utilization. In L. S. Cermak (Ed.), *Human memory and amnesia*. New York: Erlbaum, 1982.

Winocur, G., & Kinsbourne, M. Contextual cueing as an aid to Korsakoff amnesics. *Neuropsychologia*, 1978, *16*, 671–682.

Winocur, G., Kinsbourne, M., & Moscovitch, M. The effect of cueing on release from proactive interference in Korsakoff amnesic patients. *Journal of Experimental Psychology: Human Learning and Memory*, 1981, *7*, 56–65.

Winograd, T. Understanding natural language. In D. Bobrow & A. Collins (Eds.), *Representation and understanding*. New York: Academic Press, 1975.

Winston, P. H. *Artificial intelligence*. Reading, Mass.: Addison-Wesley, 1977.

Wood, F., Ebert, V., & Kinsbourne, M. The episodic–semantic distinction in memory and amnesia: Clinical and experimental observations. In L. S. Cermak (Eds.), *Human memory and amnesia*. New York: Erlbaum, 1982.

Woods, R. T., & Piercy, M. A similarity between amnesic memory and normal forgetting. *Neuropsychologia*, 1974, *12*, 437–445.

Zangwill, O. L. The amnesic syndrome. In C. W. M. Whitty & O. L. Zangwill (Eds.), *Amnesia*. London: Butterworths, 1966.

Zola-Morgan, S., Cohen, N. J., & Squire, L. R. Recall of remote episodic memory in amnesia. *Neuropsychologia*, 1983, *21*, 487–500.

Zola-Morgan, S., Dabrowska, J., Moss, M., & Mahut, H. Enhanced perceptual novelty in the monkey after fornix sections, but not after hippocampal ablations. *Neuropsychologia*, 1983, *21*, 433–454.

Zola-Morgan, S., & Squire, L. R. Two forms of amnesia in monkeys: Rapid forgetting after medial temporal lesions but not diencephalic lesions. *Society for Neuroscience Abstracts*, 1982, *8*, 24.

Zola-Morgan, S., & Squire, L. R. Towards an animal model of human amnesia: Resolution of anomalous findings with visual discrimination tasks. *Journal of Neuroscience*, 1983.

Zola-Morgan, S., & Squire, L. R. Preserved learning in monkeys with medial temporal lesions: Sparing of motor and cognitive skills. *Journal of Neuroscience*, 1984, *4*, 1072–1085.

Zola-Morgan, S., Squire, L. R., & Mishkin, M. The neuroanatomy of amnesia: amygdala–hippocampus vs. temporal stem. *Science*, 1982, *218*, 1337–1339.

CHAPTER TWO

Memories and Habits: Two Neural Systems

MORTIMER MISHKIN / BARBARA MALAMUT / JOCELYNE BACHEVALIER

The term "global anterograde amnesia" implies the rapid forgetting of all new experiences, yet investigators agree that persons suffering from this syndrome readily retain new experiences of a certain type or in a certain way. Characterizing the essential difference between the lost and spared retention abilities has become one of the major goals of both clinical and animal amnestic research.

Beginning with Milner's (1962) dramatic demonstration of a nearly normal rate of improvement of mirror-drawing skill in the severely amnesic patient H. M., the steadily mounting evidence for the dissociation of retention processes in amnesia has generated numerous theoretical interpretations of this dissociation. Among the labels that have been applied to the lost versus spared abilities are recognition versus associative memory (Gaffan, 1974), episodic versus semantic memory (Kinsbourne & Wood, 1975), working versus reference memory (Olton, Becker, & Handelmann, 1979), vertical versus horizontal associative memory (Wickelgren, 1979), declarative versus procedural knowledge (Cohen & Squire, 1980), elaborative versus integrative processing (Graf, Mandler, & Haden, 1982), and automatic versus effortful encoding (Hirst, 1982). All of these distinctions and numerous others (Huppert & Piercy, 1976; Cermak & Butters, 1972; O'Keefe & Nadel, 1978; Cutting, 1978; Cormier, 1981; Stern, 1981; Warrington & Weiskrantz, 1982) postulate, in essence, that the retention of experience entails two widely differing processes, a more and a less cognitive one (or a more and a less flexible one), only the first of which is affected in global amnesia.

The present report is written from this same theoretical perspective but adopts still another set of labels for the two types of retention: "memories" versus "habits." This particular functional distinction, which is deliberately drawn more sharply than any of those listed above, is essentially the one that was advanced by Hirsh in 1974 and later elaborated by him (Hirsh, 1980). A

Mortimer Mishkin, Barbara Malamut, and Jocelyne Bachevalier. Laboratory of Neuropsychology, National Institute of Mental Health, Bethesda, Maryland. Present address for Barbara Malamut: Department of Psychology, City College, New York, New York.

quote helps give the flavor of his position. "The present theory views the hippocampus as the gateway to memory. . . . In the absence of the hippocampus . . . learning is a matter of habit formation. Readers familiar with learning theory will realize that the behavior of normal animals is treated in a neo-Tolmanian framework, while that of hippocampally ablated animals is held to be everything for which early S–R theorists could have wished" (Hirsh, 1974, p. 439). He later modified this view slightly, as follows: "The [S-R] associative system must have been present all along if it is free to express itself following hippocampal ablation" (Hirsh, 1980, p. 181). In short, according to Hirsh, both sides in the great debate between behaviorism and cognitivism must ultimately be declared the winners, since the evidence from the study of amnesia demonstrates that both types of processes must be constantly present in normal behavior.

If this radical resolution of that long and difficult debate proves correct, it will have enormous implications for both psychological and neuropsychological research. First, every piece of learning will have to be analyzed and reanalyzed carefully for contributions to it by not just one but two qualitatively different types of retention processes. And second, two different types of retention processes implies two different storage mechanisms, or even two entirely different neural systems. The data reported in this chapter appear to us to lend support to Hirsh's provocative proposal and therefore to encourage the further development of a two-systems theory of learning.

MEMORIES AND A CORTICO-LIMBIC SYSTEM

The first form of learning to be considered, the one here labeled memory formation, is the one that by nearly universal agreement has been attributed to the hippocampal system exclusively. This attribution is explicit in the quotes from Hirsh. The evidence from our research on the monkey, however, suggests that memory formation has a broader limbic substrate than this, one that includes the amygdaloid system as well (Mishkin, Spiegler, Saunders, & Malamut, 1982). The discovery that memory functions may be shared jointly by the amygdala and the hippocampus grew out of work on the role of cortico-limbic interaction in the mnemonic process of linking neutral sensory stimuli with rewards.

Recognition and Associative Memory

As detailed elsewhere (Jones & Mishkin, 1972; Mishkin & Aggleton, 1981), studies on discrimination learning in the monkey had led to the suggestion that each primary sensory area together with its modality-specific association areas form a hierarchical system devoted to processing the purely physical qualities of the stimuli in that modality. Consequently, the attachment of reward value, and of affective qualities generally, to a stimulus that would otherwise remain emotionally and motivationally neutral would require an additional neuronal step. The additional step was postulated to be activation, by the sensory modality's highest-order processing area, of an amygdalo-hypothalamic pathway. This two-stage neural model of stimulus–reward association received its strongest support from a study that compared the effects of inferior temporal and amygdaloid lesions on the performance of two different visual-memory tests, each of which utilized easily discriminable trial-unique objects (Spiegler & Mishkin, 1981). One was a test of object recognition, that is, the ability to remember from a single trial whether or not an object had been seen before; the other was a test of object–reward association, that is, the ability to remember from a single trial whether or not an object had been baited before. On the recognition test, only the inferior temporal lesion produced marked impairment; on the association test, by contrast, both lesions produced marked impairment, and the two impairments in this case were equally severe. The pattern of results thus fit the scheme that stimulus–reward association is indeed a two-stage process entailing, first, a stimulus-recognition mechanism heavily dependent on inferior temporal cortex (viewed as the highest-order processing station in vision) and, second, a reward-attachment mechanism heavily dependent on the amygdala (viewed as a multimodal gateway to the hypothalamus).

But proof that the amygdala's role in stimulus–reward association depends directly on the visual input from inferior temporal cortex requires an additional demonstration, namely, that the association can be prevented by anatomical disconnection of the two structures. Before such a disconnection test was attempted, however, it seemed desirable to amplify the memory deficits if possible by enlargement of the two lesions to include, in the one case, more of the cortical visual system, and in the other, more of the temporal lobe limbic system. It was the latter extension of lesions that led to the discovery of global amnesia in the monkey (Mishkin *et al.*, 1982).

Whereas hippocampal removal alone had failed to yield a notable effect on either of the memory tests described above, its combination with an amygdaloid removal turned out to have a profound effect, not only on stimulus–reward association, which was the original goal, but on stimulus recognition as well (Mishkin, 1978); and not only on stimulus recognition in vision but also in touch (Murray & Mishkin, 1983). Furthermore, visual recognition was found to depend on the anatomical connections between the visual and limbic systems (Mishkin, 1982), on the further connections of the limbic system with the diencephalon (Bachevalier, Parkinson, Aggleton, & Mishkin, 1982), and, finally, on the medial thalamic portion of the diencephalon, specifically (Aggleton & Mishkin, 1983).

The Cortico-Limbo-Diencephalic System

At this point, it would be well to step back and consider briefly how this multitude of structures and interconnections could constitute a single system critical for memory formation. The model that has been proposed (Mishkin, 1982) views the storage of the neural representations of sensory stimuli as a fundamental ingredient of memory. The storage is conceived as taking place within the higher-order sensory processing areas of the cortex whenever stimulus activation of these areas triggers a cortico-limbo-thalamo-cortical circuit. Once triggered, this circuit is presumed to serve as an automatic rehearsal or imprinting mechanism, strengthening the cortical connections whose activation triggered the circuit in the first place. The strengthened cortical network of higher-order sensory neurons may be viewed as the stored representation of the stimulus, which, whenever reactivated through the original sensory pathway, would result in stimulus recognition. In addition, through the interconnections that this stored representation would establish with the stored representations of other stimuli and events, it could evoke them or be evoked by them through the process of associative recall.

The foregoing is consistent with numerous anatomical and neurological facts and also satisfies some important theoretical considerations. For example, with regard to the anatomy, each sensory modality appears to be served by a hierarchically organized set of cortical areas and connections that are directed outward from its primary projection area toward the anterior temporo-insular region (Turner, Mishkin, & Knapp, 1980). This region, which encompasses the highest-order processing areas for each of the sensory modalities, is reciprocally connected with the amygdala directly (Turner *et al.*, 1980) and with the hippocampus indirectly via entorhinal cortex (Van Hoesen & Pandya, 1975). The amygdala and hippocampus are connected in turn, also often reciprocally, with various medial and midline thalamic nuclei, including the nucleus anterior medialis and ventralis, the magnocellular portion of the nucleus medialis dorsalis, and the nucleus paraventricularis, parataenialis, and reuniens. (For a recent review of the relevant anatomical literature, see Mishkin & Aggleton, 1981.)

As for the neurological evidence, the two subcortical regions comprising the proposed circuit—namely, the medial temporal and medial thalamic regions—are also the two major sites of neuropathology associated with global amnesia in humans (Milner, 1959; Victor, Adams, & Collins, 1971; McEntee, Biber, Perl, & Benson, 1976). Furthermore, as with our findings in animals, the severity of the amnesia in clinical cases appears to be correlated with the total amount of conjoint damage sustained by the amygdalo-thalamic and hippocampo-thalamic portions of the system (Mishkin *et al.*, 1982). In addition, it is the evidence from the clinical cases that has dictated the proposal contained in the neural model that the stored stimulus representations are located in the cerebral cortex, that is, distal to the site of the neuropathology, since memories that the patients formed prior to their limbo-diencephalic injury or disease onset are so often spared (Milner, 1970; Cohen & Squire, 1981).

Sequential Neural Processing

Finally, with regard to the theoretical considerations that the model attempts to satisfy, all relate to the notion of a sequential neural order in perception and memory. To deal with the issue of perception first, there is strong evidence to suggest that an integrated percept depends on the sequential processing of sensory information through the several tiers of cortical areas composing each sensory system (Turner *et al.*, 1980; Ungerleider & Mishkin, 1982). By the time the activity related to the stimulus has reached the modality's final, or highest-order, processing station in the anterior temporo-insular cortex, the various perceptual constancies are most likely to have been achieved (Gross & Mishkin, 1977; Mishkin, 1979). As a result, the neural activity representing the stimulus at that station would also remain relatively constant despite wide variations in such exposure conditions as intensity, background, proximity, and position on the receptor surface, variations that would necessarily evoke markedly differing neural activity at earlier stations of the system. Once a relatively invariant neural representation of a stimulus has been achieved, it seems plausible to assume that this is the representation that would be stored, thereby providing for constancy of stimulus recognition under widely varying perceptual conditions.

By extension of the notion of a sequential neural order to the memory process, it also seems plausible that the stored stimulus representation is the neural entity that would be linked to subsequent neural events. In this way, not only stimulus perception and recognition but associative recall as well would benefit from the various stimulus-equivalence mechanisms that were present earlier in the sensory systems. The associative connection would thereby have to be formed only once, with a single invariant representation of the stimulus, rather than repeatedly with each of its numerous possible representations that would be evoked under varying perceptual conditions at earlier sensory stations. As already indicated, the subsequent neural events with which the stored stimulus representation could become connected would likewise be stored representations, although these would be not only of other stimuli but also of places in the environment, or behavioral acts, or, finally, affective states.

This last aspect of the model brings us back to the theoretical question that initiated our line of memory research, but with a new appreciation of the role of cortico-limbic interaction in stimulus–reward association—that is, the limbic system appears to participate in this specific memory process in at least two different ways. First, the amygdala contributes equally with the hippocampus in bringing about the cortical storage of the stimulus representation, thereby allowing for stimulus recognition. And second, the amygdala contributes on its own to the attachment of affective value to the recognized stimulus. As a result, in the absence of the hippocampus alone, there is little impairment in either one of these processes, since the amygdala can mediate both of them effectively; and in the absence of the amygdala alone, there is an impairment only in appreciating the significance of the stimulus, for although the hippocampus cannot mediate that function effectively, it can support stimulus recognition. But in the absence of both of these limbic structures, that is, when both of the alternative pathways for storing stimulus representations are destroyed, there is a profound impairment in recognizing the stimulus itself and, consequently, in acquiring any mnemonic association with it.

HABITS AND A CORTICO-STRIATAL SYSTEM

Little has been said yet about the level of learning that the memory system affords a normal monkey or, conversely, the degree of learning impairment that follows destruction of this system. Although research on one-trial visual discrimination in this species can be traced back at least to the early work of Harlow (1944), the monkey's truly remarkable visual memory capacity was uncovered only recently in studies by Gaffan (1974, 1979) and Sands and Wright (1982). Two of the animal's memory skills in particular are pertinent here: One is its ability to recognize among distractor items each of a long list of objects that were presented successively just once each; and the other is its ability to remember which objects in such a list were baited and which were not, also after they were presented successively just once each. Normal monkeys can perform both of these memory feats, that is, both recognition and associative recall, with object lists of 10 or more items, at better than 90% accuracy. Monkeys with combined amygdalo-hippocampal removals, by contrast, fail almost completely either to recall which one of a single pair of objects had been baited just a few seconds ago (Mishkin *et al.*, 1982) or even to recognize which object in a pair had been presented only a minute or two earlier (Mishkin, 1978). Clearly, the impressive memory ability of the monkey is totally eliminated by extensive limbic lesions.

Spared Learning Abilities

Yet there is abundant evidence from another source that appears to contradict this conclusion. For example, it has been known for decades that monkeys with limbic lesions can learn a difficult visual-pattern discrimination presented with repeated trials, and that they can do so at about the normal rate (Mishkin, 1954; Zola-Morgan, Squire, & Mishkin, 1982). Furthermore, although monkeys with such lesions fail completely on tests with trial-unique objects, they are clearly able to learn repeated-trial object discriminations at a nearly normal rate, even though the successive trials are separated by the same 1- to 2-minute intervals that cause difficulty in the one-trial tests of recognition and associative recall (Orbach, Milner, & Rasmussen, 1960). These results in amnesic monkeys present the same paradox of normal learning in the face of rapid forgetting that is exhibited by amnesic patients. Indeed, the paradox in the case of the amnesic monkeys appears to be even sharper, since the materials, the rules, and even the responses are all essentially the same in the tasks that are failed as they are in the ones that are mastered.

A particularly dramatic example of this paradox was uncovered in a recent series of experiments that were designed to resolve it. The most obvious explanation for the amnesic monkeys' successful learning is that, despite their rapid forgetting on one-trial memory tests, they can still retain sufficient information after each trial that even a 1- to 2-minute intertrial interval is simply too short a separation to prevent the steady accumulation of information over trial repetitions. In an attempt to demonstrate that this was indeed the case, we trained monkeys with limbic lesions on object discriminations in which the successive trials were separated by intervals that would greatly exceed their putative memory span; and to be as certain as possible that the separation would exceed their span, we chose intervals of 24 hours.

The experimental design (Malamut, Saunders, & Mishkin, 1980) was as follows: A set of 20 different pairs of easily discriminable objects was presented for concurrent learning; but these 20 different pairs were presented just once a day, on successive days, until the animals attained the criterion of 90 correct responses in five 20-trial sessions, that is, in 100 trials distributed over 5 days. Within each pair, the baited (positive) object and the unbaited (negative) object remained constant across the daily sessions, as did the serial order of the pairs. The left–right position of the objects in the pair, however, was varied pseudorandomly from day to day. When the animals reached criterion on the first set, they were next trained in the same way on a second, completely different set, and then, once again, on a third set. Given all the evidence of their rapid forgetting, the results were a total surprise. Animals with the combined amygdalo-hippocampal lesions succeeded in learning the three object discrimination sets in about 10 sessions each, a period of training exactly the same as the period required by their normal controls.

To be certain that the operated animals had not somehow compensated for their memory loss, we subsequently tested them on both a one-trial recognition test involving the principle of delayed matching-to-sample (Gaffan, 1974) and a one-trial object–reward association test involving the principle of win–stay, lose–shift (Gaffan, 1979). A variant of the recognition task will be described later, but a description of the association task is particularly pertinent here. In the latter task, a baited and an unbaited object were presented successively in a central position, with a 10-second interval between them. Ten seconds later the two objects were presented again, but this time simultaneously, with one on the left and one on the right. The animal found the reward only if it chose the previously baited object (hence, win–stay, lose–shift). The same procedure was repeated with a new pair of objects on every trial, the order of the positive and negative stimuli in the acquisition phase of the trial as well as their left–right positions in the choice phase having been determined pseudorandomly. Twenty such trials were presented each day until the animals achieved the criterion of 90 correct choices in 100 trials. The results on these tests with trial-unique objects (Malamut *et al.*, 1980; Malamut & Mishkin, 1981) confirmed our earlier findings in detail. On both measures, the animals with limbic lesions were profoundly impaired, requiring double presentation of the samples to learn the recognition task at short delays of a few seconds, falling sharply in performance at longer delays of a minute or two, and then failing completely in object–reward association learning even at the short delay.

The latter failure is particularly instructive, since the object–reward association task is nearly identical to the concurrent discrimination task with 24-hour intertrial intervals, on which the operated animals were completely unimpaired. That is, both tests utilize 20 pairs of easily discriminable objects each day; both employ reward contingencies that call for learning the response strategy of win–stay, lose–shift; and both require the animal to make its choice between two simultaneously presented stimuli. Yet if this choice must be made on the basis of a single acquisition trial, even though this trial was presented just a few seconds earlier, the operated animal, unlike the normal, fails; conversely, if the choice can be made on the basis of at least a few acquisition trials, even though these were separated from each other by 24-hour intervals, the operated animal is just as successful as the normal.

Slow versus Rapid Learning

We had initially assumed that if monkeys with limbic lesions have not only forgotten an object's reward value but have even forgotten the object itself after a minute or two, then either they should be unable to learn at all across 24-hour intervals, or if they do learn, they should be so seriously handicapped in comparison with control animals that their retardation would be obvious. Neither of these results was obtained. There appear to be two possible solutions to this remarkable puzzle. The first is that all of the products of memory that we enumerated earlier can be formed either through a rapid-learning system, which makes use of single experiences, or through a slow-learning system, which requires repetition, and that only the former type of learning is dependent on the limbo-thalamic circuit. According to this view, the two systems are distinct, but their final products are not. Consequently, in the absence of the limbo-thalamic circuit, the remaining, or slow-learning, system can yield essentially the same memories as the other; the slow-learning system simply requires several repetitions of the experience to form the memories. In short, once animals with limbic lesions have had a few trials, as in the 24-hour concurrent-learning task, they can both recognize all the objects in the test and recall each object's reward value, just as normal animals can. There is a major difficulty with this interpretation, however, in that humans who have become profoundly amnesic as a result of medial temporal or medial diencephalic damage apparently cannot learn to remember in a cognitive sense even with many repetitions of an experience. Rather, as was indicated at the outset, the learning ability that is spared in amnesic humans appears to most investigators to be qualitatively different from the learning ability that has been lost. If so, then the final products of the two learning systems cannot be the same.

Single versus Repeated Experiences

This consideration leads to the second possible solution to our puzzle of normal discrimination learning in the face of abnormally rapid forgetting. According to this second alternative, both the learning process *and* its product are divisible into two qualitatively distinct forms. One is the memory process that has already been described and for which the limbo-thalamic circuit is critical; the process subsumes both recognition memory and associative recall, an example of which is object–reward association. Object–reward association is viewed as being built on recognition memory and as involving the rapid formation of an association between a recognized but affectively neutral cue object and a recognized as well as affectively potent food object. The product of this first learning process is a new piece of information regarding the reward value of a previously neutral object. The second learning process, on the other hand, is completely independent not only of the limbo-thalamic circuit but also of recognition and associative memory; it is viewed as involving instead the more gradual development of a connection between an unconditioned stimulus object and an approach response, as an automatic consequence of reinforcement by food. The product of this process is not cognitive information but a non-cognitive stimulus–response bond, that is, not a memory but a habit. Finally, what is stored in the habit-formation system is not the neural representations of such items as objects, places, acts, emotions, and the learned connections between them but simply the changing probability that a given stimulus will evoke a specific response due to the reinforcement contingencies operating at that time (Mishkin & Petri, 1984).

If the foregoing solution to our puzzle is correct, that is, if discrimination learning does involve both a memory system and a habit system, then these two systems must have properties differing in numerous ways other than in learning rate. In particular, the memory system, although it can yield discrimination mastery in a single trial, appears to provide no advantage to monkeys when they are required to remember long lists of objects over 24-hour intervals. Otherwise, the normal animals, with an intact limbic memory system, should have far surpassed the amnesic monkeys on the 24-hour concurrent-learning task. The finding that they did not surpass them indicates, conversely, that the nonlimbic habit system is an especially powerful one, which does permit the simultaneous acquisition of a long list of stimulus–response bonds despite 24-hour intertrial intervals. The contrast implies a trade-off between short-term flexibility afforded by the memory system and long-term reliability afforded by the habit system.

Habits: A Primitive Process

Earlier we pointed out that if both habits and memories are constantly being formed by experience in normal animals, then the great debate between behaviorists and cognitivists will have finally been resolved in favor of both positions. There is one area, however, in which the behaviorist position will always remain unchallenged, and this is in its applicability across the entire phyletic scale. Even animals with the simplest nervous systems are capable of response adaptation; the acquisition of information or knowledge, by contrast, may require the evolution of a system analogous to the cortico-limbo-thalamic pathway of mammals. The supposition that the memory system is a more recent development than the habit system phylogenetically raises the related question of how these two systems compare ontogenetically.

To examine that question, we tested monkeys of different ages—3 months, 6 months, and 12 months—for both memory formation and habit formation, using our tasks of visual recognition and 24-hour concurrent learning (Bachevalier & Mishkin, 1983). The particular recognition task we chose was delayed non-matching-to-sample with trial-unique objects, since among all the one-trial memory tasks that we have tried, we found this one to be the easiest for normal animals to learn (Mishkin & Delacour, 1975). In this task, a single object of a pair is presented as the sample in a central position, and the animal displaces it for food reward. Ten seconds later, the sample and the novel object in the pair are presented simultaneously in lateral positions, and the animal finds the reward if it displaces the novel object. The same procedure is then repeated at 30-second intertrial intervals, with a new pair of objects presented on every trial. As in the tasks described earlier, the animals are trained at the rate of 20 trials a day to a criterion of 90 correct responses in 100 trials.

It seems that the task is quickly learned for at least two reasons. First, monkeys are naturally curious and so prefer to investigate the novel object. And second, the design is such that the animal is rewarded for responding to novelty on every occasion, that is, both on the sample presentation as well as on the choice test. Once the animals have mastered the principle of delayed nonmatching, thereby demonstrating their ability to recognize the sample on the basis of a single familiarization experience, their memory can be taxed further by prolongation of the delays between familiarization and test and by extension of the sample list to more than one object (Gaffan, 1974). In the latter case, all the samples in the list are first presented one at a time, and then each is paired with a novel object in a series of choice tests.

Adult monkeys that are experimentally naive can learn the delayed nonmatching principle in fewer than 100 trials, and as indicated earlier, they can then perform at better than 90% accuracy on delays of up to two minutes and on lists of up to 10 objects. Despite the apparent simplicity of the test, however, infant monkeys could not learn the basic principle until they were 4 to 5 months of age; and further, once they did learn, they could not achieve adult levels of proficiency on the performance test with longer delays and lists until they were close to two years of age. In sharp contrast, the data on the 24-hour concurrent learning task revealed that even 3-month-old infants were as proficient as fully mature animals in learning long lists of discrimination problems. These lists the infants mastered at the same rate as adults despite the 24-hour intertrial intervals.

As in the case of mature monkeys rendered amnesic by limbic lesions, the success of the normal infant monkeys in 24-hour concurrent learning demonstrates that their failure in one-trial learning cannot be attributed to any inadequacies of perception, attention, motivation, or general learning ability. The simplest interpretation is to appeal again to the distinction between habits and memories. According to this interpretation, whereas infants can readily acquire habits, they are seriously deficient in forming memories, presumably because the cortico-limbo-thalamic circuit that constitutes the memory system undergoes a relatively slow ontogenetic development.

The Cortico-Striatal System

The question to which these arguments lead, of course, is what are the neural structures that constitute the postulated habit system. Here the evidence is still relatively sparse, and so our proposal must remain tentative. Nevertheless, data from a number of sources point to the possibility that habit formation in primates and other mammals depends in large part on the second major cortico-subcortical system of the forebrain, namely, the cortico-striatal system. The striatal complex or basal ganglia is an obvious candidate from an evolutionary standpoint in that it antedates both the cerebral cortex and the limbic system in phylogenesis (MacLean, 1977). Consequently, it seems reasonable to suppose that the striatal complex precedes the others in ontogenesis, too, and there is evidence from ablation studies in infant monkeys to support this notion (Goldman & Rosvold, 1972). A second reason to look to the cortico-striatal system as a major participant in habit formation is its neuroanatomical organization. The caudate and putamen together receive a heavy and, to some extent, topographically organized input from most of the cerebral cortex, and the two striatal nuclei project in turn to the globus pallidus and its associated structures within the extrapyramidal system (Grofova, 1979; Kemp & Powell, 1970; Johnson, Rosvold, & Mishkin, 1968; Turner *et al.*, 1980; Van Hoesen, Yeterian, & Lavizzo-Mourey, 1981). This system of projections therefore provides a mechanism through which cortically processed sensory inputs could become associated with motor outputs generated in the pallidum and so yield the stimulus–response bonds that constitute habits.

Whether or not the cortico-striatal system actually serves such a function is still unknown, since critical tests of the proposal have not been made. The data that are available, however, are clearly consistent with the proposal. For example, visual-pattern-discrimination habits, which are unaffected by limbic lesions, are markedly affected by damage along the cortico-striatal pathway. Thus, pattern-discrimination learning and retention can be impaired by lesions either of the inferior temporal cortex (Mishkin, 1954) or of some of the striatal regions to which this cortex projects, including the tail of the caudate nucleus (Divac, Rosvold, & Szwarcbart, 1967) and the ventral portion of the putamen (Buerger, Gross, & Rocha-Miranda, 1974). Furthermore, the same impairment can be reproduced by transections of the white matter of the temporal stem that presumably interrupt this cortico-striatal pathway (Horel, 1978; Zola-Morgan *et al.*, 1982).

The role of sensory inputs to the striatum has not received much emphasis before. As a result, the proposal that the striatum serves as an essential link in the formation of stimulus–response connections may seem highly improbable. Yet recent results obtained with the 2-deoxyglucose technique (Macko *et al.*, 1982) have revealed that, at least in the visual modality, sensory input is surprisingly effective in activating widespread portions of the striatum. This new finding, together with the developmental, connectional, and behavioral evidence just cited, indicate that the hypothesis of a cortico-striatal habit system existing alongside a cortico-limbic memory system may be sufficiently plausible to merit direct testing. If the hypothesis should hold up, the intriguing new questions will be how the learning process is actually shared by the two systems (Mishkin & Petri, 1984) and how the two systems might both cooperate and conflict.

ACKNOWLEDGMENT

Jocelyne Bachevalier is a Postdoctoral Fellow, Conseil de la Recherche en Santé du Québec, Canada.

REFERENCES

Aggleton, J. P., & Mishkin, M. Visual recognition impairment following medial thalamic lesions in monkeys. *Neuropsychologia*, 1983, *21*, 189–197.

Bachevalier, J., & Mishkin, M. The development of memories vs habits in infant monkeys. *International Journal of Psychophysiology*, 1983, *1*, 116.

Bachevalier, J., Parkinson, J. K., Aggleton, J. P., & Mishkin, M. Severe recognition impairment after combined but not separate transection of the fornix and the amygdalofugal pathways. *Society for Neuroscience Abstracts*, 1982, *8*, 23.

Buerger, A. A., Gross, C. G., & Rocha-Miranda, C. E. Effects of ventral putamen lesions on discrimination learning by monkeys. *Journal of Comparative and Physiological Psychology*, 1974, *86*, 440–446.

Cermak, L. S., & Butters, N. The role of interference and encoding in the short-term memory deficits of Korsakoff patients. *Neuropsychologia*, 1972, *10*, 89–95.

Cohen, N. J., & Squire, L. R. Preserved learning and retention of pattern-analyzing skill in amnesia: Dissociation of knowing how and knowing that. *Science*, 1980, *210*, 207–210.

Cohen, N. J., & Squire, L. R. Retrograde amnesia and remote memory impairment. *Neuropsychologia*, 1981, *19*, 337–356.

Cormier, S. M. A match–mismatch theory of limbic system function. *Physiological Psychology*, 1981, *19*, 3–36.

Cutting, J. A cognitive approach to Korsakoff's syndrome. *Cortex*, 1978, *14*, 485–495.

Divac, I., Rosvold, H. E., & Szwarcbart, M. K. Behavioral effects of selective ablation of the caudate nucleus. *Journal of Comparative and Physiological Psychology*, 1967, *63*, 184–190.

Gaffan, D. Recognition impaired and association intact in the memory of monkeys after transection of the fornix. *Journal of Comparative and Physiological Psychology*, 1974, *86*, 1100–1109.

Gaffan, D. Acquisition and forgetting in monkeys' memory of informational object–reward associations. *Learning and Motivation*, 1979, *10*, 419–444.

Goldman, P. S., & Rosvold, H. E. The effects of selective caudate lesions in infant and juvenile rhesus monkeys. *Brain Research*, 1972, *43*, 53–66.

Graf, P., Mandler, G., & Haden, P. E. Simulating amnesic symptoms in normal subjects. *Science*, 1982, *218*, 1243–1244.

Grofova, I. Extrinsic connections of the neostriatum. In I. Divac & R. G. E. Oberg (Eds.), *The neostriatum*. Oxford and New York: Pergamon Press, 1979.

Gross, C. G., & Mishkin, M. The neural basis of stimulus equivalence across retinal translation. In S. Harnad, R. Doty, J. Jaynes, L. Goldstein, & G. Krauthamer (Eds.), *Lateralization in the nervous system*. New York: Academic Press, 1977.

Harlow, H. F. Studies in discrimination learning by monkeys: II. Discrimination learning without primary reinforcement. *Journal of General Psychology*, 1944, *30*, 13–21.

Hirsh, R. The hippocampus and contextual retrieval of information from memory: A theory. *Behavioral Biology*, 1974, *12*, 421–444.

Hirsh, R. The hippocampus, conditional operations, and cognition. *Physiological Psychology*, 1980, *8*, 175–182.

Hirst, W. The amnesic syndrome: Descriptions and explanations. *Psychological Bulletin*, 1982, *91*, 435–460.

Horel, J. A. The neuroanatomy of amnesia: A critique of the hippocampal memory hypothesis. *Brain*, 1978, *101*, 403–445.

Huppert, F. A., & Piercy, M. Recognition memory in amnesic patients: Effect of temporal context and familiarity of material. *Cortex*, 1976, *12*, 3–20.

Johnson, T. N., Rosvold, H. E., & Mishkin, M. Projections from behaviorally-defined sectors of prefrontal cortex to the basal ganglia, septum, and diencephalon of the monkey. *Experimental Neurology*, 1968, *21*, 20–34.

Jones, B., & Mishkin, M. Limbic lesions and the problem of stimulus–reinforcement associations. *Experimental Neurology*, 1972, *36*, 362–377.

Kemp, J. M., & Powell, T. P. S. The cortico-striate projection in the monkey. *Brain*, 1970, *93*, 525–546.

Kinsbourne, M., & Wood, F. Short-term memory processes and the amnesic syndrome. In D. Deutsch & J. A. Deutsch (Eds.), *Short term memory*. New York: Academic Press, 1975.

Macko, K. A., Jarvis, C. D., Kennedy, C., Miyaoka, M., Shinohara, M., Sokoloff, L., & Mishkin, M. Mapping the primate visual system with [2-^{14}C]deoxyglucose. *Science*, 1982, *218*, 394–397.

MacLean, P. D. On the evolution of three mentalities. In S. Arieti & G. Chrzanowski (Eds.), *New dimensions in psychiatry: A world view* (Vol. 2). New York: Wiley, 1977.

Malamut, B. L., & Mishkin, M. Differences between limbic and nonlimbic retention processes. *Society for Neuroscience Abstracts*, 1981, *7*, 236.

Malamut, B. L., Saunders, R. C., & Mishkin, M. Successful object discrimination learning after combined amygdaloid–hippocampal lesions in monkeys despite 24-hour intertrial intervals. *Society for Neuroscience Abstracts*, 1980, *6*, 191.

McEntee, W. J., Biber, M. P., Perl, D. P., & Benson, D. F. Diencephalic amnesia: A reappraisal. *Journal of Neurology, Neurosurgery and Psychiatry*, 1976, *39*, 436–441.

Milner, B. The memory defect in bilateral hippocampal lesions. *Psychiatric Research Reports*, 1959, *11*, 43–58.

Milner, B. Les troubles de la mémoire accompagnant des lésions hippocampiques bilatérales. In P. Passouant (Ed.), *Physiologie de l'hippocampe*. Paris: Centre National de la Recherche Scientifique, 1962.

Milner, B. Memory and the medial temporal regions of the brain. In K. H. Pribram & D. E. Broadbent (Eds.), *Biology of memory*. New York: Academic Press, 1970.

Mishkin, M. Visual discrimination performance following partial ablations of the temporal lobe: II. Ventral surface vs. hippocampus. *Journal of Comparative Physiology and Psychology*, 1954, *47*, 187–193.

Mishkin, M. Memory in monkeys severely impaired by combined but not by separate removal of amygdala and hippocampus. *Nature*, 1978, *273*, 297–298.

Mishkin, M. Analogous neural models for tactual and visual learning. *Neuropsychologia*, 1979, *17*, 139–151.

Mishkin, M. A memory system in the monkey. *Philosophical Transactions of the Royal Society of London*, 1982, *B298*, 85–95.

Mishkin, M., & Aggleton, J. Multiple functional contributions of the amygdala in the monkey. In Y. Ben-Ari (Ed.), *The amygdaloid complex*. Amsterdam: Elsevier, 1981.

Mishkin, M., & Delacour, J. An analysis of short-term visual memory in the monkey. *Journal of Experimental Psychology: Animal Behavior Processes*, 1975, *1*, 326–334.

Mishkin, M., & Petri, H. L. Memories and habits: Some implications for the analysis of learning and retention. In N. Butters & L. R. Squire (Eds.), *Neuropsychology of memory*. New York: Guilford Press, 1984.

Mishkin, M., Spiegler, B. J., Saunders, R. C., & Malamut, B. L. An animal model of global amnesia. In S. Corkin, K. L. Davis, J. H. Growden, E. Usdin, & R. J. Wurtman (Eds.), *Alzheimer's disease: A report of progress*. New York: Raven Press, 1982.

Murray, E. A., & Mishkin, M. Severe tactual memory deficits in monkeys after combined removal of the amygdala and hippocampus. *Brain Research*, 1983, *270*, 340–344.

O'Keefe, J., & Nadel, L. The amnesic syndrome. In *The hippocampus as a cognitive map*. New York: Oxford University Press, 1978.

Olton, D. S., Becker, J. T., & Handelmann, G. E. Hippocampus, space, and memory. *Behavioral and Brain Sciences*, 1979, *2*, 313–317.

Orbach, J., Milner, B., & Rasmussen, T. Learning and retention in monkeys after amygdala–hippocampus resection. *Archives of Neurology*, 1960, *3*, 230–251.

Sands, S. F., & Wright, A. A. Monkey and human pictorial memory scanning. *Science*, 1982, *216*, 1333–1334.

Spiegler, B. J., & Mishkin, M. Evidence for the sequential participation of inferior temporal cortex and amygdala in the acquisition of stimulus–reward associations. *Behavioural Brain Research*, 1981, *3*, 303–317.

Stern, L. D. A review of theories of human amnesia. *Memory and Cognition*, 1981, *9*, 247–262.

Turner, B., Mishkin, M., & Knapp, M. Organization of the amygdalopetal projections from modality-specific cortical association areas in the monkey. *Journal of Comparative Neurology*, 1980, *191*, 515–543.

Ungerleider, L. G., & Mishkin, M. Two cortical visual systems. In D. J. Ingle, M. A. Goodale, & R. J. W. Mansfield (Eds.), *Analysis of visual behavior*. Cambridge, Mass.: MIT Press, 1982.

Van Hoesen, G. W., & Pandya, D. N. Some connections of the entorhinal (area 28) and perirhinal (area 35) cortices of the rhesus monkey: I. Temporal lobe afferents. *Brain Research*, 1975, *95*, 1–24.

Van Hoesen, G. W., Yeterian, E. H., & Lavizzo-Mourey, R. Widespread corticostriate projections from temporal cortex of the rhesus monkey. *Journal of Comparative Neurology*, 1981, *199*, 205–219.

Victor, M., Adams, R. D., & Collins, G. H. *The Wernicke–Korsakoff syndrome*. Oxford: Blackwell, 1971.

Warrington, E. K., & Weiskrantz, L. Amnesia: A disconnection syndrome? *Neuropsychologia*, 1982, *20*, 233–248.

Wickelgren, W. A. Chunking and consolidation: A theoretical synthesis of semantic networks, configuring in conditioning, S-R versus cognitive learning, normal forgetting, the amnesic syndrome, and the hippocampal arousal system. *Psychological Review*, 1979, *86*, 44–60.

Zola-Morgan, S., Squire, L. R., & Mishkin, M. The neuroanatomy of amnesia: Amygdala–hippocampus versus temporal stem. *Science*, 1982, *218*, 1337–1339.

CHAPTER THREE

Advances in Cognitive Neurosciences: The Problem of Information Storage in the Human Brain

MICHAEL S. GAZZANIGA

INTRODUCTION

Traditionally, the study of human memory and cognition has fallen to the experimental psychologist. In the search for insights on the workings of the human mental system, psychologists have, among other methodologies, subjected normal individuals to experiments that tax the information-processing system and then examined the manner in which the system breaks down. This approach has produced rich insights into the normal workings of mind and has served as the groundwork for the modern-day cognitive sciences. The cognitive neurosciences take a different tack. The objective of this approach is to study and to model human cognition by the careful examination of cognitive processes following brain injury. The field includes neuroscientists, psychologists, linguists, biophysicists, and neurologists. Cognitive neuroscientists believe that their interdisciplinary efforts will produce models of normal human cognition based on biological systems.

These two experimental approaches should come to contribute heavily to framing the future questions of the cellular biologist. At present, however, there are wide gaps that exist between those seeking a cellular understanding of memory and those seeking a systems understanding. As a result, a major challenge facing biology is to achieve an understanding of how these two levels interact (see Churchland, 1982). Consider the following problem.

My pet dog is let out of my apartment door. It knows that a dish of milk is waiting every morning at the same time at the deli just south on First Avenue, off 63rd Street. I also know the same deli is waiting for me (a little later) with a quart of milk. To maintain that the neural representation of this knowledge for the dog and for me is the same is like claiming that the Cathedral of Notre Dame in Paris and a farmhouse are the same just because they are both built of stone. At some level the dog's brain and my brain function because neurons function, or even more basically, because molecules function. Yet the questions one asks about the brain for the two species would be quite different.

Michael S. Gazzaniga. Division of Cognitive Neuroscience, Department of Neurology, Cornell University Medical College, New York, New York.

Human memory is a vast and complex phenomenon, with the physical instantiation of the responsible processes being particularly troublesome for the neurobiologist on the prowl. A case in point is told by George Miller and concerns the human's ability to remember a tone. In an experiment carried out some years back by Bachem (1954), subjects were given a tone of particular frequency to remember. Moments later they were to match the tone by adjusting an oscillator. This proved to be rather easy, and the variance around the tone was small. Through time, however, the variance grew. When they were asked to do the same thing an hour later, the variance increased, and when they were asked a day later, the variance increased even more.

On the other hand, if the task was given to someone with perfect pitch, the initial measure was like that of the neophyte group, but the subsequent memories remained accurate, with no increase in variance. Clearly, when first hearing the tone, the subjects with perfect pitch were able to classify it as, say, "B flat," and when they went to perform the memory task, they called on quite different processes than those called on by the neophyte. I don't think anyone seriously claims the underlying neurobiology that supports these behaviors is the same for these two cases. The way the information is represented in the brain has to be totally different for the two cases.

In what follows, I present the lines of thought that have come out of my laboratory and represent some aspects of the systems-oriented approach. I begin with a general statement of the issue in question, memory, and then attempt to set forth the data base emphasizing our views. I have organized the data around a set of principles that, if true, would have to be taken into account by anybody who attempts to study how the human brain stores information.

MECHANISMS OF HUMAN INFORMATION STORAGE

General Background

The central issue for neurobiologists interested in human-memory research is how experience is represented and stored in the nervous system. A deeply ingrained idea is that there are basic memory units called "engrams." These are thought to be neural circuits or synaptic sites that modify their organization so as to store specific experiences. The mechanism by which they do so remains unspecified. Confounding this puzzle is the fact that while changes in synaptic organization are commonly proposed, there is no need to make such assumptions when considering how the brain could store information. The patterning of impulses, for example, in existing circuits could be the crucial code, and patterns could easily change without structural synaptic change occurring. Still, the idea that synaptic change is involved in information storage persists as the dominant theory.

Neuropsychologically oriented views of the biologic basis of information storage have deemphasized the neuronal units of memory. Such approaches are conceptually oriented toward distinguishing memory "systems," with the most pervasive distinction being the difference between short-term and long-term memory. In this vein, observations of case H. M. have been particularly influential. Brenda Milner (1974) and her colleagues over the years have carefully carried out a series of now classic studies of this patient, which have demonstrated that bilateral lesion of the hippocampus (and amygdala) produces a dense anterograde amnesia. H. M. can access past memories but is completely unable to encode new information. Experimental psychologists have been fascinated with this observation, and a plethora of supportive observations have reinforced the notion that the brain honors the distinction between short- and long-term memory (Atkinson & Juola, 1974). At about the same time, the cellular neurobiologist discovered that the hippocampus was delightfully easy to study because of its intrinsic cellular organization and its accessibility to neurophysiologic and chemical analysis. This, combined with its possible role in memory processes, made it a natural structure for cellular analysis. The stage was thus set for the systematic investigation of the brain structures managing memory processes.

In recent years, however, a wide variety of new discoveries and reassessments of earlier interpretations has come about. New work at the psychological level has, on the whole, suggested that the eloquently simple two-stage model of long- and short-term memory does not adequately describe the process of information storage. At the neurologic level, other neural structures have emerged that appear to be central to the management of memory.

At the psychological level, the importance of process has dominated current theoretical models (Craik & Tulving, 1975). Memory is no longer viewed as consisting of discrete components such as short-term memory (STM) and long-term memory (LTM) but as a reflection of processing. Problems are now addressed in terms of accessing, encoding, and organizing information. It is one thing to store information; it is quite another to find it and use it. This change is also reflected in neuropsychological studies, in which the density (or more accurately, the lack of density) of the amnesia is being better understood. Information is getting into the brain in amnesics. Motor skills are being learned, as are perceptual skills (Milner, 1974). Even cognitive skills can be learned by the amnesic (Cohen & Squire, 1980; Hirst & Volpe, 1984b). If instead of asking an amnesic patient to recall prior information, he or she is only requested to recognize it, performance may change dramatically (Warrington & Weiskrantz, 1974). Recognition scores are consistently higher than recall measures. Although there are changes in interpretation (Warrington & Weiskrantz, 1982) with each new experiment, it is as if the ability of the human brain to encode at least some aspects of experience is much more difficult to disrupt than was once expected.

The notion that the neurology of amnesia was going to be difficult also emerged from the neurological clinic. Clearly different pathologies were revealing behavioral patterns that were not unlike those found for the focal case, H. M. Thalamic lesions produce amnesias (Squire & Moore, 1979) as do a variety of more diffuse diseases (Volpe & Hirst, 1983). As a result of all these recent studies, the stage is now set for new views and new ideas about the psychological and biological basis of information storage (Squire, 1980, 1982; Hirst, 1982).

PSYCHOLOGICAL STUDIES

Recent studies of brain-damaged humans suggest that there are important superordinate organizing systems active in the acquisition and management of new information. Superordinate systems are those processes that are essential to the initial apprehension and to the orderly placement of new information in a functional network. Without these processes, information can be successfully stored but not easily accessed. The new information, if it registers in the system, lacks needed tags that deal with such key factors as what time the event occurred and how important the information is for the organism. In the following, I will be describing three superordinate systems active in the storage process. I start with studies that examine the system that puts limits on information apprehension.

Attentional Considerations

Always closely tied to the process of information storage is the mechanism of stimulus selection, which serves to direct the organism's processing capacity to one source of stimulation as opposed to others. How effectively a stimulus is processed depends both on the efficiency of processing strategies and the degree of effort or resource that is committed to a particular task.

It has proved particularly difficult to distinguish between these two aspects of information processing in the functionally intact brain. It has, however, been possible to do so in the split-brain patient. Studies to date confirm that these are, in fact, distinguishable processes. We have shown that, under the appropriate stimulus condition, the amount of information that can be apprehended in a moment's time is enhanced by creating a brain lesion (Gazzaniga, 1968; Gazzaniga & Young, 1967; Holtzman & Gazzaniga, 1984). At the same time, the total resources available to carry out data processing remain limited and fixed even in a brain system with double cognitive agency (Holtzman & Gazzaniga, 1982).

In one study (Holtzman & Gazzaniga, 1984), it was found that two disconnected half-brains of a patient bilaterally organized for language created a brain milieu that allowed for information processing activities that cannot be carried out by a normal brain; that is, there was an increase in the capacity to process information. The test conditions require the subject to fixate a point and subsequently, *each* hemisphere is exposed to the successive presentation of four *x*'s, each appearing in any one of nine cells in a 3×3 grid. Thus, each half-brain had been exposed to four pieces of information or eight for botn hemispheres. In one condition, the four pieces appeared in the same squares in each hemifield, and thus in each half-brain. In the other condition, they did not, which made this condition extremely difficult for neurologically intact observers. The results were clear. The split-brain patient was able to carry out the difficult task, whereas the control observers could not. These results suggest that when information is presented to the human brain within a fixed time constraint, the perceptual organization of a stimulus is limited by the sensory systems committed to processing comparable stimuli. By isolating one part of a sensory system from another part of the same system, as is done with callosal surgery, the organism's overall data-acquisition capacity is enhanced.

A second set of experiments demonstrated that the brain has a fixed amount of resources it can activate for cognitive tasks, which also put limits on short-term memory performance (Holtzman & Gazzaniga, 1982). In these studies, the memory-performance capacity of one hemisphere was examined as a function of whether the opposite half-brain was working on a "hard" or an "easy" problem. If the resource-allocation mechanism is cortically driven, one would predict no interaction on the task. If, however, the brain mechanisms that manage resources are subcortical, one would predict interactions between the hemispheres as a function of task difficulty. We found the latter to be the case. Working on a hard problem in one hemisphere diminished the performance of the other half-brain at a concurrent task, whereas an easy task had little effect.

Spatial–Temporal Coding

Another superordinate mechanism deals with the coding of spatial and temporal referents. Temporal encoding consists of those processes that distinguish event A from event B in terms of when in the history of the organism the two events occurred. In an ecological context, for example, the Reagan assassination attempt is easily recognized at a later point in time as having occurred before the Sadat assassination. In recent studies, it has been demonstrated that it is precisely these kinds of spatial–temporal referents that are disrupted in human amnesia (Hirst & Volpe, 1982, 1984a). Although two prior events can be recognized as having occurred, the amnesic patient is unable to tell which occurred first. It is easy to imagine how a brain system that fails to time-lock automatically all new events might be severely impaired when required to recall past experience. When such a brain is queried on its past history, it would have no basis for recreating a coherent order of events.

Preference-Encoding Mechanisms

When new information is stored in the human brain, it usually has associated with it an affective component (Rozin, 1976). An important issue would be to determine whether or not the brain system assigning affective labels to new information can be demonstrated. Recent studies of ours would suggest this is the case. The amnesic syndrome includes the loss of a feeling of familiarity for recently experienced events, especially for personal experiences. There is no sense of continuity with the past. Even when subjects solve a problem correctly or learn a new cognitive strategy, there is no feeling of familiarity associated with their response (Cohen & Squire, 1980).

One way of influencing familiarity in nonamnesic subjects is to increase the frequency of occurrence of a stimulus. Repeated exposure to a stimulus enhances the attractiveness of that stimulus: The more often a novel stimulus is seen, the greater the positive affect associated with it. Zajonc (1980) recently performed a series of experiments in which he manipulated the stimulus frequency and subsequently required subjects to rate the stimuli. Stimuli that were seen most often were rated as the most pleasant, and those seen least often were least preferred. Once these preferences were established, they persisted over several rating sessions.

In a recent study (Redington, Volpe, & Gazzaniga, 1984), a group of amnesics and a group of control subjects were exposed to stimuli that were presented at different frequencies. Following presentation of all the stimuli, subjects gave a preference rating for each stimulus. There was a marked difference between control and amnesic subjects. Although the amnesics were able to recognize the pictures they had been exposed to, they showed no modulation of preference as a function of stimulus frequency. In contrast, the ratings of age-matched control subjects were highly correlated with stimulus frequency.

Taken together, these studies argue for the presence of superordinate systems in normal human memory. Some kinds of amnesia are not necessarily due to a breakdown of information storage but rather reflect impairments in these superordinate systems that organize incoming information. In this light, the questions that the neurobiologist might ask about some kinds of human amnesia become different. The search for the engram becomes the search for a system breakdown, not the reorganization of dendrites at the synaptic level.

NEUROLOGICAL CONSIDERATIONS

A cardinal feature of working with brain-damaged patients is the great variability in performance associated with supposedly similar brain injuries. Conversely, one sees common behavioral deficits produced by a variety of different brain lesions. Working in the clinic, one comes to appreciate that the single-case method, although always provocative, is sometimes fraught with disappointment. The diversity of behavioral profiles is much more prevalent than the consistencies, especially when dealing with cognitive capacities following focal and diffuse brain injury.

This problem is particularly apparent when the psychological studies of split-brain patients are considered. If the psychological profile of case P. S.'s right hemisphere, which possesses rich language, were considered the rule (Gazzaniga, LeDoux, Smylie, & Volpe, 1979), our picture of right-hemisphere functions would be quite different than if we considered the psychological profile of case J. W., who possesses less (Sidtis, Volpe, Wilson, Rayport, & Gazzaniga, 1981). In the same vein, there are probably few who would predict that the memory deficits of all patients with bilateral hippocampal damage would be identical to the profile that has been so carefully described for case H. M. It is a bothersome notion, but it should not be trivialized; there are enormous variations in the functional organization of the human brain.

Perhaps an even more striking example of variations in brain organization is the interhemispheric transfer capacities that exist following complete callosotomy. In patients in whom the anterior commissure has been spared from surgical intervention, sectioning the corpus callosum alone usually blocks the interhemispheric transfer of visual information. That is the case for most of the patients. Yet there is a small number, approximately five, who do transfer information interhemispherically, and presumably they do so through the remaining anterior commissure (Risse, LeDoux, Wilson, & Gazzaniga, 1975). The variation in function is explicit in this instance and yet underlies the well-known truth in functional anatomical studies that there are significant physical variations in anatomical structures.

The problem of brain and behavioral correlates is compounded when considering patients suffering from disorders of memory. Amnesia, the catchall phrase that describes a class of cognitive disorders associated with poor memory, is a disease that has multiple causes and multiple densities. For example, while all amnesics, by definition, have difficulty recalling new information, their recall deficit is not necessarily tied to an equally dense deficit in recognition memory. Gaining an understanding of the mechanisms responsible for such variations is greatly enhanced by considering the dynamic processes that might be impaired in the amnesic patient. In the following, I will report on two sets of studies carried out on amnesics that use brain science techniques to examine this issue. The first study examines the possible relation between a spared hippocampus and global recognition skills as measured by the P300. The second study, which includes positron emission tomography (PET) scanning, considers how metabolic processes that track the biologic energy of an organism might possibly relate to resources that exist at a psychological level and that are important for the normal maintenance of the superordinate organizational systems described above.

The Hippocampus as a General Neuroregulator

In a previous paper, I argued that the clear distinction between the efficiency and amount of information that can be accessed through recognition memory, as opposed to recall memory, might well reflect a basic principle of brain organization (Gazzaniga, 1976). I hypothesized that the brain is organized into separate mental modules, each with its own integrity, most of which function in nonverbal terms. These separate modules are each capable of storing a limited amount of information, just as the verbal module has a limited amount it can access. When a recall demand is in order, only the verbal system can respond, because the recall method is a verbal response calling on the information encoded within this domain. Since it is probably the case that there are specialized processors for producing drawings, recall responses through this avenue would also be limited. When a recognition demand is in order, however, all of the other nonverbal modules are free to respond. Since they are, by definition, only able to point to suggested stimuli, these nonverbal modules are now free to demonstrate the information in their stores. And with many separate modules available, the recognition skills could be enormously rich, as they in fact seem to be.

There is, however, a paradox. Although amnesics vary enormously in their capacity to recognize information, the lesions that produce amnesic states can be relatively specific, as in case H. M. Following his bilateral hippocampectomy, H. M. stands as a benchmark case on how poor recognition skills can be. He has little recognition memory for episodic events, word pairs, picture series, and the like. Other patients with less-defined lesions, who are comparably impaired at recall, are much less impaired at recognition memory. Some even perform at normal levels. In an ongoing study, we are examining whether such behavioral variations might be attributable to variations in the extent of hippocampal damage (Milner, 1974). Such a correlation would be expected if the hippocampus served to regulate the storage of all new information for all the mental modules.

In this regard, Pamela Greenwood, Bruce Volpe, and I chose to study the electrophysiological response known as the P300. This event-related potential, which is associated with mnestic function, is now thought to be generated in the hippocampus (Okada, Kaufman, & Williamson, 1983). We looked for a correlation between the presence and magnitude of the P300 and recognition skills. In the amnesic group, there were three subclasses of memory disorder: One patient had a severe recognition deficit; one had a milder deficit; and several had no discernible deficits. In studies to date, case L. K., who suffers from a dense amnesia with poor recognition skills, did not have a P300 response. The patients with no recognition deficits displayed a normal P300, whereas a patient with a weak recognition impairment showed a weak P300.

These findings suggest a possible resolution to the dilemma raised concerning the variety of brain lesions that produce the amnesic syndrome. The data suggest that the hippocampus plays a primary role in the regulation of the mnemonic processes of all brain systems that are free to encode information. Perhaps in much the same sense that there are regulator genes, there are neural regulators that manage and control the data-processing capacity of many information-processing modules. Furthermore, it could be argued that more diffuse lesions that spare the hippocampus yield a system that allows the nonverbal modules to store information but finds verbal recall impaired because of other dimensions of the system breakdown. How this might work is discussed in the next section.

Biologic Energy and Psychological Resources

PET scanning allows for the exploration of metabolic and basic energy requirements of cerebral processes in both the normal and abnormal brain (see Phelps, Huang, Hoffman, Selin, Sokoloff, & Kuhl, 1979). This relatively new technique provides a staggering amount of data on any given subject and also reveals pathologies that heretofore have remained hidden to neurologic examination from imaging techniques such as CT scan. In short, the PET scan is proving to be so sensitive a measure of differential brain function in humans, current investigators can look at a scan that shows regional pathologies and exclaim, "That's the answer—now what's the question?"

Currently, there are two main approaches used in delineating energy correlations of psychological processes. There are simple activation studies where steady-state visual or auditory stimuli are presented during metabolic studies (with accumulation time of 40 minutes) using ^{18}F-2-fluoro-2-deoxyglucose (Mazziotta, Phelps, Carson, & Kuhl, 1982). More recently, there have been activation studies using psychological and hemispheric-specific stimuli that can be carried out in 2–4 minutes and make use of blood-flow markers such as $CO^{15}O$ (Kearfott, Rottenberg, & Volpe, 1983; Sidtis, Rottenberg, & Gazzaniga, 1983). These studies also indicate the sensitivity of the technology and suggest that dynamic psychological processes can be analyzed with PET scanning. A second approach is to examine the neurologically impaired patient. Here, cognitive deficits have been established "off line" as it were, through extensive neuropsychological assessment. In this fashion, possible new insights into brain mechanisms responsible for demonstrating cognitive disorders might be possible.

When studies are carried out on potentially abnormal brains, there are strict requirements. Unlike normal studies, where blood-flow measurements are sufficient, under many conditions studies on the abnormal brain require markers for blood flow, blood volume, and cerebral metabolism. With all these markers in place, it is possible to look at subtle pathological states by the examination of decoupling processes between blood flow and metabolism.

We have recently had the opportunity to study an amnesic patient using such techniques (Volpe, Herscovitch, Raichle, & Gazzaniga, 1982; Volpe, Herscovitch, Raichle, Gazzaniga, & Hirst, in press). The patient, who suffers from a marked amnesia, was found to have two brain abnormalities. In the region of the mesial temporal lobe, there was a significant decoupling between flow and metabolism. This finding is consistent with the hippocampal model for memory dysfunction. The patient did possess, however, an intermediate capacity for recognition memory. Perhaps as interesting is the concurrent observation that the patient suffered from an overall decrease in global flow and metabolism in addition to the regional decoupling abnormality in the mesial temporal lobes. Put differently, the overall energy sources available for psychological processes, which in turn call on neuronal systems for successful execution, were dramatically reduced. This raises the interesting possibility that the deficit seen in some kinds of amnesia could reflect deficits in overall biologic energy available to the brain. With abnormalities here, the normal extensive supporting systems that are activated in the storage of information cannot all be automatically summoned, because of a limitation in overall biological resources. As a consequence, although there might be enough energy to encode the content of the event, the more automatic processes that tag information for affect, time, and place, might not be functioning normally, thereby producing the clinical state of amnesia. It remains for future studies to explore these possibilities more fully.

DISCUSSION

The neurobiological and psychological understanding of information storage in the human brain is progressing at a rapid rate, and at the present time there would appear to be many points of contact between these two very different disciplines. I have reviewed some of the ongoing studies associated with our Division of Cognitive Neuroscience at Cornell that attempt to address these points of contact.

The foregoing studies carried out at both the psychological and neurological levels indicate that episodic information exposed to a neural system must not only be recorded but also must establish clear tags with such key factors as space, time, affect, and most likely a host of other psychological dimensions. It would appear that the superordinate systems that are responsible for these processes can be specifically damaged and thereby produce a clinical state of amnesia. Both focal and diffuse damage can produce memory disorders. In some forms of brain damage, the biologic energy requirements for the automatic participation of the superordinate systems in the act of information storage may not be sufficient to sustain their normal functioning. Experiments are being planned to pursue this possibility.

It is also apparent that while many different kinds of focal lesions and diffuse lesions can produce amnesic states, mesial temporal lobe damage seems particularly to affect the ability to recognize episodic events. In case H. M., it is reported that he has virtually no recognition memory. Other amnesics, most likely suffering less hippocampal involvement, appear to have some recognition memory, and some appear virtually normal. This suggests that hippocampal mechanisms might be generally involved in the storage of new information in all of the independent modules available for information storage.

Obtaining a more fundamental cellular understanding of the processes propounded herein remains as a challenge to future research. Indeed, it could be argued that given the existence of the kind of superordinate organizing system I have described, a fair question for the cellular neurobiologist might well be "What is it you are looking for and how might that fit into a systems understanding of information storage in the human central nervous system?" The answer to that ought to keep the best of us busy for a very long time indeed.

ACKNOWLEDGMENTS

This work was aided by USPHS Grant 5P01 NS 17778-01A1, the Alfred P. Sloan Foundation, and the McKnight Foundation.

I would like to gratefully acknowledge the help of Drs. Jeffrey Holtzman, Bruce Volpe, John Sidtis, and William Hirst in preparing the manuscript.

REFERENCES

Atkinson, R. C., & Juola, J. Search and decision processes in recognition memory. In D. H. Krantz, R. C. Atkinson, R. D. Luce, & P. Suppez (Eds.), *Contemporary developments in mathematical psychology* (Vol. 1: *Learning, memory and thinking*). San Francisco: Freeman, 1974.

Bachem, A. Time factors in relative and absolute pitch determination. *Journal of the Acoustical Society of America*, 1954, *26*, 751–753.

Churchland, P. S. Mind–brain reduction: New light from the philosophy of science. *Neuroscience*, 1982, *7*, 1041–1047.

Cohen, N., & Squire, L. Preserved learning and retention of pattern and analyzing skills in amnesia: Dissociation of knowing how and knowing that. *Science*, 1980, *210*, 207–210.

Craik, F. I. M., & Tulving, E. Depth of processing and the retention of words in episodic memory. *Journal of Experimental Psychology: General*, 1975, *104*, 268–294.

Gazzaniga, M. S. Short term memory and brain bisected man. *Psychonomic Science*, 1968, *12*, 161–162.

Gazzaniga, M. S. The biology of memory. In M. Rosenzweig & E. Bennett (Eds.), *Neural mechanisms of learning and memory*. Cambridge, Mass.: MIT Press, 1976.

Gazzaniga, M. S., LeDoux, J. E., Smylie, C. S., & Volpe, B. T. Plasticity in speech organization following commissurotomy. *Brain*, 1979, *102*, 805–815.

Gazzaniga, M. S., & Young, E. D. Effects of commissurotomy on the processing of increasing visual information. *Experimental Brain Research*, 1967, *3*, 368–371.

Hirst, W. The amnesic syndrome: Description and explanation. *Psychological Bulletin*, 1982, *91*, 435–460.

Hirst, W., & Volpe, B. T. Temporal recognition in anterograde amnesia. *Brain and Cognition*, 1982, *1*, 294.

Hirst, W., & Volpe, B. T. Automatic and effortful encoding in amnesia. In M. S. Gazzaniga (Eds.), *Handbook of cognitive neuroscience*. New York: Plenum, 1984. (a)

Hirst, W., & Volpe, B. T. *Skills and strategies in amnesic syndromes: A study of metamemory*. Manuscript submitted for publication, 1984. (b)

Holtzman, J. D., & Gazzaniga, M. S. Dual task interaction due exclusively to limits in processing resources. *Science*, 1982, *218*, 1325–1327.

Holtzman, J. D., & Gazzaniga, M. S. *Enhanced dual task performance after corpus commissurotomy*. Manuscript submitted for publication, 1984.

Kearfott, K., Rottenberg, D., & Volpe, B. T. Design of steady-state PET protocols for neurobehavioral studies: $CO^{15}O$, Ne^{19}. *Journal of Computer Assisted Tomography*, 1983, *7*, 51–58.

Mazziotta, J. C., Phelps, M. E., Carson, R. E., & Kuhl, D. E. Tomographic mapping of human cerebral metabolism: Auditory stimulation. *Neurology*, 1982, *32*, 921–937.

Milner, B. Hemispheric specialization: Scope and limits. In F. O. Schmitt & F. G. Worden (Eds.), *The neurosciences: Third study program*. Cambridge, Mass.: MIT Press, 1974.

Okada, Y. C., Kaufman, L., & Williamson, S. J. The hippocampal formation as a source of the slow endogenous potentials. *Electroencephalography and Clinical Neurophysiology*, 1983, *55*, 417–426.

Phelps, M., Huang, S. C., Hoffman, E. J., Selin, C., Sokoloff, L., & Kuhl, D. E. Tomographic measurement of local cerebral glucose metabolic rate in humans with (F-18) 2-fluoro-2-deoxyglucose: Validation of method. *Annals of neurology*, 1979, *6*, 371–388.

Redington, K. M., Volpe, B. T., & Gazzaniga, M. S. Failure of preference formation in amnesics. *Neurology*, 1984, *34*, 536–538.

Risse, G., LeDoux, J. E., Wilson, D. H., & Gazzaniga, M. S. The anterior commissure in man: Functional variation in a multisensory system. *Neuropsychologia*, 1975, *16*, 23–31.

Rozin, P. The psychobiological approach to human memory. In M. Rosenzweig & E. Bennett (Eds.), *Neural mechanisms of learning and memory*. Cambridge, Mass.: MIT Press, 1976.

Sidtis, J. J., Rottenberg, D. A., & Gazzaniga, M. S. Unpublished observations, 1983.

Sidtis, J. J., Volpe, B. T., Wilson, D. H., Rayport, M., & Gazzaniga, M. S. Variability in right hemisphere language function after callosal section: Evidence for a continuum of generative capacity. *Journal of Neuroscience*, 1981, *1*, 323–331.

Squire, L. R. The anatomy of amnesia. *Trends in Neurosicence*, 1980, *3*, 52–54.

Squire, L. R. The neuropsychology of human memory. *Annual Review of Neuroscience*, 1982, *5*, 241–273.

Squire, L. R., & Moore, R. Dorsal thalamic lesion in a noted case of human memory dysfunction. *Annals of Neurology*, 1979, *6*, 503–506.

Volpe, B. T., & Hirst, W. Characterization of three patients with an amnesic syndrome following hypoxic–ischemic injury. *Archives of Neurology*, 1983, *40*, 436–440.

Volpe, B. T., Herscovitch, P., Raichle, M., and Gazzaniga, M. S. A neurologic basis for human amnesia: The metabolic approach. *Society for Neuroscience*, 1982. (Abstract)

Volpe, B. T., Herscovitch, P., Raichle, M. Gazzaniga, M. S., & Hirst, W. Positron emission tomography defines metabolic abnormalities in two patients with amnesic syndromes. *Neurology*, in press.

Warrington, E. K., & Weiskrantz, L. The effect of prior learning on subsequent retention in amnesic patients. *Neuropsychologia*, 1974, *12*, 419–428.

Warrington, E. K., & Weiskrantz, L. Amnesia: A disconnection syndrome? *Neuropsychologia*, 1982, *20*, 2, 233–248.

Zajonc, R. B. Feeling and thinking: Preferences need no inferences. *American Psychologist*, 1980, *35*, 2, 151–175.

CHAPTER FOUR

Selective Attention and the Storage of Information

MICHAEL I. POSNER

INTRODUCTION

There are really two very different languages for discussing the problems of information processing in the nervous system. One language is used by neuroscience. It is most often concerned with the localization of function. The methods used are designed to discover the parts of the brain that might be active or altered during attention or memory. Studies of brain injury are used to associate parts of the brain with psychological functions. A second language comes from cognitive psychology. Its emphasis is on the logical stages or elementary mental operations involved in tasks. In cognitive psychology, studies of brain injury are most often used to explore dissociations between these elementary components. Most of these cognitive studies emphasize careful timing because they seek to understand the flow of information processing.

There is considerable dispute about the relationship of these two languages. Some believe they must remain independent alternative descriptions at different levels of analysis (Fodor, 1975). An extreme version of this view holds that the knowledge that a process is instantiated in a brain rather than in a computer or some other system is irrelevant to understanding at the cognitive level. Classical views of reductionism argue that cognitive theories will be replaced by neurophysiological ones as our understanding of the relevant neurophysiology grows. The view represented in this chapter is that of cognitive neuroscience, with attempts to map elementary cognitive operations into the relevant neural systems that support them (Posner, Pea, & Volpe, 1982). This view proposes that joint constraints arising from the use of both languages will be needed to aid us in understanding such complex process as human memory.

One of the most remarkable findings of the last dozen years of cognitive psychology is our ability to separate automatic unattended processing of information from attended, active processing of information (Marcel, 1983; Posner, 1978; Shiffrin & Schneider, 1977). The distinction appears to be a

Michael I. Posner. Department of Psychology, University of Oregon, Eugene, Oregon; Cognitive Neuropsychology Laboratory, Department of Neurology, Good Samaritan Hospital and Medical Center, Portland, Oregon.

fundamental one and one that may illuminate problems of information storage and retrieval that are the concerns of this conference. Let me highlight these findings by citing three examples from the literature. All of them are to some degree disputed, but all are important in demonstrating joint contributions of neuroscience and cognitive science approaches to mental processing.

The first arises from neuropsychology and deals with the study of visual stimuli presented within an occipital scotoma. Pöppel, Held, and Frost (1973) reported that a light presented within the occipital scotoma can lead to orienting to a visual stimulus that the subject cannot consciously see. This phenomenon has been studied in some detail in several patients (Weiskrantz, 1980) and has been the source of studies of rehabilitation (Zihl, 1980). Marcel (1983) reports preliminary evidence that the perception of the form of these unseen stimuli is sufficient to guide the shape of the hand as the subject reaches for a target. There has, of course, been dispute about the occurrence of blindsight, its physiological basis, and whether it might be accounted for by light scattered into the sighted field (Campion, Latto, & Smith, 1983). Insofar as the phenomenon is real, it provides concrete instance of dissociation between the subject's awareness of the presence of a stimulus and restricted actions of orienting toward that stimulus.

A second, and in many ways equally striking, phenomenon has been studied in cognitive psychology. It goes back as far as Pavlov, but the recent studies have been inspired by the work of Meyer, Schvaneveldt, and Ruddy (1975). These studies involve priming one target word by a prior semantically related word. What is most remarkable about this phenomenon is that facilitation of the processing of the target word occurs even in circumstances in which the subject does not desire it. For example, if subjects are asked to name the color of ink in which the target is written, the prime, by facilitating the processing of the word *name*, actually interferes with the ability of the subject to name the ink color (Warren, 1972). There is evidence that relatively little conscious attention to the prime need occur. For example, Fischler and Goodman (1978) found that primes of insufficient duration to be remembered even 1 or 2 seconds later still produce savings in reaction time to the target sometimes larger than those primes that could be reported. Marcel (1980) reported that even when the prime is masked so that subjects are unable to discriminate the prime from the mask alone, there is evidence of semantic priming. Though some of these latter observations have been disputed, there seems little doubt that the prime automatically activates sets of internal representations that stand for its physical, phonological, and semantic characteristics, and such activation has consequences on stimuli that follow it.

A third phenomenon has already been well described, namely, the distinction between those things that amnesics are capable of learning and those they are not (Squire & Cohen, Chapter 1, this volume). There are many ways to make this distinction. One way of talking about this distinction suggests that the amnesic is unable to store the record of active attention. If a stimulus could have its effect on the nervous system without currently being attended, as in the performance of a habitual skill or in priming, then an amnesic does seem to be able to learn in a relatively normal way. However, when the learning requires a summoning of information into active attention, the amnesic is able to attend but does not seem to be able to store the products of attention.

It may appear to neuroscientists that the distinction between attended and unattended or conscious and unconscious processes provides little help in the analysis of the striking dissociations found in amnesia. Only 15 years ago (Worden, 1966), there was no scientific approach, particularly no physiological approach, to an understanding of attention. This seems to have changed dramatically in the last few years, partly because of accumulating results from single-cell recording (Mountcastle, 1978; Wurtz, Goldberg, & Robinson, 1980). These studies have begun to bring order to our understanding of the neural systems that support aspects of attention. It seems now more appropriate to view attention as the concrete outcome of the activities of particular neural systems.

To aid in this enterprise, I have studied the component mental operations involved in one of the simplest of all cognitive acts, attending to a luminance increment in an otherwise dark field. This is an act that humans share with other animals. It is cognitive in the sense that it requires an alert organism capable both of scanning the environment and of perceiving the presence of a stimulus. We can divide this cognitive act into a number of components. Our goal is to define these components in studies with normal human subjects, to explore the brain mechanisms that control them through the study of patient populations, and to relate our results to those arising from anatomical (Mesulam, 1981), single-cell (Wurtz *et al.*, 1980), and other neuroscience techniques.

I outline the components of the act of orienting in Figure 4-1. Our first division is between detection, that is, the ability to make arbitrary responses such as saying, "I see it," or pressing a key based on the occurrence of the target

Figure 4-1. Components of visual orienting as discussed in this chapter.

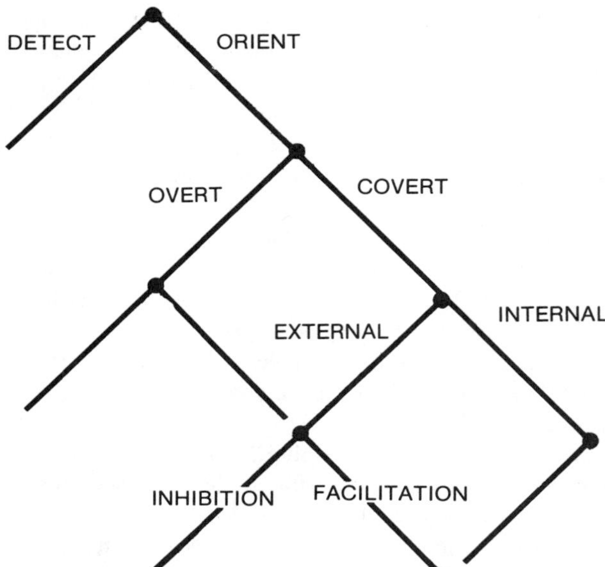

and orienting or aligning a central attentional system with a sensory pathway to be stimulated. The orienting reflex (Sokolov, 1963), as it is often discussed in psychology and neuroscience, confounds both detection and orienting as we define them here. Our reason for separating the two as mental operations is that normal subjects given advanced information about where in visual space the stimulus will occur are able to shift attention to that location and improve the efficiency of detecting stimuli that occur there. The ability to orient prior to the occurrence of the target separates the act of aligning attention from the act of perceiving the presence of the target. Similarly, brain injury cases can also dissociate these two components. In blindsight (Weiskrantz, 1980), there is severe interference with the ability to note the presence of the stimulus, with some sparing of the ability to align eyes or head with the stimulus. In parietal damage, one may get a sparing of the ability to note the presence of the stimulus when orienting is easy, along with a severe deficit in the ability to orient under some conditions (Weinstein & Friedland, 1977).

We divide orienting into covert and overt changes. It is clear that one frequently orients by moving head and eyes in the direction of the stimulus event. However, it is also possible to orient without any concomitant change in eye position or postural response (Posner, 1980). The important question is how to measure such covert changes in orienting. We have done so by time-locked changes in the efficiency of detecting or reporting target stimuli following cues that tell the subject where in an empty field the stimulus is most likely to occur (Posner, 1980; Posner & Cohen, 1984).

For eye movements it has often been argued that voluntary and reflexive control are mediated separately. In covert orienting we use either peripheral cues that are near the target, or central arrows telling the subject on which side the target is most likely to occur (Posner & Cohen, 1984). Central commands produce internal control over orienting, whereas peripheral cues induce the change in covert orienting more rapidly and automatically from the external stimulus itself.

Both central or peripheral cues will produce facilitation or time-locked improvements in the efficiency of detecting stimuli that occur at the cued position in comparison with uncued positions. We usually measure these changes by the latency of reporting the target (Posner, 1980; Posner & Cohen, 1984), but threshold measures (Bashinski & Backrach, 1980; Remington, 1980) or electrical activity (Von Voorhis & Hillyard, 1977) can also be used.

Inhibition arises when attention has been summoned by a peripheral cue to a position eccentric from the fixation point. It is seen most clearly if attention is then summoned back to fixation. The previously facilitated location is now inhibited in comparison to other locations (Posner & Cohen, 1984). Thus, it is possible by use of peripheral cues to study time-locked facilitation followed by inhibition of the position that has been cued.

In recent work, Posner and Cohen (1984) have studied the functional significance of these time-locked phasic changes in facilitation and inhibition. We have found that facilitation occurs in the first 50 to 150 milliseconds following the presentation of a peripheral cue and precedes movement of the eyes to that peripheral event by 100 to 200 milliseconds. We believe this facilitation is achieved by the alignment of a central attentional system with the pathway indicated by the cued event. We think that the same detection mechanism is involved, regardless of whether the cue is presented in the neighborhood of the stimulus or by a central cue. In short, facilitation is achieved by a phasic, time-locked turning of attention or orienting in the direction of the cue.

On the other hand, inhibition depends primarily on the sensory information presented in the cue. There is no inhibition following a central cue but only with peripheral cues. In our studies, inhibition is outweighed by the simultaneously present facilitation until attention is reoriented away from the cued event.

According to our current thinking, facilitation and inhibition work together in the process of visual orienting in the following way: When the eyes are fixed, a peripheral visual stimulus tends to summon attention rapidly to its location. Attention serves to mark out this area and will usually result in movement of the eyes in the direction of the facilitated area. As the eyes move, attention is reoriented back to the fovea. This is not necessary, since we have found conditions in which facilitation transfers to nonfoveal locations, but it is usual, since it serves to keep attention and the fovea coordinated during successive changes of eye position. When one reorients away from the target by an eye movement, the previously facilitated target location is now inhibited so that there is a bias against returning the eyes to the previously cued environmental location. The inhibition effect works both with and without eye movement, but we believe that it is closely related in a functional sense to the eye movement system. This effect serves as one of the many neural systems designed to favor novelty over repetition.

Some evidence favoring this model has been obtained for normal subjects. We have shown that the inhibition effect stays at the same location in space as the eye moves from one position to another. This contrasts markedly with the facilitation effect that can move in retinotopic coordinates but can be controlled voluntarily. The inhibition effect lasts up to 1.5 seconds following an event that would be two to three eye movements in normal subjects. We have shown in as yet unpublished work that subjects given a forced choice move their eyes in the direction of the noninhibited position more often than in the direction of the inhibited position.

This discussion, together with Figure 4-1, illustrates the relatively complex cognitive components that underlie even so simple-appearing a skill as shifting visual attention. These components can be dissociated by methods that carefully time-lock internal events to critical stimuli and carefully measure performance. They provide a concrete reality to the events that accompany covert shifts of attention. We believe that such a cognitive analysis of components of a skill is a necessary condition for investigating its neural substrate.

NEURAL SYSTEMS OF SPATIAL ATTENTION

My colleagues and I at the Cognitive Neuropsychology Laboratory at Good Samaritan Hospital in Portland, Oregon, have been examining the effects of damage to different regional brain systems on the components of covert orienting (Posner, Cohen, & Rafal, 1982; Posner, Walker, Friedrich, & Rafal, in press). In agreement with the data presented by Wurtz *et al.* (1980) and by Mountcastle (1978), we have found that lesions of the parietal lobe produce a dramatic loss in the ability to orient to the side contralateral to the lesion under some circumstances. This occurs in cases where attention has been cued to the side ipsilateral to the lesion by a peripheral cue, as in the case of extinction in clinical neurology. However, it also occurs when a central cue at fixation orients attention away from the target event and even when a central cue calls attention to the fixation position without providing any information on target location. In all of these cases, there is dramatic increase in the reaction time to target events that occur contralateral to the lesion in comparison to ipsilateral targets (Posner *et al.*, in press).

The dramatic effects of parietal lobe lesions are not duplicated by large-scale degeneration of the superior colliculus and surrounding areas that takes place in progressive supranuclear palsy (Posner, Cohen, & Rafal, 1982) nor by temporal or frontal lesions in our current experiments (Posner *et al.*, in press). The results of our studies fully confirm the suggestions from single-cell recording that the parietal lobe is importantly involved in the act of selective attention. We have established that the parietal patients seem to show a large difficulty in detecting a target contralateral to their lesion when orienting is made difficult by cues that direct their attention to some other position. The conflicting information may be information about where to shift attention or may be a cue coming from some other place in the visual field. These effects can be large enough to produce a complete lack of awareness of the target. With longer time intervals and weaker cues, parietal patients show large differences in reaction time rather than complete loss from awareness. These results confirm suggestions from our work with normals that the delays in reaction time we find with miscues have to do with the time required for the stimulus to enter a processing system related to awareness.

The effects of parietal lesions clearly cannot be accounted for by difficulty in the detection component, since presentation of a cue on the side of the target greatly reduces the difference between contralateral and ipsilateral targets. Although many subjects show the contralateral–ipsilateral difference even when cued to the target, we have several patients who have shown no difference under valid trial conditions (i.e., when cued to the correct target position) who still show a large loss in information when attention is misdirected. The ability to compensate, in some cases completely, for the difference in reaction time by a valid cue suggests that the parietal lobe is not itself the seat of the detection system. Rather, it seems to be a pathway instrumental in producing the cognitive act of orienting. The magnitude of the difference between contralateral and ipsilateral targets depends on the difficulty of orienting. If orienting is successfully produced, it appears that, at least in some patients, detection occurs in an equivalent fashion on the ipsilateral and contralateral sides.

These results tend to produce a much more concrete view of selective attention than has existed in either the cognitive or the neuroscience literature. Clearly, we can exquisitely time-lock the direction of visual attention to the presentation of cues. Moreover, there is very considerable evidence that the results obtained with spatial attention are not at all unique in this regard. Somewhat similar constellations of facilitatory and inhibitory processes have been described in situations in which subjects orient to internal concepts stored in semantic memory. For example, we (Posner & Snyder, 1975) have proposed that presentation of any word activates a pathway in the nervous system that corresponds to the physical, phonological, and semantic representation of that word. These widespread activation patterns can go on in parallel, so that there is no inhibitory consequence of activating any pathway. However, when told to attend to a particular word or code, subjects orient attention to that code. Other possible pathways, although activated by relevant information, have no access to consciousness, memory, or arbitrary responses that are dependent on active attention. Although there are differences in detail between orienting to positions in visual space and orienting to semantic memory, there seems to be considerable commonality in the way in which attention operates in the two domains.

A particularly striking relationship between memory and attentional explanations of deficit arises in the case of conduction aphasia. Conduction aphasics have great difficulty repeating back verbal items (Warrington & Shallice, 1972). This deficit has been characterized as a loss in short-term memory ability. An older and more anatomical description of the same deficit has been in terms of a disconnection between auditory receptive areas (temporal lobe) and speech production (frontal lobe) (Geschwind, 1965). Recently, work in our laboratory (McLeod & Posner, 1984; Friedrich, Glenn, & Marin, in press) suggests how these views might relate. Normal subjects can repeat auditory words while performing another task simultaneously with little decrement in performance on either task. This sparing of shadowing from the usual effects of divided attention seems to represent a privileged relationship between auditory reception and speech production. Friedrich *et al.* (in press) argue from intensive study of a conduction aphasic that the patient has lost the privileged loop between temporal and frontal areas and thus the ability to form phonological codes directly from auditory input. As a result of this loss, the patient is unable to do the necessary recoding that underlies an efficient short term memory. In this view, loss of the ability to form an automatic phonological code results in the necessity to use attention in order to achieve a phonological code and produces a radical loss to memory ability.

Friedrich's patient also illustrates that the formation of the phonological code underlying short-term retention of an item can be quite independent of access to semantic memory. The patient clearly understands the meaning of the words she cannot repeat, and indeed her errors are semantically related to the word presented. Since the amnesic patients discussed by Squire and Cohen (Chapter 1, this volume) have relatively normal short-term memories and comprehension, their problem must lie beyond the processes that form the phonological and semantic codes of words. Nonetheless, the conduction aphasic serves to illustrate how a particular deficit requiring attention for code production can result in a memory disorder.

We have not yet been able to do studies necessary to determine how different neural systems affect orienting in semantic memory. However, there is considerable evidence that forms of dyslexia and aphasia may be due to difficulties the subjects have in orienting attention toward particular codes activated by linguistic stimuli (Posner & Friedrich, in press). Thus, there is hope that the developing cognitive neuroscience approach to attention will be able to incorporate both the relatively simple orienting in visual space and much more complex tasks in which attention is employed to select information from semantic memory.

SELECTIVE ATTENTION AND MEMORY

It has been recognized for a long time that storage of information in memory must be linked in important ways to the information reaching consciousness. Although there may be no identity between information to which we attend and that which is stored, there is a considerable correlation between the two. Jacoby (1982) says, "When conditions are such that normal subjects can answer automatically, they show poor retention of the question or its answer." Recent work by Fisk and Schneider (1984) shows quite clearly the importance of this relationship. They trained subjects to categorize information automatically by approximately 5000 trials in which words were classified as to whether they were animal names. As the ability to make the categorization developed, subjects showed a loss of the ability either to report the frequency with which the words occurred or to recognize the actual words themselves. This result taken with the amnesic findings suggest that automatic processing can lead to the storage of information sufficient to perform skills (Squire & Cohen, Chapter 1, this volume) but does not leave the kind of memory that allows subjects to recognize that they have encountered the words previously.

The distinction between learning due to automatic activation and learning due to cognitive mediation via active attention is also suggested in a study of amnesics by Warrington and Weiskrantz (1982). They argue that amnesics can strengthen already existing associations in semantic memory. However, when learning requires the use of fresh associations that might require active attention, amnesics are at a disadvantage. Or as they put it, "We suggest that the amnesic subject is impaired not in his ability to engage in cognitive mediation as such, but in those memory tasks in which the stored benefits of mediation are normally important." In my terms, the amnesic can bring information to attention but has a problem in storing the products of that attentive act. Anatomically, Warrington and Weiskrantz (1982) argue that the temporal lesion might serve to dissociate semantic memory systems that involve temporal lobes from areas of the frontal lobe that subserve the storage of attended information. Thus, memories can be based on automatic activation of pathways or, alternatively, on the record of current attentional acts.

If attention and memory are closely linked, some of the results that we have presented in our effort to understand orienting and detecting ought to apply also to the next step in the information sequence, namely, storing the record of current attention. In particular, the ability to time-lock the orienting of attention to external and internal signals argues that some time-locked "write" signal ought to be available that would convert the current contents of attention to some more permanently stored record. It is, of course, quite possible that this signal only initiates a complex sequence of events that might last for many hours, days, or months (i.e., "consolidation"). However, since attention is rapidly oriented from one thing to another, the initiating signal must be very close in time to the events that occupy conscious attention at any moment in order to keep storage aligned with the proper content.

Is there any evidence that such time-locked "write" signals might be slaved to the orienting of attention? There have been suggestions that late components of the event-related potential—for example, the P300s that frequently follow the occurrence of responses to stimuli—might be crucial in the updating of memory (Demetrios, Fabiani, & Donchin, 1984; Donchin, Ritter, & McCollum, 1978). It has been suggested (Halgren *et al.*, 1980) that the generator potential for the P300 may involve the medial temporal area that Squire and Cohen (Chapter 1, this volume) has shown is so critically important in information storage. The variability of the latency of P300 (despite its rather precise name) suggests that it may be more time-locked to the occurrence of orienting or detecting the signal than to the actual physical occurrence of the stimulus itself. In situations where subjects are asked to concentrate on stimuli, the P300 is increased in amplitude. In situations where the subjects' attention is deflected from the stimuli, it is decreased in amplitude and/or increased in latency.

When subjects are presented with the same stimulus item twice in a row, their memory for the experience is much less strong than when the two stimulus occasions are spaced apart. This effect of massed versus spaced practice has been shown to arise because the second of the two presentations of the stimulus is simply not well stored (Hintzman, 1974). It is also true that the second occurrence of the same stimulus produces a much more efficient response in terms of reaction time, is handled far more automatically than its first occurrence, and produces smaller P300s (Donchin *et al.*, 1978). Once again, more efficient processing leads to poorer storage than when processing is more difficult.

The P300 is only one possible candidate for a time-locked signal that indicates storage of information currently being attended. Other candidates might be found from further analyses of event-related potential or single-cell data. I argue only that we ought to look carefully for some time-locked event, probably arising from the temporal lobe, that could serve as a "write" signal. Studies recently reported by Wood, McCarthy, Allison, Goff, Williamson, and Spencer (1982) and current studies in our lab are examining temporal lobectomy cases with the hopes of making further observations along these lines. Unfortunately, Wood *et al.* (1982) found no clear reduction in P300 in lobectomy cases. However, recent reports (Gazzaniga, Chapter 3, this volume) suggest possible P300 reduction in clear cases of amnesia.

CONSOLIDATION

How can speculations about a time-locked "write" signal following attentive acts deal with evidence for the long-term dynamics of memory presented by Squire, Cohen, and Nadel (1983) in their recent paper on the medial temporal region and memory consolidation? They put considerable emphasis on the finding that following ECT, events in the preceding year are remembered less well than events that occurred 2 or even 4 years prior to the series of shocks. These results have led Squire to postulate a long-term consolidation process that may last some years after the occurrence of the original memory. One might emphasize instead, as Squire and Cohen (1979) did, that traces are strengthened every time they are retrieved or activated by new input. They argue:

> The suggestion that resistance to amnesia develops gradually for years after learning requires that gradual alterations occur in memory storage during this period of time. At the psychological level, such changes might depend on frequent rehearsal of some memories or on the recruitment of some memories into "schemas" (Bartlett, 1932; Norman & Rumelhart, 1975). Since forgetting also occurs during the years after learning, considerable reorganization apparently takes place within the long term memory. (p. 124)

Any input activates a range of associations. It is more likely that a trace will be reactivated by input when context is most like it was when the item was originally presented. Thus, new memories may appear to be consolidating autonomously, because during a period of time they are subject to reactivation by new input. This principle clearly applies to the test of television shows reported by Squire and Cohen (Chapter 1, this volume). During the year that a television show was prominent and perhaps for several years thereafter, there is a likelihood that its memory will be reactivated by fresh input. Suppose ECT interferes with the "write" signal. Thus, the ability of reactivated memory to be strengthened by relevant input will be reduced. Traces that are recent will not receive the usual strengthening from reactivation and thus will be weaker than they would be if ECT had not occurred. Traces that have occurred within the last year or so could actually be worse off than those that were a year older, because old memories would have already undergone strengthening from retrievals prior to ECT. Thus, they would be little affected by ECT. Traces that have not been so repeatedly strengthened would be more vulnerable to ECT or other forms of insult. It seems to me that consolidation may be simply the result of repeated activation of prior traces by new memories. If this view were correct, it might seem strange that memories a year old would suffer so severely from a 2-week period of ECT if the only effect of the ECT was to prevent strengthening of the memories through reactivation. However, it is possible that reduced reactivation in subjects who receive ECT begins well before the start of the ECT. It is well known that depression often leads to a reduced exposure to stimulation and to reduced learning ability. In some of Squire's papers, patients tested prior to ECT show no difference or even an advantage for programs 2–3 years before ECT compared to 1 year before ECT, whereas normals often show the more expected monotonic reduction of memory with time prior to test. This difference between normals and pre-ECT patients could be due to the period of depression that leads to the decision to administer ECT. If that were the case, the memories that were formed during the depressive period would have had less chances for relearning and thus could be more vulnerable to the shock.

It seems to me to be less difficult to suppose that new memories are increasing in strength because the context in which they are learned remains similar for a long period of time than to suppose that an internal autonomous biochemical process is taking several years to complete.

I present these ideas not because I feel they are necessarily likely to be correct, but because I believe that the remarkable time-locking of active attention to external cues suggests that the search for signs of memory in close temporal proximity to the presentation of an event may be most fruitful for an understanding of processes leading to information storage. Theories that lead us too far away from a precise analysis of the sequence of information processing that follows the occurrence of an event may miss those processes most crucial for storage. Indeed, I was struck in reading the Squire *et al.* (1983) paper that their discussion of the mechanisms by which consolidation might occur referred to relatively permanent changes in the hippocampus following brief stimulation (Baudry & Lynch, Chapter 28, this volume). It seems to me that these findings may be even more reason to suppose that relatively permanent changes in memory are initiated by events that occur very briefly after the signal. The dendritic changes that produce the relatively permanent potentiation in the hippocampus appear to be complete within about a minute after the brief stimulus that initiates them.

SUMMARY

I introduced this chapter by suggesting that this volume, like many others, contains chapters written in two rather different languages. First, the language of neuroscience with its emphasis on specific locations, cellular and subcellular mechanisms; and second, the language of cognitive science, with its emphasis on processing stages, codes, and conscious and unconscious operations. I have tried to present a certain amount of evidence that in at least a limited area of attention, that of spatial attention, it has become increasingly possible to examine the mapping of the language of neuroscience and the language of cognition. We have begun to understand the way in which parietal cortex and midbrain work together to control the smooth, cognitive act of orienting attention in visual space. I have faith that many of the same processes that underlie the physiology of visual attention will illuminate problems of orienting and bringing information to consciousness in semantic memory. I have speculated that some of the same time-locked components that seem to illuminate processes of selective attention may also be helpful in understanding the mechanisms of memory. In particular, the remarkable dissociations shown first by Corkin (1968) and most recently by Squire and Cohen (Chapter 1, this volume) between those memories that are impaired by amnesia and those that are not seem to fit rather well with the distinction between the strengthening of automatic pathways and the storing of the records of conscious attention. I speculated that the record of conscious attention is stored consequent on some discrete "write" signal that follows shortly after orienting. The "write" signal may be related to medial temporal areas important in amnesia. I have tried to illustrate how a system that stores information at the time of orienting toward external or internal events might appear to undergo a long consolidation process and might seem to have the kind of spontaneous dynamic reorganizations that have frequently been postulated by psychoanalytic and Gestalt thinkers. Finally, I pointed to the heuristic value of a close examination of the time course of information processing that follows the presentation of signals as a way of mapping the neural systems that may be responsible for storage of information.

ACKNOWLEDGMENTS

To an unusual degree this chapter reflects the active collaboration and help of a number of people. I am especially grateful to John Walker, Lisa Choate, Robert Rafal, Fran Friedrich, Alan Allport, Tony Marcel, Mary Rothbart, and Oscar Marin for their advice and help.

REFERENCES

Bashinski, H. S., & Backrach, V. R. Enhancement of perceptual sensitivity as the result of selectively attending spatial locations. *Perception and Psychophysics*, 1980, *28*, 241–248.

Campion, J., Latto, R., & Smith, Y. M. Is blindsight an effect of scattered light spared cortex and near threshold vision. *Behavioral and Brain Sciences*, 1983, *6*, 423–437.

Corkin, S. Acquisition of motor skill after bilateral medial temporal lobe excision. *Neuropsychologia*, 1968, *6*, 255–265.

Demetrios, K., Fabiani, M., & Donchin, E. "P300" and memory: Individual differences in the von Restorff effect. *Cognitive Psychology*, 1984, *16*, 217–242.

Donchin, E., Ritter, W., & McCollum, W. C. Cognitive psychophysiology: The endogenous components of the ERP. In E. Calloway, P. Tuetins, & S. H. Koslow (Eds.), *Event related potentials in man.* New York: Academic Press, 1978.

Fischler, I., & Goodman, G. O. Latency of associative activation in memory. *Journal of Experimental Psychology: Human Perception and Performance*, 1978, *4*, 455–470.

Fisk, A. D., & Schneider, W. Memory as a function of attention, level of processing and automatization. *Journal of Experimental Psychology: Learning, Memory, and Cognition*, 1984, *10*, 181–197.

Fodor, J. A. *The language of thought.* Cambridge, Mass.: Harvard University Press, 1975.

Friedrich, J., Glenn, C. G., & Marin, O. S. M. Interruption of phonological coding in conduction aphasia. *Brain and Language*, in press.

Geschwind, N. Disconnection syndromes in animals and man: Part II. *Brain*, 1965, *88*, 585–644.

Halgren, E., Squires, N. C., Wilson, C. L., Rohrbaugh, J. W., Babb, T. C., & Crandall, P. H. Endogenous potentials generated in the human hippocampal formation and amygdala by infrequent event. *Science*, 1980, *210*, 803–805.

Hintzman, D. L. Theoretical implications of the spacing effect. In R. L. Solso (Ed.), *Theories in cognitive psychology.* Hillsdale, N.J.: Erlbaum, 1974.

Jacoby, L. L. Knowing and remembering: Some parallels in the behavior of Korsakoff patients and normals. In L. E. Cermak (Ed.), *Human memory and amnesia.* Hillsdale, N.J.: Erlbaum, 1982.

Marcel, A. J. Conscious and preconscious recognition of polysemous words. In R. S. Nickerson (Ed.), *Attention and performance VII.* Hillsdale, N.J.: Erlbaum, 1980.

Marcel, A. J. Conscious and unconscious perception: An approach to the relations between phenomenal experience and perceptual processes. *Cognitive Psychology*, 1983, *15*, 238–300.

McLeod, P., & Posner, M. I. Privileged loops from perception to act. In H. Bouma & D. Bowhuis (Eds.), *Attention and performance X.* Hillsdale, N.J.: Erlbaum, 1984.

Mesulam, M. A. A cortical network for directed attention and unilateral neglect. *Archives of Neurology*, 1981, *10*, 304–325.

Meyer, D. E., Schvaneveldt, R. W., & Ruddy, M. G. Loci of contextual effects on visual word recognition. In P. M. A. Rabbitt & S. Dornic (Eds.), *Attention and performance V.* Hillsdale, N.J.: Erlbaum, 1975.

Mountcastle, V. Brain mechanisms for directed attention. *Journal of the Royal Society of Medicine*, 1978, *71*, 14–27.

Pöppel, E., Held, R., & Frost, D. Residual visual function after brain wounds involving the central visual pathways in man. *Nature*, 1973, *243*, 295–296.

Posner, M. I. *Chronometric explorations of mind: The third Paul M. Fitts lectures.* Hillsdale, N.J.: Erlbaum, 1978.

Posner, M. I. Orienting of attention: The VIIth Sir Frederic Bartlett Lecture. *Quarterly Journal of Experimental Psychology*, 1980, *32*, 3–25.

Posner, M. I., & Cohen, Y. Facilitation and inhibition in shifts of visual attention. In H. Bouma & D. Bowhuis (Eds.), *Attention and performance X.* Hillsdale, N.J.: Erlbaum, 1984.

Posner, M. I., Cohen, Y., & Rafal, R. D. Neural systems control of spatial orienting. *Philosophical Transactions of the Royal Society of London*, 1982, *B298*, 187–198.

Posner, M. I., & Friedrich, F. Attention and the control of cognition. In S. L. Friedman & K. A. Klivington (Eds.), *Brain cognition and education.* New York: Academic Press, in press.

Posner, M. I., Pea, R., & Volpe, B. Cognitive neuroscience: Developments toward a science of synthesis. In J. Mehler, E. Walker, & M. Garrett (Eds.), *Perspectives on mental representation.* Hillsdale, N.J.: Erlbaum, 1982.

Posner, M. I., & Snyder, C. R. R. Attention and cognitive control. In R. Solso (Ed.), *Information processing and cognition: The Loyola symposium.* Hillsdale, N.J.: Erlbaum, 1975.

Posner, M. I., Walker, J. A., Friedrich, F. J., & Rafal, R. D. Effects of parietal lobe injury on covert orienting of visual attention. *Journal of Neuroscience*, in press.

Remington, R. W. Attention and saccadic eye movement. *Journal of Experimental Psychology: Human Perception and Performance*, 1980, *6*, 726–744.

Shiffrin, R. W., & Schneider, R. M. Controlled and automatic human information processing: II. Perceptual learning, automatic attending and a general theory. *Psychological Review*, 1977, *84*, 127–190.

Sokolov, Y. N. *Perception and the conditioned reflex.* New York: Macmillan, 1963.

Squire, L. R., & Cohen, N. Memory and amnesia: Resistance to disruption develops for years after learning. *Behavioral and Neural Biology*, 1979, *25*, 115–125.

Squire, L. R., Cohen, N. J., & Nadel, L. The medial temporal region and memory consolidation:

A new hypothesis. In H. Weingartner & E. Parker (Eds.), *Memory consolidation*. Hillsdale N.J.: Erlbaum, 1983.

Von Voorhis, S., & Hillyard, S. A. Visual evoked potentials and selection attention to points in space. *Perception and Psychophysics*, 1977, *22*, 54–62.

Warren, R. E. Stimulus encoding and memory. *Journal of Experimental Psychology*, 1972, *94*, 90–100.

Warrington, E. K., & Shallice, T. Neuropsychological evidence of visual storage in short term memory tasks. *Quarterly Journal of Experimental Psychology*, 1972, *24*, 30–40.

Warrington, E. K., & Weiskrantz, L. Amnesia: A disconnection syndrome? *Neuropsychologia*, 1982, *20*, 233–247.

Weinstein, E. A., & Friedland, R. P. *Hemi-inattention and hemispheric specialization*. New York: Raven Press, 1977.

Weiskrantz, L. Varieties of residual experience. *Quarterly Journal of Experimental Psychology*, 1980, *32*, 365–386.

Wood, C. C., McCarthy, G., Allison, T., Goff, W. R., Williamson, P. D., & Spencer, D. D. Endogenous event related potentials following temporal lobe excisions in humans. *Neuroscience Abstracts*, 1982, *12*, Abstract No. 279.10.

Worden, F. G. Attention and auditory electrophysiology. In E. Stellar & J. Sprague (Eds.), *Progress in physiological psychology* (Vol. 1). New York: Academic Press, 1966.

Wurtz, R. H., Goldberg, M. E., & Robinson, E. L. Behavioral modulation of visual responses in the monkey: Stimulus selection for attention and movement. *Progress in Psychobiology and Physiological Psychology*, 1980, *9*, 43–83.

Zihl, J. "Blindsight": Improvement of visually guided eye movements by systematic practice in patients with cerebral blindness. *Neuropsychologia*, 1980, *18*, 71–77.

Critical Commentaries

CHAPTER FIVE

Amnesia and a Theory for Dating Memories

J. ANTHONY DEUTSCH

It is indeed flattering to be reinstated as an expert on the neurology of memory after a very brief and temporally remote episode in this role. As most readers will undoubtedly not recall, I was propelled into the anatomical limelight by showing that anticholinesterase injections into the hippocampus produced amnesia, thus proving to some that the hippocampus was the seat of memory. However, my notoriety was short-lived, as a few months later we showed the same amnesia by injecting anticholinesterase into the peritoneum. As the peritoneum has never been as popular as the hippocampus as a candidate for the seat of memory (or any other mental faculty for that matter), our evidence was conveniently forgotten by those who specialize in the anatomy of memory as they shrank from drawing the obvious conclusion. It is thus very agreeable to be rescued from such prolonged oblivion. However, do not worry—I shall not succumb to the temptation of arguing for the mental functions of the peritoneum. Instead, as an amateur in the field, I shall attempt the equally quixotic task of arguing that memories and habits are a single system. I shall begin by showing that the arguments for two systems are less than persuasive. I shall end by showing that the evidence can be accommodated by a unitary system, analogous to the one found in vision in the coding of color and brightness.

First of all, let me deal with the assertion that there are two types of memory, the declarative and the procedural. How is such a distinction defined? "The critical feature that is procedural here is that there can develop in memory a representation based on experience that changes the way an organism responds to the environment, without affording access to the specific instances that led to this change. Accordingly, procedural learning applies to more than just the acquisition of motor skills" (Squire, 1982, p. 260). "Declarative learning includes specific facts and data that are the subject of most contemporary memory studies" (Squire, 1982, p. 262). "Thus the ability to develop and store declarative memory (all the bits of specific-item information that are the subject of conventional memory experiments like faces, words, and shapes) depends on the integrity of the particular bitemporal and diencephalic brain structures affected in amnesia" (Squire, 1982, p. 260).

However, such a procedural–declarative dichotomy leads to some strange consequences. Consider celebrating Thanksgiving or just having lunch. Each

J. Anthony Deutsch. Department of Psychology, University of California, San Diego, La Jolla, California.

experience of these events consists of faces, words, and shapes and would individually be classed as a subject to be dealt with by declarative memory. However, the specific instances of lunch or Thanksgiving are soon lost or denied to access, which would make one's memory of eating lunch or celebrating Thanksgiving a procedural memory and so place it in a different neural structure. There seem to be much simpler and direct explanations of why frequently repeated events cannot be individually recalled, based on experimentally verified principles of experimental psychology. On a more detailed level, let us look at the tasks that are spared in anterograde amnesia and that are also classified as procedural. There is mirror-tracing skill, a pursuit rotor task, fragmented-drawing recognition, and conditioned eye blink. A visual discrimination can be learned by amnesic monkeys even when the trials are spaced at 24-hour intervals, when such monkeys cannot use the memory of similar material after about 30 seconds in a recognition task (Mishkin, Spiegler, Saunders, & Malamut, 1982).

Other examples of learning in amnesics are the ability to learn to solve a puzzle (the Tower of Hanoi) and a numerical rule. Another example (Jacoby & Witherspoon, 1982) shows a capacity to retain specific information. Patients with the Korsakoff syndrome and normals were asked a question containing a homophone (e.g., What is an example involving a reed instrument?). When asked later to spell "reed–read," both groups were equally biased toward the low-frequency spelling. Similar results have been obtained by Graf, Squire, and Mandler (1984) in a modified word-fragment completion task. Now, some of these tasks could be termed procedural in its original meaning in that they refer to the acquisition of a skill; others are no more procedural than our memory of Thanksgiving dinner or everyday lunch. In some sense it is true that all knowledge is procedural as it is a guide to further action, but that does not mean that it is not declarative. Take remembering someone's name. We generally have no "access to the specific instances that led to this change" in our behavior when we meet that person. If amnesics had been shown to be incapable of learning the Tower of Hanoi puzzle, could it not have been plausibly argued that declarative memory was involved in its learning?

Is the primary defect then in semantic memory? Amnesics, on the whole, seem to be inferior in learning tasks that can easily be rehearsed, such as verbal tasks, but equally as good as normals at learning tasks that cannot. We would expect amnesics to forget to rehearse, and this would give normals an edge in a verbal task. But this does not mean that a deficit of semantic memory is a primary defect. It could easily be a secondary consequence of an overall defect of episodic memory. On this interpretation, a defect in verbal tasks would only be apparent; the amnesic should be no worse than a normal prevented from rehearsing. A subsidiary point I would like to make concerns another distinction, namely, that between diencephalic and bitemporal amnesia. This has been made on the basis of presumed differences in rates of forgetting. The basis for the distinction is the claim that subject H. M., a bitemporal amnesic, forgot at a higher rate than Korsakoff patients and normals, between 10 minutes and 7 days. I would like to draw your attention to the fact that this difference in the rate of forgetting is not in fact supported by the original paper by Huppert and Piercy (1979). H. M. falls 21%, Korsakoffs 17%, and the difference is not significant.

In any case, an attempt to dichotomize amnesics on the basis of rates of forgetting in an attempt to obtain anatomical differentiation is unpromising. Squire (1981) has shown that rates of forgetting are different in ECT patients simply as a function of time since treatment. It would seem implausible to argue that such changes are due to shifts in the anatomical or other substrate of the amnesia within the same class of patient. To return to my main theme, if we then reject the distinction between declarative and procedural knowledge as it applies to the amnesic deficit, and with it different neural homes for the two types of memory, how can we explain the preservation of some types of memory and not others in the amnesic patient?

A plausible view that has been around for a long time, and that has been given recent strong support by Gazzaniga's group (Hirst & Volpe, 1982), is that anterograde amnesia is due to a loss of the temporal ordering of events. If this is the case, then it is possible to account for anterograde amnesia in terms of a failure within a single system. This was suggested to me in the following way.

Some while ago, I did a series of experiments in which a cholinergic drug was administered to rats at various times after initial learning but at the same time before retest (Deutsch, 1971). The general result showed that memories were differentially sensitive to the effects of the drugs depending on their age. Taking the period after the habit was more than 3 days old, it seemed that its synaptic substrate increased in strength up to some maximum and thereafter declined. Subsequent careful measurement confirmed the pattern of waxing and waning of habit strength even when no drugs were used and only the passage of time was used as a variable. So far emerged a pattern of consolidation followed by forgetting. However, inspection of the results before the 3-day mark revealed another curve similar to the one already described, but which ran its up-and-down course much more quickly—days rather than weeks. These findings show two things: first, that the course of consolidation is not monotonic; instead it looks like a hump—first it goes up and then down; and second, that there is not a single process that represents each memory trace. There are at least two with different time constants that seem to occur in parallel.

What would be the reason for such an arrangement? For memory to be efficient, the organism should show not only that something happened but also when it happened. Consequently, some information about the time, relative or absolute, that a memory trace was laid down must be made available. One way to do this would be to have the memory trace change with time since it was laid down and then to measure the amount of this change once it became necessary to determine how long ago such a trace was originally laid down. Such information could in principle be derived by measuring the degree of consolidation. The first problem with this is that the relation of this process with time is not monotonic. There would be a systematic confusion between new and old traces. The second problem is that the dynamic range between zero and maximum trace strength is probably quite narrow in comparison with the number of different ages the system should ideally represent, and so such a system would give only a rather coarse indication of when something had happened. The third problem lies in memory strength. It is plausible to assume that memory strength is represented in the nervous system by an increase in synaptic efficiency or strength. It is also plausible to assume that memory consolidation is also represented by changes in synaptic efficiency or strength. Consequently, the changes in synaptic state would be ambiguous. These problems could be satisfactorily resolved if each event gave rise to a number of parallel processes, each proceeding at its own different rate. By comparing the height or intensity of each process that represented a single event, it would be possible to pinpoint its age as accurately as desired, to eliminate the ambiguity inherent in reading off a single inverted-U-shaped curve and to dissociate age from strength of memory.

To explain how such a system would work, it is perhaps best to point out that it is basically the same system that is known to operate in vision in the discrimination of wavelength and light intensity. The eye can sense where on the spectral continuum a particular wavelength lies, almost independent of its intensity, and can simultaneously sense its intensity. The eye employs inputs from three inverted-U curves that have different maxima and that partially overlap. Each wavelength thus assumes a value on each of the inverted-U curves. Such values on each of these three curves are then fed into two different mechanisms. One mechanism, which gives information about brightness, sums the values, and in so doing loses information about position on the spectrum while measuring intensity. On the other hand, the second mechanism is composed of opponent cells, in which one of the inputs from the values on one of the curves is excitatory and the other inhibitory. Such opponent cells give information about the position of the monochromatic light on the spectrum while discarding information about its intensity. In the memory system proposed, a memory trace is represented by a number of values, each on a separate curve. As the memory ages, such values shift, much as if there was a steady drift in the wavelength of a monochromatic light. This generates the signals that are then fed into the two types of cells that are used by the eye. The first, by summing the intensities that increase and decrease at different rates would signal the strength of a memory or habit, while losing all information about when the memory was laid down. The second mechanism, analogous to that which extracts color information, would extract the ratio between the strength of the signals that had been simultaneously initiated, thus measuring the age of the memory while losing information about its strength.

If these two systems, analogous to the ones in the visual system, are employed in processing information about the past, then the somewhat paradoxical data from anterograde amnesia can be economically explained. If the amnesic does not possess the opponent system that enables him to date his memories, while the system that sums trace strength is unimpaired, he will be able both to learn habits and be primed by past experience at a normal rate but unable to tell when such learning or experience took place.

How would such a disorder of the opponent system come about? We have to suppose that such an opponent process is normally connected up at the time that memory registration occurs, but that in anterograde amnesia, such a connection no longer occurs. Some trophic influence from some other brain structures may be absent. A particular balance of transmitter or neuromodulator influence may be necessary to increase the probability of connection of inhibitory inputs to the comparator mechanism. The transmitter reduction that causes such a deficiency in connection in the opponent system may tentatively be identified as acetylcholine. Lowered acetylcholine levels exist in diseases such as Alzheimer disease (Bartus, Dean, Beer, & Lippa, 1982), and anterograde amnesia can be produced by anticholinergics (Berger & Stein, 1969; Deutsch & Rogers, 1979).

A simple interference with such a mechanism could also account for the deficits and strengths of Mishkin's (1982) globally amnesic monkeys. If formation of the trace comparator was prevented by the lesion, the monkey could not place the exposure of a given object in time in his visual-recognition task. On the other hand, the traces laid down could still mediate a standard object discrimination. However, such damage could leave events recorded before the lesion more or less intact. Such a theory would not necessitate the presence of two anatomically separable stores duplicating each other in order to account for the existing data. In Mishkin's (1982) matching task, success is predicated on memory of when a given object was seen. Success was only possible for the experimental monkeys for about 30 seconds after exposure. However, such monkeys could learn discrimination of objects that were presented 24 hours apart at almost the normal rate. To explain this, one has to assume that there is a short-term memory that is outside the scheme I discussed above. However, after this, if the curves that increase and decrease at different rates are not compared by opponent cells, no dating of the event that set them in motion will be possible. On the other hand, such curves still can contain information that is as good as usual for the retrieval of a discrimination habit. In this sense, the system behaves correctly. It preserves procedural information along with Thanksgiving dinners and everyday lunches, and is capable of doing this with normal efficiency. But the system no longer can use the order of events in storage, except when the time between them is very short, or only for very brief periods, or when reconstruction of the sequence is possible from general information.

The theory so far cannot explain one very prominent symptom of anterograde amnesia, which is the inability to recognize the sensory inputs that have occurred before. As the theory postulates that the patient is left with a synaptic memory store, accessible through the summator system, he or she should be capable of matching sensory input against the contents of the memory store, and so to make a recognition judgment, but without being able to date previous occurrence. However, the assumption that sensory input is matched with the contents of the memory store via the summator system is not one that is necessary. A more plausible assumption is that the matching of sensory input takes place via the comparator or opponent system, while output from the memory store that generates command signals is transmitted via the summator system. On such an assumption, the system in anterograde amnesia is still capable of initiating output based on the contents of the memory store, while incapable of recognizing such output as having occurred before or recognizing sensory input as having occurred before. Therefore, tasks whose correct performance depends on the recognition that the output matches a part of the contents of the memory store should not be learnable by the system. Such tasks have been variously characterized as semantic, declarative, or a part of "knowing that." On the present theory their common denominator is that their correct performance rests on a match between the present performance and content of the memory store. Though the system can produce the correct response beyond chance via the summator system, recognition of the match between such a response and the content of the memory store cannot take place. Without such recognition, the act of remembering does not occur introspectively to the subject. On the other hand, there are tasks whose correct performance can be recognized by the amnesic subject not by reference to his memory but by reference to a solution of the task at the time. Such tasks have been called procedural, episodic, or involving "knowing how." The amnesic patient, according to the present theory, can produce output determined by the contents of the memory system. What he lacks is the ability to recognize when that output matches something in the memory store. In the tasks involving skill, knowing how and procedures that have been tried so far, correct performance hinges on the recognition that success has been attained by the application of a rule. For instance, in mirror drawing, the subject knows he has made the right move as soon as he has made it even if he has made no such move before or without any memory of its previous occurrence. This is not true in the paired-associate learning paradigm. This leads to the prediction on the present hypothesis that there should be a large number of procedural "knowing how" tasks that would not be learnable by the amnesic. All that would be necessary is to use procedural tasks, where the order of moves is arbitrary, or in other words, where the correctness of a move cannot be determined by reference to a rule. Similarly, declarative or semantic tasks should pose no problem if the subject can determine that he has been successful in performing the task by reference to the situation in front of him, as in a word-completion or priming task.

The scheme for memory dating or tagging suggests a substrate for a view of anterograde amnesia that has been around for a long time, which holds that such amnesia is due to a loss of the temporal ordering of events. Finally, let me end by expressing my total agreement with John Garcia's message that learning is too important to be left to the experts. But this means that I have produced an impasse, because I have probably proved to you that it cannot be left to the amateurs either.

REFERENCES

Bartus, R. T., Dean, R. L., Beer, B., & Lippa, A. S. The cholinergic hypothesis of geriatric memory dysfunction. *Science*, 1982, *217*, 408–417.

Berger, B. D., & Stein, L. An analysis of learning deficits produced by scopolamine. *Psychopharmacologia*, 1969, *14*, 271–283.

Deutsch, J. A. The cholinergic synapse and the site of memory. *Science*, 1971, *174*, 778–794.

Deutsch, J. A., & Rogers, J. B. Cholinergic excitability and memory: Animal studies and their clinical implications. In K. L. Davis & P. A. Berger (Eds.), *Brain acetylcholine and neuropsychiatric disease*. New York: Plenum, 1979.

Graf, P., Squire, L. R., & Mandler, G. The information that amnesic patients do not forget. *Journal of Experimental Psychology: Learning, Memory, and Cognition*, 1984, *10*, 164–178.

Hirst, W., & Volpe, B. T. Temporal order judgments with amnesia. *Brain and Cognition*, 1982, *1*, 294–306.

Huppert, F. A., & Piercy, M. Normal and abnormal forgetting in organic amnesia: Effect of locus of lesion. *Cortex*, 1979, *15*, 385–390.

Jacoby, L. L., & Witherspoon, D. Remembering without awareness. *Canadian Journal of Psychology*, 1982, *36* (2), 300–324.

Mishkin, M., Spiegler, B. J., Saunders, R. C., & Malamut, B. L. An animal model of global amnesia. In S. Corkin (Ed.), *Alzheimer's disease: A report of progress* (*Aging*, Vol. 19). New York: Raven Press, 1982.

Squire, L. R. Two forms of human amnesia: An analysis of forgetting. *Journal of Neuroscience*, 1981, *1*, 635–640.

Squire, L. R. The neuropsychology of human memory. *Annual Review of Neuroscience*, 1982, *5*, 241–273.

CHAPTER SIX

The Neurobiology of Memory: Implicit and Explicit Assumptions

RAYMOND P. KESNER

The study of the neurobiological basis of memory has entered an extremely exciting era with the advent of new methods of detecting brain damage in humans and improved behavioral methodology for studying cognition in both animals and humans. The major issues to be addressed concern (1) the psychological and neurobiological nature of the structural organization of memory and (2) the behavioral processes and neurobiological mechanisms that can utilize or alter the structure of memory (learning and plasticity). In this brief discussion I will discuss the major issues by making explicit some of the underlying theoretical assumptions and proposing some alternative assumptions.

The first issue is the identification of the critical psychological and neurobiological units of memory representation and the organization of these units. Two major approaches have been presented. The first approach resembles the view made popular by Lashley (1950) that memory is represented as a unitary trace and is subserved by a set of neural circuits that are functionally equivalent (Gold & McGaugh, 1975). The psychological unit of analysis is a single entity labeled memory, which can be measured by the selection of a critical set of responses (usually one) that represents the strength of the memory trace. The neural unit of analysis is represented by the central nervous system as a whole, since memory is assumed to be uniformly distributed throughout the brain.

The second approach assumes that there is a dual memory system that is represented by anatomically different circuits. These dual systems have been labeled episodic versus semantic (Kinsbourne & Wood, 1982; Tulving, 1972), working versus reference (Olton, Becker, & Handelmann, 1980), verbal versus nonverbal (Gazzaniga & LeDoux, 1978), procedural versus declarative (Cohen & Squire, 1980), and habit versus recognition (Mishkin, 1982). The psychological unit of analysis is represented by a dual trace and presumably encompasses a set of procedures and response outcomes. The critical neural unit of analysis usually is represented by a single or a set of interconnected neural circuits. In most of the models, the two systems are assumed to be relatively independent, with only minor interactions.

Raymond P. Kesner. Department of Psychology, University of Utah, Salt Lake City, Utah.

I have proposed an alternative view, namely, that memory is represented as a multidimensional trace (Kesner, 1982; Kesner & DiMattia, 1984). It is assumed that the structure of memory contains a set of traces, each representing some attribute of a memory. Many theoreticians studying human memory have adopted this view of memory representation (Bower, 1967; Tulving, 1972; Underwood, 1969). The unit of memory analysis is represented by an attribute, which is often not directly observable but is derived from a set of operations that incorporate the critical attribute(s). It is assumed that specific neural units subserve different attributes. The neural unit of analysis can vary depending to a great extent on the complexity of the neuronal network or system being studied as well as on the sophistication of techniques in studying brain–behavior functions. Thus, the neural unit of analysis subserving classical conditioning of the siphon-withdrawal response in *Aplysia* might be a single or set of interconnected neurons, whereas the unit of analysis subserving order memory in the rat might be a set of specific neural regions (such as the hippocampus, amygdala, and prefrontal cortex) comprising a large set and variety of interconnected neurons.

How are memories organized within this multidimensional framework? First, it is possible that attributes are organized in a hierarchical fashion, based on importance. Thus, the most important attributes may be stored at one level of the hierarchy and determine the storage of less important attributes at different levels. Second, it is possible that attributes are organized independently, all attributes being of equal importance. The third possibility suggests that attributes are organized in a heterarchical network employing both sequential and independent systems. As an example of the last possibility, one could envision that sensory, affective, spatial, temporal, and response attributes might be represented independently as a subset of both declarative knowledge (ability to remember and report on specific experiences) and procedural knowledge (ability to remember rules, skills, and procedures). Within the declarative knowledge system, sensory, affective, temporal, and autonomic response attributes might combine to represent the internal context, while sensory, spatial, temporal, and somatic response attributes might combine to represent the external context. Within the procedural system, there might be perceptual, affective, spatial, temporal, and response-selection rules, which might combine to represent schemas, scripts, and moods. This working model of the organization of memory representation is shown in Figures 6-1 and 6-2. The organization of these attributes within this heterarchical framework, and thus memory representation, is largely determined by the anatomical and functional nature of the interconnections of the critical neural units (regions) subserving the important attributes. As an example, I have postulated in previous papers (Kesner, 1980, 1982) that the hippocampus subserves the coding of the external environmental context (coding of sensory, temporal, spatial, and somatic response attributes), while the amygdala subserves the coding of the internal environmental context (coding of sensory, temporal, affect, and autonomic response attributes). Both the hippocampus and amygdala would be part of a system subserving declarative knowledge (see Figures 6-1 and 6-2). To the extent that one can dissociate the internal from the external context, one should be able to dissociate amygdala and hippocampus function. For example, in tasks with distinctive external environmental contexts, electrical stimulation or lesions of the hippocampus disrupt memory for one-trial appetitive learning,

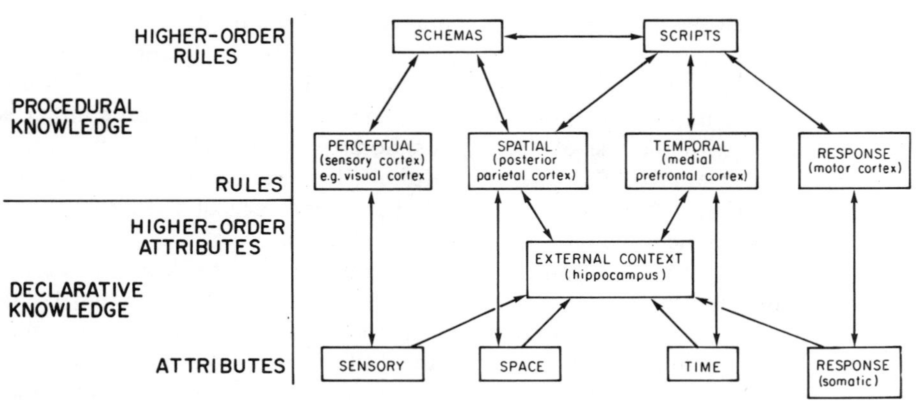

Figure 6-1. Psychological and neural network organization of memory emphasizing the importance of attributes (e.g., sensory, somatic, response, spatial, and temporal), higher-order attributes (e.g., external context mediated by hippocampus), rules (e.g., spatial mediated by posterior parietal association cortex and temporal mediated by medial prefrontal context), and higher-order rules (e.g., schemas and scripts).

delayed spatial matching-to-sample performance, and radial-arm maze performance. In contrast, electrical stimulation or lesions of the amygdala do not produce any impairment in the above situations (Berman & Kesner, 1976; Bierley, Kesner, & Novak, 1983; Kesner & Andrus, 1982; Olton & Wolf, 1981; Olton *et al.*, 1980). The reverse is true in tasks that emphasize the importance of the internal environmental context. For example, in taste-aversion learning, lesions or electrical stimulation of the amygdala produce retention impairments, whereas comparable manipulations of the hippocampus are ineffective (Best & Orr, 1973; Kesner & Berman, 1977; Kesner, Berman, Burton, & Hankins, 1975; McGowan, Hankins, & Garcia, 1972; Nachman & Ashe, 1974).

Using a within-task analysis of passive avoidance learning, it can be shown that electrical stimulation of the amygdala, but not the hippocampus, impairs

Figure 6-2. Psychological and neural network organization of memory emphasizing the importance of attributes (e.g., sensory, autonomic response, affect, and temporal), higher-order attributes (e.g., internal context mediated by amygdala), rules (e.g., affect mediated by insular-orbital prefrontal cortex), and higher-order rules and states (e.g., moods).

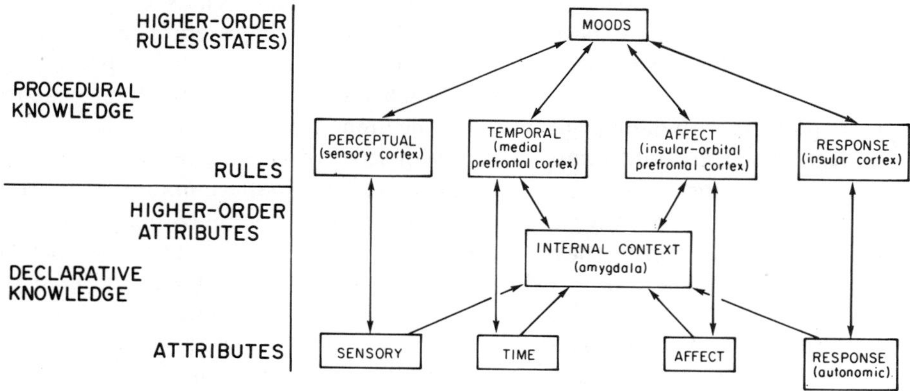

retention when the internal environmental context is manipulated with the use of an aversive experience (footshock) as a reminder cue (Baker, Kesner, & Michal, 1981). In contrast, electrical stimulation of the hippocampus, but not the amygdala, impairs retention when the external environmental context is manipulated with the use of green phosphorescent paint (Kesner & Hardy, 1983). Thus, it appears that there is a double dissociation between amygdala and hippocampus depending on the relative importance of the internal and external environmental context components of a task.

Elsewhere, I have assumed that different parts of the cerebral cortex mediate different kinds of procedural knowledge (Kesner & DiMattia, 1984). For example, medial prefrontal cortex in the rat or dorsolateral prefrontal cortex in the human might mediate the utilization of temporal rules, the insular-orbital prefrontal cortex in humans and animals might subserve affect-laden rules, and posterior parietal association cortex in humans and animals might be involved in processing of spatial rules (see Figures 6-1 and 6-2). Thus, to the extent that one can differentiate the contribution of spatial versus temporal rules, one should be able to dissociate the functions of medial prefrontal and posterior parietal association cortex. Experimental evidence in support comes from the observation that patients with prefrontal cortex damage can remember that specific items have been experienced, but they cannot discriminate the more from the less recent (i.e., order information is impaired) (Milner, 1982). In contrast, patients with posterior parietal association cortex lesions have problems dealing with spatial aspects of their environment. They have a difficult time drawing maps or diagrams of familiar spatial locations and have a general loss of "topographic" sense, which may involve the loss of long-term geographic knowledge, as well as an inability to form a "cognitive map" of the environment (De Renzi, 1982).

In recent research in my laboratory, rats with medial prefrontal cortex lesions have been presented with a list of four items (arms within an eight-arm maze). On subsequent recognition tests these animals can remember which item was presented, but they cannot remember the serial order of item presentation. This finding is similar to what has been found in humans with prefrontal cortex damage. Also, in a comparable situation, rats with posterior parietal association cortex lesions have been found to be impaired in processing of spatial information.

Since it is proposed that the amygdala and hippocampus mediate different kinds of declarative knowledge and that the medial prefrontal cortex and posterior parietal association cortex mediate different kinds of procedural knowledge, one might expect that specific lesions within cerebral cortex versus amygdala or hippocampus might result in a dissociation between procedural and declarative knowledge. Support for such a dissociation is based on evidence from patients with damage primarily in the hippocampus plus amygdala. These patients can learn and retain a variety of rules of specific perceptual–motor (tracking, mirror tracing, eyelid conditioning) and pattern-analyzing (mirror reading, rule-based verbal paired-associate learning, rules of card games) skills, while not remembering having previously performed the task, the specific contingencies of the task, or when and where they learned the task. There are many recent examples of this dissociation. To mention a few, Weiskrantz and Warrington (1979) demonstrated that amnesic patients could acquire and retain classical eyelid conditioning, but they could neither remember performing the task nor describe the apparatus or the procedure. Cohen and Squire (1980) demonstrated that amnesic patients could acquire and retain a mirror-reading skill, but between sessions could not remember repeated words that made up the reading task.

I have shown that animals with small hippocampus lesions can remember a serial order rule but can apply this rule only to recent information (Kesner & Novak, 1982). Furthermore, some preliminary work in my laboratory suggests that hippocampus-lesioned animals can learn to anticipate a sequence of repeatedly occurring events (procedural knowledge) but on a subsequent test cannot recognize having experienced the events (declarative knowledge).

The second issue is the identification of the critical process(es) that can affect learning (plasticity) and alter, establish, or restructure the organization of memory. There are a number of important subquestions. To what extent can one differentiate the operation of a process that alters the storage and retrieval of a memory from the structure of the memory representation itself? Because it is operationally and empirically very difficult to separate these two, it is not surprising that most researchers have emphasized either the importance of a process or a structure but have not attempted to differentiate between the two. I have proposed notions based on Hebb (1949) and Lewis (1976) that existing memory is normally in an inactive state but that critical neural regions will be changed into an active state when in the presence of an appropriate set of attributes (Kesner & DiMattia, 1984). This active state can then be influenced by intrinsic or extrinsic processes that increase the probability of an enduring change in the organization of memory.

What processes, then, are critical for producing a change in the structure of memory? Processes such as consolidation, storage, or retrieval are assumed to be intrinsic or directly associated with the processing of attribute information. Other processes are assumed to be extrinsic or indirectly associated with the encoding of attribute information. These latter processes tend to have more general effects and include attention (automatic versus controlled) and arousal.

With respect to intrinsic processes, it is generally assumed that some form of consolidation must take place in order to restructure existing memory and to establish a new memory (McGaugh & Herz, 1972). The first two views of memory organization would propose that there is only one consolidation process, whereas I would propose that there is activation of each neural region mediating a critical attribute, providing for the possibility of multiple consolidation processes.

With respect to extrinsic processes, it is generally assumed that attention can affect memory, but only a few researchers have discussed the nature of this influence.

I have proposed that the duration and degree (e.g., number of local circuits) of activation of critical neural circuits is greatly influenced by attention (automatic and controlled) processes (Kesner & DiMattia, 1984). Automatic attention processes would result in short duration and less extensive activation of critical neural circuits providing for accessibility to (1) information at short time delays in the case of temporal attributes, (2) information of the immediate spatial environment in the case of spatial attributes, and (3) information concerning the short-term aspects of the external context in the case of temporal–spatial attributes.

In contrast, controlled attention (e.g., rehearsal and mnemonic strategies) would increase the duration and the number of activated critical neural circuits and thus increase the probability that (1) in the case of temporal attributes information might be accessible at longer time delays, (2) in the case of spatial attributes information might have access to multiple relationships between spatial components of the immediate environment, (3) in the case of temporal-spatial attributes information might be accessible to long-term aspects of the external context, and (4) there will be an enduring change in existing memory. Furthermore, it should be noted that implicit in this formulation is the assumption that temporal attributes employ largely duration of activation, whereas spatial attributes employ largely extent of activation of critical neural circuits as a means of coding information.

Arousal can also influence memory. Some have assumed that arousal serves as a system that "gels" the memory. There are others that assume that arousal modulates consolidation (Gold & McGaugh, 1975). I have stated that arousal not only modulates consolidation but other processes (retrieval, attention) as well. Furthermore, I have assumed that this modulation takes the form of a single monotonic increasing function, where increases in the level of arousal produce increases in the rate of information processing (Kesner, 1973). Often, however, one obtains an inverted-U function for performance as a function of increased arousal. It is assumed that the ascending part of the inverted-U function is due to arousal but that the descending part is due to the activation of decremental processes (e.g., fatigue, hyperactivity, distractability) that mask the arousal function. Support for this view has been presented elsewhere (Kesner, 1973), but the most striking observation is that increased arousal induced by peripheral injections of amphetamine or electrical stimulation of the midbrain reticular formation disrupt performance at short-retention delays but facilitate performance at long-retention delays (Bierley & Kesner, 1980; Bloch, 1970; Kesner & Conner, 1972; Kesner, Bierley, & Pebbles, 1981; Krivanek & McGaugh, 1969). If one assumes that decremental mnemonic processes dominate performance at short-term retention tests, while incremental mnemonic processes dominate performance at long-term retention tests, then a rate-determining effect of arousal can easily account for the above observations.

In summary, my view is that multiple consolidation processes of varying duration, extent, and rate as influenced by attention and arousal occur simultaneously within different neural regions mediating specific attributes of a memory.

In conclusion, this short discussion made explicit some of the assumptions that encompass different theoretical approaches concerning the psychological and neurobiological organization of memory representation and the processes that can utilize or alter this organization. A special emphasis is placed on the importance of a multidimensional approach to memory organization primarily because such an approach is more consistent with the extant data and represents an alternative view not previously discussed. It is proposed that an attribute (e.g., affect) might represent the psychological unit of analysis and that for complex systems a neural region (e.g., amygdala) might represent the neural unit of analysis. Memory representations are largely determined by the organization of critical attributes and the anatomical and functional interconnections of the critical neural regions that mediate these attributes. The neural network representing memory is normally in an inactive state until it is activated by the triggering of appropriate attributes. During the state of activation, the duration, extent, and rate of activation are determined by arousal and attention processes. Prolonged and extensive activation can trigger consolidation processes, which, in turn, can alter the neural network representation of memory.

REFERENCES

Baker, L. J., Kesner, R. P., & Michal, R. E. Differential effects of a reminder cue on amnesia induced by stimulation of amygdala and hippocampus. *Journal of Comparative and Physiological Psychology*, 1981, *95*, 312–321.

Berman, R. F., & Kesner, R. P. Posttrial hippocampal, amygdaloid and lateral hypothalamic electrical stimulation: Effects upon memory of an appetitive experience. *Journal of Comparative and Physiological Psychology*, 1976, *90*, 260–267.

Best, P. J., & Orr, J., Jr. Effects of hippocampal lesions on passive avoidance and taste aversion conditioning. *Physiological Behavior*, 1973, *10*, 193–196.

Bierley, R. A., & Kesner, R. P. Short-term memory: The role of the midbrain reticular formation. *Journal of Comparative and Physiological Psychology*, 1980, *94*, 519–529.

Bierley, R. A., Kesner, R. P., & Novak, K. J. Episodic long-term memory in the rat: Effects of hippocampal stimulation. *Journal of Comparative and Physiological Psychology*, 1983, *97*, 42–48.

Bloch, V. Facts and hypothesis concerning memory consolidation. *Brain Research*, 1970, *24*, 561–575.

Bower, G. A multicomponent theory of the memory trace. In K. W. Spence & J. T. Spence (Eds.), *The psychology of learning and motivation* (Vol. 1). New York: Academic Press, 1967.

Cohen, N. J., & Squire, L. R. Preserved learning and retention of pattern-analyzing skill in amnesia: Dissociation of knowing how and knowing that. *Science*, 1980, *210*, 207–210.

De Renzi, E. Memory disorders following focal neocortical damage. *Philosophical Transactions of the Royal Society of London*, 1982, *298*, 73–83.

Gazzaniga, M. S., & LeDoux, J. E. *The integrated mind*. New York: Plenum Press, 1978.

Gold, P. E., & McGaugh, J. L. A single-trace, two-process view of memory storage processes. In D. Deutsch & J. A. Deutsch (Eds.), *Short-term memory*. New York: Academic Press, 1975.

Hebb, D. O. *The organization of behaviour*. New York: Wiley, 1949.

Kesner, R. P. A neural system analysis of memory storage and retrieval. *Psychological Bulletin*, 1973, *80*, 177–203.

Kesner, R. P. An attribute analysis of memory: The role of the hippocampus. *Physiology Psychology*, 1980, *8*, 189–197.

Kesner, R. P. Mnemonic function of the hippocampus: Correspondence between animals and humans. In C. D. Woody (Ed.), *Conditioning: Representation of neural functions*. New York: Plenum Press, 1982.

Kesner, R. P., & Andrus, R. G. Amygdala stimulation disrupts the magnitude of reinforcement contribution to long-term memory. *Physiological Psychology*, 1982, *10*, 55–59.

Kesner, R. P., & Berman, R. F. Effects of midbrain reticular formation, hippocampal and lateral hypothalamic stimulation upon recovery from neophobia and taste aversion learning. *Physiology and Behavior*, 1977, *18*, 763–768.

Kesner, R. P., Berman, R. F., Burton, B., & Hankins, W. G. Effects of electrical stimulation of amygdala upon neophobia and taste aversion. *Behavioral Biology*, 1975, *13*, 349–358.

Kesner, R. P., Bierley, R. A., & Pebbles, P. Short-term memory: The role of *d*-amphetamine. *Pharmacology Biochemistry and Behavior*, 1981, *15*, 673–676.

Kesner, R. P., & Conner, H. S. Independence of short- and long-term memory: A neural system analysis. *Science*, 1972, *176*, 432–434.

Kesner, R. P., & DiMattia, B. V. Posterior parietal association cortex and hippocampus: Equivalency of mnemonic function in animals and humans. In N. Butters & L. R. Squire (Eds.), *Neuropsychology of memory*. New York: Guilford, 1984.

Kesner, R. P., & Hardy, J. D. Long-term memory for contextual attributes: Dissociation of amygdala and hippocampus. *Behavioural Brain Research*, 1983, *8*, 139–149.

Kesner, R. P., & Novak, K. J. Serial position curve in rats: Role of the dorsal hippocampus. *Science*, 1982, *218*, 173–174.

Kinsbourne, M., & Wood, F. Theoretical considerations regarding the episodic-semantic memory distinction. In L. S. Cermak (Ed.), *Human memory and amnesia*. Hillsdale, N.J.: Erlbaum, 1982.

Krivanek, J. A., & McGaugh, J. L. Facilitating effects of pre- and post-trial amphetamine administration on discrimination learning in mice. *Agents and Actions*, 1969, *1*, 36–42.

Lashley, K. S. In search of the engram. *Symposium of the Society for Experimental Biology*, 1950, *4*, 454–482.

Lewis, D. J. A cognitive approach to experimental amnesia. *American Journal of Psychology*, 1976, *89*, 51–80.

McGaugh, J. L., & Herz, M. J. *Memory consolidation*. San Francisco: Albion, 1972.

McGowan, B. K., Hankins, W. G., & Garcia, J. Limbic lesions and control of the internal and external environment. *Behavioral Biology*, 1972, *7*, 841–852.

Milner, B. Some cognitive effects of frontal-lobe lesions in man. *Philosophical Transactions of the Royal Society of London*, 1982, *298*, 211–226.

Mishkin, M. A memory system in the monkey. *Philosophical Transactions of the Royal Society of London*, 1982, *298*, 85–95.

Nachman, M., & Ashe, J. H. Effects of basolateral amygdala lesions on neophobia, learned taste aversions, and sodium appetite in rats. *Journal of Comparative Physiological Psychology*, 1974, *87*, 622–643.

Olton, D. S., Becker, J. T., & Handelmann, G. E. Hippocampal function: Working memory or cognitive mapping? *Physiological Psychology*, 1980, *8*, 239–246.

Olton, D. S., & Wolf, W. A. Hippocampal seizures produce retrograde amnesia without a temporal gradient when they reset working memory. *Behavioral and Neural Biology*, 1981, *33*, 437–452.

Tulving, E. Episodic and semantic memory. In E. Tulving & W. Donaldson (Eds.), *Organization of memory*. New York: Academic Press, 1972.

Underwood, B. J. Attributes of memory. *Psychological Review*, 1969, *76*, 559–573.

Weiskrantz, L., & Warrington, E. K. Conditioning in amnesic patients. *Neuropsychology*, 1979, *17*, 187–194.

CHAPTER SEVEN

Is the Distinction between Procedural and Declarative Memory Useful with Respect to Animal Models of Amnesia?

RICHARD G. M. MORRIS

The Conference on the Neurobiology of Learning and Memory at Irvine in 1982, of which this volume is an outgrowth, was held on the 50th anniversary of the publication of Sir Frederick Bartlett's book *Remembering*. It was a fitting, if coincidental anniversary. Questions such as whether information in memory changes over the passage of time, a theme of some of Bartlett's experiments, recurred in discussion. Admittedly some of Bartlett's ideas, such as his concept of "effort after meaning," seem only barely relevant to infrahuman studies of memory. But in other respects, Bartlett's ideas were prescient, as in the following passage:

> In remembering proper, the psychological material which persists is itself capable of being *described*. It does not merely help to produce a certain reaction, but its descriptive characteristics are utilised by the subject, and in well articulated cases, its mode of organisation is alleged to be known. Thus, taking any particular detail, a person who remembers can set it into relation with other detail, stating its setting in time and place. (Bartlett, 1932, p. 196; original emphasis)

In this brief discussion, I shall pursue Bartlett's theme and concentrate on the nature of *representation* in animal memory, an issue explicitly addressed by Squire and Cohen (Chapter 1, this volume; see also Squire & Zola-Morgan, 1983; Squire & Cohen, 1983; Squire, 1983).

Squire and Cohen (1983) distinguish between two distinct forms of representation: (1) procedural knowledge, including perceptual–motor skills, mirror-reading, learning numerical rules, and certain complex puzzles; and (2) declarative knowledge, including specific information about both time and place and general knowledge, as well as the "facts and data of conventional memory experiments" (Squire, 1983, p. 21). Having drawn this distinction, they then argue that procedural knowledge is spared in amnesia (in fact, amnesic patients may learn such material at relatively normal rates), whereas at least the acquisi-

Richard G. M. Morris. Psychological Laboratory, University of St. Andrews, St. Andrews, Fife, Scotland.

tion and consolidation of new declarative knowledge is severely impaired. Developed in the context of human neuropsychological studies, the question arises of whether the procedural–declarative distinction can be applied, in part or in whole, to animal models of amnesia. There are a number of problems to consider.

To avoid circularity, it appears to be essential to establish in advance which of the various learning and memory tests developed for animals are "procedural" and which are "declarative." I shall argue that matters are not quite as simple as this and that it is with good reason that Squire hedges his bets with respect to the appropriate categorization of certain procedures (e.g., his reference to "certain kinds of" classical conditioning being spared in amnesia [Squire, 1983, p. 21]). As it happens, a thoughtful discussion of how the procedural–declarative distinction may be applied to animal learning has recently been published (Dickinson, 1980); unfortunately, Dickinson's treatment differs in at least one crucial respect from Squire and Cohen's interpretation of the distinction. Dickinson defines declarative knowledge as that "which corresponds to a statement or proposition describing a relationship between events in the animal's world," a form of representation that does not imply any particular course of action. He presents persuasive evidence, particularly from "blocking" experiments, that classical conditioning may, though not exclusively, involve animals' learning that events are correlated in time. Such information may then be represented as the proposition "the light causes food," that is, as a declarative proposition. He contrasts this form of description with the traditional view that the antecedent stimulus merely comes to evoke a particular "conditioned" response. With procedural knowledge, on the other hand, the "structure of the representation directly reflects the use to which the knowledge will be put in controlling the animal's behavior." Thus, in Dickinson's sense of a procedural representation, the relationship between two events in an instrumental conditioning paradigm might be described by the proposition "when the light comes on, move toward the food hopper." The crucial respect in which the uses of the term "procedural" differ is in Dickinson's linking procedural knowledge so closely to behavior. Thus, he writes: "The procedural model . . . is clearly compatible with the behaviorist's idea that learning consists of a change in behavior" (1980, p. 75). For Squire and Cohen (1983), on the other hand, procedures may be learned independently of behavior in any overt sense, as in mirror reading.

Thus, the first problem with the procedural–declarative distinction is that it is being used in different ways by different theorists. One ingenious experiment that illustrates this was reported by Gaffan (1977), primarily to demonstrate differential access to some but not other stored representations of a stimulus, depending on the precise testing procedures employed. Monkeys were seated in front of a 3×3 array of panels that could be back illuminated with different colors. They were trained on a conditional same–different matching-to-sample task in which there were three colored samples—red, amber, and blue—and four possible responses. Samples were presented on the central panel. On the choice trial several seconds later, a color (same or different) occurred on only one of the three (appropriate) response panels, whereas the fourth panel was illuminated white. The monkey had to press the color panel if it was the same as the sample and the fourth panel if it was different. An important feature of the experiment was the arrangement of the blue and red panels close together on one side of the array, and the amber and "different" panels on the other side. Gaffan found a significantly higher number of errors on the red response panel when the sample had *not* been red after blue samples than after amber samples, a puzzling result as red and amber are perceptually more confusable than red and blue. The implication, Gaffan argues, is that at the retention test, the monkeys were not recalling the sample color directly but rather the appropriate recall response associated with it. The logic of this assertion is that responses to the red and blue panels, put in close physical proximity, were more confusable than responses to the red and amber panels, which were further apart.

Gaffan's experiment was part of a series in which he had earlier demonstrated efficient recognition of sample colors. Thus, the failure to observe confusions reflecting the similarity of colors cannot be due solely to the nature of the stored representations. On the contrary, it suggests that monkeys may be able to *recognize* colors but not *recall* them. Thus, the task is declarative in the sense that the monkey has to remember a particular sample (Squire and Cohen's definition), but at least on the recall measure, it is revealed to be partly procedural in the sense that the error confusions reflect the presence of some response coding in memory (Dickinson's definition).

A second problem is distinct from but follows from the first. If certain aspects of some behavioral tasks are procedural and other aspects declarative, to what extent can there be any simple mapping of experimental *operations* onto types of stored *representations*? The answer is, surely, very little. In fact, it is abundantly clear from the animal learning literature (reviewed by Dickinson, 1980) that there is no simple relationship between many common behavioral tasks used to study learning and either the learning "subsystems" they engage or, in turn, the forms of representation they employ in memory.

Within physiological psychology, the distinction between learning and performance has never been as well respected, or possibly as well understood, as in the animal learning literature. Texts are replete with claims such as "hippocampal lesions cause improvements in active avoidance," which are descriptively adequate but only the first step in analysis. The mental or neural processes recruited during a learning task may depend critically on features of the apparatus or details of procedure, and on these grounds I take issue with Squire and Zola-Morgan's (1983) assertion that visual discrimination tasks are "procedural." Such categorization is unduly restrictive, and the study of backward learning curves (Sutherland & Mackintosh, 1971, p. 88) has shown that choice performance in visual discrimination learning is not, in individual subjects, the slow incremental process purportedly characteristic of procedural learning. Squire and Zola-Morgan (1983) argue that the procedural components of visual discrimination are *not* exclusive but *are* rate-limiting; unfortunately, data on rates of learning and overnight forgetting (which they discuss) are not sufficient to separate out subcomponents determining performance.

Squire and his colleagues have marshalled a substantial body of evidence in favor of their hypothesis, with striking demonstrations such as the successful completion of the Tower of Hanoi puzzle by H. M. However, I am fearful that the procedural–declarative distinction, at least as applied to studies of animal amnesia, may go the way of other binary distinctions that have emerged out of the clinical literature. On the one hand, the hypothesis captures an important distinction between spared and impaired memory capability; on the other hand,

(1) the distinction properly applies to forms of representation rather than task procedures, and (2) at least the declarative component of the equation looks vulnerable to further subdivision as new ways of testing (and accessing) animal memory are developed. For animal models afford an opportunity that is not necessarily presented in clinical material—namely, of looking at breakdowns in performance that rarely or never arise as a consequence of the accidents of nature. With further research, a straightforward binary classification may be of diminishing usefulness or even validity. Moreover, such research may eventually turn up the double dissociation—impaired procedural learning but intact declarative memory—that has so far failed to materialize in either the animal or human literature (but see Flowers, 1978).

However, it is surely premature to dismiss the relevance of the procedural–declarative distinction to studies of animal amnesia. On the contrary, Françoise Schenk and I have recently obtained data to which it is relevant (Morris & Schenk, 1983). Groups of rats ($n = 12$ per group) were given entorhinal cortex (radiofrequency) lesions, small lesions restricted to the overlying visual cortex (of necessity partly damaged in making the EC lesions), or no surgery. We then trained these (and other groups) to find a hidden platform in a large pool of water (Morris, 1981). Normal rats learn this task quickly (4–10 trials) and soon escape by means of relatively direct paths to the hidden platform. The entorhinal but not the small cortical lesion group showed a deficit relative to controls, but our interest focused on the pattern of recovery observed toward the end of training.

Transfer tests were conducted both early and toward the end of extensive postoperative training. In these tests, the platform was removed from the apparatus and the rats placed into the water for 60 seconds. Normal rats react to this test by swimming to the former location of the platform initially and then searching there and in its immediate vicinity (Figure 7-1). The small cortical lesion group behaved similarly. After the training, during which performance by the entorhinal cortex lesion group stabilized, rats swam through the former platform location several times during the transfer test but rarely stopped to search (Figure 7-1). Unlike normals, "recovered entorhinals" would swim around large areas of the pool before returning to go through the "correct" location. The subjective but striking impression created by this pattern of recovery was of a rat that could accurately swim through the place where a platform should be located (and during training trials *was* present) but which did not appear to "know" that a platform should be there.

There are several ways in which these findings may be interpreted, but the distinction between procedural and declarative knowledge seems particularly relevant. Using Dickinson's terminology, and Squire and Cohen's hypothesis, we might consider that the procedural representation "when in pool, swim toward place X" would have been spared; whereas the declarative proposition, "there is a hidden escape platform at place X," would either not have been stored or was inaccessible. It is a reasonable assumption that turning around repeatedly to search in a particular place, a type of behavior that necessarily cannot occur during training (because the platform is only absent in the transfer test) would be the very type of spontaneous behavior dependent on an accessible declarative database. A full report of this and several related experiments has been submitted for publication.

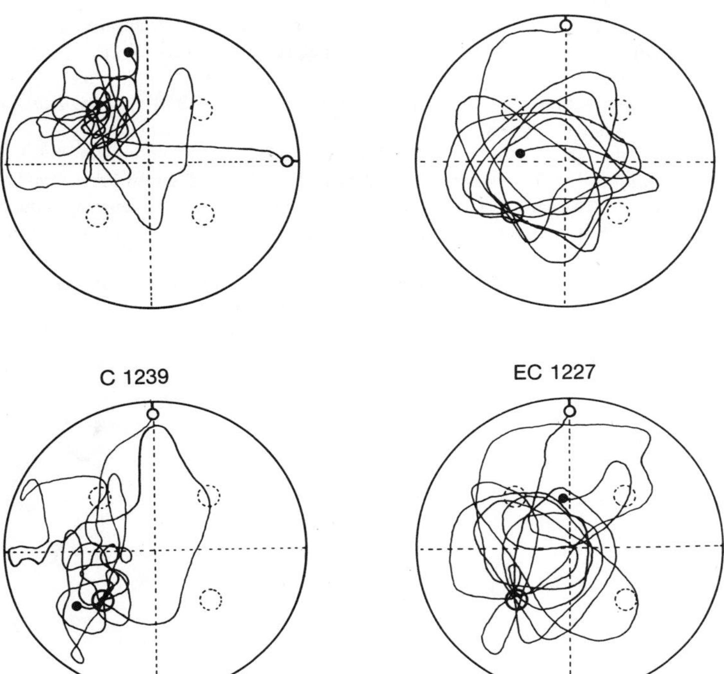

Figure 7-1. Paths taken by rats transcribed from videorecordings filmed from directly above the pool (1.3-meter diameter) during the final transfer test. The exact former position of the escape platform is shown in the center of one quadrant (NW for C1240, shown by complete circle), while the dotted circles show other possible positions of the platform for different animals. Rats were placed in the water at ○ and allowed to swim for 60 seconds; they were taken out at ●. Rats C1240 and EC1235 illustrate the different behavior of control and entorhinal cortex lesion rats particularly well. Note that both animals pass through the "correct" position often, but only the control rat stops to search in its vicinity. Rats C1239 and EC1227 also show the same pattern but are more typical of the two groups as a whole.

ACKNOWLEDGMENTS

I am grateful to the Wellcome Trust and the Guarantors of Brain for travel grants to attend the Irvine meeting in October 1982; to the European Science Foundation (ETPBBR) for supporting the work that Françoise Schenk and I have done in Switzerland and Scotland; and to Drs. M. D. Rugg and L. R. Squire for discussing some of the ideas in this commentary with me.

REFERENCES

Bartlett, F. C. *Remembering: An experimental and social psychological study*. Cambridge: Cambridge University Press, 1932.

Dickinson, A. *Contemporary animal learning theory*. Cambridge: Cambridge University Press, 1980.

Flowers, K. A. Some frequency response characteristics of parkinsonism on pursuit tracking. *Brain*, 1978, *101*, 19–34.

Gaffan, D. Response coding in recall of colors by monkeys. *Quarterly Journal of Experimental Psychology*, 1977, *29*, 597–605.

Morris, R. G. M. Spatial localisation does not require the presence of local cues. *Learning and Motivation*, 1981, *12*, 239–260.

Morris, R. G. M., & Schenk, F. Dissociation between procedural and declarative aspects of spatial memory after recovery from retrohippocampal lesions by rats. *Society for Neuroscience Abstracts*, 1983, *9*, 332.

Squire, L. R. Memory and the brain. In S. Friedman (Ed.), *Brain, cognition and education.* New York: Academic Press, 1983.

Squire, L. R., & Cohen, N. J. Human memory and amnesia. In R. F. Thompson & J. L. McGaugh (Eds.), *Handbook of behavioral neurobiology*. New York: Plenum Press, 1983.

Squire, L. R., & Zola-Morgan, S. The neurology of memory: The case for correspondence between the findings for human and nonhuman primates. In J. A. Deutsch (Ed.), *The physiological basis of memory* (2nd ed.). New York: Academic Press, 1983.

Sutherland, N. S., & Mackintosh, N. J. *Mechanisms of animal discrimination learning*. London: Academic Press, 1971.

CHAPTER EIGHT

Neurobiology, Representations, and Memory

LYNN NADEL / KENNETH WEXLER

One of the major aims of modern neuroscience has been to provide a biological understanding of learning and memory. As such, it would be expected to stress diverse adaptations and how they are realized in genetically fixed and flexible programs. Neuroscience does indeed study a rich cross-section of biological systems. However, the ideas that underlie neuroscientific research on learning have been drawn primarily from traditional psychology and rarely reflect a concern with adaptation. This chapter (1) discusses the incompatibility between biological and psychological approaches to learning, (2) outlines a biological orientation compatible with a major stream in contemporary cognitive science, and (3) attempts to integrate the study of learning into this framework.

What is learning, in the traditional psychological view? Imagine a child born into the world with no knowledge of that world (the "blank slate"). Experience impinges on the child in the form of an initially chaotic array of sensory impressions. Some of these impressions the child connects with other impressions—forming "associations." These learned associations are the primitives from which complex thoughts and behaviors are generated. Though there are important differences of opinion concerning the exact "laws" governing learning, two key assumptions have been widespread. The first asserts that there is a single kind of process—association—that accounts for all learning. This assumption is so deeply embedded into psychological tradition that being "associated," typically through the agency of temporal contiguity, has been taken as part of the definition of what it is to be "learned." Though early theorists differed as to the kinds of associations permitted, and the types of procedures needed to bring these about, few questioned the centrality of association itself. It is the seemingly nonassociative nature of many of the adaptive phenomena studied by the biologist that disqualifies them as examples of learning in the eyes of the psychologist. The second assumption is that any stimuli, responses, and/or consequences can be associated with one another by the action of this principle. This "equivalence" assumption has been held in one form or another by most traditional psychological theorists.

In addition to these separate commitments to a general learning process and its general applicability, a rather restrictive definition of learning has been

Lynn Nadel and Kenneth Wexler. Program in Cognitive Science, School of Social Science, University of California, Irvine, California.

adopted. It is asserted that learning involves more than just a change in behavior. Change alone would fail to distinguish learning from maturation, which has very little of an associative nature about it. To call an event an instance of learning, the change must reflect some specific environmental experience. By these (and other) exclusionary tactics the psychologist sought to study "pure associations"—the atoms in an eventual mental chemistry of learning.

Biologists since Darwin have taken a rather different view of the matter. An interest in selection directed their attention to forms of behavior expressed with high reliability by all successful members of a species. Such "species-typical" behaviors reflect considerable "knowledge" about the world, and it is legitimate to inquire as to how this knowledge is acquired—whether hard-wired into the genome to unfold during development (in a wide range of possible environments) or "learned" in the course of exposure to the environment typical for an organism of a particular species and age. The variety of ways in which knowledge can be shown to unfurl, with very little or even no significant (e.g., nonmetabolic) input from the external environment, has led biologists to the other extreme from psychologists; rather than reify associative learning they are surprised to see pure examples of it when it occurs. This view need not preclude an interest in the mechanisms by which knowledge is acquired during the lifetime of any given organism; it simply refuses to accept the idea that associative learning, as defined above, is the only means by which this can be accomplished.

For much of this century contact between these approaches consisted of little more than the learning–instinct debate. Not that traditional learning theory was uninterested in biology. Beginning with Hartley, the concept of association itself has been rooted in neural function. Sechenov located reflexes in the brain, Pavlov extended this view to conditioning, and Bekhterev made the connection between conditioning and association through contiguity (cf. Gormezano & Kehoe, 1981). The reductionism of modern neuroscience is heir to this tradition, and it blends quite effectively with the atomistic assumptions common to traditional learning theory. Whereas contemporary research is concerned with a diverse range of biological systems, most neuroscientists who study learning nevertheless seem to accept the generality and central importance of associative laws, and seek appropriate "model" systems in which to study them (e.g., Thompson, 1976).

But are assumptions about general laws in fact tenable? The observations of the Brelands (1961) concerning the apparent "misbehavior" of the animals they were trying to shape (without due regard for their natural behavior) and the early work of Garcia and his associates (e.g., Garcia & Koelling, 1966) on flavor-aversion conditioning suggested that both of the central tenets of traditional learning theory were incorrect. That is, not all that was once called learning is associative, and that which is associative need pay little heed to the equivalence assumption. In the ensuing years much research has made it clear that the assumption of "equivalence" of associability would not hold across all, or even most, learning situations. Organisms seem to be "prepared" to make certain kinds of associations quite easily, and others only with great difficulty, if at all. Such data evoked considerable interest in the so-called "constraints" or "biological boundaries" on learning (Seligman & Hager, 1972; Hinde & Stevenson-Hinde, 1973). As Bateson (1981) and others have noted, the very choice of the term "constraint" implies a continued allegiance to traditional learning theory—but with a twist. Now associative principles were to be considered in light of the biological makeup of the organism. In this way even Skinner could be held to take the biological nature of learning into account.

Domjan and Galef (1983) document the reasons why, in the face of considerable data demonstrating the important role of selective biological factors, general process assumptions were not replaced. The biologically based views suggested at that time were vaguely specified and often circular (e.g., Schwartz, 1974). At the same time, apparently anomalous phenomena found new interpretations within modernized learning theory (e.g., Rescorla & Wagner, 1972; Mackintosh, 1975), still resting on associationist foundations. Finally, fresh arguments in favor of the assumption of "general" laws were offered. Even if learning was an adaptive specialization (Kalat & Rozin, 1971), providing a basis for acquiring knowledge about ecologically relevant aspects of the environment, one would expect to find some generality in terms of what is being represented, as there are many aspects of the environment that are relevant for a wide range of species (e.g., gravity, space–time, causality; see Wyers, 1976). And even if the ability to form arbitrary, unprepared associations is not the pervasive mechanism it was once thought to be, it still exists and plays a central role in some kinds of learning.

In the absence of theoretically coherent alternatives to traditional accounts of learning, neuroscientists have felt comfortable with what appear to be two conflicting assumptions. First, as noted above, it is assumed by many that the study of any form of biological plasticity will contribute to our understanding of learning and memory. At the same time, it is still held that to study true learning one must study association formation, as defined above. Some bring these two underlying commitments into concert by assuming that identical molecular processes subserve the general associative mechanism wherever it is properly observed (e.g., Kandel, 1982). In this way, the study of any "model" system suffices for an understanding of all learning. It may indeed turn out to be the case that the cellular basis of associative learning is everywhere the same; this is an empirical issue, and the data are currently far from conclusive. Yet consideration of the biological diversity brought to the "acquisition of knowledge" suggests that such a simplifying assumption will not be adequate for understanding learning and memory in terms of the whole organism—or even in terms of neural systems rather than neurons and synapses.

We suggest here an alternative way to think about these matters. It begins by asserting that talk about learning and memory is misleading. These terms bias one toward the view that there are discrete memories ("traces" or "engrams") that could be easily recognized if one could but peer into the brain in the right way, or with the right tool. Nearly 50 years of persistent failure to pin down an engram suggests that "memories" will not be found encapsulated in isolable chunks. Nor does it make sense to assume that a particular "memory" is "represented" throughout the brain, embedded somehow in patterns of activity independent of where they occur. These opposed positions, which dominated neural approaches to learning–memory for much of this century, depend on adherence to the strict associative view of learning outlined earlier. We propose to focus on "knowledge"—its form and content, its acquisition and utilization—rather than on learning or memory (cf. Plotkin & Odling-Smee, 1979; 1981). Knowledge is to be distinguished from the notion of "information" used within cybernetics. Here information has no content precisely because it ignores the relevance of knowledge to its bearer. By focusing our attention on knowledge, we seek to take into account the biological content of information, as well as to connect our ideas to a broad current in contemporary cognitive science. Predicated in large measure on a biological view of cognition, this emerging perspective makes the following claims:

1. Organisms have knowledge, which they put to use in specific situations. This implies that something (representations) intervenes between observable stimuli and responses which is decoupled from both. These representations are realized in the organism's nervous system.

2. There are different kinds of knowledge, and these are represented within different "modules." These modules are defined by their centrality to the behavior and or mental processes of the species. Examples would be such things as vision, language, bird song, spatial mapping, etc.

3. There is no necessary relation between what is being represented in a module, and the form of its representation. In some cases it will be one of resemblance (e.g., images), in others not (e.g., linguistic representations).

4. The content of knowledge of any particular module is not determined by experience alone. The extensive acquisition seen in degenerate environments (Chomsky, 1980) is strong evidence of built-in knowledge. Hard-wiring of preferential connectivity within the neural system underlying a particular cognitive module provides the biological basis for this built-in knowledge. It gives to a module a structure that imposes itself on inputs. This structure plus relevant experience combine to determine the content of knowledge.

5. Knowledge is generative—that is, a small set of principles can be applied to a very large set of specific pieces of knowledge. For example, these principles allow for the generation of new routes (in spatial behavior) or sentences (in language).

6. The principles guiding the operation of a particular module could be specific to that module. The rules governing interactions among, say, linguistic representations, might be quite different from those for spatial representations.

This perspective leads one to the conclusion that there are no "general laws" of learning. Rather, learning is one form of knowledge acquisition within a specific module (e.g., learning the words of a language, or one's way about town).

The recent study of the neurobiology of human learning and memory offers an example of the utility of the ideas discussed above. In the mid-1950s when the classic patient H. M. was first studied extensively, his defect was interpreted in terms of then-current notions of a dichotomy between short-term memory (STM) and a general long-term memory system (LTM). H. M. was said to be unable to get information from STM into LTM, and this was assumed to hold across modality and material. Subsequent patients are considered to be more or less good amnesics in relation to how global and all-encompassing their defect was. Little was made of the exceptions indicating that H. M. could show some learning and retention (e.g., Corkin, 1968). At this time, attempts to replicate the amnesic defect with controlled brain lesions in experimental animals met with failure because such attempts assumed that a parallel memory defect would have to be global. The demonstration of any preserved learning capacity after appropriate damage to hippocampus (and sometimes amygdala) was taken as evidence against the role of these regions in memory function. More recent views of hippocampal function in nonhumans propose that it is involved in learning and memory but only for a restricted form of knowledge (Nadel & O'Keefe, 1974; Hirsh, 1974; O'Keefe & Nadel, 1978; Olton, Becker, & Handelmann, 1979; Parkinson & Mishkin, 1982). By concentrating on preserved capacities, research with amnesic patients has converged with this view, supporting the notion that only certain memory capacities are lost in amnesia (cf. Cohen & Squire, 1980; Parkin, 1982; Squire & Cohen, Chapter 1, this volume; Nadel, 1980). Patients can be shown to benefit considerably from experience, though the right tests must be employed, if only because the patient is typically unaware of having had any particular experience. The learning of skills, both motor and cognitive, seems intact. Normal discrimination and classical conditioning have been reported. Though there is considerable disagreement over the details, it is generally felt that knowledge about specific episodes, and their time and place of occurrence, is selectively affected in amnesia (Kinsbourne & Wood, 1975; Nadel & O'Keefe, 1974; Schacter & Tulving, 1982). Similar distinctions are drawn by others, though the terms may differ (e.g., Mishkin, Malamut, & Bachevalier, Chapter 2, and Squire & Cohen, Chapter 1, this volume). This selectivity of the amnesic defect, when looked at in the light of the modular approach to memory described above, indicates that reasonably pure cases of organic disease, such as H. M., can tell us a great deal about the compartments of the mind.

Different modules are concerned with different kinds of knowledge. It would be natural for the neuroscientist to study the function of various forms of knowledge in the life history of the organism. Such a strategy led O'Keefe and Nadel (1978) to formulate the spatial map theory on the evidence of "place" cells in the hippocampus. It could be argued that an emphasis on representational systems is misplaced, and that one should focus instead on "information processing." Computer models provide analytic tools, which, it is argued, might prove useful in the detailed study of cognition. However, information-processing psychology, for the most part, concentrates its attention on processes, in a way that assumes that representations have no empirical content. It is natural within this approach to suppose that all manner of qualitatively different cognitive abilities could be accounted for by the same set of processes. Thus, language (speech and comprehension, including grammar, phonology, and the like), problem solving and general world knowledge, spatial knowledge and facial recognition are all to be explained in terms of the same kind of procedures (see, e.g., Anderson, 1976). Biologically this view makes little sense. Moreover, it has had limited success in dealing with cognitive function (Wexler, 1978). The modularity alternative we propose is exemplified by a number of research programs, among them those concerned with vision (Marr, 1982), linguistic theory (Chomsky, 1980), language learning (Wexler & Culicover, 1981), and spatial mapping (O'Keefe & Nadel, 1978).

In addition to specifying the kinds of representational modules we can expect to find, a satisfying neurobiological approach to learning–memory would detail the ways in which representations are acquired, manipulated, and utilized. And it would specify how these modules and their principles of operation change throughout the life of the organism (cf. Nadel & Zola-Morgan, 1984; Barnes, McNaughton, & O'Keefe, 1982). We cannot address these issues directly here. In the remainder of the chapter we briefly outline what we take to be a sensible way of talking about knowledge acquisition. The implications of such a view for an analysis of ontogenetic (and phylogenetic) variations in "learning and memory" remain to be spelled out in greater detail.

An early, severe challenge to traditional learning theory was provided by the demonstration of imprinting (Hess, 1959; see Bateson, 1966, 1979, and Columbo, 1982, for reviews). This phenomenon, with its high degree of regularity and acute selectivity, fails to satisfy the basic criteria established for associative learning—"it simply involves exposing a bird to a single stimulus without explicit pairing of neutral and significant events" (Bateson, 1979, p. 472). However, by our broader definition, imprinting is a perfect example of highly constrained knowledge acquisition. Similarly, the changes seen in sensory function as a result of early experience (e.g., Pettigrew, 1978; Banks, Aslin, & Letson, 1975)—involving a kind of "tuning" or "parameter-setting" process—are also examples of knowledge acquisition. The classical conditioning demonstrated in a variety of invertebrates, with all the earmarks of associative conditioning (e.g., Carew, Hawkins, & Kandel, 1983; Sahley, Rudy, & Gelperin, 1981; Crow & Alkon, 1978; Mpitsos, Collins, & McClellan, 1978), is another example of preprogrammed learning.[1] The neural changes underlying such conditioning are intrinsic to already existing pathways interconnecting conditioned stimulus and unconditioned stimulus "representations"—pathways within which nonassociative changes such as habituation and sensitization also occur.

This picture of learning is quite consistent with the emerging account of language and language acquisition (Chomsky, 1981). The claim is that language acquisition involves a highly constrained process of parameter setting (different languages differ in the particular values of parameters). Importantly, small changes in the values of parameters cause major changes in the structure of the acquired system, due to the tightly interconnected nature of the acquisition system.

In all these cases "learning" occurs within narrow limits, involving the modification of preexisting, functional circuits. Are there general principles guiding this form of knowledge acquisition, which brings into concert contributions from both nature and nurture? Most pervasive are the mechanisms guaranteeing the canalization of development. This concept refers to the way in which the development of some trait, be it structural or behavioral, necessarily follows a certain path to a foreordained conclusion.

Consider the problem of learning who is or is not a conspecific. One nativist possibility is that the animal is born with an image or template of its conspecifics already built in; the problem then reduces to one of specifying the neural development involved. But this is quite inflexible, allowing for little or no variability in the environment nor for individual recognition. Suppose some single feature, or small set of features, is prewired so as to attract the organism's attention. Through attending to this "guide," the organism is brought (in its natural environment) into contact with aspects of its world about which it "needs" to acquire knowledge. Thus, the visual features of the to-be-imprinted

1. We do not imply that conditioning in invertebrates is all that it is in vertebrates. In the latter, for example, recent work shows that environmental context assumes an importance in both learning and performance.

conspecific could serve to draw the young bird's attention to its remaining features (cf. Eiserer, 1980). These could then serve in turn to guide the young organism as it acquires knowledge about species-typical acts such as appropriate song (Marler, 1978). Other examples of this are provided by cases where a complex pattern of species-typical behavior comes under the variable control of a number of different kinds of knowledge (e.g., bird navigation and orientation). Prior to any relevant experience, the ability to navigate using one set of environmental features (say, the sun's rays) could be prewired. By following these cues, and thereby behaving correctly, knowledge about other relevant features of the situation could be acquired. Of course, the kinds of knowledge that could be acquired in this way will also be constrained by biological structure (see Plotkin & Odling-Smee, 1981). Such a "developmental bootstrapping" mechanism seems to characterize accurately much perceptual "learning." Similarly, it finds natural application to forms of play behavior and other kinds of guided practice, "learning" by imitation, and learning that occurs within a cultural–social context.

Hogan (1973) describes a cascade of canalized learning experiences by which chicks could find out about food. Imprinting has already gotten the chicks to follow the mother hen. She attracts their direct attention when she discovers a new food source. In so doing she not only helps to feed them but also familiarizes them with that food source—familiar foods are much more readily eaten later. It is important to note the fundamentally nonassociative nature of these examples, which see learning as "one of many mechanisms whereby an organism comes to develop back-up strategies for meeting environmental challenges when prewired solutions become outmoded or ineffective" (Smith & Bogomolny, 1983). What is observed rather than associative learning involves changes in the "salience" of stimuli—habituation and sensitization. These changes affect where, and to what, organisms will attend, and by so doing they channel experience (or our interpretation of it) along well-worn developmental paths.

In the absence of events that elicit changes in prepared circuits of the type just described, organisms can form associations about spatial–temporal contiguity and/or contingency relations. Indeed, it is precisely in these most arbitrary situations that what has been called "grade-A certified learning" (Miller, 1967) occurs. Yet even here it would be a mistake to ignore the biological facts. One could view this "arbitrary" learning system as highly prepared to establish representations of things that co-occur in time and space—right down to the provision of a behavioral component, the neophilic exploration system, which guides the organism's information gathering. Described in this way, the module responsible for such knowledge could well, by its absence, explain the selective nature of organic amnesia. That a syndrome first thought to be globally devastating should turn out to involve dysfunction in a relatively specialized system encourages us in applying modular notions to the study of memory and other cognitive functions.

We began with the assertion that the study of learning and memory needed to be placed in an appropriate biological context. Attempts to reformulate general-process learning theories along biologically constrained lines have resulted only in modified general-process, or information-processing, theories. In its place much of contemporary cognitive science would put the analysis of knowledge. The study of "learning" then becomes the study of how different kinds of knowledge are acquired, and data from studies ranging quite widely across the nonassociative–associative continuum are pertinent. Several forms of knowledge acquisition within highly prepared circuits seem amenable to interpretation in terms of specific prewired components serving to canalize further acquisition of knowledge. The strong consistency of species-typical behavior and its ability to adapt to local circumstances (as in bird-song dialects or individual neighbor recognition) can both be accounted for within this kind of developmental system. True associative learning, in which there is interchangeability between arbitrarily chosen (merely contingently related) objects and/or events, appears to transpire within a knowledge module concerned with co-occurrence in space and time. Such a function attributed to the hippocampal formation makes sense of the amnesic syndrome and suggests that analyses based on the functions of separate knowledge modules could prove important in fulfilling the promise of neuroscience—to provide biological accounts of psychological phenomena.

ACKNOWLEDGMENTS

This chapter attempts to summarize an emerging consensus in cognitive neuroscience and credits far fewer sources than it could. We thank our colleagues at Irvine and elsewhere. In particular, we thank those whose ideas we've borrowed freely: Seligman (1970); Kalat and Rozin (1971); Marler (1978); Bateson (1979); Domjan and Galef (1983); and Shettleworth (1983) are noteworthy. Not least of the pleasures of our line of work is the collegiality that pervades most interactions. During the preparation of the chapter, Nadel was supported by Grant No. NS17712 (NINCDS) and Wexler was supported by Grant No. BNS78-27044 (NSF).

REFERENCES

Anderson, J. R. *Language, memory and thought*. Hillsdale, N.J.: Erlbaum, 1976.

Banks, M. S., Aslin, R. N., & Letson, R. D. Sensitive period for the development of human binocular vision. *Science*, 1975, *190*, 675–677.

Barnes, C. A., McNaughton, B. L., & O'Keefe, J. Loss of place specificity in hippocampal complex-spike cells of senescent rat. *Society for Neuroscience Abstracts*, 1982, *8*, 840.

Bateson, P. The characteristics and context of imprinting. *Biological Reviews*, 1966, *41*, 177–220.

Bateson, P. How do sensitive periods arise and what are they for? *Animal Behavior*, 1979, *27*, 470–486.

Bateson, P. Linking the biological functions and the mechanisms of learning: Uses and abuses. *Behavioral and Brain Sciences*, 1981, *4*, 142.

Breland, K., & Breland, M. The misbehavior of organisms. *American Psychologist*, 1961, *16*, 681–684.

Carew, T. J., Hawkins, R. D., & Kandel, E. R. Differential classical conditioning of a defensive withdrawal reflex in *Aplysia californica*. *Science*, 1983, *219*, 397–400.

Chomsky, N. Rules and representations. *Behavioral and Brain Sciences*, 1980, *3*, 1–61.

Chomsky, N. *Lectures on government and binding*. Dordrecht, Holland: Foris, 1981.

Cohen, N. J., & Squire, L. R. Preserved learning and retention of pattern-analyzing skill in amnesia: Dissociation of knowing how and knowing that. *Science*, 1980, *210*, 207–210.

Columbo, J. The critical period concept: Research, methodology, and theoretical issues. *Psychological Bulletin*, 1982, *91*, 260–275.

Corkin, S. Acquisition of motor skill after bilateral medial temporal-lobe excision. *Neuropsychologia*, 1968, *6*, 255–265.

Crow, T. J., & Alkon, D. L. Retention of an associative behavioral change in *Hermissenda*. *Science*, 1978, *201*, 1239–1241.

Domjan, M., & Galef, B. S., Jr. Biological constraints on instrumental and classical conditioning: Retrospect and prospect. *Animal Learning and Behavior*, 1983, *11*, 116–121.

Eiserer, L. A. Development of filial attachment to static and visual features of an imprinting object. *Animal Learning and Behavior*, 1980, *8*, 159–166.

Garcia, J., & Koelling, R. A. Relation of cue to consequence in avoidance learning. *Psychonomic Science*, 1966, *4*, 123–124.

Gormezano, I., & Kehoe, E. J. Classical conditioning and the law of contiguity. In P. Harzem & M. D. Zeiler (Eds.), *Advances in analysis of behavior* (Vol. 2). New York: Wiley, 1981.

Hess, E. The relationship between imprinting and motivation. In *Nebraska Symposium on Motivation*. Lincoln: University of Nebraska Press, 1959.

Hinde, R. A., & Stevenson-Hinde, J. (Eds.). *Constraints on learning: Limitations and predispositions*. New York: Academic Press, 1973.

Hirsh, R. The hippocampus and contextual retrieval of information from memory: A theory. *Behavioral Biology*, 1974, *12*, 421–444.

Hogan, J. A. How young chicks learn to recognize food. In R. A. Hinde & J. Stevenson-Hinde (Eds.), *Constraints on learning: Limitations and predispositions*. New York: Academic Press, 1973.

Kalat, J. W., & Rozin, P. Specific hungers and poison avoidance as adaptive specializations of learning. *Psychological Review*, 1971, *78*, 459–486.

Kandel, E. R. *Steps towards a molecular grammar for learning: Explorations into the nature of memory*. Paper read at Bicentennial Symposium, Harvard Medical School, 1982.

Kinsbourne, M., & Wood, F. Short term memory and pathological forgetting. In D. Deutsch & J. A. Deutsch (Eds.), *Short term memory*. New York: Academic Press, 1975.

Mackintosh, N. J. A theory of attention: Variation in the associability of stimuli with reinforcement. *Psychological Review*, 1975, *82*, 276–298.

Marler, P. Perception and innate knowledge. In W. H. Heidcamp (Ed.), *The nature of life: 13th Nobel conference*. Baltimore: University Park Press, 1978.

Marr, D. *Vision*. San Francisco: Freeman, 1982.

Miller, N. E. Certain facts of learning relevant to the search for its physical basis. In G. C. Quarton, T. Meinechuk, & F. O. Schmitt (Eds.), *The neurosciences: A study program*. New York: Rockefeller University Press, 1967.

Mpitsos, G. J., Collins, S. D., & McClellan, A. D. Learning: A model system for physiological studies. *Science*, 1978, *199*, 497–502.

Nadel, L. Cognitive and neural maps. In P. W. Juscyzk & R. M. Klein (Eds.), *The nature of thought: Essays in honor of D. O. Hebb*. Hillsdale, N.J.: Erlbaum, 1980.

Nadel, L., & O'Keefe, J. The hippocampus in pieces and patches: An essay on modes of explanation in physiological psychology. In R. Bellairs & E. G. Gray (Eds.), *Essays on the nervous system: A festschrift for J. Z. Young*. Oxford: Clarendon Press, 1974.

Nadel, L., & Zola-Morgan, S. Infantile amnesia: A neurobiological perspective. In M. Moscovitch (Ed.), *Infant memory*. New York: Plenum Press, 1984.

O'Keefe, J., & Nadel, L. *The hippocampus as a cognitive map*. Oxford: Clarendon Press, 1978.

Olton, D. S., Becker J. T., & Handelmann, G. E. Hippocampus, space and memory. *Behavioral and Brain Sciences*, 1979, *2*, 313–365.

Parkin, A. J. Residual learning capacity in organic amnesia. *Cortex*, 1982, *18*, 417–440.

Parkinson, J. K., & Mishkin, M. A selective mnemonic role for the hippocampus in monkeys: Memory for the location of objects. *Society for Neuroscience Abstracts*, 1982, *8*, 23.

Pettigrew, J. D. The paradox of the critical period for striate cortex. In C. W. Cotman (Ed.), *Neuronal plasticity*. New York: Raven Press, 1978.

Plotkin, H. C., & Odling-Smee, F. J. Learning, change and evolution: An enquiry into the teleonomy of learning. *Advances in the Study of Behavior*, 1979, *10*, 1–41.

Plotkin, H. C., & Odling-Smee, F. J. A multiple-level model of evolution and its implications for sociobiology. *Behavioral and Brain Sciences*, 1981, *4*, 225–268.

Rescorla, R. A., & Wagner, A. R. A theory of Pavlovian conditioning: Variations in the effectiveness of reinforcement and non-reinforcement. In A. H. Black & W. F. Prokasy (Eds.), *Classical conditioning II*. New York: Appleton, 1972.

Sahley, C., Rudy, J. W., & Gelperin, A. An analysis of associative learning in a terrestrial mollusc: 1. Higher-order conditioning, blocking and a transient US pre-exposure effect. *Journal of Comparative Physiology*, 1981, *144*, 1–8.

Schacter, D. L., & Tulving, E. Amnesia and memory research. In L. S. Cermak (Ed.), *Human memory and amnesia*. Hillsdale, N.J.: Erlbaum, 1982.

Schwartz, B. On going back to nature. *Journal of the Experimental Analysis of Behavior*, 1974, *21*, 183–198.

Seligman, M. E. P. On the generality of the laws of learning. *Psychological Review*, 1970, *77*, 406–418.

Seligman, M. E. P., & Hager, J. L. (Eds.). *Biological boundaries of learning*. Englewood Cliffs, N.J.: Prentice-Hall, 1972.

Shettleworth, S. Function and mechanism in learning. In M. D. Zeiler & P. Harzem (Eds.), *Advances in analysis of behavior* (Vol. 3: *Biological factors in learning*). New York: Wiley, 1983.

Smith, G. J., & Bogomolny, A. Appetitive instrumental training in preweanling rats: I. Motivational determinants. *Developmental Psychobiology*, 1983, *16*, 119–128.

Thompson, R. F. The search for the engram. *American Psychologist*, 1976, *31*, 209–227.

Wexler, K. A review of John R. Anderson's *Language, memory, and thought*. *Cognition*, 1978, *6*, 327–351.

Wexler, K., & Culicover, P. *Formal principles of language acquisition*. Cambridge, Mass.: MIT Press, 1981.

Wyers, E. J. Learning and evolution. In L. Petrinovich & J. L. McGaugh (Eds.), *Knowing, thinking and believing: Festschrift for Professor David Krech*. New York: Plenum Press, 1976.

SECTION TWO

Systems Neurophysiology of Learning and Memory

CHAPTER NINE

Neuronal Substrates of Learning and Memory: A "Multiple-Trace" View

RICHARD F. THOMPSON / GREGORY A. CLARK / NELSON H. DONEGAN / DAVID G. LAVOND / JANN S. LINCOLN / JOHN MADDEN IV / LAURA A. MAMOUNAS / MICHAEL D. MAUK / DAVID A. MCCORMICK / JUDITH K. THOMPSON

In this chapter we will argue that when an animal learns even a relatively simple task, several memory trace systems may become established in the brain. Indeed, evidence to date suggests that in simple aversive learning, at least three memory trace systems may develop. One involves the basic association between the "neutral" conditioned stimulus (CS) and the aversive unconditioned stimulus (UCS), a process often termed conditioned emotional state or conditioned fear (Mowrer, 1947). This is revealed by rapid learning of *nonspecific* responses, such as heart rate change, that indicate the development of an associative process but do not deal effectively with the UCS (Weinberger, 1982). Such responses are generally believed to reflect incentive or learned motivation.

Specific, adaptive responses such as eyelid closure or leg flexion are learned more slowly and do deal specifically and effectively with the aversive UCS. This might be termed the *specific*, adaptive memory trace system. We suggest that the nonspecific trace system must first be established in order for the specific trace to develop, but once developed, the specific trace system may acquire some degree of functional autonomy (see, e.g., Rescorla & Solomon, 1967).

A third memory trace system might be called "cognitive" or recognition memory. In terms of the current distinction between "procedural" and "declarative" memory (see, e.g., Squire, 1982), acquisition of a simple conditioned

Richard F. Thompson, Nelson H. Donegan, David G. Lavond, Jann S. Lincoln, Laura A. Mamounas, Michael D. Mauk, and Judith K. Thompson. Department of Psychology, Stanford University, Stanford, California.

Gregory A. Clark. Center for Neurobiology and Behavior, College of Physicians and Surgeons, Columbia University, New York, New York.

John Madden IV. Departments of Physiology and of Psychiatry and Behavioral Sciences, Stanford University Medical School, Stanford, California.

David A. McCormick. Department of Neurology, Stanford University Medical School, Stanford, California.

response is procedural learning. However, higher brain systems such as the hippocampus become engaged even in these simple tasks and may develop a "declarative" trace system.

It is reasonable to suggest that these memory trace systems are hierarchically organized within the mammalian brain. Damage to the "declarative" trace system may abolish higher-order "declarative" forms of memory while sparing the specific and nonspecific trace systems. Destruction of the specific trace system would abolish memories for specific adaptive responses and might impair some aspects of "declarative" memory but spare the nonspecific memory system. However, impairment of the nonspecific system, particularly early in learning, might be expected to impair all three forms of memory. Evidence presented in this chapter supports these tentative suggestions.

In recent years the "model system" approach to analysis of the neuronal substrates of learning and memory has been valuable and productive. The basic notion is to utilize a preparation showing a clear form of associative learning in which neuronal analysis is possible. When a suitable preparation has been developed, the first issue that must be addressed is that of identifying the neuronal structures and systems that are involved in a given form of learning. Most typically, this has been approached using lesions, electrophysiological recording, and anatomical methods. A critical aspect is circuit analysis—tracing the neuronal pathways and systems from the CS channel to the motor neurons. As the essential structures and pathways are defined it becomes possible to localize and analyze cellular mechanisms underlying learning and memory (Cohen, 1980; Ito, 1982; Kandel & Spencer, 1968; Thompson & Spencer, 1966; Thompson *et al.*, 1976; Thompson, Berger, & Madden, 1983; Thompson, McCormick, *et al.*, 1983; Tsukahara, 1981; Woody, Yarowsky, Owens, Black-Cleworth, & Crow, 1974). One of the many advantages of utilizing a few well-defined model systems for analysis of brain substrates of learning and memory is that knowledge is cumulative and can be generalized across laboratories.

We adopted a particularly clear-cut and robust form of associative learning in the intact mammal as a model system: Classical conditioning of the rabbit nictitating membrane (NM) and eyelid response to an acoustic CS, using a corneal airpuff USC. This simple form of learning, first developed for behavioral analysis by Gormezano (1972), is very well characterized behaviorally, has proved extremely valuable for analysis of theoretical issues in learning by Wagner and associates (Donegan & Wagner, in press; Wagner, 1969, 1981), and is particularly well suited for neurobiological analysis (Disterhoft, Kwan, & Low, 1977; Thompson *et al.*, 1976). A number of laboratories are now using this preparation for the study of neuronal substrates of learning and memory (see, e.g., Thompson *et al.*, in press).

A word is in order about the nature of the conditioned response (CR). Investigators typically record either extension of the NM, which is a largely passive consequence of eyeball retraction (Cegavske, Thompson, Patterson, & Gormezano, 1976), or closure of the external eyelid. However, with standard procedures for NM conditioning, both become conditioned simultaneously and synchronously, together with some degree of contraction of the periorbital facial musculature (McCormick, Lavond, & Thompson, 1982). The major components are NM extension (eyeball retraction) and eyelid closure. In recent work we have measured and/or observed both. When we refer to the CR below, we mean both the NM and eyelid. All effects reported here occur equally for both. This fact maps very nicely into the large animal and human behavioral literature on eyelid conditioning. Indeed, eyelid conditioning exhibits the same basic laws of learning in a wide range of mammalian species, including humans, and is prototypic of classical conditioning of striated muscle responses (Hilgard & Marquis, 1940). It may be viewed as but one instance of the general class of specific adaptive CRs learned to deal with an aversive UCS.

Localization of the memory trace(s) has proved to be one of the most baffling questions in science (Hebb, 1949; Lashley, 1929). In order to analyze neuronal–synaptic mechanisms of memory storage and retrieval, it is first necessary to identify and localize the brain systems, structures, and regions that are critically involves (Thompson, Berger, & Madden, 1983). An obvious distinction must be made between the learned-response circuit—the necessary structures from CS receptors to CR effectors—and the memory trace itself, which is the essential neuronal plasticity that codes the learned response. The latter is included within the former but is only a part of it.

INITIAL LOCALIZATION OF THE MEMORY TRACE FOR THE SPECIFIC, ADAPTIVE LEARNED RESPONSE: THE CEREBELLUM

The major focus of this chapter is on localization of the memory trace for the specific, adaptive learned response. Excluding possible sites for the specific, adaptive memory trace is a necessary part of localizing critical sites. We have presented evidence elsewhere that, for classical conditioning of the NM–eyelid response to an acoustic stimulus, the memory trace is not in the CS channel (primary auditory relay nuclei), the reflex pathways, the alpha or startle response pathways, or the motor nuclei and neurons (Kettner & Thompson, 1982; Thompson, Berger, & Madden, 1983; Thompson, McCormick, *et al.*, 1983; Thompson *et al.*, in press).

Other laboratories have shown that animals can learn the standard NM–eyelid CR following ablation of all brain tissue above the level of the thalamus (Norman, Buchwald, & Villablanca, 1977; Enser, 1974). Several inferences are possible from this result, perhaps the most parsimonious being that a "primary memory trace" circuit exists below the level of the thalamus for the standard CR. This is not to say that higher brain structures do not normally play important roles and develop substantial learning-induce neuronal plasticity. Indeed, the hippocampus does so (see below and Thompson *et al.*, 1980, 1982).

Over the past 4 years, we have been in the process of completing an extensive and detailed mapping of the midbrain–brain stem, recording neuronal-unit activity in already trained animals (McCormick, Lavond, & Thompson, 1983; Thompson *et al.*, in press). Learning-related increases in unit activity are prominent in certain regions of the cerebellum, both in cortex and deep nuclei, in certain regions of the pontine nuclei, and in the red nucleus. Such unit activity is also seen in certain regions of the reticular formation and, of course, in the cranial motor nuclei engaged in generation of the behavioral response—portions of the 3rd, 5th, 6th, accessory 6th, and 7th nuclei. The results to date of the mapping studies point to substantial engagement of the cerebellar system in the generation of the CR.

Current studies in which we have recorded neuronal-unit activity from the deep cerebellar nuclei (dentate and interpositus nuclei) over the course of training have in some locations revealed a striking pattern of learning-related

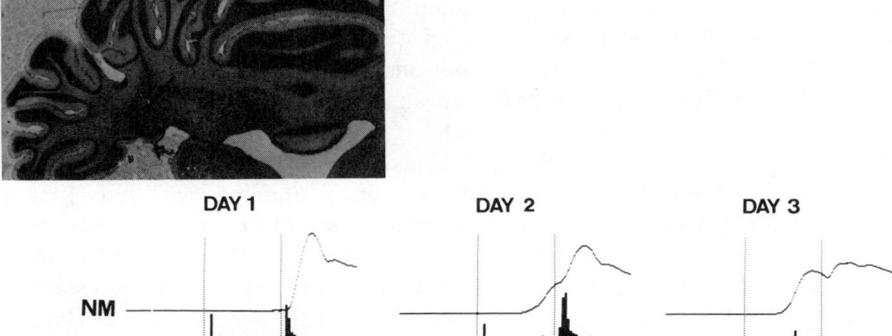

Figure 9-1. Histograms of unit cluster recordings obtained from the medial dentate nucleus during classical conditioning of NM–eyelid response. The recording site is indicated by the arrow. Each histogram bar is 9 msec in width and each histogram is summed over an entire day of training. The first vertical line represents the onset of the tone and the second vertical line represents the onset of the airpuff. The trace above each histogram is the averaged movement of the animal's NM for an entire day, with "up" being the extension of the NM across the cornea. The total duration of each histogram and trace is 750 msec. The pattern of increased discharges of cerebellar neurons appears to develop a neuronal "model" of the amplitude–time course of the learned behavioral response. (From McCormick, Clark, Lavond, & Thompson, 1982.)

growth in activity (McCormick, Clark, Lavond, & Thompson, 1982). In the example shown in Figure 9-1, the animal did not learn on Day 1 of training. Unit activity showed evoked responses to tone and airpuff onsets but no response in association with the reflex NM response, in marked contrast to unit recordings from the cranial motor nuclei. On Day 2, the animal began showing CRs, and the unit activity in the medial dentate nucleus developed a "model" of the CR. On Day 3, the learned behavioral response and the cerebellar model of the learned response are well developed, but there is still no clear model of the reflex behavioral response. The cerebellar-unit model of the learned response precedes the behavioral response significantly in time.

Another example is shown in Figure 9-2. This animal was given unpaired training before acquisition began. Average histograms reveal that the unit activity showed only minimal responses to the tone and airpuff during the unpaired day of training. However, during acquisition, as the animal learned, the unit activity developed a model of the CR. Again, there is no clear model of the unconditioned response (UCR). *A neuronal model of the learned behavioral response appears to develop de novo in the cerebellum.* The course of development of the conditioned behavioral NM–eyelid response and the concomitant growth in the neuronal unit "model" of the CR in the ipsilateral dentate–interpositus nuclear region are shown for a group of animals in Figure 9-3. The correlation between the two measures is +.90.

In current work, we have found that lesions ipsilateral to the trained eye in several locations in the neocerebellum (Figure 9-4)—large ablations of the

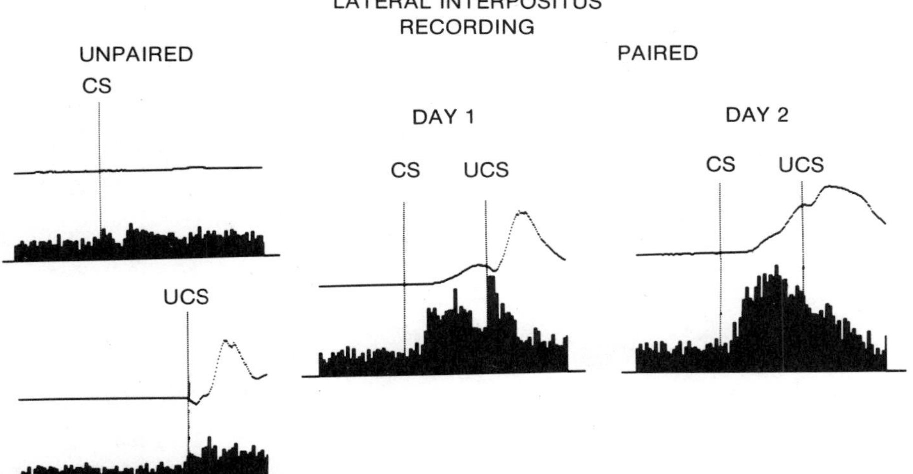

Figure 9-2. Histograms of unit recordings obtained from a chronic electrode implanted on the border of the dentate–interpositus nuclei in one animal. The animal was first given random, unpaired presentations of the tone and airpuff (104 trials of each stimulus) and then trained with 2 days of paired training (117 trials each day). Each histogram is an average over the entire day of training indicated. The upper trace represents movement of the NM, with "up" being closure. The first vertical line represents the onset of the CS; the second line represents the onset of the UCS. Each histogram bar is 9 msec in duration. Notice that these neurons develop a model of the CR, but not the UCR, during learning. (From McCormick & Thompson, unpublished observations.)

lateral portion of the hemisphere (Figure 9-5), localized electrolytic lesions of the dentate–interpositus nuclei and surrounding fibers (Figure 9-6), and discrete lesions of the superior cerebellar peduncle (Figure 9-7)—permanently abolish the CR but have no effect on the UCR and do not prevent subsequent learning by the contralateral eye (Clark, McCormick, Lavond, Baxter, Gray, & Thompson, 1982; Clark, McCormick, Lavond, & Thompson, 1984; McCormick, Lavond, Clark, Kettner, Rising, & Thompson, 1981; McCormick, Clark, Lavond, & Thompson, 1982; McCormick, Guyer, & Thompson, 1982). The electrolytic lesion result has recently been replicated exactly by Yeo, Hardiman, Glickstein, and Russell (1982) using light as well as tone CSs and a periorbital shock rather than corneal airpuff UCS. If training is given after unilateral cerebellar lesion, the ipsilateral eye cannot learn, but the contralateral eye learns normally (Figure 9-8) (Lincoln, McCormick, & Thompson, 1982). Lesions in several locations in the ipsilateral pontine brain stem produce a similar selective abolition of the CR (Desmond & Moore, 1982; Lavond, McCormick, Clark, Holmes, & Thompson, 1981). Although some uncertainty still exists, the learning-effective lesion sites in the pontine brain stem apear to track the course of at least a part of the superior cerebellar peduncle.

Taken together, these results indicate that the cerebellum is an obligatory part of the learned-response circuit for eyelid–NM conditioning. Since decerebrate animals can learn the response, this would seem to localize an essential component of the memory trace to the ipsilateral cerebellum and/or its major

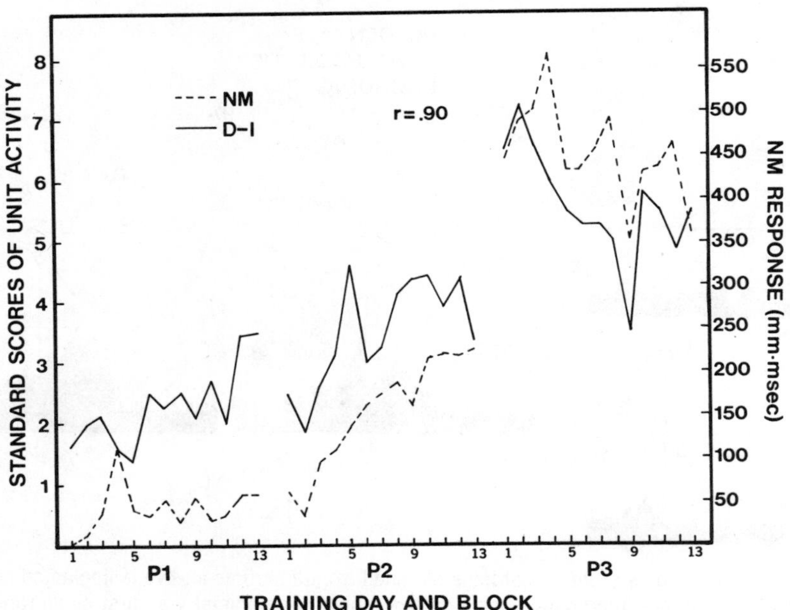

Figure 9-3. Amplitude of the CR in comparison to the magnitude of the dentate–interpositus neuronal activity in the second half of the CS period over the course of learning. Seven of the recording sites that developed larger-type responses were utilized for this figure. Standard scores were calculated by finding the mean number of action potentials counted for the block of training trials in question, subtracting the number of counts in the corresponding half of the pre-CS period for that block, and dividing by the standard deviation over the entire training session: $(\overline{CS}_{block} - \overline{PCS}_{block})/SD\ PCS_{session}$. The magnitude of the CS was measured as the area under the curve described by the amplitude–time course of the NM response in mm · msec. (From McCormick & Thompson, unpublished observations.)

Figure 9-4. Reconstructions of cerebellar lesions effective in abolishing the ipsilateral conditioned NM–eyelid response. A is a typical unilateral aspiration of the lateral cerebellum and dentate–interpositus nuclei. B represents a unilateral electrolytic lesion of the dentate–interpositus nuclei (DIX) in which the overlying cortex is spared. C is a localized unilateral lesion of the superior cerebellar peduncle (SPX). All reconstructions are through the broadest extent of each lesion. Abbreviations: ANS, ansiform lobe; CN, cochlear nucleus; D, dentate nucleus; F, fastigial nucleus; ANT, anterior lobe; FL, flocculus; I, interpositus nucleus; IC, inferior colliculus; IO, inferior olive; IP, inferior cerebellar peduncle; PF, paraflocculus; SC, superior colliculus; SP, superior cerebellar peduncle; VM, vermal lobes; VII, seventh nucleus. (From Clark *et al.*, 1982; McCormick *et al.*, 1981, McCormick, Clark, Lavond, & Thompson, 1982; McCormick, Guyer, & Thompson, 1982.)

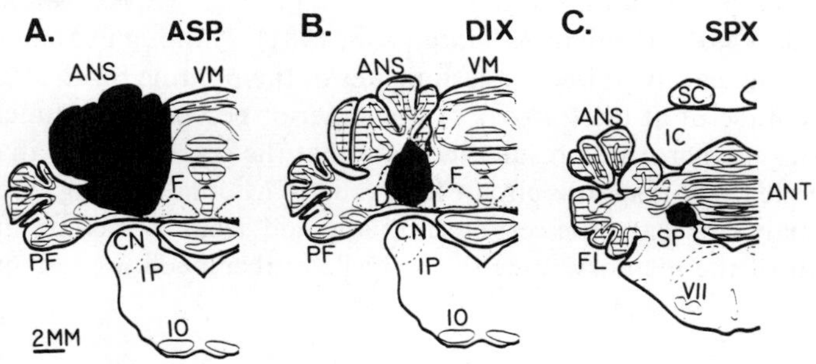

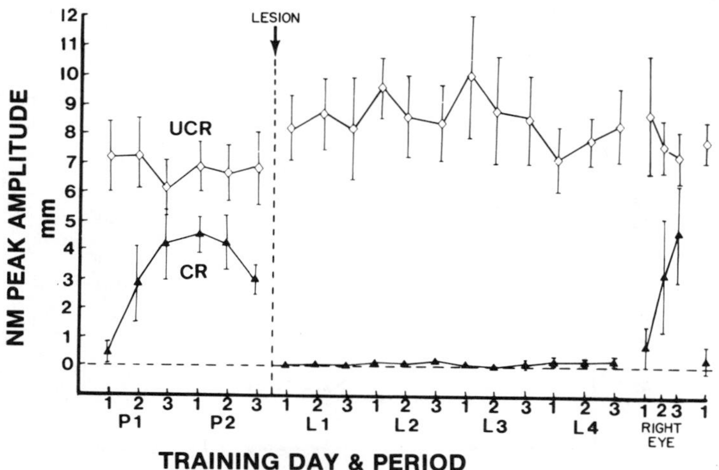

Figure 9-5. Effects of ablation of left lateral cerebellum on the learned NM–eyelid response (six animals). Solid triangles indicate the amplitude of the CR; open diamonds indicate the amplitude of the UCR. All training was to left eye (ipsilateral to lesion), except where labeled "right eye." The cerebellar lesion completely and permanently abolished the CR of the ipsilateral eye, but had no effect on the UCR. P_1 and P_2 indicate initial learning on the 2 days prior to the lesion. L_1–L_4 are 4 days of postoperative training to the left eye. The right eye was then trained and learned rapidly. The left eye was again trained and showed no learning. Numbers on abscissa indicate 40-trial periods, except for "right eye," which are 24-trial periods. (From McCormick, Clark, Lavond, & Thompson, 1982.)

Figure 9-6. Effects of unilateral lesions of cerebellar nuclei on NM CRs and UCRs (mean amplitude, $n = 14$). Animals received 3 days of training (P1–P3) on the left eye prior to lesioning. After lesioning (left cerebellar nuclei), animals were trained for 4 days (L1–L4) to test for retention and recovery of the conditioned responses. On the fifth postlesion session (L5), training was switched to the right (nonlesioned) side, then returned to the left eye ($n = 13$). Results of each training day are represented in four periods of trials, approximately 27 trials per period. Note that CR amplitude was almost completely abolished by the lesion, but UCR amplitude was unaffected. Note also the right (nonlesioned) side learned quickly, controlling for nonspecific lesion effects, but that conditioned responding on the left side showed essentially no recovery. (From Clark *et al.*, 1982, 1984.)

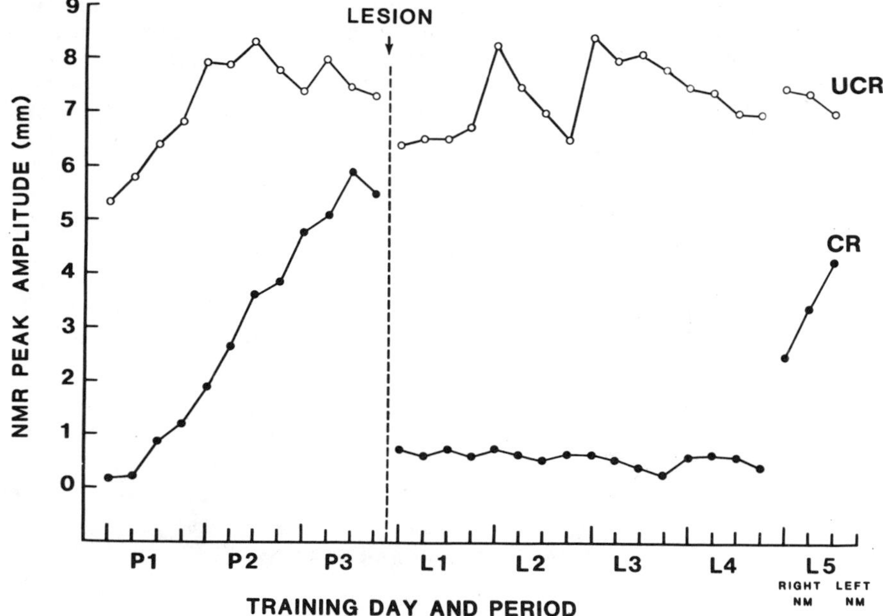

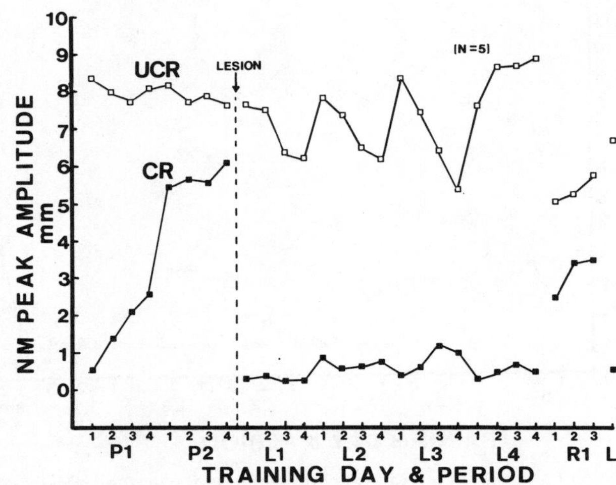

Figure 9-7. Effect of lesion of the ipsilateral superior cerebellar peduncle (SCP) on retention and reacquisition of the NM (and eyelid) responses, averaged for five animals. Solid squares indicate the amplitude of the CR; open squares indicate the amplitude of the UCR. All training was to the left side except where labeled R1. The lesion abolished or severely impaired the ipsilateral CR, with no effect on the UCR. P1–P2 indicate the 2 days of training prior to the lesion. L1–L4 indicate the 4 days of training after the lesion. The contralateral (right) eye was then trained and learned quite rapidly (R1). The left eye was again trained (L) and still showed only very small responses. Numbers on abscissa represent approximately 27-trial blocks. (From McCormick, Guyer, & Thompson, 1982.)

Figure 9-8. Effects of ablation of left lateral cerebellum on learning of the NM (and eyelid) responses (six animals). Solid triangles indicate the amplitude of the CR; open diamonds indicate the amplitude of the UCR. All training was to left eye (ipsilateral to lesion) except where labeled R1. The cerebellar lesion prevented conditioning of the ipsilateral eye but had no effect on the UCR. P1–P4 indicate the 4 days of postlesion training to the left eye. The right eye was then trained and learned at a rate comparable to that of initial learning of nonlesioned animals. The left eye was again trained (P5) and showed no learning. Numbers on abscissa indicate 40-trial blocks. (From Lincoln *et al.*, 1982.)

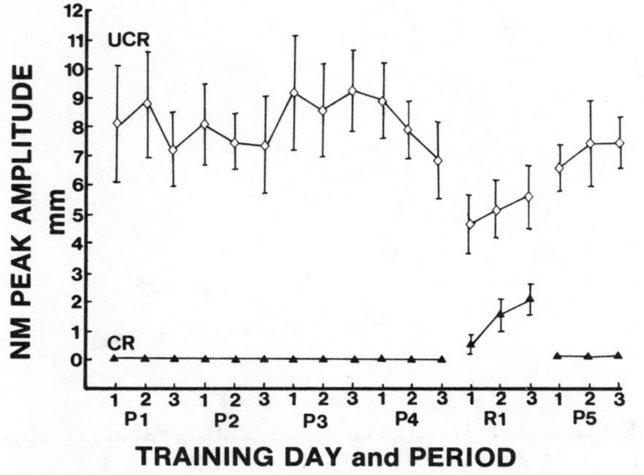

afferent–efferent systems. The fact that a neuronal unit "model" of the learned behavioral response develops in the cerebellar deep nuclei and may precede the behavioral response by as much as 50 msec or more would seem to localize the process to cerebellum or its afferents for which the cerebellum is a mandatory relay. This time period is consistent with the minimum onset latency for CRs in well-trained animals (about 80 msec) and is very close to the minimum CS-UCS interval that can support learning.

The possibility that unilateral cerebellar lesions produce a modulatory disruption of a memory trace localized elsewhere in the brain seems unlikely. If so, it must be efferent from the cerebellum, since discrete lesions of the superior cerebellar peduncle abolish the learned behavioral response. Yet the neuronal model of the learned response is presesnt within the ipsilateral cerebellum. In current studies, we have trained animals with both eyes and made bilateral ablations of the lateral cerebellum (Lavond, Lincoln, McCormick, & Thompson, 1983). The lesions permanently abolish the conditioned NM–eyelid response on both sides. (The smallest effective bilateral lesions do not produce any persisting signs of motor dysfunction.) Such animals have been repeatedly retrained for as long as 3 months postoperatively and show no relearning at all of the CR with either eye (see Figure 9-9).

In a related project we have found that the lateral ipsilateral cerebellum is also essential for classical conditioning of the hindlimb flexion reflex (Donegan, Lowry, & Thompson, 1983). Rabbits are initially trained with a shock UCS to the left hindpaw; using the same conditions otherwise as in NM–eyelid training

Figure 9-9. Effects of bilateral neocerebellar lesion on the conditioned NM–eyelid response of one animal. Before lesion, the animal's left NM–eyelid was trained (L), with subsequent training of the right NM–eyelid (R). Each data point is an average of 30 trials. A bilateral cerebellar aspiration was performed, and the animal was allowed to recover 1 full week. The animal was then given 4 full days of training (120 trials each day) to the left and then the right NM–eyelid followed by 1 additional day of training on the left. At 1 month postlesion the animal was again trained 2 days on each side. At 3 months postlesion, the animal again received 4 days of training per side followed by 1 final day on the left. Each data point after (L) and (R) represents 1 full day of training. Histology revealed that the ansiform and paramedian lobes and the dorsal aspect of the dentate–interpositus nuclei were removed bilaterally. Note that although the animal learned the response initially in fewer than 90 trials, subsequent training of 1440 trials on the left side and 1200 trials on the right over a period of 3 months failed to reinstate this learned response. (From Lavond, Lincoln, McCormick, & Thompson, unpublished observations.)

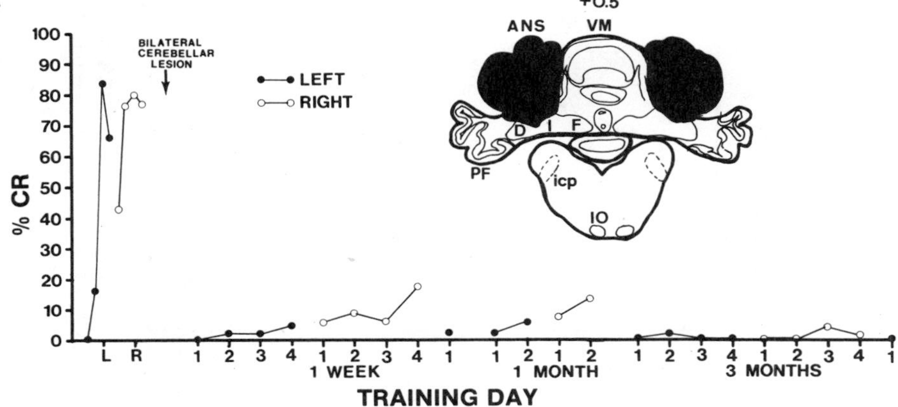

(i.e., tone CS) and EMG activity recorded from flexor muscles of both hindlimbs. Both hindlimbs develop an equivalent learned flexor response, consistent with the rabbit's normal mode of locomotion. Ablation of the left lateral cerebellum permanently abolishes this CR in both hindlimbs (see Figure 9-10). Training (i.e., paw shock UCS) is then given to the right hindlimb, and both hindlimbs relearn. When training is then shifted back to the left hindlimb, the learned response in both hindlimbs rapidly extinguishes. These results demonstrate that the left cerebellar lesion does not simply prevent the animal from making the learned response in the left hindlimb and support the view that the memory trace for learning of the hindlimb flexion response, like the NM–eyelid learned response, is established unilaterally in the cerebellum. There is an earlier Soviet report (Karamian, Fanaralijian, & Kosareva, 1969) indicating that complete removal of the cerebellum in dogs well trained in leg-flexion conditioning permanently abolished the discrete leg-flexion response.

Finally, electrical stimulation through recording microelectrodes in the medial dentate–lateral interpositus nuclear region elicits a clear NM–eyelid response in every animal in which a neuronal unit "model" of the behavioral learned response is recorded. This response (measurement is of NM extension) has an onset latency from cerebellar nuclear stimulation of approximately 40 msec (see Figure 9-11).

From these results we infer that the cerebellum is essential for the learning of all discrete, adaptive motor responses, at least for classical conditioning with an aversive UCS. In terms of localization of the putative memory trace for the conditioned NM–eyelid response, our evidence at present is most consistent

Figure 9-10. Example of the effects of lesioning the cerebellar deep nuclei ipsilateral to the side of training on leg-flexion CRs and UCRs in the rabbit. In each session, 30 training trials were presented wherein a 350-msec auditory CS overlapped and terminated with a 100-msec paw shock UCS. During sessions 1–12 and 16–18, the shock UCS was delivered to the left paw (ipsilateral to the side of the lesion) and during sessions 13–15, the shock UCS was shifted to the right paw. (The bilateral leg-flexion UCRs to the paw shock UCS were measured by means of a stabilimeter device.) (From Donegan *et al.*, 1983.)

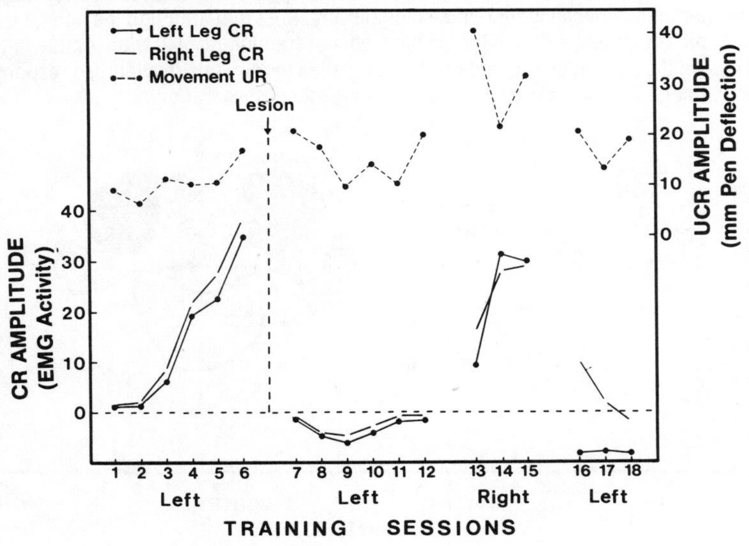

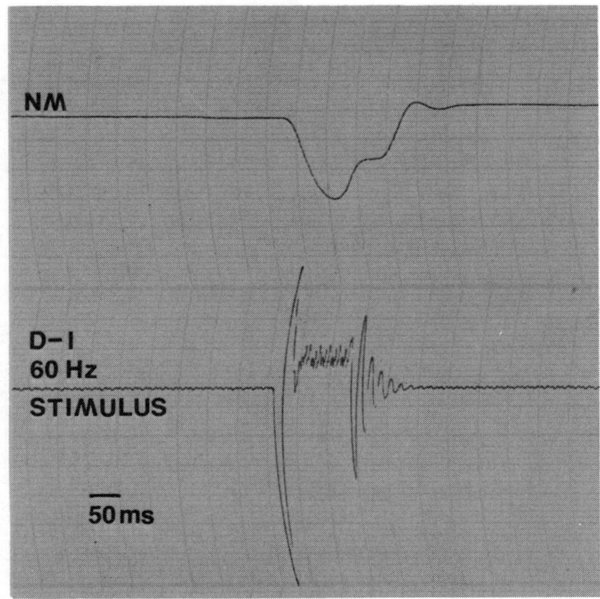

Figure 9-11. Example of 60-Hz dentate–interpositus stimulation-induced NM extension and eyelid closure response. Stimulus was 60 Hz AC, 150 msec, 75 μA. Each small division represents .5 mm of NM movement across the eyeball. (From McCormick & Thompson, unpublished observations.)

with localization to the medial dentate–lateral interpositus nuclei. Composite diagrams are shown in Figure 9-12, indicating regions of the ipsilateral cerebellar deep nuclei from which the neuronal unit "model" of the learned behavioral response can be recorded (A—solid dots), regions from which electrical stimulation evokes an NM–eyelid response (B—solid dots), the locus of lesions that permanently abolish the conditioned NM–eyelid response (C), and cerebellar lesions that do not abolish the conditioned NM–eyelid response. Note that the sites of the neuronal model, the sites of effective electrical stimulation, and the effective lesion site are essentially identical, involving the most medial portion of the dentate nucleus and the most lateral portion of the interpositus nucleus. Large cortical cerebellar lesions are ineffective in abolishing the learned response; the small critical region of the dentate–interpositus must be damaged (see also Figure 9-4). We do not yet know if the cerebellar cortex plays an important role in initial learning; it does not appear to be essential for the memory of the learned response.

In current work in progress (Mamounas, Madden, Barchas, & Thompson, 1983), we have found that microinjection of as little as 2 nmol of bicuculline methiodide directly into this same region—medial dentate–lateral interpositus nuclear area—causes a selective and reversible abolition of both the behavioral CR and the neuronal model of the CR (recorded with a microelectrode .75 mm ventral to the tip of the microinfusion cannula) (see Figure 9-13). This selective bicuculline abolition of the learned response occurs regardless of how well trained or overtrained the animal is. The fact that high concentrations of gamma-aminobutyric acid (GABA) have been localized to these nuclear regions (Okada, Nitsch-Hassler, Kim, Bak, & Hassler, 1971), coupled with the observa-

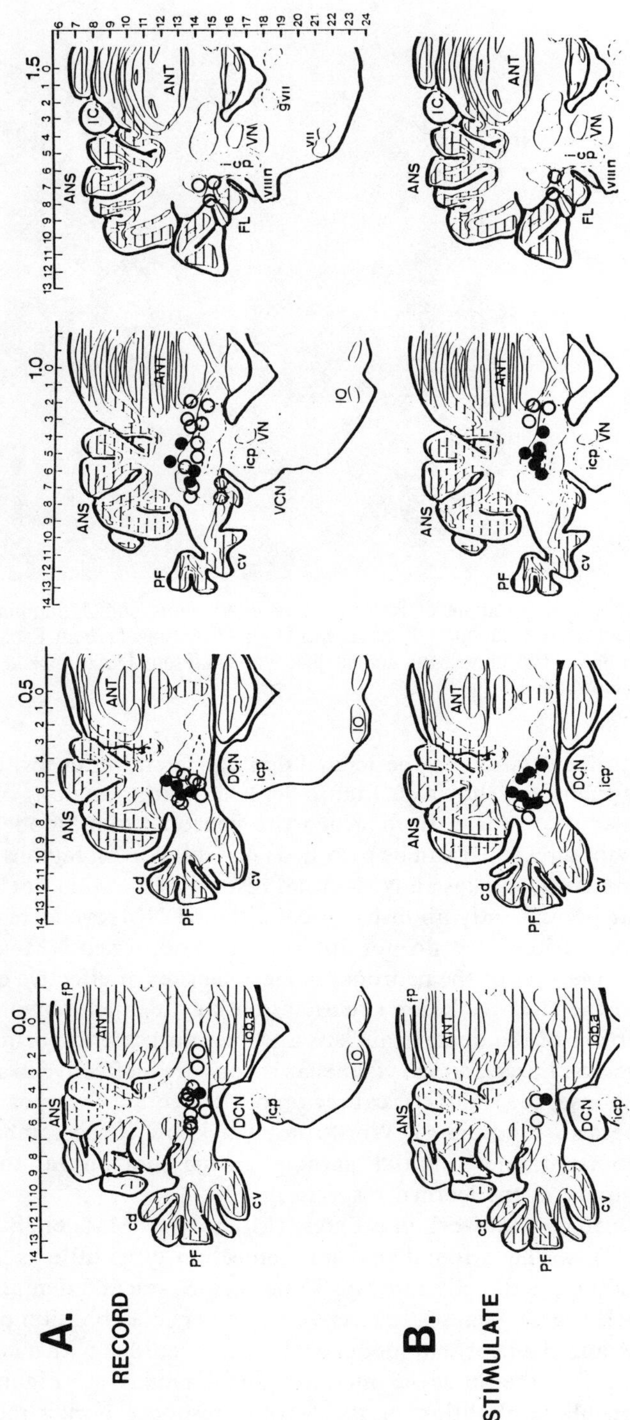
A.
RECORD
B.
STIMULATE
0.0
0.5
1.0
1.5
ANS
ANT
fp
PF
cd
cv
lob.a
DCN
icp
IO
VCN
VN
FL
IC
gvii
vii
viiin

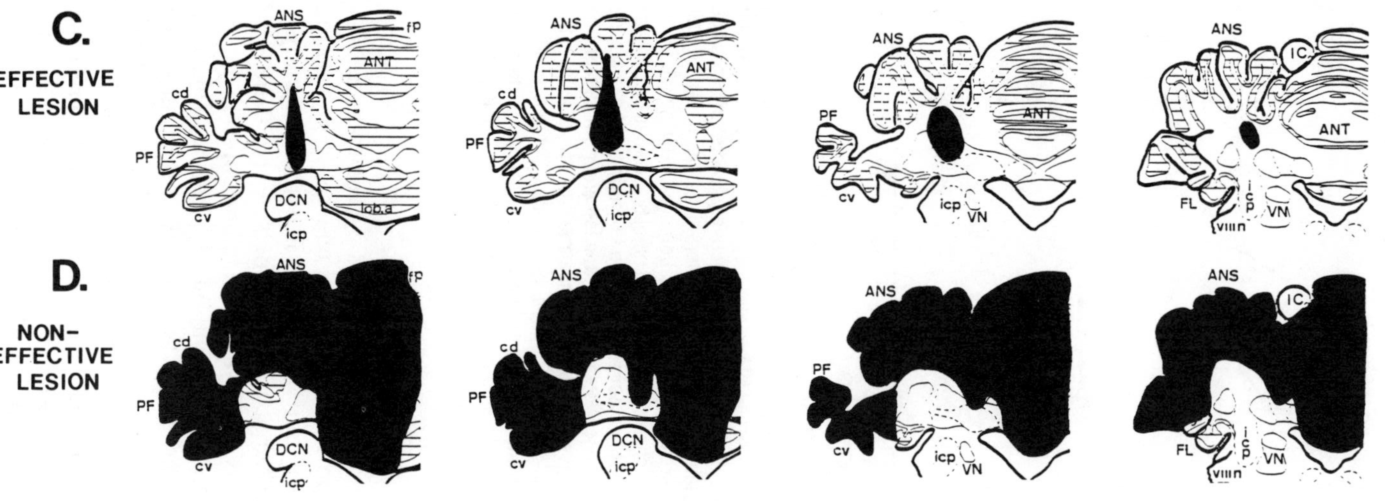

Figure 9-12. Summary diagram of the chronic recordings, stimulation, dentate-interpositus lesions, and noneffective lesions of the cerebellar cortex. (A) The recording sites (●) that developed neuronal responses within the CS period that were greater than 2 standard scores, as well as the recording sites (○) that did not develop a neuronal response within the CS period. (B) The sites at which 60-Hz stimulation at 100 μA or the onset of direct current stimulation at 100 μA produced ipsilateral NM extension and eyelid closure. The sites that were ineffective in eliciting eyelid responses are represented by open dots (○). (C) A typical stereotaxic lesion of the medial dentate-lateral interpositus nuclear region that abolished the CR. (D) A composite drawing of aspirations of 3 animals that were ineffective in abolishing the learned eyelid response. Note that the medial dentate-lateral interpositus region not only develops neuronal responses related to the performance of the learned response during training but, when stimulated, will elicit an eyelid response that is dependent, as is the learned response, on the intactness of the superior cerebellar peduncle. Furthermore, lesioning of this region of the deep cerebellar nuclei permanently abolishes the learned response, while cortical lesions that circumscribe this region do not. Abbreviations: ANS, ansiform lobule (Crus I and Crus II); ANT, anterior lobe; FL, flocculus; DCN, dorsal cochlear nucleus; IO, inferior olive; Lob. a, lobulus A (nodulus); Lob. b, lobulus B (uvula); Lob. c, lobulus C (pyramis and medius medianus); PF, paraflocculus; VN, vestibular nuclei; cd, dorsal crus; cv, ventral crus; g vii, genu of the tract of the seventh nerve; icp, inferior cerebellar peduncle; vii, seventh (facial) nucleus; vii n, nerve of the seventh nucleus. (From McCormick & Thompson, in press.)

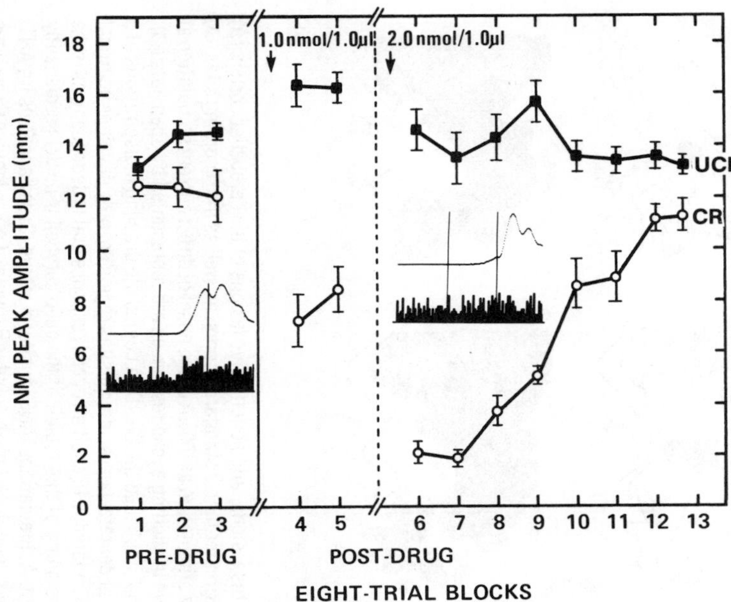

Figure 9-13. Effects of localized microinjection of bicuculline methiodide into the medial dentate–lateral interpositus region on the well-learned NM–eyelid response. Closed squares and open circles represent the peak amplitude of the UCR and CR, respectively. Each training block consists of eight averaged trials with a variable 30-sec intertrial interval. Left panel: Mean NM-response amplitude during three blocks of predrug baseline conditioning. Center panel: Mean NM-response amplitude for two blocks following microinjection of 1 nmol bicuculline methiodide into dentate–interpositus. Right panel: Mean NM-response amplitude for eight blocks following microinjection of 2 nmol of bicuculline methiodide. Note inserts within left and right panels: The upper trace in each histogram represents the averaged NM response; the lower trace depicts the corresponding dentate–interpositus multiple-unit peristimulus histogram. The bin width is 9 msec. The first vertical line in each histogram indicates tone onset; the second vertical line indicates airpuff onset. The predrug histogram is an average of blocks 2 and 3; the postdrug histogram is an average of blocks 6 and 7. (From Mamounas *et al*., 1983.)

tions by Chan-Palay (1977, 1978) demonstrating autoradiographic localization of GABA receptors in this region provides a basis for tentatively postulating that bicuculline produces its selective abolition of the CR in a traditional way—through blockage of inhibitory GABAergic transmission. Note that there is no increase in spontaneous unit activity following bicuculline infusion in the recordings shown in Figure 9-13—thus, the abolition of both the behavioral and the neuronal learned responses seems not to be due to abnormally increased cellular activity. Instead, it seems more likely to be blocking inhibitory synaptic transmission that is in some way essential for the generation of the learned responses. One calls to mind Eugene Roberts's notion of GABA-ergic processes playing a key role in learning (Roberts, 1976, 1980). This result also demonstrates that abolition of the CR by lesions in this region cannot be due to nonspecific persisting effects of the lesion. The bicuculline abolition of the CR dissipates over time, with CRs returning to baseline levels by the end of the test session (see Figure 9-13).

It seems a very reasonable possibility that the memory trace for learning of classical (and instrumental?) discrete, adaptive motor responses occurs in the cerebellum. Perhaps the most prominent feature of such learned responses is their precise timing. At least in aversive learning, the CR is under very strong control by the CS-UCS interval in terms of onset latency and temporal morphology and is always timed to be at maximum at or shortly before the time when then onset of the UCS occurs. The cerebellum is very well designed to provide such precise timing (Eccles, Ito, & Szentagothai, 1967). Indeed, the cerebellum has been suggested by several authors as a possible locus for the coding of learned motor responses (Albus, 1971; Eccles, 1977; Eccles *et al.*, 1967; Gilbert, 1974; Ito, 1970; Marr, 1969). A number of stimulation, recording, and lesion studies utilizing several behavioral paradigms (e.g., electrical stimulation of the cerebellum as a UCS, plasticity of the vesetibuloocular reflex, signaled arm-wrist movements, recovery from hemilabyrinthectomy) have implicated the cerebellum as being involved in the learning and/or retention of these motor responses (Brogden & Gantt, 1942; Brooks, 1979; Brooks, Kozlovskaya, Atkin, Horvath, & Uno, 1973; Chapman, Spidalieri, & Lamarre, 1982; Gilbert & Thach, 1977; Ito, 1982; Kaplan & Aronson, 1969; Llinas, Walton, Hillman, & Sotelo, 1975; Miles & Lisberger, 1981; Thach, 1970, 1975).

THE NONSPECIFIC MEMORY-TRACE SYSTEM

A number of authors have distinguished between two classes of conditioned responses, diffuse or nonspecific preparatory CRs and precise, specific, adaptive CRs (see Konorski, 1967; Mowrer, 1947; Rescorla & Solomon, 1967; Schlosberg, 1937). A similar distinction has recently been made by Weinberger (1982) in his survey of aversive conditioning between "nonspecific" and "specific" CRs. Nonspecific responses are usually autonomic but also include generalized body movements, are learned rapidly, and prepare the organism to do something. Such responses are often viewed as manifestations of a "conditioned emotional state" or "acquired drive," e.g., conditioned fear (Brown & Jacobs, 1949; Brush, 1971; Frey & Ross, 1968; Miller, 1948; Mowrer, 1947; Konorski, 1967; Rescorla & Solomon, 1967). They presumably reflect the basic association between the neutral CS and the "emotogenic" properties of the UCS. Conditioning of specific responses, for example, eyelid closure or leg flexion, involves learning precise, adaptive CRs that deal specifically with the UCS and requires more extensive training. Prokasy (1972) suggested a similar dichotomy based on occurrence of learned responses. In his terms, the first phase, lasting until the occurrence of the first CR, consists in detection of the CS-UCS contingency and initial selection of the appropriate adaptive response, and the second phase concerns the increase in relative frequency of the specific, adaptive learned response.

We proposed (see above and Thompson, McCormick, *et al.*, 1983; Thompson, Berger, & Madden, 1983; Thompson *et al.*, 1984, in press) that in aversive learning, initial development of the nonspecific "conditioned fear" trace system may be essential for the subsequent development of the specific adaptive memory trace and that the neuronal substrates of the two trace systems differ, at least in part. A large body of literature suggests that morphine and the endogenous opioids act on learned fear or anxiety as well as on pain per se (e.g., Jaffe & Martin, 1980; Julien, 1981; Wikler, 1958). Indeed, opiate and endogenous opioid actions have been implicated in aversive learning in a variety of

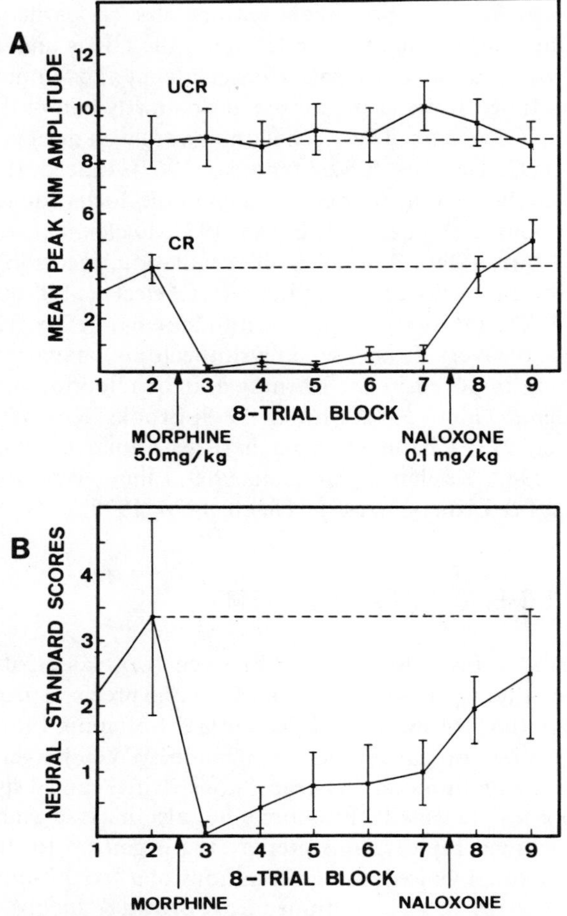

Figure 9-14. (A) Mean ($n = 13$) NM-response peak amplitude during the CS period (for CR) and UCS period (for UCR). Dashed lines represent the baseline before morphine was given. (B) Mean hippocampal unit standard scores during the CS period. Dashed line represents the baseline. (From Mauk, Warren, & Thompson, 1982.)

studies (Martinez, Jensen, Messing, Rigter, & McGaugh, 1981). If our suggestion has merit, then it might be expected that opiates would interfere with learning of the NM–eyelid response, at least in the earlier phases of learning. This is indeed the case.

Systemic administration of morphine (i.v. 5.0 mg/kg) to animals that have just learned the NM–eyelid response to criterion causes an immediate and naloxone-reversible (i.v. 0.1 mg/kg) abolition of the CR but has no effect on the UCR (Mauk, Warren, & Thompson, 1982) (see Figure 9-14). Morphine has no effect on tone CS–evoked neuronal unit activity in the central nucleus of the inferior colliculus. The abolition of the CR occurs on the trial immediately after injection, prior to presentation of the next UCS. It would seem that morphine is acting directly on some aspect of the associative process. In a series of studies using both central and peripheral administration of highly specific opiate analogues (e.g., morphiceptin), it was shown that the opiate abolition of the CR is entirely a central action and can be obtained by activation of *mu* receptors (see Figures 9-15 and 9-16) (Mauk, Madden, Barchas, & Thompson, 1982). The most immediate and profound effects are obtained with administration to the rostral region of the fourth ventricle, suggesting involvement of opiate-receptor-rich systems in this region. Application of the same kind and amount of opiate in the fourth ventricle also selectively abolishes the classically conditioned heart-rate-slowing response to periorbital shock in the rabbit (Figure 9-17) (Lavond, Mauk, Madden, Barchas, & Thompson, 1983; Lavond, Lincoln, McCormick, & Thompson, 1983, in press).

We suggested that this selective fourth ventricle opiate abolition of both the learned NM–eyelid response and the learned heart rate response might be due to a common action on some part of the "conditioned fear" system in the brain stem (Thompson *et al.*, in press; Thompson, McCormick, *et al.*, 1983). Consistent with this interpretation is the fact that overtraining protects against the effects of opiates on the NM–eyelid CR (Mauk, Castellano, Rideout, Madden, Barchas, & Thompson, 1983) (see Figure 9-18). It is as though the presumed cerebellar system develops some degree of "functional autonomy" when the specific adaptive response is well learned; conditioned fear is no longer so critical. There are, of course, other essential neuronal substrates for the learned heart rate response, including portions of the amygdala and the hypothalamus (Cohen, 1980; Kapp, Gallagher, Applegate, & Frysinger, 1982; Smith, Astley, DeVit, Stein, & Walsh, 1980). Interestingly, administration of opiates to the central nucleus of the amygdala abolishes the conditioned heart-rate-slowing response in the rabbit (Kapp *et al.*, 1982) but has no effect on the just learned NM–eyelid response (Mauk, Madden, Barchas, & Thompson,

Figure 9-15. The effect of intracerebroventricular (ICV) infusion (fourth ventricle) of the potent and highly selective *mu* receptor agonist [N-MePhe^3, D-Pro^4]morphiceptin on NM CRs. Animals were trained to criterion baseline conditioning (left panel). ICV infusion of [N-MePhe^3, D-Pro^4]morphiceptin produced a dose-dependent abolition of CRs (center panel). This effect was reversed in animals given i.v. injections of naloxone 2.5 mg/kg (right panel). (From Mauk, Madden, Barchas, & Thompson, 1982.)

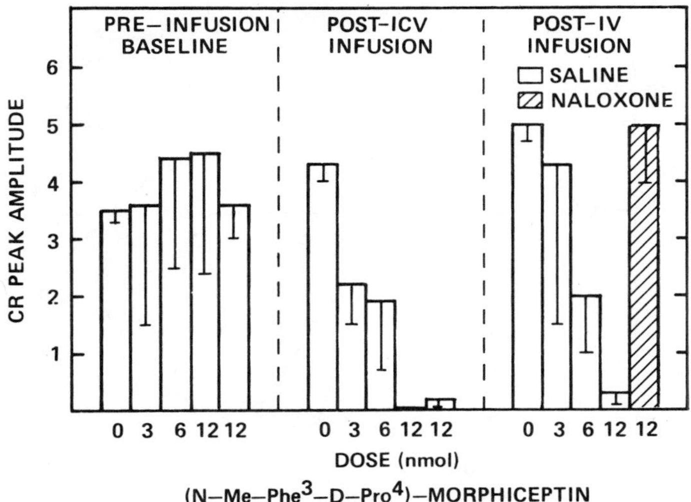

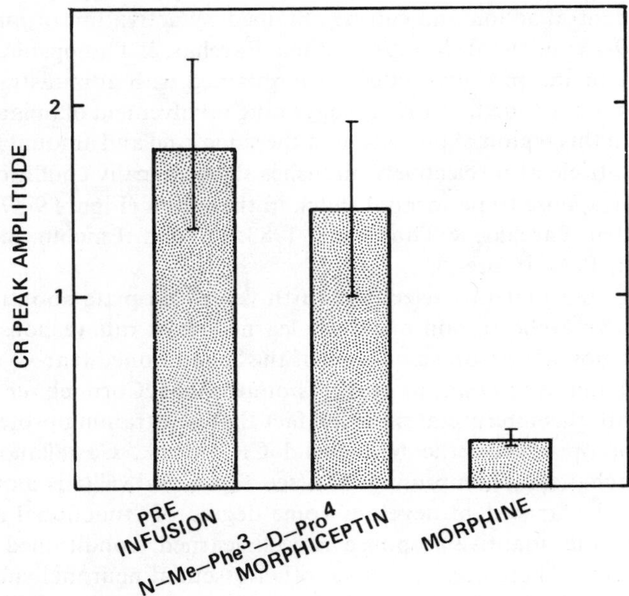

Figure 9-16. Systemic administration of [N-MePhe[3], D-Pro[4]]morphiceptin has no effect on CRs, supporting a central site of action. Each animal was given serial systemic doses of [N-MePhe[3], D-Pro[4]]morphiceptin in doses ranging from .1 to 10 times those effective via central administration (i.e., 1.2 to 120 nmol; see Figure 9-15). (From Mauk, Madden, Barchas, & Thompson, 1982.)

Figure 9-17. Mean percentage differences of heart rate for two groups (opiate alone: open circle; opiate–naltrexone: closed circle) over the course of adaptation, paired training, and drug conditions. Positive percentage scores (100% × (PreUCS–PreCS)/PreCS) reflect heart-rate acceleration. The substances were infused into the fourth ventricle when animals had just learned the conditioned bradycardia. (From Lavond, Mauk, Madden, Barchas, & Thompson, 1983.)

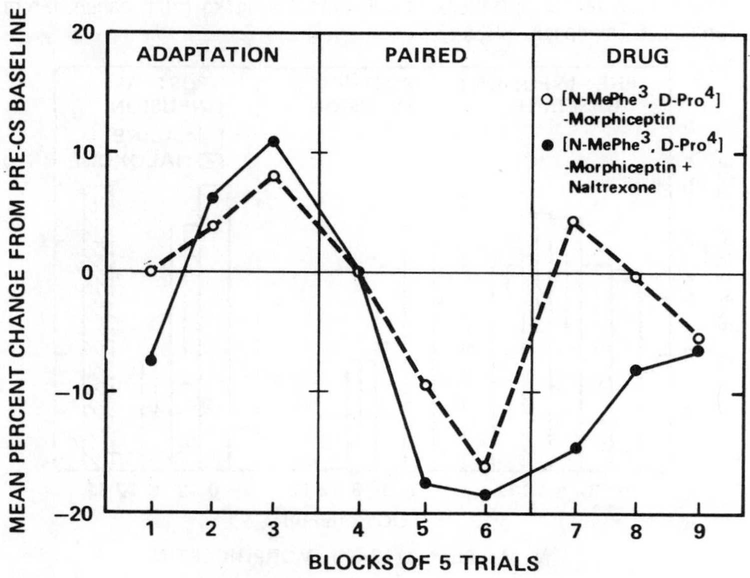

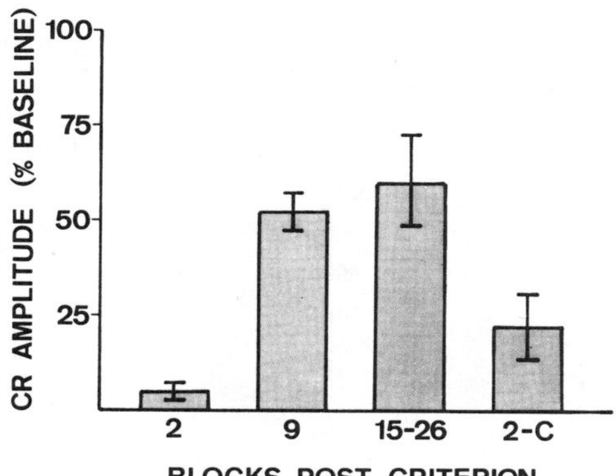

Figure 9-18. The effect of additioning baseline conditioning blocks (overtraining) on morphine abolition of CRs. CR amplitudes following a 5 mg/kg injection of morphine are presented in terms of preinjection baseline. Each group received different amounts of overtraining before injection: 2 blocks (n = 13), 9 blocks, (n = 4), 15–20 blocks (n = 7). The final group (2-C) was a control for consolidation effects (n = 6). (From Mauk *et al.*, 1983.)

1982). We only suggest that there may be localized (and possibly common) opiate actions on some part of the conditioned fear circuitry in the vicinity of the fourth ventricle necessary for both responses: learned heart rate and the initial learning of the NM–eyelid response.

In current work, we have found that bilateral lesions of the deep cerebellar nuclei (dentate–interpositus region) that completely prevent learning of the NM–eyelid response with either eye do not prevent learning of the conditioned heart-rate-slowing response (Figure 9-19) (Lavond, Lincoln, McCormick, & Thompson, 1983). In short, the "fear" system appears to be essential for initial learning of the discrete, adaptive response, with its memory trace presumably established in the cerebellar system, but the cerebellar trace system is not essential for learning of nonspecific "fear" responses.

THE HIPPOCAMPUS: PROCEDURAL AND DECLARATIVE MEMORY

One of the more striking aspects of neuronal plasticity induced by simple conditioning procedures is the marked engagement of unit activity in the hippocampus (Swanson, Teyler, & Thompson, 1982). In a series of studies Berger, Thompson, and associates (Berger, Alger, & Thompson, 1976; Berger & Thompson, 1978a, 1978b, 1978c, 1982; Berger, Laham, & Thompson, 1980; Berry & Thompson, 1978; Hoehler & Thompson, 1980; Thompson *et al.*, 1980, 1982) found that the majority of identified pyramidal neurons sampled in the CA3–CA1 region of the dorsal hippocampus developed a very clear neuronal "model" of the learned behavioral NM–eyelid response in the rabbit (see Figure 9-20). Over a wide range of conditions that impair or alter acquisition, maintenance, or extinction of the learned NM–eyelid response, the learning-induced increase in hippocampal unit activity precedes and accurately predicts subsequent behavioral learning performance (Berger & Thompson, 1978b; Berger *et al.*, 1980; Thompson *et al.*, 1980, 1982). The hippocampal response has

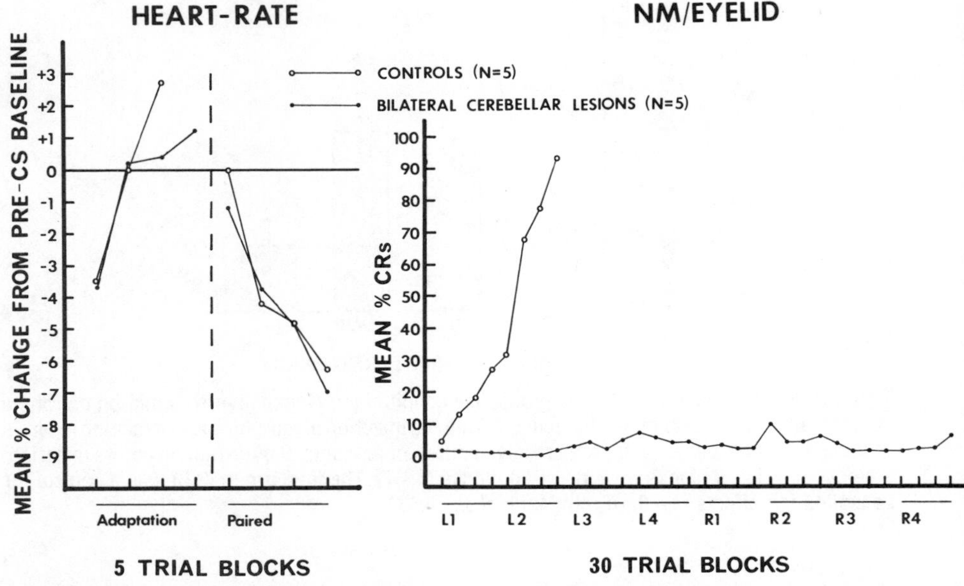

Figure 9-19. Control animals and those with bilateral cerebellar lesions both learn heart-rate conditioning but subsequent training on the NM–eyelid response shows that the controls learn rapidly, but animals with cerebellar lesions fail completely to learn with extensive training on each eye. (From Lavond *et al.*, in press.)

all the properties one would wish of a direct measure of the inferred process of learning in the brain. Yet, as noted above, animals can learn simple conditioned responses without a hippocampus.

This is not the place to review the vast literature on effects of hippocampal lesions on learning and more generally on behavior (see, e.g., O'Keefe & Nadel, 1978; Olton, Becker, & Handelmann, 1979). However, it is to be emphasized that the hippocampus does become essential even in simple conditioning paradigms when greater demands are placed on the memory system, as in latent inhibition, discrimination reversal and trace conditioning (Berger & Orr, in press; Orr & Berger, 1981; Solomon & Moore, 1975; Thompson *et al.*, 1982; Thompson, Berger, & Madden, 1983; Thompson, McCormick, *et al.*, 1983; Weisz, Solomon, & Thompson, 1980). Where it has been studied in such paradigms, unit activity in the hippocampus becomes markedly engaged (Thompson, Berger, & Madden, 1983).

A number of authorities in the field of human learning and memory have distinguished two "kinds" of memory, which Squire (1982) has recently termed "procedural" and "declarative." Damage to diencephalic or hippocampal–temporal structures in humans results in marked deficits in formation of declarative memory but not procedural memory. Squire and associates have proposed that declarative memory may be a new development in evolution that corresponds with the elaboration of the hippocampus and other higher brain systems (e.g., regions of the thalamus and cerebral cortex).

Simple classical conditioning paradigms would seem to be instances of procedural memory. However, when the tasks are made more complex it is possible that "declarative" memory becomes involved, and the hippocampus then plays a more critical role. In the context of Squire's theory, it might be suggested that declarative memory developed from the more ancient procedural memory system, the latter involving the cerebellum. If so, then one might expect the hippocampal system to become engaged in all learning paradigms, even though it is essential only in situations that require some aspect of "declarative" memory. A further expectation would be that the cerebellar system may itself play a role in the engagement of the hippocampal system, at least in procedural learning.

In current work we have obtained precisely this result (Clark *et al.*, 1982, 1984). In well-trained animals exhibiting the hippocampal neuronal response model of the behavioral response (both CR and UCR components—see Figures 9-20, 9-21, and 9-22), ipsilateral electrolytic lesions of the medial dentate–lateral intepositus region that abolish the learned behavioral response also abolish the neuronal model *in the CS period* and reduce the response in the UCS period in the hippocampus (see Figures 9-21 and 9-22). When the animal is then trained on the other eye, which learns, the learning-predictive neuronal response in the CS period in the hippocampus returns. When training is then

Figure 9-20. Example of the discharge pattern of a hippocampal pyramidal neuron responding during trial periods in a rabbit well trained in the NM–eyelid CR. Upper trace: Single trace of spontaneous discharges of the unit at a fast sweep (calibrations: 50μV and 5 msec). Middle trace: Behavioral NM response averaged over a number of trials. Lower trace: Peristimulus histogram of the cell discharges cumulated over the same trials as for the averaged NM response (calibration: 25 unit counts per 15-msec time bin). For middle and lower traces, total trace duration is 750 msec; first cursor, tone CS onset; second cursor, corneal airpuff UCS onset. (From Berger & Thompson, 1978a.)

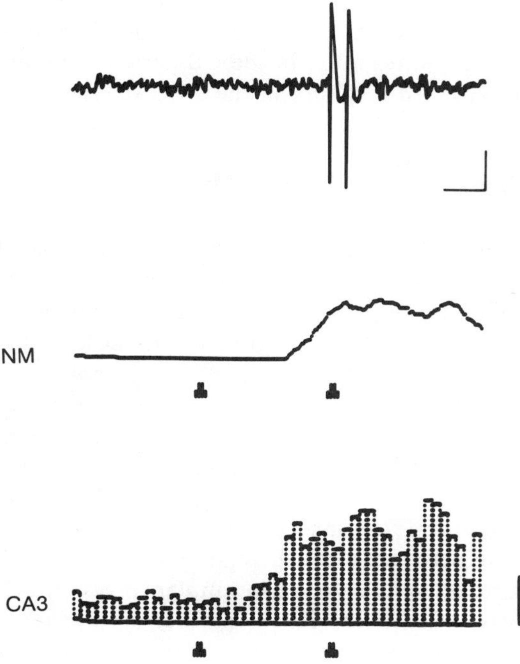

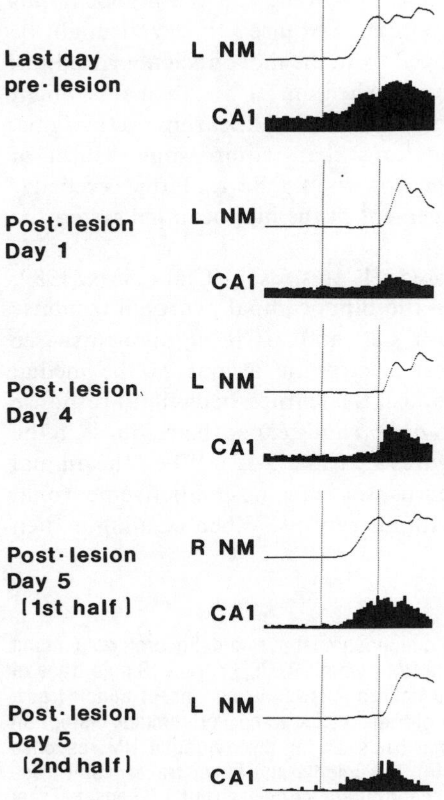

Figure 9-21. NM and hippocampal unit (CA1) responses before and after lesions of the dentate–interpositus nuclei and surrounding fibers. Top trace: NM response. Bottom trace: Peristimulus histogram of hippocampal multiple-unit discharges (15-msec time bins). First vertical line represents tone onset; second vertical line represents airpuff onset. Total trace length: 750 msec. Prelesion, postlesion Day 1–4 represent averages from the entire 117-trial training session; on postlesion Day 5 training was switched to the right (nonlesioned side) eye, then returned to the left side. Lesion of the dentate–interpositus nuclei was found to abolish both the learned NM–eyelid and hippocampal unit responses. However, training on the right (nonlesioned) side reinstated this hippocampal response as well as the right NM–eyelid response. Subsequent training on the left again failed to produce CRs on the left, although the hippocampal response remained. (From Clark *et al.*, 1982.)

shifted back to the eye ipsilateral to the cerebellar lesion, which still cannot relearn, the hippocampal response in the CS period gradually extinguishes as the previously conditioned response in the contralateral eye extinguishes.

HIERARCHICAL MEMORY-TRACE SYSTEMS

Our notion that memory-trace systems in the brain may be hierarchically organized implies that the nonspecific trace system is necessary for the development of the specific and declarative trace systems and that the specific trace system may be necessary for the development of at least some aspects of the declarative trace system but that the converse is not the case; that is, the declarative system is not necessary for the nonspecific and specific systems, and the specific trace system is not necessary for the nonspecific trace system. Assume for purposes of argument that conditioned heart rate reflects the nonspecific trace system, well-learned, conditioned NM–eyelid (and leg flexion) responses reflect primarily the specific trace system, and conditioned increases in hippocampal unit activity are a neuronal reflection of the "declarative" trace system, at least as it becomes engaged in simpler "procedural" learning tasks.

All the data reported here and from other laboratories to date are consistent with these assertions. Ablation of the cerebral cortex and hippocampus

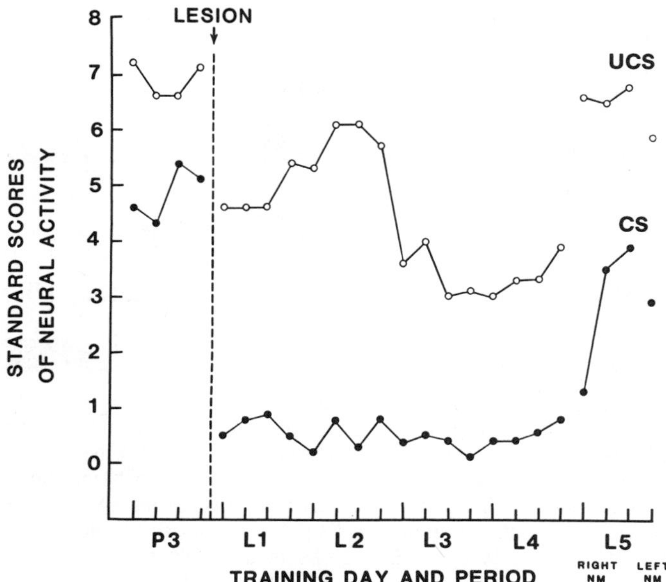

Figure 9-22. Effects of cerebellar lesions on hippocampal neuronal activity (mean standard scores, $n = 10$). Lesions caused complete or near-complete abolition of hippocampal responding in the CS period (solid circles) and a significant reduction in the UCS period (open circles). Both responses recovered when training was switched to the nonlesioned (right) side on L5 (and the right NM response was learned rapidly), even though NM CRs on the left side remained severely reduced. (From Clark *et al.*, 1982, 1984.)

do not prevent learning of nonspecific or specific, adaptive responses but do impair learning in more complex paradigms (Thompson, Berger, & Madden, 1983). Destruction of the appropriate region of the cerebellar nuclei abolishes specific, adaptive conditioned responses and the learning-induced increase in hippocampal neuron activity in the CS period (Figure 9-21) but does not impair learning of the nonspecific conditioned heart-rate response (Figure 9-19). Administration of opiates abolishes both the nonspecific conditioned heart rate response and the specific, adaptive NM–eyelid response if the latter is not very well learned (Figures 9-14, 9-17, 9-18). It also abolishes the learning-induced response in hippocampal neuron activity in the CS period (Figures 9-14 and 9-23).

One of the unresolved questions in the field of learning is how many "kinds" of learning occur. Our hierarchical trace notion and the empirical results to date, both from our laboratory and others, suggests that the mammalian brain may have its own definitions of the kinds or categories of learning that occur. These categories may or may not agree with the conventional operationally defined categories in use today.

ACKNOWLEDGMENTS

The work reported here was supported in part by research grants from the National Science Foundation (BNS 81-17115), the National Institutes of Health (NS23368), the National Institute of Mental Health (MH26530), the McKnight Foundation, and the Office of Naval Research to

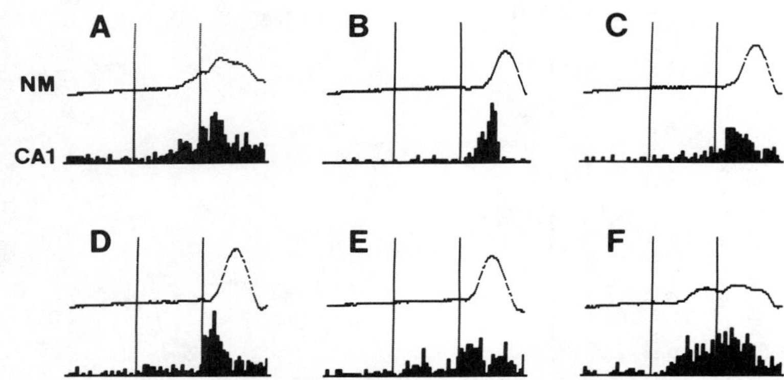

Figure 9-23. Examples of eight-trial averaged behavioral NM responses (upper trace) and associated multiple-unit histograms of hippocampal activity (lower trace, 12-msec time bins) for a single animal. The early vertical line indicates tone onset, and the later line, airpuff onset. Total trace length is 750 msec. (A) Block of eight trials immediately preceding the injection of morphine. Note the (conditioned) increase in hippocampal activity in the CS period (CS-UCS interval), which is completely absent immediately after the injection of morphine (B). The unit increase begins to redevelop in the later blocks 3 to 5 (C–E). Both the behavioral and unit CRs recover fully after an injection of naloxone (F). (From Mauk, Warren, & Thompson, 1982.)

Richard F. Thompson; the National Institute of Mental Health (MH23861) to John Madden IV; Predoctoral Fellowships from the National Institute of Mental Health (IF31 MH08513-01 5F31 MH08673-02) to Gregory A. Clark and David A. McCormick; Neuroscience Training Grant (IT32 MH17047-01) to Laura A. Mamounas; Postdoctoral Fellowships from the National Institute of Mental Health (1F32 MH08576-01 and 2F32 MH08233-03) to Nelson H. Donegan and David G. Lavond. We would like to extend our gratitude to Jack Barchas for his support and guidance in our collaborative efforts.

REFERENCES

Albus, J. S. A theory of cerebellar function. *Mathematical Biosciences*, 1971, *10*, 25–61.

Berger, T. W., Alger, B. E., & Thompson, R. F. Neuronal substrate of classical conditioning in the hippocampus. *Science*, 1976, *192*, 483–485.

Berger, T. W., & Orr, W. B. Hippocampectomy selectively disrupts discrimination reversal in conditioning of the rabbit nictitating membrane response. *Behavioural Brain Research*, in press.

Berger, T. W., & Thompson, R. F. Identification of pyramidal cells as the critical elements in hippocampal neuronal plasticity during learning. *Proceedings of the National Academy of Sciences, USA*, 1978a, *75*, 1572–1576.

Berger, T. W., & Thompson, R. F. Neuronal plasticity in the limbic system during classical conditioning of the rabbit nictitating membrane response: I. The hippocampus. *Brain Research*, 1978b, *145*, 323–346.

Berger, T. W., & Thompson, R. F. Neuronal plasticity in the limbic system during classical conditioning of the rabbit nictitating membrane response. II. Septum and mammillary bodies. *Brain Research*, 1978c, *156*, 293–314.

Berger, T. W., & Thompson, R. F. Hippocampal cellular plasticity during extinction of classically conditioned nictitating membrane behavior. *Behavioural Brain Research*, 1982, *4*, 63–76.

Berger, T. W., Laham, R. I., & Thompson, R. F. Hippocampal unit–behavior correlations during classical conditioning. *Brain Research*, 1980, *193*, 229–248.

Berry, S. D., & Thompson, R. F. Prediction of learning rate from the hippocampal EEG. *Science*, 1978, *200*, 1298–1300.

Brogden, W. J., & Gantt, W. H. Interneural conditioning: Cerebellar conditioned reflexes. *Archives of Neurology and Psychiatry*, 1942, *48*, 437–455.

Brooks, V. B. Control of intended limb movements by the lateral and intermediate cerebellum. In D. P. C. Lloyd & V. D. Wilson (Eds.), *Integration in the nervous system*. Tokyo–New York: Igaku-Shoin, 1979.

Brooks, V. B., Kozlovskaya, I. B., Atkin, A., Horvath, F. E., & Uno, M. Effects of cooling the dentate nucleus on tracking-task performance in monkeys. *Journal of Neurophysiology*, 1973, *36*, 974–995.

Brown, J. S., & Jacobs, A. The role of fear in the motivation and acquisition of responses. *Journal of Experimental Psychology*, 1949, *39*, 747–759.

Brush, R. F. (Ed.). *Aversive conditioning and learning*. New York: Academic Press, 1971.

Cegavske, C. F., Thompson, R. F., Patterson, M. M., & Gormezano, I. Mechanisms of efferent neuronal control of the reflex nictitating membrane response in the rabbit. *Journal of Comparative Physiological Psychology*, 1976, *90*, 411–423.

Chan-Palay, V. *Cerebellar dentate nucleus, organization, cytology and transmitters*. Berlin: Springer, 1977.

Chan-Palay, V. Autoradiographic localization of γ-aminobutyric acid receptors in the rat central nervous system by using [^{3}H]muscimol. *Proceedings of the National Academy of Sciences, USA*, 1978, *75*, 1024–1028.

Chapman, C. E., Spidalieri, G., & Lamarre, Y. A study of sensorimotor properties of dentate neurons during conditioned arm movements in the monkey. *Society for Neuroscience Abstracts*, 1982, *8*, 830.

Clark, G. A., McCormick, D. A., Lavond, D. G., Baxter, K., Gray, W. J., & Thompson, R. F. Effects of electrolytic lesions of cerebellar nuclei on conditioned behavioral and hippocampal neuronal responses. *Society for Neuroscience Abstracts*, 1982, *8*, 22.

Clark, G. A., McCormick, D. A., Lavond, D. G., & Thompson, R. F. Effects of lesions of cerebellar nuclei on conditioned behavioral and hippocampal neuronal responses. *Brain Research*, 1984, *291*, 125–136.

Cohen, D. H. The functional neuroanatomy of a conditioned response. In R. F. Thompson, L. H. Hicks, & B. V. Shryrkov (Eds.), *Neural mechanisms of goal-directed behavior and learning*. New York: Academic Press, 1980.

Desmond, J. E., & Moore, J. W. A brain stem region essential for classically conditioned but not unconditioned nictitating membrane response. *Physiology and Behavior*, 1982, *28*, 1029–1033.

Disterhoft, J. F., Kwan, H. H., & Low, W. D. Nictitating membrane conditioning to tone in the immobilized albino rabbit. *Brain Research*, 1977, *137*, 127–144.

Donegan, N. H., Lowry, R., & Thompson, R. F. *Ipsilateral cerebellar lesions severely impair or abolish retention of classically conditioned leg-flexion responses in the rabbit*. Manuscript in preparation, 1983.

Donegan, N. H., & Wagner, A. R. Conditioned diminution and facilitation of the UCR: A sometimes-apparent-process interpretation. In I. Gormezano, W. F. Prokasy, & R. F. Thompson (Eds.), *Classical conditioning III: Behavioral, neurophysiological and neurochemical studies in the rabbit*. Hillsdale, N.J.: Erlbaum, in press.

Eccles, J. C. An instruction-selection theory of learning in the cerebellar cortex. *Brain Research*, 1977, *127*, 327–352.

Eccles, J. C., Ito, M., & Szentagothai, J. *The cerebellum as a neuronal machine*. New York: Springer, 1967.

Enser, D. Personal communication, 1974.

Frey, P. W., & Ross, L. E. Classical conditioning of the rabbit eyelid response as a function of interstimulus interval. *Journal of Comparative and Physiological Psychology*, 1968, *65*, 246–250.

Gilbert, P. F. C. A theory of memory that explains the function and structure of the cerebellum. *Brain Research*, 1974, *70*, 1–8.

Gilbert, P. F. C., & Thach, W. T. Purkinje cell activity during motor learning. *Brain Research*, 1977, *128*, 309–328.

Gormezano, I. Investigations of defense and reward conditioning in the rabbit. In A. H. Black & W. F. Prokasy (Eds.), *Classical conditioning II: Current research and theory*. New York: Appleton-Century-Crofts, 1972.

Hebb, D. O. *The organization of behavior*. New York: Wiley, 1949.

Hilgard, E. R., & Marquis, D. G. *Conditioning and learning*. New York: Appleton, 1940.

Hoehler, F. K., & Thompson, R. F. Effect of the interstimulus (CS-UCS) interval on hippocampal unit activity during classical conditioning of the nictitating membrane response of the rabbit (*Oryctrolagus cuniculus*). *Journal of Comparative and Physiological Psychology*, 1980, *94*, 201–215.

Ito, M. Neurophysiological aspects of the cerebellar motor control system. *International Journal of Neurology*, 1970, *7*, 162–176.

Ito, M. Cerebellar control of the vestibulo-ocular reflex: Around the flocculus hypothesis. *Annual Review of Neuroscience*, 1982, *5*, 275–296.

Jaffe, J. H., & Martin, W. R. Opioid analgesics and antagonists. In A. G. Goodman, L. S. Goodman, & A. Gilman (Eds.), *The pharmacological basis of therapeutics*. New York: Macmillan, 1980.

Julien, R. M. *A primer of drug action*. San Francisco: Freeman, 1981.

Kandel, E. R., & Spencer, W. A. Cellular neurophysiological approaches in the study of learning. *Physiology Review*, 1968, *48*, 65–134.

Kaplan, H., & Aronson, L. R. Function of forebrain and cerebellum in learning in the teleost *Tilapia Heudelotii Macrocephala. Bulletin of the Museum of Natural History*, 1969, *142*, 142–208.

Kapp, B. S., Gallagher, M., Applegate, C. D., & Frysinger, R. C. The amygdala central nucleus: Contributions to conditioned cardiovascular responding during aversive pavlovian conditioning in the rabbit. In C. D. Woody (Ed.), *Conditioning: Representation of involved neural functions*. New York: Plenum Press, 1982.

Karamian, A. I., Fanaralijian, V. V., & Kosareva, A. A. The functional and morphological evolution of the cerebellum and its role in behavior. In R. Llinas (Ed.), *Neurobiology of cerebellar evolution and development: First international symposium*. Chicago: American Medical Association, 1969.

Kettner, R. E., & Thompson, R. F. Auditory signal detection and decision processes in the nervous system. *Journal of Comparative and Physiological Psychology*, 1982, *96*, 328–331.

Konorski, J. *Integrative activity of the brain*. Chicago: University of Chicago Press, 1967.

Lashley, K. S. *Brain mechanism and intelligence*. Chicago: University of Chicago Press, 1929.

Lavond, D. G., Lincoln, J. S., McCormick, D. A., & Thompson, R. F. Effect of bilateral lesions of the lateral cerebellar nuclei on conditioning of heart-rate and nictitating membrane/eyelid responses in the rabbit. *Neuroscience Abstracts*, 1983, *9*, 636.

Lavond, D. G., Lincoln, J. S., McCormick, D. A., & Thompson, R. F. Effect of bilateral lesions of the lateral cerebellar nuclei on conditioning of heart-rate and nictitating membrane/eyelid responses in the rabbit. *Brain Research*, in press.

Lavond, D. G., Mauk, M. D., Madden, J., IV, Barchas, J. D., & Thompson, R. F. Central opiate effect on heart-rate conditioning. *Pharmacology Biochemistry and Behavior*, 1983, *19*, 379–382.

Lavond, D. G., McCormick, D. A., Clark, G. A., Holmes, D. T., & Thompson, R. F. Effects of ipsilateral rostral pontine reticular lesions on retention of classically conditioned nictitating membrane and eyelid responses. *Physiological Psychology*, 1981, *9*, 335–339.

Lincoln, J. S., McCormick, D. A., & Thompson, R. F. Ipsilateral cerebellar lesions prevent learning of the classically conditioned nictitating membrane/eyelid response. *Brain Research*, 1982, *242*, 190–193.

Llinas, R., Walton, K., Hillman, E. D., & Sotelo, C. Inferior olive: Its role in motor learning. *Science*, 1975, *190*, 1230–1231.

Mamounas, L. A., Madden, J., IV, Barchas, J. D., & Thompson, R. F. Microinfusion of bicuculline into dentate/interpositus region abolishes classical conditioning of the well-trained rabbit eyelid response. *Neuroscience Abstracts*, 1983, *9*, 830.

Marr, D. A theory of cerebellar cortex. *Journal of Physiology*, 1969, *202*, 437–470.

Martinez, J. L., Jensen, R. A., Messing, R. B., Rigter, H., & McGaugh, J. L. (Eds.). *Endogenous peptides and learning and memory processes*. New York: Academic Press, 1981.

Mauk, M. D., Castellano, T. G., Rideout, J. A., Madden, J., IV, Barchas, J. D., & Thompson, R. F. Overtraining reduces opiate abolition of classically conditioned responses. *Physiology and Behavior*, 1983, *30*, 493–495.

Mauk, M. D., Madden, J., IV, Barchas, J. D., & Thompson, R. F. Opiates and classical conditioning: Selective abolition of conditioned responses by activation of opiate receptors within the central nervous system. *Proceedings of the National Academy of Sciences, USA*, 1982, *79*, 7598–7602.

Mauk, M. D., Warren, J. T., & Thompson, R. F. Selective, naloxone-reversible morphine depression of learned behavioral and hippocampal responses. *Science*, 1982, *216*, 434–435.

McCormick, D. A., Clark, G. A., Lavond, D. G., & Thompson, R. F. Initial localization of the memory trace for a basic form of learning. *Proceedings of the National Academy of Sciences, USA*, 1982, *79*, 2731–2742.

McCormick, D. A., Guyer, P. E., & Thompson, R. F. Superior cerebellar peduncle selectively abolish the ipsilateral classically conditioned nictitating membrane/eyelid response of the rabbit. *Brain Research*, 1982, *244*, 347–350.

McCormick, D. A., Lavond, D. G., Clark, G. A., Kettner, R. E., Rising, C. E., & Thompson, R. F. The engram found? Role of the cerebellum in classical conditioning of nictitating membrane and eyelid responses. *Bulletin of the Psychonomic Society*, 1981, *18*(3), 103–105.

McCormick, D. A., Lavond, D. G., & Thompson, R. F. Concomitant classical conditioning of the rabbit nictitating membrane and eyelid responses: correlations and implications. *Physiology and Behavior*, 1982, *28*, 769–775.

McCormick, D. A., Lavond, D. G., & Thompson, R. F. Neuronal responses of the rabbit brainstem during performance of the classically conditioned nictitating membrance (NM) eyelid response. *Brain Research*, 1983, *271*, 73–88.

McCormick, D. A., & Thompson, R. F. Responses of the rabbit cerebellum during acquisition and performance of a classically conditioned nictitating membrane eyelid response. *Journal of Neuroscience*, in press.

Miles, F. A., & Lisberger, S. G. Plasticity in the vestibulo-ocular reflex: A new hypothesis. *Annual Review of Neuroscience*, 1981, *4*, 273–299.

Miller, N. E. Studies of fear as an acquirable drive: I. Fear as motivation and fear-reduction as reinforcement in learning of new responses. *Journal of Experimental Psychology*, 1948, *38*, 89–101.

Mowrer, O. H. On the dual nature of learning—a reinterpretation of "conditioning" and "problem-solving." *Harvard Educational Review*, 1947, *17*, 102–148.

Norman, R. J., Buchwald, J. S., & Villablanca, J. R. Classical conditioning with auditory discrimination of the eyeblink in decerebrate cats. *Science*, 1977, *196*, 551–553.

Okada, Y., Nitsch-Hassler, C., Kim, J. S., Bak, I. J., & Hassler, R. Role of gamma-aminobutyric acid (GABA) in the extrapyramidal motor system: I. Regional distribution of GABA in rabbit, rat guinea pig and baboon CNS. *Experimental Brain Research*, 1971, *13*, 514–518.

O'Keefe, J., & Nadel, L. *The hippocampus as a cognitive map*. New York: Oxford University Press, 1978.

Olton, D. S., Becker, J. T., & Handelmann, G. E. Hippocampus, space and memory. *Behavioral and Brain Sciences*, 1979, *2*, 313–365.

Orr, W. B., & Berger, T. W. Hippocampal lesions disrupt discrimination reversal learning of the rabbit nictitating membrane response. *Neuroscience Abstracts*, 1981, *7*, 648.

Prokasy, W. F. Developments with the two-phase-model applied to human eyelid conditioning. In A. H. Black, & W. R. Prokasy (Eds.), *Classical conditioning II: Current research and theory*. New York: Appleton-Century-Crofts, 1972.

Rescorla, R. A., & Solomon, R. L. Two process learning theory: Relationships between Pavlovian conditioning and instrumental learning. *Psychological Review*, 1967, *74*, 151–182.

Roberts, E. Disinhibition as an organizing principle in the nervous system—the role of the GABA system. In E. Roberts, T. N. Chase, & D. B. Tower (Eds.), *GABA in nervous system function*. New York: Raven Press, 1976.

Roberts, E. Epilepsy and antiepileptic drugs: A speculative synthesis. In G. H. Glaser, J. K. Penny, & D. M. Woodbury (Eds.), *Antiepileptic drugs: Mechanisms of action*. New York: Raven Press, 1980.

Schlosberg, H. The relationship between success and the laws of conditioning. *Psychological Review*, 1937, *44*, 379–394.

Smith, O. A., Astley, C. A., DeVit, J. L., Stein, J. M., & Walsh, K. E. Functional analysis of hypothalamic control of the cardiovascular responses accompanying emotional behavior. *Federation Proceedings*, 1980, *39*, 2487–2494.

Solomon, P. R., & Moore, J. W. Latent inhibition and stimulus generalization for the classically conditioned nictitating membrane response in rabbits (*Cryctolagus cuniculus*) following dorsal hippocampal ablation. *Journal of Comparative and Physiological Psychology*, 1975, *89*, 1192–1203.

Squire, L. The neurophysiology of human memory. *Annual Review of Neuroscience*, 1982, *5*, 241–273.

Swanson, L. W., Teyler, T. J., & Thompson, R. F. (Eds.). Hippocampal LTP: Mechanisms and functional implications. *Neuroscience Research Program*, 1982, *20*(5).

Thach, W. T. Discharge of cerebellar neurons related to two maintained postures and two prompt movements: I. Nuclear cell output. *Journal of Neurophysiology*, 1970, *33*, 527–536.

Thach, W. T. Timing of activity in cerebellar dentate nucleus and cerebral motor cortex during prompt volitional movement. *Brain Research*, 1975, *88*, 233–241.

Thompson, R. F., Barchas, J. D., Clark, G. A., Donegan, N., Kettner, R. E., Lavond, D. G., Madden, J., Mauk, M. D., & McCormick, D. A. Neuronal substrates of associative learning in the mammalian brain. In D. L. Alkon & J. Farley (Eds.), *Primary neural substrates of learning and behavioral change*. Princeton, N.J.: Princeton University Press, in press.

Thompson, R. F., Berger, T. W., Berry, S. D., Clark, G. A., Kettner, R. E., Lavond, D. G., Mauk, M. D., McCormick, D. A., Solomon, P. R., & Weisz, D. J. Neuronal substrates of learning and memory: Hippocampus and other structures. In C. D. Woody (Ed.), *Conditioning: Representation of involved neural functions*. New York: Plenum Press, 1982.

Thompson, R. F., Berger, T. W., Berry, S. D., Hoehler, F. K., Kettner, R. E., & Weisz, D. J. Hippocampal substrate of classical conditioning. *Physiological Psychology*, 1980, *8*, 262–279.

Thompson, R. F., Berger, T. W., Cegavske, C. F., Patterson, M. M., Roemer, R. A., Teyler, T. J., & Young, R. A. A search for the engram. *American Psychologist*, 1976, *31*, 209–227.

Thompson, R. F., Berger, T. W., & Madden, J., IV. Cellular processes of learning and memory in the mammalian CNS. *Annual Review of Neuroscience*, 1983, *6*, 447–491.

Thompson, R. F., Clark, G. A., Donegan, N. H., Lavond, D. G., Madden, J., IV, Mamounas, L. A., Mauk, M. D., & McCormick, D. A. Neuronal substrates of basic associative learning. In N. Butters & L. Squire (Eds.), *Neuropsychology of memory*. New York: Guilford Press, 1984.

Thompson, R. F., McCormick, D. A., Lavond, D. G., Clark, G. A., Kettner, R. E., & Mauk, M. D. The engram found? Initial localization of the memory trace for a basic form of associative learning. In J. M. Sprague & A. N. Epstein (Eds.), *Progress in psychobiology and physiological psychology*. New York: Academic Press, 1983.

Thompson, R. F., & Spencer, W. A. Habituation: A model phenomenon for the study of neuronal substrates of behavior. *Psychological Review*, 1966, *173*, 16–43.

Tsukahara, N. Synaptic plasticity in the mammalian central nervous system. *Annual Review of Neuroscience*, 1981, *4*, 351–379.

Wagner, A. R. Stimulus selection and "modified continuity theory." In G. H. Bower & J. T. Spence (Eds.), *Psychology of learning and motivation* (Vol. 3). New York: Academic Press, 1969.

Wagner, A. R. SPO: A model of automatic memory processing in animal behavior. In N. E. Spear & R. R. Miller (Eds.), *Information processing in animals: Memory mechanisms*. Hillsdale, N.J.: Erlbaum, 1981.

Weinberger, N. M. Effects of conditioned arousal on the auditory system. In A. L. Beckman (Ed.), *The neural basis of behavior*. Jamaica, N.Y.: Spectrum, 1982.

Weisz, D. J., Solomon, P. R., & Thompson, R. F. The hippocampus appears necessary for trace conditioning. *Bulletin of the Psychonomic Society*, 1980, *193*, 244. (Abstract)

Wikler, A. *Mechanisms of action of opiates and opiate antagonists: A review of their mechanisms of action in relation to clinical problems* (Public Health Monograph No. 52). Washington, D.C.: U.S. Government Printing Office, 1958.

Woody, C. D., Yarowsky, P., Owens, J., Black-Cleworth, P., & Crow, T. Effect of lesions of coronal motor areas on acquisition of conditioned eye blink in the cat. *Journal of Neurophysiology*, 1974, *37*, 385–394.

Yeo, C. H., Hardiman, M. J., Glickstein, M., & Russell, I. S. Lesions of cerebellar nuclei abolish the classically conditioned nictitating membrane response. *Society for Neuroscience Abstracts*, 1982, *8*, 22.

CHAPTER TEN

Classical Conditioning Mediated by the Red Nucleus: An Approach Beginning at the Cellular Level

NAKAAKIRA TSUKAHARA

One of the major goals of the study of neuroscience is to understand the neuronal mechanisms underlying learning and memory. To understand the neuronal basis of learning, it is not unreasonable to investigate the "modifiable element" of the network involved in learning behavior. One way to achieve this is, first, to characterize the mode of behavioral modification; then, to identify the neuronal circuit involved in the behavior to localize the possible sites that are responsible for the behavioral modification; and finally, to study the cellular mechanisms underlying the behavioral modification. This "top-down" approach has been successfully employed by Kandel (1978) in the invertebrate nervous system.

In the mammalian central nervous system, however, it is not an easy task to identify particular neuronal circuits involved in any form of complex learning behavior. An alternative way of approaching this problem is to analyze a modifiable element of the system first and then to reconstruct in "bottom-up" fashion the modification of behavior produced by a pathway that contains the modifiable element.

As an example of such an approach, we first analyzed the plasticity of the red nucleus and found that cortico-rubral synapses from the cerebral cortex onto the red nucleus (RN) have remarkable plasticity; that is, sprouting and formation of new functional synapses occurs in several circumstances. Then we tried to use this sprouting synapse as a modifiable element and attempted to reconstruct classical conditioning. We could reproduce classical conditioning by stimulating the cortico-rubral fibers as the conditioned stimulus (CS) and the forelimb electric shock as an unconditioned stimulus (UCS). By training the cat by CS-UCS pairing, it was possible to induce classical conditioning by using these monosynaptic cortico-rubral synapses. Here we have a better chance to

Nakaakira Tsukahara. Department of Biophysical Engineering, Faculty of Engineering Science, Osaka University, Toyonaka, Osaka, Japan; National Institute for Physiological Sciences, Okazaki, Japan.

analyze the primary site at which the conditional change takes place, because it is monosynaptic and we know that it is modifiable; and indeed it turned out that the primary site was at the cortico-rubral synapses.

LESION-INDUCED SPROUTING

The most remarkable example of plasticity in the brain is the formation of new synaptic connections, a process called "sprouting." Sprouting is now recognized as a widespread phenomenon in the central nervous system (Tsukahara, 1981). In the peripheral nervous system, it was already known in the 1950s that collateral sprouting of intact motor nerve fibers reinnervates muscles after partial transection of the motor nerve. The experimental evidence for sprouting in the brain is mostly of recent origin. Liu and Chambers (1958), using a light microscope, demonstrated that dorsal root fibers can sprout in the cat spinal cord. A decade later, Raisman and Field showed that new synapses are formed by the sprouting of fibers in the rat brain (Raisman, 1969; Raisman & Field, 1973). Now there is a growing list of investigations dealing with the formation of central synapses by sprouting of fibers, and it is clear that the phenomenon is widespread in the brain (Tsukahara, 1981).

The large size and ready identifiability of RN neurons, together with the unique synaptic organization of the RN, make it a particularly favorable target for electrophysiological investigation of synaptic plasticity. Of particular importance is the discrete segregation of the two major synaptic inputs: those from the nucleus interpositus (IP) of the cerebellum, terminating on the somatic portions of the cell membranes, and those from the cerebral cortex that form synapses on the distal dendrites. Analysis of the spatial characteristics of the synaptic potentials has been greatly aided by recent advances in neuronal modeling made possible by computer technology.

Stimulation of the two excitatory inputs of an RN neuron produces monosynaptic excitatory postsynaptic potentials (EPSPs) with different time courses, as shown in Figure 10-1A. Stimulation of the IP produces fast-rising EPSPs, whereas stimulation of the efferent fibers of the neurons of the cerebral cortex at the cerebral peduncle (CP) produces slow-rising EPSPs. Also, it has been shown that the EPSPs induced from the CP are less sensitive to membrane potential displacement than those induced from the IP (not illustrated). These phenomena have been interpreted by assuming a qualitative difference between synaptic sites on the somatic and dendritic membrane of the RN cells, a view that is supported by electron-microscopic evidence (Murakami, Katsumaru, Saito, & Tsukahara, 1982).

Our question is whether, when we destroy one of the inputs—IP, for example—do the cortico-rubral fibers sprout? If sprouting takes place at the proximal portion of the soma-dendritic membrane, then we can expect that the time course of the cortico-rubral EPSPs might change, because the electrotonic distortion would be much smaller due to its proximal location. So we should have a fast-rising EPSP superimposed on the preexisting slow-rising cortico-rubral EPSPs. It turned out that this is indeed the case.

After chronic lesions of the IP in adult cats, a new fast-rising EPSP appears superimposed on the slow-rising cortico-rubral EPSPs as shown in Figure 10-1B. The histogram of Figure 10-1C illustrates frequency distribution of CP-EPSPs induced by stimulating the cortico-rubral fibers at the CP in normal cats. The inset diagram shows how we measured the time-to-peak. Figure 10-1D shows the frequency distribution of CP-EPSPs in cats with lesions of IP. It is noted that the time-to-peak is shorter in D than in C. These data were taken to indicate that new, functionally active synapses are formed at the proximal portion of the soma-dendritic membrane of the RN cells. It should be noted that a change of cable properties of RN neurons after IP lesion accounts for only a minor portion, less than 5%, of the observed changes in time-to-peak of the cortico-rubral EPSPs.

Rall's (1964) theoretical analysis of the shape of the EPSPs predicts that the EPSPs produced by the proximal synapses are larger in amplitude and shorter in rise time than those of the distal ones. Are the newly appeared cortico-rubral EPSPs consistent with this prediction? We analyzed the unitary EPSPs and found that the relation of the time-to-peak and the amplitude of the cortico-rubral unitary EPSPs before and after chronic lesions of IP can be fitted to the theoretical calculation derived from Rall's compartment model (1964). The time course of the theoretical EPSPs generated at each of five

Figure 10-1. Lesion-induced sprouting in the adult feline red nucleus (RN). (A) Synaptic organization of the normal RN. Monosynaptic excitatory input from ipsilateral sensorimotor cortex (SM) through the cerebral peduncle (CP) impinges on the distal dendrites and that from the contralateral nucleus interpositus (IP) of the cerebellum on the soma. Stimulation of the CP produces a slow-rising EPSP in an RN cell and stimulation of the IP produces a fast-rising EPSP as shown in the inset. (B) After IP lesion a fast-rising component appears superimposed on the slow-rising CP-EPSPs as shown in the inset. (C) Frequency distribution of the time-to-peak of the CP-EPSPs of normal cats measured as in the inset of A. (D) Same as C but CP-EPSPs of cats with chronic IP lesions measured as in the inset of B. (Modified from Tsukahara, Hultborn, Murakami, & Fujito, 1975.)

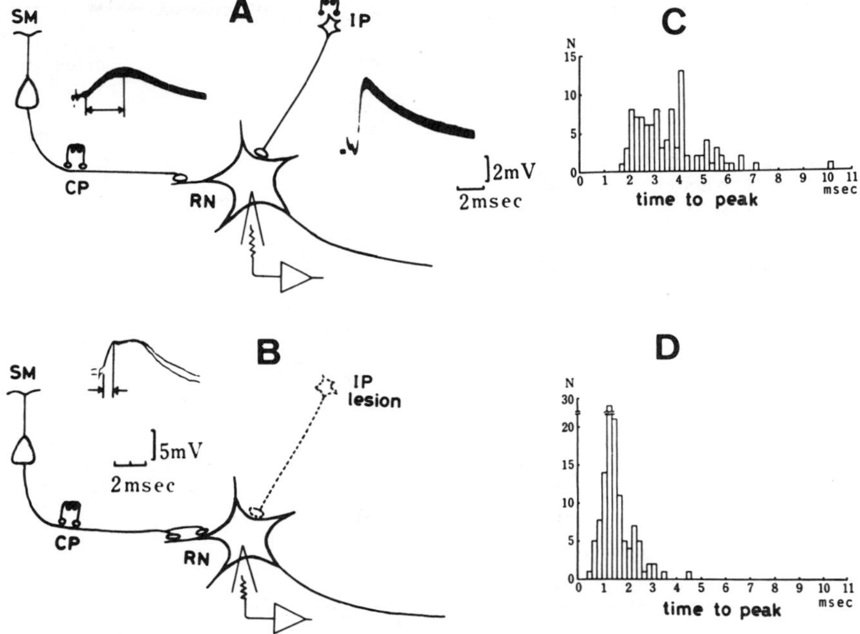

compartments is illustrated in Figure 10-2D. The theoretical relation between time-to-peak and amplitude is shown by the dotted curve. The experimental data are well fitted to this curve; the points derived from normal cats are concentrated on the distal compartment and those from cats with lesions of the IP are scattered in all compartments. It is likely that the new synapses are formed at the proximal compartments.

How fast does sprouting occur? This is an important question, because in order to correlate the sprouting phenomenon with learning behavior, it is necessary to have some idea of the time course of development of sprouting. The time course of development of the newly formed cortico-rubral synapses, as investigated by the time-to-peak of CP-EPSPs is illustrated in Figure 10-3.

Figure 10-2. Cortico-rubral unitary EPSPs. (A) Intracellular EPSP evoked by stimulation of the CP in an RN cell of a cross-innervated cat. (B) Same as A but evoked by stimulation of the SM in a cat with a lesion of the IP 27 days before acute experiment. (C) Same as B but in a normal cat. (A–C) Upper traces, intracellular potentials; lower traces, extracellular field potential corresponding to the upper traces. (D) Relation between time-to-peak and amplitude of the unitary EPSPs. ○, unitary EPSPs of IP-lesioned cats; ★, those of cross-innervated cats more than 2 months before recording; ●, those of normal cats; ①–⑤ time-to-peak and amplitude of theoretical EPSPs derived from Rall's compartment model initiated at each compartment of a five-compartment chain. The time course of the theoretical EPSPs generated in these compartments is shown in the inset of the figure. (From Tsukahara, 1981.)

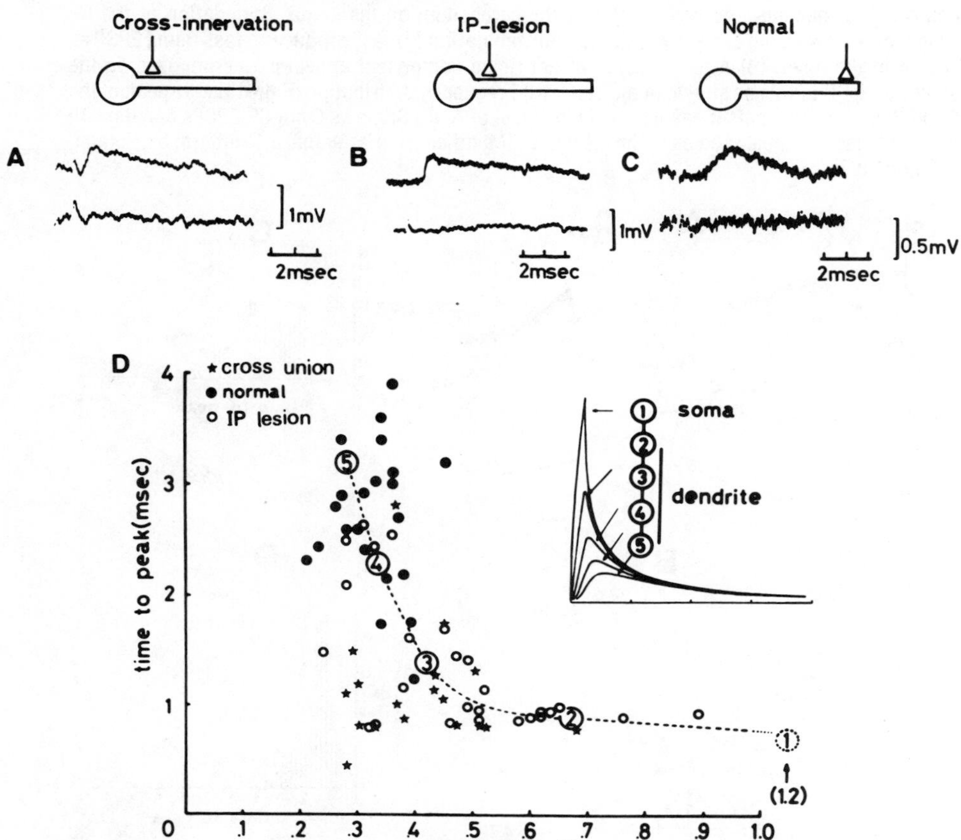

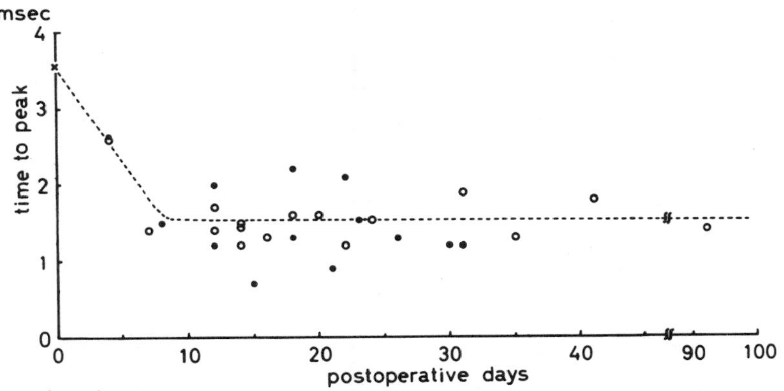

Figure 10-3. Time course of the change in the rise time of the CP-EPSPs after IP lesion. Ordinate: time-to-peak of the CP-EPSPs; abscissa: days after IP lesion; ○, mean time-to-peak of the CP-EPSPs of more than six RN cells; ●, mean time-to-peak of the CP-EPSPs of two to five RN cells. Each point represents data from one cat. A cross indicates the mean time-to-peak of the CP-EPSPs of 100 RN cells in normal cats. (From Tsukahara, Hultborn, Murakami, & Fujito, 1975.)

Here the relationship between the average time-to-peak of the cortico-rubral EPSPs and the number of days after lesions of the IP for each experimental animal is shown. Four days after the lesion of the IP, there is already a significant shortening of the time-to-peak. After 10 days, the shortening reaches its maximum.

Are there any morphological correlates for these physiological findings? Electron-microscopic studies (Nakamura, Mizuno, Konishi, & Sato, 1974; Hanaway & Smith, 1978; Murakami *et al.*, 1982) provided evidence in support of the physiological conclusion of sprouting. Previous electron-microscopic studies of the RN were not able to survey the whole neuronal surface because of the extended nature of the dendritic tree of neurons from the RN region. However, intracellular horseradish peroxidase (HRP) injection with microelectrodes has made it possible to survey whole labeled neurons electron-microscopically. This technique combined with techniques involving degeneration of the presynaptic terminals has enabled us to locate the site of termination of the two major inputs of the RN: inputs from the cerebral cortex and those from the IP of the cerebellum.

Quantitative measurement of the dendritic tree by a computer-assisted image-processing system developed in our laboratory revealed that the diameters of dendritic branches decrease monotonically. Therefore, it is possible to estimate the position of synapses on RN cell dendrites by measuring the minor diameter of cross-sections of dendritic branches in electron micrographs of HRP-stained RN cells. Furthermore, cortico-rubral synapses can be distinguished by the degeneration of their terminals after lesions of the cerebral sensorimotor cortex.

The degeneration of terminal boutons after destruction of the cerebral sensorimotor cortex was found mainly on dendritic branches with small diameters, that is, 1–4 μm. Figure 10-4 shows the frequency distribution of the diameters of the dendritic cross-sections of HRP-stained RN neurons. We used the shorter diameter of the cross-section when the shape of the cross-section

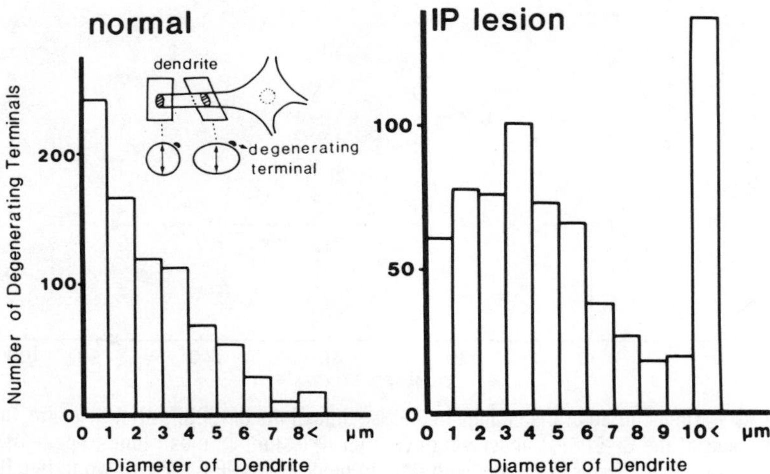

Figure 10-4. Frequency distribution of the dendritic diameters where degeneration terminals of cortico-rubral synapses were found. (A) Normal cat. (B) Cats with chronic destruction of the IP. Ordinate: number of degeneration presynaptic terminals; abscissa: minor diameters of dendrites on which the cortico-rubral degeneration terminals were found. (Modified from Murakami, Katsumaru, Saito, & Tsukahara, 1982.)

was not round. These histological findings therefore support the results of the electrophysiological studies discussed earlier. They show that cerebral inputs terminate on the distal dendrites of RN neurons, whereas inputs from IP terminate on the soma.

Murakami *et al.* (1982) studied the degenerated terminals of cortico-rubral fibers on the dendritic surface of RN cells stained by intracellular injection of HRP. These terminals end on dendrites with diameters of 1–4 μm. Degenerated cortico-rubral terminals were also studied in cats in which the IP had been destroyed about 3 months previously. In these animals, in accordance with the physiological findings, the cerebral synapses were found to terminate not only on the distal dendrites but also on the proximal dendrites and on the somatic portion of the RN cells (Figure 10-4).

SPROUTING IN NORMAL CENTRAL NEURONS

Although much evidence has been provided to show that sprouting can and does take place after denervation in the mammalian central nervous system, we still have little idea of what triggers this process. For example, does the presence of degenerating fibers initiate the process of sprouting? In this context, we might ask to what extent sprouting occurs in circumstances other than denervation.

Published attempts to use controlled cross-innervation of peripheral nerves for the purpose of investigating central reorganization are quite old. Sperry (1947) investigated the functional compensation of movement disorders that followed cross-innervation of nerves innervating flexor and extensor muscles in various species of mammals. He found that in monkeys motor "reeducation" occurs and that the reversed action is inhibited while new, correct, and smoothly coordinated movements are learned.

Eccles, Eccles, Shealey, and Willis (1962) investigated possible changes in the synaptic connections of spinal motoneurons after cross-innervation of the flexor and extensor nerves of the hindlimbs in the cat. Although they found evidence indicative of the formation of new synapses on motoneurons after cross-innervation, this was restricted to the groups of motoneurons in which axons had been severed. Thus, the extent of the reorganization was very limited. Subsequently, motivated by these experiments, we performed cross-innervation experiments in cats to determine whether synaptic reorganization occurred at the supraspinal level. The cortico-rubro-spinal system is one of the major motor outflows from the cerebrum to the spinal cord. Therefore, if synaptic reorganization at the supraspinal level should occur, the cortico-rubro-spinal system might well be affected. If so, it should be possible to detect the changes using techniques similar to those described previously.

For cross-innervation of the forelimb nerves, the musculocutaneous, median, radial, and ulnar nerves were cut at the axillary region, and the central stumps of the radial nerve were united with the peripheral stumps of the musculocutaneous, median, and ulnar nerves by suturing the nerve sheaths. A similar procedure was applied to the peripheral stumps of the radial nerve which were united with the central stumps of the musculocutaneous, median and ulnar nerves.

These studies (Tsukahara, Fujito, Oda, & Maeda, 1982) showed that 2 to 6 months after cross-innervation, the rise time of the cortico-rubral EPSPs induced by stimulating the CP became shorter than those of normal cats. A typical slow EPSP evoked by stimulating the CP in a normal cat is illustrated in Figure 10-5C. In contrast, the EPSPs shown in Figure 10-5A are from a cat with cross-innervation of the forelimb nerves. Recordings are from cells innervating the upper spinal segments (C cells). The EPSPs had a much faster-rising time course than those in normal cats. In these experiments, C cells were identified by the antidromic excitation produced by stimulating the C_1 spinal segment. The frequency distribution of the time-to-peak of the CP-EPSPs of C cells in cross-innervated cats is shown in Figure 10-5B. The mean time-to-peak of CP-EPSPs of C cells in cats cross-innervated more than 2 months previously (1.9 ± 0.9 msec, $n = 160$) was significantly shorter than that of the normal cats (3.6 ± 1.4 msec, $n = 100$). The slower time to peak in C cells was also found when recordings were performed less than 2 months after cross-innervation. In contrast, the EPSPs of the RN cells in normal cats had a much slower rise time than those of C cells in cross-innervated cats, as shown in Figure 10-5D.

Furthermore, a fast-rising component appeared in the cortico-rubral unitary EPSPs of the cross-innervated cats. This was not accompanied by an appreciable change in the dendritic cable properties of the RN neurons, and there was no change in the number of synapses of the interposito-rubral terminals, as estimated physiologically (Fujito, Tsukahara, Oda, & Yoshida, 1982). By analogy with previous experiments, these findings all suggest that new synapses had formed on the proximal portions of the soma-dendritic membrane of the RN cells by cortico-rubral fibers that normally terminate on the distal dendrites. It appears, therefore, that sprouting can occur in central neurons without lesions of the synaptic inputs.

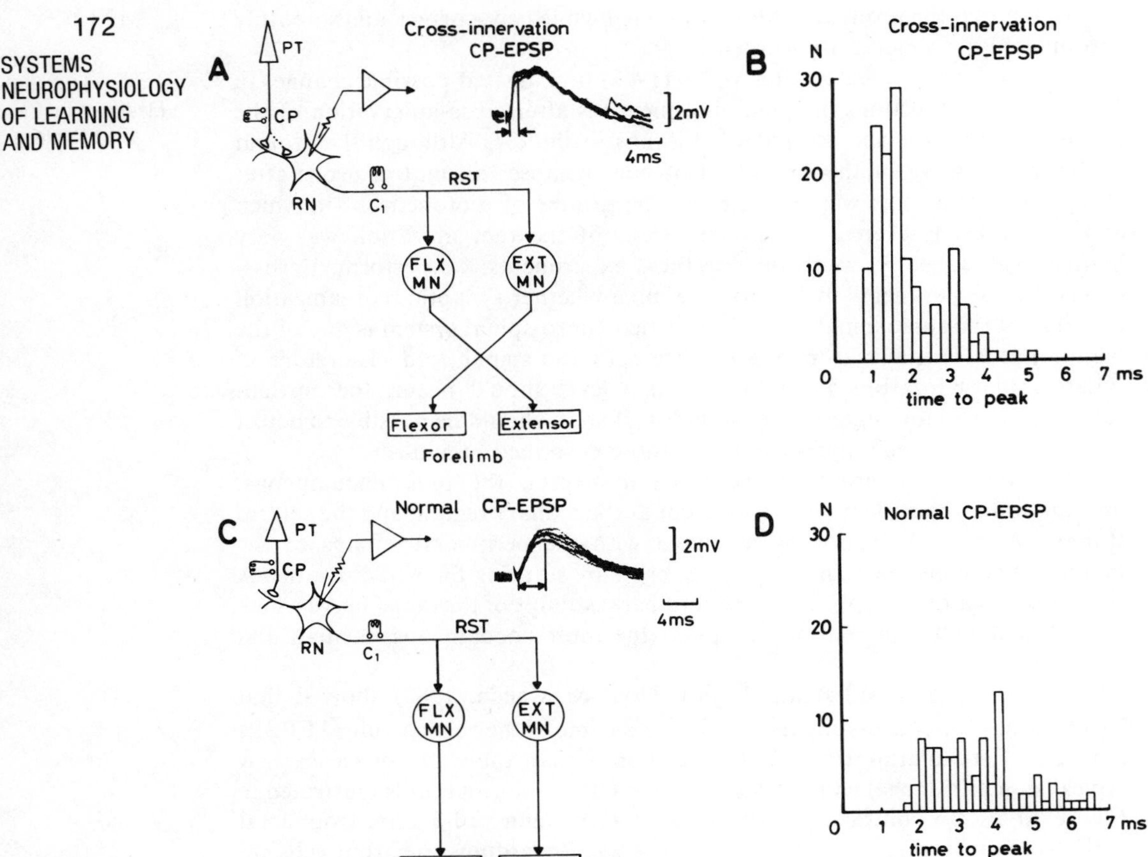

Figure 10-5. Cortico-rubral EPSPs in cross-innervated cats. (A) Traces are intracellular responses in RN neurons, from a cross-innervated cat 176 days before acute experiments. (B) Traces are intracellular responses in an RN cell in a normal cat. (A, B) Diagram illustrates the experimental arrangements. PT, pyramidal tract cell; RST, rubro-spinal tract; FLX MN, flexor motoneuron; EXT MN, extensor motoneuron; C_1, C_1 spinal segment; RN, red nucleus; CP, cerebral peduncle. (B) Frequency distribution of time-to-peak of CP-EPSPs in cross-innervated cats. Ordinate: number of cells; abscissa: time-to-peak of CP-EPSPs (in msec). (D) Same as B but with CP-EPSPs in normal cats. (Modified from Tsukahara, Fujito, Oda, & Maeda, 1982.)

SPROUTING AND THE NEURONAL BASIS OF CLASSICAL CONDITIONING

There has been a large body of studies dealing with the neuronal correlates of classical conditioning. In the mammalian central nervous system, it is not easy to distinguish local neuronal changes at the sites of the recording from that occurring at a distant site. One strategy for isolating the primary site of change is to simplify afferent pathways for the conditioned responses. Hitherto, the mammalian RN has been used to investigate neuronal plasticity such as sprouting. In an extension of these studies, an attempt was made to use the plasticity of cortico-rubral synapses as an element in the reconstruction of a simplified learning paradigm.

There are experiments indicating that midbrain structures play an important role for the conditioned avoidance response. Smith (1970) has reported that rubral lesions abolished the conditioned forelimb flexion responses established by pairing tone as the CS with forelimb electric shock as the UCS.

A classical conditioning paradigm was therefore used in our study. Our question is whether or not known synaptic plasticity, such as sprouting, constitutes a neuronal basis for classical conditioning. In order to facilitate the identification of the primary site of conditioning, the CS was delivered to the left CP as an electric shock. Furthermore, the cortical outflow was restricted mainly to the cortico-rubral fibers by lesions of cortico-fugal fibers below the level of the red nucleus. This procedure eliminates the contribution of the pyramidal tract as well as the cortico-ponto-cerebellar and some other cortico-bulbar fibers in this reflex (Figure 10-6). The CS was the electric pulse train to the CP, and forelimb electric shock was used as the UCS. It was found that after pairing the CS-UCS in close temporal association, initially ineffective stimulus intensities of the CS gave rise to flexion of the contralateral forelimb (Tsukahara, Oda, & Notsu, 1981).

Figure 10-6. Associative learning mediated by the RN. Arrangement of experimental setup. CS, conditioned stimulus; US, unconditioned stimulus; CP, cerebral peduncle; IP, nucleus interpositus of the cerebellum; INT, interneuron; Flex. MN, flexor motoneuron. Diagram of histological sections illustrates the lesions of the cortico-fugal fibers at the CP.

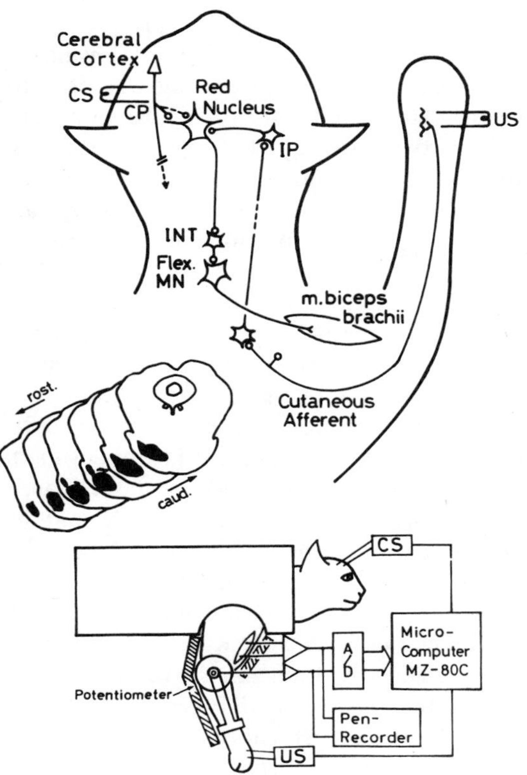

Cats were kept in bags with holes from which their heads and right forelimb protruded. They were mounted on a frame, and the shoulder was fixed to the frame to maintain the forelimb at the predetermined resting position. The movement of the elbow joint was measured by a potentiometer attached to the joint. Electromyograms of the biceps brachii muscle and the triceps brachii muscle were recorded.

A series of stimuli was given daily during the training session. The CS was a train of five pulses at 2-msec intervals. The UCS was an electric shock that preceded the CS by from 60 to 200 msec, mostly 100 msec. CS-UCS pairing of 120 trials with an intertrial interval of 30 sec constituted the training of the day. Once every five trials, only the CS was given. The ratio of positive responses of 24 such trials without the UCS gives the score of performance of the day. The extinction procedure was CS alone, or reversing the sequence of the stimuli as UCS-CS. At the end of the training session, the flexion responses were tested by changing the stimulus intensities for the CS, and the relation between the score of performance and applied current was determined.

After training, the score of performance gradually increased, and after about 1 week, the score attained a plateau. Figure 10-7B shows the mechanogram of elbow flexion at the first day and seventh day of training. CS (S_1) is the CS to the CP, and UCS (S_2) is the UCS to the forearm. At the first day, the CS alone produced no response. After the seventh day, the CS produced elbow flexion.

Figure 10-7C shows the time course of acquisition and extinction of conditioned responses. The score of performance increased gradually, attaining the plateau after about 1 week. In parallel with the increase in the score of performance, the minimum current intensity for producing 100% performance (100% performance current) decreased. After establishing the conditioned response by CS-UCS pairing, backward pairing was used to extinguish the conditioned responses, as shown in Figure 10-7C. Random control experiments were also performed in two cats, and the results from these two cases are illustrated in Figure 10-8. The CS presented at regular intervals of 30 sec was followed by the UCS presented randomly as determined by the microcomputer-controlled stimulating system. With this mode of stimulation, neither the score of performance nor the current intensity for producing 100% performance changed appreciably with training. In a third cat, the UCS was presented by itself for 10 days. In this case, the 100% performance current did not show any appreciable change. Therefore, it seems likely that the behavioral modification is to be considered as an example of classical conditioning.

The pathway mediating the conditioned response in this experimental paradigm is considered to be relatively simple in view of the fact that corticofugal fibers are surgically eliminated just caudal to the RN, and also because the CS electrodes were implanted within the CP, which contains cortico-rubral fibers that are presynaptic to the cells in the RN.

The latency of electrical activity elicited in the biceps muscle in response to the CS also supports this view; the shortest latency recorded in the electromyograms from the biceps brachii muscle was 8 msec, which is in accord with the shortest time required for the transmission of impulses along the cortico-rubro-spinal pathway to the muscle. Therefore, it is likely that the conditioned responses are mediated by the cortico-rubro-spinal system.

The primary site of the neuronal change in this pathway was tested. The RN cells receive another excitatory input from the IP of the cerebellum. So if

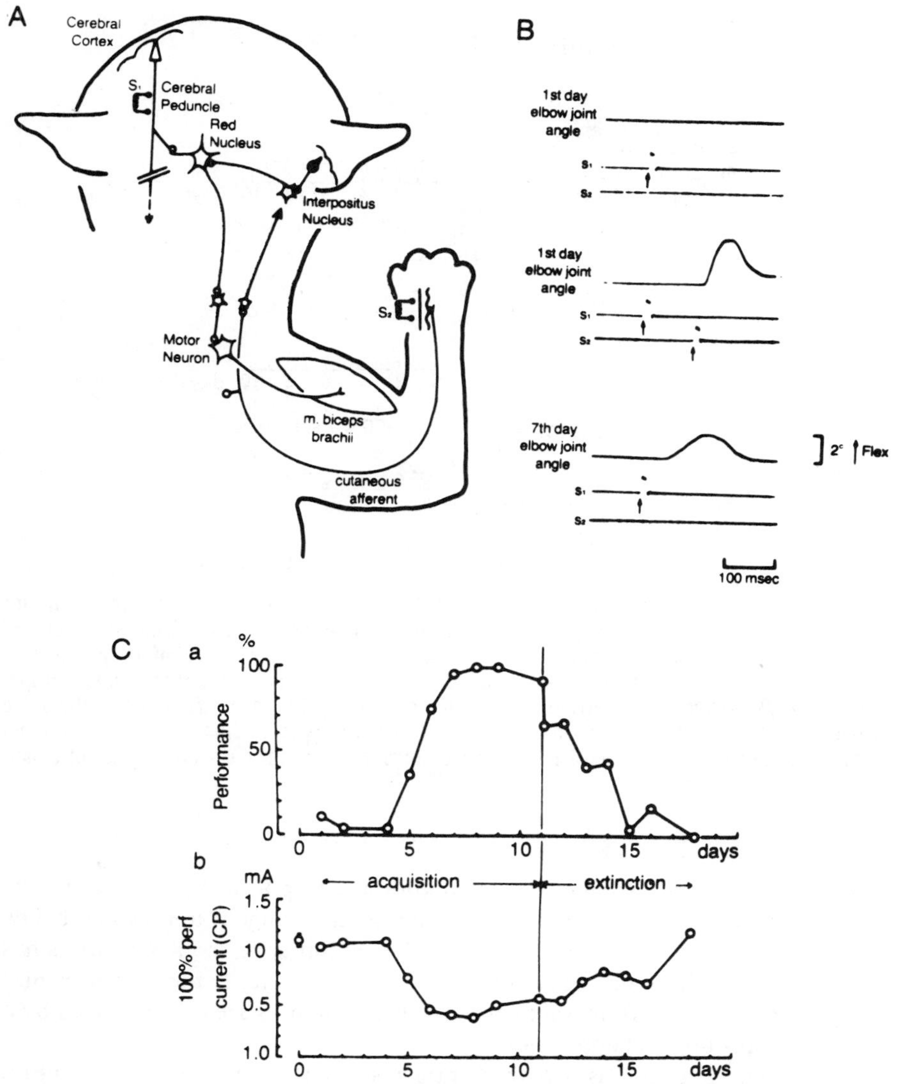

Figure 10-7. Associative conditioning mediated by the RN. (A) Arrangement of experimental setup. S_1, conditioned stimulus (CS); S_2, unconditioned stimulus (UCS). (B) Specimen record of elbow flexion (uppermost traces) on the 1st day and 7th days after conditioning. Upward arrows of middle and lowermost traces indicate the onset of the stimulus. (C) Change in performance (a) and change in minimum current for eliciting 100% performance (100% performance current) (b) during forward and backward pairing (ordinates). Abscissa: days after onset of training, CS-UCS interval of 100 msec. After the 11th day, the stimulus sequence was reversed to UCS-CS with an interval of 900 msec. (Modified from Tsukahara, Oda, & Notsu, 1981.)

the primary sites of the neuronal change are below the RN, we should be able to have a similar change in the increase of the score of performance by stimulating the IP or a decrease in the current intensity, which gives the same score of performance. This possibility was tested, and the results are summarized in Figure 10-9 from nine cats. There is no appreciable decrease of current intensities for eliciting the same score of performance by stimulating the IP, although

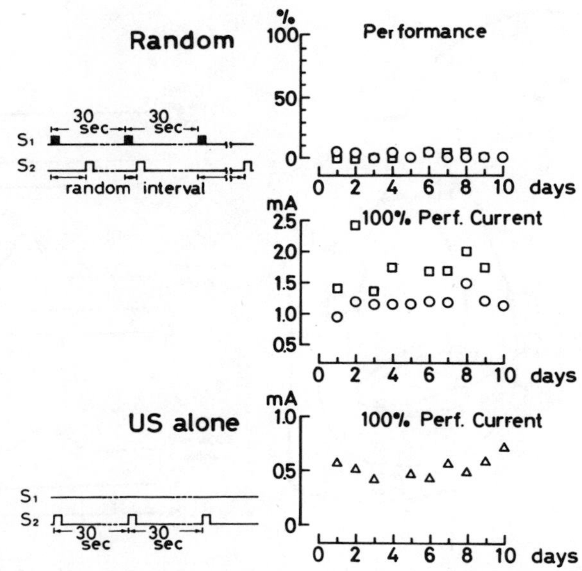

Figure 10-8. Random control and control with UCS alone. Uppermost and middle graphs for random control. Lowermost graph for UCS alone. Uppermost graph: Ordinate, score of performance during random control experiments in two cats with the stimulus parameters shown in the inset; abscissa, days after CS-UCS pairing with random intervals. Middle graph: Ordinate, 100% performance current in the same cats as in the upper graph, using the same symbols for the two cats; abscissa, days after CS-UCS pairing with random intervals. Lowermost graph: UCS alone. Ordinate, 100% performance current; abscissa, days after onset of conditioning with UCS alone.

there is already establishment of the conditioned responses by stimulating the CP. This result indicates that the site of neuronal change is not located below the RN. It is also unlikely that the general excitability of the RN neurons has changed by conditioning. Therefore, the most likely site is the cortico-rubral synapses. We already know that cortico-rubral synapses are characterized by a prominent sprouting phenomenon.

The next question is whether transmission through the cortico-rubral synapses was indeed facilitated after conditioning. We tested this by counting the extracellular unitary spikes of RN cells in awake conditioned cats. Figure 10-10 shows a comparison of the firing probability of RN neurons to the same CS before and after the establishment of conditioned reflex. The firing probability, as measured by the number of spikes to the stimuli to the CP, increased in some RN neurons after conditioning. This result is consistent with the interpretation reached from the behavioral experiment hitherto mentioned; that is, transmission through the cortico-rubral pathway increases after conditioning.

There still remains a question of whether or not the sprouting of cortico-rubral fibers is the anatomical basis of observed conditioned responses. If the sprouting is really the cause, then one would expect to see changes in cortico-rubral EPSPs after the establishment of the conditioned reflex that are similar to those observed after lesions of the IP, or after cross-innervation. We tested this by intracellular recording from RN neurons in conditioned as well as in control cats. It was found that after the establishment of the conditioned reflex, a new fast-rising component appears in the cortico-rubral dendritic EPSPs (Tsukahara & Oda, 1981).

The training procedures used in our experiments were the same as before. Control cats had cortico-fugal lesions like the conditioned animals but were not subjected to any training regime. As shown in Figure 10-11A, in conditioned animals, it was found that indeed a fast-rising component is superimposed on the slow-rising cortico-rubral dendritic EPSPs. A similar fast-rising component is also evident in EPSPs induced by stimulating the sensorimotor cortex as shown in Figure 10-11B. In contrast, the CP-EPSP shown in Figure 10-11C from a control, nonstimulated cat shows only a slow-rising time course as is seen in normal nonlesioned cat as shown in Figure 10-11D. The time-to-peak of the CP-EPSPs was measured in both conditioned and control cats, and the frequency distributions of the time-to-peak of CP-EPSPs are illustrated in Figures 10-11E and F. Data are from anesthetized cats. If dual peaks occurred, the first peak was measured to determine the time-to-peak of the EPSPs. The time-to-peak of CP-EPSPs in conditioned cats appears shorter than that of control, nonstimulated cats, which, according to our test, was significant statistically ($p < .01$). In Figure 10-11G, the frequency distribution of the CP-EPSPs in normal nonlesioned cats from our previous experiments is illustrated. It should be noted that in some nonstimulated peduncular-lesioned cats, time-to-peak of the CP-EPSPs is faster than that in the nonlesioned control cats.

Figure 10-9. Primary site of conditioned changes. (A) INT, interneurons interpolated in the rubrospinal system; MN, flexor motoneurons. (B) Current intensity of CP stimulation for producing 100% performance to CS. (C) Current intensity producing 100% performance by stimulation of IP with the same train of pulses and the same cats used in B. The data from nine cats are illustrated with mean and *SD*. Abscissa: days after onset of conditioning of CS to CP and UCS to the skin of the forelimb.

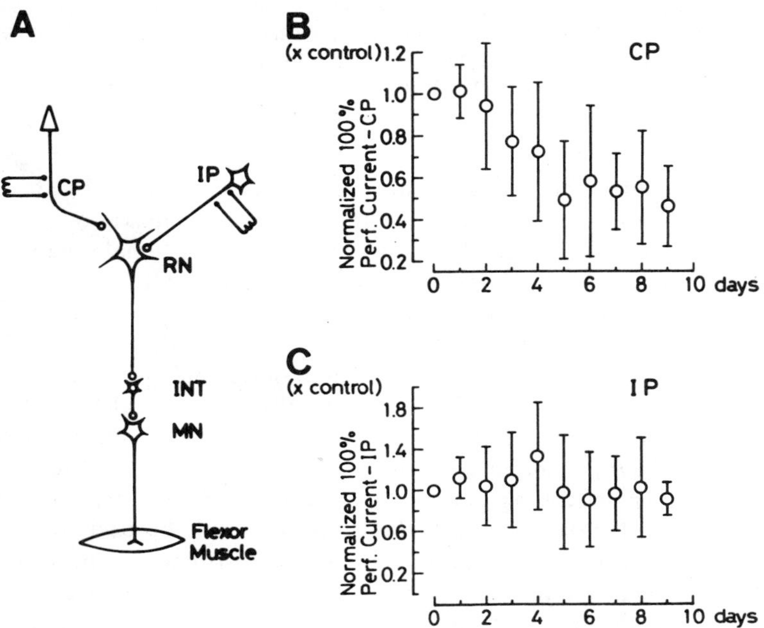

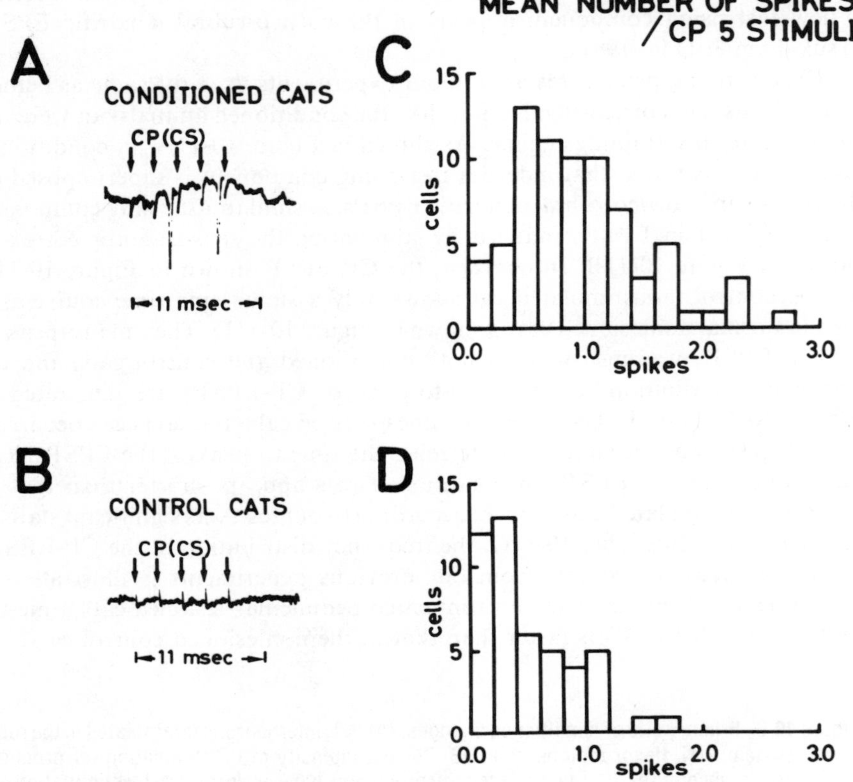

Figure 10-10. RN unit responses to the conditioned stimulus (CS). (A) Specimen RN unit responses in a conditioned cat on the 9th day after conditioning. CS consisting of five pulses (marked by downward arrows) was delivered to the cerebral peduncle (CP). (B) No spike response in a control cat, in which the conditioned response was extinguished by presenting the CS alone for 6 days. (C, D) Histogram of the number of spikes induced in each RN unit by the CS. Abscissa: mean number of spikes during initial 11 msec after onset of the CS in each unit; ordinate: number of RN cells. (C) Conditioned cats. (D) Control cat. (From Oda, Kuwa, Miyasaka, & Tsukahara, 1981.)

The most likely interpretation of these results seems to be that, by analogy with the previous experiments using IP lesions or cross-innervation, the cortico-rubral fibers sprout after conditioning to form new functional synapses on the proximal portion of the soma-dendritic membrane of RN cells. However, another possibility exists. For example, shortening of the spine where cortico-rubral terminals are located could be possible, because shortening of the spine can result in shortening of electrotonic length of transmission of cortico-rubral synaptic currents as recorded from the RN cell soma. We calculated the effect of morphological changes in spines on the postsynaptic potential using the Butz and Cowan (1974) theorem and found that the effect of this morphological change on the time-to-peak of the cortico-rubral EPSPs is very small (Kawato & Tsukahara, 1984). Therefore, this possibility can be excluded. Another possibility for the increased transmission of cortico-rubral synapses after establishment of conditioning, is the possible increase of postsynaptic potentials due to prolonged increase of transmitters. At the present moment, this is the primary unsolved issue in the RN.

In discussing the nature of these changes of CP-EPSPs and the possible mechanisms of conditioning, I believe that the sprouting of cortico-rubral synapses that we have discovered constitutes one of the neuronal bases of conditioning for the following reasons: (1) The experiment that sprouting occurs without nerve degeneration added considerable strength to this view. (2) The site of conditional changes is at the cortico-rubral synapses where sprouting was found. (3) The change of the cortico-rubral EPSPs that one would expect from sprouting of the cortico-rubral synapses at the proximal portion of the soma-dendritic membrane of RN cells was indeed observed after establishment of conditioning. (4) Finally, the time course of acquisition and extinction of conditioning is a slow process, requiring one week or so. And at least for the acquisition process, the time course is similar to that of sprouting, which takes about one week. Unfortunately, at present we do not know

Figure 10-11. Cortico-rubral EPSPs from conditioned and nonconditioned cats. (A) Cerebral peduncle (CP)-EPSPs induced in a red nucleus (RN) cell after the 8th day of conditioning, when conditioning is fully established. (B) Same cell as in A but an EPSP induced by stimulating the sensorimotor cortex (SM). (C) CP-EPSPs induced in an RN cell in a nonconditioned control cat. (D) CP-EPSPs induced in an RN cell in a normal cat. (From Tsukahara, Hultborn, Murakami, & Fujito, 1975.) Upper traces: intracellular potential. Lower traces: extracellular records corresponding to the upper traces. Time and voltage calibration of B also applies to A. (E, F) Frequency distribution of the time-to-peak of CP-EPSPs in the conditioned (E) and nonconditioned (F) cats. (G) Same histogram but taken from CP-EPSPs of normal cats. (Modified from Tsukahara, Hultborn, Murakami, & Fujito, 1975.) Ordinate: number of cells; abscissa: time-to-peak of CP-EPSPs (in msec). (From Tsukahara & Oda, 1981.)

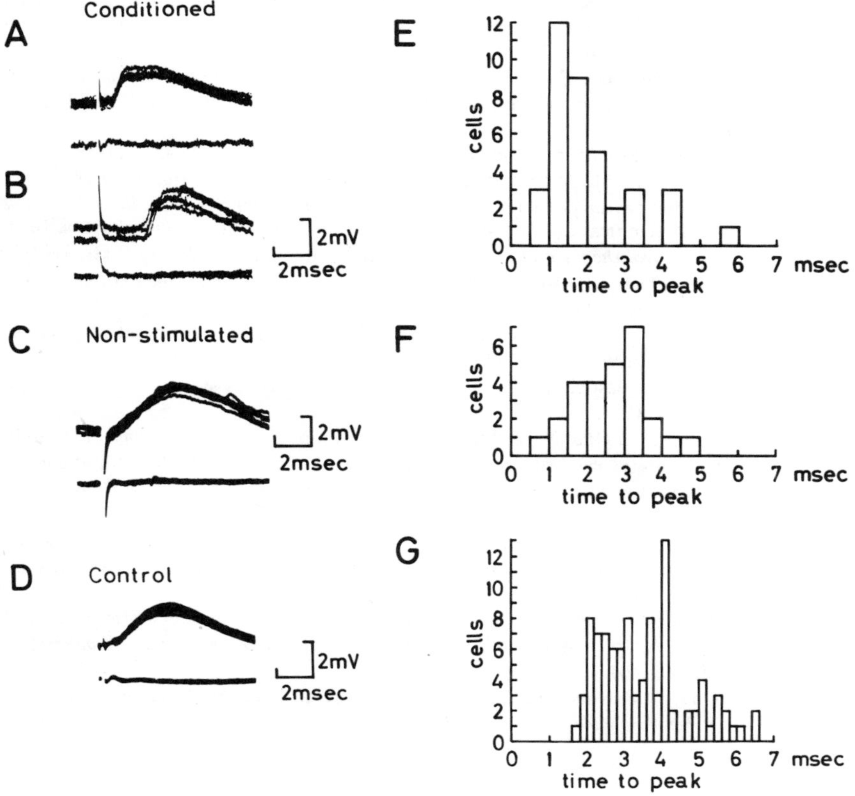

anything about whether synaptic retraction corresponding to extinction occurs as it does in some peripheral synapses. In spite of our belief that sprouting is responsible, we are aware that the experimental evidence listed above is not sufficient and that it requires future experimental efforts before the final conclusion can be drawn.

REFERENCES

Butz, E. G., & Cowan, J. D. Transient potentials in dendritic system of arbitrary geometry. *Biophysical Journal*, 1974, *14*, 661–689.

Eccles, J. C., Eccles, R. M., Shealey, C. N., & Willis, W. D. Experiments utilizing monosynaptic excitatory action on motoneurons for testing hypothesis relating to specificity of neuronal connection. *Journal of Neurophysiology*, 1962, *25*, 559–579.

Fujito, N., Tsukahara, N., Oda, Y., & Yoshida, M. Formation of functional synapses in the adult cat red nucleus from the cerebrum following cross-innervation of forelimb flexor and extensor nerves: II. Analysis of newly-appeared synaptic potentials. *Experimental Brain Research*, 1982, *45*, 13–18.

Hanaway, J., & Smith, J. Sprouting of corticorubral terminals in the cerebellar deafferented cat red nucleus. *Society for Neuroscience Abstracts*, 1978, *4*, 473.

Kandel, E. R. *A cell-biological approach to learning*. Bethesda, Md.: Society for Neuroscience, 1978.

Kawato, M., & Tsukahara, N. Theoretical study of electrical properties of dendritic spines. *Journal of Theoretical Biology*, 1984, *103*, 507–522.

Liu, C. N., & Chambers, W. W. Intraspinal sprouting of dorsal root axons. *Archives of Neurology and Psychiatry*, 1958, *79*, 46–61.

Murakami, F., Katsumaru, H., Saito, K., & Tsukahara, N. A quantitative study of synaptic reorganization in red nucleus neurons after lesion of the nucleus interpositus of the cat: An electron microscopic study involving intracellular injection of horseradish peroxidase. *Brain Research*, 1982, *242*, 41–53.

Nakamura, Y., Mizuno, N., Konishi, A., & Sato, M. Synaptic reorganization of the red nucleus after chronic deafferentation from cerebellorubral fibers: An electron microscope study in the cat. *Brain Research*, 1974, *82*, 298–301.

Oda, Y., Kuwa, K., Miyasaka, S., & Tsukahara, N. Modification of rubral unit activities during classical conditioning in the cat. *Proceedings of the Japan Academy*, 1981, *57*, Series B, 402–405.

Raisman, G. Neuronal plasticity in the septal nuclei of the adult rat. *Brain Research*, 1969, *14*, 25–48.

Raisman, G., & Field, P. M. A quantitative investigation of the development of collateral re-innervation after partial deafferentation of septal nuclei. *Brain Research*, 1973, *50*, 241–264.

Rall, W. Theoretical significance of dendritic trees for neuronal input–output relations. In R. F. Reiss (Ed.), *Neural theory and modeling*. Stanford: Standard University Press, 1964.

Smith, A. M. The effects of rubral lesions and stimulation on conditioned forelimb flexion responses in the cat. *Physiology and Behavor*, 1970, *5*, 1121–1126.

Sperry, R. W. Effect of crossing nerves to antagonistic limb muscles in the monkey. *Archives of Neurology and Psychiatry*, 1947, *58*, 452–473.

Tsukahara, N. Synaptic plasticity in the mammalian central nervous system. *Annual Review of Neuroscience*, 1981, *4*, 351–379.

Tsukahara, N., Fujito, Y., Oda, Y., & Maeda, J. Formation of functional synapses in adult cat red nucleus from the cerebrum following cross-innervation of forelimb flexor and extensor nerves: I. Appearance of new synaptic potentials. *Experimental Brain Research*, 1982, *45*, 1–12.

Tsukahara, N., Hultborn, H., Murakami, F., & Fujito, Y. Electrophysiological study of formation of new synapses and collateral sprouting in red nucleus neurons after partial denervation. *Journal of Neurophysiology*, 1975, *38*, 1359–1372.

Tsukahara, N., & Oda, Y. Appearance of new synaptic potentials at cortico-rubral synapses after the establishment of classical conditioning. *Proceedings of the Japan Academy*, 1981, *57*, series B, 398–401.

Tsukahara, N., Oda, Y., & Notsu, T. Classical conditioning mediated by the red nucleus in the cat. *Journal of Neuroscience*, 1981, *1*, 72–79.

CHAPTER ELEVEN

Studies of Pavlovian Eye-Blink Conditioning in Awake Cats

CHARLES D. WOODY

INTRODUCTION

The last decade has seen the realization of scientists' attempts to link learned behavior with its cellular and molecular substrates. This chapter, per request, concerns my efforts and those of my immediate colleagues toward this goal. Due to limitations of space, the material will be presented in somewhat abbreviated form. Further details may be found in the referenced publications.

HISTORICAL PERSPECTIVE

Studies of conditioning began with the well-known work of Pavlov (1910, 1927) and Thorndike (1913) early in this century. Some subsequent advances are listed in Table 11-1. Among these, the ability of Jasper and colleagues (see Ricci, Doane, & Jasper, 1957) to obtain extracellular recordings of cortical unit activity during conditioning and habituation in the monkey represents the first unequivocal linkage of patterns of single-neuron activity to learned behavior. A few other highlights include (1) careful assessment of optimal interstimulus intervals for acquisition of conditioned behavior by Gormezano and colleagues (1966, 1972); (2) investigation of vertebrate habituation at the cellular level by Spencer and coworkers (1966a, 1966b, 1966c); (3) linkage of presynaptic inhibition to invertebrate habituation (see Kandel, 1976); (4) investigation of Pavlovian conditioning at the intracellular level in awake vertebrates with demonstration of two underlying processes: one controlling the type of movement performed (Woody & Black-Cleworth, 1973) and the other supporting discriminative reception of the conditioned stimulus (CS) (Woody, Knispel, Crow, & Black-Cleworth, 1976); and (5) direct demonstration of nerve membrane conductances underlying associative behavioral change in an invertebrate preparation (Alkon, 1979).

Charles D. Woody. Brain Research Institute, Mental Retardation Research Center, Departments of Anatomy and Psychiatry, University of California, Los Angeles Medical Center, Los Angeles, California.

Table 11-1. A few milestones[a] of salience in the search for a physiologic understanding of conditioning

1910–1929	Early discoveries	Pavlov (1910, 1927), Thorndike (1913), Graham-Brown & Sherrington (1912)
1930–1939	Major extensions, plus early studies of eyelid conditioning	Skinner (1938), Konorski & Miller (1936), Konorski (1948), Hilgard & Marquis (1940)
1940–1949	Early studies of sensitization	Grant (1943)[b], Grant & Norris (1947)[b]
1950–1959	Latencies of eyelid CRs; use of brain stimulation as CS; sensory preconditioning (interstimulus intervals—ISIs); extracellular, single unit studies of conditioning and habituation; effects of unpaired CS and US presentations; intertrial intervals (ITIs) for optimal eyelid CRs	Boneau (1958), Doty, Rutledge, & Larsen (1956), Hoffeld, Thompson, & Brogden (1958)[b], Kimble & Dufort (1956) (also see Kimble & Ost, 1961), Ricci, Doane, & Jasper (1957), Spence & Norris (1950), Yoshii *et al.* (1958) (also see Yoshii & Ogura, 1960)
1960–1969	Conditioning of single units in the brain with chemical stimuli; pigeon heart-rate conditioning; extracellular unit activity of the motor cortex during wrist flexion; optimal ISIs for nictitating membrane conditioning; cellular role in learning; unit correlates of conditioning; hypothalamic stimulation as a reinforcer; physiologic basis of habituation; neural changes at the facial nucleus with eye-blink conditioning	Bures & Buresova (1967), Cohen & Pitts (1968), Evarts (1966), Gormezano (1966), Kandel & Spencer (1968)[b], O'Brien & Fox (1969a, 1969b), Olds (1962), Olds & Hirano (1969), Spencer, Thompson, & Neilson (1966a, 1966b, 1966c)[b], Woody & Brozek (1969a, 1969b)
1970–1979	Membrane conductances linked to associative learning; unit correlates of sensory preconditioning; physiological studies of sensitization; unit correlates of nictitating membrane conditioning; cellular basis of habituation; effects of glucoreceptors in conditioning; unit correlates of pupillary conditioning; unit correlates of rabbit nictitating membrane conditioning; acceleration of conditioning; postsynaptic correlates of invertebrate conditioning; postsynaptic correlates of eye-blink conditioning from intracellular cortical recordings; neural evidence for dual-process conditioning	Alkon (1979), Buchhalter, Brons, & Woody (1978)[b], Carew, Castellucci, & Kandel (1979)[b], Disterhoft, Kwan, & Lo (1977), Kandel (1976)[b], Kotlyar & Yeroshenko (1971), Oleson, Ashe, & Weinberger (1975), Thompson *et al.* (1976), Voronin, Gerstein, Ioffe, & Kudrioshov (1973), Woolacott & Hoyle (1976), Woody & Black-Cleworth (1973), Woody, Knispel, Crow, & Black-Cleworth (1976)
1980–	Cellular studies of conditioning in other invertebrates besides *Hermissenda*; synaptic plasticity of the red nucleus in conditioning	Carew, Hawkins, & Kandel (1983), Hawkins, Abrams, Carew, & Kandel (1983), Tsukahara, Oda, & Notsu (1981), Walters & Byrne (1983), Walters, Carew, Hawkins, & Kandel (1982)

[a]Many relevant reports concerning other forms or studies of conditioning have been omitted for lack of space (e.g., see elsewhere in the present volume and Woody, 1982b, 1982c).

[b]Some relevant reports concerning habituation, sensitization, and sensory preconditioning are included.

AIMS AND STRATEGIES

My own efforts began in the 1960s, first with attempts to trace "engrams" as field potentials within the neural circuitry of the brain (Nahvi, Woody, Ungar, & Sharafat, 1975; Woody, 1967; Woody, 1970; Woody & Nahvi, 1973) and then with identification of neural circuitry involved in the elaboration of a specific conditioned eye-blink response in an unanesthetized mammalian preparation. This was done by tracing the circuit from the orbicularis oculi muscles centrally to the cortical region at which production of the movement was controlled (Woody & Brozek, 1969a, 1969b; Woody, 1970). Establishment that neurons of the coronal–pericruciate cortex were involved in the mediation of eye-blink conditioning was accomplished at the single unit level by 1972 (Engel & Woody, 1972; Woody & Engel, 1972; Woody, Vassilevsky, & Engel, 1970). Patterns of unit activity were found to be isomorphic with acquisition, extinction, and latency of performance of the conditioned blink response. Production of the conditioned response (CR), but not the unconditioned response (UCR), was shown to depend on the intactness of the motor cortex (Figures 11-1 and 11-2), using cortical spreading depression (Woody & Brozek, 1969a) and ablation techniques (Woody, Yarowsky, Owens, Black-Cleworth, & Crow, 1974) in which the CR was abolished while the UCR was retained.[1] Also, an electrical CS introduced directly into the motor cortex in association with presentation of glabella tap unconditioned stimulus (UCS) sufficed for development of a blink CR of the proper latency for transmission along the same motor circuitry (Figure 11-3) involved in the other blink-conditioning experiments. Development of the CR was not prevented by removal of the posterior, sensory and sensory-association regions of the cortex (Woody & Yarowsky, 1972; Woody *et al.*, 1974). A detailed review of these findings appeared in 1974 (Woody, 1974).

CHARACTERIZATION OF THE CONDITIONED BEHAVIOR

The short-latency (20-msec) onset of the blink CR elicited by click CS was of great advantage in tracing the involved neural circuitry, since much of the 20-msec response latency could be accounted for by known nerve conduction times along established cortico-bulbar motor pathways (Figure 11-3). The short-latency CR was elicited discriminatively by a click CS that had been explicitly paired with glabella tap UCS, and not by an explicitly unpaired hiss discriminative stimulus (DS). "Random" presentations of the CS, UCS, and DS failed to produce conditioning, behaviorally.

Earlier investigations of eyelid conditioning raised the possibility that short-latency (alpha) responses to a CS might represent sensitization rather than conditioning (Grant & Norris, 1947). Our studies indicated that it was possible to separate sensitized from conditioned blink responses even when the latencies of both types of responses were less than 20 msec. Differences were found in the numbers of responses elicited by the CS and DS early and late in training (Figure 11-4). Most behavioral responses that occurred early in training represented sensitization because they were elicited nonspecifically by the DS as well as by the CS and appeared without need of forward pairing of CS and UCS. Most behavioral responses that appeared later in training represented conditioning because they were elicited specifically by the CS (as opposed to the DS) and depended on forward, associative pairings of the CS and UCS for their emergence.

1. Paradoxically, the long-latency conditioned eye-blink and nictitating membrane responses do not need the neocortex or hippocampus for their elaboration (Norman, Villablanca, Brown, Schwafel, & Buchwald, 1974; Moore, Desmond, & Berthier, 1982) but instead depend on brain stem pathways involving the cerebellar peduncles (Thompson *et al.*, 1982, and elsewhere herein).

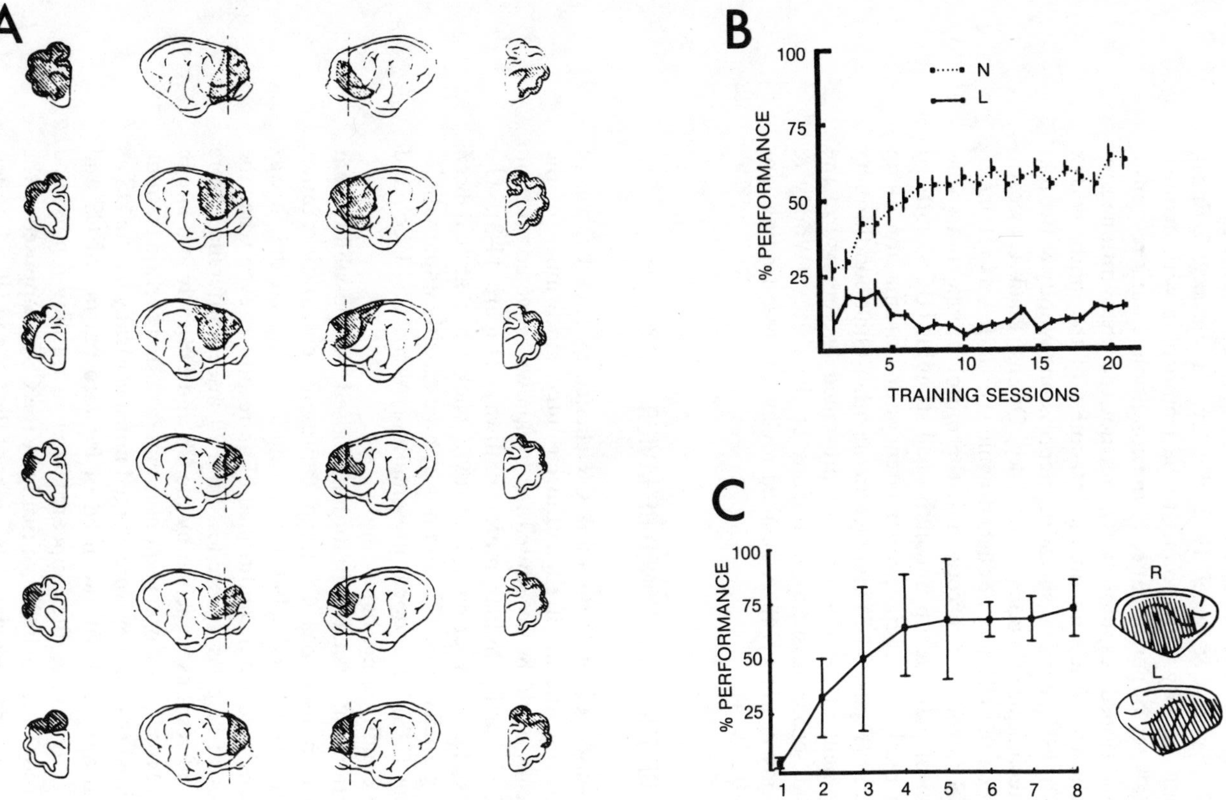

Figure 11-1. (A) Areas (shaded) of cortex removed from six lesioned cats. Data from cats 1–5 are shown in B. (B) Performance levels of normal (N) and lesioned (L) cats, $n = 6$ and $n = 5$, respectively, during training of classically conditioned eye blink. Group averages and standard deviations shown are compiled from averages of response performance by each animal for the respective training session. Each training session consisted of 150 trials of paired CS and UCS. The CS-UCS interval was 400 msec; the intertrial interval was 10 sec. (C) Averaged conditioned blink performance levels with standard deviations for seven cats with extensive bilateral ablation of caudal cortex. An example is shown of regions of right (R) and left (L) cortex removed in one animal that reached 75% response performance. (From Woody, Yarowsky, Owens, Black-Cleworth, & Crow, 1974.)

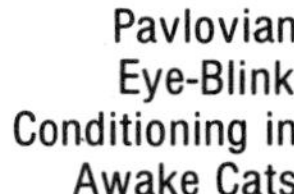

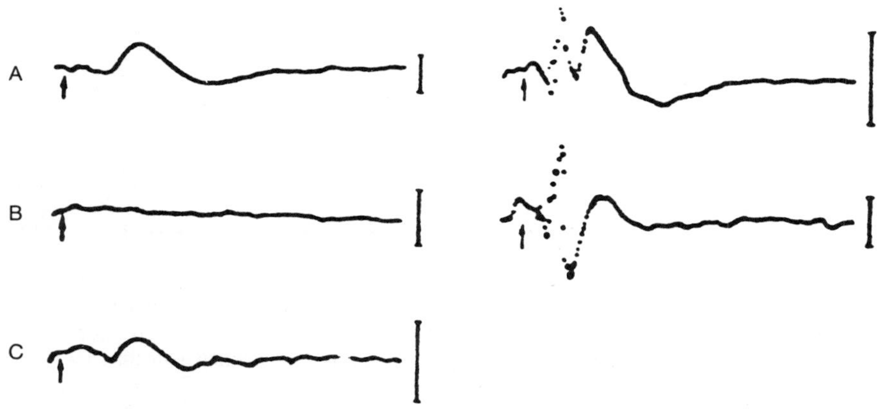

Figure 11-2. Effect of application of 25% KCl to rostral cortex on conditioned (I) and unconditioned (II) blink response. The traces show averaged field potentials at the facial nucleus: (A) before KCl, (B) after KCl, during presumed depression of cortex, and (C) after recovery of the conditioned response. The presence or absence of a response in these traces was isomorphic with the presence or absence of conditioned and unconditioned eye blinks. 50-μV calibrations are shown. Length of response averages is 102 msec. Arrows designate stimulus delivery. I and II are from different animals. (From Woody & Brozek, 1969a.)

Figure 11-3. (A) Typical averaged responses to suprathreshold glabella tap recorded from trigeminal (V) and facial (VII) nuclei. Evoked-response averages of bipolar recordings from facial (VII) nerve at the level of the zygoma and from orbicularis oculi (EMG) are also shown. All traces begin 1.5 msec after stimulus delivery. Note differences in responses recorded superiorly (S) and inferiorly (I) in facial nucleus. Calibrations are below. (B) Response onset latencies at different loci along efferent pathway for production of conditioned blink response. Standard deviations of 3–4 msec are associated with the above means. (C) Three successive (bipolar) EMG responses in orbicularis oculi muscle evoked by electrical microstimulation at ipsilateral coronal-pericruciate cortex. Beginning of stimulation coincident with beginning of trace. Response onset latencies are 7–9 msec. (From Woody & Brozek, 1969b; Woody, Vassilevsky, & Engel, 1970.)

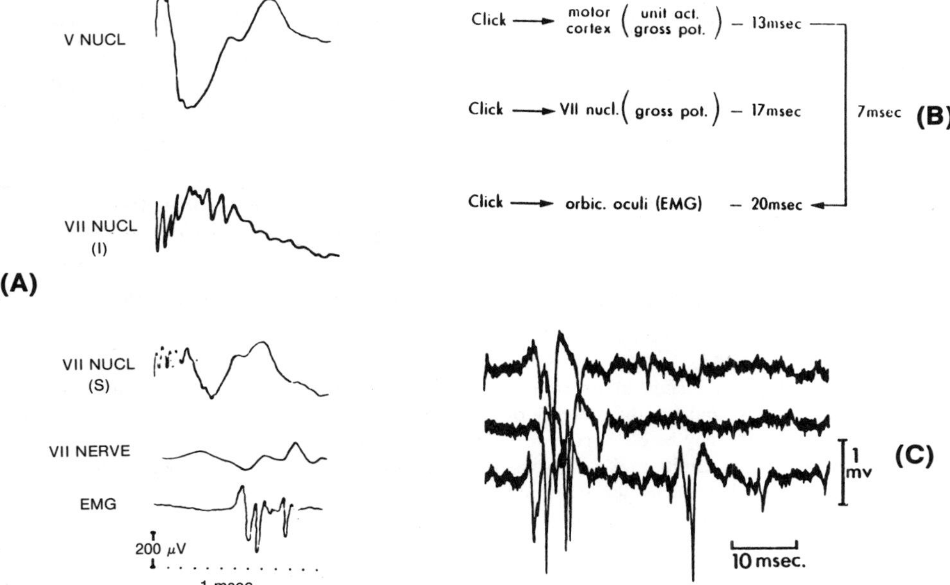

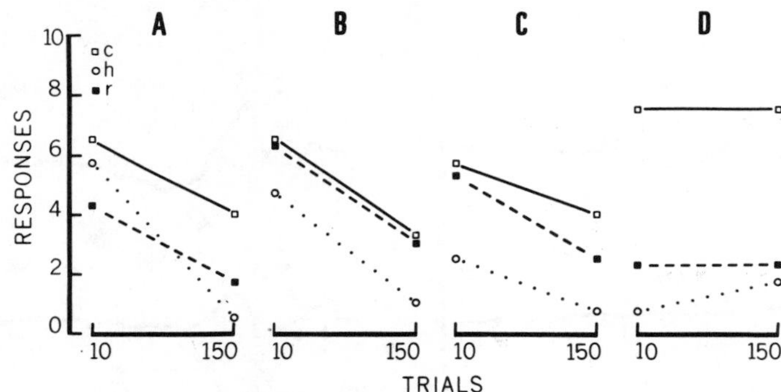

Figure 11-4. Averaged levels of blink performance to click CS in a group of cats given associative (c) or pseudorandom (r) pairings of the click with glabella tap UCS. The level of performance to concurrent presentation of an explicitly unpaired hiss DS (h) of equal intensity to the click is also shown. Each training session consists of 150 stimulus-presentation trials. The mean number of blink responses are shown for the first 10 and last 10 stimulus presentations in the first (A), second (B), third (C), and last (D) training session. Initially, sensitization results in increased levels of blink responses to all stimuli. These responses do not show stimulus specificity (i.e., the eye blinks were elicited by the click irrespective of its associative presentation and also by the explicitly unpaired DS). There appears to be adaptation or habituation of the sensitized response within each of the first three training sessions, as indicated by the reduced performance levels during the last 10 trials of each session. In sessions A and C, the CR emerges sufficiently from the background to be distinguished in the last 10 trials. By the last training session, a stable CR has emerged. (Some cats do not show any early sensitized behavioral responses.)

Others (Kandel, 1976; Kandel & Spencer, 1968) suggested that conditioning might be atypical if some motor response analogous to that subsequently conditioned could be elicited by the CS prior to associative pairing with the UCS, calling the phenomenon "alpha" conditioning.[2] In fact, detection of CRs and UCRs to the CS depends on the sensitivity of the measurement technique—for example, field potential detection at VII nucleus > EMG detection > observer detection by experienced observer > observer detection by inexperienced observer. Also, the presence or absence of an unconditioned blink response to the CS or DS prior to training depends on (1) the intensity and physical character of the CS and (2) levels of arousal, alertness, and fear in the preparation. That weak click presentations result in extracellular field potentials at the level of the facial nucleus (see Figure 11-5) with or without associated blinking suggests that even the weakest peripheral stimuli can produce physiologic responses at the near extreme of motor pathways, with or without the association of conspicuous movement. Much the same may happen to invertebrates, where postsynaptic potential (PSP) activity in response to initial CS presentations has been measured directly in single neurons (cf. Carew, Hawkins, & Kandel, 1983; Hawkins, Abrams, Carew, & Kandel, 1983).

2. Calling this phenomenon alpha conditioning is ill-advised. The term properly refers to the latency of response and not the presence or absence of response before training. (Both sensitized responses and CRs may be of short latency.) The suggestion that conditioning in which the CRs after training resemble initial UCRs or sensitized responses to the CS is atypical of most conditioning may be rejected on the fallacy of the implied assumption that most investigators have employed the same accuracies or sensitivities of response detection. They have not.

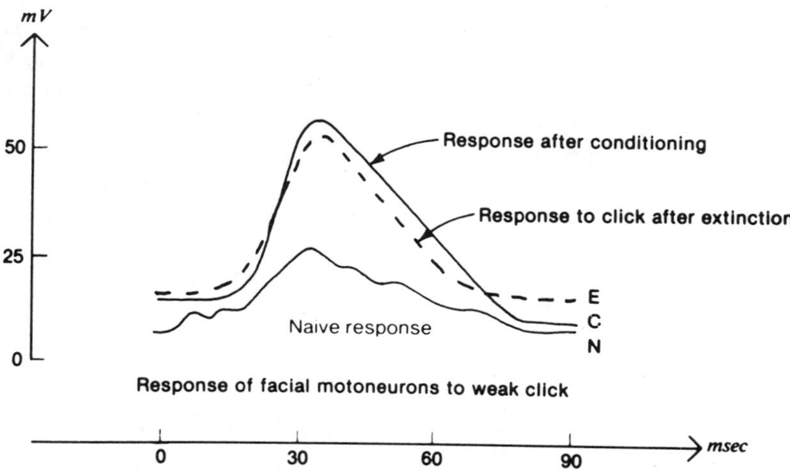

Figure 11-5. Evoked potentials recorded monopolarly from the facial nucleus during development and extinction of a conditioned eye blink in a cat. Each trace is the average of 128 responses to a 70-db, 1-msec click (CS): N, initially in naive animal; C, after establishment of the conditioned reflex; E, after extinction. The traces begin 8.4 msec before arrival of the click at the ears of the animal. Calibrations are as shown; positive up. Note that a response to the stimulus is present in the naive animal. The facial nucleus contains the motoneurons for producing the eye blink. (From Woody & Brozek, 1969a.)

RESULTS OF FURTHER INVESTIGATIONS

Further studies of short-latency eye-blink conditioning in the awake cat (Brons & Woody, 1980; Woody, 1970; Woody & Black-Cleworth, 1973; Woody & Engel, 1972; Woody, Knispel, Crow, & Black-Cleworth, 1976; Woody *et al.*, 1970) showed that the excitability of cortical neurons increased with conditioning. Neural excitability increased in such a way[3] as to support:

1. Performance of the *specific* conditioned motor response as opposed to some other motor response (for review see Woody, 1982a).
2. Discrimination of the CS from the DS—that is, the ability of the CS to elicit the CR discriminatively (for review see Woody, 1977).

We now know that the changes in neural excitability supporting motor performance of the specific CR (*Type I*) can be induced nonassociatively by repetitive presentations of the UCS. The phenomenon is termed "latent facilitation" (see Woody, 1982d). These neural changes are found postsynaptically in neurons of the motor cortex (Brons & Woody, 1980; Woody & Black-Cleworth, 1973) as well as in neurons of the facial nucleus (Matsumura & Woody, 1982).

3. That is, excitability increased selectively in those groups of projective or receptive neurons that would support the aspects of conditioning listed.

The increases in neural excitability last for periods longer than a month if a CS is paired associatively with the UCS (Tables 11-2 and 11-3).

The increases in neural excitability supporting discriminative reception of the CS (*Type II*) are induced associatively (see the material in Table 11-4). Their duration of persistence has not yet been studied. These neural changes have been found in the (auditory) association cortex—that is, in the midlateral and posterior suprasylvian gyri (Woody, Knispel, Crow, & Black-Cleworth, 1976).

Still other changes in neural excitability have been found in the motor cortex after repeated UCS presentations (Brons, Woody, & Allon, 1982). These changes consist of reductions in neural excitability in response to weak, extracellularly applied electrical stimuli. Details of these changes have been discussed recently, elsewhere (Berthier & Woody, 1984; Woody, in press).

IMPLICATIONS OF OUR FINDINGS

Our findings indicate that more than one cellular mechanism mediates Pavlovian conditioned behavior. The associative feature of this type of conditioning appears to depend mainly on the mechanism influencing CS reception (cf. Tables 11-2, 11-3, and 11-4). Because of the ablation findings shown in Figure 11-1C, that mechanism should be represented subcortically as well as cortically. The type of movement that is conditioned depends, at least in its early stages, on nonassociative presentations of the UCS and on a postsynaptic mechanism represented in the neurons of the motor cortex and in motoneurons.

Although our findings suggest that a two-stage, two-mechanism process suffices to support the type of eye-blink conditioning that was studied, it is likely that additional stages and mechanisms are involved. This is not only due to the elegant complexity of the neural mechanisms already shown to control associative conditioning in invertebrate molluscs (Alkon, 1982) but also because the presentations of CS, UCS, and DS during training may lead to sensitization,

Table 11-2. Threshold currents required to discharge neurons of pericruciate cortex in awake cats exposed to six behavioral situations

Group	Both	Eye	Nose	$\overline{0}$	Number of cells
CS only	1.1	0.9	1.1	0.9	50
UCS only	0.7[a]	0.6	0.9	0.7	63
Del UCS	0.8	0.6	0.8	0.6	55
Del CS-UCS	0.6[b]	0.6	0.9	0.6	43
CS-UCS	0.5[b]	0.7	0.9	0.5[b]	35
UCS-CS	0.6[b]	0.8	1.0	1.1	44

Note. Values are means of threshold currents (nA) of all cells studied. Muscle projections (polysynaptic) are shown above; $\overline{0}$ projects to neither eye-blink nor nose-twitch muscles. (From Brons & Woody, 1980.)

[a] $p \leq .10$.

[b] Mean threshold values that were significantly ($p < .05$) different from those seen in the CS-only group.

Table 11-3. Intracellular threshold currents, per cat, required to discharge "both" cells for six behavioral groups

Group	Thresholds
CS only	0.7
	1.0
	1.2
	1.2
	1.2
	1.5
UCS only	0.5
	0.5
	0.8
Del UCS	0.5
	0.8
	0.9
	1.0
Del CS-UCS	0.4
	0.5
	0.6
CS-UCS	0.4
	0.5
	0.5
	0.8
UCS-CS	0.5
	0.5
	0.6
	0.7

Note. Values are mean intracellular threshold currents (rank-ordered in nA) per cat required to discharge "both" (i.e., both eye and nose projective) cells for the six behavioral groups—that is, cats given CS only, UCS only, UCS only and tested after a delay of 4 weeks, forward pairings of CS and UCS and tested after delay of 4 weeks, forward pairings of CS and UCS, and backward pairings of UCS and CS. Recordings from one of the four cats in the UCS-only group did not include any neurons of "both" projections. (From Brons & Woody, 1980.)

Table 11-4. Extracellular currents required to initiate discharges

	Click	Hiss	Both	$\overline{0}$
C	1.0 (2.3)	3.6 (3.8)	2.6 (3.6)	2.7 (4.0)
R	2.0 (3.1)	2.5 (3.4)	1.9 (2.8)	3.5 (5.7)
N	5.7 (5.1)	5.9 (5.1)	5.7 (5.3)	5.5 (5.2)

Note. Values are medians (in nA), with means in parentheses. (Lines separate significantly different values.) Units are from conditioned (C), randomization (R), and naive (N) animals. Medians are the average of median scores of each cat; means are the average threshold of all units in the category. Units and their corresponding means and medians have been separated according to sensory receptive property of the unit: click, increased discharge to click; hiss, increased discharge to hiss; both, increased discharge to both click and hiss; $\overline{0}$, unresponsive to click or hiss. (From Woody, Knispel, Crow, & Black-Cleworth, 1976.)

habituation, sensory preconditioning, and second-order conditioning as well as conditioning itself (see Woody, 1982c).

The neural adaptations supporting eye-blink conditioning and analogous forms of learning are distributed over a network of sensory and motor labeled lines much like those shown in Figure 11-6 (see Woody, 1982c, for further details). The adaptations influence the probability of discharge of each neural element in response to stimuli such as the CS. The loci of adaptations with respect to the neurons' motor projections influence the type(s) of motor response that the stimuli will elicit. Further discussion of this probabilistic view of information processing along the neural circuitry of the brain may be found elsewhere (Woody, 1982c).

OTHER STUDIES

Additional investigations have been directed toward the following.

Evaluation of the role of modulators of neural changes (i.e., cyclic GMP, cyclic AMP, Ca^{++}, and Ca-calmodulin-dependent protein kinase) in neurons of the motor cortex that show increased excitability, postsynaptically,[4] *after conditioning.* Preliminary findings (Swartz & Woody, 1979; Wallis, Woody, & Gruen, 1982; Woody, Alkon, & Hay, in press; Woody, Carpenter, Gruen, Knispel, Crow, & Black-Cleworth, 1976; Woody, Swartz, & Gruen, 1978) suggest that cyclic GMP (and Cacalmodulin-dependent protein kinase) may be involved in the production of the excitability changes in the motor cortex since they both produce increases in the input resistance of neurons in this region. The increases in resistance after cyclic GMP may be made to persist if depolarization-induced spike discharges coincide with application of the cyclic nucleotide (Woody *et al.*, 1978). Intracellularly injected Ca-calmodulin-dependent protein kinase requires depolarization (presumably with calcium entry) in order for an increase in input resistance to be seen. Ca-calmodulin-dependent protein kinase appears to be a major mediator of the associative effects of pairing light and rotation on the A-current of the type B photoreceptor of *Hermissenda*. There, the necessary entry of calcium in response to depolarization has been demonstrated directly together with increased input resistance to calcium-activated Ca-calmodulin-dependent protein kinase. These effects on input resistance reflect a possible commonality in mechanisms supporting conditioning in vertebrates and invertebrates. Cyclic AMP and Ca^{++}, per se, produce decreases rather than increases in neuronal input resistance when injected intracellularly into cortical cells (Wallis *et al.*, 1982; Woody & Gruen, 1980).

Rapid acquisition of eye-blink conditioning. Our previous studies of eye-blink conditioning required 750–1000 training trials for acquisition of a blink CR, thereby preventing intracellular recording from a single neuron during the process of conditioning. (Consequently, those studies compared findings in naive animals with those in conditioned animals and in animals after extinction, after presentations of UCSs alone, and so forth.)

4. Direct, intracellular studies indicated that the changes were postsynaptic (see Brons & Woody, 1980; Woody & Black-Cleworth, 1973). Unpublished studies using an adaptive filter to perform PSP analysis (as in Figure 14 of Woody, 1967) failed to disclose supersized PSPs indicative of presynaptic superfacilitation.

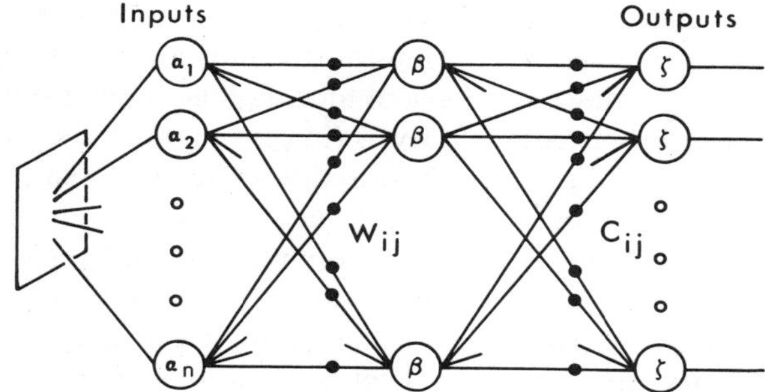

Figure 11-6. An adaptive network capable of learning (after that of Minsky & Papert, 1969). W_{ij} and C_{ij} are adaptive weightings that influence transmission and integration. Feedback circuitry is omitted from this figure, but is likely to play an important role in regulating the adaptive system (see Woody, 1982c).

Recently, using Voronin's approach (1973), it has been possible to produce eye-blink conditioning after 20 or fewer associative pairings. The manner in which electrical stimulation of the hypothalamus has been used to accelerate the development of discriminative eye-blink conditioning is described in two recent reports (Kim, Woody, & Berthier, 1983; Woody, Kim, & Berthier, 1983). The ability to record intracellularly during the conditioning process (e.g., Figure 8 of Woody *et al.*, 1983), though technically difficult, should permit us to measure input resistance directly during conditioning and test our hypothesis (Woody & Black-Cleworth, 1973) that a decrease in postsynaptic conductance occurs during conditioning that results in an increased neuronal excitability.

EFFECTS OF TECHNICAL PROCEDURES ON STUDIED CELLS

Investigators' concern over the possibility of cell injury arising from procedures used to measure cells' membrane properties intracellularly is entirely justified. Those who have studied neuronal membrane properties in single invertebrate neurons impaled with multiple electrodes or in *in vitro* preparations wherein cut or cultured sections of brain tissue are maintained artificially have, understandably, been particularly concerned with this question. So have we.

Fortunately, the chronic, awake mammal, studied *in vivo*, readily lends itself to tests of cell injury. For example, one can evaluate functionally significant cell injury by comparing patterns of unit activity elicited by weak auditory stimuli in penetrated versus unpenetrated neurons (Woody, Gruen, & McCarley, 1984). When this is done, one finds that, with the exception of intracellularly recorded units with action potentials of < 30 mV, the patterns of extracellularly (unpenetrated cells) and intracellularly (penetrated cells) recorded activity are similar. Specifically, the amounts and latency of unit activity evoked in response to click are comparable in intracellular and extracellular recordings, and the rates of baseline discharge are similar, except in cells with action potentials of < 30 mV in which baseline rates of "spontaneous" discharge are slightly higher than those of extracellularly recorded units.

All cells that are penetrated are damaged, by definition, but in most stable cortical recordings, sealing of the membrane around the penetrating electrode is such that we cannot detect injury sufficient to alter the cells' normal transfer properties. Studies examining electrophysiologic indications of injury (e.g., response to ramp depolarizing currents) and morphologic assessments of injury at both light and electron-microscopic levels (in cells marked with horseradish peroxidase) have also not disclosed abnormalities (Sakai, Sakai, & Woody, 1978; Sakai & Woody, 1980; Woody & Gruen, 1978; Woody & Vrensen, unpublished data). Recordings with action potentials of 30–50 mV and stable resting potentials are found most often to reflect penetration of dendrites remote from regions of active spike propagation. Recordings with action potentials of 70–80 mV are found to reflect penetrations of somas or, rarely,

Table 11-5. Comparison of four different conditioning preparations

	Vertebrate (eye blink)	Vertebrate (nictitating membrane)	*Hermissenda* (light avoidance)	*Aplysia* (siphon withdrawal)
Associative conditioning	Yes	Yes	(Yes)	Yes
Single cells identified	Yes	No	Yes	Yes
Relevance of neural correlates to production of conditioned behavior	Demonstrated[a]	Demonstrated[b]	Demonstrated	Not demonstrated
Training with CS and DS	Yes	+/–[c]	No	Yes
Testing with CS and DS	Yes	Yes	(Yes)	Yes
Species	Cat	Rabbit	Mollusc	Mollusc
Fixed-latency behavioral CR	Yes	Partially	Partially	No
Unit activity locked to latency and duration of behavioral response	Yes	(Yes)	(Qualitatively)	No
Intracellular (electrophysiological) studies	Yes	No	Yes	Yes
Cyclic nucleotides linked	(cGMP)	—	(cAMP)	cAMP
Ca^{++} linked	—	—	Directly demonstrated	Indirectly demonstrated
Protein-kinase-active	(Ca-calmodulin-dependent)	—	Ca-calmodulin-dependent	(cAMP-dependent)
Voltage clamp	No	No	Yes	Indirect (somatic clamp for studies of distant terminals)
Neural correlates meet lesion test	Yes[a]	Yes[b]	—	?
Protein isolates	No	No	Yes[d]	No
Analogues of conditioning studied electrophysiologically (e.g., Elec CS)	Yes[e]	No	Yes[e, f]	Yes[f]
Multiple neural mechanisms supporting conditioning demonstrated	Yes	—	[g]	?
Pre–postsynaptic	(Post)	—	Post	(Pre)

[a] For motor cortex but not for auditory association cortex.

[b] For cerebellar peduncle but not for hippocampus.

[c] Not for most electrophysiological studies.

[d] 20,000 mol. wt. protein.

[e] Intact animal.

[f] Isolated nervous system.

[g] A single, complex mechanism involving mutual interactions between decreased K^+ conductance and increased Ca^{++} conductance.

axons. Application of hyperpolarizing current results in abrupt blockage of somatic spike production and in an increase in amplitude of axonally produced spikes prior to blockage of their production.

COMPARATIVE MODELS

A comparison of the findings in our preparation with those in three other conditioning preparations is provided in Table 11-5. Detailed information concerning the other preparations and studies may be found elsewhere herein and in Woody (1982b, 1982c). Since this field of research is progressing so rapidly, some of the information in Table 11-5 compiled at the time of the preparation of this chapter will probably be out of date by the time this volume has been published.

ACKNOWLEDGMENTS

I thank my many collaborators (see references) and gratefully acknowledge the support of NSF (BNS 78-24146), AFOSR (AFOSR 81-1079), and NINCHD (HD 05958-12) in this research.

REFERENCES

Alkon, D. L. Voltage-dependent calcium and potassium ion conductances: A contingency mechanism for an associative learning model. *Science*, 1979, *205*, 810–816.

Alkon, D. L. A biophysical basis for molluscan associative learning. In C. D. Woody (Ed.), *Conditioning: Representation of involved neural functions*. New York: Plenum Press, 1982.

Berthier, N. E., & Woody, C. D. An essay on latent learning. In N. Butters & L. R. Squire (Eds.), *Neuropsychology of memory*. New York: Guilford Press, 1984.

Boneau, C. A. The interstimulus interval and the latency of the conditioned eyelid response. *Journal of Experimental Psychology*, 1958, *56*, 464–472.

Brons, J. F., & Woody, C. D. Long-term changes in excitability of cortical neurons after Pavlovian conditioning and extinction. *Journal of Neurophysiology*, 1980, *44*, 605–615.

Brons, J. F., Woody, C. D., & Allon, N. Changes in the excitability to weak intensity electrical stimulation of units of the pericruciate cortex in cats. *Journal of Neurophysiology*, 1982, *47*, 377–388.

Buchhalter, J. S., Brons, J., & Woody, C. D. Changes in cortical neuronal excitability after presentations of a compound auditory stimulus. *Brain Research*, 1978, *156*, 162–167.

Bures, J., & Buresova, O. Plastic changes of unit activity based on reinforcing properties of extracellular stimulation of single neurons. *Journal of Neurophysiology*, 1967, *30*, 98–113.

Carew, T. J., Castellucci, V. F., & Kandel, E. R. Sensitization in *Aplysia*: Restoration of transmission in synapses inactivated by long-term habituation. *Science*, 1979, *205*, 417–419.

Carew, T. J., Hawkins, R. D., & Kandel, E. R. Differential classical conditioning of a defensive withdrawal reflex in *Aplysia californica*. *Science*, 1983, *219*, 397–400.

Cohen, D. H., & Pitts, L. H. Vagal and sympathetic components of conditioned cardioacceleration in the pigeon. *Brain Research*, 1968, *9*, 14–31.

Disterhoft, J. F., Kwan, H. H., & Lo, W. D. Nictitating membrane conditioning to tone in the immobilized albino rabbit. *Brain Research*, 1977, *137*, 127–143.

Doty, R. W., Rutledge, L. T., Jr., & Larsen, R. M. Conditioned reflexes established to electrical stimulation of cat cerebral cortex. *Journal of Neurophysiology*, 1956, *19*, 401–415.

Engel, J., Jr., & Woody, C. D. Effects of character and significance of stimulus on unit activity at coronal–pericruciate cortex of cat during performance of conditioned motor response. *Journal of Neurophysiology*, 1972, *35*, 220–229.

Evarts, E. V. Pyramidal tract activity associated with a conditioned hand movement in the monkey. *Journal of Neurophysiology*, 1966, *31*, 14–27.

Gormezano, I. Classical conditioning. In J. B. Sidowski (Ed.), *Experimental methods and instrumentation in psychology*. New York: McGraw-Hill, 1966.

Gormezano, I. Investigations of defense and reward conditioning in the rabbit. In A. H. Black & W. F. Prokasy (Eds.), *Classical conditioning II: Current research and theory*. New York: Appleton-Century-Crofts, 1972.

Graham-Brown, R., & Sherrington, C. S. On the instability of a cortical point. *Proceedings of the Royal Society B*, 1912, *85*, 250–277.

Grant, D. A. Sensitization and association in eyelid conditioning. *Journal of Experimental Psychology*, 1943, *32*, 201–212.

Grant, D. A., & Norris, E. B. Eyelid conditioning as influenced by the presence of sensitized beta-responses. *Journal of Experimental Psychology*, 1947, *37*, 423–433.

Hawkins, R. D., Abrams, T. W., Carew, T. J., & Kandel, E. R. A cellular mechanism of classical conditioning in *Aplysia*: Activity-dependent amplification of presynaptic facilitation. *Science*, 1983, *219*, 400–405.

Hilgard, E. R., & Marquis, D. G. *Conditioning and learning*. New York: Appleton-Century-Crofts, 1940.

Hoffeld, D. R., Thompson, R. F., & Brogden, W. J. Effect of stimuli–time relations during preconditioning training upon the magnitude of sensory preconditioning. *Journal of Experimental Psychology*, 1958, *56*, 437–442.

Kandel, E. R. *Cellular basis of behavior*. San Francisco: Freeman, 1976.

Kandel, E. R., & Spencer, W. A. Cellular neurophysiological approaches in the study of learning. *Physiological Review*, 1968, *48*, 65–134.

Kim, E. H.-J., Woody, C. D., & Berthier, N. E. Rapid acquisition of conditioned eye blink responses in cats following pairing of an auditory CS with glabella tap US and hypothalamic stimulation. *Journal of Neurophysiology*, 1983, *49*, 767–779.

Kimble, G. A., & Dufort, R. H. The associative factor in eyelid conditioning. *Journal of Experimental Psychology*, 1956, *52*, 386–391.

Kimble, G. A., & Ost, J. W. P. A conditioned inhibitory process in eyelid conditioning. *Journal of Experimental Psychology*, 1961, *61*, 150–156.

Konorski, J. *Conditioned reflexes and neuron organization*. London and New York: Cambridge University Press, 1948.

Konorski, J., & Miller, S. Conditioned reflexes of the motor analyzer. *Trudy Laboratorii Fiziologii*, 1936, *6*, 119–278. (English summary)

Kotlyar, B. I., & Yeroshenko, T. Hypothalamic glucoreceptors: The phenomenon of plasticity. *Physiology and Behavior*, 1971, *7*, 609–615.

Matsumura, M., & Woody, C. D. Excitability changes of facial motoneurons of cats related to conditioned and unconditioned facial motor responses. In C. D. Woody (Ed.), *Conditioning: Representation of involved neural functions*. New York: Plenum Press, 1982.

Minsky, M., & Papert, S. *Perceptrons: An introduction to computational geometry*. Cambridge, Mass.: MIT Press, 1969.

Moore, J. W., Desmond, J. E., & Berthier, N. E. The metencephalic basis of the conditioned nictitating membrane response. In C. D. Woody (Ed.), *Conditioning: Representation of involved neural functions*. New York: Plenum Press, 1982.

Nahvi, M. J., Woody, C. D., Ungar, R., & Sharafat, A. R. Detection of neuroelectric signals from multiple data channels by optimum linear filter method. *Electroencephalography and Clinical Neurophysiology*, 1975, *38*, 191–198.

Norman, R. J., Villablanca, J. R., Brown, K. A., Schwafel, J. A., & Buchwald, J. S. Classical conditioning in the bilateral hemispherectomized cat. *Experimental Neurology*, 1974, *44*, 363–380.

O'Brien, J. H., & Fox, S. S. Single-cell activity in cat motor cortex: I. Modifications during classical conditioning procedures. *Journal of Neurophysiology*, 1969a, *32*, 267–284.

O'Brien, J. H., & Fox, S. S. Single-cell activity in cat motor cortex: II. Functional characteristics of the cell related to conditioning changes. *Journal of Neurophysiology*, 1969b, *32*, 285–296.

Olds, J. Hypothalamic substrates of reward. *Physiological Review*, 1962, *42*, 554–604.

Olds, J., & Hirano, T. Conditioned responses of hippocampal and other neurons. *Electroencephalography and Clinical Neurophysiology*, 1969, *26*, 159–166.

Oleson, T. D., Ashe, J. H., & Weinberger, N. M. Modification of auditory and somatosensory system activity during pupillary conditioning in the paralyzed cat. *Journal of Neurophysiology*, 1975, *38*, 1114–1139.

Pavlov, I. P. *Work of the digestive glands* (W. H. Thompson, Trans.). London: Griffin, 1910.

Pavlov, I. P. *Conditioned reflexes* (G. V. Anrep, Trans. & Ed.). London: Oxford University Press, 1927.

Ricci, G., Doane, B., & Jasper, H. Microelectrode studies of conditioning: Technique and preliminary results. *International Congress of Neurological Science*, 1957, *1*, 401–417.

Sakai, H., & Woody, C. D. Identification of auditory responsive cells in the coronal–pericruciate cortex of awake cats. *Journal of Neurophysiology*, 1980, *44*, 223–231.

Sakai, M., Sakai, H., & Woody, C. Sampling distribution of morphologically identified neurons of the coronal–pericruciate cortex of awake cats following intracellular injection of HRP. *Brain Research*, 1978, *152*, 329–333.

Skinner, B. F. *The behavior of organisms: An experimental analysis*. New York: Appleton-Century-Crofts, 1938.

Spence, K. W., & Norris, E. B. Eyelid conditioning as a function of the inter-trial interval. *Journal of Experimental Psychology*, 1950, *40*, 716–720.

Spencer, W. A., Thompson, R. F., & Neilson, D. R., Jr. Alteration in responsiveness of ascending and reflex pathways activated by iterated cutaneous afferent volleys. *Journal of Neurophysiology*, 1966a, *29*, 240–252.

Spencer, W. A., Thompson, R. F., & Neilson, D. R., Jr. Decrement of ventral root electrotonus and intracellularly recorded PSPs produced by iterated cutaneous afferent volleys. *Journal of Neurophysiology*, 1966b, *29*, 253–274.

Spencer, W. A., Thompson, R. F., & Neilson, D. R., Jr. Response decrement of the flexion reflex in the acute spinal cat and transient restoration by strong stimuli. *Journal of Neurophysiology*, 1966c, *29*, 221–239.

Swartz, B. E., & Woody, C. D. Correlated effects of acetylcholine and cyclic guanosine monophosphate on membrane properties of mammalian neocortical neurons. *Journal of Neurobiology*, 1979, *10*, 465–488.

Thompson, R. F., Berger, T. W., Berry, S. D., Clark, G. A., Kettner, R. N., Lavond, D. G., Mauk, M. D., McCormick, D. A., Solomon, P. R., & Weisz, D. J. Neuronal substrates of learning and memory: Hippocampus and other structures. In C. D. Woody (Ed.), *Conditioning: Representation of involved neural functions*. New York: Plenum Press, 1982.

Thompson, R. F., Berger, T. W., Cegavske, C. F., Patterson, M. M., Roemer, R. A., Teyler, T. J., & Young, R. A. The search for the engram. *American Psychologist*, 1976, *31*, 209–227.

Thorndike, E. L. *Educational psychology: The psychology of learning* (Vol. 2). New York: Teachers College, 1913.

Tsukahara, N., Oda, Y., & Notsu, T. Classical conditioning mediated by the red nucleus in the cat. *Journal of Neuroscience*, 1981, *1*, 72–79.

Voronin, L. L., Gerstein, G. Y., Ioffe, S. V., & Kudrioshov, I. E. A rapidly elaborated conditioned reflex with simultaneous recording of neuronal activity. *Zhurnal Vysshei Nervnoi Deiatelnosti*, 1973, *23*, 636–639.

Wallis, R. A., Woody, C. D., & Gruen, E. Effects of intracellular pressure injections of calcium ions in morphologically identified neurons of cat motor cortex. *Society for Neuroscience Abstracts*, 1982, *8*, 909.

Walters, E. T., & Byrne, J. H. Associative conditioning of single sensory neurons suggests a cellular mechanism for learning. *Science*, 1983, *219*, 405–408.

Walters, E. T., Carew, T. J., Hawkins, R. D., & Kandel, E. R. Classical conditioning in *Aplysia*: Neuronal circuits involved in associative learning. In C. D. Woody (Ed.), *Conditioning: Representation of involved neural functions*. New York: Plenum Press, 1982.

Woody, C. D. Characterization of an adaptive filter for the analysis of variable latency neuroelectric signals. *Medical and Biological Engineering*, 1967, *5*, 539–553.

Woody, C. D. Conditioned eye blink: Gross potential activity at coronal–pericruciate cortex of the cat. *Journal of Neurophysiology*, 1970, *33*, 838–850.

Woody, C. D. Aspects of the electrophysiology of cortical processes related to the development and performance of learned motor responses. *The Physiologist*, 1974, *17*, 49–69.

Woody, C. D. Changes in activity and excitability of cortical auditory receptive units of the cat as a function of different behavioral states. *Annals of the New York Academy of Sciences*, 1977, *290*, 180–199.

Woody, C. D. Acquisition of conditioned facial reflexes in the cat: Cortical control of different facial movements. *Federation Proceedings*, 1982a, *41*, 2160–2168.

Woody, C. D. (Ed.). *Conditioning: Representation of involved neural functions*. New York: Plenum Press, 1982b.

Woody, C. D. *Memory, learning, and higher function: A cellular view*. New York: Springer, 1982c.

Woody, C. D. Neurophysiologic correlates of latent facilitation. In C. D. Woody (Ed.), *Conditioning: Representation of involved neural functions*. New York: Plenum Press, 1982d.

Woody, C. D. The electrical excitability of nerve cells as an index of learned behavior. In D. L. Alkon & J. Farley (Eds.), *Primary neural substrates of learning and behavioral change*. Cambridge: Cambridge University Press, in press.

Woody, C. D., Alkon, D. L., & Hay, B. Depolarization-induced effects of Ca^{2+}-calmodulin dependent protein kinase injection, *in vivo*, in single neurons of cat motor cortex. *Brain Research*, in press.

Woody, C. D., & Black-Cleworth, P. Differences in excitability of cortical neurons as a function of motor projection in conditioned cats. *Journal of Neurophysiology*, 1973, *36*, 1104–1116.

Woody, C. D., & Brozek, G. Changes in evoked responses from facial nucleus of cat with conditioning and extinction of an eye blink. *Journal of Neurophysiology*, 1969a, *32*, 717–726.

Woody, C. D., & Brozek, G. Gross potential from facial nucleus of cat as an index of neural activity in response to glabella tap. *Journal of Neurophysiology*, 1969b, *32*, 704–716.

Woody, C. D., Carpenter, D. O., Gruen, E., Knispel, J. D., Crow, T. W., & Black-Cleworth, P. Persistent increases in membrane resistance of neurons in cat motor cortex. *AFRRI Scientific Report*, 1976, *SR 76-1*, 1–31.

Woody, C. D., & Engel, J., Jr. Changes in unit activity and thresholds to electrical microstimulation at coronal–pericruciate cortex of cat with classical conditioning of different facial movements. *Journal of Neurophysiology*, 1972, *35*, 230–241.

Woody, C. D., & Gruen, E. Characterization of electrophysiological properties of intracellularly recorded neurons in the neocortex of awake cats: A comparison of the response to injected current in spike overshoot neurons. *Brain Research*, 1978, *158*, 343–357.

Woody, C. D., & Gruen, E. Effects of cyclic nucleotides on morphologically identified cortical neurons of cats. *Proceedings of the International Union of Physiological Sciences*, 1980, *14*, 789.

Woody, C. D., Gruen, E., & McCarley, K. Intradendritic recordings from neurons of motor cortex of cats. *Journal of Neurophysiology*, 1984, *51*, 925–938.

Woody, C. D., Kim, E. H.-J., & Berthier, N. E. Effects of hypothalamic stimulation on unit responses recorded from neurons of sensorimotor cortex of awake cats during conditoning. *Journal of Neurophysiology*, 1983, *49*, 780–791.

Woody, C. D., Knispel, J. D., Crow, T. J., & Black-Cleworth, P. Activity and excitability to electrical current of cortical auditory receptive neurons of awake cats as affected by stimulus association. *Journal of Neurophysiology*, 1976, *39*, 1045–1061.

Woody, C. D., & Nahvi, M. Application of optimum linear filter theory to the detection of cortical signals preceding facial movement in cat. *Experimental Brain Research*, 1973, *16*, 455–465.

Woody, C. D., Swartz, B. E., & Gruen, E. Effects of acetylcholine and cyclic GMP on input resistance of cortical neurons in awake cats. *Brain Research*, 1978, *158*, 373–395.

Woody, C. D., Vassilevsky, N. N., & Engel, J., Jr. Conditioned eye blink: Unit activity at coronal–precruciate cortex of the cat. *Journal of Neurophysiology*, 1970, *33*, 851–864.

Woody, C. D., & Vrensen, G. Unpublished data.

Woody, C. D., & Yarowsky, P. J. Conditioned eye blink using electrical stimulation of coronal–precruciate cortex as conditional stimulus. *Journal of Neurophysiology*, 1972, *35*, 242–252.

Woody, C. D., Yarowsky, P., Owens, J., Black-Cleworth, P., & Crow, T. Effect of lesions of cortical motor areas on acquisition of eyeblink in the cat. *Journal of Neurophysiology*, 1974, *37*, 385–394.

Woolacott, M. H., & Hoyle, G. Membrane resistance changes associated with single, identified neuron learning. *Society for Neuroscience Abstracts*, 1976, *2*, 339.

Yoshii, N., Matsumoto, J., Maeno, S., Hasegawa, Y., Yamaguchi, Y., Shimokochi, M., Hori, Y., & Yamazaki, H. Conditioned reflex and electroencephalography. *Medical Journal of Osaka University*, 1958, *9*, 353–375.

Yoshii, N., & Ogura, H. Studies on the unit discharge of brainstem reticular formation in the cat: I. Changes of reticular unit discharge following conditioned procedure. *Medical Journal of Osaka University*, 1960, *11*, 1–17.

CHAPTER TWELVE

Initial Events in Conditioning: Plasticity in the Pupillomotor and Auditory Systems

NORMAN M. WEINBERGER / DAVID M. DIAMOND / THOMAS M. MCKENNA

INTRODUCTION

Scope

This chapter concerns some initial events during Pavlovian defensive conditioning in the cat. Our approach involves identification of some of the earliest behavioral and neurophysiological manifestations of associative learning, as defined by the development of a conditioned response and of discharge plasticity, respectively. We operationally define "early" associative events as those that develop rapidly, in a small number of trials during the pairing of a conditioned stimulus (CS) and unconditioned stimulus (UCS). We have not attempted to delineate all of the initial behavioral and neurophysiological plastic events during conditioning, a task far beyond our means; nor can we review here all previous reports of early events in conditioning. The behavioral manifestations of learning are taken from the pupillomotor system, in which conditioned dilation is seen to conform to all of the major Pavlovian laws of association. Neurophysiological events discussed here are limited to the auditory system, which is the sensory system of the acoustic CS. Therefore, our approach is *stimulus*-oriented rather than *response*-oriented. We view our studies as complementary to attempts to determine the neural circuitry underlying one or another conditioned response, and to inquiries into the cellular mechanisms of learning, as exemplified in the research discussed in several other chapters of this volume.

We begin with a brief historical overview, including a perspective on the lack of integration between sensory neurobiology and the neurobiology of learning and memory, followed by discussion of pioneering studies of learning

Norman M. Weinberger, David M. Diamond, and Thomas M. McKenna. Center for the Neurobiology of Learning and Memory and Department of Psychobiology, University of California, Irvine, California.

and the auditory system. After setting forth our own findings, we conclude with comments on the relationship of our approach to other approaches, and a discussion of the roles of associative physiological plasticity in sensory systems.

Some History

Sensory Sciences and Learning Sciences

The processes by which the brain acquires, stores, and uses information are central to brain function and behavioral adaptation. Discovery of the principles and mechanisms that yield learning and memory present some of the greatest challenges to neurobiology. As evident both historically and in the current literature, difficult problems, particularly those as broad and complex as the neurobiology of learning and memory, have been and continue to be attacked by various approaches; although this is not requisite, they also tend to be isolated from each other. This division of labor demands a synthesis ultimately, of course. But the empirical and conceptual isolation may also engender a heavy cost. For example, the fields of sensory neurobiology and learning have followed largely independent paths. Thus, sensory processes have been ignored in most inquiries into the neural bases of learning and memory. Incidentally, the neurobiology of learning and memory has been ignored to an even greater extent by the sensory sciences.

The study of sensory processes in neurobiology has a long, honorable, and fruitful tradition. Much fundamental knowledge of the structure and function of nervous systems has been derived directly or indirectly from sensory neurobiology. A major advantage of research in sensory physiology is that the experimenter can usually designate and control stimuli, which are then transduced by appropriate receptors. Thus, the neurons from which recordings are obtained receive the effects of normal, physiological operations, in contrast to sequelae of electrical stimulation of the brain. A second major attraction of sensory neurobiology is that the major function of the system under investigation is generally self-evident. The experimenter need only ascertain how the system accomplishes its function—a difficult task, to be sure. The same cannot be said with as much certainty for many other regions or systems within the brain.

These factors, which have provided sensory neurobiology with so solid a foundation and so sure a place, also may have promoted its isolation from the mainstream study of learning and memory. Although we cannot discuss the reasons for this situation in detail, we offer two possible explanations: successes in sensory neurophysiology and a lack of appropriate conceptual frameworks in learning.

During the past three decades, sensory physiology has found many invariant relationships between stimulus parameters and the responses of single neurons, especially in the anesthetized brain. While important, such data are not likely to promote conceptualizations about the dynamic role of sensory systems in learning. The successes of sensory neurobiology in attaining some reasonable explanations of how the nervous system represents the environment have in some sense underscored the apparent stability of sensory systems. In so doing, they have reinforced the view that learning and memory begin where sensory analysis leaves off. Plasticity as a property of sensory systems would seem to be antithetical to and incompatible with the requirement that organisms obtain a valid picture of the world in which they live.

A second possible reason for the virtual absence of sensory function in conceptualizations of the neurobiology of learning and memory is that plasticity in sensory systems fits neither into an accepted theoretical framework of learning nor even into an obvious behavioral function, beyond providing environmental information. This contrasts sharply with, for example, the hippocampus, as exemplified by the case of H. M. (Milner, Corkin, & Teuber, 1968). Rather, learning-related changes in sensory system responses have been viewed either as evidence of distributed memory systems (e.g., John, 1967) or merely as signs of learning, isolated findings. To this day, little thought and less investigation have been directed to the issue of the functional significance of learning-related sensory plasticity. What role do such changes play in the life of an organism?

The isolation of sensory physiology from the study of learning and memory is ironic, because the first neurophysiological sign of learning was the serendipitous finding of conditioned blocking of the alpha rhythm in sensory cortex, specifically in the visual cortex of man (Durup & Fessard, 1935). For almost two decades following World War II, during the initial period of intensive neurophysiological investigation of learning, virtually every relevant study of sensory systems—particularly, auditory, somatosensory, and visual cortex—reported that associative learning was accompanied by the development of alterations in the electroencephalogram (EEG) and evoked potentials (EPs) during presentation of a CS. Reviews of this early period have been provided by John (1967) and Morrell (1961).

There now appears to be renewed interest in sensory systems and learning. Recent success in the study of sites of learning-induced plasticity in two invertebrates both have implicated initial levels of sensory systems. Eric Kandel and his associates (1978) have reported that habituation of gill withdrawal in *Aplysia* is due to a presynaptic change, specifically to a decrement in transmitter release. Although most attention has been focused on the presynaptic nature of the effect, the locus of change is in first-order sensory neurons that make monosynaptic contact with motor neurons.

As for associative learning, remarkably, a peripheral sensory site has now been identified as the locus of change in another invertebrate. Daniel Alkon and his associates have found that classical conditioning to light followed by bodily rotation in *Hermissenda* involves a change in the responsivity of the photoreceptors (Alkon, 1982). Such a peripheral locus of change apparently is not the case in vertebrates. For example, during acoustic–somatic classical conditioning in the cat, the auditory system receptor potential, the cochlear microphonic, is unaffected by associative processes (Ashe, Cassady, & Weinberger, 1976), in contrast to higher levels of the auditory system (see the next section). Evolutionary encephalization of learning-related plasticity in sensory systems is consistent with these findings, but there are insufficient data to make a strong case now.

As pointed out above, there is a long history of reports that sensory system responses to signal stimuli are altered during learning in mammals. However, until the past decade, analytic studies were lacking. It is interesting that more recently, three different approaches to the study of vertebrate conditioning all have been led to focus on sensory system plasticity during associative learning.

David Cohen and his colleagues have been tracing the neural circuitry underlying the conditioned cardiac response in pigeons, using a visual CS (Cohen, 1974). They have found that the first locus of change in the circuit from the eye to the heart is in the visual system itself, in the avian lateral geniculate nucleus (Cohen, 1982).

The approach of the late James Olds and his colleagues was quite different. Instead of attempting to delineate a circuit underlying acquired behavior, they sought the loci that developed the shortest-latency associative responses during a hybrid classical–instrumental appetitive conditioning task in the rat (Olds, Disterhoft, Segal, Kornblith, & Hirsh, 1972). They were led to the sensory system of the CS, the auditory system (Disterhoft & Stuart, 1976; Olds, Nienhuis, & Olds, 1978; Birt, Nienhuis, & Olds, 1979; Birt & Olds, 1981).

Our own approach has sought brain sites in which associatively induced discharge plasticity developed in the fewest number of conditioning trials during acoustic–somatic defensive conditioning in the cat. These studies identified sites in the thalamo-cortical auditory system. Details of this line of inquiry are provided in a later section. (See also Weinberger, 1984.)

The major point we wish to emphasize at this juncture is that investigators who have sought critical sites of physiological plasticity during learning in widely differing organisms, using diverse behavioral situations and employing a variety of conceptual strategies, have implicated the sensory system of the signal stimulus. Within vertebrates the auditory system has been studied most extensively, and so we now turn to a brief review of this line of investigation.

Auditory System: Early Studies and Control Problems

Initial studies of the effects of classical conditioning reported that EPs to an acoustic CS increased at all levels of the auditory system (i.e., cochlear nucleus, superior olive, inferior colliculus, medial geniculate, and auditory cortex) during acquisition of conditioned behavioral responses (CRs), compared to a prior period of quiescence (Galambos & Sheatz, 1962; Galambos, Sheatz, & Vernier, 1955; Gerken & Neff, 1963; Hearst, Beer, Sheatz, & Galambos, 1960; Jouvet, 1956; Marsh, McCarthy, Sheatz, & Galambos, 1961; Moushegian, Rupert, Marsh, & Galambos, 1961; Popova, 1969). These findings were generally interpreted to indicate that associative learning per se causes increases in auditory system evoked activity. However, these studies failed to appreciate the need to control for (1) general level of arousal, (2) stimulus intensity, and (3) feedback from CRs.

Regarding arousal, general excitability increases when a reward or punishment (UCS) is introduced after a period of quiescence. Thus, changes in evoked activity could reflect merely an increase in arousal level during the pairing of an acoustic stimulus with a reinforcer (Berlucchi, Munson, & Rizzolatti, 1968; Hall & Mark, 1967; Mark & Hall, 1967; Wickelgren, 1968). Appropriate control procedures for changes in arousal, which could produce sensitization or pseudoconditioning, have been incorporated into recent experiments. Two major controls involve presentation of the CS and UCS in a random (Rescorla, 1967) or strictly unpaired (Furedy, 1971; Furedy, Poulos, & Schiffman, 1975) relationship, as well as CS-UCS pairing. More complex controls are also available, for example, discrimination between a reinforced (CS+) and a nonreinforced (CS−) stimulus and single or repeated reversals of the discrimination (Pavlov, 1927). These are elegant ways of demonstrating not only associative effects but additionally that the effects are not restricted to the particular combinations of CS and UCS employed (LoLordo, 1979).

Given controls for nonassociative effects, learning-induced changes in the auditory system could be secondary to changes in effective stimulus intensity at the cochlea. For example, animals often approach the sound source of a CS during training (Pavlov, 1927), and the position of the subject has a large effect on ERs (Marsh, Worden, & Hicks, 1962). Three other sources of variability have been identified: (1) sound-shadowing by the pinna (Wiener, Pfeiffer, & Backus, 1966), (2) action of the middle ear muscles (Baust, Berlucchi, & Moruzzi, 1964; Carmel & Starr, 1963; Galambos & Rupert, 1959), and (3) masking noise produced by the subjects' own movements (Baust & Berlucchi, 1964; Imig & Weinberger, 1970; Irvine & Webster, 1972; see also Starr, 1964). The use of earphones may insure stimulus constancy in the external auditory meatus but does not control for the other two major sources of variance. All four sources can be controlled simultaneously by neuromuscular paralysis. As an alternative, Disterhoft and Stuart (1976) reported extremely short-latency discriminated neuronal responses in the inferior colliculus of freely moving rats (but see Birt & Olds, 1981). These results cannot be explained by changes in effective stimulus intensity. However, such findings are extremely rare, and the stringency of the latency criterion precludes discovery of associative events with a latency greater than a few milliseconds.

Even with controls for nonassociative factors and stimulus constancy, there remains the problem of feedback from the behavioral CR itself. Almost all behaviors have sensory consequences that will be highly correlated with the development of a CR, leading to the apparent, but not real, development of a neural correlate in regions of the brain that receive the influence of such feedback. This problem can be solved by restricting the period of neuronal data analysis to a very brief interval preceding the performance of any CR (Olds *et al.*, 1972), but this excludes important neuronal events that might occur with longer latencies. An alternative is to eliminate feedback from the CR.

The problems of stimulus constancy and elimination of feedback during auditory electrophysiological experiments both have been solved by training animals under neuromuscular blockade (Buchwald, Halas, & Schramm, 1966). This is the tactic that we adopted; it led to a focus on early events in the acquisition of behavioral CRs.

RAPIDLY ACQUIRED CONDITIONED RESPONSES

Introduction

The use of neuromuscular blockade had been a valuable tool in the analysis of learning and also for neurophysiology. For example, neuromuscular blockade has been used as a critical test of the role of response-produced feedback in the acquisition of behavioral CRs (Black, 1965) and to eliminate musculoskeletal activities in the study of instrumental conditioning (Koslovskaya, Vertes, &

Miller, 1973). Neurophysiological studies of conditioning have recorded from animals trained under neuromuscular blockade and then compared these findings to behavioral skeletal CRs acquired in the absence of blockade (O'Brien & Packham, 1973). However, classically conditioned autonomic responses are acquired under blockade, so it is feasible to record neuronal discharges during the acquisition of behavioral CRs.

The restriction to autonomic response systems in this case proved to be fortuitous, because autonomic conditioning is extremely rapid. In fact, autonomic CRs develop more rapidly than do commonly recorded somatic CRs that are specific to the nature of the UCS. A more detailed discussion has been presented previously (Weinberger, 1982), but a summary at this point will prove helpful.

Two-Factor Views of Learning: A Brief Overview

There have been several theoretical positions that learning, particularly conditioning, is best understood as a nonunitary process. Earlier formulations have been reviewed by Rescorla and Solomon (1967). Briefly, Schlosberg (1937) distinguished between classical (Pavlovian) conditioning and instrumental (Thorndikian) conditioning on the basis of the nature of the CRs that developed in each situation. The former were said to be "diffuse," "preparatory," and of an "emotional" character, whereas the latter were characterized as "precise" and "adaptive." Mowrer's original two-factor theory distinguished between "visceral" and "skeletal motor," the former being "problem posing," the latter, "problem solving." Furthermore, he asserted that the former are classically conditioned and are necessary for the subsequent acquisition of instrumental problem-solving CRs (Mowrer, 1947). Solomon and Wynne (1954) pointed out that both visceral and skeletal motor responses are elaborated during classical conditioning, and subsequent research on specific somatic responses, such as the nictitating membrane (NM) response (Gormezano, Schneiderman, Deaux, & Fuentes, 1962), clearly established that skeletal motor responses are readily established during classical conditioning, in the absence of detectable instrumental contingencies.

The rate of acquisition of CRs is of interest for both behavioral and neurobehavioral reasons, not the least of which is that the most rapidly developing learning-induced changes in brain function are candidates for causal roles in physiological plasticity that develops more slowly. In a brief review of defensive classical conditioning, Weinberger (1982) pointed out that one cluster of CRs is acquired more rapidly than another cluster. However, the distinction was not purely along the lines of a visceral–somatic cleavage. Rather, rapidly acquired CRs all could be characterized as being "nonspecific" to the particular nature of the UCS. In other words, these CRs were found to develop in all classical conditioning studies in which they were recorded, regardless of whether the UCSs were electrodermal stimulation (EDS) to the leg or body, EDS or airpuff to the eye, and so forth. Such nonspecific CRs include all visceral (autonomic) CRs—that is, pupillary dilation, the galvanic skin response (GSR), and changes in heart rate and blood pressure, and also some skeletal motor responses such as changes in respiration and general motor "restlessness." In contrast, more slowly acquired CRs proved to be somatomotor and were all highly specific to the particular UCS employed. These responses include the NM response, eye blink, nose twitch, and leg flexion (Table 12-1). Thus, EDS to the leg results in leg-flexion CRs, not eye-blink CRs; airpuff to the eye results in acquisition of an eye-blink or NM anticipatory response, but not flexion. However, the nonspecific responses are acquired in both cases, and they are acquired first. This is seen most clearly when both types of responses are recorded simultaneously (e.g., Schneiderman, 1972). Under optimal training conditions, specific responses such as the NM response can be acquired in as few as 30 trials (Disterhoft, Chapter 15, this volume). But the issue is whether or not nonspecific responses are acquired before specific CRs under all conditions. If so, they may be necessary for the subsequent development of the specific "problem-solving" CRs, as claimed by Mowrer (1947) and elaborated by Konorski (1967).

A more precise statement of the issue is whether the central neural state(s) that is (are) reflected in the elicitation of nonspecific CRs plays a causal role in the development of specific somatic CRs. The issue remains open. Some relevant findings are provided by Thompson *et al.* (Chapter 9, this volume), who have proposed a three-factor theory, the third factor being "cognitive" or "recognition memory."

Table 12-1. Rates of classical conditioning of various response systems

Response system	Rate (trials)[a]	Subject	References[b]
"Nonspecific"			
GSR	5–10	Cat	Van Twyver & King (1969).
	5–10	Rat	Holdstock & Schwartzbaum (1965)
Pupil	5–12	Cat	Ashe, Cassady, & Weinberger (1976), Ashe, Cooper, & Weinberger (1978b), Gerall & Obrist (1962), Oleson, Westenberg, & Weinberger (1972)
Blood pressure	10–15	Rabbit	Yehle, Dauth, & Schneiderman (1967)
Nonspecific motor	10–15	Rat	deToledo & Black (1966), Parrish (1967)
Respiration	5–10	Lizard	Davidson & Richardson (1970)
	10–15	Rabbit	Yehle *et al.* (1967)
Heart	5–10	Lizard	Davidson & Richardson (1970)
	10	Rabbit	Yehle *et al.* (1967)
	11–20	Pigeon	Cohen (1974)
	24–36	Rat	deToledo & Black (1966)
"Specific"			
Nictitating membrane	70–164	Rabbit	Gormezano, Scheiderman, Deaux, & Fuentes (1962)
Eyelid (airpuff)	160–240	Rabbit	Schneiderman, Fuentes, & Gormezano (1962)
Limb flexion	125–300	Cat	Bruner (1969), O'Brien & Packham (1973)
Eyelid (glabella tap)	600–900	Cat	Woody & Brozek (1969)

[a] Earliest consistent CRs. In cases where the authors did not specify the rate of learning, estimates were obtained from the published data or authors' comments.

[b] References cited are representative and do not constitute an exhaustive list.

In any event, the fact that autonomic response systems develop CRs rapidly provides an opportunity to seek initial neurophysiological manifestations of learning during the acquisition of a behavioral CR.

Plasticity in the Pupillomotor System

The nonspecific autonomic pupillary conditioned dilation response is particularly convenient and reliable in the cat (Gerall & Obrist, 1962).[1] We chose this response system and preparation as a means simultaneously to control for nonassociative factors, insure stimulus constancy, and eliminate response-produced feedback. In addition, this preparation permits the continuous recording of the discharges of single neurons during acquisition of a behavioral CR.

Preliminary to concurrent neurophysiological studies, it was first necessary to characterize fully the pupillary dilation response, to insure that it shares with somatic CRs the properties of accepted, genuine CRs. Cats were trained using various acoustic stimuli as CSs (in some studies tactile stimuli were also used as CSs) and EDS to a forelimb as the UCS. Pupillary dilation was recorded by an infrared pupillometer of our design (Cassady, Farley, Weinberger, & Kitzes, 1982). Full characterization of this response revealed that it does indeed exhibit all of the major behavioral characteristics that were originally discovered by Pavlov: acquisition, extinction, discrimination both within and between modalities, discrimination reversal, conditioned inhibition, inhibition of delay, and also habituation and dishabituation (Ashe *et al.*, 1976; Cooper, Ashe, & Weinberger, 1978; Oleson, Westenberg, & Weinberger, 1972; Oleson, Vododnick, & Weinberger, 1973; Oleson, Ashe, & Weinberger, 1975; Ryugo & Weinberger, 1978; Weinberger, Oleson, & Haste, 1973; Weinberger, Oleson, & Ashe, 1975). An example of a group pupillary dilation learning curve is presented in Figure 12-1.

The behavioral data provided the basis for determining the extent to which early neurophysiological signs of learning develop in the system that first processes the CS, the auditory system.

DISCHARGE PLASTICITY IN THE AUDITORY SYSTEM

Multiple-Unit Studies

In order to determine if the auditory system developed response plasticity due to associative processes, our initial study was designed to obtain recordings from the highest (cortical) and lowest (cochlear nucleus) levels of the auditory system during acquisition, discrimination, and discrimination reversal. Because it is not feasible to establish all of these behavioral phenomena in a single training session, it was not possible to record the discharges of the same single neuron throughout training. Therefore, we used multiple-unit recordings, obtained with low-impedance microelectrodes, chronically implanted in primary

1. Pupillary size has been employed as a reliable measure of cognitive processes in humans, for example, in memory load (Kahneman & Beatty, 1966), problem solving (Bradshaw, 1968), and information processing (Simpson & Hale, 1969).

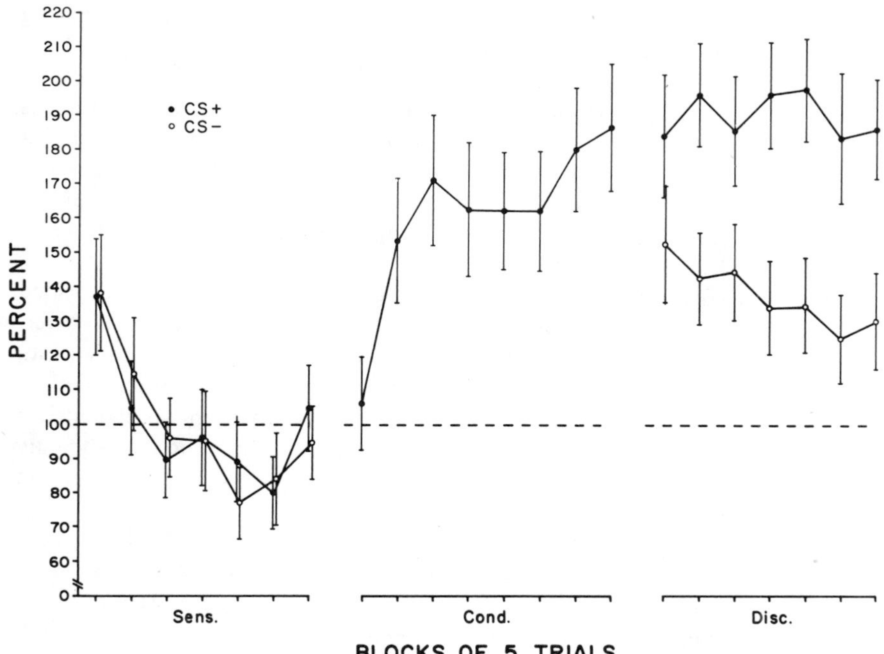

Figure 12-1. Pupillary dilation to two acoustic stimuli (CS+ and CS−) during sensitization (unpaired acoustic and electrodermal stimulation), conditioning (CS+ paired with EDS), and discrimination (reinforced CS +, unreinforced CS −). Each point is the mean (±*SE*) dilation response for a group of 12 cats. The control level of 100% is the mean sensitization value. Note the rapid acquisition of the pupillary CR during the first 10 trials (two blocks) of conditioning. (From Ashe, Cooper, & Weinberger, 1978a.)

auditory cortex (AI) and the ventral cochlear nucleus (VCN). In AI, differential plasticity of evoked discharges developed rapidly, to reinforced (CS+) and nonreinforced (CS−) acoustic stimuli during the acquisition of a differential pupillary dilation CR (Oleson *et al.*, 1975). These effects underwent reversal 1 week later, when the reinforcement contingencies were reversed. The VCN displayed similar effects, but its discharge plasticity developed after that of AI on a within-subject basis. Interestingly, the effects of differential conditioning were still evident in both pupillary behavior and evoked discharges in the auditory cortex 1 week after initial training but were no longer present in the cochlear nucleus. The rates of acquisition to criterion were not significantly different: median trials = 9 for pupil and 14 for auditory cortex.

These findings indicated that the responses of the auditory system to physically constant acoustic stimuli are governed by their associative value. Further, discharge plasticity at the highest level of the system and the behavioral CR both develop rapidly and so comprise some of the initial events during classical conditioning.

Although these findings under highly controlled conditions strongly indicated that the associative effects in the auditory system were due to central processes, a more direct test was to measure the receptor potential, the cochlear microphonic, during pupillary conditioning. We found no systematic changes in this potential during conditioning (Ashe *et al.*, 1976), thus excluding peripheral sources of response change during learning.

Having identified the AI as a site of rapidly developing associative changes, we next investigated its thalamic sources of input, the medial geniculate nucleus (MGN). The organization of this nucleus is complex. It has three major subdivisions—the ventral, dorsal, and magnocellular (medial)—on the basis of cyto- and myeloarchitectonics, Golgi impregnation, afferents, and efferents (Morest, 1964, 1965a, 1965b; Ramón y Cajal, 1966; Oliver & Hall, 1975; Ryugo & Killackey, 1974).

The ventral division (MGv) is characterized by (1) neurons with restricted receptive fields (Aitkin & Webster, 1972), (2) tonotopic (Aitkin & Webster, 1972; Calford & Webster, 1981) and laminar (Morest, 1965a) organization, (3) a functionally homogeneous and topographic input from the central nucleus of the inferior colliculus (Jones & Rockel, 1971), (4) medium-sized neurons with "tufted" dendrites (Morest, 1964) typical of specific thalamic sensory relay nuclei (Scheibel & Scheibel, 1966), and (5) a dense and topographic projection to AI (Colwell & Merzenich, 1975; Niimi & Naito, 1974).

In contrast, the magnocellular division (MGm) is characterized by (1) neurons with wide receptive field properties (Erickson, Jane, Waite, & Diamond, 1964; Erickson, Hall, Jane, Snyder, & Diamond, 1967; Poggio & Mountcastle, 1960; Wepsic, 1966), (2) a lack of tonotopic (Aitkin, 1973; Love & Scott, 1969) or laminar (Morest, 1965a) organization, (3) a functionally heterogeneous input, including medial lemniscal (Jane & Schroeder, 1971; Schroeder & Jane, 1971), and brachial from the inferior colliculus (Moore & Goldberg, 1963, 1966), (4) large neurons with "radiate" or isodendrites, characteristic of regions receiving heterogeneous input (Morest, 1964; Ramon-Moliner, 1962; 1975), and (5) projections throughout the auditory cortex in a diffuse and widespread fashion (Heath & Jones, 1971; Rose & Woolsey, 1958; Ryugo & Killackey, 1974; Winer, Diamond, & Raczkowski, 1977; Herkenham, 1980).

The dorsal division (MGd) has (1) medium-size neurons with evenly spaced radiating dendrites (Morest, 1964), (2) cells that are responsive to acoustic stimulation (Aitkin & Webster, 1972; Lippe & Weinberger, 1973), (3) input from the diffusely arranged lateral tegmental system (Morest, 1965b), nucleus sagulum, and external nucleus of the inferior colliculus (Calford & Aitkin, 1983), and (4) cortical targets in auditory fields other than AI (Raczkowski, Diamond, & Winer, 1975; Rose & Woolsey, 1958).

The anatomical and physiological characteristics of these subdivisions indicate that the MGv is part of the lemniscal auditory system, whereas the MGm and MGd are lemniscal adjuncts (Calford & Aitkin, 1983; Graybiel, 1972, 1974). Figure 12-2 presents a camera lucida reconstruction of the MGN from three adjacent Golgi sections.

We recorded multiple-unit activity within the MGN during acquisition and discriminative conditioning of the pupillary dilation response. Only the MGm developed discharge plasticity during acquisition and discrimination learning involving two acoustic stimuli (Ryugo & Weinberger, 1976, 1978). The restriction of plasticity to the MGm was clearly established, because simultaneous recordings from the MGv and MGd yielded no plasticity. A histological summary of these findings is presented in Figure 12-3; open circles denote plastic sites. Note that plasticity was obtained only in the MGm.

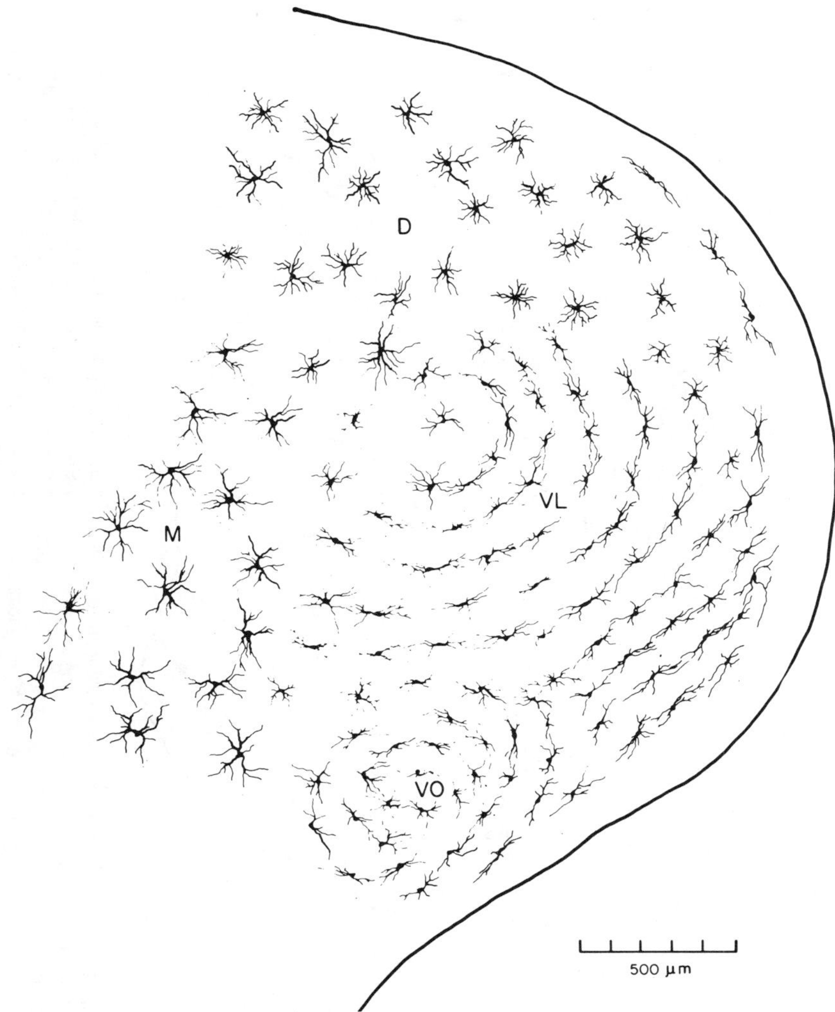

Figure 12-2. Camera lucida reconstruction of the medial geniculate nucleus from Golgi material. Typical distribution of neuronal types through the middle of the MGN of the adult cat. Coronal section, Golgi-Cox. Abbreviations: D, dorsal; M, magnocellular; VL, ventral pars lateralis; VO, ventral pars ovoida. (From Ryugo & Weinberger, 1978.)

In two cases, plasticity failed to develop in the MGm, but these were the only cats in which a pupillary CR did not develop. Therefore, these particular negative findings were obtained from "inadequate" (stupid?) preparations and cannot be interpreted simply as examples of nonplasticity in the MGm. These findings illustrate the importance of having a behavioral control for interpreting negative findings and demonstrate a close relationship between structure and functional plasticity during classical conditioning.

Similar results have been obtained in two other laboratories. Gabriel, Miller, and Saltwick (1976) found multiple-unit CRs in the MGm but not in the MGv of the MGN of the rabbit during instrumental conditioning. M. Olds and

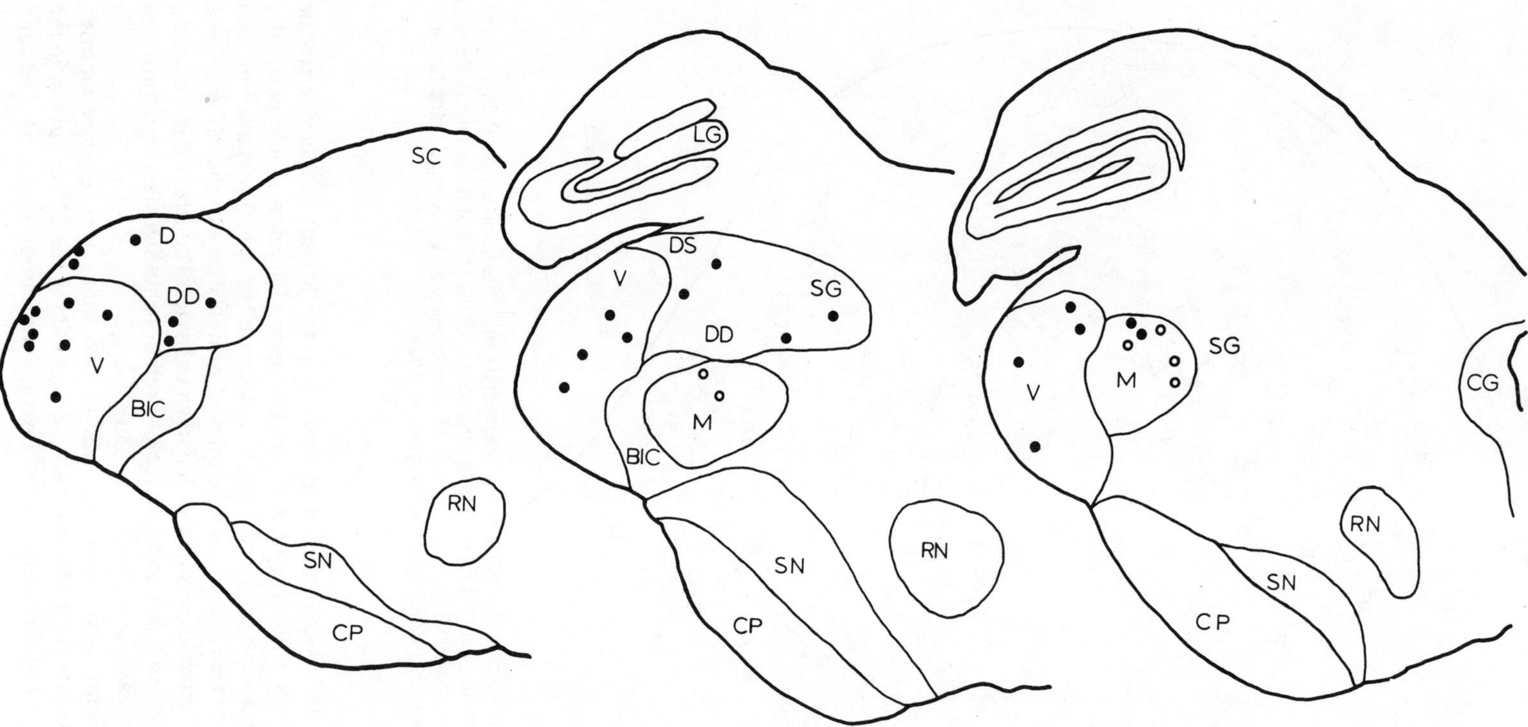

Figure 12-3. Histological verification of recording sites in the MGN. Open circles indicate placements in which plasticity developed; closed circles, sites in which response plasticity did not develop. All of the plastic loci were confined to the magnocellular division; two animals failed to develop plasticity in MGm, but these two animals also failed to acquire a conditioned pupillary response. Abbreviations: BIC, brachium of inferior colliculus; CG, central gray; CP, cerebral peduncles; D, dorsal, DD, deep dorsal, DS, superficial dorsal, M, magnocellular, and V, ventral divisions of MGN; RN, red nucleus; SC, superior colliculus; SG, suprageniculate nucleus; SN, substantia nigra. (From Ryugo & Weinberger, 1978.)

her colleagues reported the same findings in the rat using a training regimen that is a hybrid classical–instrumental conditioning situation (Birt *et al.*, 1979; Birt & Olds, 1981).[2]

The replication of findings across species, tasks, and laboratories strongly supports the view that cells within the MGm of the MGN are especially plastic during learning. Furthermore, physiological plasticity can be produced in the MGm by means other than learning paradigms. Long-term potentiation of a monosynaptic response in the hippocampus was first described by Bliss and Lomo (1973), who linked this phenomenon to learning. Its duration far outlasts that of posttetanic potentiation. See also Baudry and Lynch (Chapter 28, this volume) for details. Recently, we have found that long-term potentiation is easily established in the MGm of the MGN following brief, high-frequency stimulation of its major ascending auditory input, the brachium of the inferior colliculus (Gerren & Weinberger, 1983). Figure 12-4 presents relevant data.

Finally, it is interesting that the tripartate organization of the MGN is essentially the same across a very wide and diverse range of mammals. In addition to the rat, cat, and rabbit, there are the tree shrew (Oliver & Hall, 1975), the squirrel monkey (Jordan, 1973), the owl monkey (Fitzpatrick & Imig, 1978), and the opossum (Robards, unpublished data). The MGm may be an especially conditionable substrate of an evolutionarily conservative nature.

Single-Unit Studies

Multiple-unit recordings may be adequate for locating signs of discharge plasticity but they are inadequate for making inferences about the characteristics of plasticity in single neurons. As it turns out, they may also be misleading. Therefore, we extended the previous study to record the discharges of single neurons in the MGm, one neuron per training session. The discharges of 34 neurons were recorded continuously during conditioning and a prior sensitization control period. Evoked discharge plasticity developed in most neurons, and background activity increased in the rest (Weinberger, 1982). We found both increases and decreases in evoked activity; the latter had been masked in multiple-unit records previously obtained in our laboratory and in those of other investigators as well. Discharge plasticity developed very rapidly, usually within 6–10 trials (Figure 12-5).

We now returned to the AI, using single-unit recordings to provide information about the characteristics of individual neurons. The AI receives convergent input from the plastic MGm and the nonplastic MGv (Anderson, Knight, & Merzenich, 1980). Discharge plasticity developed quickly during acquisition of the pupillary CR (Hopkins & Weinberger, 1980; Weinberger, Hopkins, & Diamond, 1984). Decreases as well as increases, and a lack of change, were found for evoked activity (Figure 12-6). As in the case of the MGm, multiple-unit recordings that indicate only one direction of change apparently mask these diverse effects. Thus, conclusions about the functional significance of changes in sensory cortex during learning must begin with the

2. Disterhoft and Stuart (1976) failed to find discharge plasticity in the MGN of the rat using a virtually identical training paradigm, but they pooled the data from the magnocellular and ventral subdivisions, possibly masking plasticity in the former.

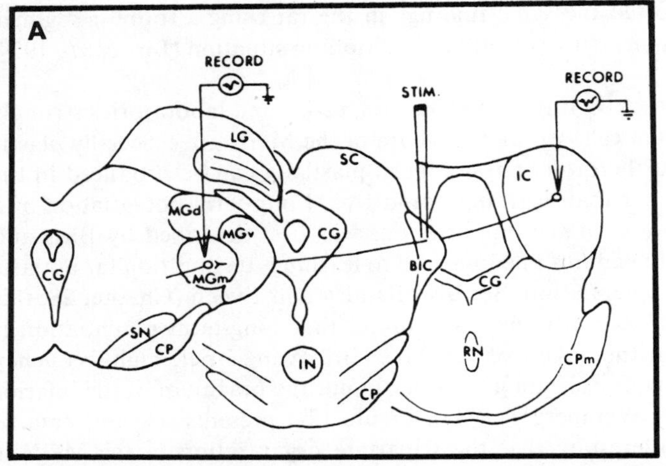

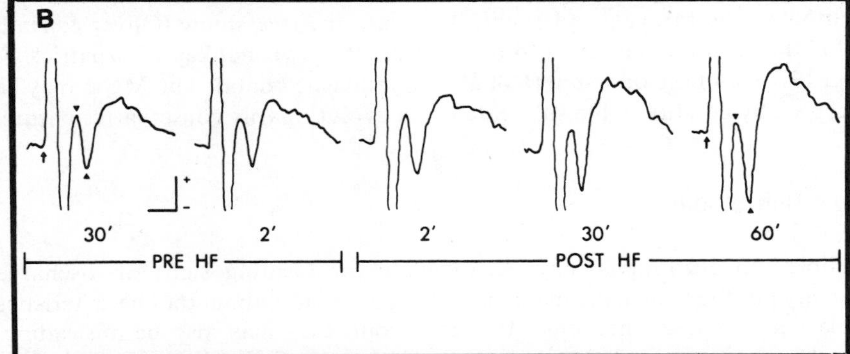

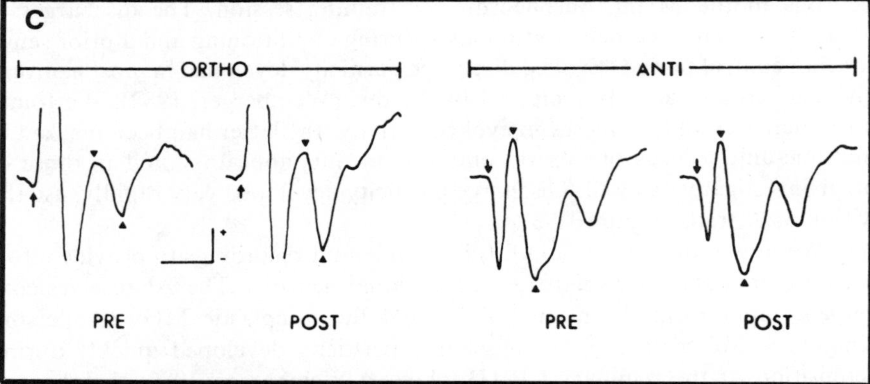

Figure 12-4. Long-term potentiation of monosynaptic response in the magnocellular medial geniculate nucleus. (A) Schematic representation of electrode placements in medial geniculate magnocellularis (MGm), brachium of the inferior colliculus (BIC), and inferior colliculus (IC). (B) Representative MGm responses to BIC stimulation at various times before (PRE) and after (POST) high-frequency (HF) stimulation of the BIC. Note increased responses following HF, amplitude continuing to increase after 60 min. (C) Representative MGm (ORTHOdromic) and IC (ANTIdromic) responses to BIC stimulation 5 min before (PRE) and 40 min after (POST) HF stimulation of the BIC. Note potentiation of orthodromic response in the absence of change in the antidromic response. Markers: horizontal bars = 1 msec; vertical bars = 100 μV; arrows indicate time of stimulus; triangles = points used for amplitude and latency measurements. (From Gerren & Weinberger, 1982.)

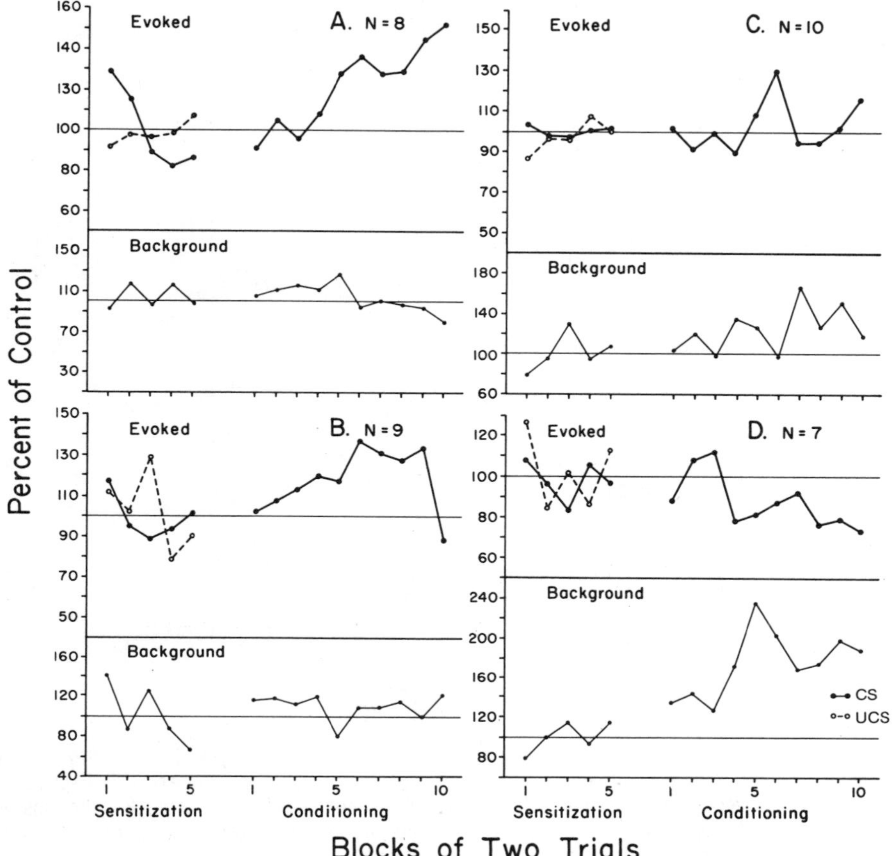

Figure 12-5. Evoked and background activity for single neurons in the magnocellular medial geniculate during acquisition of the pupillary dilation CR. (A) Cells developing maintained increased evoked discharges; (B) cells developing increased discharges not maintained beyond 18th conditioning trial; (C) cells that did not exhibit plasticity of evoked activity but did develop increased background discharges; (D) cells that developed decreased evoked and increased background discharges. Control level (100%) is the mean value during the sensitization period. Note rapid development of evoked plasticity in 10 or fewer trials (A, B, D). (From Weinberger, 1982.)

prime data (i.e., the records from single neurons) to avoid simplistic generalizations (e.g., that meaningful stimuli only elicit greater responses).

We next studied the so-called secondary auditory cortical field (AII). This area receives no input from the MGv but does receive input from the MGm. In contrast to AI, the AII is not organized in a tonotopic manner, and its neurons have broad tuning functions. Thus, AI would seem to be the highest level of the lemniscal auditory system, whereas AII appears to be a component of the nonlemniscal auditory system at the level of cerebral cortex.

As in the case of other single-unit studies, we recorded the discharges of one neuron per training session during the acquisition of the pupillary dilation CR. Data were obtained from 22 cells. The pairing of an acoustic stimulus with EDS resulted in the rapid development of discharge plasticity in AII, as for AI and MGm. However, the probability of obtaining physiological plasticity was

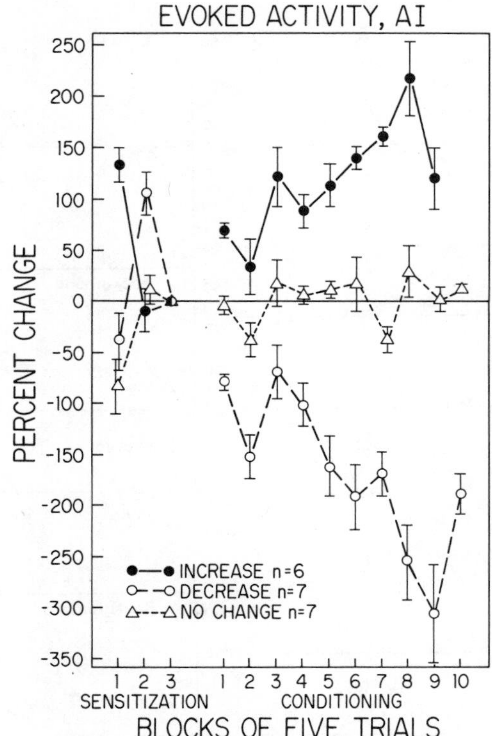

Figure 12-6. Evoked discharge plasticity of single neurons in primary auditory cortex during pupillary conditioning for increases ($n = 6$), decreases ($n = 7$), and no change ($n = 7$). Each point is the mean percent change in evoked discharges relative to the last five-trial block of the sensitization period ($\pm$ *SE*). Note the rapid development of discharge plasticity during the first 5–15 trials. (From Weinberger, Hopkins, & Diamond, 1984.)

higher than for AI. In fact, it was about as high as possible; 21 of 22 neurons exhibited statistically significant changes in evoked discharges, and 22 of 22 cells developed alterations in background discharges (Diamond & Weinberger, 1982, 1984). This extraordinary degree of plasticity has not been widely reported for other brain regions, to the best of our knowledge. The rate of change was rapid, requiring 10–15 trials or less for evoked activity (Figure 12-7).

Changes in background discharges were related to the rate of acquisition of the pupillary dilation CR and to the level of tonic arousal, as indexed by the diameter of the pupil during intertrial intervals. The background activity in AII decreased at the time that pupillary CRs were first seen. Further details are provided in Diamond and Weinberger (1984).

Possible Mechanisms of Plasticity in Auditory Cortex

Because the MGv does not develop discharge plasticity during conditioning, auditory cortex plasticity cannot be attributed to a change in thalamo-cortical ascending lemniscal activity. If there is a thalamic source or contribution to cortical plasticity, the MGm is the most likely candidate, for several reasons. First, the MGm does develop discharge plasticity and at a rate that is equal to or greater than auditory cortex. Simultaneous recordings from the MGm and the auditory cortex should be done to provide more detailed information on the relative time courses of plasticity. Second, the MGm projects to all auditory cortical fields, and the two fields studied both develop plasticity. If MGm promotes or regulates cortical discharge plasticity in the auditory system, then one might expect other auditory fields also to be affected by associative processes. Third, the mode of termination of MGm afferents is conducive to a regulatory or modulatory role that could result in increased or decreased responses to acoustic input. Thus, the MGm projects mainly to upper layers (e.g., Herkenham, 1980), where it could bias the excitability of underlying pyramidal neurons via contacts on apical dendrites; of course, other elements with processes in the superficial layers of cortex could be affected as well (e.g., Steriade, 1970).

Clearly, this formulation is speculative but it is not premature. It may at least have heuristic value in promoting investigations of the mechanisms of cortical plasticity during learning.

The model that all of these findings suggests is one in which primary sensory information—that is, the physical parameters of acoustic stimulation—are projected on AI in a highly organized, relatively direct fashion via the lemniscal pathway through the MGv, unmodified by learning. On the other hand, the responses of cortical cells to such information are affected by stimulus significance. Their plasticity may involve the lemniscal-adjunct magnocellular

Figure 12-7. Development of evoked discharge plasticity for single neurons in secondary cortical field (AII) during acquisition of the pupillary dilation conditioned response. Each point is the mean percent change for blocks of two trials relative to the mean of the last five trials of the sensitization period (± *SE*). Data are for 21 of 22 neurons that developed plasticity of evoked activity. Note the rapid development of plasticity, evident by trial 8 (block 4).

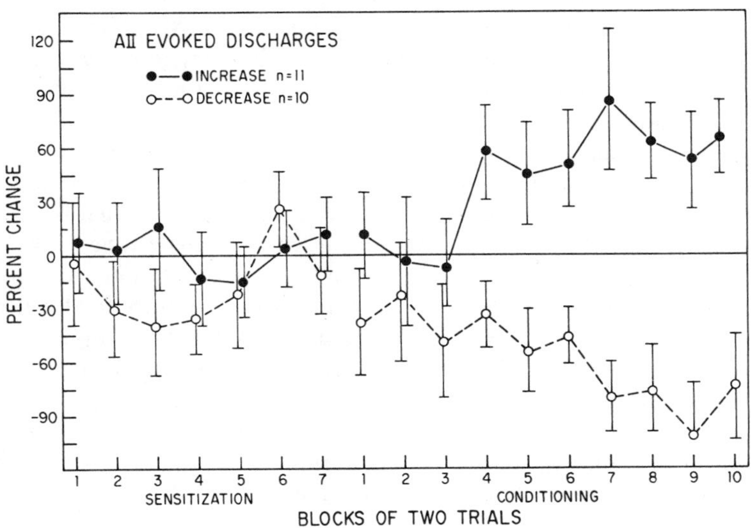

medial geniculate, the discharges of which are controlled rapidly by associative processes.

This schema would help explain how the auditory system simultaneously conveys information regarding the physical nature of acoustic stimuli and also their behavioral significance. The two types of analysis are carried on in parallel paths, the separation of which has been demonstrated in the thalamus. The two aspects of stimulus analysis converge in the cortex. In a sense, sensory auditory cortex might better be considered to be "cognitive auditory cortex."

It is not yet known whether learning-induced changes in the responses of auditory cortical neurons reflect changes in their general excitability or a more specific alteration of information processing, such as indexed by changes in frequency tuning. Our preliminary studies point to the latter.

Preliminary Findings on Associative Learning and Tuning Functions

In order to determine the effects, if any, of associative learning on the tuning of auditory cortical neurons, it is first necessary to demonstrate that tuning functions—that is, the responses of cells as a function of frequency—are stable in the absence of associative learning. Isointensity tones at various frequencies were presented under computer control to generate frequency response functions. The acoustic delivery system was calibrated during each recording session, using a technique and a computer program generously provided by Professor L. Kitzes, Department of Anatomy, University of California at Irvine, to compensate for the nonlinearities inherent in the acoustic coupling of a speaker to the tympanic membrane. Frequency response functions, defined as the responses of a given cell to frequencies between .1 and 25 kHz, were determined for a single intensity (e.g., 75 db, SPL) twice before training (separated by 15–20 minutes of silence), immediately after sensitization, and also after conditioning.

In the absence of any other variables, except the passage of time, the tuning of single neurons in auditory cortex was stable prior to training (Diamond & Weinberger, 1984). Acquisition of the pupillary CR was rapid, as found previously, and the final frequency function was obtained after only 20 trials of pairing. The findings to date are preliminary, but they do indicate that associative learning results in changes in the tuning of cortical cells. Figure 12-8 shows poststimulus histograms, and Figure 12-9 depicts the frequency functions taken at four times: twice before sensitization, after sensitization, and after conditioning. Note that the functions show a peak at 2.8 kHz and are essentially the same for the first three determinations, that is, are stable even after the period of sensitization during which a single tone (.7 kHz) was presented unpaired with EDS. However, following conditioning, in which the tone was followed by EDS, the tuning function changed. Specifically, it shifted to lower frequencies; the peak shifted to 1.4 kHz, and responses to higher frequencies were decreased. Note that the breadth of tuning has increased, and overall the function is not as "sharp." Of special interest, the frequency selected to be the CS (.7 kHz) was picked because it was initially ineffective in driving the cell prior to training. Following conditioning, the responses to the CS were augmented, to a statistically significant degree.

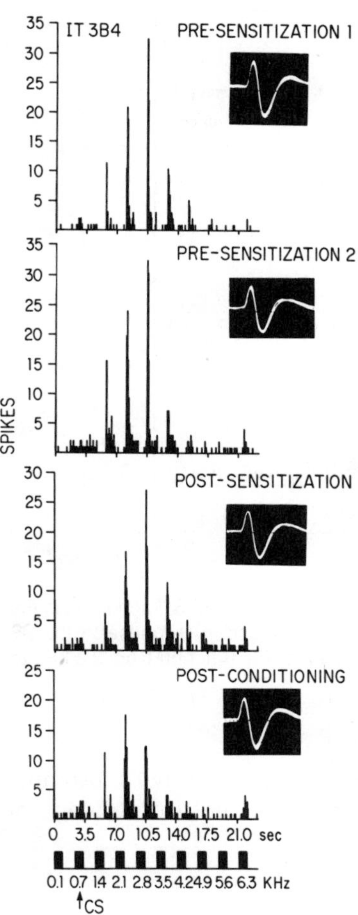

Figure 12-8. Poststimulus histograms for ascending-frequency series for a single neuron in auditory cortex before and after training. Tone duration = 900 msec, intensity = 80 db SPL, intertone intervals = 1100 msec. Each histogram is the sum of discharges for 10 consecutive frequency series. Each set of frequency series was given four times: "presensitization 1," 20 min before the start of sensitization; "presensitization 2," immediately before sensitization; "postsensitization," immediately after 20 trials of unpaired presentation of a tone (.7 kHz) and EDS; "postconditioning," immediately after 20 trials of paired tone and EDS. Inset shows that the waveform of the cell was constant throughout the period of recording. Note that the histograms for the series preceding conditioning were similar to each other, in contrast to the postconditioning histogram, which shows a shift to lower frequencies.

The data for the CS frequency are precisely those to which prior studies of learning have confined themselves, that is, demonstrating that the responses to the CS are changed (in this case augmented) due to conditioning. However, this is only a fragment of the larger picture, which is that this change in response to the CS is merely a part of the change in the tuning function engendered by conditioning. It is particularly interesting that the shift in the tuning function was toward the frequency of the CS, that is, toward lower frequencies than the original best frequency. Whether this was fortuitous or not remains to be determined in more extensive experiments.

These and similar data suggest that the actual effects of learning on the responses of individual cells in auditory cortex transcend the CS frequency and result in a change in the tuning response function of the cell. Such an effect presumably is not restricted to the one cell that happened to be near the tip of the recording microelectrode, so that the "retuning" may occur on a large scale within auditory cortex. In short, the representation of frequency on auditory cortex may reflect the meaning of stimuli rather than be restricted to a fixed representation of the frequency organization of the cochlea and the subcortical

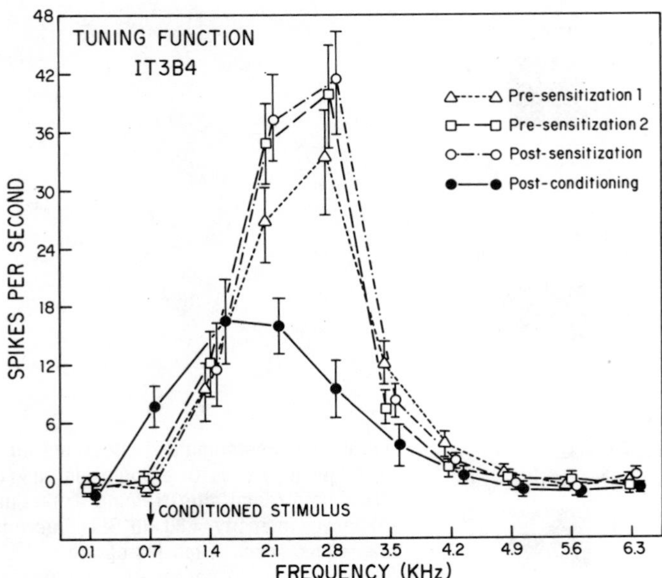

Figure 12-9. Frequency tuning functions for the data presented in Figure 12-8. Each point is the mean evoked response (± SE) for each frequency. Note the increase in response to the CS (.7 kHz) after conditioning, and especially the shift of the peak of the function from 2.8 kHz to 1.4 kHz. The breadth of tuning also increased.

lemniscal auditory system. These types of findings also suggest that substantial links may be found between the sensory sciences and the neurobiology of learning and memory.

RELATIONS TO OTHER APPROACHES

As this volume so aptly attests, there are many approaches to the neurobiology of learning and memory. Differences include differing techniques and also various levels of inquiry, that is, molecular, neural systems, behavioral. These distinctions do not imply that the approach of a single investigator or a group of investigators is limited to one technique or level of inquiry, but implicit in each approach is the "goal" of each research program. This is because the nature of the answers that an approach seeks are to a large extent constrained by the experimental designs and methods that are employed. A thorough analysis of all of the conceptual frameworks, strategies, and tactics employed in pursuit of the understanding of the neurobiology of learning and memory has not yet been written. The task is formidable, more so because there is no consensus on what would constitute such an "understanding." Indeed, an explicit delineation of alternative "understandings" is still wanting. One may legitimately ask whether or not clarification of these conceptual issues even has been a major concern.

The plurality of approaches and the absence of commonly agreed-on goals may be indicative of the extreme difficulty of the problems involved and may be symptomatic of relatively early stages of inquiry. We have not yet developed a satisfactory theoretical framework for our findings but believe it would be helpful to consider the problem explicitly at this point.

The rapid development of discharge plasticity in the auditory system during pupillary conditioning generally elicits two types of questions. The first concerns the effects of lesions of the magnocellular MGN or of auditory cortex—do such lesions impair or abolish acquisition or retention of the pupillary dilation CR? The second concerns the cellular and synaptic mechanisms involved in the rapidly acquired discharge plasticity obtained in the MGm and the auditory cortex. We have undertaken studies on neither of these issues, but these questions raise some conceptual problems. Both seem to be based on the assumption that it is essential to determine the locus and nature of cellular events that underlie the acquisition of a specific learned response, in this case the pupillary dilation CR. The implicit position seems to be that the neural circuit that underlies the acquisition of an associatively acquired response must be delineated. Lesions are strong inference tests that the region in question is essential for the acquisition of the response in question. Cellular investigations would then be applied to the neurons so identified to determine the biophysical and biochemical changes that are responsible for the associatively induced neuronal plasticity. This strategy has been employed with profit, as several other chapters in this volume attest.

Although we agree that this approach provides essential information on the nature of the neurobiological processes responsible for learning and memory, we doubt that it will yield the entire understanding of these processes, nor even that it is more compelling than all other lines of inquiry. There are two major reasons for holding this view. First, animals acquire many CRs, not merely one CR, in any situation. Second, the response-circuit approach provides no place for neuronal plasticity that is involved in learning but is not essential for a particular CR.

It is now clear that associative processes lead to the development of many CRs, even when restricting investigation to classical conditioning. As pointed out above, several CRs that are not specific to the nature of the UCS develop rapidly, prior to the acquisition of the CR that is specific to the UCS. It is this latter, more slowly acquired response that is generally considered as "the conditioned response" and is the one response to which neural tracing approaches usually have been applied. (An exception is the work of Cohen, 1982, who has been tracing the cardiac CR in the pigeon.) These rapidly acquired responses can hardly be ignored, unless one can demonstrate that they have no adaptive role. Whether such nonspecific CRs also develop in invertebrates has not been thoroughly investigated, so it would be premature to assume that the problem of multiple CRs is circumvented by the use of these animals.

But the problem is even more complex. Is there only one specific somatic CR? Few investigators have addressed this question explicitly. Anokhin (1961) is a notable exception. In order to study the acquisition of limb flexion during defensive conditioning in the dog, Anokhin constructed a platform consisting of four sprung sections, one under each paw, providing for the recording of limb extensions that otherwise would not be detected. He found that prior to the elaboration of the conditioned flexion response to shock applied to a specific leg, the animal developed a conditioned crossed-extension response.

This makes perfectly good sense in that flexion in the absence of the crossed-extension response would result in an unstable posture. Anokhin also found that the first somatic CR to emerge was a general motor restlessness, as indexed by unpatterned jiggling of all platforms. But the main point of these findings is that the acquisition of a commonly used specific somatic CR is preceded by the emergence of another specific somatic CR that is ordinarily not measured or even detected. Therefore, it seems reasonable to exercise caution in developing conceptual frameworks that encompass only a single CR, in particular the one response that the experimenter measures.

Given that multiple CRs develop, does an adequate understanding of learning require that the underlying neuronal circuitry and cellular mechanisms be determined for each? This is not a pleasant prospect, and perhaps not even a reasonable requirement, but this issue awaits detailed consideration.

A second reason for our reluctance to consider neurobehavioral circuit analysis to be sufficient in the study of learning and memory is that it leaves no place for associatively induced neuronal plasticity unless such plasticity is necessary for the behavioral response that the experimenter chooses to measure. For example, Woody and his associates (1974), in their elegant studies of short-latency eye-blink and nose-twitch CRs, reported that although an area of the posterior suprasylvian gyrus developed discharge plasticity to an acoustic CS, ablations of this region had no effect on the conditioned blink response. They concluded, quite correctly, that this area is not necessary for acquisition of the blink response (Woody, Yarowsky, Owens, Black-Cleworth, & Crow, 1974).

As for the effects of lesions of the magnocellular MGN or auditory cortex on pupillary conditioning, we have not studied this question. Le Doux and his colleagues have recently found that destruction of the entire medial geniculate abolishes CRs (but not unconditioned responses) during fear conditioning in the rat; ablations of auditory cortex are without effect (Le Doux, Sakaguchi, & Reis, 1984). These data are highly interesting, but they do not indicate that the auditory cortex is less involved in learning than is the MGN.

One way to view the negative effects of lesions is to assume that the "wrong" response was measured and that the lesions could be shown to impair the learning of some acquired response, either in the initial training situation or in another, more complex situation. But even if either of these alternatives were true, the tissue in question still would be relegated to being part of a response circuit. Past formulations of general learning theories that have actually been restricted to theories of response acquisition have not been successful, so there seems to be no compelling reason to attack the neurophysiological bases of learning only with respect to particular CRs, even when Pavlovian conditioning is the vehicle for inquiry. Much adaptive behavior that is based on learning involves motor equivalence, the use of nonidentical patterns of muscular contraction to attain a goal. Furthermore, the effects of classical conditioning are not limited to the acquisition of classically conditioned responses, but also to the acquisition of information that is employed in subsequent instrumental situations (Rescorla & Solomon, 1967).

These comments are not meant to imply that all brain regions are only loosely coupled to particular patterns of muscular contraction but only that some brain tissue that plays a critical role in learning and memory is not intimately tied to particular response circuits. The latter are especially advantageous for reductionistic studies of the sites and cellular mechanisms of plasticity in learning. Associative processes that have other functional characteristics need to be understood from other viewpoints. So if plasticity in the auditory system, or any other region of the brain, is not essential for the performance of a particular acquired response, what roles do these processes play in learning? We consider this problem in the final section.

FUNCTIONS OF SENSORY SYSTEM PLASTICITY

Several roles have been proposed for the physiological plasticity that develops in the sensory system of a conditioned or signal stimulus during learning. These include stimulus significance, control of overt movements, early stage of processes linking particular responses to particular stimuli (Birt & Olds, 1981), and stimulus set (Krasne, Chapter 14, this volume).

In discussing discharge plasticity in the MGN, Birt and Olds (1981) suggested that sensory plasticity in the auditory system is related to the linking of particular responses to particular stimuli. This conclusion is based largely on rejecting explanations in terms of stimulus significance and movement control. We readily agree with the elimination of the latter, because indeed there appears to be no close relation between the development of discharge plasticity in the auditory system and the expression of acquired responses during conditioning. Not only are the data of Birt and Olds (1981) incompatible with such an interpretation, but Gabriel *et al.* (1976) also found a poor correspondence between neural plasticity and avoidance responding. Furthermore, as we have previously pointed out, auditory system plasticity develops rapidly, whereas specific somatic CRs appear more slowly. Additionally, although evoked auditory plasticity develops at the same rapid rate as do pupillary CRs, the two have a low within-animal correlation (Oleson *et al.*, 1975; Ryugo & Weinberger, 1978; Weinberger *et al.*, 1984; Diamond & Weinberger, 1984). The only high intercorrelations we have found are in accessory oculomotor nuclei, specifically the interstitial nucleus of Cajal and the nucleus of Darkschewitsch (Ashe, Cooper, & Weinberger, 1978b; see also Ashe *et al.*, 1978a, and Ashe & Cooper, 1978), which are involved in the efferent control of pupillary diameter. Hence, it seems reasonable to reject a "motor" role for auditory system plasticity during learning.

In contrast, we find arguments against stimulus significance less convincing. Birt and Olds (1981) argue that auditory plasticity does not reflect stimulus significance, because the distribution of plasticity within the medial geniculate nucleus and adjacent areas apparently is not identical in their studies of rat appetitive conditioning, the studies of Gabriel and associates (1976) for rabbit avoidance conditioning, and our studies of Pavlovian conditioning in the cat. They reason that the methods for "making the tone important should presumably result in similar changes, if these changes are strictly related to stimulus significance" (Birt & Olds, 1981, p. 1051). But there is great similarity in findings among the three laboratories, especially when considering initial or early plasticity in the MGN. All three laboratories reported rapidly developing response plasticity in the magnocellular division and a lack of such plasticity in the ventral and dorsal divisions (Gabriel, Saltwick, & Miller, 1975; Gabriel *et al.*, 1976; Ryugo & Weinberger, 1976, 1978; Birt & Olds, 1981).[3] Furthermore, we do not understand why one should expect acoustic signals to acquire the same significance for cats, rats, and rabbits that are in different motivational states and training situations. Given the variations in species and training situation, it seems remarkable that the same effects have been found in the MGN. Finally, reports of discharge plasticity in auditory cortex from various laboratories and training situations are highly consistent (Buchwald *et al.*, 1966; Halas, Beardsley, & Sandlie, 1970; Disterhoft & Olds, 1972; Cassady, Cole, Thompson, & Weinberger, 1973; Oleson *et al.*, 1975; Disterhoft & Stuart, 1976; Gasanov, Galashina, & Bogdanov, 1979; Kraus & Disterhoft, 1982; Weinberger *et al.*, 1983; Diamond & Weinberger, 1984). Therefore, we see little justification for rejecting the possibility that auditory system plasticity during learning does reflect stimulus significance.

Krasne (Chapter 14, this volume) argues that sensory systems cannot be the sites at which representations of stimuli are linked to particular responses. He suggests that sensory plasticity might represent a predisposition or set that increases the likelihood that a particular stimulus might result in a particular response in a given situation. Stimulus set appears closely related to the notion of stimulus significance, except that it attempts to tie sensory system plasticity more closely to responses than does the latter.

While stimulus significance and stimulus set both are compatible with extant data and are reasonable roles for sensory system plasticity during learning, we suggest that a more detailed understanding of such plasticity is necessary to clarify its role in learning. Our preliminary data, discussed previously, suggest that conditioning causes a change in the tuning function of neurons in auditory cortex. Further, they indicate that the tuning can shift toward the frequency of the CS (Figures 12-8, 12-9). If the effect occurs in many neurons across auditory cortex, the number of neurons that become responsive or more responsive to a significant stimulus would increase. This implies that cortical maps of receptor surfaces are plastic. The specific details of the cochleotopic, retinotopic, and somatotopic organization of the auditory, visual, and somatosensory cortices, respectively, actually may be maps of stimulus significance for individual animals. Thus, when an experimenter "maps" a sensory cortex, the result may be a "snapshot" of the effects of experience with stimuli in that modality. One might then expect to find the same general organization in various animals, but also obtain clear differences in details between individual

3. A brief report from Gabriel's lab (Foster, Orona, Lambert, & Gabriel, 1980) claimed late-developing plasticity in the MGv, which has since been retracted (Gabriel, personal communication, and Gabriel, Orona, Foster, & Lambert, 1982). Plasticity in the dorsal division occurs only after extensive training (Gabriel *et al.*, 1982). Other differences emphasized by Birt and Olds (1981) were that they found associative changes only in the caudal one-third of the MGm, in a transition zone between its caudal pole and the lateral midbrain tegmentum, and in the parabrachial region. The areas outside of the MGm have not been studied by other laboratories, so these data cannot substantiate a claim of differing results. As for possible differences within regions of the MGm, we think it is unwarranted to attempt such fine-grain distinctions when detailed anatomical comparisons of the MGm of the rat and cat have not yet been done. Birt and Olds (1981) focus on differences among the laboratories, whereas we emphasize similarities; this is a bit like two thirsty men in the desert—one anguishes that the water bottle is half-empty while the other is pleased that it is half-full. Given the vast differences in species, training conditions, criteria used to establish plasticity, and the use of various acoustic stimuli, we believe it is highly significant that the magnocellular MGN rapidly develops discharge plasticity in all cases.

animals. In line with this, Merzenich, Knight, and Roth (1975) found large individual differences in tonotopic maps of auditory cortex in the cat and emphasized the danger of pooling maps from various animals, because the resultant composite yields a highly "blurred" organizational schema. Plasticity in the somatosensory cortical representation of the hand in monkeys may also be related to a learning effect (Merzenich, 1982; Merzenich, Kaas, Wall, Nelson, Sur, & Felleman, 1983).

A change in "tuning" and "mapping" of sensory cortex consequent to learning could play a larger role than that of increasing the probability that a significant stimulus woud elicit a particular response. The allocation of more neurons to a given stimulus parameter would increase the resolution in the analysis of, for example, a CS and similar stimuli. Such an effect could be involved in stimulus equivalence, that is, the process by which animals treat variations in the exact pattern of receptor stimulation as functionally equivalent. This process is essential to learning, because an identical pattern of receptor stimulation does not occur from one experience to the next. Thus, if there are more neurons allocated to the domain of an important stimulus, then slight variations in the reception of this stimulus on the next occasion will find more neurons likely to respond to it. The change in tuning of a cell would then be expected to involve not merely a shift in the peak of the tuning curve but also a broadening of the function. This is what we have found to date (Figures 12-8, 12-9).

CONCLUSIONS

During classical defensive conditioning, the earliest behavioral manifestations of learning are the development of CRs that are not specific to the nature of the UCS; these are all autonomic and general somatic CRs. Somatic CRs that are specific to the US develop more slowly, and are generally the responses on which neurophysiological analyses of learning have focused. Concomitant with the expression of, for example, the pupillary dilation CR, discharge plasticity develops in the magnocellular MGN, a nonspecific part of the auditory thalamus, but not in the ventral MGN, the lemniscal component. Auditory cortical fields AI and AII also develop discharge plasticity rapidly, the latter having all sampled neurons exhibiting plasticity. All of these events may be considered among the initial manifestations of conditioning as they all develop within a small number of trials following a preceding sensitization control period. These data suggest that the auditory system processes the two aspects of acoustic stimuli separately, subcortically: Physical stimulus parameters are analyzed by the lemniscal system, represented by the ventral MGN, whereas stimulus meaning, or its associative value, is related to the magnocellular MGN. These two stimulus dimensions converge at the auditory cortex. Preliminary findings indicate that cortical discharge plasticity actually reflects a change in the tuning function of neurons due to associative processes. Such effects, if proved to be general, may indicate that the organization of sensory cortical fields is plastic and reflects the acquired significance of stimuli. This mechanism could be a substrate for stimulus equivalence. These and other considerations emphasize the benefits of a rapprochement between sensory physiology and the neurobiology of learning and memory, and underscore the need to develop conceptual frameworks that include a dynamic role for the plasticity that undeniably is a major feature of sensory systems during learning.[4]

ACKNOWLEDGMENTS

This work has been supported in part by research grants BNS76-81924, NS16108, fellowships MH 05424, 05440, and 51324, an unrestricted grant from the Monsanto Company, and the University of California Irvine Focused Research Program on Cooperative Brain Function. We wish to thank Paul E. Gold and James L. McGaugh for helpful discussions and comments on an earlier version of the manuscript. We also thank Jacqueline D. Weinberger for invaluable secretarial assistance.

REFERENCES

Aitkin, L. M. Medial geniculate body of the cat: Responses to tonal stimuli of neurons in medial division. *Journal of Neurophysiology*, 1973, *36*, 275–283.

Aitkin, L. M., & Webster, W. R. Medial geniculate body of the cat: Organization and responses to tonal stimuli of neurons in ventral division. *Journal of Neurophysiology*, 1972, *35*, 365–379.

Alkon, D. L. A biophysical basis for molluscan associative learning. In C. D. Woody (Ed.), *Conditioning: Representation of involved neural function*. New York: Plenum, 1982.

Anderson, R. A., Knight, P. L., & Merzenich, M. M. The thalamocortical and corticothalamic connections of AI, AII and AAF in the cat: Evidence for two segregated systems of connections. *Journal of Comparative Neurology*, 1980, *194*, 663–701.

Anohkin, P. K. A new conception of the physiological architecture of conditioned reflex. In A. Fessard, R. W. Gerard, & J. Konorski (Eds.), *Brain mechanisms and learning*. Oxford: Blackwell, 1961.

Ashe, J. H., Cassady, J. M., & Weinberger, N. M. The relationship of the cochlear microphonic potential to the acquisition of a classically conditioned pupillary dilation response. *Behavioral Biology*, 1976, *16*, 45–62.

Ashe, J. H., & Cooper, C. L. Multifiber efferent activity in postganglionic sympathetic and parasympathetic nerves related to the latency of spontaneous and evoked pupillary dilation response. *Experimental Neurology*, 1978, *59*, 413–434.

Ashe, J. H., Cooper, C. L., & Weinberger, N. M. Mesencephalic multiple-unit activity during acquisition of conditioned pupillary dilation. *Brain Research Bulletin*, 1978a, *3*, 143–154.

Ashe, J. H., Cooper, C. L., & Weinberger, N. M. Role of the parasympathetic pupillomotor system in classically conditioned pupillary dilation of the cat. *Behavioral Biology*, 1978b, *23*, 1–13.

Baust, W., & Berlucchi, G. Reflex response to clicks of cat's tensor tympani during sleep and wakefulness and the influence thereon of the auditory cortex. *Archives Italiennes de Biologie*, 1964, *102*, 686–712.

Baust, W., Berlucchi, G., & Moruzzi, G. Changes in the auditory input during arousal in cats with tenotomized middle ear muscles. *Archives Italiennes de Biologie*, 1964, *102*, 675–685.

Berlucchi, G., Munson, J. B., & Rizzolatti, G. Auditory-evoked responses in cats with tenotomized middle ear muscles during sleep. *Pflügers Archiv für die Gesamte Physiologie*, 1968, *292*, 80–82.

Birt, D., Nienhuis, R., & Olds, M. Separation of associative from non-associative short latency changes in medial geniculate and inferior colliculus during differential conditioning and reversal in rats. *Brain Research*, 1979, *167*, 129–138.

Birt, D., & Olds, M. Associate response changes in lateral midbrain tegmentum and medial geniculate during differential appetitive conditioning. *Journal of Neurophysiology*, 1981, *46*, 1039–1055.

4. Limitations of space precluded a review of physiological plasticity during learning other than the auditory system. Examples of such findings include: olfactory system (Freeman, 1980), somatosensory (Voronin, Gerstein, Kudryashov, & Ioffe, 1975), and visual (Kotlyar & Frolov, 1971; Kotlyar & Mayorov, 1971; Shinkman, Bruce, & Pfingst, 1974). We also wish to call attention to Whitfield's provocative hypothesis regarding the role of sensory neocortex as a substrate for the internal construction of the external sensory environment (Whitfield, 1979). Our hypothesis regarding stimulus equivalance appears to be broadly compatible with this formulation.

Black, A. H. Cardiac conditioning in curarized dogs. The relationship between heart rate and skeletal behaviour. In W. F. Prokasy (Ed.), *Classical conditioning: A symposium*. New York: Appleton-Century-Crofts, 1965.

Bliss, T. V. P., & Lomo, T. Long lasting potentiation of synaptic transmission in the dentate area of the anaesthetized rabbit following stimulation of the perforant path. *Journal of Physiology*, 1973, *232*, 331.

Bradshaw, J. L. Pupil size and problem solving. *Quarterly Journal of Experimental Psychology*, 1968, *20*, 116–122.

Bruner, A. Reinforcement strength in classical conditioning of leg flexion, freezing, and heart rate in cats. *Conditional Reflex*, 1969, *4*, 24–31.

Buchwald, J. S., Halas, E., & Schramm, S. Changes in cortical and subcortical unit activity during behavioral conditioning. *Physiology and Behavior*, 1966, *1*, 11.

Calford, M. B., & Aitkin, L. M. Ascending projections to the medial geniculate body of the cat: Evidence for multiple parallel auditory pathways through the thalamus. *Journal of Neuroscience*, 1983, *11*, 2365–2380.

Calford, M. B., & Webster, W. R. Auditory representation within principal division of cat medial geniculate body: An electrophysiological study. *Journal of Neurophysiology*, 1981, *45*, 1013–1028.

Carmel, P. W., & Starr, A. Acoustical and nonacoustical factors modifying middle ear muscle activity in waking cats. *Journal of Neurophysiology*, 1963, *26*, 598–616.

Cassady, J. M., Cole, M., Thompson, R., & Weinberger, N. M. Neural correlates of asymptotic avoidance and classical conditioned leg flexion. *Experimental Neurology*, 1973, *40*, 207–215.

Cassady, J. M., Farley, G. R., Weinberger, N. M., & Kitzes, L. M. Pupillary activity measured by reflected infra-red light. *Physiology and Behavior*, 1982, *28*, 851–854.

Cohen, D. H. The neural pathways and informations flow mediating a conditioned autonomic response. In L. V. DiCara (Ed.), *Limbic and autonomic nervous system research*. New York: Plenum, 1974.

Cohen, D. H. Central processing time for a conditioned response in a vertebrate model system. In C. D. Woody (Ed.), *Conditioning: Representation of involved neural function*. New York: Plenum, 1982, 517–534.

Colwell, S. A., & Merzenich, M. M. Organization of thalamocortical and corticothalamic projections to and from physiologically defined loci within primary auditory cortex in the cat. *Anatomical Record*, 1975, *181*, 336.

Cooper, C. L., Ashe, J. H., & Weinberger, N. M. Effects of stimulus omission during habituation of the pupillary dilation reflex. *Physiological Psychology*, 1978, *6*, 1–6.

Davidson, R. E., & Richardson, A. M. Classical conditioning of skeletal and autonomic responses in the lizard. *Physiology and Behavior*, 1970, *5*, 589–594.

deToledo, L., & Black, A. H. Heart rate: Changes during conditioned suppression in rats. *Science*, 1966, *152*, 1404–1406.

Diamond, D. M., & Weinberger, N. M. Physiological plasticity of single neurons in secondary cortex (AII) during pupillary conditioning in cat. *Society for Neuroscience: Proceedings of the Twelfth Annual Meeting*, 1982, *8*, 317. (Abstract)

Diamond, D. M., & Weinberger, N. M. Physiological plasticity of single neurons in auditory cortex of cat during acquisition of the pupillary conditioned response: II, secondary field (AII). *Behavioral Neuroscience*, 1984, *98*, 189–210.

Disterhoft, J., & Olds, J. Differential development of conditioned unit changes in thalamus and cortex of rat. *Journal of Neurophysiology*, 1972, *35*, 665–679.

Disterhoft, J., & Stuart, D. Trial sequence of changed unit activity in auditory system of alert rat during conditioned response acquisition and extinction. *Journal of Neurophysiology*, 1976, 39, 266–281.

Durup, G., & Fessard, A. L'électroencephalogramme de l'homme. *Année Psychologique*, 1935, *36*, 1–32.

Erickson, R. P., Hall, W. C., Jane, J., Synder, M., & Diamond, I. T. Organization of the posterior dorsal thalamus of the hedgehog. *Journal of Comparative Neurology*, 1967, *131*, 103–130.

Erickson, R. P., Jane, J., Waite, R., & Diamond, I. T. Single neuron investigation of sensory thalamus of the opossum. *Journal of Neurophysiology*, 1964, *27*, 1026–1047.

Fitzpatrick, K. A., & Imig, T. J. Projections of auditory cortex upon the thalamus and midbrain in the owl monkey. *Journal of Comparative Neurology*, 1978, *177*, 537.

Foster, K., Orona, E., Lambert, R., & Gabriel, M. Neuronal activity in the auditory system during differential conditioning in rabbits. *Society for Neurosciences Abstracts*, 1980, *6*, 424.

Freeman, W. J. Evidence for an olfactory search image or representation in the EEG of conditioned cats and rabbits. *Advancement in Physiological Sciences*, 1980, *16*, 421–429.

Furedy, J. J. Explicity-unpaired and truly-random CS-controls in human classical differential autonomic conditioning. *Psychophysiology*, 1971, *8*, 497–503.

Furedy, J. J., Poulos, C. X., & Schiffman, K. Contingency theory and classical autonomic excitatory and inhibitory conditioning: Some problems of assessment and interpretation. *Psychophysiology*, 1975, *12*, 98–105.

Gabriel, M., Miller, J. D., & Saltwick, S. E. Multiple unit activity of the rabbit medial geniculate nucleus in conditioning, extinction and reversal. *Physiological Psychology*, 1976, *4*, 124–134.

Gabriel, M., Orona, E., Foster, K., & Lambert, R. W. Mechanism and generality of stimulus significance in a mammalian model system. In C. D. Woody (Ed.), *Conditioning: Representation of involved neural function*. New York: Plenum, 1982.

Gabriel, M., Saltwick, S. E., & Miller, J. D. Conditioning and reversal of short-latency multiple-unit responses in rabbit medial geniculate nucleus. *Science*, 1975, *189*, 1108–1109.

Galambos, R., & Rupert, A. Action of middle ear muscles in normal cats. *Journal of the Acoustical Society of America*, 1959, *31*, 349–355.

Galambos, R., & Sheatz, G. C. An electroencephalograph study of classical conditioning. *American Journal of Physiology*, 1962, *203*, 173–184.

Galambos, R., Sheatz, G. C., & Vernier, B. Electrophysiological conditioned response in cats. *Science*, 1955, *123*, 376–377.

Gasanov, A. G., Galashina, A. G., & Bogdanov, A. V. A study of neuron systems in learning. In R. F. Thompson, L. E. Hicks, & V. B. Shvyrokov (Eds.), *Neural mechanisms of goal-directed behavior and learning*. New York: Academic Press, 1980.

Gerall, A. A., & Obrist, P. A. Classical conditioning of the pupillary dilation response of normal and curarized cats. *Journal of Comparative and Physiological Psychology*, 1962, *55*, 486–491.

Gerken, G. M., & Neff, W. D. Experimental procedures affecting evoked responses recorded from auditory cortex. *Electroencephalography and Clinical Neurophysiology*, 1963, *15*, 947–957.

Gerren, R., & Weinberger, N. M. Long term potentiation in the magnocellular medial geniculate nucleus of the anesthetized cat. *Brain Research*, 1983, *265*, 138–142.

Gormezano, I., Schneiderman, N., Deaux, E., & Fuentes, I. Nictitating membrane: Classical conditioning and extinction in the albino rabbit. *Science*, 1962, *138*, 33–34.

Graybiel, A. M. Some fiber pathways related to the posterior thalamic region in the cat. *Brain, Behavior and Evolution*, 1972, *6*, 363–393.

Graybiel, A. M. Studies on the anatomical organization of posterior association cortex. In F. O. Schmitt, & F. G. Worden (Eds.), *The neurosciences: Third study program*. Cambridge, Mass.: MIT Press, 1974.

Halas, E., Beardsley, J., & Sandlie, M. Conditioned neuronal responses at various levels in conditioning paradigms. *Electroencephalography and Clinical Neurophysiology*, 1970, *28*, 468–477.

Hall, R. D., & Mark, R. Fear and the modification of acoustically evoked potentials during conditioning. *Journal of Neurophysiology*, 1967, *30*, 893–910.

Hearst, E., Beer, B., Sheatz, G., & Galambos, R. Some electrophysiological correlates of conditioning in the monkey. *Electroencephalography and Clinical Neurophysiology*, 1960, *12*, 137–152.

Heath, C. J., & Jones, E. G. An experimental study of ascending connections from the posterior group of thalamic nuclei in the cat. *Journal of Comparative Neurology*, 1971, *141*, 397–426.

Herkenham, M. Laminar organization of thalamic projections to the rat neocortex. *Science*, 1980, *207*, 532–535.

Holdstock, T. L., & Schwartzbaum, J. S. Classical conditioning of heart rate and galvanic skin response in the rat. *Psychophysiology*, 1965, *2*, 25–38.

Hopkins, W., & Weinberger, N. M. Modification of auditory cortex single unit activity during pupillary conditioning. *Society for Neurosciences: Proceedings of the tenth annual meeting*, Cincinnati, 1980. (Abstract)

Imig, T. J., & Weinberger, N. M. Auditory system multi-unit activity and behavior in the rat. *Psychonomic Science*, 1970, *18*, 164–165.

Irvine, D. R. F., & Webster, W. R. Studies of peripheral gating in the auditory system of cats. *Electroencephalography and Clinical Neurophysiology*, 1972, *32*, 545–556.

Jane, J. A., & Schroeder, D. M. A comparison of dorsal column nuclei and spinal afferents in the European hedgehog *Erinaceus europaeus*. *Experimental Neurology*, 1971, *30*, 1–17.

John, E. R. *Mechanisms of memory*. New York: Academic Press, 1967.

Jones, E. G., & Rockel, A. J. The synaptic organization in the medial geniculate body of afferent fibers ascending from the inferior colliculus. *Zeitschrift für Zelforschung*, 1971, *113*, 44–66.

Jordan, H. The structure of the medial geniculate nucleus (MGN): A cyto- and myeloarchitectonic study in the squirrel monkey. *Journal of Comparative Neurology*, 1973, *148*, 469–479.

Jouvet, M. Analyse électroencephalographique de quelques aspects du conditionnement chez le chat. *Acta Neurologica Latinoamericana*, 156, *2*, 107–115.

Kahneman, D., & Beatty, J. Pupil diameter and load on memory. *Science*, 1966, *154*, 1583–1585.

Kandel, E. R., *A cell-biological approach to learning*. Bethesda, Md.: Society for Neuroscience, 1978.

Konorski, J. *Integrative activity of the brain: An interdisciplinary approach*. Chicago: University of Chicago Press, 1967.

Koslovskaya, I. B., Vertes, R. P., & Miller, N. E. Instrumental learning without proprioceptive feedback. *Physiology and Behavior*, 1973, *10*, 101–107.

Kotlyar, B. I., & Frolov, A. G. Reorganization of unit activity in the lateral geniculate body during sound–light association. *Journal of Higher Nervous Activity*, 1971, *21*, 827–835.

Kotlyar, B. I., & Mayorov, V. I. Activity of the visual cortex units in rabbits in the course of association of sound with rhythmic light. *Journal of Higher Nervous Activity*, 1971, *21*, 157–163. (In Russian)

Kraus, N., & Disterhoft, J. F. Response plasticity of single neurons in rabbit auditory association cortex during tone-signalled learning. *Brain Research*, 1982, *246*, 205–215.

Le Doux, J. E., Sakaguchi, A., & Reis, D. J. Subcortical efferent projections of the medial geniculate nucleus mediate emotional responses conditioned to acoustic stimuli. *Journal of Neuroscience*, 1984, *4*, 683–698.

Lippe, W. R., & Weinberger, N. M. The distribution of sensory evoked activity within the medial geniculate body of the unanesthetized cat. *Experimental Neurology*, 1973, *40*, 207–215.

LoLordo, V. M. Constraints on learning. In M. E. Bitterman, V. M. LoLordo, J. B. Overmier, & M. E. Rashotte. *Animal learning: Survey and analysis*. New York: Plenum, 1979.

Love, J. A., & Scott, J. W. Some response of characteristics of cells of the magnocellular division of the medial geniculate body of the cat. *Canadian Journal of Physiology and Pharmacology*, 1969, *47*, 881–888.

Mark, R., & Hall, R. D. Acoustically evoked potentials in the rat during conditioning. *Journal of Neurophysiology*, 1967, *30*, 875–892.

Marsh, J. T., McCarthy, D. A., Sheatz, G., & Galambos, R. Amplitude changes in evoked auditory potentials during habituation and conditioning. *Electroencephalography and Clinical Neurophysiology*, 1961, *13*, 224–234.

Marsh, J. T., Worden, F. G., & Hicks, L. Some effects of room acoustics on evoked auditory potentials. *Science*, 1962, *137*, 280–282.

Merzenich, M. M. Organization of primate sensory forebrain structures: A new perspective. In R. A. Thompson & J. R. Green (Eds.), *New perspectives in cerebral localization*. New cortex in the cat. *Journal of Neurophysiology*, 1975, *38*, 231–249.

Merzenich, M. M., Kaas, J. H., Wall, J., Nelson, R. J., Sur, M., & Felleman, D. Topographic reorganization of somatosensory cortical areas 3b and 1 in adult monkeys following restricted deafferentation. *Neurosciences*, 1983, *8*, 33–55.

Milner, B., Corkin, S., & Teuber, H. L. Further analysis of the hippocampal-amnesic syndrome: 14 year followup study of H. M. *Neuropsychologia*, 1968, *6*, 215–234.

Moore, R. Y., & Goldberg, J. M. Ascending projections of the inferior colliculus in the cat. *Journal of Comparative Neurology*, 1963, *121*, 109–136.

Moore, R. Y., & Goldberg, J. M. Projections of the inferior colliculus in the cat. *Experimental Neurology*, 1966, *14*, 429–438.

Morest, D. K. The neuronal architecture of the medial geniculate body of the cat. *Journal of Anatomy*, 1964, *98*, 611–630.

Morest, D. K. The laminar structure of the medial geniculate body of the cat. *Journal of Anatomy*, 1965a, *99*, 143–160.

Morest, D. K. The lateral tegmental system of the midbrain and the medial geniculate body: Study with Golgi and Nauta methods in cat. *Journal of Anatomy*, 1965b, *99*, 611–634.

Morrell, F. Electrophysiological contributions to the neural basis of learning. *Physiological Review*, 1961, *41*, 443–494.

Moushegian, G., Rupert, A., Marsh, J. T., & Galambos, R. Evoked cortical potentials in absence of middle ear muscles. *Science*, 1961, *133*, 582–583.

Mowrer, O. H. On the dual nature of learning—a re-interpretation of "conditioning" and "problem-solving." *Harvard Educational Review*, 1947, *17*, 102–148.

Niimi, K., & Naito, F. Cortical projections of the medial geniculate body in the cat. *Experimental Brain Research*, 1974, *19*, 326–342.

O'Brien, J. H., & Packham, S. C. Conditioned leg movement in the cat with massed trials, trace conditioning, and weak US intensity. *Conditional Reflex*, 1973, *8*, 116–124.

Olds, J., Disterhoft, J. F., Segal, M., Kornblith, C., & Hirsh, R. Learning centers of rat brain mapped by measuring latencies of conditioned unit responses. *Journal of Neurophysiology*, 1972, *35*, 202–219.

Olds, J., Nienhuis, R., & Olds, M. E. Patterns of conditioned unit responses in the auditory system of the rat. *Experimental Neurology*, 1978, *59*, 209–228.

Oleson, T., Ashe, J., & Weinberger, N. M. Modification of auditory and somatosensory activity during pupillary conditioning in the paralyzed cat. *Journal of Neurophysiology*, 1975, *38*, 1114–1139.

Oleson, T. D., Vododnick, D. S., & Weinberger, N. M. Pupillary inhibition of delay during Pavlovian conditioning in paralyzed cat. *Behavioral Biology*, 1973, *8*, 337–346.

Oleson, T. D., Westenberg, I. S., & Weinberger, N. M. Characteristics of the pupillary dilation response during Pavlovian conditioning in paralyzed cats. *Behavioral Biology*, 1972, *7*, 829–840.

Oliver, D. L., & Hall, W. C. Subdivisions of the medial geniculate body in the tree shrew (*Tapaiai glis*). *Brain Reserach*, 1975, *86*, 217–227.

Parrish, J. Classical discrimination conditioning of heart rate and bar-press suppression in the rat. *Psychonomic Science*, 1967, *9*, 267–268.

Pavlov, I. P. *Conditioned reflexes*. London: Oxford University Press, 1927.

Poggio, G. F., & Mountcastle, V. B. A study of the functional contributions of the lemniscal and spinothalamic systems to somatic sensibility. *Bulletin of the Johns Hopkins Hospital*, 1960, *106*, 266–316.

Popova, N. S. Changes in auditory evoked potentials during defensive conditioning in dogs. *Neuroscience Translations*, 1969, *8*, 903–911.

Raczkowski, D., Diamond, I. T., & Winer, J. Organization of thalamocortical auditory system in the cat studied with horseradish peroxidase. *Brain Research*, 1975, *101*, 345–354.

Ramon-Moliner, E. An attempt at classifying nerve cells on the basis of their dendritic patterns. *Journal of Comparative Neurology*, 1962, *119*, 211–227.

Ramon-Moliner, E. Specialized and generalized dendritic patterns. In M. Santini (Ed.), *Golgi centennial symposium: Perspectives in neurobiology*. New York: Raven Press, 1975.

Ramón y Cajal, S. *Studies on the diencephalon*. Springfield, Ill.: Thomas, 1966.

Rescorla, R. A. Pavlovian conditioning and its proper control procedures. *Psychological Review*, 1967, *74*, 71–80.

Rescorla, R. A., & Solomon, R. L. Two-process learning theory: Relationships between Pavlovian conditioning and instrumental learning. *Psychological Review*, 1967, *74*, 151–182.

Rose, J. E., & Woolsey, C. N. Cortical connections and functional organization of the thalamic auditory system of the cat. In H. F. Harlow & C. N. Woolsey (Eds.), *Biological and biochemical bases of behavior*. Madison, Wisc.: University of Wisconsin Press, 1958.

Ryugo, D. K., & Killackey, H. P. Differential telencephalic projections of the medial and ventral divisions of the medial geniculate body of the rat. *Brain Research*, 1974, *82*, 173–177.

Ryugo, D. K., & Weinberger, N. M. Differential plasticity of morphologically distinct neuron populations in the medial geniculate body of the cat during classical conditioning. *Society for Neuroscience: Proceedings of the sixth annual meeting*, Toronto, 1976. (Abstract)

Ryugo, D. K., & Weinberger, N. M. Differential plasticity of morphologically distinct neuron populations in the medial geniculate body of the cat during classical conditioning. *Behavioral Biology*, 1978, *22*, 275–301.

Scheibel, M. E., & Scheibel, A. B. Patterns of organization in specific and nonspecific thalamic fields. In D. P. Purpura & M. D. Yahr (Eds.), *The thalamus*. New York: Columbia University Press, 1966.

Schlosberg, H. The relationship between success and the laws of conditioning. *Psychological Review*, 1937, *44*, 379–394.

Schneiderman, N. Response system divergencies in aversive classical conditioning. In A. H. Black & W. F. Prokasy (Eds.), *Classical conditioning II: Current research and theory*. New York: Appleton-Century-Crofts, 1972.

Schneiderman, N., Fuentes, I., & Gormezano, I. Acquisition and extinction of the classically conditioned eyelid response in the albino rabbit. *Science*, 1962, *136*, 650–652.

Schroeder, D. M., & Jane, J. A. Projections of dorsal column nuclei and spinal cord to brainstem and thalamus in the tree shrew, *Tupia glis*. *Journal of Comparative Neurology*, 1971, *142*, 309–350.

Shinkman, P. G., Bruce, C. G., & Pfingst, B. E. Operant conditioning of single-unit response patterns in visual cortex. *Science*, 1974, *184*, 1194–1196.

Simpson, H. M., & Hale, S. M. Pupillary changes during a decision-making task. *Perceptual and Motor Skills*, 1969, *29*, 495–498.

Solomon, R. L., & Wynne, L. C. Traumatic avoidance learning: The principles of anxiety conservation and partial irreversibility. *Psychological Review*, 1954, *61*, 353–385.

Starr, A. Influence of motor activity on click-evoked responses in the auditory pathway of waking cats. *Experimental Neurology*, 1964, *10*, 191–204.

Steriade, M. Ascending control of thalamic and cortical responsiveness. *International Review of Neurobiology*, 1970, *12*, 87–144.

Van Twyver, H. B., & King, R. L. Classical conditioning of the galvanic skin response in immobilized cats. *Psychophysiology*, 1969, *5*, 530–535.

Voronin, L. L., Gerstein, G. L., Kudryashov, I. E., & Ioffe, S. V. Elaboration of a conditioned reflex in a single experiment with simultaneous recording of neural activity. *Brain Research*, 1975, *92*, 385–403.

Weinberger, N. M. Effects of conditioned arousal on the auditory system. In A. L. Beckman (Ed.), *The neural basis of behavior*. New York: Spectrum, 1982.

Weinberger, N. M. The neurophysiology of learning: A view from the sensory side. In N. Butters & L. R. Squire (Eds.), *Neuropsychology of memory*. New York: Guilford Press, 1984.

Weinberger, N. M., Hopkins, W., & Diamond, D. M. Physiological plasticity of single neurons in auditory cortex of cat during acquisition of the pupillary conditioned response: I. Primary fields (AI). *Behavioral Neuroscience*, 1984, *98*, 171–188.

Weinberger, N. M., Oleson, T. D., & Ashe, J. H. Sensory system neural activity during habituation of the pupillary orienting reflex. *Behavioral Biology*, 1975, *15*, 283–301.

Weinberger, N. M., Oleson, T. D., & Haste, D. Inhibitory control of conditional pupillary dilation response in the paralyzed cat. *Behavioral Biology*, 1973, *9*, 307–316.

Wepsic, J. G. Multimodal sensory activation of cells in the magnocellular medial geniculate nucleus. *Experimental Neurology*, 1966, *15*, 299–318.

Whitfield, I. C. The object of sensory cortex. *Brain, Behavior and Evolution*, 1979, *16*, 129–154.

Wickelgren, W. A. Effect of state of arousal on click-evoked responses in cats. *Journal of Neurophysiology*, 1968, *31*, 757–768.

Wiener, J. M., Pfeiffer, R. R., & Backus, A. S. M. On the sound pressure transformation by the head and auditory meatus of the cat. *Acata Oto-Laryngologica*, 1966, *61*, 255–269.

Winer, J. A. Diamond, I. T., & Raczkowski, D. Subdivisions of the auditory cortex of the cat: Retrograde transport of horseradish peroxidase to the medial geniculate body and posterior thalamic nuclei. *Journal of Comparative Neurology*, 1977, *176*, 387–418.

Woody, C. D., Aspects of the electrophysiology of cortical processes related to the development and performance of learned motor responses. *The Physiologist*, 1974, *17*, 49.

Woody, C. D., & Brozek, G. Gross potential from facial nucleus of cat as an index of neural activity in response to glabella tap. *Journal of Neurophysiology*, 1969, *64*, 704–716.

Woody, C., Yarowsky, P., Owens, J., Black-Cleworth, P., & Crow, T. Effect of lesions of cortical motor areas on acquisition of conditioned eye blink in the cat. *Journal of Neurophysiology*, 1974, *37*, 385–394.

Yehle, A., Dauth, G., & Schneiderman, N. Correlates of heart-rate classical conditioning in curarized rabbits. *Journal of Comparative Physiological Psychology*, 1967, *64*, 98–104.

Critical Commentaries

CHAPTER THIRTEEN

Premises in Neurophysiological Studies of Learning

WALTER J. FREEMAN

The diversity of detail and the specialty of promise in the approaches of Thompson, Tsukahara, Weinberger, and Woody present a challenge to perceive their interrelatedness and define their context in the research endeavor we and they share. I have elected to comment on certain premises, which appear to be held in common by these four investigators, which materially shape the direction and scope of their work, and which I no longer share.

1. The neuron is the elementary functional module of the brain, and the neural pulse train represents its complement of neural information.
2. The conditioned reflex is the optimal form of behavior for the study of neural basis of learning.
3. Feed-forward neural connections suffice for the study of brain function relating to learning.

Taking the first premise, there is no question that the neuron doctrine of Deiters, Sherrington, and Ramón y Cajal will remain, in the larger context of the cellular doctrine of Virchow, one of the key organizing concepts comprising our basis for understanding the brain. The integrity of the single neuron as an element of trophic and transactional function is not at issue. My skepticism on this premise takes two forms. The weaker statement is, the neuron is not the only functional module in the brain; the stronger statement is, the neuron is not the module of expression and transformation of behaviorally related information in the cerebral cortex. By corollary, the unit pulse train is not the only vector of information; more strongly, it does not by itself manifest the information maintained routinely in the cerebral cortex.

Generally speaking, the brain can be viewed as a hierarchy of modules ranging from molecules through organelles to neurons and beyond to assemblies of neurons in varying forms and degrees of complexity. The nerve cell is a starting point both for brain growth and for our understanding of brain function, but the neuron doctrine should not be taken too literally to the exclusion of other kinds of organization. Cell biologists are quite familiar with

Walter J. Freeman. Department of Physiology-Anatomy. University of California, Berkeley, California.

the semiautonomous functional properties of subneuronal components such as ATPase (the "sodium pump"), the node of Ranvier, gap junctions, the dendrites of spikeless neurons, and so forth. It is my view that these modules participate in behaviorally related informational transactions (so also do axons, mitochondria, and ribosomes), but the information is not expressed at those levels, nor at the level of neurons. I believe that it exists at the level of assemblies of neurons, minimally tens of thousands, and more likely in the cooperative activity of hundreds of millions.

By corollary, while the axon and the action potential are the dominant (and I believe only significant) means for distance transmission in the brain, the "message" is not in the medium (the pulse train) but in the organization of pulse trains in neural assemblies. One way to characterize such organization for an ensemble is to define a pulse density function (the number of pulses per second per unit volume of a particular cell type); (Freeman, 1975). More generally the pulse train should be viewed as a sample from a certain neural set, and the significance of the sample depends on the scope and meaning established *a priori* for the set. The pulse rate of a unit is (metaphorically speaking) one letter on a printed page.

Taking the second premise, the conditioned reflex is unquestionably one of the most effective technical means for establishing control over animal behavior and for inducing changes that manifest learning. But the conditioned reflex is not the only model for learning; more strongly, in my view, it is inappropriate as a model for brain function in learning.

Perhaps the most persuasive case was made by John Dewey against the reflex (1896) and the conditioned reflex (1912) in psychology, and I will not attempt to recapitulate it. Suffice it to restate his conclusion that even in the laboratory an animal subject initiates action "into the stimulus" in a manner of incorporation for the guidance of future action. We might reformulate this view in contemporary terms of images (Freeman, 1981). At each stage of the imposed conditioning process the subject sustains a sensory search image, which tests the environment and conditions the emergence of a motor image for some action that modulates the probability of recurrence of an expected stimulus. The conclusion for the physiologist is that neural activity of the brain does not manifest responses to stimuli but rather images of expected input and expectant output.

Another way to express this is to recall the brilliant contribution of J. Y. Lettvin and his colleagues (Lettvin, Maturana, McCulloch, & Pitts, 1959) characterizing the performance of single neurons in the frog retina as "feature detectors." Whereas this conceptual approach has been successful in vision, it has not in olfaction (Lettvin & Gesteland, 1965). I believe that the reason for this failure is that the proper referent (content of meaning) of the olfactory neural activity is not the externally imposed stimulus, but the subject's expectancy of input or some combination of input and expectancy (Freeman, 1981). What insight can stimulus–response determinism offer regarding the neural mechanism of expectancy?

Taking the third premise, the circuit diagrams used by the above four authors, and by the majority of investigators in our field to present their inferences and conclusions in the form of "models," do not show feedback connections. Most weakly we can say that feed-forward projections are not the only form of neural connection. More strongly, unless the existence and functional properties of neural feedback are fully accounted for, the properties of feed-forward circuits that incorporate feedback cannot be properly understood.

All of us are aware of the existence of neural feedback and of its importance in the generation and control of action. We are also constrained by the need to simplify in order to understand and communicate. The presence of feedback in a neural circuit can complicate things unbearably. Immediately, there is an indeterminacy regarding relations between input and output, especially if the system is nonlinear (which it usually is), with the existence of indefinite numbers of state spaces. The difficulties of evaluating the properties of open-loop components can be baffling. The evaluation of closed-loop feedback gains (interaction intensities) from system transfer functions requires a quantal leap in the complexity of calculations and measurement (Freeman, 1979).

It is easier to sweep this complexity under the rug, which I do now by resorting to anecdote. Three years ago in a workshop at Irvine I presented some data on the properties of mitral cells in the olfactory bulb, from which I inferred that they formed a mutually excitatory neural population (i.e., one having positive feedback). I cited this as confirmation of Ramón y Cajal's (1909) hypothesis of "avalanche conduction," in which a weak olfactory stimulus might undergo "amplification" (as we would say now). Rafael Lorente de Nó, in the audience, stated that I was in error; Cajal had in mind feed-forward recruitment of mitral cells and disavowed the notion of feedback. Lorente later recalled (personal communication) that in the mid-1920s he prepared a manuscript on the cytoarchitecture of the cerebral cortex, in which he concluded that feedback relations were a prominent feature. After reading the manuscript, Cajal strongly urged Lorente not to publish it because it would be unacceptable to the scientific community and might blight his career. Out of respect for his mentor, Lorente elected not to publish the material while Cajal lived; when he did publish (Lorente de Nó, 1934), the work established itself as one of the enduring classics in neuroanatomy. Its influence on neuropsychology (through Donald Hebb), on neural modeling (through Warren McCulloch), and on computer design (through John von Neumann by way of McCulloch) has been incalculably great.

Why was the neuroscience community in the first third of this century so reluctant to face feedback? Why is it now? The answer is clear; feedback makes things too complicated. One cannot and should not fault the present generation of investigators for simplifying this property out of their circuit diagrams. The computer technology required to deal with it effectively has only recently become widely available. But future neuroscientists, who are among those principally to whom this volume is directed, should be aware that the most fearsome dragons they will face on the uncharted seas of neuroscience will be neural feedback loops in their numerous forms and guises.

REFERENCES

Dewey, J. The reflex arc concept in psychology. *Psychological Review*, 1896, *3*, 357–370.

Dewey, J. Perception and organic action. *Journal of Philosophy*, 1912, *9*, 645–668.

Freeman, W. J. *Mass action in the nervous system*. New York: Academic Press, 1975.

Freeman, W. J. Nonlinear dynamics of paleocortex manifested in the olfactory EEG. *Biological Cybernetics*, 1979, *35*, 21–37.

Freeman, W. J. A physiological hypothesis of perception. *Perspectives in Biology and Medicine*, 1981, *24*, 561–592.

Lettvin, J. Y., & Gesteland, R. C. Speculations on smell. *Cold Spring Harbor Symposia on Quantitative Biology*, 1965, *30*, 217–225.

Lettvin, J. Y., Maturana, H. R., McCulloch, W. S., & Pitts, W. H. What the frog's eye tells the frog's brain. *Proceedings of the Institute of Radio Engineering* (*IRE*), 1959, *47*, 1940–1951.

Lorente de Nó, R. Studies on the structure of the cerebral cortex: I. The area entorhinalis. *Journal fuer Psychologie und Neurologie* (Leipzig), 1934, *45*, 381–438.

Ramón y Cajal, S. *Histologie du système nerveux de l'homme et des vertébrés* (2 Vols.) (L. Azoulay, Trans.). Paris: A. Maloine, 1909–1911; Madrid: Instituto Ramón y Cajal (Vol. 2), 1972.

CHAPTER FOURTEEN

Stimulus–Response Relationships: A Simplistic View

FRANKLIN B. KRASNE

As an invertebrate neurobiologist, I am going to take license to entertain a rather simplistic view of the processes and circuitry that mediate learned stimulus–response relationships, because by so doing, I believe I can help clarify the significance of the findings reported in the chapters by Thompson, Tsukahara, Woody, and Weinberger.

When a conditioned reflex is evoked, activity in a specific set of sensory neurons must result in a specific spatial–temporal pattern of motoneuron activity. My simplistic assumption will be that this involves at one end circuitry that serves strictly for the analysis of stimuli, at the other end circuitry whose sole job is storing and generating patterns of motor response, and in-between circuitry that joins the sensory and motor apparatus together (Figure 14-1, top).

With this kind of framework in mind, I was struck by the list of structures in which preceding contributors found selective alterations of unit responses to the conditioned stimuli they had employed (Figure 14-1, bottom). For with the exception of the hippocampus, each of these sites is in an area of the brain that a classical neuroanatomy text would classify rather emphatically as either sensory-analyzing or motor-production circuitry.

In one sense this is no surprise. We can find things only where we look for them, and we tend to look in places that we feel we to some extent understand, which tends to be at the left and right sides of Figure 14-1. For when we find an altered response in, for example, auditory cortex, we can say, "Of course, that makes sense in relation to the fact that the animal is now responding in a new way to certain sounds." But by contrast, when we find an altered response somewhere like hippocampus, most of us really don't know quite what to think, because despite a lot of good ideas, which have been extensively discussed in the first section of this volume, it still remains uncertain what that magnificent structure really does. So we are a little like the drunk looking for his lost keys at night. He thinks he remembers he lost them in a hopelessly dark alley, but he decides to look for them under the lamp post where there is light to find them by. Most of us are probably inclined to believe that stimulus–response associations should be in the box called sensory–motor transformation in Figure 14-1,

Franklin B. Krasne. Department of Psychology and Brain Research Institute, University of California, Los Angeles, California.

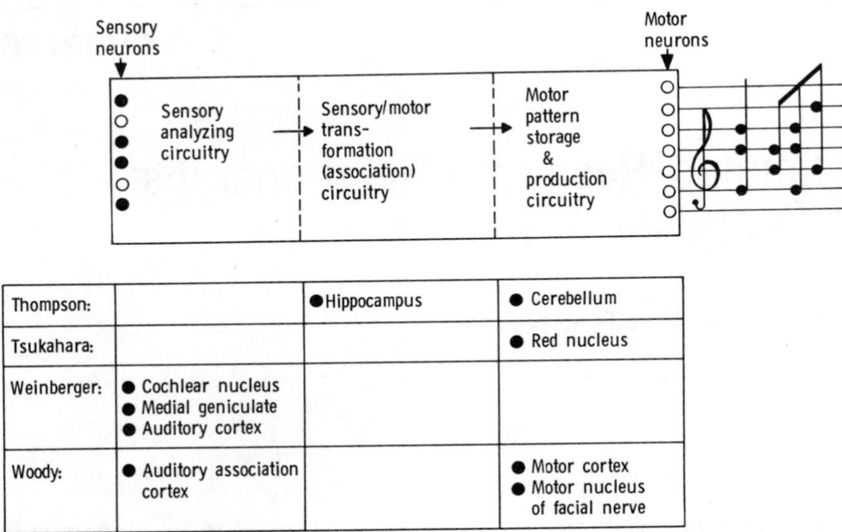

Thompson:		● Hippocampus	● Cerebellum
Tsukahara:			● Red nucleus
Weinberger:	● Cochlear nucleus ● Medial geniculate ● Auditory cortex		
Woody:	● Auditory association cortex		● Motor cortex ● Motor nucleus of facial nerve

Figure 14-1. Top: Processes and circuitry that mediate between stimulus and response. Bottom: The types of circuitry in which changed unit responses have been found by the authors contributing to this section.

but we still tend to look for associations in the left- and right-hand compartments.

What then do we make of these relatively peripheral alterations? Whenever we find a classically conditioned alteration in a unit response, we must ask about the origin of that alteration, and there are always three possibilities (Figure 14-2): (1) The alteration may be due to change in the *intrinsic state* of the neuron being recorded or the presynaptic terminals making contact with it. (2) The alteration may be due to *antecedent change* in the pathway leading from the sensors of the conditioned stimulus to the neuron under observation. (3) The alteration may be due to changes in the kind or amount of *tonic modulation* being imposed on the neuron under observation or neurons antecedent to it.

Consider first the possibility of antecedent change for the unit response alterations described in the communications under discussion. Alterations of unit responses in motor areas are, of course, always especially to be suspected of being due to this cause, because movement production is at the tail end of the series of events leading to a behavioral response. Tsukahara seems to have ruled out antecedent change as the basis for his observations by using a monosynaptic input to his target cells. Woody has acknowledged that his altered facial motor neuron and motor cortex responses are partly due to antecedent change, but by using local test shocks he has bypassed such antecedent routes and still finds important changes. Thompson, however, has not yet dealt with this problem for his altered cerebellar responses.

On the afferent side—the medial geniculate, auditory cortex, and the like—changes found by Weinberger and others might well be due to antecedent change, but so long as the latency from the conditioned stimulus to those altered unit responses is sufficiently short, these antecedents can only be in even more peripheral sensory processing circuitry. Weinberger is not alone in having found altered transmission at very early sensory relay stations; several laboratories have reported it and have established that the changed responses can have such a short latency that they must be due to altered success of transmission somewhere along the shortest available pathway between sensory neurons and the units under observation (Disterhoft & Stuart, 1977; Gabriel, Saltwick, & Miller, 1975). We are therefore probably safe in concluding that altered sensory and motor unit responses of the kind under discussion both do reflect, in at least some measure, local changes in net success of synaptic transmission.

However, this still leaves open the crucial question of whether these changes in success of transmission are due to intrinsic changes in the recorded neurons or terminals on them, or whether they are due to these neurons being tonically modulated from afar. Here we are on much more treacherous ground. Both Tsukahara and Woody have recorded intracellularly from their postsynaptic target neurons, and neither reports seeing signs of tonic modulation. But such signs might be very difficult to detect even if they were there, and signs of presynaptic modulation would be impossible to detect by postsynaptic recording; thus, in this situation negative evidence cannot be very convincing. Tsukahara, however, has provided one intriguing piece of positive evidence for intrinsic change by establishing that augmented EPSPs are not only larger, as they would be whatever the cause of augmented transmission effectiveness, but are also altered in shape; their rates of rise are increased precisely as would be expected if the synapses producing them were new ones closer to the cell body recording site than those of controls. Other explanations for this shape change could surely be advanced, and anatomical evidence may be needed to make Tsukahara's arguments fully convincing. But I must say that Tsukahara has come close to convincing me that he has his electrodes on cells whose population of presynaptic inputs has intrinsically changed.

I will consider below some other ways of discovering the nature of the changes under discussion, but I wish to turn first to a consideration of just what the function of the alterations in sensory and motor unit responses under discussion might be.

The most discouraging, and perhaps also the most likely, possibility is that these changes, far from being of local origin, are due to centrifugal modulation originating from the locus of a more central engram (Figure 14-3A) and that

Figure 14-2. Possible loci of change responsible for alterations in the responses of a unit to a stimulus.

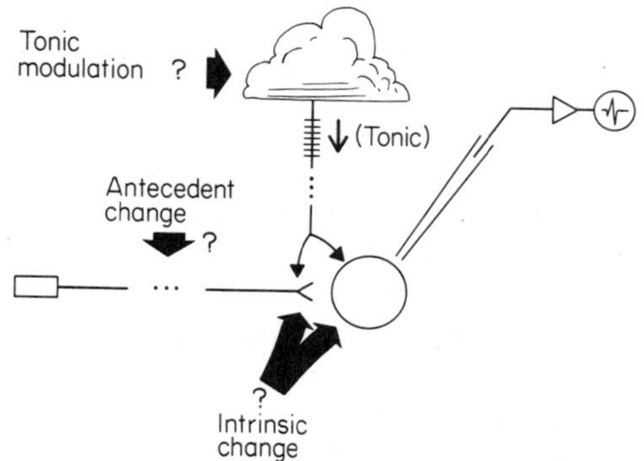

they serve merely to "bias" or "tune" the sensory and motor pathways (see Gabriel, 1976). In this view, the sensory and motor "sets" thus produced would be turned on only when the animal was in a situation where the conditioned reflex would be likely to be called for, and they would serve to increase the likelihood of detection of the conditioned stimulus, to reduce chances of erroneous perceptions, to increase the strength or rapidity of motor responses, and so forth. However, they would in no sense be a part of the engram.

Finding a plausible function for intrinsic change, particularly rather peripheral intrinsic change, is not quite so easy. We must start by recognizing that, whatever the role such intrinsic change might have, there is one thing it almost certainly does *not* do. And that is to associate the conditioned stimulus with the conditioned response! For it is axiomatic that the selective joining of the conditioned stimulus and conditioned response can occur only where units that are innately capable of signaling which of various possible conditioned stimuli have occurred meet units that can selectively promote the various responses of the animal's repertoire. But sensory areas have little or no known response representation, whereas motor areas, though they receive kinds of sensory information needed for feedback during response production, do not seem likely to receive sufficient sensory information to allow them to be the site of joining of arbitrarily chosen conditioned stimuli to responses.

Insofar as these presumptions are correct, the most that changes in pure sensory circuitry or pure motor circuitry can do is to establish sensory or response "sets"—that is, to increase the probability that an animal will react to a particular stimulus or execute a particular response. The association between stimulus and response cannot occur in such circuitry. Note, however, that if in attempting to train an animal in a single association, we were to do nothing more than establish strong stimulus and response sets, the animal would in all regards behave as though it had associated the stimulus and response. We could discover otherwise only if we then tried to teach the animal a *second* association. For this animal would then make both responses to each stimulus (or perhaps choose indiscriminately if the responses were incompatible). In thinking about the contributions under discussion, it occurred to me that it is only very rarely that we verify that we have a real association by adding a second association to the first.

Now, although the most that changes in pure sensory and motor circuitry can do is to produce sensory and motor predispositions, this function can be crucial for the successful design of associative circuitry. For the sake of seeing why this is so, let us suppose that any given stimulus is represented by activity of n out of a large population of feature detectors, and any response of the animal's repertoire is elicitible by the firing of a particular motor command cell. Then the associative process would have to be able to cause the coupling of any possible stimulus feature set to any command neuron.

The most straightforward, though by no means the most plausible, way one could imagine of arranging this is illustrated in Figure 14-3, B_1: Here, a very large population of "superfeature" cells is prewired to the feature detectors in such a way that the firing of any particular combination of n feature cells can be represented by the firing of a single, unique "superfeature" cell. This is accomplished by the convergence of n feature cells on each superfeature cell in all possible combinations, with activity in all n of the feature cells converging on a particular superfeature cell being needed to excite that superfeature cell to

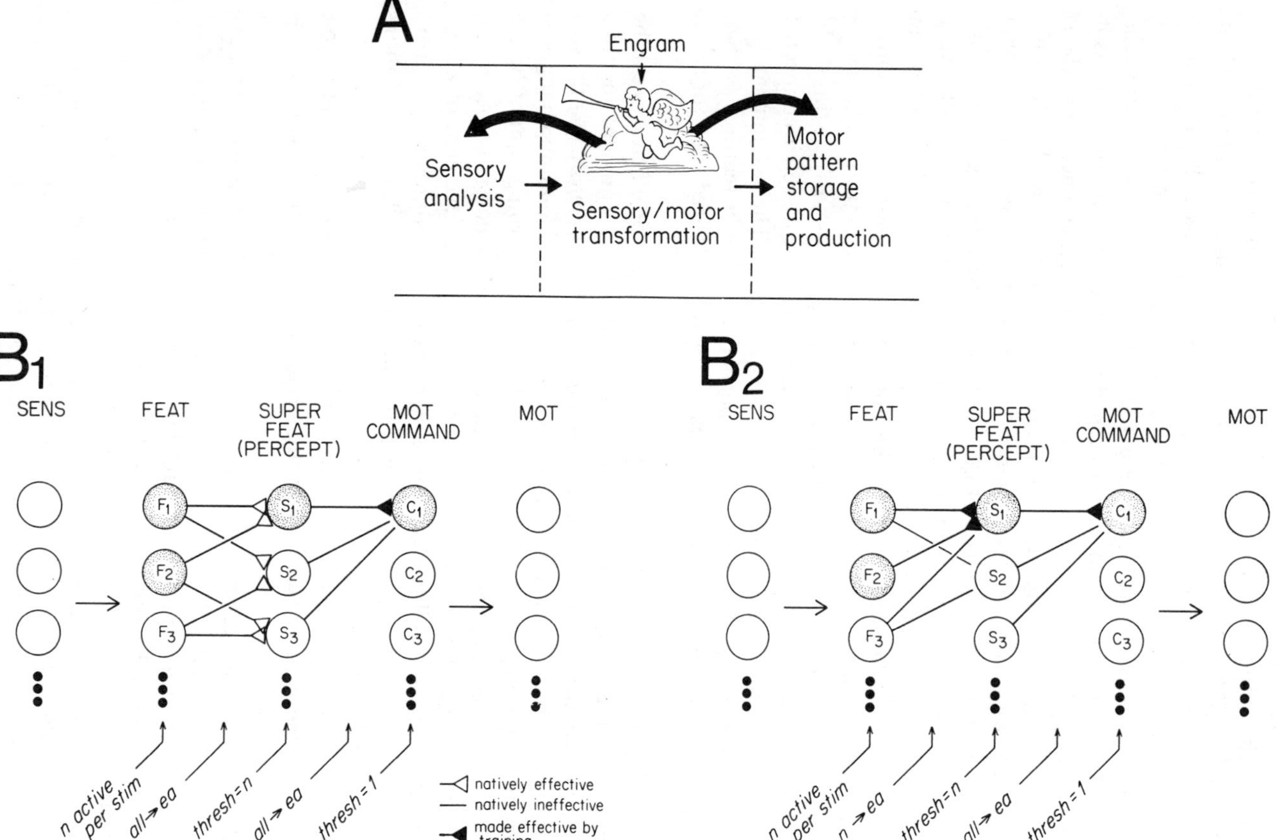

Figure 14-3. Possible roles of tonic modulation and intrinsic change. (A) A centrally located engram could be the origin of tonic modulating signals producing centrifugal control of sensory analysis and motor pattern generating circuitry. (B) Capability for intrinsic change within sensory analyzing circuitry could reduce the number of neurons needed to produce large numbers of arbitrary associations between stimuli and responses. B_1, an arrangement that does not utilize such change; B_2, an arrangement that does. In B_1, the coincident firing of units F_1 and F_2 drive unit C_1 by virtue of prewired connections to S_1 and learned potentiation of the synapse between S_1 and C_1. In B_2, the firing of S_1 depends on the learned potentiaion of the synapse joining F_1 and F_2 to S_1 (see text). Shaded neurons are active.

firing threshold. Each superfeature cell in turn projects to every motor command cell via an ineffective but potentiatable synapse. The selective association between any stimulus and any response is then formable by potentiating the synapse that joins the superfeature cell representing the stimulus to the motor command cell that drives the response. Such a scheme would work well but would have the hopeless liability that a separate, prewired superfeature or "percept" cell would be required for every conceivable stimulus that just might someday be the conditioned stimulus for a learned response; the number of such cells would far exceed the number of neurons in a human brain.

However, this absurdity could be avoided if the set of superfeature cells were initially uncommitted and were assigned to specific feature sets only as it became necessary in the course of an animal's learning experiences. For then, instead of needing a separate superfeature cell for every possible stimulus, only a number corresponding to the number of stimuli that any individual can actually learn to recognize in its lifetime would be needed (see e.g., Konorski's concept of "gnostic" units; Konorski, 1967). And although this is still a very large number, it is no longer astronomical nor even absolutely unacceptable in terms of the number of neurons available for the task. Figure 14-3, B_2 shows an arrangement that would permit uncommitted superfeature cells to be assigned arbitrarily to particular feature sets. As in Figure 14-3, B_1, the threshold of each superfeature cell is n. However, here every superfeature cell is connected to *every* feature cell, but via initially ineffective synapses. The assignment of a previously unused superfeature cell to a particular set of n features is then accomplished by potentiating the synapses between the desired n feature cells and the designated superfeature cell.

The assignment of superfeature cells to particular sets of n features can be thought of as the formation of a "percept," and such assignment involves learning entirely within sensory–perceptual circuitry. It is therefore just the sort of learning that the observations of Weinberger and others on unit changes in sensory analyzers might reflect. And while this sort of learning cannot be the basis for the association between stimuli and responses, which must occur at a slightly later stage of processing, it can be essential to achievement of a high level of associational ability, for it greatly decreases the number of neurons required for the establishment of a very large number of arbitrary associations between stimuli and responses.

These considerations begin, I think, to provide some possible adaptive role for intrinsic change in sensory-analyzing circuitry (and by analogy, in motor-production circuitry as well).

But in the specific scheme indicated in Figure 14-3, B_2 change would make sense only at the highest levels of sensory circuitry. To what use, if any, could intrinsic change at lower levels be put? The scheme we have been discussing is not the only approach to establishing sensory percepts that can ease the load on associational circuitry. A quite different kind of scheme that can be considered is one in which the changes leading to the formation of percepts occur in a distributed fashion throughout broad reaches of sensory-processing circuitry. In such distributed schemes the assignment of a previously uncommitted "superfeature" or "percept" cell to a particular pattern of sensory neuron activity is accomplished by enhancing the effectiveness of virtually every synapse in the system that can promote the driving of the designated superfeature cell by the sensory pattern in question. Increases of efficacy at lower levels would presumably be modest, lest the hard-wired analyzing capabilities of the circuitry be disrupted, whereas those at the highest levels would be more profound. In a network that works this way synapses that were potentiated in establishing a superfeature cell for one stimulus would often be traversed when other stimuli are presented. But if *not too many* percepts have been established, the odds are that any given superfeature cell would be much more strongly excited by its "proper" stimulus than by any other. Relevant calculations of error probabilities for this sort of scheme are to my knowledge few. But those that I have been able to find (Brindley, 1969) suggest that if the network interposed between sensory neurons and superfeature cells is properly designed and is rich in neurons with receptive fields with *substantial but not total* overlap, then one can do realistically well with surprisingly small numbers of neurons. Moreover, using the same general strategy, the layer of superfeature cells can be replaced with a substantially smaller set of neurons, none of which has a receptive field that is entirely unique for a particular stimulus, without seriously degrading the associative capacity of the network as a whole.

This kind of scheme could explain a finding of intrinsic changes throughout sensory-analyzing circuitry. Its advantage would be still greater economy than the scheme of Figure 14-3, B_2. Moreover, it would have the advantage that misfortunes befalling a few neurons would not have major consequences.

Having now considered plausible functional roles for intrinsically and extrinsically imposed alterations in excitability of units in sensory and motor circuitry, we are left with two broad hypotheses: (1) Altered responses of such units are due to centrifugal control used for "tuning" the stimulus and response systems; or (2) such alterations are due to intrinsic changes that code for sensory percepts and their motor equivalents. I believe that determining which (if either) of these hypotheses is correct by trying to look for direct physiological signs of modulation is likely to be hopeless. Absence of such signs will mean little, given the resolution of our ability to detect them, whereas presence of them would still not rule out the concomitant occurrence of intrinsic change. However, I think there are two slightly more "psychological" approaches that might well allow discrimination of the hypotheses.

The first such approach is based on the fact that centrifugal control as opposed to intrinsic change makes sense only if the control is situational. Therefore, if the kinds of relatively peripheral transmission alterations under discussion here are due to extrinsic modulaton, they should *not* be manifest when the animal is removed from the context of his training. A formal test of this might involve a conditional discrimination paradigm. In one context a subject would be trained to associate one response, R_1, with a stimulus, S_1, and in another context an association between a different stimulus and response, S_2 and R_2, would be reinforced. The crucial question would then be whether the kinds of sensory analyzer and motor circuitry effects described in the communications under discussion do or do not depend on the contextual cue. Insofar as they do, it is likely that they are due to centrifugal control; insofar as they do not, they are probably due to local, intrinsic change.

The other kind of experiment I believe would perhaps allow discrimination of our two hypotheses uses special training procedures to see whether one can establish local changes of transmission effectiveness that are in fact more specific and more selective than one thinks could be produced by a realistic centrifugal control system. Suppose, for example, that we were to use *direct* stimulation of a single postsynaptic cell, *x*, as an unconditioned stimulus in a classical conditioning paradigm, and were to find that *x* increased its responses to the conditioned stimulus. We would then, as usual, not know whether the synapses onto *x* had changed intrinsically or whether distant circuitry had received information that activity of *x* and its afferents had been paired, had stored this information, and had begun tonically facilitating the pathway from the conditioned stimulus to *x*. However, suppose that *only x* and no other neuron of similar type were to have become conditioned. Then, the centrifugal control hypothesis would have to postulate that the distant control circuitry could on a neuron-by-neuron basis discriminate and remember exactly which single postsynaptic cell had been fired by the unconditioned stimulus and could, with perfect selectivity, augment transmission to that neuron and that neuron alone. At this juncture we would probably find it more plausible to conclude that the changes responsible for the altered activity of *x* were due to changes intrinsic to *x* or the synapses on it.

This general type of experiment has been done a number of times on motor neurons and pyramidal tract neurons (Loucks, 1933; Doty, 1969; Black-Cleworth, Woody, & Niemann, 1975; Mis, Gormezano, & Harvey, 1979). But for the most part the question at issue has not been that of specificity. Rather, it has simply been whether an unconditioned stimulus that directly activates a response pathway can produce any conditioning at all. However, there is one experiment, by O'Brien and collaborators (O'Brien, Wilder, & Stevens, 1977), that actually conformed closely to the format of the experiment just proposed, and the results suggest that there may indeed be perfect specificity of conditioning to the units directly activated by the unconditioned stimulus.

One problem with this general paradigm has almost always been a degree of weakness and unreliability of conditioning obtained when the unconditioned stimulus was direct stimulation of the conditioned response pathway. And the reason for this has long been suspected to be the lack of a substantial emotional component in such training paradigms. Thus, the joint firing of a neuron and some of its afferents may not be a sufficient condition for potentiating the synapses between them; there may also be a requirement for an additional "plasticizing" modulatory influence stemming from emotional processes. This view is tremendously reinforced by Woody's contribution to this section and is also reinforced by Chapter 26, by Hawkins and Kandel, in this volume. Thus, the experiment suggested here might be greatly aided by using hypothalamic stimulation in the way that Woody describes, along with the conditioned and unconditioned stimuli.

To conclude, it seems to me that this and the preceding experiment could go a long way toward resolving whether or not the engrams responsible for the observations reported today are or are not local ones. However, until the outcomes of these experiments or other new kinds of evidence are obtained, I believe it is fair to say that we have yet to demonstrably have gotten our hands on the cells holding bits of a mammalian engram, and we might still be a long way away.

REFERENCES

Black-Cleworth, P., Woody, C. D., & Niemann, J. A conditioned eyeblink obtained by using electrical stimulation of the facial nerve as the unconditioned stimulus. *Brain Research*, 1975, *90*, 45–56.

Brindley, G. S. Nerve net models of plausible size that perform many simple learning tasks. *Proceedings of the Royal Society of London B*, 1969, *174*, 173–191.

Disterhoft, J. F., & Stuart, D. K. Differentiated short latency response increases after conditioning in inferior colliculus neurons of alert rat. *Brain Research*, 1977, *130*, 315–333.

Doty, R. W. Electrical stimulation of the brain in behavioral context. *Annual Review of Psychology*, 1969, *20*, 289–320.

Gabriel, M. Short-latency discriminative unit response: Engram or bias? *Physiological Psychology*, 1976, *4*, 275–280.

Gabriel, M., Saltwick, S. E., & Miller, J. D. Conditioning and reversal of short latency multiple-unit response in the rabbit medial geniculate nucleus. *Science*, 1975, *189*, 1108–1109.

Konorski, J. *Integrative activity of the brain*. Chicago: University of Chicago Press, 1967.

Loucks, R. B. An appraisal of Pavlov's systematization of behavior from the experimental standpoint. *Journal of Comparative Psychology*, 1933, *15*, 1–47.

Mis, F. W., Gormezano, I., & Harvey, J. A. Stimulation of abducens nucleus supports classical conditioning of the nictitating membrane response. *Science*, 1979, *206*, 473–475.

O'Brien, J. H., Wilder, M. B., & Stevens, C. D. Conditioning of cortical neurons in cats with antidromic activation as the unconditioned stimulus. *Journal of Comparative and Physiological Psychology*, 1977, *91*, 918–929.

CHAPTER FIFTEEN

Systems Neurophysiology of Learning and Memory: Some Comments

JOHN F. DISTERHOFT

N. M. WEINBERGER *ET AL.*, "INITIAL EVENTS IN CONDITIONING: PLASTICITY IN AUDITORY AND PUPILLOMOTOR SYSTEMS"

Dr. Weinberger covered several areas in his chapter. The two that I would like to comment on specifically concern differential rates of conditioning in specific and nonspecific motor systems and the plasticity of auditory cortex single neurons during conditioning.

Weinberger made the interesting and important point that various response systems show different rates of change during learning. The table he used included representative learning rates for "nonspecific" systems such as GSR or pupil and "specific" systems such as nictitating membrane (NM) or limb flexion. Nonspecific systems were shown to condition within 5–10 trials. The specific systems conditioned markedly more slowly, taking 70–600 trials to condition.

I have no problem with Weinberger's conclusion; nonspecific systems do condition more quickly than specific ones. I would merely point out that the dichotomy may not be as marked as his table suggests. When we chose conditioning parameters to optimize speed of acquisition (250-msec CS-UCS interval, average 60-sec intertrial interval), we found asymptotic NM conditioning in a group of rabbits by trial 40 of acquisition (Disterhoft, Kwan, & Lo, 1977, Figure 3). Most rabbits showed well-defined CRs by trial 30.

Speed of conditioning is of some practical significance in choosing a conditioning paradigm in which to study the single-neuron events underlying conditioned response acquisition. This is one of the reasons Weinberger has chosen conditioning of a nonspecific system, pupillary dilation, in his multiple-unit and single-unit studies of conditioning. But "specific" response systems, such as NM extension, may be useful for such studies as well. Since NM conditioning is generally acquired in less than 40 trials, we have been able to monitor responsivity of single auditory cortex neurons during the learning

John F. Disterhoft. Department of Cell Biology and Anatomy, Northwestern University Medical School, Chicago, Illinois.

process (Kraus & Disterhoft, 1982) from the naive to conditioned state. Since we are beginning to understand the final output pathway subserving NM conditioning (Thompson *et al.*, Chapter 9, this volume; Disterhoft, Shipley, & Kraus, 1982), we may be able to describe the neural events and circuitry underlying the acquisition of "specific" as well as "nonspecific" CRs from CS input to CR output.

Weinberger's differentiation of learning rates between systems raises another interesting point about correlations of neural events and behavioral learning. As he pointed out, it would appear that changes occur sequentially in different sytems during learning. Thus, while we are conditioning a "specific" system such as the NM, "nonspecific" response systems such as pupillary dilation and heart rate no doubt condition first in the trial sequence. In this case, we may monitor CNS changes related to a nonspecific system change and mistakenly correlate it to a specific system. Is it possible that the hippocampal multiple units that Berger, Alger, and Thompson (1976) observed to change at eight to nine trials in NM conditioning were correlated with pupillary, heart rate, or respiration conditioning rather than preceding the much slower NM response acquisition? This possibility comes to mind since so many of the nonspecific responses in Weinberger's (1982) table appear to change within 10 conditioning trials. Weinberger's compilation of data stresses the importance of monitoring more than one type of response system during acquisition, when possible, and of being sensitive to the limitations of correlative neural–behavioral data.

Weinberger's data on auditory cortex single neurons during pupillary conditioning suggest that sensory system changes may be independent of the type of behavioral response system being monitored. I make this point because Weinberger's data and conclusions are so similar to those that we reported on single auditory association cortex neurons plasticity in rabbit during NM conditioning (Kraus & Disterhoft, 1982).

We isolated single neurons and defined their best frequency. We then used that frequency tone as the CS during NM conditioning. We found that neurons in conditioned rabbits were more than twice as likely to show significant alterations in response to the CS during the conditioning trial sequence as neurons in pseudoconditioned rabbits (51% vs. 19%); that neurons were equally likely to show significant increases or decreases in CS-evoked responses; and finally, that auditory association cortex neurons, as a group, changed after behavioral learning. This suggests, of course, that acquisition of the behavioral NM CR is not dependent on auditory cortex. Figure 15-1 shows examples of response increases recorded in two single neurons to the tone CS after conditioning.

The one major difference between our data and Weinberger's concerns the percentage of cells that changed. He found that almost 100% of the cells he recorded in AII cortex changed after learning. Our report of 51% change in auditory association cortex is more similar to the 60% figure he found in AI. The subareas of rabbit auditory cortex have not been as well defined as those in cat. So it is certainly possible that we recorded neurons in an association area not strictly homologous with cat AII. There were some procedural differences in the way data were taken in the two studies as well.

These differences notwithstanding, the overwhelming similarity between auditory cortex single-neuron plasticity in rabbits learning a "specific" motor task, NM extension, and cats learning a "nonspecific" task, pupillary dilation, seems theoretically significant. It suggests that plasticity and information storage ("engrams"?) may be going on quite separately in auditory cortex and motor systems. The fact that neurons in both studies changed after behavioral learning supports this. It is also true that rabbits can learn NM conditioning (Moore, Yeo, Oakley, & Russell, 1980), and cats can learn eye-blink conditioning (Norman, Buchwald, & Villablanca, 1977) without their auditory cortex. To my knowledge, pupillary dilation has not been studied after cortical lesions, but I see no reason why it would be impaired. In addition, Woody has suggested that the mechanisms of plasticity in auditory and motor cortices are quite different (Woody, Chapter 11, this volume; Woody, Knispel, Crow, & Black-Cleworth, 1976). The relative independence of neural events in auditory cortex from those in motor systems found in both Weinberger's and our studies support the idea that auditory system plasticity obeys different rules from motor system plasticity.

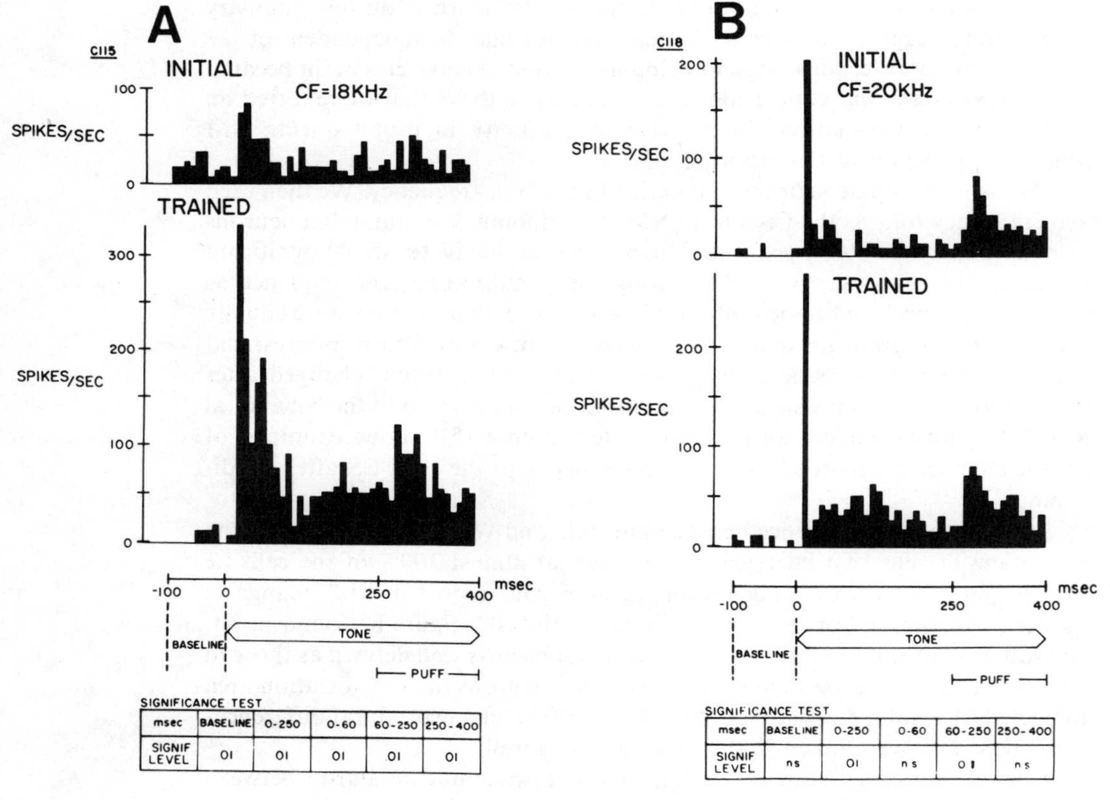

msec	BASELINE	0-250	0-60	60-250	250-400
SIGNIF LEVEL	01	01	01	01	01

msec	BASELINE	0-250	0-60	60-250	250-400
SIGNIF LEVEL	ns	01	ns	01	ns

Figure 15-1. Neural activity occurring during "initial" trails (rabbit behaviorally naive) is shown for comparison with that occurring during "trained" trials (CR has been learned). Each histogram consists of firing rate summed over 20 trials. The stimulus configuration and statistical changes in neural activity occurring during various components are illustrated. The critical frequency (CF) of each unit is indicated. (A) Generalized increase in CS-evoked firing rate with training. Note the accompanying decrease in spontaneous firing rate. (B) Increase in CS-evoked activity selective to the late (60–250 msec) portion of the CS-UCS interval. (From Kraus & Disterhoft, 1982.)

Some Comments

Dr. Thompson summarized the progress he has made on experiments aimed at analyzing the NM conditioned reflex arc in rabbit. He properly emphasized his finding that dentate–interpositus lesions eliminate the conditioned, but not unconditioned, NM response on the side of the lesion (Lincoln, McCormick, & Thompson, 1982; McCormick, Lavond, Clark, Kettner, Rising, & Thompson, 1981). He also reported preliminary experiments that indicate that such lesions eliminate classically conditioned leg-flexion responses in rabbits as well.

I share Thompson's enthusiasm about the importance of these data for focusing the analysis of the rabbit NM reflex arc. Woody made a similar breakthrough when he showed that motor cortex lesions or spreading depression eliminate the conditioned, but not unconditioned, eye-blink response in cats (Woody & Brozek, 1969; Woody, Yarowsky, Owens, Black-Cleworth, & Crow, 1974). The progress Woody has made in analyzing the cortical substrates of cat eye-blink conditioning, summarized in his presentation in this volume, attests to the practical importance of knowing where in the brain to search. Thompson has shown that lesions in the dentate–interpositus disrupt a critical portion of the circuit required for acquisition or performance of the NM CR (and possibly of the leg-flexion CR). But whether dentate–interpositus is the site of plastic changes necessary for conditioning, or of "engrams" (McCormick *et al.*, 1981), remains an open question. The possibility remains that dentate–interpositus is afferent to, or efferent from, the locus of such plastic alterations.

Vestibular ocular reflex (VOR) plasticity is also eliminated by cerebellar lesions, and the engram for this gain change has also been proposed to lie within cerebellum (Ito, Shiida, Yagi, & Yamamoto, 1974; Robinson, 1976). Direct tests of this hypothesis indicate that the locus of VOR plasticity is in the brain stem outside the cerebellum (Miles & Lisberger, 1981; Demer & Robinson, 1982), although Ito remains committed to the cerebellar hypothesis for rabbit (Ito, 1982). The extensive VOR system data suggest that analyzing the cerebellum's role in rabbit NM conditioning remains to be resolved and may be a bit more complicated than it would appear at first glance. There is the very real possibility that cerebellum is part of a loop through brain stem where the *primary* plastic changes underlying NM conditioning reside. But as mentioned above, Thompson's demonstration that dentate–interpositus is in the conditioned reflex arc is an important step in unraveling it.

REFERENCES

Berger, T. W., Alger, B., & Thompson, R. F. Neuronal substrate of classical conditioning in the hippocampus. *Science*, 1976, *192*, 483–485.

Demer, J. L., & Robinson, D. A. Effects of reversible lesions and stimulation of olivocerebellar system on vestibuloocular reflex plasticity. *Journal of Neurophysiology*, 1982, *47*, 1084–1107.

Disterhoft, J. F., Kwan, H. H., & Lo, W. D. Nictitating membrane conditioning to tone in the immobilized albino rabbit. *Brain Research*, 1977, *137*, 127–143.

Disterhoft, J. F., Shipley, M. T., & Kraus, N. Analyzing the rabbit NM conditioned reflex arc. In C. D. Woody (Ed.), *Conditioning: Representation of involved neural functions*. New York: Plenum, 1982.

Ito, M. Cerebellar control of the vestibulo-ocular reflex—around the flocculus hypothesis. *Annual Review of Neuroscience*, 1982, *5*, 275–296.

Ito, M., Shiida, T., Yagi, N., & Yamamato, M. The cerebellar modification of rabbits horizontal vestibulo-ocular reflex induced by sustained head rotation combined with visual stimulation. *Proceedings of the Japan Academy*, 1974, *50*, 85–89.

Kraus, N., and Disterhoft, J. F. Response plasticity of single neurons in rabbit auditory association cortex during tone-signalled learning. *Brain Research*, 1982, *246*, 205–215.

Lincoln, J. S., McCormick, D. A., & Thompson, R. F. Ipsilateral cerebellar lesions prevent learning of the classically conditioned nictitating membrane/eyelid response. *Brain Research*, 1982, *242*, 190–193.

McCormick, D. A., Lavond, D. G., Clark, G. A., Kettner, R. E., Rising, C. E., & Thompson, R. F. The engram found? Role of the cerebellum in classical conditioning of nictitating membrane and eyelid responses. *Bulletin of Psychonomic Science*, 1981, *18*, 103–105.

Miles, F. A., & Lisberger, S. G. Plasticity in the vestibulo-ocular reflex: A new hypothesis. *Annual Review of Neuroscience*, 1981, *4*, 273–299.

Moore, J. W., Yeo, C. H., Oakley, D. A., & Russell, I. S. Conditioned inhibition of the nictitating membrane response in neodecorticate rabbits. *Behavioural Brain Research,* 1980, *1*, 397–410.

Norman, R. J., Buchwald, J. S., & Villablanca, J. R. Classical conditioning with auditory discrimination of the eye blink in decerebrate cat. *Science*, 1977, *196*, 551–553.

Robinson, D. A. Adaptive gain control of vestibuloocular reflex by the cerebellum. *Journal of Neurophysiology*, 1976, *39*, 954–969.

Weinberger, N. M. Effects of conditioned arousal on the auditory system. In A. L. Beckman (Ed.), *The neural basis of behavior*. New York: Spectrum, 1982.

Woody, C. D., & Brozek, G. Changes in evoked responses from facial nucleus of cat with conditioning and extinction of an eye blink. *Journal of Neurophysiology*, 1969, *32*, 717–726.

Woody, C. D., Knispel, J. D., Crow, T. J., & Black-Cleworth, P. A. Activity and excitability to electrical current of cortical auditory receptive neurons of awake cats as affected by stimulus association. *Journal of Neurophysiology*, 1976, *39*, 1045–1061.

Woody, C. D., Yarowsky, P., Owens, J., Black-Cleworth, P., & Crow, T. Effect of lesions of cortical motor areas on acquisition of conditioned eye blink in the cat. *Journal of Neurophysiology,* 1974, *37*, 385–394.

CHAPTER SIXTEEN

Facts and Hypotheses Related to the Search for the Engram

VINCENT BLOCH / SERGE LAROCHE

For the neurobiologist interested in memory, as well as for the layman, the central concern is to know how and in what form the trace of an event can be stored in the brain. The essential condition for the validity of a brain model is that it should be compatible with both psychological and physiological knowledge. Though disagreements about the legitimacy of reductionism are over, we are still facing different levels of inquiry, and the scientific approach to physiological knowledge is based on techniques different from those of approaches at the behavioral level. Psychological and physiological levels are not reducible, but the first requirement is that in each discipline studies must lead to models that are consistent with the laws of functioning observed at both levels. This has not always been the case in the past for memory models.

So what are the main data on memory shown by behavioral studies? First, memory traces are not built up instantaneously, and sensory encoding of information seems to be followed by a perseveration of brain activity on which subsequent storage and retrieval are dependent. This has been shown by the abundant literature on so-called consolidation, which would be better named "the phase of information processing," because consolidation contradictorily implies some sort of priming mechanism acting on an already established trace (Bloch, 1970).

The second aspect of memory is the fact that access to memory is highly variable and retrieval is dependent on many external and internal factors.

The third principle, emphasized by Spear (1978), is that the memory trace is multidimensional. Memory of an event is not limited to the target memory built up under the control of the experimenter but is composed of an ensemble of elements taken into account by the subject during acquisition. At the physiological level, this means that the trace cannot be localized in a particular brain area but depends on functioning of as many circuits as there are elements.

Fourth, reactivation of the memory trace can be triggered by different strategies, and retrieval can occur after the presentation of a partial and apparently secondary element of the initial situation. Moreover, the delivery of a "reminder" not only reactivates the memory trace but also reintroduces a

Vincent Bloch and Serge Laroche. Department of Psychophysiology, University of Paris XI and C.N.R.S., Gif-sur-Yvette, France.

period of susceptibility of the brain during which the same kind of treatments, amnesic or hypermnesic commonly used in postacquisition, perturb or facilitate the performance in the next retention test (De Vietti, Conger, & Kirkpatrick, 1977). The essential point is that the effectiveness of postevent treatments is time-dependent and that temporal gradients are similar to those that exist during the so-called consolidation period. Thus, several lines of experimental evidence suggest that retrieval may be based on the reactivation of the same physiological events as those on which the initial formation of the trace was based.

We have discussed elsewhere (Bloch, Hennevin, & Leconte, 1979) the possibility that reactivation of these events could also take place during paradoxical sleep that follows acquisition. Recent unpublished data show that a reminder can be introduced during paradoxical sleep and modify the performance on the subsequent retention test in wakefulness. If such a stimulus can be integrated in the memory trace, it seems to imply that this trace has been reactivated during paradoxical sleep.

Now, regarding what we know about the physiological level, it is evident that a memory model must take into account the main aspects of brain function. That is to say, a neuron is nothing by itself but a component of networks in which definite traffic patterns of impulses are activated by the situation to be memorized and reactivated during retrieval in order to produce a behavioral response or a mental event. However, from time to time, models are proposed that are no more than a form of extreme extension of Lashley's (1950) principle of equipotentiality and which search for a storage mechanism in the individual neuron. An example of this approach is to be found in the attempts—and failure—to found the biochemistry of memory, based on the search for a macromolecular coding of the memory trace. More recently, Sinz, Grechenko, and Sokolov (1983) have defended an endoneuronal localization of memory processes. This concept is based on experiments performed on isolated and synapse-free neurons of the snail that show evidence of true conditioning and which suggest that membranal *plasticity* is not limited to synaptic sites. For these authors, the memory neuron concept is necessary to account for rapid storage in a stable memory form in one trial learning (although it is not the case in their experiments using numerous conditioning trials), and for fast retrieval with time intervals not compatible with circuit labeling. However, their model, taken as a *memory* neuron model, is not entirely compatible with the laws of memory that we quoted above and, physiologically, is hardly compatible with the laws of neuronal function in an intact animal. In such an organism, how can a neuron be conditioned without being stimulated by other neurons synaptically connected, and how can the animal behaviorally retrieve its memory without activating a complex response circuit? How can its response be even slightly different from one time to another without assuming some possibility of *modulation* through some synapses?

It is therefore easier to accept that memory encoding depends on the establishment of specific spatiotemporal patterns of activation in neural networks. Moreover, Hebb's (1949) dual-trace hypothesis following the perseveration theory of Müller and Pilzecker (1900), as well as Lashley's (1950) notion of the neurodynamic engram, are now widely accepted. Hebb proposed that a short-lasting labile trace was the basis for short-term memory as well as for preparing the long-term one. Despite the fact that this view was based on the assumption of reverberating activity, the point is that it is not necessary to admit such a controversial view in order to adopt the idea that some sort of *perseveration* is going on after the registration of information. Perseveration could be based on transient changes of neuron excitability, transmitter availability, and the like. There is enough evidence as to the lability of the immediate postacquisition trace to allow us to assume that activation of a specific neuronal configuration triggered by the initial stimulus complex persists for some time. In addition, as we have described above, reactivation of the trace by a reminder reintroduces a period of susceptibility of the brain that obeys the same temporal law as that during the postacquisition period. This is an important point, because it suggests that readout of a trace is based on the same sort of events as its registration. Incidentally, it is amazing to consider that the kind of evidence that was needed to support the consolidation theory came from experiments originally designed to reject this hypothesis.

We can summarize these views in Figure 16-1 (upper left), in which the brain is schematically represented by a multiinputs–outputs matrix. This model tries to take into account psychological as well as physiological data discussed above.

On the upper left, registration of information is represented by the action of the stimuli (S_1), controlled by the experimenter, as well as the actions of other stimuli (s_2, s_3, s_4), referring to different attributes of memory and its multidimensional aspect. These stimuli trigger a pattern of activity that is assumed to persist for some time. During this persistence, the action of several kinds of modulators (reticular activation, hormones, etc.) is possible only on the points of connection within which excitation is maintained.

Possibly, this pattern of activity is replayed during paradoxical sleep (Figure 16-1, upper right), and again points of connection are reinforced by reticular activation, which is one of the characteristics of this stage of sleep. A major argument in favor of the implied functional similarity of reticular action in sleep and wakefulness is the finding that an increase in the duration of paradoxical sleep that normally occurs after acquisition can be suppressed by electrical stimulation of the reticular formation (Bloch *et al.*, 1979).

Long-term memory (Figure 16-1, lower left) is characterized by the absence of activity in the specific network which is only *potentially* maintained by permanent marking of the connection points. A memory trace does not truly exist but rather is based on the probability of its being reinstalled as a dynamic event of circulating impulses when the initial stimuli trigger it.

In this kind of model, the storage of information is associated with the network as a whole. However, whatever its nature and cause, a disruption taking place in part of the whole connectivity does not prevent the retrieval of either the target memory or responses associated with it, provided that the firing of parts of the initial pattern occurs as a result of activation from relevant input stimuli (Figure 16-1, lower right). This would account, for example, for the reinstatement of a target memory (R) when contextual cues (e.g., s_4) are presented after experimentally induced amnesia or spontaneous forgetting. Similarly, if some disruption has prevented reactivation of the whole trace, only a secondary response (r) may occur, as has been shown, for instance, in the maintenance of autonomic responses to a stimulus that has lost its capacity to evoke the motor response (Hine & Paolino, 1970).

In this view, activity patterns that are "read out" during retrieval constitute an internal representation of memory, such as John (1972) conceived of and succeeded in investigating with evoked potential techniques. It also becomes

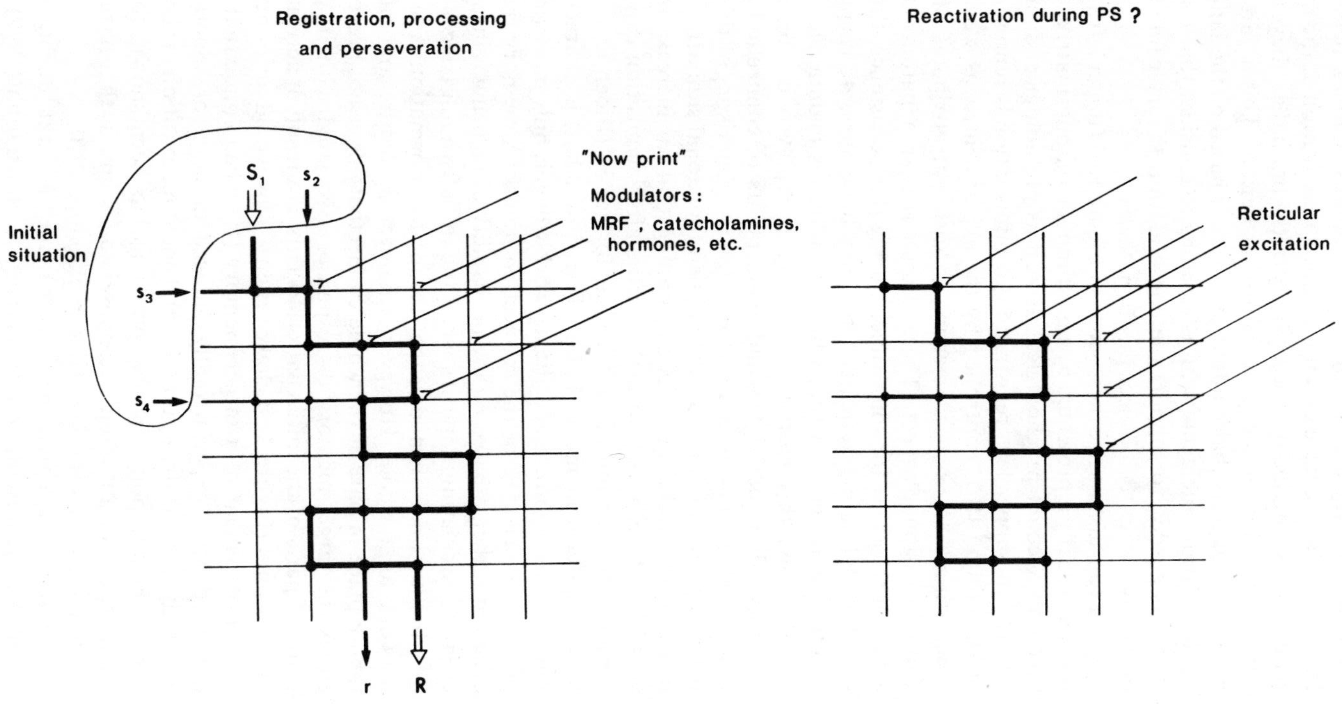

Registration, processing
and perseveration
Initial
situation
S_1
s_2
s_3
s_4
"Now print"
Modulators :
MRF , catecholamines,
hormones, etc.
r
R
Reactivation during PS ?
Reticular
excitation

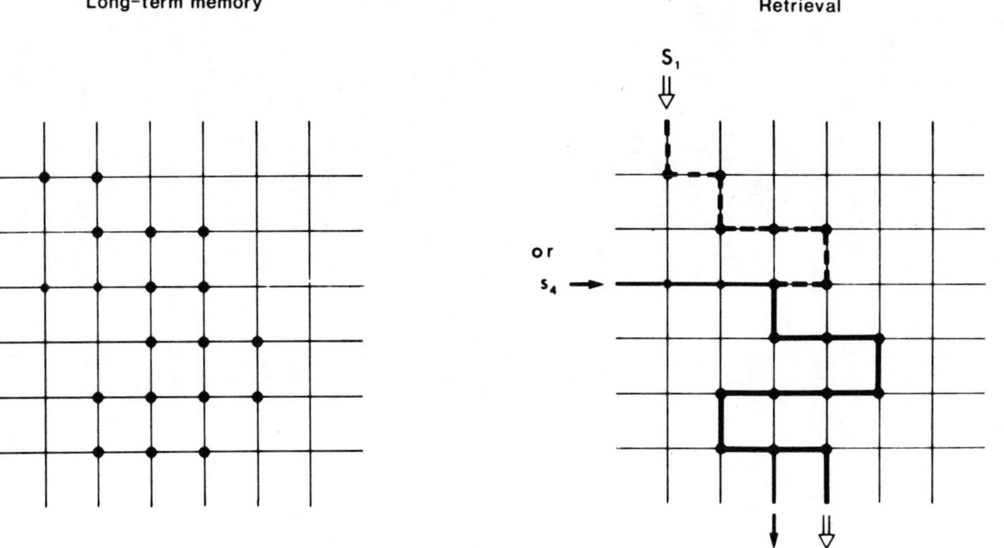

Figure 16-1. Schematic representation of a memory model discussed in text. Brain is represented as a simple matrix. Intersections stand for synaptic connections. Heavy lines represent activation pattern. Points represent relevant synapses or set of synapses.

easier to understand why brain stimulation, such as that used by Penfield in his classical studies, could result in retrieval of memories when it was delivered to brain regions that contained a main part of the neural circuit.

Now let us turn to possible mechanisms through which temporary neurodynamic engrams can be established and transformed into structural engrams.

An audacious hypothesis would be to assume cell neurogenesis. It has been shown by Altman, Das, and Anderson (1968) that neuronal mitosis continued after birth in rats and that handling could prolong this process. Although the first observation has been verified, the second has not yet been confirmed, and it is extremely difficult to conceive how a specific experience could induce neuronal birth and how new neurons could mark a specific network.

Another hypothesis is based on the phenomenon of central sprouting, which nowadays represents an important field of research. Collateral sprouting is being extensively studied, but so far the only existing evidence comes from experimental damage to the neural tissue. Thus, to use the term "plasticity," as is often done in designating both postlesion phenomena and memory changes, does not seem appropriate. Nevertheless, it is possible that terminal sprouting may be initiated in the absence of degeneration through changes in the activity pattern of neural pathways. At least, Tsukahara (Chapter 10, this volume) provided indirect but striking evidence that in the red nucleus classical conditioning could produce synaptic growth similar to that caused by lesions. It should be added that the possibility of such growth seems implicitly accepted as a presynaptic correspondence of postsynaptic growth of new dendritic spines invoked as a candidate mechanism in the formation of engrams (see Greenough, Chapter 32, this volume).

The third kind of hypothesis rests on the idea that the number of synapses in the mammalian brain is so considerable that specific networks could be formed, rather than by addition, by regression or repression of synapses not used in the matrix of circulating impulses produced by the initial situation. Changeux (Changeux & Danchin, 1976) has developed the idea of a selective elimination of irrelevant connections. This view is based on evidence showing that during development primitive peripheral multi-innervation disappears progressively and that central cell death occurs according to a timed programming. Although it has been shown that environmental conditions can modulate these processes during early life, there is no evidence of such a possibility in adulthood. More audaciously, Mark (1975) has suggested the possibility of *repression* of irrelevant synapses. This hypothesis was based on his experimental work on the motor end plate, which demonstrated that sprouting axonal elements occupy vacated synaptic sites as a result of cut neighboring axons, subsequent regeneration of the latter producing a repression of the new synapses. However, here again we have no evidence of such a mechanism in the central nervous system in the absence of an initial lesion.

The fourth kind of hypothesis considers that the consolidation of the trace results from an increase in the transmission factor at the synapses involved in the initial activation of the network. In our opinion, this hypothesis is supported by a great deal of experimental evidence. First, we have already stressed the importance of behavioral data concerning the time of perseveration. These data would imply the existence of an intermediate process that prepares lasting modifications at the synaptic level. The reality of such synaptic modifications consequent to learning is now supported by numerous data, referred to in this volume. These include not only biochemical but also structural modifications, such as the increase in the surface area of synaptic apposition, the curvature of contacts, and the increase in the volume of dendritic spines. Although Fifkova and Van Harreveld (1975) have shown that the latter modifications are correlated with the phenomenon of long-term potentiation (LTP), it is nevertheless unlikely that we are facing with a causality relationship. In contrast, LTP constitutes an excellent candidate, which may reflect an intermediate mechanism that, in turn, may prepare more lasting changes. It should be added that the artificial establishment of LTP by trains of short, repeated stimulations no doubt re-creates the same type of circulating impulses as those that are triggered in the networks activated by natural stimuli.

An argument in favor of this conception seems to be linked to the parallelism between the effects of a memory modulator at three levels: behavioral learning, cellular conditioning, and synaptic potentiation. Since 1966 we have been using the same facilitating agent, posttrial reticular stimulation, in our work on memory. In all of our experiments, stimulation is delivered during the first 90 seconds after training sessions or trials, with current intensity below cortical arousal threshold. It has been shown that posttrial stimulation of the mesencephalic reticular formation (MRF) facilitates learning in a great variety of experimental situations in rodents and cats (see the example given in Figure 16-2A). This led us to interpret the facilitatory effect of MRF stimulation in terms of an intensification of neural events that follow sensory encoding of information, that is to say, within the framework of the perseveration theory. This is schematically represented in Figure 16-1 (upper left), in which diffuse reticular activation acts only at synapses that have been previously excited by stimuli of the initial situation and responses evoked by them. This view that diffuse reticular activation might be a prerequisite for early changes in connectivity is supported by Singer's (1979) work on the visual system. This author showed that visual responses are reinforced at the same time by reticular inhibition of the inhibitory interneurons of one of the nonspecific thalamic nuclei and by heterosynaptic facilitation of synaptic transmission at the cortical level.

Since hippocampal cells have been reported to show clear changes in activity during classical conditioning (Olds, Disterhoft, Segal, Kornblith, & Hirsh, 1972; Thompson, Berger, Berry, Hoehler, Kettner, & Weisz, 1980), we examined the effect of the same posttrial MRF stimulation on Pavlovian conditioning of hippocampal cells in awake, freely moving rats (Laroche & Bloch, 1982). We found that this stimulation given immediately after each conditioning trial (1) facilitates the development of associative changes in CA3 and dentate (see Figure 16-2B) multiunit activity, and (2) results in long-term enhancement of hippocampal responsiveness to the conditioned stimulus. We also noted that in the entorhinal cortex, where no conditioning was found, MRF stimulation had no effect on multiunit activity, thus showing the specific nature of posttrial MRF stimulation on learning-induced plasticity, as it was hypothesized above for the behavioral studies.

If posttrial MRF activation facilitates perseveration of neural processes triggered in networks by incoming information, it could be assumed that this perseverative process might help long-lasting modifications to occur at the synaptic level. Therefore, the third step was to mimic natural trains of impulses in the perforant pathway by using short tetanizing trains of stimuli, and to look

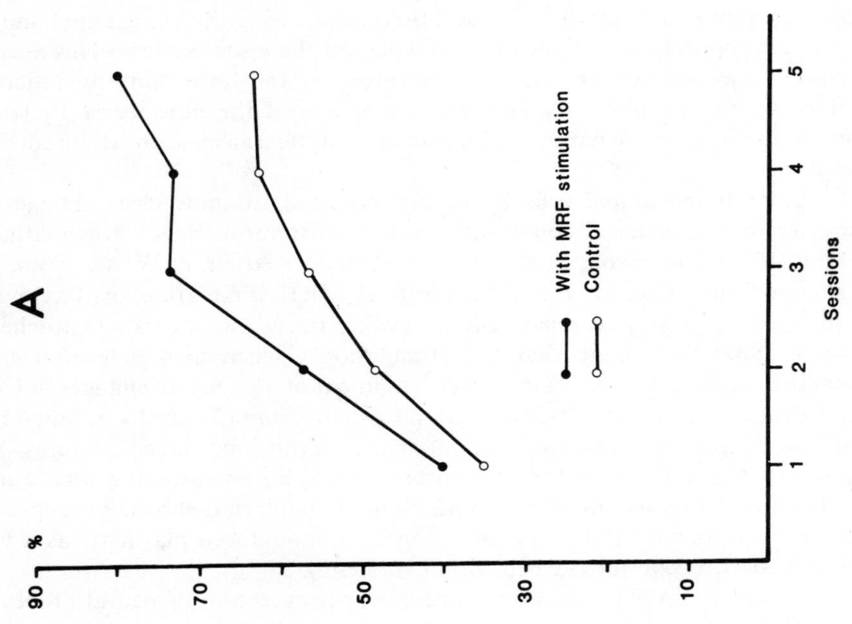
A
%
90
70
50
30
10
1
2
3
4
5
Sessions
With MRF stimulation
Control

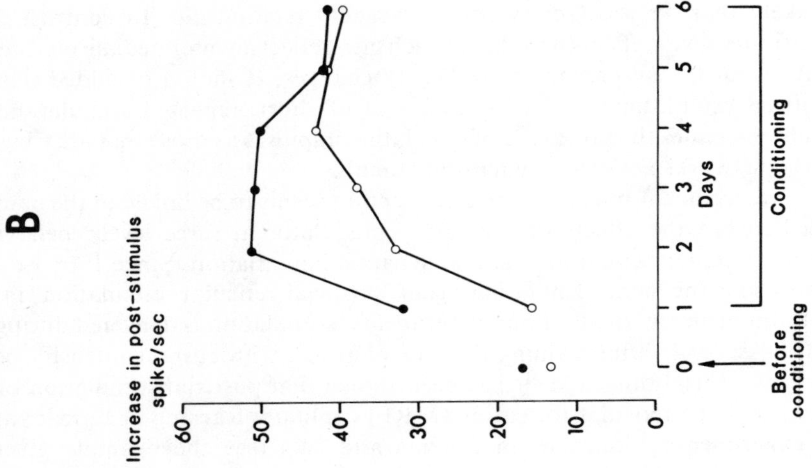
B
Increase in post-stimulus spike/sec
60
50
40
30
20
10
0
0
1
2
3
4
5
6
Days
Before conditioning
Conditioning

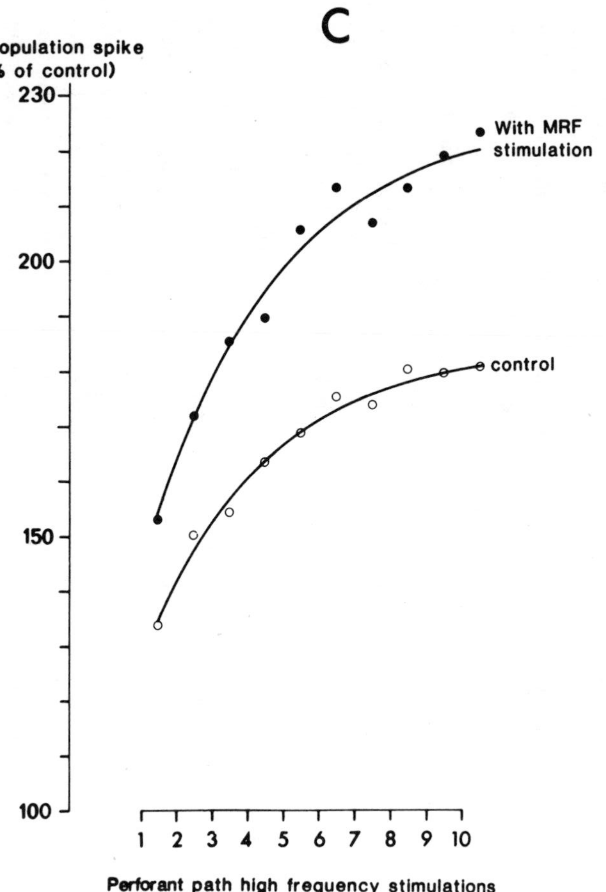

Figure 16-2. Effect of postevent MRF stimulation. Parallel studies in behavior (A), conditioning of dentate multiunit activity (B), and long-term potentiation (C). (A) Posttrial MRF facilitation of a positively reinforced brightness discrimination task in a T-maze. (B) Post-trial MRF facilitation of associative changes in dentate multiunit activity in a tone–footshock classical conditioning situation. Note the early development of dentate neuronal responses to the conditioned stimulus in the stimulated group compared with the control group. (C) Facilitation of the development of LTP in the dentate gyrus when animals are given MRF stimulation immediately after each of the perforant-path high-frequency stimulations (20 msec, 400 Hz). In A, B, and C, postevent MRF stimulation has the same parameters: 300 Hz sine wave current, 4.5 μA, 10 periods of 6 sec on and 3 sec off.

for the effects of posttrain MRF stimulation on LTP. MRF stimulation was exactly the same as those used in learning studies and was delivered *after* each LTP-inducing stimulus, with the assumption that neural events initiated by incoming stimuli must persist over a sufficient period of time so that MRF stimulation can act on these events. The results showed that postevent MRF stimulation greatly enhanced the magnitude of LTP at the synapses of the perforant path on dentate granular cells (Figure 16-2C). Thus, it appeared plausible that the effect of posttrial MRF stimulation, which facilitates conditioned neuronal responses, might be mediated through an enhancement of LTP.

Moreover, postevent MRF stimulation was shown to prolong LTP duration for several days (Figure 16-3A). Therefore, the question to be raised concerns the existence of LTP-like phenomena in the normal activity of the brain following learning. There is some direct or indirect evidence that synaptic evoked potentials could be enhanced after learning, and Thompson and associates (Chapter 9, this volume) have provided such an example. We thought, however, that linkage between LTP and learning could be provided more convincingly by looking at an actual change in LTP itself provoked by learning and modulated by a treatment that acts in a parallel manner on learning rather than at an enhanced single evoked potential.

Thus, our last step was to compare LTP development in control rats with that of rats whose training had been completed 48 hours earlier in a situation in which we used dentate multiunit conditioning. In a third group of rats, we studied LTP development with conditioning facilitated by posttrial MRF stimulation. It can be seen in Figure 16-3B that the amount of LTP was increased after the learning experience. Moreover, this effect was greatly enhanced in rats in whom learning was facilitated by posttrial MRF stimulation. Appropriate control groups ensured that it was the association of learning experience with MRF stimulation and not the total amount of MRF stimulation that had this effect on subsequent LTP.

Thus, it appears that all the existing evidence clearly implicates LTP mechanisms in memory consolidation. Memorizing activity has been shown to be followed by a modification of the synaptic transmission factor, which can be clearly detected 2 days later. Moreover, this transmission factor is still more enhanced when memory registration has been facilitated by a modulating agent.

More generally, this implies that hypermnesic agents exert their facilitatory effects on processes of conversion of short-term memory into long-term memory. This is precisely the hypothesis advanced by consolidation theorists, particularly by McGaugh (1966), who was the first to use facilitating drugs with posttrial injections.

To summarize, we would like to emphasize four points that appear to us essential for the elaboration of neural memory models. The first concerns the requirement to take into account the existence of short-term perseveration of neural activation triggered by the initial situation. The second stresses the importance of the use of memory modulators, particularly when they produce parallel effects at the three levels—behavioral, cellular, and synaptic. The third suggests that between registration and retrieval of memory, it is not necessary to assume a specific mechanism of storage. In the absence of memory reactivation, the engram may exist only potentially, in an inactive form, based upon the

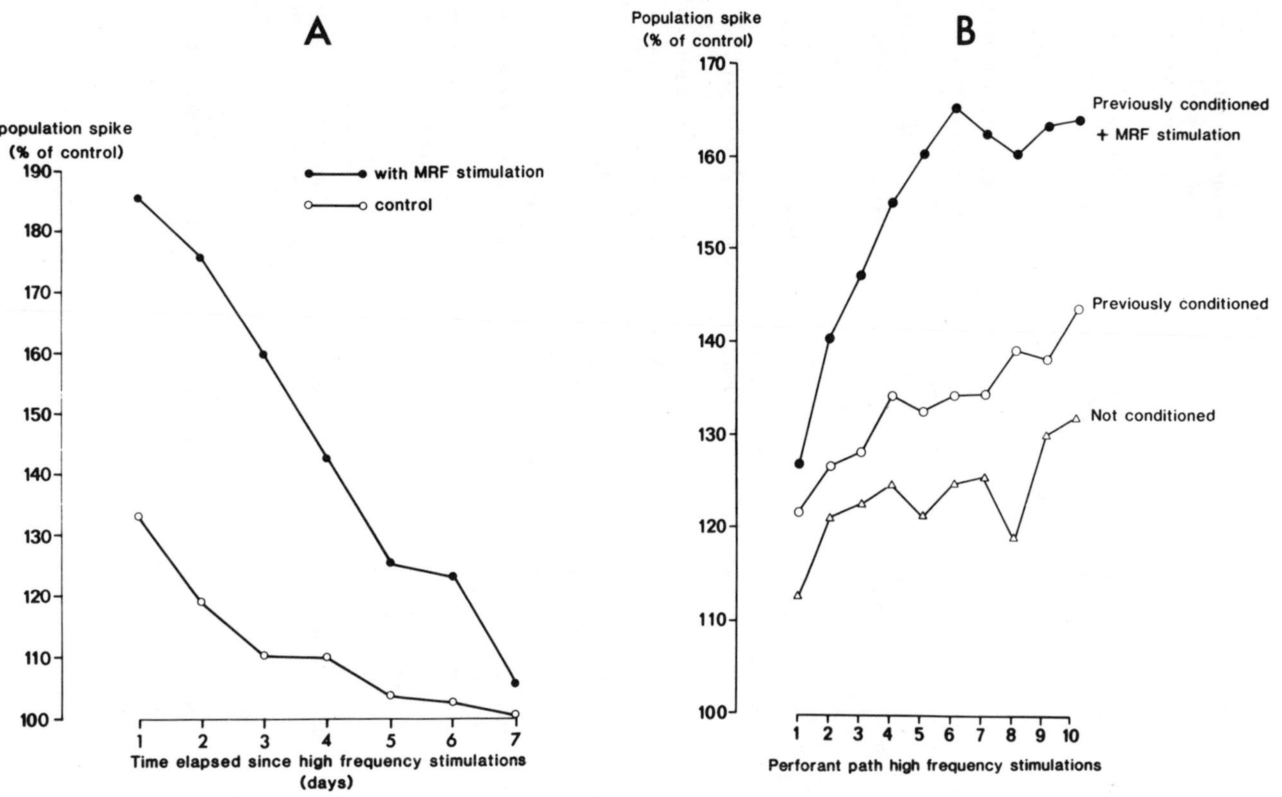

Figure 16-3. Long-term effects of postevent MRF stimulation. (A) Average amplitude of LTP as a function of time since its establishment (illustrated in Figure 16-1C). Note longer duration of LTP when animals received MRF stimulation after each perforant-path high-frequency stimulation. (B) Development of LTP 48 hr after the last session of dentate multiunit conditioning. LTP was induced by 10 perforant-path high-frequency stimulations with 5-min intervals. Note the increased amount of LTP in conditioned animals compared with controls, and the enhancing effect of MRF stimulation given immediately after each trial of the classical conditioning phase of the experiment.

modifications of the points of connection within the network. Fourth, it is important to stress that a neural memory model must be compatible with behavioral as well as physiological data.

REFERENCES

Altman, J., Das, D. G., & Anderson, W. J. Effects of infantile handling on morphological development of the rat brain: An exploratory study. *Developmental Psychobiology*, 1968, *1*, 10–20.

Bloch, V. Facts and hypotheses concerning memory consolidation processes. *Brain Research*, 1970, *24*, 561–575.

Bloch, V., Hennevin, E., & Leconte, P. Relationship between paradoxical sleep and memory processes. In M. A. B. Brazier (Ed.), *Brain mechanisms in memory and learning: From the single neuron to man*. New York: Raven Press, 1979.

Changeux, J.-P., & Danchin, A. Selective stabilization of developing synapses as a mechanism for the specification of neuronal networks. *Nature*, 1976, *264*, 705–712.

De Vietti, T. L., Conger, G. L., & Kirkpatrick, B. R. Comparison of the enhancement gradients of retention obtained with stimulation of the mesencephalic reticular formation after training or memory reactivation. *Physiology and Behavior*, 1977, *19*, 549–554.

Fifkova, E., & Van Harreveld, A. Morphological correlates of long-lasting potentiation of synaptic transmission in the dentate gyrus following stimulation of the entorhinal area. *Anatomical Record*, 1975, *181*, 355–356.

McGaugh, J. L. Time-dependent processes in memory storage. *Science*, 1966, *153*, 1351–1358.

Hebb, D. O. *The organization of behavior*. New York: Wiley, 1949.

Hine, B., & Paolino, R. M. Retrograde amnesia: Production of skeletal but not cardiac response gradient by electroconvulsive shock. *Science*, 1970, *109*, 1224–1226.

John, E. R. Switchboard versus statistical theories of learning and memory. *Science*, 1972, *177*, 850–864.

Laroche, S., & Bloch, V. Conditioning of hippocampal cells and long-term potentiation: An approach to mechanisms of posttrial memory facilitation. In C. Ajmone Marsan & H. Matthies (Eds.), *Neuronal plasticity and memory formation*. New York: Raven Press, 1982.

Lashley, K. S. In search of the engram. *Symposium of the Society for Experimental Biology*, 1950, *4*, 454–482.

Mark, R. *Memory and nerve cell connections*. Oxford: Oxford University Press, 1975.

Müller, G. E., & Pilzecker, A. Experimentelle Beiträge zur lehre von Gedachtniss. *Zeitschrift für Psychologie*, 1900, *1*, 1–300.

Olds, J., Disterhoft, J. F., Segal, M., Kornblith, C. L., & Hirsh, R. Learning centers of rat brain mapped by measuring latencies of conditioned unit responses. *Journal of Neurophysiology*, 1972, *35*, 202–219.

Singer, W. Central-core control of visual-cortex functions. In O. Schmitt & F. G. Worden (Eds.), *The neurosciences: Fourth study program*. Cambridge, Mass.: MIT Press, 1979.

Sinz, R., Grechenko, T. N., & Sokolov, E. N. The memory neuron concept: A psychophysiological approach. In R. Sinz & M. R. Rosenzweig (Eds.), *Memory, motivation and event-related potentials in mental operations*. Jena: VEB Gustav Fischer, and Amsterdam: Elsevier Biomedical Press, 1983.

Spear, N. E. *The processing of memories: Forgetting and retention*. Hillsdale, N.J.: Erlbaum, 1978.

Thompson, R. F., Berger, T. W., Berry, S. D., Hoehler, F. K., Kettner, R. E., & Weisz, D. J. Hippocampal substrate of classical conditioning. *Physiological Psychology*, 1980, *8*, 262–279.

SECTION THREE

Modulation of Memory

CHAPTER SEVENTEEN

Basic Processes and Modulatory Influences in the Stages of Memory Formation

MARK R. ROSENZWEIG / EDWARD L. BENNETT

INTRODUCTION

This chapter and the current research of our group deal with attempts to identify the neurochemical processes that must occur between the input of information to the nervous system and its eventual recall. This is an active and productive area of research, but it is characterized by divergent approaches and findings rather than by convergence on acknowledged constructs and findings. The activity and productivity of the field are reflected and recorded in a number of symposia that have appeared in recent years (e.g., Rosenzweig & Bennett, 1976; Brazier, 1979; Ajmone Marsan & Matthies, 1982). Yet although each of these meetings has demonstrated interesting and probably important new findings, there is still much disagreement about the basic concepts of the field. The unsettled state of this area was noted by Adrian Dunn in his 1980 *Annual Review of Psychology* chapter from which we quote some comments here:

> The logical constructs of the formation of memory are presently in a confused state. Most researchers . . . believe that there is more than one temporal stage of memory, but the nature and number of these stages are not agreed upon. [Others, however, claim that the apparent] multiple stages may reflect characteristics of the amnestic agent[s] rather than fundamental stages in the biological processing of memory. . . .
>
> The relationships between the various stages are also unclear. Parallel trace models in which separate memory traces [of different durations] are formed and decay independently (McGaugh, 1966) are currently in disfavor, and many prefer a single-trace multiple process model (Gold & McGaugh, 1975) in which the same trace goes through different stages during which [its strength] can be modulated. . . .
>
> There is an enduring dispute over the nature of the . . . processes [that are susceptible to manipulation]—are they part of memory storage or memory retrieval? . . .
>
> The absence of a solid conceptual framework has not precluded continuation of studies on the biochemistry of memory. Indeed, there is some hope that biochemical data may help unravel some of the problems. . . . (pp. 343–344)

Mark R. Rosenzweig. Department of Psychology, University of California, Berkeley, California.
Edward L. Bennett. Melvin Calvin Laboratory, Lawrence Berkeley Laboratory, Berkeley, California.

Some investigators see the task of delineating the processes involved in formation of memory as much more complex than Dunn suggests. Thus Mark (1979) supposes that these processes are about as complex and varied as those involved in carbohydrate metabolism, with numerous parallel pathways and shunts. In this case there may be no single steps that are crucial to the formation of memory, no bottlenecks at which the whole process can be halted. Kety (1976) has argued strongly for a multiplicity of underlying processes:

> So profound and powerful an adaptation as learning or memory is not apt to rest upon a single modality. Rather, I suspect that advantage is taken of every opportunity provided by evolution. There were forms of memory before organisms developed nervous systems, and after that remarkable leap forward it is likely that every new pathway and neural complexity, every new neurotransmitter, hormone, or metabolic process that played upon the nervous system and subserved a learning process was preserved and incorporated.
>
> Invertebrate learning has much to teach us, especially since it can be studied more rigorously than the processes occurring in the mammalian brain. We must be aware, however, that it gives us only one part of a remarkable concert of memory processes that are possible and that have come into play in nervous systems of greater complexity and with more varied behavioral options.
>
> I would suggest that many different memory processes have adapted the large range of species for survival, and that in any single species, especially those that are later in evolution, a variety of mechanisms are employed. (pp. 321–322)

Note that Kety's position may also raise problems about the use of some animal models for study of human memory processes.

Our own work, and that of others, has convinced us that there is at least one obligatory process: The formation of long-term memory requires synthesis of proteins. Blocking synthesis of proteins in the nervous system does not prevent learning, nor does it interfere with short-term memory (STM) or intermediate-term memory (ITM), but it does prevent formation of long-term memory (LTM). More specifically, it appears that the formation of LTM requires a pulse of protein synthesis (lasting on the order of minutes) that occurs somewhere within the posttraining period (lasting on the order of hours). Influenced both by this finding and our review of the literature, we would like to test hypotheses according to which formation of the earlier stages of memory (STM and ITM) also depends on obligatory processes. This should also permit us to assign specific modulatory influences to particular stages of memory formation.

EXPLICATION OF ASSUMPTIONS EMBEDDED WITHIN THIS LINE OF INQUIRY

Before reviewing some of the findings that seem to us to support the positions taken in the previous paragraph, let us state some of the concepts and assumptions that we believe are embedded in this line of inquiry:

1. Concept of the memory trace: Memory is stored in the nervous system by physicochemical alteration of neurons and/or neural circuits. The same information can be stored in successive transformations of the trace.
2. Much information is lost rather rapidly, but in some cases the chemical stages in memory formation lead eventually to structural changes that underlie LTM storage.

3. Formation of the memory trace involves both necessary or basic processes (sometimes called intrinsic) and also modulatory (or extrinsic) influences that affect the rate or level of the direct processes.

4. Behavior on a retention test is related to the strength of the memory trace and also to conditions at the time of retention (e.g., motivation, ambient stimuli, and the like). Valid measurement of strength of memory therefore requires careful control of the surrounding conditions.

5. Even if conditions at the time of a memory test are well controlled, the behavior will be affected by the operation of random factors. One way of overcoming random variation within the subject involves the use of repeated training and testing of the same subjects on equivalent items. (We have done some experiments of this sort using subjects well trained on the radial maze, where items are similar and strength of training brings animals to a plateau; Mizumori, Rosenzweig, & Bennett, in press.) Another approach uses groups of similar subjects treated as identically as possible. Results for such a group provide an estimate of the probability of response for a single animal.

SURVEY OF SOME RELEVANT FINDINGS

In this survey we will take up research that bears on four topics: (1) the necessity of protein synthesis for formation of LTM; (2) modulation of formation of memory; (3) processes that may underlie the earlier stages of memory formation; and (4) synergistic effects from combined administration of memory-active agents.

Before undertaking the reviews, we should comment that attempts to survey and understand this field are complicated by a number of deficiencies in the literature. We pointed out several of these shortcomings in 1971 when we reviewed a related topic: chemical alterations produced in brain by environment and training (Bennett & Rosenzweig, 1971). For example, we made the following comment: "It is surprising and worrisome that some of the most interesting studies have appeared as isolated reports with no follow up, to date, from either the originating laboratory or by others. We would like to urge greater attention to replication of results, especially before publication, so that experimental results in the literature can be relied on as being factually correct" (p. 196). In the ensuing decade, many additional investigators have joined the study of neurochemical processes in learning and memory, and the number of publications has increased greatly. Nevertheless, Dunn (1980) in his recent review still stressed the prevailing lack of replication: "The most obvious deficit in the literature reviewed is the rarity with which experiments from one laboratory are replicated in another . . . there is also some persisting doubt as to the consistency of effects found within a laboratory" (p. 360).

The Necessity of Protein Synthesis for Formation of Long-Term Memory

The hypothesis that protein synthesis is required for memory storage goes back to Katz and Halstead (1950). Tests of this hypothesis were initiated by Flexner, Flexner, and Stellar (1963) and Flexner, Flexner, Stellar, de la Haba, and Roberts (1962, 1965), and much current research follows their basic approach. The design involves these components: (1) giving animal subjects brief training that, without further treatment, would yield evidence of retention at a later test (e.g., 1 day, 7 days); (2) administering to some subjects an inhibitor of protein synthesis at various times close to training; and (3) comparing test performance of experimental and control subjects. Both active and passive behavioral tests have been used in order to obviate certain problems of interpretation of results.

Our review of research on this hypothesis will include the following sections: (1) development of research on the protein-synthesis hypothesis of formation of LTM; (2) consideration of whether memory for tasks that involve positive reinforcements are blocked by inhibition of protein synthesis; (3) alternative interpretations to the protein-synthesis hypothesis of formation of LTM; and (4) possible roles of proteins in the storage of memory.

Development of Research on the Protein-Synthesis Hypothesis of Formation of Long-Term Memory

The early studies on this hypothesis employed puromycin (PM) as the inhibitor of protein synthesis (e.g., Flexner *et al.*, 1963; Agranoff & Klinger, 1964; Barondes & Cohen, 1966). Soon cycloheximide (CXM) and acetoxycycloheximide (AXM) were introduced into this research (e.g., Barondes & Cohen, 1967a, 1967b). Questions were raised as to whether PM was producing amnesic effects because it inhibits protein synthesis or because of side effects. Cohen, Ervin, and Barondes (1966) showed that PM causes abnormal electrical activity in the hippocampus, and Cohen and Barondes (1967) suggested that PM's effect on memory may be due to occult seizures. Furthermore, PM was found to affect memory if administered 24 hours or more after training, suggesting that it might affect retrieval instead of, or in addition to, consolidation of memory. Other inhibitors of protein synthesis, on the contrary, had to be administered close to the time of training in order to affect memory. For these reasons, PM has largely been abandoned in research on formation of memory, and it will not be considered further in this chapter.

By the early 1970s considerable evidence had been obtained indicating that protein synthesis during or soon after training is necessary for formation of LTM. Nevertheless, the interpretation of these findings was still clouded by serious problems such as the following: (1) The inhibitors of protein synthesis that were available for research (PM, AXM, and CXM) were rather toxic; this impeded experiments and complicated interpretation of results. (2) It appeared that inhibition of protein synthesis could prevent memory formation after weak training but not after strong training (Barondes, 1970). The discovery by Bennett, Orme, and Hebert (1972) that anisomycin (ANI) is an effective amnestic agent in rodents paved the way to resolution of the main challenges to the protein-synthesis hypothesis of memory formation. ANI blocks protein synthesis at the level of translation (Vazquez, 1979; see especially pp. 136–138). It does not alter the electrical activity of neurons in *Aplysia* (Schwartz, Castellucci, & Kandel, 1971) nor does it affect synaptic transmission in rats (Jonec & Wasterlain, 1979).

We found ANI to be of much lower toxicity than other protein-synthesis inhibitors; in mice 25 times the effective amnestic dose was not lethal, whereas CXM had to be used at close to a lethal dose. Since ANI has low toxicity and an appropriate dose can be used to produce 80% inhibition in brain for about 2 hours, it can be given repeatedly at 2-hour intervals to vary the duration of cerebral inhibition at the amnestic level. Several of the experiments to be described will involve repeated administration of ANI. Using this technique in his doctoral research with us and extending inhibition to as long as 14 hours, James Flood found that the stronger the training, the longer the inhibition had to be maintained to prevent formation of memory for one-trial passive avoidance training (Flood, Bennett, Orme, & Rosenzweig, 1975b).

Although the earlier studies on protein synthesis and memory formation had employed multiple-trial active avoidance training (e.g., learning to go to the correct end compartment in a T-maze to avoid footshock), many investigators began in the 1970s to rely on single-trial passive avoidance (e.g., learning to remain in the start compartment rather than stepping onto a grid). The one-trial training allowed more precise timing of training and of administration of drugs with regard to training. Moreover, while strength of multiple-trial training could be varied in terms of the number of trials and number of successful responses, the strength of single-trial learning in a two-compartment apparatus could also be graded in terms of such variables as footshock intensity, step-through latency, and escape latency (Flood, Bennett, Rosenzweig, & Orme, 1972). A possible problem with regard to passive-avoidance training (sometimes also referred to as active inhibition) is that the subject shows that it retains memory for the shock by refusing to leave the start compartment. Critics noted that an animal made ill by a drug might also remain in the start position because it was too ill to move. Actually, the animals in such tests often poke their heads through the doorway frequently but refuse to enter the shock compartment, showing that they are lively but remember the shock. Also, tests for memory are often conducted 7 days after training and injection, when any illness caused by injection would have long been over. Other aspects of the illness interpretation will be considered below. Some experimenters have followed the precaution of testing hypotheses by using both active and passive avoidance in their research designs. Thus, we have shown that the relation between strength of training and duration of cerebral protein synthesis holds not only for one-trial passive avoidance training but also for multiple-trial active-avoidance training (Flood *et al.*, 1975a).

If the inhibition of protein synthesis is to prevent formation of memory, most results of investigators using rodent subjects show that inhibition must be initiated within a very few minutes after training. When mice were given strong one-trial passive-avoidance training, inhibition of protein synthesis had to reach 80% within 2–3 minutes of training to prevent formation of LTM (Bennett, Flood, Orme, Rosenzweig, & Jarvik, 1975; Bennett, Rosenzweig, & Flood, 1977). To achieve this required administering ANI more than 30 seconds prior to training. "These results are interpreted as indicating that under appropriate training conditions protein necessary for establishing long-term memories can be synthesized within minutes after training. This eliminates an obligatory mechanism involving synthesis of new messenger RNA because such synthesis in the mammal requires 10 to 20 minutes. It thus appears that under certain conditions of strong training, the synthesis of memory-related proteins can start within a minute or two by utilizing existing messenger RNA" (Rosenzweig, 1976, p. 20). Work with chicks indicates that the inhibitor can be administered as long as 20 minutes after training and still be amnestic (Gibbs & Ng, 1977). Once the brief critical period is past (and its exact time course may vary with task and species), we have not found even prolonged subsequent inhibition with ANI to prevent formation of memory.

Although memory-related proteins are usually synthesized in the minutes following training, this synthesis can be deferred during a period of inhibition of protein synthesis. As previously noted, we found that the stronger the training, the longer the synthesis can be deferred but still take place (Flood *et al.*, 1975b). In order to study how this call for protein synthesis might vary during the period of inhibition, we performed experiments in which we permitted intervals of partial recovery by delaying one or another of the four successive injections of ANI needed to produce a high proportion of amnesic mice under specific training conditions. The results showed that the longer such a window of controlled synthesis lasted, and the closer to training it occurred, the greater the percentage of the subjects remembering at the time of testing (Flood *et al.*, 1975b). In other words, the "templates" or "promoters" for protein synthesis that are formed during training fade out in a regular fashion during prolonged inhibition of synthesis. Below, in the section on Possible Roles of Protein in the Storage of Memory, we will see evidence of a somewhat similar phenomenon in dendritic spines: Activation of neurons leads to enlargement of spines involving the addition of protein in the spine membrane; during inhibition of protein synthesis caused by ANI such enlargement does not occur, but it then takes place as the ANI wears off and protein synthesis again becomes possible (Fifkova, Anderson, Young, & Van Harreveld, 1982).

Before concluding this section, we should note the possibility that there is a second critical period a few hours after training when inhibition of protein synthesis can also prevent formation of LTM. This was suggested by some early work with streptovitacin A, a powerful inhibitor of protein synthesis that must be administered intracranially. We found that it could be given to rats a few hours posttraining and still produce amnesia (Bennett *et al.*, 1972). We plan to test this in mice and chicks. It may be that streptovitacin A affects a later phase of the synthesis of memory-related proteins than do other inhibitors that we have tested so far. Indeed Brecher-Fride, Ben-Or, and Allweis (1979) and Matthies (1982) have independently suggested that there may be two temporally distinct and qualitatively different periods of memory-related protein synthesis.

Is Memory for Positive as Well as Negative Reinforcements Blocked by Inhibition of Protein Synthesis?

Some investigators have asked whether inhibition of protein synthesis might block formation of memory for negatively reinforced behavior but not for positive reinforcement. A brief review of studies bearing on this question is therefore in order. We can preface this by stating that most of the evidence appears to support the conclusion that protein-synthesis inhibition blocks formation of LTM for positive as well as for negative reinforcement. Such evidence goes back at least to 1968; it comes from studies by investigators in the United States, Europe, and Australia and from experiments employing rats, mice, and chicks; it is based on a variety of tasks and on reinforcements that include water, food, heat in a cold chamber, and presence of a stimulus that induces imprinting. Nevertheless, there are difficulties in interpreting the results of these experiments, just as there are problems in experiments with negative consequences. Most of the studies with positive reinforcement have not included the necessary control studies, so it seems to us that no firm conclusion can yet be reached on this question.

Apparently the first studies conducted to determine whether inhibition of protein synthesis would prevent formation of LTM for an appetitive task were two papers by Barondes and Cohen (Barondes & Cohen, 1968; Cohen & Barondes, 1968). In these experiments, water-deprived mice learned rapidly which of the arms of a T-maze provided water reward. Mice injected with CXM 30 minutes before training retained well at 3 hours but showed almost no retention at 6 hours or 7 days in that they did not go to the water reward. Subcutaneous injection of the drug immediately after training produced a small but significant impairment at 7 days, but injections at 30 minutes or 24 hours after training had no effect on retention. The investigators concluded that these results were identical to those they had obtained with AXM in a task motivated by escape from footshock. They also commented on the temporal aspects in a manner closely similar to that of the present chapter: "It appears, as suggested previously, that the protein synthesis apparently required for 'long-term' memory storage occurs during training and/or within minutes after training" (Cohen & Barondes, 1968, p. 339).

Although Daniels (1972) cited other 1968 papers of Barondes and Cohen, he seems not to have known of the two just discussed, because he also set out to determine whether inhibition of protein synthesis would prevent storage of LTM for appetitive learning as it does for avoidance learning. To do so, he administered either saline or AXM through implanted cannulas into the hippocampus of water-deprived rats. The rats learned in a single trial to obtain water by thrusting the head into a small box that contained a water tube; the box was in an experimental chamber to which the rats had been adapted previously. Administration of AXM 5 hours before the learning trial did not prevent acquisition or retention over 3 hours after training, but thereafter the head entries were significantly fewer than those of the control group. Some animals received the injections immediately after training; this did not affect retention. Daniels (1972) concluded that effects of inhibition of protein synthesis or formation of memory for this appetitive task were similar to the effects that he had reported previously (1971) on aversively motivated tasks.

Ungerer was apparently the first to publish doubts about such experiments. In her first studies on this topic (Ungerer, 1972, 1973), she concluded that AXM blocked memory for a task rewarded by access to a novel food. But then she wondered whether associating the food with AXM might not set up an aversion for the food and whether this might not be misinterpreted as blockage of memory for the task. Her tests demonstrated that such an aversion was indeed formed (Ungerer, Marchi, Roportz, & Weil, 1975). Moreover, when a familiar rather than a novel food was used as the reward, there was no evidence that AXM blocked memory for training in the food-acquisition behavior.

In unpublished experiments performed in 1971 by Bennett *et al.*, we had found that coupling CXM with saccharine-flavored water led to avoidance of this fluid, especially if CXM had followed access to the sweetened water. For this reason we abandoned experiments testing whether CXM could block memory for acquisition reinforced by fluid rewards. Other experimenters continued, however, to report that inhibitors of protein synthesis blocked formation of memory for positively reinforced performances, but they did not test for possible aversive effects of the inhibitor—effects that could have given the incorrect appearance of blockage of memory. It may be, however, that the results of Barondes and Cohen (1968) mentioned above are not susceptible to this criticism because of their concern for the temporal parameter. That is, they showed that the inhibitor had to be given in immediate temporal proximity to the training in order to cause amnesia, whereas induction of taste aversion is well known to show wide latitude for temporal pairing.

Having shown that an inhibitor of protein synthesis blocks formation of LTM for aversive consequences of pecking in the chick, Mark and associates designed a task employing positive reinforcement: young chicks learned to discriminate bits of grain from pebbles among which they were scattered (Rogers, Drennen, & Mark, 1974). The chicks learned this visual discrimination in about 20 pecks. The learning was not impaired by intracranial injection of CXM 10 minutes before the trial, but 24 hours later the CXM-injected chicks showed no retention of the discrimination, whereas saline-injected chicks showed good retention. In a later paper, Rogers, Oettinger, Szer, and Mark (1977) replicated these findings and also compared them with those on other tasks. These included one-trial passive avoidance (learning not to peck a bead coated with a bitter substance) and operant training (learning to peck a bead to turn on a heat lamp for 2-second intervals when the chicks were placed in a cold chamber). Whether the training involved aversive or positive reinforcement, CXM appeared to prevent establishment of LTM.

Imprinting was chosen by Gibbs and Lecanuet (1981) as an appetitive task with which to study effects of several agents on short-term, intermediate-term and long-term phases of memory in the chick. In a 10-minute training session, a chick was exposed to and allowed to follow a colored ball that moved jerkily 4 centimeters above floor level, following a circle 120 centimeters in diameter. In the test session 48 hours later, the amount of following behavior was measured. Intracranial injection of CXM markedly reduced following in those chicks to whom the drug had been administered either immediately or 5 minutes after the initial exposure period; injection of CXM 10 minutes after training had no effect on retention. The investigators concluded that it is important that CXM and other inhibitors of memory formation that have been used in previous experiments involving avoidance have been shown here to have similar effects for learning that involves approach.

Thus, most investigators who have sought to determine whether inhibitors of protein synthesis can block formation of LTM for appetitively motivated tasks have reported significant blockage. We believe that the evidence is not conclusive, however, unless and until it can be demonstrated that the apparent blockage of memory formation cannot be accounted for by aversive associations formed between the reinforcer and the protein-synthesis inhibitor. This would appear to be a problem that requires further research.

Some Alternative Interpretations

Alternative interpretations of the amnesic effects of inhibition of cerebral protein synthesis have been offered by some investigators. Let us consider here briefly four such hypotheses: (1) Inhibitors of protein synthesis may cause nonspecific side effects such as illness, and it is these side effects that interfere with formation of memory. (2) Inhibition of protein synthesis blocks formation of memory not because of its direct effects but rather because it modifies concentrations of catecholamine neurotransmitters. (3) Protein-synthesis inhibition blocks formation of memory because it interferes with paradoxical sleep, and in rodents paradoxical sleep must occur within a few hours of learning if LTM is to be formed. (4) Inhibition of protein synthesis interferes with retrieval rather than blocking consolidation.

THE ILLNESS INTERPRETATION

Barondes and Cohen (1967b, 1968) considered the hypothesis that inhibitors of protein synthesis might interfere with formation of LTM not through their primary effect but by causing nonspecific side effects such as illness around the time of training or in the posttraining period. This possibility was of serious concern with an agent like CXM, because many investigators observed that amnestic doses made rodent subjects visibly sick. In an attempt to test this hypothesis, investigators tested the amnesic effects of CXM given minutes before training with the same dosage given hours before training (Barondes & Cohen, 1967b; Squire & Barondes, 1976). Since injections given hours before training did not interfere with later retention but those given minutes before did cause amnesia, it was concluded that the specific effect (inhibition of protein synthesis) must be the cause of the amnesia.

We have noted that ANI is relatively nontoxic at the low doses usually employed (30 mg/kg), but it may cause some reduction of locomotor activity. At a high dose (210 mg/kg), some mice show such symptoms as watery eyes, lethargy, diarrhea, piloerection, and unresponsiveness to handling. We therefore tested the illness hypothesis by administering different doses of ANI at different times prior to training, and we made assessments of the nonspecific side effects, which had not been done in the earlier studies. Specifically, we gave a high dose (210 mg/kg ANI) 5 hours prior to training or a low dose (30 mg/kg) 20 minutes prior to training (Davis, Rosenzweig, Bennett, & Squire, 1980). Three kinds of measures were taken on equivalent groups of mice: (1) level of inhibition of cerebral protein synthesis at the time of training, (2) amount of locomotor activity and ratings of sickness at the time of training, and (3) retention either 24 hours or 7 days after training. Inhibition of synthesis at the time of training had declined to about 80% for the mice that had received the higher dose 5 hours earlier but was about 90% for those that had received the lower dose 20 minutes previously. Although they showed less inhibition of synthesis, the mice that had received the higher dose nevertheless showed a significant reduction of locomotion and significant ratings of illness, whereas the mice with the lower dose did not differ significantly on these measures from the saline controls. Amnesia, however, was greater for the mice that had received the lower dose just 20 minutes before training. Thus, amnesia was determined by the level of inhibition of protein synthesis at training and for the next few hours rather than by the degree of illness or other nonspecific side effects caused by the inhibitory agent.

THE CATECHOLAMINE INTERPRETATION

The hypothesis has been advanced by some investigators (e.g., Flexner & Goodman, 1975; Quartermain & Botwinick, 1975) that protein-synthesis inhibition blocks formation of memory not because of its direct effects but rather because it modifies concentrations of catecholamine neurotransmitters. We verified that ANI does reduce catecholamine concentrations, but only by 15–20%—far less than the 50–80% claimed in some reports. Then, in a series of experiments we demonstrated that although catecholamine inhibitors can cause amnesia for weak training, they are not effective against strong training, whereas ANI is effective (Bennett, *et al.*, 1977). Furthermore, in conditions where three successive injections of ANI are required to block memory formation, replacing one of these injections by a catecholamine inhibitor abolishes the amnesia, whereas substituting an injection of CXM (a protein-synthesis inhibitor) maintains amnesia. This provides a clear demonstration that the effects of inhibition of protein synthesis on memory cannot be attributed to effects on catecholamine systems.

Further evidence on this question has come from experiments investigating amnesic effects of catecholamine inhibitors or protein-synthesis inhibitors injected directly into various brain structures. The results demonstrated specific and differential regional effects of protein-synthesis inhibitors on memory formation that cannot be attributed to their effects on catecholamine systems (Flood, Smith, & Jarvik, 1980). These findings and those described in the previous paragraph seem to us to be among the strongest evidence that protein-synthesis inhibition acts by a different route from catecholamine inhibition in affecting memory.

When the temporal constraints for blocking formation of LTM by inhibiting protein synthesis are compared to the time courses of changes in catecholamine systems caused by inhibition of protein synthesis, it becomes apparent that effects on catecholamine levels are not critically involved in such amnesia. Specifically, experiments show that a few minutes of protein synthesis in the posttraining period are sufficient to guarantee formation of an LTM, whereas changes in catecholamine levels caused by inhibition of protein synthesis are much slower to develop (on the order of an hour).

THE PARADOXICAL SLEEP INTERPRETATION

Consider now the hypothesis that protein-synthesis inhibition prevents formation of LTM because it interferes with the occurrence of paradoxical sleep (PS; also called rapid-eye-movement [REM] sleep). Bloch and collaborators (1976) reported that the amount of REM sleep increased after learning in the rat, and that preventing REM sleep for a period of 3 hours after shuttlebox training impaired formation of LTM (Leconte & Hennevin, 1973). Pearlman and Greenberg (1973), using shuttlebox learning and discrimination learning, confirmed that deprivation of REM sleep for 3 hours after training impaired long-term retention. Fishbein and Gutwein (1977) then found that ANI in amnestic doses prevents the occurrence of REM sleep for several hours; these results were corroborated by Rojas-Ramirez and associates (Rojas-Ramirez, Aguilar-Jiminez, Posada-Andrews, Bernal-Pedraza, & Drucker-Colin, 1977). It is such findings that suggested the hypothesis stated at the start of this paragraph. This REM–memory hypothesis has gained some currency, but we believe that a more searching review of the work in this area raises some problems about it. In the first place, whereas Bloch and his associates (1976) and Pearlman and Greenberg (1973) reported that occurrence of REM sleep during the first 3 hours after training is critical for formation of LTM, Fishbein (who started his work on this topic with Bloch) now states that PS in the 3 hours after training is not essential for memory formation but that stability and maintenance of memory is dependent on PS occurring over a protracted time period (Gutwein, Shiromani, & Fishbein, 1980; Fishbein & Gutwein, 1981). Thus, the basic observation about posttraining REM sleep and memory formation is still in question. Even if REM sleep somewhere in the hours following training is definitely found to affect memory formation, it is clear that this effect does not have the precise time requirements that have been found for the amnesic effect of inhibition of protein synthesis. Furthermore, in experiments involving injections of ANI, a dose of 40 mg/kg was as effective as one of 120 mg/kg in delaying onset of REM sleep, but the larger dose was clearly the more amnestic (Gutwein *et al.*, 1980). Thus, attributing the amnesic effects of protein inhibition to effects on REM sleep does not bear up under critical examination.

THE RETRIEVAL INTERPRETATION

Some workers have suggested that the use of inhibitors of protein synthesis may impair retrieval process(es) rather than interfering with formation of LTM. Reports of spontaneous recovery of memory in animals previously classified as amnesic and reports of reminder-induced recovery have been used as evidence that memory deficits can be caused by impairment of retrieval. We believe that the possibility of spontaneous recovery after experimental amnesia is often exaggerated. Thus Barraco and Stettner (1976, p. 267) thank an anonymous reviewer of their manuscript for pointing out the following facts: When recovery has been reported to occur, it is usually from an amnesia present at 24 hours after training; no studies have reported amnesia present at a longer posttraining interval, such as 1 week, and then subsequent spontaneous recovery.

Although not denying that retrieval may account for some cases of performance deficit, we believe that there are many conditions in which inhibition of protein synthesis does prevent consolidation of memory. Thus, we have demonstrated that when amnesia for a learned task is sufficiently severe, as a result of either use of inhibitors or passage of time, a reminder procedure does not lead to recovery; on the other hand, animals exhibiting a weak memory for the task will improve when given the reminder procedure (Davis, Rosenzweig, Bennett, & Orme, 1978).

Possible Roles of Proteins in the Storage of Memory

Memory-related protein(s) synthesized in the posttraining period may be involved in several different ways in the storage of memory. They may be involved in either functional or structural mechanisms. As an example of a functional mechanism, alterations in amounts of certain enzymes may effect change in the rate of synthesis or metabolism of neurotransmitters. For example, Rose (1979) has shown prompt increases of cerebral acetylcholinesterase following exposure to light. Our previous research has also provided examples of structural changes such as those in numbers of dendritic spines (Globus, Rosenzweig, Bennett, & Diamond, 1973) and in synaptic dimensions (Diamond, Lindner, Johnson, Bennett, & Rosenzweig, 1975). Such structural changes could participate in the formation of new or modified synaptic connections.

Many people think of structural changes as occurring rather slowly, so the question has arisen whether they could take place rapidly enough to account for the onset of LTMs. As early as the 1960s it had been shown that changes in synaptic size and number could occur in a matter of hours in the brains of adult rats: Cragg (1967, 1968) had reported that when dark-reared rats were exposed to light for 1 hour, changes in size and number of synapses in the occipital cortex could be observed 24 hours later. Then Cragg (1969) found that in retinal synapses several changes occur when dark-reared rats are exposed to light for as little as 3 minutes.

An interesting example of rapid structural changes that appear to involve protein synthesis comes from recent research of Fifkova and colleagues. Fifkova and Van Harreveld (1977) reported that tetanic stimulation of the perforant path of mice for 30 seconds caused enlargement of dendritic spines in the distal third of the dentate molecular layer of the hippocampus; at 2–6 minutes, the enlargement was 15%; at 10–60 minutes, 38%; at 4–8 hours, 35%; and at 23 hours, 23%. In a further study (Fifkova *et al.*, 1982) some animals were given ANI 15 minutes before the tetanic stimulation, and measures were taken either 4 minutes or 90 minutes poststimulation. In the absence of stimulation, ANI did not affect the size of dendritic spines. But when ANI preceded stimulation, it suppressed the stimulation-induced spine enlargement at 4 minutes but not at 90 minutes poststimulation. This was a surprise to the investigators who had supposed that protein synthesis would be involved at 90 minutes but not at 4 minutes.

In discussing these results, Fifkova and collaborators (1982) noted that, according to values we have published (Flood, Rosenzweig, & Bennett, 1973), inhibition caused by the dose of ANI employed reaches 90% within 15 minutes after administration and remains high for another 75 minutes and then wears off rapidly. Since ANI was given 15 minutes prestimulation, at 4 minutes poststimulation the inhibition would be at its height, whereas at 90 minutes poststimulation (105 minutes after administration of the drug) inhibition would be declining. Thus, little protein synthesis could occur at 4 minutes poststimulation, but once inhibition of protein synthesis began to wear off, protein synthesis could occur selectively in the previously stimulated spines, provided some kind of internal recognition mechanism served to identify these spines (Fifkova *et al.*, 1982, pp. 205–207). This is similar to our proposal that activation of neural pathways during training sets up "templates" or "promoters," which normally are used promptly to direct synthesis of proteins but which may last up to hours during inhibition of synthesis and still be able to direct synthesis of protein thereafter, if the inhibition has not lasted too long.

It was originally supposed that the initial enlargement of spines was due to influx of ions and water and that this change of size was later consolidated by protein synthesis. But the elastic properties of the membrane would allow for only 2–5% expansion (Stahaelin, personal communication to Fifkova *et al.*), and this is smaller than the 15% observed in the 2–6 minutes following stimulation, so the insertion of new membrane material is favored as the main mechanism for increasing the perimeters of the activated spines. Furthermore, calculations based on the rate of protein synthesis and its transport from sites of synthesis in the perikaryon and large dendrites "suggest that changes in spine dimensions observed 4 min after stimulation can be caused by protein synthesis" (Fifkova *et al.*, 1982, p. 206).

Rapid changes in synaptic dimensions have also been reported and related to protein synthesis by Baudry and Lynch (Chapter 28, this volume).

Of course, even though some structural changes in neural circuits may occur rapidly and serve to store memories immediately after the short-term and intermediate-term phases are over, this does not preclude other memory-related structural changes from occurring over considerably longer periods of time. Even increases in the stability of some memories that continue up to years, as Squire and Cohen (1979) have demonstrated, may involve structural changes in neural circuits, but that is not the focus of this chapter.

With the evidence that protein synthesis is required for formation of LTM, several investigators have been attempting to identify specific proteins involved in memory formation. This question is included in the extensive review of neurochemistry of learning by Kometiani, Aleksidze, and Klein (1982) which surveys Russian-language as well as English-language reports.

Modulation of the Formation of Memory

The formation and expression of memory can be modulated by several sorts of processes and treatments. For example, the level of arousal of the subject modulates memory formation, with a moderate level being optimal and too low or too high levels impairing memory formation. Activity of the hippocampus may modulate the formation of memory traces that is occurring in other regions of the brain. Agents that act on the cholinergic system have been used by many investigators to modulate formation and/or retrieval of memory. For example, in a relatively early investigation in this field, Deutsch (1971) showed that an anticholinesterase agent administered just before a retention test could improve recall of a weak memory trace but impaired recall of a strong trace. Flood, Landry, and Jarvik (1981) studied the effects on memory formation of a large number of agents that affect the cholinergic system; they administered the agents intraventricularly just after mice were given active avoidance training in a T-maze, and they tested for recall 1 week later. Drugs that decreased acetylcholine (ACh) receptor activity were found to impair retention, the impairment increasing monotonically with the dose. On the other hand, drugs that increase ACh receptor activity or ACh levels in the brain improved memory up to an optimal dosage but impaired retention at high doses. Thus these cholinergic agents could modulate memory in either direction, depending upon the dose, in conformity with the old dictum of Paracelsus that the dose makes the drug. Later in this chapter (section on Synergistic Effects from Combined Administration of Memory-Active Agents) we will see evidence that administering two or three cholinergic agents together yields strong synergistic effects.

Any of several excitant agents given during the posttraining period reduces the degree of amnesia caused by a protein-synthesis inhibitor, whereas any of several depressants further impairs the memory. Two kinds of evidence indicate that these effects are properly called "modulatory." One is that memory strength can be altered in either direction and by graded amounts. The other is that the excitants or depressants do not affect the strength or duration of inhibition of protein synthesis (Flood, Jarvik, Bennett, Orme, & Rosenzweig, 1977). In other words, these agents do not affect the direct process of protein synthesis, but they may act by facilitating or inhibiting the transmission of neural impulses in circuits involved in processing information leading to memory formation (Rosenzweig, Bennett, & Flood, 1981).

Much of the research on modulation has not considered what stage or stages of memory formation might be affected by the modulatory treatment. In at least some of the cases mentioned in the last paragraph we have evidence that the modulatory treatment affected the formation of LTM rather than earlier stages. For example, *d*-amphetamine significantly counteracted the amnesic effect of ANI even when the amphetamine was given as late as 90 minutes posttraining. By this time, both STM and ITM were probably over. On the other hand, picrotoxin could not counteract the amnesic effects if it was administered later than 30 minutes posttraining, so it may act on the intermediate-term stage. We believe that attempting to relate modulatory influences to stages of memory formation will yield increased understanding of both modulation and stages of memory formation. Let us turn now to the hypothesized earlier stages.

Processes Underlying Earlier Stages of Memory Formation

The hypothesized earlier stages—STM and ITM—have tended to be neglected except for an active program of investigation headed by Marie E. Gibbs (M. E. Watts in her earlier publications) and recent work by Allweis and collaborators. Gibbs and colleagues, from their findings with chicks, support a three-stage model in which each stage depends on the previous one (Gibbs & Ng, 1977). Frieder and Allweis (1982), from their research with rats, support a four-stage model in which later stages of memory may develop even though experimental treatment has suppressed an earlier one. Because of the extensive work and numerous publications of the Gibbs group, research with the chick has provided an influential current analogue to the hypothesized stages of human learning. The main stages of memory formation and underlying processes, as hypothesized by Gibbs and Ng, are shown in Figure 17-1. Some of the agents reported to facilitate or inhibit each stage are shown in Table 17-1. It should be noted that Gibbs and Ng have concluded from these experiments with chicks that protein synthesis is required for formation of LTM.

The method used by Gibbs and colleagues with chicks has been mainly one-trial aversive training, a technique adapted from Cherkin (Cherkin & Lee-Teng, 1965; Lee-Teng & Sherman, 1966; Cherkin, 1969). Chicks peck spontaneously at small targets, and shiny targets such as a metal bead are especially attractive. If the target has been coated with a bitter liquid, one peck suffices to train lasting avoidance behavior. Cherkin's training method was somewhat modified by Mark and Watts, and they showed that it was suitable for testing the effects of intracranial injection of drugs in chicks (Mark & Watts, 1971; Watts & Mark, 1971a, 1971b). To overcome possible sources of confounding, chicks have been trained in successive as well as simultaneous discrimination tasks (Gibbs & Barnett, 1976), in multiple-trial aversive discrimination (Gibbs & Ng, 1977), and in a positively reinforced discrimination that requires less than 5 minutes of training (Rogers *et al.*, 1974; Gibbs & Ng, 1977).

STM is hypothesized by Gibbs and Ng to occur as a result of neuronal hyperpolarization which, under normal circumstances, results from increased potassium conductance across neuronal membranes following neuronal stimulation. Indeed, intracerebral injections of depolarizing agents such as glutamate and lithium chloride have been found to disrupt the STM phase of memory formation (Gibbs & Ng, 1979). The magnitude of potassium conductance has been found to be a function of the concentration of extracellular and intracellular calcium (Jansen & Nicholls, 1973). Based on this finding, Gibbs,

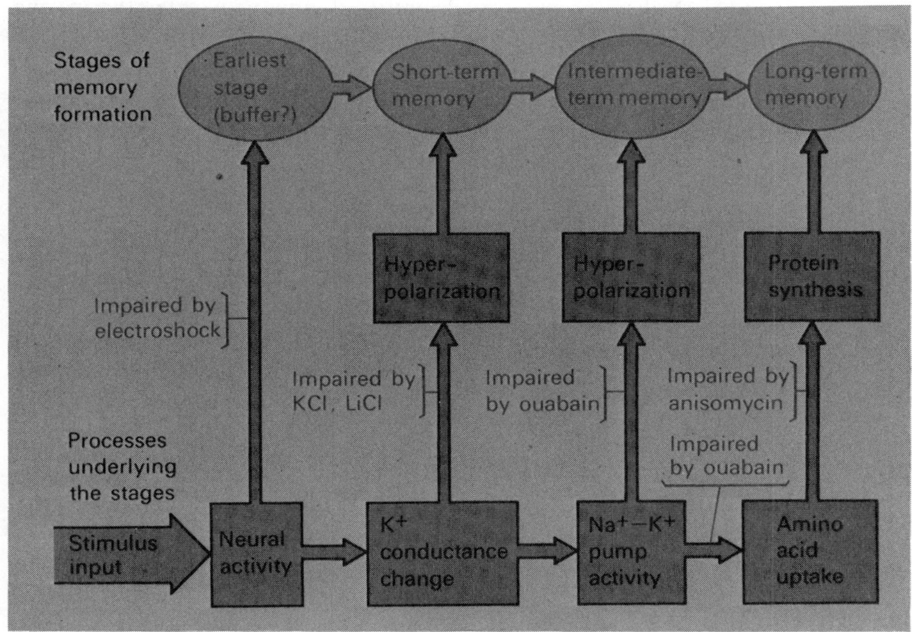

Figure 17-1. Stages of memory formation and processes that may underlie each stage. For each stage, a treatment is indicated that appears to impair the putative underlying processes of memory formation. (From Rosenzweig & Leiman, 1982, after Gibbs & Ng, 1977.)

Gibbs, and Ng (1979) recently tested their proposed mechanism of STM by administering calcium chloride in day-old chick forebrain just prior to passive-avoidance training. Results demonstrated that when $CaCl_2$ was injected 5 minutes before training, STM lasted four times as long as normally. In another part of the same study, lanthanum chloride injected intracerebrally into chicks prevented calcium flux across neuronal membranes, and this abolished the STM phase of memory formation. The chick data indicate that STM is in its most active phase from 5 to 10 minutes after one-trial training, and then it declines rapidly.

Table 17-1. Stages of memory in the chick and agents that affect their formation

Stage	Maximum duration	Processes hypothesized to mediate	Agents that facilitate	Agents that inhibit
Short-term	30 min	Hyperpolarization involving K^+ conductance change	Calcium chloride	Lithium chloride Potassium chloride
Intermediate-term	90 min	Hyperpolarization involving Na^+-K^+ pump activity	Diphenylhydantoin Pargyline	Ouabain Ethacrynic acid
Long-term	Days	Protein synthesis	Pargyline Amphetamine	Anisomycin Cycloheximide Aminoisobutyrate

Note. From studies of Gibbs and Ng, (1977).

During the ITM phase of memory formation, Gibbs and Ng hypothesize, the affected neurons are hyperpolarized as in the STM phase, but the hyperpolarization is produced by activation of the sodium pump. Evidence supporting this hypothesis comes from studies in which sodium pump inhibitors (ouabain or ethacrynic acid) were injected into chick forebrain. Such injections resulted in a decline in memory 10–15 minutes after passive-avoidance training, that is, at the end of the STM phase (see Figure 17-2). These results were interpreted as indicating that ouabain did not alter STM formation and function but abolished the ITM phase. Subsequent LTM did not form, as was evidenced by amnesia on testing 24 hours posttraining. These findings supported the sequentially dependent, multistage model of memory formation. It has been found that *d*-amphetamine and norepinephrine (NE) counteract ouabain-induced amnesia via stimulation of NE release, which in turn acts to increase the activity of the sodium pump (Gibbs, 1976; Gibbs & Ng, 1977). Ouabain-induced amnesia has also been reversed by an injection of the sodium pump stimulator diphenylhydantoin (DPH) shortly after training. The fact that DPH did not overcome KCl-induced amnesia suggested that STM does not rely on sodium pump activity for normal functioning (Gibbs & Ng, 1976). The intermediate phase of memory is reported to be most active between 15 and 30 minutes posttraining in the chick, after which ITM decays (Gibbs & Ng, 1977).

The LTM phase is reported by Gibbs and Ng (1977) to become functionally optimal in the chick about 60 minutes posttraining. Formation of LTM is sensitive to disruption by administration of protein-synthesis inhibitors such as CXM or ANI. With injections of such inhibitors close to the time of training, memory remains strong for about 30 minutes after training in the chick; then it begins to decline, and by 60 minutes posttraining it is significantly weaker than that of controls. Thus, these observations on the chick accord with findings by us and others that formation of LTM in the mouse requires protein synthesis.

It is encouraging to see that the relatively small amount of work on formation of LTM in the chick conforms to the results of extensive work on

Figure 17-2. Time courses of decline of memory of chicks after various treatments. The graphs show percentages of chicks that gave learned avoidance responses on tests conducted at different training–testing intervals. Percentage of recall varied with both the substances injected into the brain and the time intervals. Each point is based on data from a different group of chicks. (From Rosenzweig & Leiman, 1982; adapted from Gibbs & Ng, 1977.)

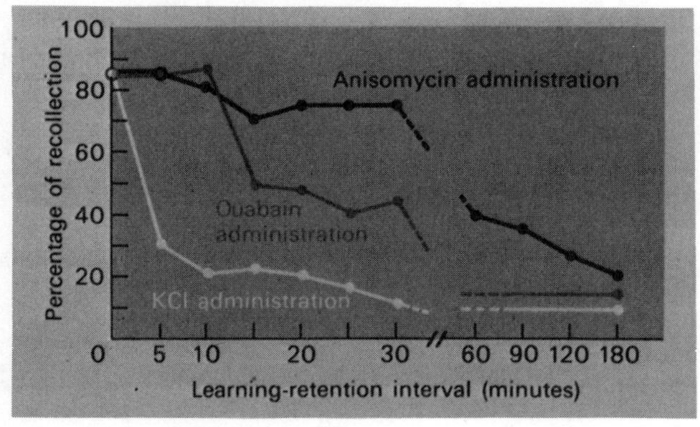

LTM in the mouse. But in regard to the STM and ITM phases, there are relatively few observations with rodents that can be used to check the generality of the findings made with the chick. Furthermore, we can hardly consider the results on STM and ITM in the chick to be well established, since they almost all come from a single laboratory, with little independent confirmation. There are, in fact, some discrepant results from other laboratories. For example, other investigators have reported that ouabain blocks access to short-term or "labile" memory rather than preventing STM or ITM from being established (Rogers *et al.*, 1977). They have conjectured that the discrepancy between their results and those of Gibbs and Ng might be accounted for by assuming that the roles of ouabain may be different in their multiple-trial appetitive task from one-trial passive-avoidance task used by Gibbs and Ng. No further work to test this suggestion or to resolve the discrepancy appears to have been done.

There are also some gaps and puzzling features in the reports from Gibbs laboratory. For example, although Gibbs and colleagues have used CXM, and more recently, ANI in their behavioral research, they have published only fragmentary data on the inhibitory effects of CXM in chick brain and apparently no data on the efficacy of ANI. Such data are not difficult to obtain and are important in the interpretation of experiments. The data that Gibbs and coworkers have published concerns the asymmetric inhibition of protein synthesis by administration of microgram quantities of CXM unilaterally (Gibbs *et al.*, 1979). Demonstration of asymmetrical inhibition of protein synthesis is of interest for the interpretation of studies in which impairment of monocular learning by the appropriate administration of CXM has been reported (Bell & Gibbs, 1979). Both the results of Woolston, Morgan, and Hambley (1979) and recent results we have obtained indicate that it is very difficult to get high inhibition in one hemisphere of the chick and not the other with either inhibitor. Somewhat more data on inhibition in chick brain using these two inhibitors come from Bull, Ferrera, and Orrego (1976). They have reported that CXM is more toxic than ANI in chicks, as we have previously reported for mice.

Thus, although Gibbs should be credited with a creative and productive program of research, there is great need for replication, extension, tests of generality with mammalian subjects, and related neurochemical research.

There has been relatively little research to explore in rodents the neurochemical phases of memory formation that precede LTM. Tucker and Gibbs (1976, 1979) have tried to extend their chick model to rats. They reported that CXM or ouabain could impair formation of memory for taste aversion that was caused by illness induced by injection of lithium chloride. Their results have been challenged, however, by Bolas, Bellingham, and Martin (1979). Also, taste aversion induced by illness has been characterized as being so different in its neural bases from other kinds of learning that it may not be valid to generalize from it to other kinds of learning, according to Bures and Buresova (1979). A different three- or four-stage model has been proposed by Frieder and Allweis (1978, 1982) as the basis of experiments with rats. Their 1978 paper reported that hypoxia prevented transcription from STM to "medium-term" memory (MTM) but that LTM later appeared, so MTM and LTM were held to be independent parallel processes, both derived from STM. Later they reported (1982) that ethacrynic acid prevented the formation of STM but that MTM and LTM later appeared, both apparently derived from very-short-term memory (VSTM). They do not refer to the fact that Gibbs and associates have claimed that ethacrynic acid interferes with ITM and not STM. There is obviously much to be done to replicate and extend observations with both chicks and rodents as well as in considering similarities and differences in results across classes of animals.

The radial-arm maze (Olton, 1978; Olton & Samuelson, 1976) may provide a useful situation for investigating the neurochemistry of the early stages of memory formation. This positively motivated test has been used in studies of brain mechanisms of learning (e.g., effects of hippocampal lesions), and it is thought to tap ecologically important processes of search strategies in foraging for food. An animal can be used as its own control in repeated tests of memory when delays are interposed during trials. Olton (1978) has presented evidence that only working memory is formed during a trial (not LTM) and that memory for the previous trial is "reset" when a new trial begins. On the other hand, Kesner and Novak (1982) have reported evidence indicating that rats show both STM and LTM during trials in the radial maze. We have confirmed that rats learn this task easily and perform well, but we have found that mice perform poorly in the radial maze (Mizumori, Rosenzweig, & Kermisch, 1982). Recently we have tested rats with implanted cerebral cannulas in this apparatus, imposing delays of various durations between the first 6 choices and the last 6 choices in a 12-arm maze. The results show that when working memory exceeds a few minutes in duration, there is an LTM (anisomycin-sensitive) component (Mizumori, Rosenzweig, & Bennett, in press).

Synergistic Effects from Combined Administration of Memory-Active Agents

A few investigators have tried combining agents that are each effective on memory in order to look for additive or synergistic effects (e.g., Bartus, Dean, Beer, & Lippa, 1982; Flood & Cherkin, 1981; Flood, Smith, & Cherkin, 1983). Usually this work has not been planned to shed any light on hypotheses of stages of memory formation, but we intend to investigate effects of combinations that may work on a single stage as well as combinations in which different agents may act on different stages of memory formation.

An example of the remarkable potentiation that can be achieved by combining cholinergic drugs has been offered by Flood and Cherkin (1981; see also Flood, Smith, & Cherkin, 1984). They trained mice on active avoidance on a T-maze and injected the drugs intraventricularly immediately after the end of brief training. Dose–response curves were determined for several agents to find their optimal doses for improving retention. With the weak training employed, use of either no drug or low drug levels yielded rather poor retention. As dosage of the posttraining injection increased, retention improved, up to an optimal dosage. Animals that received still larger doses showed successively lower levels of retention, as shown in Figure 17-3 for two ACh receptor agonists, arecoline and oxotremorine. When these two drugs were combined, each at 1/40 of its optimal dosage, the combination was as effective as either drug at its optimal dosage. Thus there was a 20-fold potentiation of effectiveness. Using three ACh agonists, a 60-fold potentiation was obtained.

The mechanism of this strong synergistic effect is not yet known. Arecoline and oxotremorine are both ACh receptor agonists. Perhaps they work on different subpopulations of receptors. Both work on muscarinic receptors, which make up most of the cholinergic receptors in the brain, but there are also

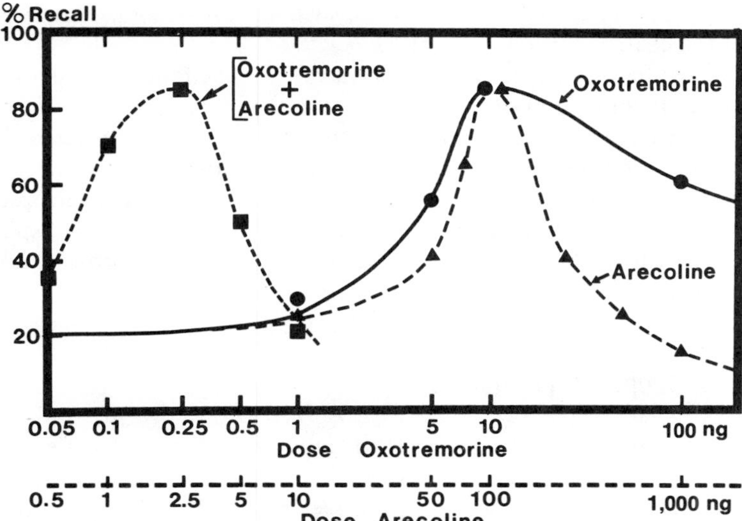

Figure 17-3. Synergistic effects of two acetylcholine receptor agonists on formation of long-term memory in mice. The graphs show percentages of groups that recalled weak training that had been coupled with various doses of either oxotremorine or arecoline or a combination of oxotremorine and arecoline. Note that the dosage scales are logarithmic. Use of saline solution in control groups produced 20% recall, so this can be considered baseline performance. Sufficiently high doses (5000 ng oxotremorine or 1000 ng arecoline) drove recall down to 15%. (From data of Flood *et al.*, 1983.)

some nicotinic receptors in the brain, and there is evidence that arecoline works on these too. It is also possible that the time courses of action of the agents differ, so that combined administration could prolong the effects at receptors. Flood *et al.*, (1984) showed that prolonged cholinergic stimulation obtained by repeated posttraining injections of arecoline significantly aided memory formation.

Synergistic effects of this sort may be helpful in clinical efforts to aid memory. Use of reduced dosages could minimize toxicity and side effects, help to prevent the development of tolerance, and also reduce the cost of drugs used in treatments.

Study of synergistic effects may also aid the investigation of stages of memory formation. If there is sequential dependence among stages, then combinations of agents with quite different actions that modulate different stages might well produce synergistic effects. On the other hand, if there are parallel but independent memories of different durations, then modulating the strength of one would not affect the others and no synergy would be expected.

PROGRAM OF RESEARCH

From our review of research in this field, we conclude that there are valuable findings and promising hypotheses. We also see three kinds of gaps in the existing research in this field: (1) lack of replication by other investigators so that even basic facts are not clear; (2) lack of generalizability from one species to another, especially in regard to the earlier steps of memory formation, and

(3) lack of parallel neurochemical studies, such as dose–response curves of the agents in the central nervous system.

Before listing specific studies that appear to be called for, we wish briefly to discuss the following points: (1) specific questions being addressed by investigators in this area, (2) an explanation of strategies employed in this research, and (3) the nature of findings that would constitute satisfactory answers. After listing studies to be carried out, we will then come to the final topic: relationships between these findings and other levels of inquiry. Limitation of space has forced us to write the final section in terser, more economical form than the rest of the chapter.

Specific Questions Being Addressed

Some of the main questions being asked by investigators in this field are the following:

1. Are different neurochemical processes required for retention of memories over different lengths of time, so that it may be meaningful to speak of stages—for example, STM processes, ITM processes, and LTM processes? It may be possible to solve in neurochemical terms the question of separate stages of memory that has long been of concern to behavioral scientists.

2. If different stages are found, are the later ones sequentially dependent on the earlier ones, or do they operate in parallel, or is there some more complex relationship among them?

3. If different stages are found, how can each be modulated? How do various modulatory treatments interact (additively, canceling, or potentiating), both within a stage and across stages?

4. If different stages are found, can individual variations in ability to remember (e.g., unusually good memory, deficient memory, rapid loss of memory) be related to behavioral tests for specific stages and/or physiological indices of different stages?

An Explanation of Strategies Employed in This Research

1. Although investigators must use published results from other laboratories for guidance, we also recommend that they should not hesitate to attempt to replicate important results in order to test their reliability. One of the problems in this field is the lack of results that are well established by replication in independent laboratories.

2. Investigators are measuring temporal courses of effects of a relatively large number of agents and treatments on memory in order to find whether they tend to fall into a small number of temporal periods. If the results show only a small number of temporal periods, this is evidence of a corresponding number of stages of memory formation.

3. Investigators are attempting to modulate each putative stage of memory formation in both directions, that is, by enhancement as well as impairment. If this can be done, it will provide further evidence for the existence of stages.

4. It is important to manipulate learning strength appropriately for particular experiments so that either enhancement or inhibition can be detected without running into ceiling or floor effects.

5. Use of animal subjects of different classes (e.g., birds and mammals) and of different genera (e.g., rats and mice) makes it possible to test the generality of formulations over animal forms.

6. Use of several kinds of behavioral tests—active and passive avoidance, positive and negative reinforcement—is essential, both to test generality of findings and to overcome difficulties and limitations of interpretation that characterize each test when used in isolation.

7. With each species and task, it is imperative that investigators explore the parameters sufficiently, in terms of both the behavioral and pharmacological levels, to provide a systematic picture of results.

8. Combinations of effective agents should be employed in attempts to explore possible synergies of effects both within and among stages of memory formation.

The Nature of Findings That Would Constitute Satisfactory Answers

The nature of some of the findings that would constitute satisfactory answers to some of the questions addressed above, are indicated here:

1. If the results of a wide variety of memory-affecting treatments all fall within a small number of time courses, this would be strong support for the existence of a small number of stages of memory, corresponding to the time courses. Some evidence of this sort has been presented (e.g., by M. E. Gibbs and K. Ng), but to establish such results will require not only independent replication but also use of a wider variety of treatments and also extension to other classes and genera of animals.

2. If time courses of the putative stages and of modulatory effects are similar (but not necessarily identical) across strains and species, this would provide evidence of the generality of the stages.

3. If enhancing, depressing, or inhibiting earlier putative stages (STM or ITM) produces clear effects in the same direction on memory strength at later stage(s) (ITM + LTM, or LTM), this would provide evidence that the stages are linked sequentially. (But such results would also be expected in the case of a single-trace mechanism with multiple kinds of modulation, as hypothesized by Gold & McGaugh, 1975.)

4. If modulation of different putative stages yields positive combinatory effects (additive or potentiating), this would provide evidence that the stages are linked sequentially. (This could also be accounted for by the Gold & McGaugh, 1975, hypothesis of a single trace mechanism with multiple kinds of modulation.)

Studies to Be Carried Out

We intend to fill, in part at least, each of the gaps in the literature noted at the beginning of this section. Thus, we will attempt to replicate some of the most important reports for the chick; to replicate and extend research with chick, mouse, and rat models; and to conduct appropriate parallel neurochemical studies, as we have done in past research with the mouse. There is certainly plenty of work to be done in this area to occupy several research groups, and as indicated above, we believe that attempts to replicate major findings among laboratories is important to solid advances. Substantial progress toward demonstrating and defining successive stages in the formation of memory should provide rational bases for ameliorating both deficient and normal memory process.

Relationships between These Findings and Other Levels of Inquiry (More Molecular or More Molar Approaches to Learning and Memory)

Research at this level can draw on findings and concepts at other levels, and it can suggest related investigations that might be fruitful at other levels. A few examples of each kind are noted here:

1. This research can draw on established pharmacology and neurochemistry for selection of agents that may be effective as modulators of memory.

2. Recent progress of molecular biology, including the synthesis and processing of hormones from larger precursors, following earlier advances in the synthesis and metabolism of neurotransmitters, opens up new possibilities for the selection and modification of agents that may modulate memory.

3. For development of suitable behavioral tests for the research described in this paper, it is important that tests be devised and run by behavioral psychologists who are aware of many aspects of animals' responses and of the problems of studying learning and memory. Automation can come later.

4. This behavioral–neurochemical research could be related to electrophysiological studies of intact nervous systems and of explants by studying effects of memory-active agents on such preparations. That is, it might be fruitful to test whether and how the temporal characteristics of effectiveness of agents in intact animals (i.e., on STM, ITM, and LTM) will be related to their effectiveness on model systems for learning that are studied by electrophysiological recording in brain regions or in brain explants. We have recently discussed some research on long-term potentiation in this regard (Rosenzweig, 1984, p. 371).

5. The chemical processes being considered here are very likely related to the neuroanatomical plasticity that we have demonstrated (e.g., Bennett, Diamond, Krech, & Rosenzweig, 1964; Globus *et al.*, 1973) and that others are showing in further ways (e.g., the work of Nottebohm described by Marx, 1982). Additional exchanges between behavioral, neurochemical, and neuroanatomical levels of inquiry should prove to be fruitful in studying neural processes in learning and memory.

ACKNOWLEDGMENTS

This project has received support from National Institute of Mental Health grant 1 R01 MH36042-01A1 and from the Office of Energy Research, Office of Health and Environmental Research, Department of Energy, under Contract No. DE-AC03-76SF00098. Helpful comments on a draft of this chapter were made by Marie Alberti, Susan Benloucif, James F. Flood, Sheri J. Y. Mizumori, Teresa Patterson, and Michael J. Renner.

REFERENCES

Agranoff, B. W., & Klinger, P. D. Puromycin effect on memory fixation in the goldfish. *Science*, 1964, *146*, 952–953.

Ajmone Marsan, C., & Matthies, H. (Eds.). *Neuronal plasticity and memory formation*. New York: Raven Press, 1982.

Barondes, S. H. Some critical variables in studies of the effect of inhibitors of protein synthesis on memory. In W. L. Byrne (Ed.), *Molecular approaches to learning and memory*. New York: Academic Press, 1970.

Barondes, S. H., & Cohen, H. D. Puromycin effect on successive stages of memory storage. *Science*, 1966, *151*, 594–595.

Barondes, S. H., & Cohen, H. D. Arousal and the conversion of "short-term" to "long-term" memory. *Proceedings of the National Academy of Sciences, USA*, 1968, *61*, 923–929.

Barondes, S. H., & Cohen, H. D. Comparative effects of cycloheximide and puromycin on cerebral protein synthesis and consolidation of memory in mice. *Brain Research*, 1967a, *4*, 44–51.

Barondes, S. H., & Cohen, H. D. Delayed and sustained effect of acetoxycycloheximide on memory in mice. *Proceedings of the National Academy of Sciences, USA*, 1967b, *58*, 157–164.

Barraco, R. A., & Stettner, L. J. Antibiotics and memory. *Psychological Bulletin*, 1976, *83*, 242–302.

Bartus, R. T., Dean, R., Beer, B., & Lippa, A. S. The cholinergic hypothesis of geriatric memory dysfunction. *Science*, 1982, *217*, 408–417.

Bell, G. A., & Gibbs, M. E. Interhemispheric engram transfer in chick. *Neuroscience Letters*, 1979, *13*, 163–168.

Bennett, E. L., Diamond, M. C., Krech, D., & Rosenzweig, M. R. Chemical and anatomical plasticity of brain. *Science*, 1964, *146*, 610–619.

Bennett, E. L., Flood, J. F., Orme, A., Rosenzweig, M. R., & Jarvik, M. Minimum duration of protein synthesis needed to establish long-term memory. *Abstracts of the Fifth International Meeting of the International Society for Neurochemistry*, Barcelona, 1975, 476.

Bennett, E. L., Orme, A., & Hebert, M. Cerebral protein synthesis inhibition and amnesia produced by scopolamine, cycloheximide, streptovitacin A, anisomycin and emetine in rat. *Federation Proceedings*, 1972, *31*, 838.

Bennett, E. L., & Rosenzweig, M. R. Chemical alterations produced in brain by environment and training. In A. Lajtha (Ed.), *Handbook of neurochemistry* (Vol. 6). New York: Plenum, 1971.

Bennett, E. L., Rosenzweig, M. R., & Flood, J. F. Protein synthesis and memory studied with anisomycin. In S. Roberts, A. Lajtha, & W. H. Gispen (Eds.), *Mechanisms, regulation and special functions of protein synthesis in the brain.* Amsterdam: Elsevier/North-Holland Biomedical Press, 1977.

Bloch, V. Brain activation and memory consolidation. In M. R. Rosenzweig & E. L. Bennett (Eds.), *Neural mechanisms of learning and memory*. Cambridge, Mass.: MIT Press, 1976.

Bolas, K. E., Bellingham, W. P., & Martin, G. M. Aversive properties of cycloheximide versus memory inhibition in chickens' formation of visually cued food aversions. *Pharmacology Biochemistry and Behavior*, 1979, *10*, 251–254.

Brazier, M. A. B. (Ed.). *Brain mechanisms in memory and learning*. New York: Raven Press, 1979.

Brecher-Fride, E., Ben-Or, S., & Allweis, C. The effect of chloramphenicol and anisomycin on memory consolidation and cerebral protein synthesis in the rat. *Abstracts of the Seventh International Meeting of the International Society of Neurochemistry*, Jerusalem, 1979.

Bull, R., Ferrera, E., & Orrego, F. Effects of anisomycin on brain protein synthesis and passive avoidance learning in newborn chicks. *Journal of Neurobiology*, 1976, *7*, 37–49.

Bures, J., & Buresova, O. Neurophysiological analysis of conditioned taste aversion. In M. A. B. Brazier (Ed.), *Brain mechanisms in memory and learning*. New York: Raven Press, 1979.

Cherkin, A. Kinetics of memory consolidation: Role of amnesic treatment parameters. *Proceedings of the National Academy of Sciences, USA*, 1969, *63*, 1094–1101.

Cherkin, A., & Lee-Teng, E. Interruption by halothane of memory consolidation in chicks. *Federation Proceedings*, 1969, *24*, 328.

Cohen, H. D., & Barondes, S. H. Puromycin effect on memory may be due to occult seizures. *Science*, 1967, *157*, 333–334.

Cohen, H. D., & Barondes, S. H. Cycloheximide impairs memory of an appetitive task. *Communications in Behavioral Biology*, 1968, *1*, 337–339.

Cohen, H. D., Ervin, F., & Barondes, S. H. Puromycin and cycloheximide: Different effects on hippocampal electrical activity. *Science*, 1966, *154*, 1557–1558.

Cragg, B. G. Changes in the visual cortex on first exposure of rats to light: Effect on synaptic dimensions. *Nature*, 1967, *215*, 251–253.

Cragg, B. G. Are there structural alterations in synapses related to functioning? *Proceedings of the Royal Society, London*, 1968, *171*, 319–323.

Cragg, B. G. Structural changes in naive retinal synapses detectable within minutes of first exposure to daylight. *Brain Research*, 1969, *15*, 79–96.

Daniels, D. Actinomycin-D: Effects on memory and brain RNA synthesis in an appetitive learning task. *Nature*, 1971, *231*, 395–397.

Daniels, D. Effects of acetoxycycloheximide on appetitive learning and memory. *Quarterly Journal of Experimental Psychology*, 1972, *24*, 102–114.

Davis, H. P., Rosenzweig, M. R., Bennett, E. L., & Orme, A. E. Recovery as a function of the degree of amnesia due to protein synthesis inhibition. *Pharmacology Biochemistry and Behavior*, 1978, *8*, 701–710.

Davis, H. P., Rosenzweig, M. R., Bennett, E. L., & Squire, L. R. Inhibition of cerebral protein synthesis: Dissociation of nonspecific effects and amnesic effects. *Behavioral and Neural Biology*, 1980, *28*, 99–104.

Deutsch, J. A. The cholinergic synapse and the site of memory. *Science*, 1971, *174*, 788–794.

Diamond, M. C., Lindner, B., Johnson, R., Bennett, E. L., & Rosenzweig, M. R. Differences in occipital cortical synapses from environmentally enriched, impoverished, and standard colony rats. *Journal of Neuroscience Research*, 1975, *1*, 109–119.

Dunn, A. J. Neurochemistry of learning and memory: An evaluation of recent data. *Annual Review of Psychology*, 1980, *31*, 343–390.

Fifkova, E., Anderson, C. L., Young, S. J., & Van Harreveld, A. Effect of anisomycin on stimulation-induced changes in dendritic spines of the dentate granule cells. *Journal of Neurocytology*, 1982, *11*, 183–210.

Fifkova, E., & Van Harreveld, A. Long-lasting morphological changes in dendritic spines of dentate granular cells following stimulation of the entorhinal area. *Journal of Neurocytology*, 1977, *6*, 211–230.

Fishbein, W., & Gutwein, B. M. Paradoxical sleep and memory storage processes. *Behavioral Biology*, 1977, *19*, 425–464.

Fishbein, W., & Gutwein, B. M. Paradoxical sleep and a theory of long-term memory. In W. Fishbein (Ed.), *Sleep, dreams, and memory*. New York: Spectrum, 1981.

Flexner, J. B., Flexner, L. B., & Stellar, E. Memory in mice as affected by intracerebral puromycin. *Science*, 1963, *141*, 57–59.

Flexner, J. B., Flexner, L. B., Stellar, E., de la Haba, G., & Roberts, R. B. Inhibition of protein synthesis in brain and learning and memory following puromycin. *Journal of Neurochemistry*, 1962, *9*, 595–605.

Flexner, J. B., Flexner, L. B., Stellar, E., de la Haba, G., & Roberts, R. B. Loss of memory as related to inhibition of cerebral protein synthesis. *Journal of Neurochemistry*, 1965, *12*, 535–541.

Flexner, L. B., & Goodman, R. H. Studies on memory: Inhibitors of protein synthesis also inhibit catecholamine synthesis. *Proceedings of the National Academy of Sciences, USA*, 1975, *72*, 4660–4663.

Flood, J. F., Bennett, E. L., Orme, A. E., & Rosenzweig, M. R. Effects of protein synthesis inhibition on memory for active avoidance training. *Physiology and Behavior*, 1975a, *14*, 177–184.

Flood, J. F., Bennett, E. L., Orme, A. E., & Rosenzweig, M. R. Relation of memory formation to controlled amounts of brain protein synthesis. *Physiology and Behavior*, 1975b, *15*, 97–102.

Flood, J. F., Bennett, E. L., Rosenzweig, M. R., & Orme, A. E. The influence of training strength on amnesia induced by pre-training injections of cycloheximide. *Physiology and Behavior*, 1972, *9*, 589–600.

Flood, J. F., & Cherkin, A. Cholinergic drug interactions: Enhancement and impairment of memory retention. *Society for Neuroscience Abstracts*, 1981, *7*, 369.

Flood, J. F., Jarvik, M. E., Bennett, E. L., Orme, A. E., & Rosenzweig, M. R. Protein synthesis inhibition and memory for pole jump avoidance and extinction. *Pharmacology Biochemistry and Behavior*, 1977, *7*, 71–77.

Flood, J. F., Landry, D. W., & Jarvik, M. E. Cholinergic receptor interactions and their effects on long-term memory processing. *Brain Research*, 1981, *215*, 177–185.

Flood, J. F., Rosenzweig, M. R., Bennett, E. L., & Orme, A. E. The influence of duration of protein synthesis inhibition on memory. *Physiology and Behavior*, 1973, *10*, 555–562.

Flood, J. F., Smith, G. E., & Cherkin, A. Memory retention: Potentiation of cholinergic drug combinations in mice. *Neurobiology of Aging*, 1983, *4*, 37–43.

Flood, J. F., Smith, G. E., & Cherkin, A. Memory retention: Effect of prolonged cholinergic stimulation in mice. *Pharmacology Biochemistry and Behavior*, 1984, *20*, 161–163.

Flood, J. F., Smith, G. E., & Jarvik, M. E. A comparison of the effects of localized brain administration of catecholamine and protein synthesis inhibitors on memory processing. *Brain Research*, 1980, *197*, 153–165.

Frieder, B., & Allweis, C. Transient hypoxic-amnesia: Evidence for triphasic memory-consolidating mechanism with parallel processing. *Behavioral Biology*, 1978, *22*, 178–189.

Frieder, B., & Allweis, C. Memory consolidation: Further evidence for the four-phase model from the time courses of diethyldithiocarbamate and ethacrinic acid amnesias. *Physiology and Behavior*, 1982, *29*, 1071–1075.

Gibbs, M. E. Effects of amphetamine on short-term, protein independent memory in day-old chicks. *Pharmacology Biochemistry and Behavior*, 1976, *4*, 305–309.

Gibbs, M. E., & Barnett, J. M. Drug effects on successive discrimination learning in young chickens. *Brain Research Bulletin*, 1976, *1*, 295–299.

Gibbs, M. E., Gibbs, C. L., & Ng, K. T. The influence of calcium on short-term memory. *Neuroscience Letters*, 1979, *14*, 355–360.

Gibbs, M. E., & Lecanuet, J. Disruption of imprinting by memory inhibitors. *Animal Behaviour*, 1981, *29*, 572–580.

Gibbs, M. E., & Ng, K. T. Diphenylhydantoin facilitation of labile, protein-independent memory. *Brain Research Bulletin*, 1976, *1*, 203–208.

Gibbs, M. E., & Ng, K. T. Psychobiology of memory: Towards a model of memory formation. *Biobehavioral Reviews*, 1977, *1*, 113–136.

Gibbs, M. E., & Ng, K. T. Neuronal depolarization and the inhibition of short-term memory formation. *Physiology and Behavior*, 1979, *23*, 369–375.

Globus, A., Rosenzweig, M. R., Bennett, E. L., & Diamond, M. C. Effects of differential experience on dendritic spine counts. *Journal of Physiological and Comparative Psychology*, 1973, *82*, 175–181.

Gold, P. E., & McGaugh, J. L. A single-trace, two-process view of memory storage process. In D. Deutsch & J. A. Deutsch (Eds.), *Short-term memory*. New York: Academic Press, 1975.

Gutwein, B. M., Shiromani, J., & Fishbein, W. Paradoxical sleep and memory: Long-term disruptive effects of anisomycin. *Pharmacology Biochemistry and Behavior*, 1980, *12*, 377–384.

Jansen, J. K. S., & Nicholls, J. G. Conductance changes, an electrogenic pump and the hyperpolarization of leech neurones following impulses. *Journal of Physiology* (London), 1973, *229*, 635–655.

Jonec, V., & Wasterlain, C. G. Effect of inhibitors of protein synthesis on the development of kindled seizures in rats. *Experimental Neurology*, 1979, *66*, 524–532.

Katz, J. J., & Halstead, W. G. Protein organization and mental function. *Comparative Psychology Monographs*, 1950, *20*, 1–38.

Kesner, R. P., & Novak, J. M. Serial position curve in rats: Role of the dorsal hippocampus. *Science*, 1982, *218*, 173–175.

Kety, S. S. Biological concomitants of affective states and their possible roles in memory processes. In M. R. Rosenzweig & E. L. Bennett (Eds.), *Neural mechanisms of learning and memory*. Cambridge, Mass.: MIT Press, 1976.

Kometiani, P. A., Aleksidze, N. G., & Klein, E. E. The neurochemical correlates of memory. *Progress in Neurobiology*, 1982, *18*, 181–229.

Leconte, P., & Hennevin, E. Caractéristiques temporelles de l'apprentissage chez le rat. *Physiology and Behavior*, 1973, *11*, 677–686.

Lee-Teng, E., & Sherman, S. M. Memory consolidation of one-trial learning in chicks. *Proceedings of the National Academy of Sciences, USA*, 1966, *56*, 926–931.

Mark, R. F. Concluding comments. In M. A. B. Brazier (Ed.), *Brain mechanisms in memory and learning*. New York: Raven Press, 1979.

Mark, R. F., & Watts, M. E. Drug inhibition of memory formation in chickens. I. Long-term memory. *Proceedings of the Royal Society, London* (*Biology*), 1971, *178*, 439–454.

Marx, J. L. How the brain controls birdsong. *Science*, 1982, *217*, 1125–1126.

Matthies, H. Plasticity in the nervous system—an approach to memory research. In C. Ajmone Marsan & H. Matthies (Eds.), *Neuronal plasticity and memory formation*. New York: Raven Press, 1982.

McGaugh, J. L. Time-dependent processes in memory storage. *Science*, 1966, *153*, 1351–1358.

Mizumori, S. Y. J., Rosenzweig, M. R., & Bennett, E. L. Long-Term working memory in the rat: Effects of hippocampally applied anisomycin. *Behavioral Neuroscience*, in press.

Mizumori, S. Y. J., Rosenzweig, M. R., & Kermisch, M. G. Failure of mice to demonstrate spatial memory in the radial maze. *Behavioral and Neural Biology*, 1982, *35*, 33–45.

Olton, D. S. Characteristics of spatial memory. In S. H. Hulse, H. Fowler, & W. K. Honig (Eds.), *Cognitive processes in animal behavior*. Hillsdale, N.J.: Erlbaum, 1978.

Olton, D. S., & Samuelson, R. J. Remembrance of places passed: Spatial memory in rat. *Journal of Experimental Psychology: Animal Behavior Processes*, 1976, *2*, 97–116.

Pearlman, C. A., & Greenberg, R. A. Posttrial REM sleep: A critical period for consolidation of shuttle-box avoidance. *Animal Learning and Behavior*, 1973, *1*, 49–51.

Quartermain, D., & Botwinick, C. Y. The role of biogenic amines in the reversal of cycloheximide-induced amnesia. *Journal of Physiological and Comparative Psychology*, 1975, *88*, 386–401.

Rogers, J. L., Drennen, H. D., & Mark, R. F. Inhibition of memory formation in the imprinting period: Irreversible action of cycloheximide in young chickens. *Brain Research*, 1974, *79*, 213–233.

Rogers, J. L., Oettinger, R., Szer, J., & Mark, R. F. Separate chemical inhibitors of long-term and short-term memory: Contrasting effects of cycloheximide, ouabain, and ethacrynic acid on various learning tasks in chickens. *Proceedings of the Royal Society, London*, 1977, *96*, 171–195.

Rojas-Ramirez, J. A., Aguilar-Jiminez, E., Posada-Andrews, A., Bernal-Pedraza, J. G., & Drucker-Colin, R. R. The effects of various protein synthesis inhibitors on the sleep–wake cycle of rats. *Psychopharmacology*, 1977, *53*, 147–150.

Rose, S. P. R. Transient and lasting biochemical responses to visual deprivation and experience in the rat visual cortex. In M. A. B. Brazier (Ed.), *Brain mechanisms in memory and learning*. New York: Raven Press, 1979.

Rosenzweig, M. R. Recent developments in the neurobiology of memory. *Society for Neuroscience Fifth Annual Meeting*. Brain Information Service Conference Report No. 43, 1976.

Rosenzweig, M. R. Experience, memory, and the brain. *American Psychologist*, 1984, *39*, 365–376.

Rosenzweig, M. R., & Bennett, E. L. (Eds.), *Neural mechanisms of learning and memory*. Cambridge, Mass.: MIT Press, 1976.

Rosenzweig, M. R., Bennett, E. L., & Flood, J. F. Pharmacological modulation of formation of long-term memory. In G. Adam, I. Meszaros, & E. I. Banyai (Eds.), *Brain and behavior* (Vol. 17: *Advances in physiological sciences*). London: Pergamon Press, 1981.

Rosenzweig, M. R., & Leiman, A. L. *Physiological psychology*. Lexington, Mass.: D. C. Heath, 1982.

Schwartz, J. H., Castellucci, V. F., & Kandel, E. R. Functioning of identified neurons and synapses in abdominal ganglion of *Aplysia* in absence of protein synthesis. *Journal of Neurophysiology*, 1971, *34*, 939–953.

Squire, L. R., & Barondes, S. H. Amnesic effect of cycloheximide not due to depletion of a constitutive brain protein with short half-life. *Brain Research*, 1976, *103*, 183–190.

Squire, L. R., & Cohen, N. Memory and amnesia: Resistance to disruption develops for years after learning. *Behavioral and Neural Biology*, 1979, *25*, 115–125.

Tucker, A. R., & Gibbs, M. E. Cycloheximide-induced amnesia for taste aversion memory in rats. *Pharmacology Biochemistry and Behavior*, 1976, *7*, 181–184.

Tucker, A. R., & Gibbs, M. E. Saccharine aversion memory in rats: Inhibition of cycloheximide-resistant memory by ouabain. *Physiology and Behavior*, 1979, *23*, 341–346.

Ungerer, A. Effets comparés de l'acétoxycycloheximide et de la kétamine sur la rétention d'un apprentissage instrumental. *Comptes Rendus de l'Académie des Sciences, Paris*, 1972, *274*, 2692–2695.

Ungerer, A. Nature et ampleur des effets de l'acétoxycycloheximide sur la rétention d'un apprentissage instrumental chez la souris. *Physiology and Behavior*, 1973, *11*, 323–327.

Ungerer, A., Marchi, D., Ropartz, P., & Weil, J. Aversive effects and retention impairment induced by acetoxycycloheximide in an instrumental task. *Physiology and Behavior*, 1975, *15*, 55–62.

Vazquez, D. *Inhibition of protein synthesis* (Vol. 30: *Molecular biology, biochemistry and biophysics*). New York: Springer, 1979.

Watts, M. E., & Mark, R. F. Drug inhibition of memory formation in chickens: II. Short-term memory. *Proceedings of the Royal Society, London*, 1971a, *178*, 455–464.

Watts, M. E., & Mark, R. F. Separate actions of ouabain and cycloheximide on memory. *Brain Research*, 1971b, *25*, 420–423.

Woolston, M. E., Morgan, I. G., & Hambley, J. W. Biochemical effects of cycloheximide in developing chick brain. *Pharmacology Biochemistry and Behavior*, 1979, *10*, 245–249.

CHAPTER EIGHTEEN

Neurohypophyseal Hormone Influences on Learning and Memory Processes

DAVID DE WIED

INTRODUCTION

In the early 1960s we found that the removal of the posterior–intermediate lobe of the pituitary in rats interfered with the maintenance of shuttle-box avoidance behavior, which could be amended by treatment with pitressin or by purified [Lys^8]-vasopressin (LVP) (de Wied, 1965). These observations originated a large series of studies that were aimed at the elucidation of the behavioral action of posterior pituitary principles (see de Wied, 1983).

Soon after the studies in posterior lobectomized rats, it appeared that pitressin and vasopressin also affected acquisition and extinction of active- and passive-avoidance behavior in intact rats (de Wied & Bohus, 1966; de Wied, 1971; Ader & de Wied, 1972). The long-term effect that was found in active and passive avoidance and several other behavioral paradigms, the critical period for the effect to occur, and studies on experimentally induced retrograde amnesia pointed to an effect of vasopressin on memory processes. Further investigations on passive-avoidance behavior indicated that vasopressin facilitated consolidation as well as retrieval processes (Bohus, Kovács, & de Wied, 1978). Although oxytocin seemed to have similar though weaker effects than vasopressin, Schulz, Kovács, and Telegdy (1974) found that it had an effect on behavior opposite to that of vasopressin. This was confirmed, and the results suggested that oxytocin may be regarded as an amnesic neuropeptide.

After it had been found that the neurohypophyseal hormones were much more active following intracerebroventricular injection than after peripheral administration, suggesting a central effect, the next question that was addressed concerned the physiological implication of vasopressin and oxytocin in memory processes. For this, rats with a vasopressin deficiency, such as those of the Brattleboro strain with hereditary diabetes insipidus, or rats treated intracerebroventricularly with vasopressin and oxytocin antiserum, were used in order to inactivate the hormones in the brain. These studies suggested that memory processes are disturbed in the absence of the neurohypophyseal hormones. Lesions of and microinjection into particular brain areas pointed to

David de Wied. Rudolf Magnus Institute for Pharmacology, Medical Faculty, University of Utrecht, Utrecht, The Netherlands.

several limbic midbrain structures as the sites of action of neurohypophyseal hormones (van Wimersma Greidanus, Bohus, Kovács, Versteeg, Burbach, & de Wied, 1983). These regions in general appeared to correspond well with the projections of extrahypothalamic neurohypophyseal hormones containing nerve fibers (Buijs, Velis, & Swaab, 1980; Sofroniew & Weindl, 1981).

In order to explore the mode of action, the influence of the neurohypophyseal hormones was studied on monoaminergic neurotransmission in microdissected brain areas (see Versteeg, 1983). Increased norepinephrine turnover in the ceruleo-telencephalic norepinephrine system appeared to mediate the influence of these peptides on memory consolidation processes.

If vasopressin is associated with memory consolidation and retrieval, it should be released from the extrahypothalamic vasopressin-containing nerve terminals in limbic midbrain structures. Since the release from these projections is difficult to measure, release into the blood and cerebrospinal fluid (CSF) and the concentration in microdissected brain nuclei innervated by these extrahypothalamic pathways were determined during critical periods of avoidance learning and retention. These studies pointed to a remarkable association between release of vasopressin and memory consolidation and retrieval.

By the early 1970s we had found that the memory effect of vasopressin is dissociated from its peripheral endocrine effects (Lande, Witter, & de Wied, 1971; de Wied, Greven, Lande, & Witter, 1972). Structure–activity studies corroborated the view that fragments of neurohypophyseal hormones are responsible for the central nervous system (CNS) effects, and it was postulated that neurohypophyseal hormones are precursor molecules of more potent and selective neuropeptides involved in the consolidation and retrieval of memory processes (de Wied & Bohus, 1978). Structure–activity studies, however, were insufficient to determine the active core in vasopressin and oxytocin that affects memory consolidation and retrieval. Investigations into the generation of fragments from vasopressin and oxytocin in brain synaptic membranes *in vitro* revealed that these precursors may form highly potent and selective memory modulating neuropeptides (Burbach, Kovács, de Wied, van Nispen, & Greven, 1983).

More recently other CNS effects have been discovered and their effects have been studied, albeit less extensively than the memory effects of the neurohypophyseal hormones and their putative neuropeptides. Effects on development of tolerance to and physical dependence on opiates and alcohol, drug-seeking behavior, rewarded behavior, cardiovascular regulation, maternal behavior, temperature regulation, and brain development need further exploration (de Wied & van Ree, 1982). Such studies may reveal the complex physiological interaction of these hormones with brain function, and the results may provide leads for the understanding of the etiology of psychopathological syndromes.

MODULATION OF MEMORY PROCESSES BY NEUROHYPOPHYSEAL HORMONES

Vasopressin

Pitressin administered during either the acquisition or the extinction period of shuttle-box avoidance behavior results in a long-lasting resistance to extinction (de Wied & Bohus, 1966). Similar effects were found using one-way active-avoidance behavior. A single injection of vasopressin resulted in a long-term, dose-dependent, inhibitory effect on extinction of the avoidance behavior that persisted beyond the actual presence of the peptide in the body (de Wied, 1971; de Wied, van Wimersma Greidanus, Bohus, Urban, & Gispen, 1976; van Wimersma Greidanus, Bohus, & de Wied, 1973). In most of these studies a pole-jumping avoidance test was used, in which the rat had to jump onto a pole in the middle of a box in response to a light that served as the conditioned stimulus (CS). Electric footshocks delivered to the floor of the box were used as the unconditioned stimulus (UCS). Although a number of attempts to replicate our observations have met with mixed success, Schulz *et al.* (1974), Bigl, Stark, Ott, Sterba, and Matthies (1977), and Le Moal *et al.* (1981) successfully reproduced these findings.

Vasopressin and related peptides may under certain conditions affect acquisition of avoidance behavior. This can be demonstrated when acquisition is low or deficient as found in hypophysectomized rats. Acquisition of shuttle-box avoidance behavior of hypophysectomized rats improves following vasopressin administration (de Wied, 1969; Lande, Witter, & de Wied, 1971; Bohus, Gispen, & de Wied, 1973). In intact rats vasopressin generally does not affect acquisition but the vasopressin analogue [Orn^8]-vasopressin facilitates pole-jumping avoidance learning (de Wied, 1973). Additionally, a slight improvement can be observed if the tendency to respond is low (King & de Wied, 1974). Resistance to extinction of pole-jumping avoidance behavior is also demonstrable if vasopressin is injected at the first acquisition session in association with a correct avoidance response. This suggests that some measure of associative strength must be present (King & de Wied, 1974). Classical conditioning alone is a sufficient behavioral substrate, but instrumental conditioning appeared to be more effective.

Studies in which LVP was administered at different time periods during extinction of pole-jumping avoidance behavior favored the hypothesis that vasopressin facilitates memory consolidation. In general, it can be stated that vasopressin is fully active when administered in association with behavior which occurs 1 hour prior to or after injection (de Wied, 1971; Bohus, Ader, & de Wied, 1972). Administration at 3 hours before or after the behavioral session markedly decreased the effectiveness of the treatment.

Memory processes involve consolidation and retrieval of acquired information. Consolidation is a labile phase and takes place during several hours after learning (McGaugh, 1973). Substances that affect memory consolidation should be effective during this labile phase. In fact, several drugs, such as amphetamine and strychnine, enhance performance if administered shortly after training (McGaugh & Petrinovich, 1965; McGaugh & Dawson, 1971). Since consolidation takes place within a few hours after learning, modulation of this process should be limited to this phase and be ineffective when treatment is postponed. A second sensitive period is present if after completion of the consolidation process retrieval of the acquired information is tested. Thus, treatment shortly before the retention test may reveal the modulation of memory retrieval processes by drugs or neuropeptides.

Vasopressin affects consolidation as well as retrieval processes. This has been shown in experiments on passive-avoidance behavior. This was studied in a simple "step through" apparatus, which consists of a dark box to which an illuminated platform is attached. The learning trial consists of electric footshocks of short duration in the dark box. Rats are tested for retention at various hours after the learning trial. Posttrial injection of vasopressin induces a long-term facilitation of passive-avoidance behavior (Bohus, Kovács, & de Wied, 1978). Intracerebroventricular administration of [Arg^8]-vasopressin (AVP) at various time intervals after the single learning trial indicated that vasopressin facilitates consolidation as well as retrieval processes. Treatment given immediately after the learning trial is most effective, and if postponed to 3 or 6 hours after the learning trial is greatly reduced or absent. Treatment given 23 hours after the learning trial, that is, 1 hour prior to the retention test, is as effective as intracerebroventricular administration of AVP immediately after the learning trial.

Facilitation of passive-avoidance behavior by vasopressin and related peptides was also found by Lissák and Bohus (1972), Krejci, Kupkova, Metys, Barth, and Jost (1979), and Bookin and Pfeiffer (1977). However, Hostetter, Jubb, and Kozlowski (1980) and Gold and van Buskirk (1976) failed to find an effect of vasopressin on passive-avoidance behavior. This may be caused by differences in the degree to which animals are familiarized with the training situation prior to the learning trial (Rigter, 1982). This author used the experimental design as described by Ader, Weijnen, and Moleman (1972). He found that postlearning injection of vasopressin facilitated subsequent retention of the response. The effect was time-dependent. However, in the absence of pretraining, the postlearning effect of vasopressin on passive-avoidance behavior was lost. This also explains the negative results of Hostetter *et al.* (1980), since these authors omitted the pretraining trials. Vasopressin also facilitates passive avoidance behavior, in a situation where the aversive stimulus is attack by a trained fighter mouse used as a more natural behavior (Leshner & Roche, 1977). Further, [$DesGly^9$-Lys^8]-vasopressin (DGLVP) increases resistance to extinction of conditioned taste aversion (Yawter & Green, 1980).

Vasopressin and related peptides prevent or reverse retrograde amnesia for a passive-avoidance response in rats induced by CO_2 inhalation or electroconvulsive shock (Rigter, van Riezen, & de Wied, 1974; Rigter, Elbertse, & van Riezen, 1975), or by pentylenetetrazol (Bookin & Pfeiffer, 1977; Bohus, Conti, Kovács, & Versteeg, 1982) as well as puromycin-induced retrograde amnesia for a maze-learning task in mice (Lande, Flexner, & Flexner, 1972; Flexner, Flexner, Hoffman, & Walter, 1977; Flexner, Flexner, Walter, & Hoffman, 1978; Walter, Hoffman, Flexner, & Flexner, 1975). The ability of vasopressin to reverse retrograde amnesia also suggests a retrieval hypothesis. This is in agreement with findings by Asin (1979) and Judge and Quartermain (1982), who reported that pretraining and preretention administration of LVP attenuates amnesia for a passive-avoidance task as induced by diethyldithiocarbonate or anisomycin. Pretraining injection, however, was ineffective in the studies of Asin (1979).

Vasopressin does not affect extinction of a food-motivated runway response (Garrud, Gray, & de Wied, 1974), but the performance of food-deprived rats that were trained to hold a lever down to obtain a food pellet was more efficient in vasopressin-tested rats (Garrud, 1975). Vasopressin also facilitates acquisition of alcohol drinking (Finkelberg, Kalant, & LeBlanc, 1978). In contrast to food-motivated behavior, sexually motivated approach behavior is affected by vasopressin. Male rats treated with DGLVP chose the correct arm of a T-maze for reaching a receptive female significantly better than placebo-treated controls

(Bohus, 1977a, 1977b). This influence is also of a long-term nature. Copulation reward appeared to be essential for this effect, since unrewarded males did not make more correct responses. DGLVP also delayed the disappearance of intromission and ejaculatory behavior of male rats following castration. Thus, vasopressin also affects extinction of a genetically determined behavior.

Vasopressin seems to have negative effects on rewarded behavior. In a continuously reinforced schedule, LVP-treated rats were slower in reaching the learning criterion (Alliot & Alexinsky, 1982). Interestingly, this accords with other studies on rewarded behavior. Vasopressin and related peptides reduce acquisition of heroin self-administration in rats (van Ree & de Wied, 1977a, 1977b; van Ree, 1983). The same was found for electrical self-stimulation elicited from the lateral hypothalamus (Schwarzberg, Hartmann, Kovács, & Telegdy, 1976) or the ventral tegmental substantia nigra area (Dorsa & van Ree, 1979). Vasopressin reduces, whereas oxytocin and related fragments facilitate, electrical self-stimulation.

Oxytocin

Oxytocin has an effect on memory processes opposite to that of vasopressin (Schulz *et al.*, 1974; Bohus, Kovács, & de Wied, 1978; Bohus, Urban, & van Wimersma Greidanus, 1978; Kovács & Telegdy, 1982). The first reports on the role of oxytocin on avoidance behavior were rather conflicting. Injected systemically, the hormone failed to affect avoidance behavior (de Wied, 1971; Lissák & Bohus, 1972) and to prevent retrograde amnesia (Walter *et al.*, 1975). Higher doses exerted effects similar to those of vasopressin on extinction of pole-jumping avoidance behavior (de Wied & Gispen, 1977) or in equimolar doses was markedly less potent (Walter, van Ree, & de Wied, 1978). Bigl *et al.* (1977), using extremely high doses, failed to find an effect of oxytocin, although low doses of LVP and AVP increased resistance to extinction of pole-jumping avoidance behavior. Schulz *et al.* (1974) were the first to report that daily injections of rats with low doses of oxytocin (300 mU/kg) facilitated extinction of a bench-jumping active avoidance response. This was confirmed by Kovács, Vécsei, and Telegdy (1978) on passive-avoidance behavior. The concept that oxytocin and vasopressin exert opposite effects on active- and passive-avoidance behavior was confirmed and extended by Bohus, Kovács, and de Wied (1978). Intracerebroventricularly administered oxytocin was found to attenuate passive-avoidance behavior. The influence is of a long-term nature, although a bell-shaped dose–response curve was found. Whereas low doses attenuated, higher amounts facilitated passive-avoidance behavior, like vasopressin given in the same way. The effect can be elicited following postlearning as well as pre-retention administration. Thus, oxytocin attenuates consolidation as well as retrieval processes. The influence of oxytocin is also a time-dependent process (Bohus, Kovács, & de Wied, 1978). In view of these findings, oxytocin may be regarded as an amnesic neuropeptide.

The opposite effect of vasopressin and oxytocin was further explored in a series of experiments in which the influence of either peptide on passive-avoidance behavior was studied in the same animal (Drago, Bohus, & de Wied, 1981). Facilitation of passive-avoidance behavior following postlearning injection of [DesGly^9-Arg^8]-vasopressin (DGAVP) could not be reversed by preretention administration of [DesGly^9]-oxytocin. Conversely, attenuation of passive-avoidance behavior by postlearning injection of DG-oxytocin could not be counteracted by preretention injection of DGAVP. These findings need to be extended but indicate that the opposite effect of vasopressin and oxytocin cannot be explained by a simple competitive or functional antagonism.

PHYSIOLOGICAL IMPLICATION OF VASOPRESSIN IN MEMORY PROCESSES

Several approaches have been used to determine the physiological significance of the neurohypophyseal hormones in memory processes. Since most studies were performed on vasopressin, emphasis in this discussion will be focused on this hormone. The various approaches include animals with a vasopressin deficiency as induced by removal of the posterior–intermediate lobe of the pituitary (de Wied, 1965), or those having a genetic disturbance in the synthesis of vasopressin as found in homozygous diabetes insipidus rats of the Brattleboro strain (Valtin & Schroeder, 1964). Also, rats with a temporary deficit in brain vasopressin by intracerebroventricular injection of specific vasopressin antiserum have been used in this respect (van Wimersma Greidanus, Dogterom, & de Wied, 1975). The results of these studies will be reviewed in the subsequent paragraphs.

Posterior Lobectomy

The suggestion that neurohypophyseal hormones are involved in learning and memory processes came from studies on acquisition and maintenance of avoidance behavior in posterior lobectomized rats (de Wied, 1965). These initial studies showed that acquisition of shuttle-box avoidance behavior was not materially affected by the removal of the posterior–intermediate lobe of the pituitary in rats. Escape behavior also was not affected in posterior-lobectomized rats, indicating that neither sensory nor motor capacities were disturbed. However, extinction of shuttle-box avoidance behavior was markedly facilitated. This abnormal behavior could be corrected by treatment with pitressin administered as a long-acting preparation or with long-acting purified LVP. The treatment could be given either during acquisition or during extinction to be effective (de Wied, 1969). These findings showed that pitressin had a long-term effect on avoidance behavior, which was eventually also observed in other avoidance behaviors, in hypophysectomized (Bohus *et al.*, 1973) and in intact rats (de Wied & Bohus, 1966; de Wied, 1971).

In retrospect, these studies are difficult to interpret, since extrahypothalamic neurohypophyseal-hormone-containing networks have been discovered. Such networks have been demonstrated in a variety of limbic and midbrain structures such as hippocampus, septum, amygdala, medullary areas, and the vicinity of the ventricular systems (Sterba, 1974; Buijs, 1978; Buijs *et al.*, 1980; Sofroniew & Weindl, 1981). Unless the release of neurohypophyseal hormones from the terminals of these networks is disturbed due to the increased synthesis of vasopressin as a result of the mild diabetes insipidus of posterior-lobectomized rats, an explanation for the memory dysfunction of these animals cannot be given. The existence of a strain of rats with hereditary diabetes insipidus seemed to provide a better animal model, because this strain is totally deprived of vasopressin.

Homozygous Diabetes Insipidus (HoDi) Rats

A homozygous variant of the Brattleboro strain lacks the ability to synthesize vasopressin due to a mutation of a single pair of autosomal loci (Valtin & Schroeder, 1964). Memory function of HoDi rats appeared to be severely impaired, as assessed in a one-trial passive-avoidance situation compared with heterozygous control animals (HeDi), when tested for performance 24 hours after the learning trial (de Wied, Bohus, & van Wimersma Greidanus, 1975). AVP and DGLVP given immediately after the learning trial restored passive-avoidance behavior of HoDi rats. The fact that DGLVP was as active as AVP suggested that the beneficial effect of vasopressin could not be ascribed to an influence on water metabolism, since DGLVP is nearly devoid of antidiuretic activities (de Wied *et al.*, 1972). Because the HoDi rat shows avoidance comparable to that of HeDi litter mates if tested immediately after the learning trial, but not if tested 24 hours later, it was concluded that memory rather than learning processes are disturbed in the absence of vasopressin. If a multiple-trial paradigm is used, such as shuttle-box or pole-jumping avoidance behavior, HoDi rats show nearly normal acquisition, but the behavior is extinguished at a more rapid rate than that of HeDi or Wistar rats (Bohus, van Wimersma Greidanus, & de Weid, 1975). Celestian, Carey, and Miller (1975) reported that HoDi rats are inferior in acquiring shuttle-box avoidance behavior, since only 30% of the animals reached the learning criterion. However, those rats that achieved the criterion maintained the response much better than control animals. Bailey and Weiss (1979) found that passive avoidance behavior of HoDi rats is inferior to that of heterozygous controls, but the absence of vasopressin does not cause total impairment of passive-avoidance behavior. The absence of vasopressin in HoDi rats is associated with an increase in oxytocin synthesis (Valtin, Sawyer, & Sokol, 1965; Dogterom, van Wimersma Greidanus, & Swaab, 1977) and marked disturbances in the pituitary–adrenal function (Wiley, Pearlmutter, & Miller, 1974; de Wied, Bohus, & van Wimersma Greidanus, 1976; Vinson, Goddard, & Whitehouse, 1977), in growth and metabolism (Sokol & Wise, 1973; Dloumá, Křeček, & Zicha, 1977), in development (Boer, Swaab, Uylings, Boer, Buijs, & Velis, 1980), and in electrolyte balance (Laycock, 1977). There may also exist variations in the Brattleboro strain due to local breeding influences, which may explain the discrepancies in results. Recent experiments (Láczi, Fekete, & de Wied, 1982) with the strain bred by the Central Breeding Laboratories of TNO, Zeist, The Netherlands, again demonstrated the markedly disturbed passive avoidance behavior of the HoDi rat.

Electrophysiological studies showed that rhythmic slow activity (RSA) of HoDi rats contains substantially lower hippocampal theta frequencies during paradoxical sleep than that of HeDi control animals (Urban & de Wied, 1975). DGAVP nearly completely normalized the distribution of hippocampal theta frequencies of HoDi rats (Urban & de Wied, 1978). HoDi rats are also unable to maintain copulatory behavior after castration. Intromission and ejaculatory pattern disappear almost immediately after castration, whereas normal rats show a gradual decline of copulatory behavior. This can be prevented by the administration of DGLVP to HoDi rats (Bohus, 1977b). Brito, Thomas, Gingold, and Gash (1981) showed that HoDi rats adapt more slowly than normal animals in a T-maze and make fewer correct responses when learning a visual and olfactory discrimination task. In other tasks the HoDi rat was not always inferior. Brito *et al.* (1981) suggest that not all aspects of learning and memory are equally disturbed in HoDi rats.

Bioinactivation of Brain Vasopressin

Reasoning that specific vasopressin antiserum would bind and therefore temporarily inactivate brain vasopressin, the intracerebroventricular administration of vasopressin antiserum was used to study the physiological role of vasopressin in memory processes. Indeed, the administration of specific vasopressin antiserum via one of the lateral ventricles interferes with active- and passive-avoidance behavior (van Wimersma Greidanus, Dogterom, & de Wied, 1975; van Wimersma Greidanus & de Wied, 1976b). A marked deficit in passive-avoidance behavior is found if the antiserum is given immediately after the learning trial and rats are tested for retention between 6 and 24 hours later. This is not the case if the retention test is run immediately or within 2 hours after the learning trial. Intravenous injection of vasopressin antiserum in an amount a hundred times as much as that used in the lateral ventricle does not affect passive avoidance behavior, although it effectively blocks the biological effects of circulating vasopressin as assessed by urine production and excretion of vasopressin in the urine. These results also point to the importance of brain versus peripheral vasopressin in memory processes. The fact that the critical period for the antiserum to be effective is approximately 2 hours corroborates observations on the time-dependent influence of vasopressin as found in active- and passive-avoidance behavior (de Wied, 1971; Bohus, Kovács, & de Wied, 1978). These observations indicate that vasopressin is involved in memory consolidation processes.

Since the antiserum attenuates passive-avoidance behavior as well when administered 1 hour prior to the retention test, endogenous vasopressin also facilitates retrieval processes. Intracerebroventricular oxytocin antiserum has the opposite effect and facilitates passive-avoidance behavior. The same time-dependent effects as found with vasopressin antiserum were observed following oxytocin antiserum (Bohus, Kovács, & de Wied, 1978). Interestingly, if vasopressin antiserum is given 1 hour prior to the 24-hour retention test, which causes attenuation of passive-avoidance behavior, rats thus treated but tested at a second retention test 24 hours later show avoidance again. Van Wimersma Greidanus (1982) further showed that passive-avoidance performance of rats treated 1 hour before the retention test can be restored by coadministration of $ACTH_{4-10}$ but not if the antiserum had been given immediately after the learning trial. This latter procedure interferes with the consolidation of memory processes. Vasopressin antiserum also affects one-way active-avoidance behavior. Although acquisition of the behavior is somewhat delayed, extinction of the response of rats treated with the antiserum during acquisition is markedly facilitated (van Wimersma Greidanus, Dogterom, & de Wied, 1975).

VASOPRESSIN LEVELS IN BLOOD, CSF, AND BRAIN DURING AVOIDANCE BEHAVIOR

Another approach has been the measurement of vasopressin levels in blood, CSF, and various brain regions in relation to avoidance performance. Vasopressin levels (antidiuretic [AD] activity) in eye plexus blood were measured by bioassay immediately after the 24-hour retention test of a passive-avoidance response (Thompson & de Wied, 1973). Eye plexus blood contains much higher AD activity than peripheral truncal blood. A good correlation was found between shock intensity during the learning trial, avoidance latency at the 24-hour retention test, and the level of AD activity in eye plexus blood. This finding was interpreted as indicating an association between AD activity and memory formation.

Subsequent studies by our group using a radioimmunoassay (RIA) for vasopressin extracted from truncal blood could not corroborate the studies by Thompson and de Wied (1973). No change in immunoreactive (IR) AVP was found during passive-avoidance retention as measured 24 hours after the learning trial. Only if a high shock intensity was used, which caused maximal avoidance latencies, a slight increase in IR AVP was detected (van Wimersma Greidanus, Croiset, Goedemans, & Dogterom, 1979). Neither the rate of acquisition nor extinction of pole-jumping avoidance behavior were associated with a significant elevation of circulating IR AVP levels.

Release of Vasopressin into Eye Plexus Blood

Recent experiments designed to replicate and extend the findings by Thompson and de Wied (1973), however, again pointed to a relation between passive-avoidance retention and the levels of AD activity and IR AVP levels in eye plexus blood. Both assays were used. A good relation was found between plasma AD activity and IR AVP levels (Láczi *et al.*, 1982). The levels in eye plexus blood are high and can be determined without an extraction procedure. Levels were also determined immediately after the learning trial. AD activity and IR AVP levels were high in eye plexus blood in nonshocked rats, probably because of the stress of handling and exposure to the test box. In fact, the levels in rats that received footshock of various intensities were not significantly higher whether determined immediately, at 10, or at 30 minutes after the learning trial. The avoidance latencies at the 24-hour retention test, however, were related to the intensity of the electric footshock at the learning trial.

HoDi rats did not display passive-avoidance behavior at the 24-hour retention test even when subjected to the high shock intensity of 1 mA for 2 seconds. The levels of IR AVP in eye plexus blood of these rats was under the limit of detection. HeDi rats showed maximal avoidance latency at the retention test, although IR AVP in eye plexus blood was much lower than that found in Wistar animals and not significantly different from that of nonshocked HeDi controls.

Finally, the intracerebroventricular administration of vasopressin antiserum to Wistar rats one-half hour before the learning trial, which attenuates passive-avoidance behavior, hardly affected IR AVP levels of eye plexus blood, immediately after the learning trial. However, if given one-half hour before the retention test, attenuation of passive-avoidance behavior and a markedly reduced IR AVP in eye plexus blood were found.

The augmented release of vasopressin into the blood stream raises the issue of the significance of peripherally circulating hormone levels for the influence of this nonapeptide on avoidance behavior. The memory effect of vasopressin probably is a direct effect on limbic midbrain structures, since microinjection of picogram amounts of vasopressin facilitates passive-avoidance behavior (Kovács, Bohus, & Versteeg, 1979b; Kovács, Bohus, Versteeg, de Kloet, & de Wied, 1979). This view has been challenged. Le Moal *et al.* (1981), using a vasopressin receptor antagonist, have shown that pretreatment with this analogue prevents vasopressin-induced blood pressure increase and the influence on memory. They concluded that the memory effect of vasopressin in part is mediated by changes in blood pressure. This is not in accord with our findings, which show that fragments of vasopressin such as DGLVP, which are almost devoid of pressor activity, retain their effect on avoidance behavior (de Wied *et al.*, 1972). In subsequent experiments, Koob *et al.* (1981) found that the antagonist given subcutaneously by itself caused an effect on extinction of active-avoidance behavior opposite to that of exogenous AVP. Injections of the antagonist into the lateral ventricle were ineffective except at a very high dose of 10 μg.

Peripheral mechanisms may, however, play a role in the memory effect of vasopressin. Rats, adrenalectomized or adrenomedullectomized 2 days before the learning trial of a passive avoidance response, display a marked deficit in retention. Posttrial or preretention administration of AVP does not normalize the retention deficit of the operated animals (Borrell, de Kloet, Versteeg, & Bohus, 1983), whether given subcutaneously or intracerebroventricularly. Thus, the action of AVP may be mediated through adrenomedullary catecholamines or circulating catecholamines, or may be necessary for the expression of the behavioral effect of vasopressin. Postlearning administration of adrenalin restored passive-avoidance retention, but the action followed a bell-shaped dose–response curve. Borrell *et al.* (1983) found that AVP potentiated the facilitating effect of high doses of epinephrine which in themselves caused amnesia, and also of median doses, which caused maximal avoidance latencies. Following preretention administration of epinephrine in low, medium, and high doses, AVP markedly improved retention in all adrenalectomized rats that received epinephrine. These results suggest that the action of vasopressin on consolidation and retrieval of memory for a passive-avoidance response depends on peripheral catecholamines. Since intracerebroventricularly administered AVP also failed to improve retention in adrenalectomized rats, the blood–brain barrier does not seem to be the cause of the inactivity of the peptide to affect passive-avoidance behavior in adrenalectomized rats. Taking into account the important role of the dorsal noradrenergic bundle in the effect of AVP on memory processes (Kovács, Bohus, & Versteeg, 1979b; Kovács, Bohus, Versteeg, de Kloet, & de Wied, 1979), one might postulate a unique interaction between vasopressin and central and peripheral catecholamines. These together with vasopressin seem to act in a cooperative way to affect memory processes.

The relationship between vasopressin levels in eye plexus blood collected immediately after the retention test and passive-avoidance latencies as reported by Thompson and de Wied (1973) has been found again by Láczi *et al.* (1982). The augmented release of vasopressin under these conditions probably is a reflection of the activity of the supraoptic–neurohypophyseal system associated with the memory of the fearful aversive stimulation experienced by the rat during the learning trial. This augmented release may be important for retrieval processes.

However, these studies measured blood levels of vasopressin. The existence of an extrahypothalamic distribution of vasopressin-containing networks and lack of knowledge on the regulation of the release of vasopressin from the terminals of these networks require the direct measurement of vasopressin in the brain, either in the CSF or at the site of release.

Release of Vasopressin into the CSF

Mens, van Egmond, de Rotte, and van Wimersma Greidanus (1982) have been unable to find differences in the vasopressin levels in cisternal CSF of rats subjected to passive-avoidance behavior. Extensive studies on the relationship between behavioral performance during retention of a passive-avoidance response and vasopressin levels in the CSF revealed no significant effect. However, a subsequent study in which IR AVP in cisternal CSF was measured at various intervals after the learning trial showed that the levels of rats exposed to a high-intensity footshock (1 mA) are markedly elevated when measured immediately after the learning trial. Rats trained at a mild footshock of .25 mA have IR AVP levels in the CSF that are only slightly higher than those of nonshocked animals. In general, the levels of vasopressin in CSF immediately after the learning trial are related to the intensity of the electric footshock (Láczi, Gaffori, Fekete, de Kloet, & de Wied, in press). At the 24-hour retention test IR AVP levels in CSF of rats exposed to mild footshock are significantly elevated. Surprisingly, the levels of rats subjected to the highest shock intensity at the learning trial are under the limit of detection when tested 1 day later. A possible explanation for this may be that exposure to this high shock level at the learning trial releases the readily releasable pool of vasopressin from the terminals of the vasopressin-containing neurons, thus preventing spillover in the CSF. Indeed, the levels of IR AVP in the CSF when tested for avoidance performance at 5 days after the learning trial are markedly elevated. This suggests that repletion of AVP in the terminals of the extrahypothalamic network has taken place.

In conclusion, passive-avoidance behavior in rats is accompanied by the release of IR AVP into the CSF, and the levels are related to the intensity of the aversive stimulus and avoidance latencies. It is conceivable that AVP is released during passive-avoidance learning and retention at the sites of the memory effect of this neuropeptide in the brain. This local release may be reflected in changes in the CSF, but the measurement of AVP in brain nuclei involved in the CNS effect of vasopressin might provide additional evidence.

Vasopressin Levels in the Brain

Although Dogterom and Buijs (1980) did not find a change in vasopressin concentration in various brain regions during passive-avoidance behavior, we detected marked changes in IR AVP in various limbic structures 24 hours after exposure of rats to the high shock intensity. IR AVP of rats exposed to electric footshock during the learning trial of a passive-avoidance response was significantly decreased in the nucleus paraventricularis, the nucleus suprachiasmaticus, and the lateral septal nucleus and hippocampus, whereas that of the central amygdala nucleus, subfornical organ, and locus ceruleus was increased, as compared with the level in nonshocked control rats (Láczi *et al.*, in press). No significant differences in IR AVP were found in the habenular periventricular hypothalamic nucleus, organum vasculosum of the lamina terminalis, and medial and dorsal raphe nucleus.

The reason for the opposite effects on vasopressin levels in two distinct limbic regions as a result of passive-avoidance learning is not clear. AVP facilitates both consolidation and retrieval of memory. These effects seem to be localized in different limbic midbrain regions (Bohus *et al.*, 1982). A decrease in IR AVP was found in the hippocampal–septal area, which plays a role in vasopressin-induced consolidation of memory processes (Kovács, Bohus, & Versteeg, 1979b; Kovács, Bohus, Versteeg, de Kloet, & de Wied, 1979), whereas increased levels were found in the amygdala, which has been implicated in the retrieval type of action of vasopressin (Bohus *et al.*, 1982). The locus ceruleus does not seem to play a role in the influence of vasopressin in memory processes (Kovács, Bohus, Versteeg, de Kloet, & de Wied, 1979) although the concentration of IR AVP was markedly increased. However, this nucleus might exert a modulatory role on noradrenergic mechanisms that are activated by the stressful stimuli associated with learning and retention of passive avoidance behavior (Mason & Iversen, 1978). Nevertheless, the results show that passive-avoidance behavior is accompanied by a depletion in those extrahypothalamic vasopressin-containing nerve terminals that mediate the effect of the peptide on memory consolidation, whereas the concentration is increased in those terminals projecting to sites that are involved in vasopressin-induced retrieval effects.

Other hormones may be released during passive-avoidance behavior as well. For example, pituitary–adrenal activity as assessed by plasma corticosterone levels is also related to passive-avoidance behavior (de Wied, Bohus, & van Wimersma Greidanus, 1976). Determined at 15 minutes after the retention test, plasma corticosterone levels are markedly elevated when HoDi and HeDi rats are tested for retention immediately after the learning trial, when avoidance latencies are also high. However, if tested 24 hours after the learning trial, plasma corticosterone levels are low in HoDi rats that do not show avoidance, whereas those of HeDi rats that avoid maximally are high. Treatment with AVP or DGLVP restores passive-avoidance behavior of HoDi rats but not the pituitary–adrenal response at the retention test. Still other pituitary *c.q.* brain-borne hormones such as ACTH, α-MSH, and prolactin may be released during acquisition and retention of passive-avoidance behavior. These may all play a part in the complex adaptive process that is essential for the formation and maintenance of new behavior patterns.

SITE OF ACTION OF VASOPRESSIN ON MEMORY PROCESSES

Lesion studies showed that destruction of the rostral septal region and the anterodorsal hippocampus prevent the effect of vasopressin on extinction of pole-jumping avoidance behavior (van Wimersma Greidanus, Bohus, & de Wied, 1975; van Wimersma Greidanus & de Wied, 1976a). Lesions of the thalamic parafascicular area only partially prevented the influence of vasopressin, whereas transsection of the fornix and stria terminalis were ineffective in blocking vasopressin-induced resistance to extinction of pole-jumping avoidance behavior (van Wimersma Greidanus, Croiset, & Schuiling, 1979).

Microinjection of picogram amounts of vasopressin in various limbic midbrain nuclei was used to explore further the site of action of this peptide. These studies were done using passive-avoidance behavior as the paradigm. Treatments were given immediately after the learning trial and thus were indicative for consolidation processes (Kovács, Bohus, & Versteeg, 1979b; Kovács, Bohus, Versteeg, de Kloet, & de Wied, 1979; Kovács *et al.*, 1980). Local microinjection into the dorsal septal area, the hippocampal dentate gyrus, or the dorsal raphe nucleus facilitated passive-avoidance behavior, whereas microinjection into the central amygdaloid nucleus or the hippocampal subiculum were without effect. Thus, the hippocampus, septum, and raphe regions are sensitive to the memory-consolidating effect of vasopressin. Interestingly, administration of vasopressin antiserum into the dorsal raphe nucleus or the hippocampal dentate gyrus has an opposite effect and attenuates passive-avoidance performance (Kovács *et al.*, 1980; Kovács, Bohus, Versteeg, Telegdy, & de Wied, 1982). Microinjection of vasopressin into the amygdala, however, partially reversed pentylenetetrazol-induced amnesia, but only if the peptide was given shortly before the retention test (Bohus *et al.*, 1982). Microinjection into the dorsal raphe nucleus or dorsal septal area was without effect. Thus, the neuroanatomical substrate for the memory effect of vasopressin seems to be different for consolidation and retrieval processes.

EFFECTS ON BRAIN NEUROTRANSMISSION

It is conceivable that the neurohypophyseal hormones modulate monoaminergic neurotransmission. Catecholamine metabolism in HoDi rats differs from that of homozygous normal (HoNo) controls (Versteeg, Tanaka, & de Kloet, 1978). In many brain regions the differences in catecholamine turnover are opposite in vasopressin-deficient and vasopressin-treated normal animals. The same is found between vasopressin antiserum and vasopressin treatment (Versteeg, de Kloet, van Wimersma Greidanus, & de Wied, 1979).

The ceruleo-telencephalic norepinephrine system has been implicated in the acquisition, consolidation, and retrieval of a learned response (Crow, 1968; Kety, 1970; Mason & Iversen, 1977). This system is sensitive to the memory-modulating effect of the neurohypophyseal hormones. Systemic or intracerebroventricularly administered AVP appeared to affect catecholamine metabolism rather selectively in a number of restricted brain regions (Kovács, Vecsei, Szabó, & Telegdy, 1977; Tanaka, Versteeg, & de Wied, 1977). AVP-enhanced norepinephrine turnover in the hypothalamus, thalamus, and medulla oblongata, but not in the septum, preoptic area, hippocampus, and amygdala in rats pretreated with α-methyl-*p*-tyrosine. In addition, AVP facilitated dopamine turnover in the preoptic area, septum, and striatum, but not in hypothalamus and amygdala (Kovács *et al.*, 1977; Tanaka, Versteeg, & de Wied, 1977). In a subsequent experiment in nuclei selected on the basis of previous studies on the site of action of the memory effect of vasopressin (van Wimersma Greidanus & de Wied, 1976a; van Wimersma Greidanus, Croiset, & Schuiling, 1979; Kovács *et al.*, 1979b, 1980; Kovács, Bohus, Versteeg, de Kloet, & de Wied, 1979) and the distribution of the extrahypothalamic neurohypophyseal hormone-containing pathways (Buijs *et al.*, 1980; Sofroniew & Weindl, 1981) the influence of intracerebroventricular AVP on catecholamine activity was further investigated. Norepinephrine turnover was enhanced in the dorsal septal nucleus, the anterior hypothalamic nucleus, the parafascicular nucleus, the dorsal raphe nucleus, and the locus ceruleus; whereas dopamine utilization was enhanced in the caudate nucleus, the median eminence, and the dorsal raphe nucleus. The turnover of norepinephrine was reduced in the supraoptic nucleus and the nucleus ruber. No effect was found in 35 other nuclei (Tanaka, de Kloet, de Wied, & Versteeg, 1977). Recent studies by van Heuven-Nolsen and Versteeg (unpublished observations) in microdissected brain nuclei demonstrated regional effects on norepinephrine and dopamine turnover following intracerebroventricular oxytocin as well. In several nuclei the effects are opposite to those found with vasopressin except for the dorsal septal nuclei. This agrees well with the finding that vasopressin and oxytocin both facilitate passive-avoidance behavior when microinjected into this region (Kovács, Bohus, & Versteeg, 1979a).

Further evidence for the involvement of catecholamine transmission in the memory effect of the neurohypophyseal hormones was obtained by local injection into the same regions that caused facilitation of passive-avoidance behavior (Kovács *et al.*, 1979b; Kovács, Bohus, Versteeg, de Kloet, & de Wied, 1979). Microinjection of vasopressin into the dentate gyrus of the hippocampus enhanced, whereas application of AVP in the dorsal septal area decreased, norepinephrine turnover in the injected region. Microinjection of AVP into the dorsal raphe nucleus did not affect norepinephrine turnover but enhanced dopamine utilization (Kovács *et al.*, 1979a).

Destruction of the ceruleo-telencephalic norepinephrine system with the neurotoxin 6-hydroxydopamine (6-OHDA) prevents the facilitatory effect of vasopressin on passive-avoidance behavior if injected immediately after the learning trial (consolidation) but not if injected prior to the retention test (retrieval) (Kovács, Bohus, Versteeg, de Kloet, & de Wied, 1979). Although the above-mentioned neurochemical effects implicate the ceruleo-telencephalic norepinephrine system as the mediator of the effect of vasopressin on memory consolidation and point to the terminal areas rather than the cell bodies, the evidence is not conclusive. Microinjection of vasopressin into the locus ceruleus does not affect passive-avoidance behavior, but it enhances norepinephrine utilization in this region. In addition, microiontophoretic application of AVP and LVP increases the firing rate of the majority of the norepinephrine neurons in this cell body region (Olpe & Baltzer, 1981).

Although evidence for a selective interaction of vasopressin with distinct norepinephrine and dopamine-containing systems in the brain is rather convincing, other transmitter systems seem to be involved. Intracerebroventricularly administered vasopressin decreases serotonin concentration in mesencephalon and septum but not in hippocampus, hypothalamus, and striatum (Schwarzberg, Kovács, Szabó, & Telegdy, 1981). Recently, Auerbach and Lipton (1982) reported that AVP increases serotonin synthesis and release from hippocampal tissue *in vitro*. These effects were found in the dentate gyrus but not in the CA1 regions, whereas Gardner, Richards, and Möhring (1981) failed to find an effect on K^+-stimulated release of serotonin from brain stem slices. Other data also argue for an interaction with serotonergic systems. HoDi rats have a lower whole-brain concentration of serotonin than have HeDi controls (Leonard, Ramaekers, & Rigter, 1976), but Kovács *et al.* (1980) reported higher serotonin levels in septum, mesencephalon, and striatum but not in the hypothalamus of the HoDi rat. Pargyline-induced accumulation of serotonin was significantly lower in these brain regions of HoDi rats as compared to that of HeDi litter mates. This suggests a reduced turnover of serotonin in the absence of vasopressin.

STRUCTURE–ACTIVITY STUDIES

Arginine-vasopressin is rather potent in increasing resistance to extinction of pole-jumping avoidance behavior following subcutaneous administration (Table 18-1). Removal of the C-terminal amino acid residue glycinamide yields a peptide with a somewhat reduced behavioral potency (de Wied *et al.*, 1972). However, DGLVP and DGAVP have lost almost all peripheral endocrine effects. Thus, the removal of the C-terminal glycinamide dissociates the behavioral influence of vasopressin from the classical endocrine effects. These findings suggested that a fragment of vasopressin might be the behavioral principle.

Further studies with several fragments of AVP indicated that the behavioral activity is located in the covalent ring structure, although a second activity site might be present in the linear part of the molecule (de Wied, 1976). Substitution in the amino acid residues of the covalent ring structure of AVP by different amino acids generally reduces the behavioral effect. Alterations in the linear part of the molecule are less damaging (Walter *et al.*, 1978). Nevertheless, behavioral activities are more tolerant than endocrine activities to modification of the various amino acid residues in the vasopressin molecule.

Attenuation of retrograde amnesia has also been used to determine the active core of the vasopressin molecule on memory processes. DGLVP either before or after training attenuates puromycin-induced retrograde amnesia for a maze-learning task in mice (Lande *et al.*, 1972). This peptide also counteracts CO_2-induced amnesia for a passive-avoidance response in rats (Rigter *et al.*, 1974). Interestingly, the C-terminal tripeptide of oxytocin is more active in protecting against amnesia than that of vasopressin. Moreover, the covalent ring structures of vasopressin or oxytocin are inactive (Walter *et al.*, 1975). Although oxytocin slightly affects retrograde amnesia, Gly-Gly-Gly-oxytocin is fully active in this respect. The dipeptide Leu-Gly-NH_2 also is rather potent in this test. Since attenuation of retrograde amnesia measures retrieval processes, the conclusion that the active sequence for these processes is mainly present in the C-terminal part of the neurohypophyseal hormones seems justified. This hypothesis was corroborated by studies on passive-avoidance behavior. Consolidation was significantly facilitated by intracerebroventricularly administered AVP, DGAVP, the covalent ring structure, and the ring structure plus Pro^7 (Table 18-1). Surprisingly, the ring structure of oxytocin with and without Pro^7 also facilitates avoidance latency following postlearning administration. Although the linear parts of both vasopressin and oxytocin facilitate consolidation, these fragments are less active (Kovács, Bohus, Versteeg, Telegdy, & de Wied, 1982). Inhibition of consolidation was brought about by oxytocin, DG-oxytocin, and vasotocin (AVT).

Table 18-1. Amino acid sequences of various neurohypophyseal hormones and related fragments

Compound	Sequence
Arg^8-vasopressin (AVP$_{1-9}$)	H-Cys-Tyr-Phe-Gln-Asn-Cys-Pro-Arg-Gly-NH$_2$
Desglycinamide^9-Arg^8-vasopressin (AVP$_{1-8}$)	H-Cys-Tyr-Phe-Gln-Asn-Cys-Pro-Arg-OH
Pressinamide (AVP$_{1-6}$)	H-Cys-Tyr-Phe-Gln-Asn-Cys-NH$_2$
Prolyl-arginyl-glycinamide (AVP$_{7-9}$)	H-Pro-Arg-Gly-NH$_2$
Oxytocin (OXT$_{1-9}$)	H-Cys-Tyr-Ile -Gln-Asn-Cys-Pro-Leu-Gly-NH$_2$
Tocinamide (OXT$_{1-6}$)	H-Cys-Tyr-Ile -Gln-Asn-Cys-NH$_2$
Prolyl-leucyl-glycinamide (OXT$_{7-9}$)	H-Pro-Leu-Gly-NH$_2$
Arg^8-oxytocin (vasotocin; AVT$_{1-9}$)	H-Cys-Tyr-Ile -Gln-Asn-Cys-Pro-Arg-Gly-NH$_2$

Facilitation of retrieval was found with AVP and less pronounced with DGAVP, the ring structure of AVP plus Pro^7, the ring structure of oxytocin, the linear tripeptide Pro-Leu-Gly-NH$_2$ (PLG), and Leu-Gly-NH$_2$, whereas retrieval was attenuated by oxytocin, DG-oxytocin, AVT, and DGAVT. Thus, the requirement for the amnesic effect of oxytocin on consolidation and retrieval concerns practically the whole molecule. Only the C-terminal amino acid residue glycinamide can be removed without appreciable loss of activity or reversal of the effect. AVT$_{1-8}$ attenuates retrieval rather selectively. These structure–activity studies, although suggesting that consolidation and retrieval are separately located in the neurohypophyseal hormones, appeared to be insufficient to determine the active loci of the neurohypophyseal hormones in this respect.

CONVERSION OF NEUROHYPOPHYSEAL HORMONES

Studies on the biotransformation of vasopressin and oxytocin in the brain might reveal the generation of specific neuropeptides involved in consolidation and retrieval processes. Two main routes for the conversion of neurohypophyseal hormones in the brain have been identified. Aminopeptidase action cleaving the Cys^1-Tyr^2 bond of LVP was found by Pliška and Thorn (1971) using minced cerebral cortex tissue. Further evidence for an aminopeptidase-mediated pathway was provided by Marks, Abrash, and Walter (1973), who showed release of the Tyr^2 and Ile^3 residues from oxytocin and the release of Tyr^2 and Phe^3 from vasopressin by purified brain aminopeptidases. C-terminal-cleaving enzymes produced Leu-Gly-NH$_2$ and glycinamide from oxytocin (Marks *et al.*, 1973).

Burbach and colleagues (Burbach, de Kloet, & de Wied, 1980; Burbach, Schotman, & de Kloet, 1980) found evidence for the presence of aminopeptidase and C-terminal-cleaving peptidase activity in brain synaptic membranes of rat forebrain tissue. Quantification of these activities utilizing differentially ^{14}C-labeled oxytocin preparations showed that the aminopeptidase pathway strongly prevails in SPM fractions. Other subcellular preparations that contain high aminopeptidase activity are the synaptosomal and microsomal fractions.

Although C-terminal-cleaving peptidase is low in SPM preparations of the medial basal hypothalamus, the nigrostriatal area and the region of the dorsal raphe area are highest. These regions are densely innervated by neurohypophyseal hormone-containing fibers. Converting peptidase activities have also been detected in the cortex, which has a low density of vasopressinergic fibers. The activity of enzymes in that region is also the lowest of all areas tested.

During exposure of oxytocin to isolated brain synaptic membranes, a limited number of peptide fragments were found by the high-pressure liquid chromatography (HPLC) fractionation of the digest. A main metabolite was eluted with a retention time of 10.2 minutes. This peptide was obtained in pure form from the HPLC eluate. The amino acid composition of the peptide determined after performic acid treatment and acid hydrolysis was Cys(O_3H) (2.0), Asp (1.0), Glu (1.0), Gly (1.0), Tyr (<0.1), Ile (<0.1), Leu (1.0). In end-group analyses, mono-dansyl-cystine was found and identified in two-dimensional thin-layer chromatography. In addition, after treatment of the isolated peptide with pyroglutamate-aminopeptidase, dansyl-asparagin was detected, demonstrating the presence of a pyroglutamic acid residue at the N-terminus of the peptide. Based on these analyses, the oxytocin fragment appeared to be a hexapeptide with the sequence pGlu-Asn-Cys(Cys)-Pro-Leu-GlyNH_2[pGlu^4, Cyt^6]-OXT_{4-9} (Burbach, Schotman, & de Kloet, 1980). This peptide following posttrial intracerebroventricular injection appeared to be much more active in attenuating passive-avoidance behavior than oxytocin. It was effective in the order of 1 pg, whereas 100 pg of oxytocin had to be given to elicit the same response. Both peptides caused bell-shaped dose–response curves. The desglycinamide fragment had the same effect. It was somewhat less potent but more stable, since it did not show a bell-shaped dose–response relationship. The C-terminal glycinamide is therefore not required for the memory-attenuating effect of oxytocin. [Cyt^6]-OXT_{5-9} was inactive. The [pGlu^4-Cyt^6]-OXT_{4-9} peptide had no uterotonic activity in amounts a 1000 times that of oxytocin to stimulate the rat uterus *in vitro*.

These results demonstrate the existence of an enzyme system in the brain that converts oxytocin into potent neuroactive peptides, and substantiate the concept that oxytocin functions as a precursor peptide in the brain. The same has been found for vasopressin (Burbach *et al.*, 1983). A preferentially formed metabolite of AVP of similar structure was found that exerts a markedly more potent action on passive avoidance behavior than the parent peptide. These findings support the notion that the neurohypophyseal hormones are precursor molecules of the second order of neuropeptides involved in memory processes.

OTHER CENTRAL EFFECTS MODULATED BY NEUROHYPOPHYSEAL HORMONES AND RELATED PEPTIDES

In addition to their role in memory processes, vasopressin, oxytocin, and related peptides are implicated in several other centrally mediated responses, such as tolerance development to and physical dependence on opiate and ethanol, heroin addiction (van Ree, Bohus, Versteeg, & de Wied, 1978; Hoffman, Ritzmann, Walter, & Tabakoff, 1978), electrical self-stimulation (Schwarzberg *et al.*, 1976), cardiovascular regulation (Versteeg, Bohus, & de Jong, 1979), induction of maternal behavior (Pedersen, Ascher, Monroe, & Prange, 1982), control of body temperature (Cooper, Kasting, Lederis, & Veale, 1979), and brain development (Boer *et al.*, 1980).

Thus, DGLVP facilitates the development of resistance to the antinociceptive action of morphine in mice (Krivoy, Zimmermann, & Lande, 1974). The linear tripeptide of oxytocin, PLG, accelerates the development of tolerance to the antinociceptive action of intracerebroventricularly administered β-endorphin in rats (van Ree, de Wied, Bradbury, Hulme, Smyth, & Snell, 1976), as well as the development of morphine tolerance in both mice and rats (Contreras & Takemori, 1980; Székely, Miglécz, Dunai-Kovács, Tarnawa, Ronai, Gráf, & Bajusz, 1979). Physical dependence on opiates as assessed by body weight loss and hypothermia is also affected by fragments of neurohypophyseal hormones. The linear tripeptides of vasopressin and oxytocin both facilitate the development of physical dependence on morphine (van Ree *et al.*, 1978). However, the data on physical dependence are conflicting, possibly because of different test procedures and amounts of peptides used in the respective studies (van Ree & de Wied, 1981). Various fragments of vasopressin and oxytocin modulate physical dependence on ethanol. Treatment with AVP attenuates the disappearance rate of tolerance to ethanol in mice (Hoffman *et al.*, 1978). In the same animals continuously exposed to ethanol, DGAVP enhances residual tolerance to the hypothermic effect of ethanol (Rigter & Crabbe, 1980). Withdrawal convulsions were found to exacerbate in mice treated with DGAVP. Thus, DGAVP facilitates development of tolerance to and physical dependence on opioids as well as ethanol.

Acquisition of heroin self-administration of rats is reduced by the covalent ring structure of vasopressin and facilitated by PLG (van Ree & de Wied, 1977a, 1977b). The same is found for electrical self-stimulation elicited from the lateral hypothalamus or the ventral tegmental area. Oxytocin and PLG facilitate, whereas vasopressin and DGAVP have a suppressive effect (Schwarzberg *et al.*, 1976; Dorsa & van Ree, 1979).

Cardiovascular regulatory processes may also be modulated by neurohypophyseal hormones and related fragments (Versteeg, Bohus, & de Jong, 1979). A centrally evoked pressor response following electrical stimulation of the mesencephalic reticular formation was found to be attenuated by peripherally injected LVP (Bohus, 1974). The same was observed for intracerebroventricularly administered AVP, DGLVP, the covalent ring structure of AVP, and the linear tripeptide of vasopressin (Versteeg, Bohus, & de Jong, 1979). Oxytocin and PLG are also effective, but the covalent ring structure is inactive. In fact, PLG is more potent in this respect than the other peptides. However, the locus of action of this tripeptide is different from that of vasopressin.

Oxytocin is involved in maternal behavior. Administered intracerebroventricularly to virgin rats, full maternal behavior is displayed toward foster pups. This effect, which is dependent on the estrogen level, is also brought about by fragments of both oxytocin and vasopressin (Pedersen *et al.*, 1982). In primed ovariectomized rats, the ring structure of oxytocin appeared to be as active as the parent molecule, whereas PLG had a relatively weak activity (Pedersen *et al.*, 1982).

Effects of vasopressin on body temperature seem to be specific for the molecule. Oxytocin is not active in this respect (Veale, Kasting, & Cooper, 1981), and DGAVP also fails to normalize endotoxin-induced hyperthermia (Kovács & de Wied, 1983). Effects of vasopressin on brain development have not been studied with fragments of the neurohypophyseal hormones.

Ader, R., & de Wied, D. Effects of lysine vasopressin on passive avoidance learning. *Psychonomic Science*, 1972, *29*, 46–48.

Ader, R., Weijnen, J. A. W. M., & Moleman, P. Retention of a passive avoidance response as a function of the intensity and duration of electric shock. *Psychonomic Science*, 1972, *26*, 125–128.

Alliot, J., & Alexinsky, T. Effects of posttrial vasopressin injections on appetitively motivated learning in rats. *Physiology and Behavior*, 1982, *28*, 525–530.

Asin, K. E. Lysine vasopressin attenuation of diethyl-dithiocarbamate-induced amnesia. *Pharmacology, Biochemistry and Behavior*, 1979, *12*, 343–346.

Auerbach, S., & Lipton, P. Vasopressin augments depolarization-induced release and synthesis of serotonin in hippocampal slices. *Journal of Neuroscience*, 1982, *2*, 477–482.

Bailey, W. H., & Weiss, J. M. Evaluation of a memory deficit in vasopressin-deficient rats. *Brain Research*, 1979, *162*, 174–178.

Bigl, H., Stark, H., Ott, T., Sterba, G., & Matthies, H. Beeinflussing von Lernprozessen durch Hinterlappenhormone am Beispiel der Ratte. In *Hormonale und humorale Informationsübermittelung durch Peptide als Mediatoren*. Berlin: Akademie, 1977.

Boer, G. J., Swaab, D. F., Uylings, H. B. M., Boer, K., Buijs, R. M., & Velis, D. N. Neuropeptides in rat brain development. *Progress in Brain Research*, 1980, *53*, 202–227.

Bohus, B. The influence of pituitary peptides on brain centers controlling autonomic responses. *Progress in Brain Research*, 1974, *41*, 175–183.

Bohus, B. Effect of desglycinamide-lysine vasopressin (DG-LVP) on sexually motivated T-maze behavior in the male rat. *Hormones and Behavior*, 1977a, *8*, 52–61.

Bohus, B. The influence of pituitary neuropeptides on sexual behavior. In H. P. Klotz (Ed.), *Hormones et sexualité*. Paris: Expansion Scientifique Française, serie No. 21, 1977b.

Bohus, B., Ader, R., & de Wied, D. Effects of vasopressin on active and passive avoidance behavior. *Hormones and Behavior*, 1972, *3*, 191–197.

Bohus, B., Conti, L., Kovács, G. L., & Versteeg, D. H. G. Modulation of memory processes by neuropeptides: Interaction with neurotransmitter systems. In C. Ajmone Marsan & H. Matthies (Eds.), *Neuronal plasticity and memory formation*. New York: Raven Press, 1982.

Bohus, B., Gispen, W. H., & de Wied, D. Effect of lysine-vasopressin and ACTH-(4–10) on conditioned avoidance behavior of hypophysectomized rats. *Neuroendrocrinology*, 1973, *11*, 137–143.

Bohus, B., Kovács, G. L., & de Wied, D. Oxytocin, vasopressin and memory: Opposite effects on consolidation and retrieval processes. *Brain Research*, 1978, *157*, 414–417.

Bohus, B., Urban, I., van Wimersma Greidanus, Tj. B., & de Wied, D. Opposite effects of oxytocin and vasopressin on avoidance behavior and hippocampal theta rhythm in the rat. *Neuropharmacology*, 1978, *17*, 239–247.

Bohus, B., van Wimersma Greidanus, Tj. B., & de Wied, D. Behavioral and endocrine responses of rats with hereditary hypothalamic diabetes insipidus (Brattleboro strain). *Physiology and Behavior*, 1975, *14*, 609–615.

Bookin, H. B., & Pfeiffer, W. D. Effect of lysine vasopressin on pentylenetetrazol-induced retrograde amnesia in rats. *Pharmacology, Biochemistry and Behavior*, 1977, *7*, 51–54.

Borrell, J., de Kloet, E. R., Versteeg, D. H. G., & Bohus, B. The role of adrenomedullary catecholamines in the modulation of memory by vasopressin. In *Proceedings of the Symposium on Integrative Neurohumoral Mechanisms, Budapest*, 1983.

Brito, G. N., Thomas, G. J., Gingold, S. I., & Gash, D. M. Behavioral characteristics of vasopressin-deficient rats (Brattleboro strain). *Brain Research Bulletin*, 1981, *6*, 71–75.

Buijs, R. M. Intra- and extrahypothalamic vasopressin and oxytocin pathways in the rat: Pathways to the limbic system, medulla oblongata and spinal cord. *Cell and Tissue Research*, 1978, *192*, 423–435.

Buijs, R. M., Velis, D. N., & Swaab, D. F. Extrahypothalamic vasopressin and oxytocin innervation of fetal and adult rat brain. *Progress in Brain Research*, 1980, *53*, 159–168.

Burbach, J. P. H., de Kloet, E. R., & de Wied, D. Oxytocin biotransformation in the rat limbic brain: Characterization of peptidase activities and significance in the formation of oxytocin fragments. *Brain Research*, 1980, *202*, 401–414.

Burbach, J. P. H., Kovács, G. L., de Wied, D., van Nispen, J. W., & Greven, H. M. A major metabolite of arginine-vasopressin in the brain is a highly potent neuropeptide. *Science*, 1983, *221*, 1310–1312.

Burbach, J. P. H., Schotman, P., & de Kloet, E. R. Oxytocin biotransformation in the rat limbic brain: Chemical characterization of two oxytocin fragments and proposed pathway for oxytocin conversion. *Biochemical and Biophysical Research Communications*, 1980, *97*, 1005–1013.

Celestian, J. F., Carey, R. J., & Miller, M. Unimpaired maintenance of a conditioned avoidance response in the rat with diabetes insipidus. *Physiology and Behavior*, 1975, *15*, 707–711.

Contreras, P. C., & Takemori, A. E. The effects of prolyl-leucyl-glycinamide on morphine tolerance and dependence. *Federation Proceedings*, 1980, *39*, 845.

Cooper, K. E., Kasting, N. W., Lederis, K., & Veale, W. L. Evidence supporting a role for endogenous vasopressin in natural suppression of fever in the sheep. *Journal of Physiology*, 1979, *295*, 33–45.

Crow, T. J. Cortical synapses and reinforcement: A hypothesis. *Nature*, 1968, *219*, 736–737.

de Wied, D. The influence of the posterior and intermediate lobe of the pituitary and pituitary peptides on the maintenance of a conditioned avoidance response in rats. *International Journal of Neuropharmacology*, 1965, *4*, 157–167.

de Wied, D. Effects of peptide hormones on behavior. In W. F. Ganong & L. Martini (Eds.), *Frontiers in neuroendrocinology*. London–New York: Oxford University Press, 1969.

de Wied, D. Long-term effect of vasopressin on the maintenance of a conditioned avoidance response in rats. *Nature*, 1971, *232*, 58–60.

de Wied, D. The role of the posterior pituitary and its peptides on the maintenance of conditioned avoidance behavior. In K. Lissás (Ed.), *Hormones and brain function*. New York: Plenum Press, 1973.

de Wied, D. Behavioral effects of intraventricularly administered vasopressin and vasopressin fragments. *Life Sciences*, 1976, *19*, 685–690.

de Wied, D. Neuropeptides and behavior. In M. J. Parnham & J. Bruinvels (Eds.), *Discoveries in pharmacology*. Amsterdam: Elsevier/North-Holland, 1983.

de Wied, D., & Bohus, B. Long-term and short-term effects on retention of a conditioned avoidance response in rats by treatment with long acting pitressin and α-MSH. *Nature*, 1966, *212*, 1484–1486.

de Wied, D., & Bohus, B. The modulation of memory processes by vasotocin, the evolutionarily oldest neurosecretory principle. *Progress in Brain Research*, 1978, *48*, 327–334.

de Wied, D., Bohus, B., & van Wimersma Greidanus, Tj. B. Memory deficit in rats with hereditary diabetes insipidus. *Brain Research*, 1975, *85*, 152–156.

de Wied, D., Bohus, B., & van Wimersma Greidanus, Tj. B. The significance of vasopressin for pituitary ACTH release in conditioned emotional situations. In E. Endröczi (Ed.), *Cellular and molecular bases of neuroendocrine processes*. Budapest: Akadémiai Kiadó, 1976.

de Wied, D., & Gispen, W. H. Behavioral effects of peptides. In W. H. Gainer (Ed.), *Peptides in neurobiology*. New York: Plenum Press, 1977.

de Wied, D., Greven, H. M., Lande, S., & Witter, A. Dissociation of the behavioral and endocrine effects of lysine vasopressin by tryptic digestion. *British Journal of Pharmacology*, 1972, *45*, 118–122.

de Wied, D., & van Ree, J. M. Neuropeptides, mental performance aging. *Life Sciences*, 1982, *31*, 709–719.

de Wied, D., van Wimersma Greidanus, Tj. B., Bohus, B., Urban, I., & Gispen, W. H. Vasopressin and memory consolidation. *Progress in Brain Research*, 1976, *45*, 181–197.

Dloumá, H., Křeček, J., & Zicha, J. Growth and urine osmolarity in young Brattleboro rats. *Journal of Endocrinology*, 1977, *75*, 329–330.

Dogterom, J., & Buijs, R. M. Vasopressin and oxytocin distribution in rat brain: Radioimmunoassay and immunocytochemical studies. In C. Ajmone Marsan & W. Z. Traczyk (Eds.), *Neuropeptides and neural transmission*. New York: Raven Press, 1980.

Dogterom, J., van Wimersma Greidanus, Tj. B., & Swaab, D. F. Evidence for the release of vasopressin and oxytocin in cerebrospinal fluid: Measurements in plasma and CSF of intact and hypophysectomized rats. *Neuroendocrinology*, 1977, *24*, 108–118.

Dorsa, D. M., & van Ree, J. M. Modulation of substantia nigra self-stimulation by neuropeptides related to neurohypophyseal hormones. *Brain Research*, 1979, *172*, 367–371.

Drago, F., Bohus, B., & de Wied, D. Interaction between vasopressin and oxytocin in the modulation of passive avoidance retention of the rat. *Neuroscience Letters*, 1981, Suppl. 7, S260.

Finkelberg, F., Kalant, H., LeBlanc, A. E. Effect of vasopressin-like peptides on consumption of ethanol by the rat. *Pharmacology, Biochemistry and Behavior*, 1978, *9*, 453–458.

Flexner, J. B., Flexner, L. B., Hoffman, P. L., & Walter, R. Dose–response relationships in attenuation of puromycin-induced amnesia by neurohypophyseal peptides. *Brain Research*, 1977, *134*, 139–144.

Flexner, J. B., Flexner, L. B., Walter, R., & Hoffman, P. ADH and related peptides: Effect of pre- or posttraining treatment on puromycin amnesia. *Pharmacology, Biochemistry and Behavior,* 1978, *8*, 93–95.

Gardner, C. R., Richards, M. H., & Möhring, J. Arginine-vasopressin inhibits noradrenaline release from rat brain stem slices. *Archives of Pharmacology,* 1981, *316* (Suppl.), R68.

Garrud, P. Effects of lysine-8-vasopressin on punishment induced suppression of a lever-holding response. *Progress in Brain Research*, 1975, *42*, 173–186.

Garrud, P., Gray, J. A., & de Wied, D. Pituitary–adrenal hormones and extinction of rewarded behavior in the rat. *Physiology and Behavior*, 1974, *12*, 109–119.

Gold, P. E., & van Buskirk, R. Effects of posttrial hormone injections on memory processes. *Hormones and Behavior*, 1976, *7*, 509–517.

Hoffman, P., Ritzmann, R. F., Walter, R., & Tabakoff, B. Arginine vasopressin maintains ethanol tolerance. *Nature*, 1978, *276*, 614–616.

Hostetter, G., Jubb, S. L., & Kozlowski, G. P. An inability of subcutaneous vasopressin to affect passive avoidance behavior. *Neuroendocrinology*, 1980, *30*, 174–177.

Judge, M. E., & Quartermain, D. Alleviation of anisomycin-induced amnesia by pre-test treatment with lysine vasopressin. *Pharmacology, Biochemistry and Behavior*, 1982, *16*, 463–466.

Kety, S. S. The biogenic amines in the central nervous system: Their possible roles in arousal, emotion and learning. In F. O. Schmitt (Ed.), *The neurosciences.* New York: Rockefeller University Press, 1970.

King, A. R., & de Wied, D. Localized behavioral effects of vasopressin on maintenance of an active avoidance response in rats. *Journal of Comparative and Physiological Psychology*, 1974, *86*, 1008–1018.

Koob, G. F., LeMoal, M., Gaffori, O., Manning, M., Sawyer, W. H., Rivier, J., & Bloom, F. E. Arginine-vasopressin and a vasopressin antagonist peptide: Opposite effects on extinction of active avoidance in rats. *Regulatory Peptides*, 1981, *2*, 153–163.

Kovács, G. L., Bohus, B., & Versteeg, D. H. G. The effects of vasopressin on memory processes: The role of noradrenergic neurotransmission. *Neuroscience*, 1979a, *4*, 1529–1537.

Kovács, G. L., Bohus, B., & Versteeg, D. H. G. Facilitation of memory consolidation by vasopressin: Mediation by terminals of the dorsal noradrenergic bundle? *Brain Research*, 1979b, *172*, 73–85.

Kovács, G. L., Bohus, B., & Versteeg, D. H. G. The interaction of posterior pituitary neuropeptides with monoaminergic neurotransmission: Significance in learning and memory processes. *Progress in Brain Research*, 1980, *53*, 123–140.

Kovács, G. L., Bohus, B., Versteeg, D. H. G., de Kloet, E. R., & de Wied, D. Effect of oxytocin and vasopressin on memory consolidation: Sites of action and catecholaminergic correlates after local micro-injection into limbic midbrain structures. *Brain Research*, 1979, *175*, 303–314.

Kovács, G. L., Bohus, B., Versteeg, D. H. G., Telegdy, G., & de Wied, D. Neurohypophyseal hormones and memory. In H. Yoshida, Y. Hagihara, & S. Ebashi (Eds.), *Advances in pharmacology and therapeutics II* (Vol. 1: *CNS pharmacology, neuropeptides*). Oxford–New York: Pergamon Press, 1982.

Kovács, G., & de Wied, D. Hormonally active arginine-vasopressin suppresses endotoxin-induced fever in rats: Lack of effect of oxytocin and a behaviorally active vasopressin fragment. *Neuroendocrinology*, 1983, *37*, 258–261.

Kovács, G. L., & Telegdy, G. Role of oxytocin in memory and amnesia. *Pharmacology and Therapeutics,* 1982, *18*, 375–395.

Kovács, G. L., Vécsei, L., Szabo, G., & Telegdy, G. The involvement of catecholaminergic mechanisms in the behavioral action of vasopressin. *Neuroscience Letters,* 1977, *5*, 337–344.

Kovács, G. L., Vécsei, L., & Telegdy, G. Opposite action of oxytocin to vasopressin in passive avoidance behavior in rats. *Physiology and Behavior*, 1978, *20*, 801–802.

Krejci, I., Kupkova, B., Metys, J., Barth, T., & Jost, K. Vasopressin analogs: Sedative properties and passive avoidance behavior in rats. *European Journal of Pharmacology*, 1979, *56*, 347–353.

Krivoy, W. A., Zimmermann, E., & Lande, S. Facilitation of development of resistance to morphine analgesia by desglycinamide-9-lysine vasopressin. *Proceedings of the National Academy of Sciences, USA*, 1974, *71*, 1852–1856.

Láczi, F., Fekete, M., & de Wied, D. Antidiuretic activity and immunoreactive arginin-vasopressin levels in eye plexus blood during passive avoidance behavior in rats. *Life Sciences*, 1983, *32*, 577–589.

Láczi, F., Gaffori, O., Fekete, M., de Kloet, E. R., de Wied, D. Levels of Arginine-vasopressin in cerebrospinal fluid during passive avoidance behavior in rats. *Life Sciences*, in press.

Lande, S., Flexner, J. B., & Flexner, L. B. Effect of corticotrophin and desglycinamide lysine vasopressin on suppression of memory by puromycin. *Proceedings of the National Academy of Sciences, USA*, 1972, *69*, 558–560.

Lande, S., Witter, A., & de Wied, D. Pituitary peptides: An octapeptide that stimulates conditioned avoidance acquisition in hypophysectomized rats. *Journal of Biological Chemistry*, 1971, *246*, 2058–2062.

Laycock, J. F. The Brattleboro rat with hereditary hypothalamic diabetes insipidus. *General Pharmacology*, 1977, *8*, 297–302.

Le Moal, M., Koob, G. F., Koda, L. Y., Bloom, F. E., Manning, M., Sawyer, W. H., & Rivier, J. Vasopressor receptor antagonist prevents behavioral effects of vasopressin. *Nature*, 1981, *291*, 491–493.

Leonard, B. E., Ramaekers, F., & Rigter, H. Monoamines in brain and urine of rats with hereditary hypothalamic diabetes insipidus. *Experientia*, 1976, *32*, 901–902.

Leshner, A. I., & Roche, K. E. Comparison of the effects of ACTH and lysine vasopressin on avoidance-of-attack in mice. *Physiology and Behavior*, 1977, *18*, 879–883.

Lissák, K., & Bohus, B. Pituitary hormones and avoidance behavior of the rat. *International Journal of Psychobiology*, 1972, *2*, 103–115.

Marks, N., Abrash, L., & Walter, R. Degradation of neurohypophyseal hormones by brain extracts and purified brain enzymes. *Proceedings of the Society for Experimental Biology*, 1973, *142*, 455–460.

Mason, S. T., & Iversen, S. D. Behavioral basis of the dorsal bundle extinction effect. *Pharmacology, Biochemistry and Behavior*, 1977, *7*, 373–379.

Mason, S. T., & Iversen, S. D. Reward, attention and the dorsal noradrenergic bundle. *Brain Research*, 1978, *150*, 135–148.

McGaugh, J. L. Drug facilitation of learning and memory. *Annual Review of Pharmacology*, 1973, *13*, 229–241.

McGaugh, J. L., & Dawson, R. G. Modification of memory storage processes. In W. K. Honig & P. H. R. James (Eds.), *Animal Memory*. New York: Academic Press, 1971.

McGaugh, J. L., & Petrinovich, L. F. Effects of drugs on learning and memory. *International Review of Neurobiology*, 1965, *8*, 139–196.

Mens, W. B. J., van Egmond, M. A. H., de Rotte, A. A., & van Wimersma Greidanus, Tj. B. Neurohypophyseal peptide levels in CSF and plasma during passive avoidance behavior in rats. *Hormones and Behavior*, 1982, *16*, 371–382.

Olpe, H.-R., & Baltzer, V. Vasopressin activates noradrenergic neurons in the rat locus coeruleus: A microiontophoretic investigation: *European Journal of Pharmacology*, 1981, *73*, 177–178.

Pedersen, C. A., Ascher, J. A., Monroe, Y. L., & Prange, A. J., Jr. Oxytocin induces maternal behavior in virgin female rats. *Science*, 1982, *216*, 648–649.

Pliška, V., Barth, T., & Thorn, N. A. Some metabolites of specifically tritium labelled lysine-vasopressin: Identification by thin-layer chromatography and determination by the liquid scintillation technique. *Acta Endocrinologica*, 1971, *67*, 1–11.

Rigter, H. Vasopressin and memory: The influence of prior experience with the training situation. *Behavioral Neurobiology*, 1982, *34*, 337–351.

Rigter, H., & Crabbe, J. C. Neurohypophysial peptides and ethanol. In D. de Wied & P. A. van Keep (Eds.), *Hormones and the brain*. Lancaster, England: MTP Press, 1980.

Rigter, H., Elbertse, R., & Van Riezen, H. Time-dependent anti-amnesic effect of ACTH 4–10 and desglycinamide-lysine vasopressin. *Progress in Brain Research*, 1975, *42*, 163–171.

Rigter, H., van Riezen, H., & de Wied, D. The effects of ACTH- and vasopressin-analogues on CO_2-induced retrograde amnesia in rats. *Physiology and Behavior*, 1974, *13*, 381–388.

Schulz, H., Kovács, G. L., & Telegdy, G. Effect of physiological doses of vasopressin and oxytocin on avoidance and exploratory behavior in rats. *Acta Physiologica Academiae Scientarium Hungarica*, 1974, *45*, 211–215.

Schwarzberg, H., Hartmann, G., Kovács, G. L., & Telegdy, G. Effect of intraventricular oxytocin and vasopressin on self-stimulation in rats. *Acta Physiologica Academiae Scientarium Hungarica*, 1976, *47*, 127–131.

Schwarzberg, H., Kovács, G. L., Szabó, G., & Telegdy, G. Intraventricular administration of vasopressin and oxytocin effects the steady state levels of serotonin, dopamine and norepiniphrine in rat brain. *Endocrinologica Experimentales* (Bratislava), 1981, *15*, 75–80.

Sofroniew, M. V., & Weindl, A. Central nervous system distribution of vasopressin, oxytocin, and neurophysin. In J. L. Martinez Jr., R. A. Jensen, R. B. Mesing, H. Rigter, & J. L. McGaugh (Eds.), *Endogenous peptides and learning and memory processes*. New York: Academic Press, 1981.

Sokol, H. W., & Wise, J. The effect of exogenous vasopressin and growth hormone on the growth of rats with hereditary hypothalamic diabetes insipidus. *Growth*, 1973, *37*, 127–142.

Sterba, G. Ascending neurosecretory pathways of the peptidergic type. In F. Knowles & L. Vollrath (Eds.), *Neurosecretion—the final neuroendocrine pathway*. Berlin: Springer, 1974.

Székely, J. I., Miglécz, E., Dunai-Kovács, L., Tarnawa, I., Ronai, A. L., Gráf, L., & Bajusz, S. Attenuation of morphine tolerance and dependence by α-melanacyle stimulating hormone (α-MSH). *Life Sciences*, 1979, *24*, 1931–1938.

Tanaka, M., de Kloet, E. R., de Wied, D., & Versteeg, D. H. G. Arginine[8]-vasopressin affects catecholamine metabolism in specific brain nuclei. *Life Sciences*, 1977, *20*, 1799–1808.

Tanaka, M., Versteeg, D. H. G., & de Wied, D. Regional effects of vasopressin on rat brain catecholamine metabolism. *Neuroscience Letters*, 1977, *4*, 321–325.

Thompson, E. A., & de Wied, D. The relationship between the antidiuretic activity of rat eye plexus blood and passive avoidance behavior. *Physiology and Behavior*, 1973, *11*, 377–380.

Urban, I., & de Wied, D. Inferior quality of RSA during paradoxical sleep in rats with hereditary diabetes insipidus. *Brain Research*, 1975, *97*, 362–366.

Urban, I., de Wied, D. Neuropeptides: Effects on paradoxical sleep and theta rhythm in rats. *Pharmacology, Biochemistry and Behavior*, 1978, *8*, 51–59.

Valtin, H., Sawyer, W. H., & Sokol, H. W. Neurohypophysial principles in rats homozygous and heterozygous for hypothalamic diabetes insipidus (Brattleboro strain). *Endocrinology*, 1965, *77*, 701–706.

Valtin, H., & Schroeder, H. A. Familial hypothalamic diabetes insipidus in rats (Brattleboro strain). *American Journal of Physiology*, 1964, *206*, 425–430.

van Ree, J. M. The influence of neuropeptides related to pro-opiomelanocortin on acquisition of heroin self-administration of rats. *Life Sciences*, 1983, *33*, 2283–2289.

van Ree, J. M., Bohus, B., Versteeg, D. H. G., & de Wied, D. Neurohypophyseal principles and memory processes. *Biochemical Pharmacology*, 1978, *27*, 1793–1800.

van Ree, J. M., & de Wied, D. Heroin self-administration is under control of vasopressin. *Life Sciences*, 1977a, *21*, 315–320.

van Ree, J. M., & de Wied, D. Modulation of heroin self-administration by neurohypophyseal principles. *European Journal of Pharmacology*, 1977b, *43*, 199–202.

van Ree, J. M., & de Wied, D. Vasopressin, oxytocin and dependence on opiates. In J. L. Martinez, Jr., R. A. Jensen, R. B. Messing, H. Rigter, & J. L. McGaugh (Eds.), *Endogenous peptides and learning and memory processes*. New York: Academic Press, 1981.

van Ree, J. M., de Wied, D., Bradbury, A. F., Hulme, E. C., Smyth, D. G., & Snell, C. R. Induction of tolerance to the analgesic action of lipotropin C-fragment. *Nature*, 1976, *264*, 792–794.

van Wimersma Greidanus, Tj. B. MSH/ACTH-(4–10): A tool to differentiate between the role of vasopressin in memory consolidation or retrieval processes. *Peptides*, 1982, *3*, 7–11.

van Wimersma Greidanus, Tj. B., Bohus, B., & de Wied, D. Effects of peptide hormones on behavior. *Excerpta Medica International Congress Series*, 1973, *273*, 197–201.

van Wimersma Greidanus, Tj. B., Bohus, B., & de Wied, D. CNS sites of action of ACTH, MSH and vasopressin in relation to avoidance behavior. In W. E. Stumpf & L. D. Grant (Eds.), *Anatomical neuroendocrinology*. Basel: Karger, 1975.

van Wimersma Greidanus, Tj. B., Bohus, B., Kovács, G. L., Versteeg, D. H. G., Burbach, J. P. H., & de Wied, D. Sites of behavioral and neurochemical action of neuropeptides. *Neurosciences and Biobehavioral Reviews*, 1983, *7*, 453–463.

van Wimersma Greidanus, Tj. B., & de Wied, D. Dorsal hippocampus: A site of action of neuropeptides on avoidance behavior? *Pharmacology, Biochemistry and Behavior*, 1976a, *5* (Suppl. 1), 29–33.

van Wimersma Greidanus, Tj. B., & de Wied, D. Modulation of passive avoidance behavior of rats by intracerebroventricular administration of antivasopressin serum. *Behvarioal Biology*, 1976b, *18*, 325–333.

van Wimersma Greidanus, Tj. B., Dogterom, J., & de Wied, D. Intraventricular administration of anti-vasopressin serum inhibits memory consolidation in rats. *Life Sciences*, 1975, *16*, 637–644.

van Wimersma Greidanus, Tj. B., Croiset, G. Goedemans, H., & Dogterom, J. Vasopressin levels in peripheral blood and in cerebrospinal fluid during passive and active avoidance behavior in rats. *Hormones and Behavior*, 1979, *12*, 102–111.

van Wimersma Greidanus, Tj. B., Croiset, G., & Schuiling, G. A. Fornix transection: Discrimination between neuropeptide effects on attention and memory. *Brain Research Bulletin*, 1979, *4*, 625–629.

Veale, W. L., Kasting, N. W., & Cooper, K. E. Arginine vasopressin, an endogenous antipyretic: Evidence and significance. *Federation Proceedings,* 1981, *40*, 2750–2753.

Versteeg, C. A. M., Bohus, B., & de Jong, W. Inhibitory effects of neuropeptides on centrally evoked pressor responses. In Y. Yamori, W. Lovenberg, & E. D. Freis (Eds), *Prophylactic approach to hypertensive diseases.* New York: Raven Press, 1979.

Versteeg, D. H. G. Neurohypophyseal hormones and brain neurochemistry. *Pharmacology and Therapeutics,* 1983, *19*, 297–325.

Versteeg, D. H. G., de Kloet, E. R., van Wimersma Greidanus, Tj. B., & de Wied, D. Vasopressin modulates the activity of catecholamine containing neurons in specific brain regions. *Neuroscience Letters*, 1979, *11*, 69–73.

Versteeg, D. H. G., Tanaka, M., & de Kloet, E. R. Catecholamine concentration and turnover in discrete regions of the brain of the homozygous Brattleboro rat deficient in vasopressin. *Endocrinology*, 1978, *103*, 1654–1661.

Vinson, G. P., Goddard, C., & Whitehouse, B. J. Steroid profiles formed by adrenocortical tissue from rats with hereditary diabetes insipidus (Brattleboro strain) and from normal Wistar rats under different conditions of stimulation. *Journal of Endocrinology*, 1977, *75*, 31P–12P.

Walter, R., Hoffman, P. L., Flexner, J. B., & Flexner, L. B. Neurohypophyseal hormones, analogs, and fragments: Their effect on puromycin-induced amnesia. *Proceedings of the National Adademy of Sciences, USA*, 1975, *72*, 4180–4184.

Walter, R., van Ree, J. M., & de Wied, D. Modification of conditioned behavior of rats by neurohypophyseal hormones and analogues. *Proceedings of the National Academy of Sciences, USA*, 1978, *75*, 2493–2496.

Wiley, M. K., Pearlmutter, A. F., & Miller, R. E. Decreased adrenal sensitivity to ACTH in the vasopressin deficient (Brattleboro) rat. *Neuroendocrinology*, 1974, *14*, 257–270.

Yawter, M. P., & Green, K. F. Effects of desglycinamide-lysine vasopressin on a conditioned task aversion in rats. *Physiology and Behavior*, 1980, *25*, 851–854.

CHAPTER NINETEEN

Adrenergic Influences on Memory Storage: Interaction of Peripheral and Central Systems

JAMES L. MCGAUGH / K. C. LIANG / CATHY BENNETT / DEBRA B. STERNBERG

The fact that the memory of a recent experience is both strong and fragile is an interesting paradox. New memories are strong, of course, in the sense that they tend to reflect accurately the experiences that created them. They are weak in the sense that they are highly susceptible to disrupting influences. As we all know, memories fade with time. But over time, memories also become resistant to disrupting influences. Both of these facts have no doubt been known for centuries, since the experience of forgetting is ubiquitous, and memory losses produced by head injuries and diseases are fairly common occurrences. These facts are among the difficult issues that theories of memory must confront. What processes enable the vivid and accurate recollections of recent experiences? Are recent and lasting memories based on different mechanisms? What processes underlie the strengthening of memories over time?

CONCEPTS OF MEMORY CONSOLIDATION

The perseveration–consolidation hypothesis proposed by Mueller and Pilzecker (1900) was the first attempt to provide an explanation for the lability of recent memory. In so doing, the hypothesis also provided an explanation for the strengthening of memory over time. This hypothesis proposed that the neural processes initiated by an experience perseverate for some time following the experience and that the perseveration produces changes resulting in the consolidation or fixation of the neural trace of the experience. Thus, according to this hypothesis, the consolidation of the memory trace is subject to the influences of conditions affecting the perseverating neural processes. Hebb's (1949) proposal that recent memory is based on reverberating neural circuits and that long-term memory results from changes induced in the circuits by the reverberation is a more explicit form of the consolidation hypothesis. The

James L. McGaugh, Cathy Bennett, and Debra B. Sternberg. Center for the Neurobiology of Learning and Memory and Department of Psychobiology, University of California, Irvine, California.

K. C. Liang. Department of Psychology, National Taiwan University, Taipei, Taiwan, Republic of China.

common assumption is that lasting memories are not formed at the moment of an experience. The recent-memory paradox loses its mystery if it is assumed that forgetting is due to the waning of perseverative neural processes whether they are in the form of reverberating circuits or some other form of persistent activity. Things are, however, not that simple. Forgetting occurs over long intervals of time. Do the perseverative processes activated by an experience continue for days or years? It seems unlikely. Thus, the paradox persists.

Although the consolidation hypothesis has not fared well as an explanation of forgetting in laboratory studies of human memory (Keppel, 1984), the hypothesis seems to provide a reasonably good explanation for findings of clinical studies of retrograde amnesia in humans (McDougall, 1901; Squire, Cohen, & Nadel, 1984). Further, the findings of the effects of various treatments on retention in laboratory animals are generally consistent with the consolidation hypothesis. The findings by Duncan (1949) and Gerard (1949) that animals' retention of recently learned responses is impaired by posttraining treatment with electroconvulsive shock (ECS) were the first experimental demonstrations of retrograde amnesia. These studies stimulated extensive investigation of the effects on memory of posttraining administration of electrical stimulation of the brain, drugs, hormones, and other treatments (Agranoff, Chapter 21, this volume; de Wied, Chapter 18, this volume; Kesner, 1982; McGaugh, 1983a; McGaugh & Gold, 1976; McGaugh & Herz, 1972; Rosenzweig & Bennett, Chapter 17, this volume).

Research on memory consolidation has focused on two broad sets of questions (McGaugh & Gold, 1974). One set of questions concerns the characteristics of the consolidation process. That is, what do such experiments reveal about the nature of time-dependent processes in memory? A second set of questions, and the one that serves as the focus of this chapter, concerns the nature of the neurobiological processes underlying memory consolidation. What physiological processes influence consolidation; what brain structures are involved; and, ultimately, what are the cellular processes that underlie memory storage?

Initially, it was hoped that laboratory studies of retrograde amnesia would provide precise information about the length of the gradient of retrograde amnesia, and by inference, the time required for memory storage or consolidation. However, no time-constants for consolidation were found. In animal studies, the gradients range from seconds to days, depending on the particular experimental conditions used (Cherkin, 1969; McGaugh & Dawson, 1971). With electrical stimulation of the brain used as the amnestic treatment, for example, the gradient of retrograde amnesia depends on the intensity of the stimulation, as well as the region stimulated and the training conditions (Gold, Macri, & McGaugh, 1973). In humans, the extent of retrograde amnesia resulting from head injury varies directly with the degree of trauma (Russell & Nathan, 1946). Further, as Squire and his colleagues have shown, in human patients given a series of ECT treatments, the gradient of retrograde amnesia may extend for several years (Squire & Cohen, Chapter 1, this volume). These findings strongly suggest that the neuronal processes underlying memory continue to change over long periods of time. But again, it seems unlikely that the neurobiological events activated by an experience are, alone, responsible for such continuing changes (Squire *et al.*, 1984).

Amnestic treatments have also been used in an effort to reveal stages of memory storage (e.g., McGaugh, 1968; Rosenzweig & Bennett, Chapter 17, this volume). If it is assumed, for example, that a short-term memory lasts until consolidation is complete, then the length of the gradient of retrograde amnesia might provide a measure of short-term memory. The lack of time-constants in amnesia gradients clearly poses a serious problem for such efforts. This is not to say that it will not be possible to determine whether memories of different ages are based on different processes. But it is clear that the time course of memory processes is not readily indexed by amnesia gradients obtained with any specific treatment. The fact that a treatment administered after training affects the retention of the training experience indicates only that the processes underlying memory storage or consolidation are susceptible to the particular treatment used. Thus, gradients of retention produced by posttraining treatments are more appropriately viewed as "susceptibility gradients" (Gold & McGaugh, 1975).

EXPERIMENTAL AND ENDOGENOUS MODULATION OF MEMORY

It is well documented that posttraining treatments can have enhancing as well as impairing effects on retention. Enhancement is readily produced with stimulant drugs (McGaugh, 1965, 1973), electrical stimulation of the brain (Bloch, 1970; McGaugh & Gold, 1976), and pituitary and adrenergic hormones (de Wied, 1980; McGaugh, 1983b). The enhancing effects, like the impairing treatments, are most effective when administered shortly after training. Moreover, the effect of a particular treatment depends on many conditions, including the dose or intensity of the treatment as well as the training conditions used. Generally, low doses of drugs and hormones and low-intensity brain stimulation enhance retention, whereas high doses and high-intensity brain stimulation impair retention (Gold & McGaugh, 1975). Since the same treatments may either impair or enhance memory depending on the experimental conditions, it seems appropriate to refer to the treatments as "memory modulating" treatments.

The guiding assumption of neurobiological studies of memory using posttraining memory-modulating treatments is that understanding the bases of the treatments' effects on memory will contribute to the discovery of the neurobiological processes underlying memory storage. It may be that some treatments act by directly affecting the cellular mechanisms of memory storage. It might be, for example, that protein synthesis inhibitors impair memory by blocking cellular consolidation processes. Lynch and his colleagues (Baudry & Lynch, Chapter 28, this volume) have obtained evidence indicating that memory storage can be blocked by inhibiting an enzyme which, they propose, is involved in producing receptor changes underlying synaptic mechanisms of memory. However, much recent evidence indicates that many treatments affect memory through influences on endogenous physiological processes involved in the modulation of memory consolidation. That is, the treatments may influence the cellular mechanisms of memory storage through effects on physiological processes that modulate storage. As we noted above, there is extensive evidence that retention is influenced by posttraining administration of hormones, including epinephrine, ACTH, and vasopressin, that are normally released from the adrenal medulla and pituitary gland when animals are stimulated or stressed (Bohus & de Wied, 1981; de Wied, 1980; Gold & Delanoy, 1981; Gold & van Buskirk, 1975; McGaugh, 1983a). The fact that the dose–response effect is typically an inverted-U-shaped function suggests that moderate levels of these hormones have effects that are favorable for memory consolidation. Further, such findings suggest that endogenous hormonal responses to experiences may modulate the storage of the memories of the experiences. Thus, posttraining susceptibility of memory storage processes to modulating influences provides a mechanism for regulating the storage of experiences (Gold & McGaugh, 1975). Viewed from this perspective, a susceptibility to retrograde amnesia is a price paid for a memory storage system that provides a means by which the importance of an experience, as reflected in part by the hormonal consequences of the experience, modulates the strength of the memory.

Much recent evidence supports this general hypothesis (McGaugh, 1983a). Hormones are, as the hypothesis requires, released by training experiences (e.g., McCarty & Gold, 1981). Further, hormones administered after training are most effective in influencing memory if they are administered at the time at which endogenous hormones would be expected to be released by an experience. And, as we have indicated, recent findings indicate that memory consolidation is affected by treatments that alter hormonal systems. Further, recent findings have provided evidence that peripheral hormones affect memory through influences on brain systems involved in regulating memory storage. We turn now to a discussion of these recent findings.

INVOLVEMENT OF EPINEPHRINE IN MEMORY-MODULATING TREATMENTS

Studies using adrenalectomized animals were the first to suggest that treatments may affect memory storage through influences involving peripheral hormones. Adrenalectomy blocks the amnestic effect of a variety of treatments, including protein-synthesis inhibitors, ECS, and amygdala kindling (Bookin & Pfeifer, 1978; Flexner & Flexner, 1970; McIntyre, 1976). Since the adrenal cortex, as well as the adrenal medulla, was removed in these studies, it is not clear which hormone systems were involved in the effect of adrenalectomy on memory. For example, the effects might be due to a decrease in corticosterone, an increase in ACTH resulting from the decrease in corticosterone, or a loss of medullary hormones, including enkephalins as well as epinephrine and norepinephrine. It is clear, however, from more recent studies, that the effects of amnestic treatments are altered by influences affecting adrenergic systems. In a series of studies, for example, Gold and Sternberg (Gold & Sternberg, 1978; Sternberg & Gold, 1981) reported that α- and β-antagonists administered to rats prior to training attenuate the memory-impairing effects of a variety of posttrial treatments, including electrical stimulation of the frontal cortex or amygdala, and administration of pentylenetetrazol, cycloheximide, or diethyldithiocarbamate. The blocking effect of adrenergic agonists is not restricted to memory impairment. As Figure 19-1 shows, administration of the β-antagonist propranolol to rats prior to training on an active avoidance task blocked the memory-enhancing effects of cortical stimulation produced with low footshock training, as well as the memory-impairing effects of cortical stimulation found when high footshock is used in training (Sternberg, Gold, & McGaugh, 1983). Thus, the effects of

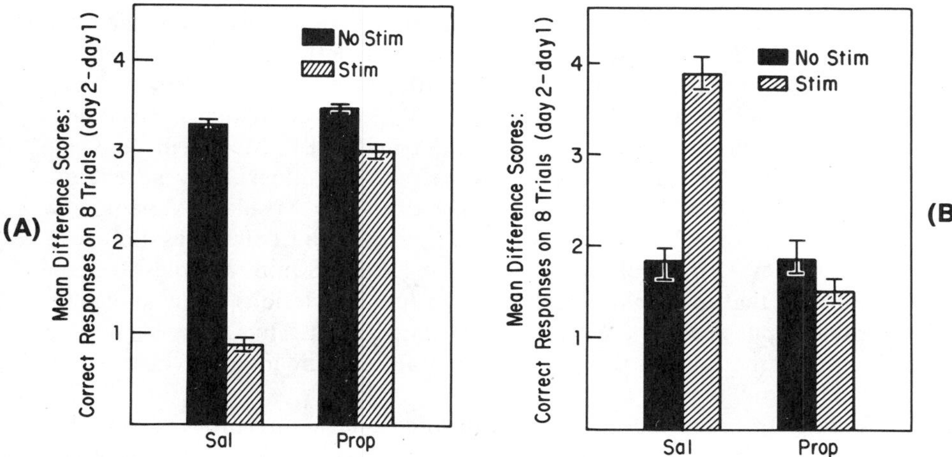

Figure 19-1. Effects of posttraining frontal cortex stimulation (5 mA/1 sec) on retention of an active-avoidance response. Saline or propranolol was administered prior to training. (A) High footshock (750 μA); (B) low footshock (500 μA).

blockers appear to be due to some general interference with the modulation of memory storage. Another finding of particular interest is that centrally administered adrenergic antagonists did not attenuate the effects of frontal cortex stimulation on memory (Sternberg & Gold, 1981). Thus, the effects appear to involve peripheral adrenergic mechanisms.

These results are consistent with other recent findings suggesting that adrenergic influences on memory act, at least in part, through peripheral effects. Posttraining administration of *d*-amphetamine enhances retention when the drug is injected intraperitoneally but not when injected intracerebroventricularly. Further, retention is also enhanced with posttraining peripheral injections of 4-hydroxyamphetamine, a drug that does not readily pass the blood–brain barrier. Adrenal demedullation attenuates the memory-enhancing effects of both drugs (Martinez, Jensen, *et al.*, 1980; Martinez, Vasquez, *et al.*, 1980; McGaugh *et al.*, 1982). Since the effects were not blocked by peripheral sympathectomy (produced by 6-hydroxydopamine [6-OHDA]), it seems likely that they involve the release of hormones from the adrenal medulla. And since medullary hormones, including epinephrine, pass the blood–brain barrier poorly, if at all, the findings also suggest that the effects of these drugs on memory may involve activation of peripheral receptors. It is possible that peripheral hormones directly influence the brain by acting on brain regions poorly protected by the blood–brain barrier. Further, on the basis of available evidence, the possibility that limited amounts of peptide and catecholamine hormones can pass the blood–brain barrier cannot be completely ruled out.

AMYGDALA INFLUENCES ON MEMORY: INTERACTION WITH EPINEPHRINE

Ultimately, of course, the effects of peripheral hormones on memory must involve influences on brain systems. Although we do not yet know how peripheral hormones affect the brain, recent findings from our laboratory suggest that peripheral hormones alter the functioning of brain systems involved in memory consolidation. Our studies have focused on the role of the amygdala in memory storage. There are several reasons for our interest in this brain region. First, there is extensive evidence that memory storage is modulated by electrical stimulation of the amygdala (Berman & Kesner, 1981; McGaugh & Gold, 1976). Second, as we noted above, such effects are blocked by adrenergic antagonists. And third, the studies of Mishkin (1982; Mishkin, Malamut, & Bachevalier, Chapter 2, this volume), and Squire and his colleagues (Squire & Cohen, Chapter 1, this volume; Squire *et al.*, 1984; Squire & Zola-Morgan, 1983) indicate that in monkeys, as well as in humans, lesions of the amygdala and hippocampus produce a severe memory impairment. Thus, there is growing evidence that the amygdala is part of a brain system involved in memory consolidation.

Findings from our laboratory provide additional support for the view that the amygdala is involved in modulating memory storage. Memory is markedly impaired in animals in which amygdala lesions were made either before or shortly after training (Liang, McGaugh, Martinez, Jensen, Vasquez, & Messing, 1982). In this study, rats were first implanted bilaterally with electrodes in their amygdalae. They were then trained on a one-trial inhibitory avoidance task and were tested for retention 12 days later. In three groups, bilateral radio-frequency lesions were made either 2 days before training, immediately after training, or 10 days after training. Retention performance (see Figure 19-2) was highly impaired in animals lesioned before or immediately after training. However, the retention performance of the animals lesioned 10 days after training was comparable to that of implanted controls. It is, of course, difficult to interpret the retention performance of animals lesioned before training. These animals may have been less sensitive to the shock or may have had an impaired ability to attend to apparatus cues. The finding that retention is impaired by lesions made immediately after training suggests that the impairment is due to interference with consolidation. Such effects may have been due either to the lesion-induced damage to brain tissue involved in consolidation or to the effects of the radio-frequency stimulation used in making the lesions. In either case, it is clear that the memory impairment is not due to loss of memory storage sites, since lesions made 10 days after training did not significantly affect retention.

Other findings from our laboratory provide additional evidence that the effects on memory of amygdala stimulation are not due to effects restricted to the amygdala. And consequently, they provide additional support for the view that the amygdala is involved in modulating memory processes located elsewhere in the brain. In one study (Liang & McGaugh, 1983a), we examined the effects of blocking major amygdaloid pathways. In different groups of rats, the stria terminalis (ST) or the ventral amygdalo-fugal (VAF) pathways were transected and the animals were then trained, successively, on inhibitory- and active-avoidance tasks. Bilateral amygdala stimulation was administered immediately after training, and retention was tested 24 hours later. As Table 19-1 shows, the ST lesions completely blocked the effects of the amygdala stimulation but did not significantly affect retention in unstimulated controls. In contrast, the VAF lesions did not block the enhancing effects of posttraining amygdala stimulation. In another study (Liang, Messing, & McGaugh, 1983) the ST was blocked by injecting naloxone into the bed nucleus of the ST immediately after training but just prior to amygdala stimulation. Naloxone

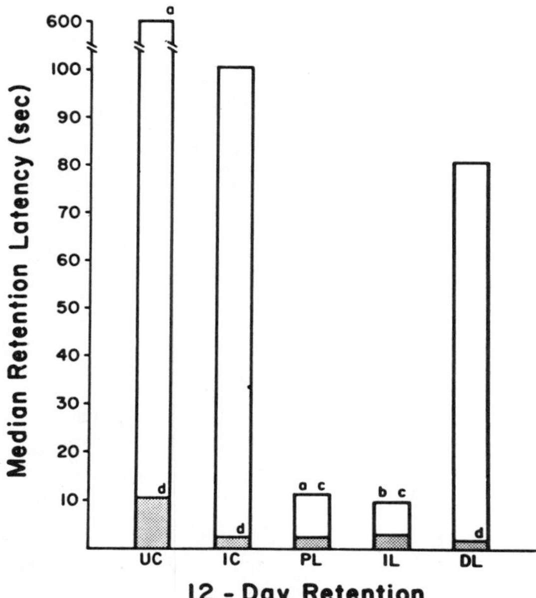

Figure 19-2. Effect of bilateral amygdala lesions on retention of an inhibitory-avoidance response. Animals received either a 2-mA, 2-sec footshock (blank bars) or no footshock (dotted bars) during training and were tested for retention 12 days later. Various groups served as unimplanted controls (UC) or implanted controls (IC) or received pretraining amygdala lesions (PL) made 2 days before training, immediate posttraining amygdala lesions (IL), or delayed posttraining amygdala lesions (DL) 10 days after training. a, b, different from the IC group, $p < .02$ and $p < .05$, respectively; c, different from the DL group, $p < .02$; d, different from the corresponding footshock groups, $p < .05$.

was selected because of evidence that Met-enkephalin fibers in the ST terminate in the bed nucleus (Uhl, Kuhar, & Snyder, 1978). The effect of the naloxone injection was comparable to that found with ST lesions: The naloxone blocked the effect of electrical stimulation on retention. The findings of these two studies strongly suggest that the effect of amygdala stimulation on memory is due to influences mediated by the ST. Since the ST contains both afferents and efferents, it is not clear from these studies whether the effect of amygdala stimulation is due to blocking of amygdala inputs or to blocking of outputs. It does seem clear, however, that the effect requires an intact ST.

An intact ST seems also to be required for the effects of peripheral epinephrine on memory (Liang & McGaugh, 1983b). Rats in this study were first given bilateral sham or ST lesions. Following recovery from the surgery, they were given epinephrine (s.c.) immediately after training on a one-trial inhibitory-avoidance task. As Figure 19-3 shows, posttraining epinephrine in doses ranging from .01 to 1.0 mg/kg enhanced retention in the sham controls. However, the same dose failed to affect retention in the ST-lesioned animals. These findings strongly suggest that the effect of epinephrine on memory involves influences mediated by the ST. It might be that epinephrine acts by stimulating amygdala afferents. It is also possible that epinephrine effects on brain systems underlying memory do not work through the amygdala but work, rather, through effects, elsewhere in the brain, that are modulated by influences

Table 19-1. Effects of posttraining amygdala stimulation on retention in ST-lesioned or VAF-transected rats

	ST+	ST−	VAF+	VAF−
	Median retention latencies (sec) (inhibitory avoidance)			
IC	366.8	298.9	246.4	21.2*
AS	27.7*	276.3	45.1[c]	45.1*
	Mean difference avoidance scores (active avoidance)			
IC	2.92	2.67	1.13	1.38
AS	1.08**	2.79	2.56***	2.57***

Note. IC, implanted controls; AS, amygdala stimulation. $*p < .01$; $**p < .02$; $***p < .05$, different from IC/ST+ or IC/VAF+. From Liang and McGaugh (1983a).

from ST efferents. Our findings do not distinguish between these two possibilities.

The hypothesis that epinephrine effects on memory involve amygdala influences is also supported by our findings that the effect of posttraining amygdala stimulation on memory is altered by adrenal demedullation and denervation (Brewton, Liang, & McGaugh, 1981). Rats in these experiments were implanted bilaterally with amygdala electrodes and were then given either sham adrenal surgery or were demedullated surgically or denervated by removing the adrenals and replacing them in the fatty tissue around the kidneys. They were then trained on an inhibitory-avoidance task and, 2 weeks later, on an active-avoidance task. Amygdala stimulation was administered immediately posttraining and retention was tested 24 hours after training. Comparable results were obtained with both tasks and with both demedullation and denervation. Figures 19-4 and 19-5 show the effects obtained with demedullation. As can be seen, the retention of amygdala-stimulated rats was poorer than that of either unimplanted or implanted controls. Further, the performance of unimplanted, but demedullated, controls was like that of the sham-operated controls. That is, under these conditions, demedullation alone did not affect retention. Retention was significantly impaired, however, in the controls that were demedullated and implanted with amygdala electrodes. Thus, while neither the implantation procedure nor the adrenal surgery alone affected retention, the combined treatments produced retention deficits comparable to those produced by posttraining amygdala stimulation. The finding of greatest relevance to our hypothesis is that demedullation markedly altered the effects of posttraining amygdala stimulation on retention. The retention performance of demedullated rats given amygdala stimulation was significantly better than that of demedullated implanted controls. These findings clearly indicate that adrenal demedullation and denervation significantly alter the effects of amygdala stimulation on memory.

As we noted above, posttraining amygdala stimulation also enhances retention in animals with intact adrenal medullae when low-intensity footshock is used in training (Gold, Hankins, Edwards, Chester, & McGaugh, 1975). And

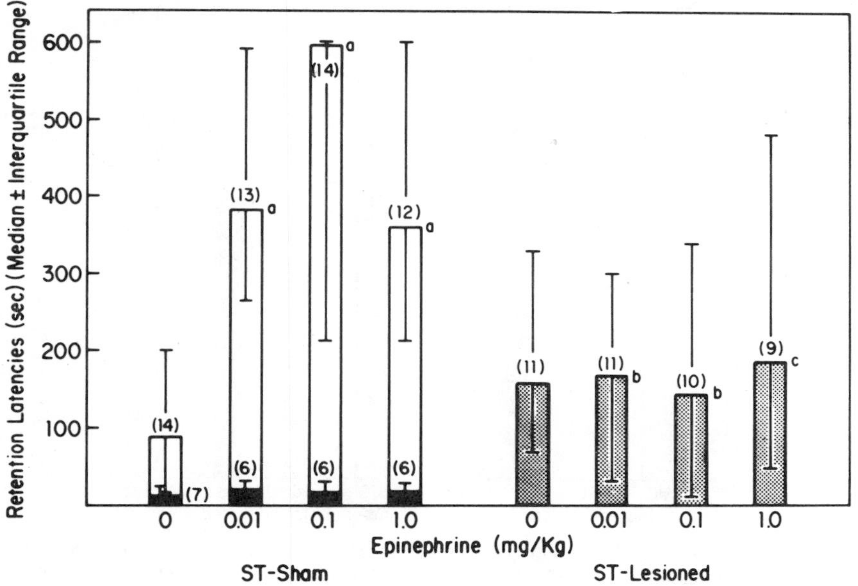

Figure 19-3. Effects of posttraining epinephrine on inhibitory avoidance retention in sham controls and ST-lesioned rats. Black bars represent the nonfootshock controls. a, different from the ST sham/saline controls, $p < .01$; b, c, different from the corresponding ST sham/epinephrine groups, $p < .05$ and $.05 < p < .10$, respectively; Mann-Whitney two-tailed *U*-tests.

Figure 19-4. Effects of posttraining amygdala stimulation (AS) on retention of inhibitory avoidance in adrenal-demedullated and sham-operated rats. a, $p < .01$ compared with UC and IC sham controls, and $p < .05$ compared with adrenal AS group; b, $p < .02$ compared with IC sham controls.

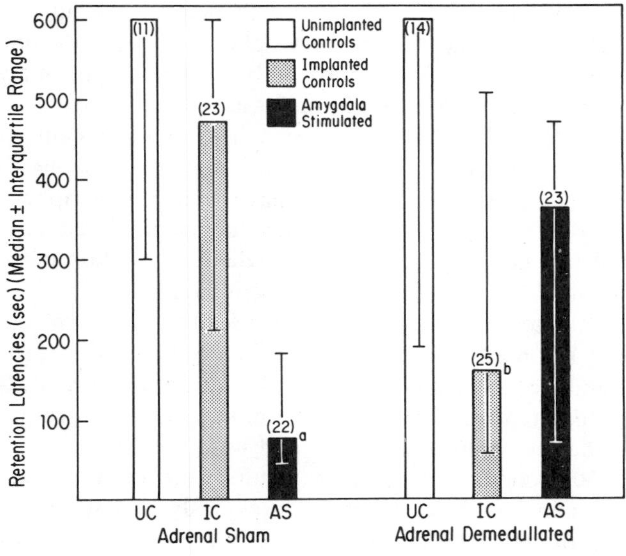

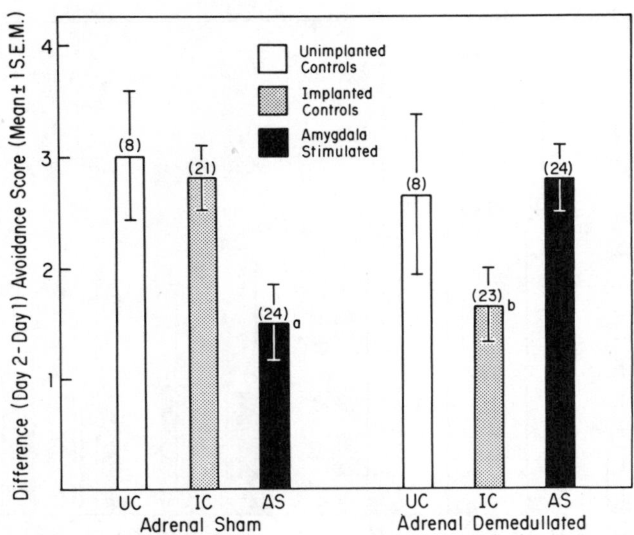

Figure 19-5. Effects of posttraining amygdala stimulation (AS) on retention of active avoidance in adrenal-demedullated and sham-operated rats. a, $p < .01$ compared with IC sham and demedullated AS groups; b, $p < .02$ compared with IC sham controls, and $p < .02$ compared with AS adrenal-demedullated group.

since plasma epinephrine levels are known to vary with footshock intensity (McCarty & Gold, 1981), our findings fit well with the view that the effect of amygdala stimulation on memory may vary depending on the amount of peripheral epinephrine released by the training experience: Retention is enhanced by amygdala stimulation when peripheral epinephrine levels are low and impaired when peripheral epinephrine levels are high. This interpretation of our findings is based on the assumption that the effect of demedullation is due specifically to a decrease in peripheral epinephrine. It is possible, of course, that the effect is due to decreases in other medullary hormones, or perhaps to a decrease in corticosterone resulting from damage to the adrenal cortex. We have found, however, that the memory deficit seen in demedullated animals with implanted electrodes is not improved by corticosterone in a wide range of doses (Bennett, Liang, & McGaugh, unpublished findings).

We have obtained additional evidence bearing on our interpretation that the effects of demedullation on memory are due to a decrease in epinephrine (Liang, McGaugh, & Bennett, 1984). We have found that peripheral epinephrine attenuates the retention impairment seen in demedullated rats. Further, in demedullated rats given epinephrine, amygdala stimulation impairs retention, as it does in animals with intact adrenal medullae. Rats in this study were first bilaterally implanted with amygdala electrodes and were then either demedullated or given sham adrenal surgery. They were then trained, successively, on inhibitory- and active-avoidance tasks. Retention was tested 24 hours after training. Immediately following training, animals in several groups were injected (s.c.) with either epinephrine or saline and were then given amygdala stimulation within 30 seconds. Comparable results were obtained with both tasks (Figures 19-6 and 19-7). As we found previously, retention was impaired in demedullated animals with implanted amygdala electrodes. Further, amygdala stimulation impaired retention in sham-operated controls but enhanced retention (in comparison with demedullated implanted controls) in demedullated animals. Both of these effects appear to be due to lowered levels of peripheral epinephrine. The retention performance of demedullated animals given posttraining epinephrine was comparable to that of animals with intact adrenal medullae. Further, amygdala stimulation impaired retention in demedullated animals, as it did in intact controls, if epinephrine was administered immediately after the training, that is, just prior to the stimulation. Animals in two other demedullated groups (shown on the right in Figures 19-6 and 19-7) were given epinephrine 3 minutes after training. One of the groups received amygdala stimulation immediately after training. The retention of both groups was better than that of demedullated implanted controls. This finding indicates that posttraining epinephrine levels influence the effects of amygdala stimulation on memory. Our experimental conditions mimic the conditions that would ordinarily occur when posttraining amygdala stimulation is administered to animals with intact adrenal medullae. Thus, our findings strongly support the interpretation that amygdala influences on retention are modulated by peripheral epinephrine.

In these studies retention was, as we noted, severely impaired in demedullated animals implanted with amygdala electrodes. With the training conditions used, neither treatment alone affected retention. In a recent study (Liang & McGaugh, unpublished findings), we found impaired retention in demedullated

Figure 19-6. Effects of posttraining amygdala stimulation and epinephrine injection (1.0 mg/kg, s.c.) on inhibitory avoidance retention in sham-operated and adrenal-demedullated rats. The demedullated/saline control group had poorer retention than the sham/saline control and the demedullated/epinephrine control groups (a, $p < .05$). Amygdala stimulation impaired retention in the sham groups and the demedullated/epinephrine group (b, $p < .05$), but had no impairing effect on the demedullated/saline and demedullated/epinephrine delay groups. However, the demedullated/epinephrine stimulated group had better retention than the sham/saline stimulated group (c, $p < .02$). All comparisons based on Mann–Whitney two-tailed *U*-tests.

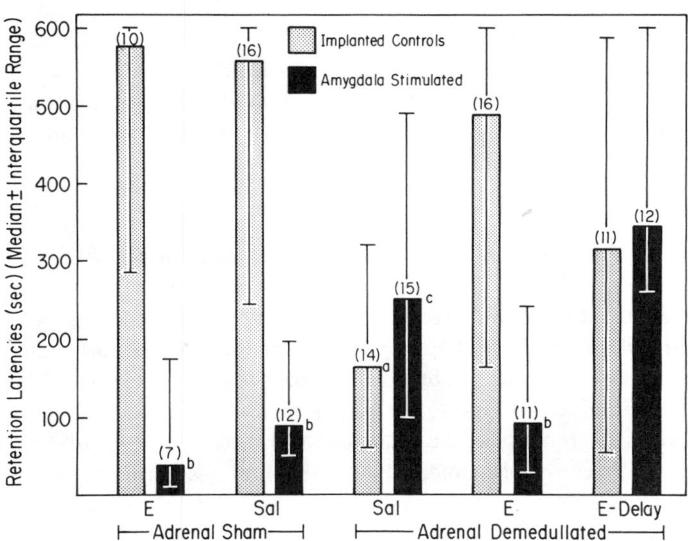

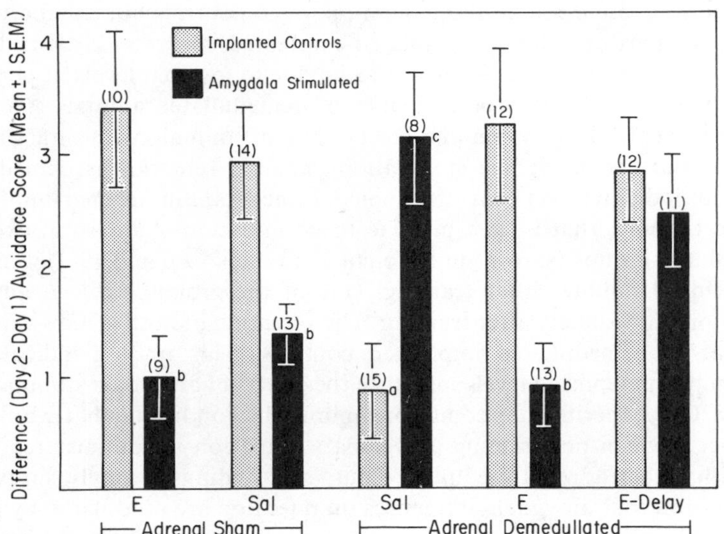

Figure 19-7. Effects of posttraining amygdala stimulation and epinephrine injection (1.0 mg/kg, s.c.) on active avoidance retention in adrenal-sham and adrenal-demedullated rats. The demedullated/saline control group had poorer retention than the sham/saline control group and the demedullated/epinephrine control as well as the demedullated/epinephrine delay control groups (a, $p < .01$). Amygdala stimulation impaired retention in the sham groups and the demedullated/epinephrine groups (b, $p < .05$), but enhanced retention in the demedullated/saline groups (c, $p < .01$) and had no effect on the demedullated/epinephrine delay group. All comparisons based on two-tailed independent *t*-tests.

rats when low footshock intensity was used in the training. Retention is also poor in animals with implanted amygdala electrodes when the training footshock levels are low (Gold *et al.*, 1975). We have obtained comparable effects in animals with ST lesions (Liang & McGaugh, unpublished findings). Thus, it seems likely that the retention impairment seen in demedullated animals with implanted electrodes is due to a summation of the impairment produced by each treatment alone. Further, the finding that the retention deficit seen in the animals given the combined treatments is attenuated by posttraining epinephrine or amygdala stimulation suggests that the deficit is due to interference with memory-modulating processes.

EFFECTS OF ADRENERGIC STIMULATION OF THE AMYGDALA

In other recent studies, we have attempted to determine the basis or bases of the interaction of amygdala and epinephrine influences on memory. One possibility is that amygdala activity involved in memory modulation is influenced either directly by epinephrine passing the blood–brain barrier or indirectly by adrenergic amygdala afferents. There are both α- and β-receptors within the amygdaloid complex (U'Prichard, Reisine, Mason, Fibiger, & Yamamura, 1980). Fibers from the locus ceruleus provide the majority of the norepinephrine input to the amygdala (Fallon, Koziell, & Moore, 1978). The innervation is probably mediated by the VAF, since ST lesions do not affect adrenergic innervation of the amygdala (Emson, Bjorklund, Lindvall, & Paxinos, 1979). As we summarized above, our studies indicate that ST lesions block the enhancing effects on memory of both amygdala stimulation and peripheral epinephrine. Thus, if epinephrine influences on memory involve adrenergic pathways to the amygdala, the memory impairment found with ST lesions is most likely due to blocking of outputs from the amygdala. VAF lesions do not block the effect of posttraining amygdala stimulation on memory. We would not expect blocking of adrenergic afferents to block the effects of amygdala stimulation on memory since we assume that the afferents serve only to modulate amygdala activity. However, if peripheral epinephrine affects memory through influences on the amygdala mediated by the VAF, since ST lesions do not affect adrenergic innervation of by VAF lesions. We have not, as yet, investigated this implication.

A number of recent studies have shown that retention can be influenced by administering adrenergic agonists and antagonists directly into the amygdala. Such findings are generally consistent with the view that memory storage is modulated endogenously by adrenergic influences in the amygdala. Gallagher and her colleagues (Gallagher, Kapp, Pascoe, & Rapp, 1981) reported that retention in an inhibitory avoidance task is impaired by intra-amygdala injections of the β-blockers *d,l*-propranolol and *d,l*-alprenolol. Further, the effects of these adrenergic antagonists were blocked by norepinephrine. Gallagher *et al.* (1981) also reported that retention was enhanced by posttraining intra-amygdala injections of the α-antagonist phentolamine and that the enhancing effects were blocked by propranolol. The doses in these experiments are quite high (>5 μg per injection) in relation to brain levels of adrenergic catecholamines. However, similar results have been obtained with somewhat lower doses. Ellis and Kesner (1983) reported that posttraining intra-amygdala injections of norepinephrine (1.0 μg) impaired retention of an inhibitory avoidance response and that the effect was blocked by propranolol (1.5 μg). Lower doses of norepinephrine were ineffective and higher doses of propranolol impaired retention.

In recent experiments we have found that posttraining norepinephrine enhances retention when administered in doses lower than those used in the above studies (Liang & McGaugh, unpublished findings). Rats in these studies were first implanted bilaterally with amygdala cannulae. Following recovery from the surgery, they were trained on an inhibitory avoidance task and given 1.0 μl injections of norepinephrine, bilaterally, 30 seconds after training. Figure 19-8 shows the dose–response effects of norepinephrine. The norepinephrine enhanced retention in doses of .1 and .3 μg. Higher doses were ineffective. As Figure 19-9 shows, the enhancing effect of posttraining norepinephrine is time-dependent: Injections given 2 hours after training were ineffective. The enhancing effects of norepinephrine (.2 μg) were blocked by propranolol (.2 and 1.0 μg). If the effects of peripheral epinephrine on memory involve activation of adrenergic receptors in the amygdala, then the epinephrine effects should be blocked by adrenergic antagonists. In support of this view, we found that intra-amygdala injections of propranolol (.2 μg) administered immediately after training, blocked the enhancing effects of epinephrine (.100 mg/kg) administered subcutaneously immediately after the propranolol injections.

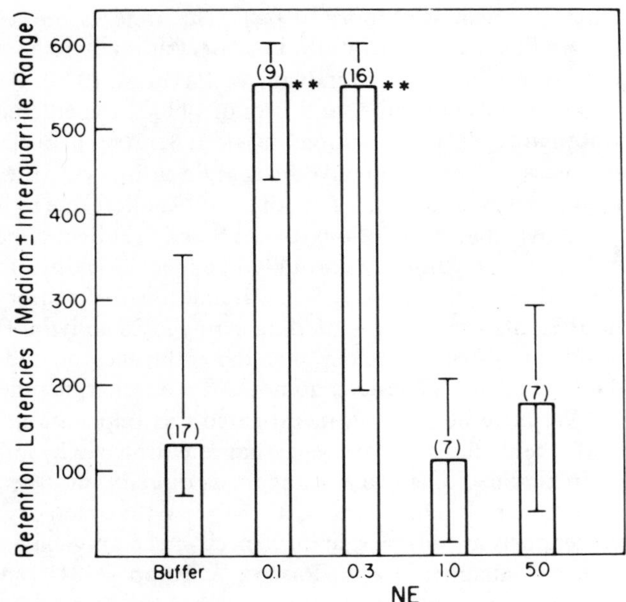

Figure 19-8. Effects of posttraining intra-amygdala administration of norepinephrine (NE) on retention of an inhibitory-avoidance response. Buffer solution or NE (dose in μg) was injected bilaterally (1.0-μl injection). **$p < .05$ compared with buffer controls.

Figure 19-9. Effects of posttraining intra-amygdala administration of norepinephrine (NE) and propranolol (doses in μg) on retention. NE was ineffective when administered 2 hours posttraining. Propranolol blocked the effect of immediate posttraining NE. **$p < .05$ compared with buffer controls.

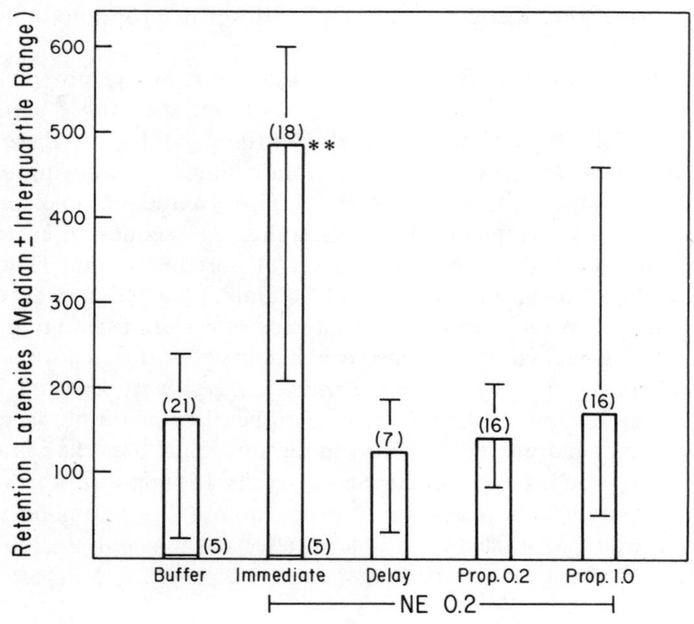

It is clear from these studies that memory can be influenced by adrenergic stimulation of the amygdala. Considered together, the findings from several laboratories suggested that retention is enhanced by low doses of agonists and impaired by high doses. The findings are thus like those obtained with peripheral administration of adrenergic agonists. The findings are also consistent with evidence that retention is enhanced by intracerebroventricular injections of norepinephrine (Haycock, van Buskirk, Ryan, & McGaugh, 1977; Meligeni, Ledergerber, & McGaugh, 1978; Stein, Belluzzi, & Wise, 1975). However, in view of these findings, it is puzzling that retention is not affected by intracerebroventricular injections of amphetamine (Martinez, Jensen, *et al.*, 1980) or epinephrine (de Almeida, Kapczinski, & Izquierdo, 1983). Further studies are needed to clarify this issue.

These conflicting findings would, no doubt, be less puzzling if we knew whether peripheral epinephrine effects on memory are mediated by adrenergic afferents from the periphery. If the effects are mediated by central adrenergic influences, then it is unclear why surgical and pharmacological treatments that deplete central norepinephrine have, at best, very modest influences on memory (Fibiger, Roberts, & Price, 1975; Ogren, Archer, & Ross, 1980). We have found that animals treated with DSP-4, a neurotoxin that selectively depletes central norepinephrine, are not impaired on active and inhibitory avoidance tasks (Bennett, McGaugh, Arnold, & Liang, 1983). The finding that, in animals with locus ceruleus lesions, retention is impaired by brain stimulation administered at intervals of greater than a week following training (Zornetzer, Abraham, & Appleton, 1978) suggests that central norepinephrine does have some influence on memory consolidation. Further, findings that 6-OHDA lesions of the dorsal adrenergic bundle block the effects of vasopressin and naloxone on memory (Bohus, Conti, Kovacs, & Versteeg, 1982; Rapp & Gallagher, 1983) also suggest that memory is influenced by activation of the locus ceruleus. It is not yet clear, however, whether activation of the locus coeruleus is involved in the effects of peripheral epinephrine on memory.

HORMONAL INTERACTIONS IN MEMORY MODULATION

There is extensive evidence that learning and memory can be influenced by a variety of hormones (McGaugh, 1983a). The findings of several recent studies suggest that the effects of several hormones on memory involve interactions with adrenergic systems. A number of studies have found that retention is enhanced by posttraining peripheral or intra-amygdala administration of naloxone (Gallagher & Kapp, 1978; Izquierdo, 1979; Messing *et al.*, 1979). As we noted above, naloxone effects on memory are blocked by lesions of the dorsal bundle (Rapp & Gallagher, 1983). Further, Izquierdo and Graudenz (1980) reported that naloxone effects on memory are blocked by propranolol. These findings have been interpreted as suggesting that naloxone affects retention by releasing central adrenergic systems from tonic inhibition. Other recent findings (Borrell, de Kloet, Versteeg, & Bohus, 1983) indicate that the effects on memory of posttraining vasopressin are blocked by adrenal demedullation. Further, in demedullated rats vasopressin potentiates the enhancing effects of peripherally administered epinephrine. Other recent findings indicate that the effects of epinephrine also interact with influences of corticosterone (Borrell, de Kloet, & Bohus, 1984). In animals adrenalectomized 2 days before training, retention was enhanced by posttraining epinephrine. However, if the animals were given corticosterone, much higher doses of epinephrine were required in order to enhance retention. Borrell *et al.* (1984) suggest that corticosterone may act to protect neural processes from deleterious effects of high levels of catecholamines.

These findings suggest the interesting possibility that the various hormones that have been found to modulate memory may work through a common effect on neural functioning that involves influences of epinephrine. It might even be the case that peripheral adrenergic influences are essential for hormonal influences on memory consolidation. Nothing is as yet known about the locus of the interaction of these hormonal influences on memory. The studies using naloxone suggest that an interaction might occur in the amygdala. It is less clear where the interaction between epinephrine and vasopressin might occur, since it is not known whether these hormones pass the blood–brain barrier in amounts sufficient to influence brain systems. Discovery of the locus of the interactions would greatly facilitate efforts to understand the mechanisms involved in hormonal modulation of memory consolidation.

ENDOGENOUS MEMORY-MODULATING SYSTEMS

Many different kinds of posttraining treatments have been found to influence retention. As we have emphasized in this chapter, studies of the effects of hormones on memory are of particular interest, since the findings of these studies strongly suggest that hormones normally released by learning experiences may play an important role in the endogenous regulation of memory storage (Gold & McGaugh, 1978, 1984; McGaugh, 1983a, 1983b). It is important to note that hormones influence retention in a variety of learning tasks and with appetitive as well as aversive motivation used in training (e.g., Sternberg, Gold, & McGaugh, unpublished findings). Typically, these studies indicate that the hormones either improve or impair retention in comparison with the retention in controls. Recently, Weinberger, Gold, and Sternberg (1984) reported that epinephrine enables animals to learn under conditions where learning would otherwise not occur. Rats under general anesthesia were stimulated with legshock paired with a sound. Retention was tested later, following recovery from the anesthesia, by measuring suppression of drinking at the onset of the sound. Animals given epinephrine prior to training showed clear evidence of learning. The epinephrine did not alter the depth of anesthesia. Obviously, it will be of considerable interest to understand how and where epinephrine acts in enabling learning to occur in an anesthetized brain.

Under most circumstances, however, hormones do not appear to be essential for learning. Removal of the adrenal medulla or pituitary does not prevent learning. Rather, as we have emphasized, hormones appear to have a modulatory role in learning. Figure 19-10 indicates some ways in which hormones might interact with brain systems involved in memory storage. We assume that sensory stimulation activates cells in a memory system in which the lasting changes underlying memory will be produced. We assume, also, that sensory stimulation activates brain systems that modulate the degree of storage that will occur in the memory system. As we have indicated, evidence from several lines

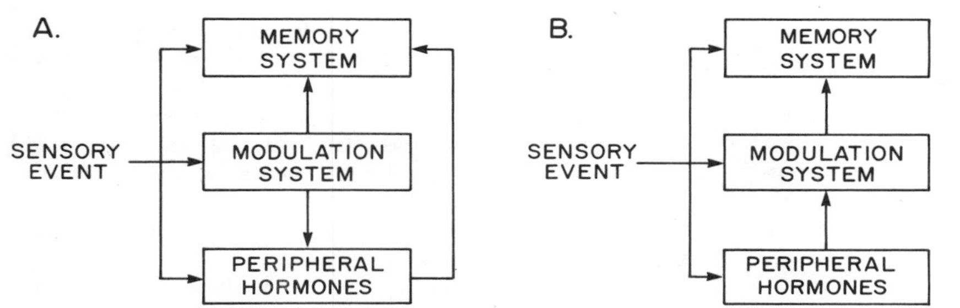

Figure 19-10. Interaction of peripheral hormones with central modulating and memory systems.

of inquiry, including our own, suggests that the amygdala may be part of a memory-modulating system. We assume, further, that sensory stimulation releases peripheral hormones. It may be, as is suggested in Figure 19-10A, that the brain systems involved in memory modulation act in part by further influencing the release of hormones, which then act on the memory system. The findings that the effects of a variety of memory-modulating treatments are blocked by adrenergic antagonists fit well with this scheme. According to the scheme shown in Figure 19-10B, hormones affect the memory system through influences on the central modulating system. The findings of our studies of the effects of epinephrine on memory generally fit well with this model. Lesions of the ST, for example, block the effects of amygdala stimulation and peripheral epinephrine by interfering with the effect of the modulating system on the memory system. Demedullation, as well as intra-amygdala administration of adrenergic antagonists, alters the effects of amygdala stimulation by reducing the peripheral hormonal influences on the central modulating system.

Viewed from this perspective, understanding the neurobiological mechanisms of memory will require an understanding of the ways in which hormones act to influence central modulating systems, as well as an understanding of how the modulating systems act to influence the cellular mechanisms of memory. It is interesting to note that hormones that are known to play important roles in homeostatic regulation may also play an important role in regulating memory. This is perhaps not surprising in view of the central role of memory in adaptation.

ACKNOWLEDGMENTS

This work was supported by USPHS Research Grants MH12526 and AG00538 (to J. L. M.) and Postdoctoral Fellowship MH08646 (to D. B. S.).

REFERENCES

Bennett, C., McGaugh, J. L., Arnold, M., & Liang, K. C. Behavioral measures after central noradrenergic depletion with the neurotoxin, DSP-4: Lack of impairment in avoidance tasks. *Neuroscience Abstracts*, 1983, *9*, 830.

Berman, R. F., & Kesner, R. P. Electrical stimulation as a tool in memory research. In M. M. Patterson & R. P. Kesner (Eds.), *Electrical stimulation research techniques*. New York: Academic Press, 1981.

Bloch, V. Facts and hypotheses concerning memory consolidation. *Brain Research*, 1970, *24*, 561–575.

Bohus, B., Conti, L., Kovacs, G. L., & Versteeg, D. H. G. Modulation of memory processes by neuropeptides: Interaction with neurotransmitter systems. In C. Ajmone Marsan & H. Matthies (Eds.), *Neuronal plasticity and memory formation.* New York: Raven Press, 1982.

Bohus, B., & de Wied, D. Actions of ACTH- and MSH-like peptides on learning, performance and retention. In J. L. Martinez, Jr., R. A. Jensen, R. B. Messing, H. Rigter, & J. L. McGaugh (Eds.), *Endogenous peptides and learning and memory processes.* New York: Academic Press, 1981.

Bookin, H. B., & Pfeifer, W. D. Adrenalectomy attenuates electroconvulsive shock-induced retrograde amnesia in rats. *Behavioral Biology*, 1978, *24*, 527–542.

Borrell, J., de Kloet, E. R., & Bohus, B. Corticosterone decreases the efficacy of adrenaline to affect passive avoidance retention of adrenalectomized rats. *Life Science,* 1984, *34*, 99–104.

Borrell, J., de Kloet, E. R., Versteeg, D. G. H., & Bohus, B. The role of adrenomedullary catecholamines in the modulation of memory by vasopressin. In E. Endroczi, D. de Wied, L. Angelucci, & V. Scapagnini (Eds.), *Integrative neurohumoral mechanisms: Developments in neuroscience.* Amsterdam: Elsevier/North Holland, 1983.

Brewton, C. B., Liang, K. C., & McGaugh, J. L. Adrenal demedullation alters the effect of amygdala stimulation on retention of avoidance tasks. *Neuroscience Abstracts*, 1981, *7*, 870.

Cherkin, A. Kinetics of memory consolidation: Role of amnesic treatment parameters. *Proceedings of the National Academy of Sciences, USA*, 1969, *63*, 1094–1101.

de Almeida, M., Kapczinski, F. P., & Izquierdo, I. Memory modulation by posttraining intraperitoneal but not intracerebroventricular administration of ACTH or epinephrine. *Behavioral and Neural Biology*, 1983, *39*, 277–283.

de Wied, D., Pituitary neuropeptides and behavior. In K. Fuxe, T. Hokfelt, & R. Luft (Eds.), *Central regulation of the endocrine system.* New York: Plenum, 1980.

Duncan, C. P. The retroactive effect of electroshock on learning. *Journal of Comparative and Physiological Psychology*, 1949, *42*, 32–44.

Ellis, M. E., & Kesner, R. P. The noradrenergic system of the amygdala and aversive memory processing. *Behavioral Neuroscience*, 1983, *97*, 399–415.

Emson, P. C., Bjorklund, A., Lindvall, O., & Paxinos, G. Contributions of different afferent pathways to the catecholamine and 5-hydroxytryptamine-innervation of the amygdala: A neurochemical and histochemical study. *Neuroscience*, 1979, *4*, 1347–1357.

Fallon, J. H., Koziell, D. A., & Moore, R. Y. Catecholamine innervation of the basal forebrain: II. Amygdala, suprahinal cortex and entorhinal cortex. *Journal of Comparative Neurology*, 1978, *180*, 509–532.

Fibiger, H. C., Roberts, D. C. S., & Price, T. C. On the role of telencephalic noradrenaline in learning and memory. In G. Jonsson, T. Malmfers, & C. Sachs (Eds.), *Chemical tools in catecholamine research.* Amsterdam: Elsevier/North Holland, 1975.

Flexner, J. B., & Flexner, L. B. Adrenalectomy and the suppression of memory by puromycin. *Proceedings of the National Academy of Sciences, USA*, 1970, *66*, 46–52.

Gallagher, M., & Kapp, B. S. Manipulation of opiate activity in the amygdala alters memory processes. *Life Sciences*, 1978, *23*, 1973–1978.

Gallagher, M., Kapp, B. S., Pascoe, J. P., & Rapp, P. R. A neuropharmacology of amygdaloid systems which contribute to learning and memory. In Y. Ben-Ari (Ed.), *The amygdaloid complex.* Amsterdam: Elsevier/North Holland, 1981.

Gerard, R. W. Physiology and psychiatry. *American Journal of Psychiatry*, 1949, *106*, 161–173.

Gold, P. E., & Delanoy, R. L. ACTH modulation of memory storage processing. In J. L. Martinez, Jr., R. A. Jensen, R. B. Messing, H. Rigter, & J. L. McGaugh (Eds.), *Endogenous peptides and learning and memory processes.* New York: Academic Press, 1981.

Gold, P. E., Hankins, L., Edwards, R. M., Chester, J., & McGaugh, J. L. Memory interference and facilitation with posttrial amygdala stimulation: Effect on memory varies with footshock level. *Brain Research*, 1975, *86*, 509–513.

Gold, P. E., Macri, J., & McGaugh, J. L. Retrograde amnesia gradients: Effects of direct cortical stimulation. *Science*, 1973, *179*, 1343–1345.

Gold, P. E., & McGaugh, J. L. A single-trace, two-process view of memory storage processes. In D. Deutsch & J. A. Deutsch (Eds.), *Short-term memory.* New York: Academic Press, 1975.

Gold, P. E., & McGaugh, J. L. Neurobiology and memory: Modulators, correlates, and assumptions. In T. Teyler (Ed.), *Brain and learning.* Stamford, Conn.: Greylock, 1978.

Gold, P. E., & McGaugh, J. L. Endogenous processes in memory consoldiation. In H. Weingartner & E. Parker (Eds.), *Memory consolidation.* Hillsdale, N.J.: Erlbaum, 1984.

Gold, P. E., & Sternberg, D. B. Retrograde amnesia produced by several treatments. Evidence for a common neurobiological mechanism. *Science*, 1978, *201*, 367–369.

Gold, P. E., & van Buskirk, R. B. Facilitation of time-dependent memory processes with posttrial epinephrine injections. *Behavioral Biology*, 1975, *13*, 145–153.

Haycock, J. W., van Buskirk, R., Ryan, J. R., & McGaugh, J. L. Enhancement of retention with centrally administered catecholamines. *Experimental Neurology*, 1977, *54*, 199–208.

Hebb, D. O. *The organization of behavior*. New York: Wiley, 1949.

Izquierdo, I. Effect of naloxone and morphine on various forms of memory in the rat: Possible role of endogenous opiate mechanisms in memory consolidation. *Psychopharmacology*, 1979, *66*, 199–203.

Izquierdo, I., & Graudenz, M. Memory facilitation by naloxone is due to release of dopaminergic and beta-adrenergic systems from tonic inhibition. *Psychopharmacology*, 1980, *67*, 265–268.

Keppel, G. Consolidation and forgetting theory. In H. Weingartner & E. Parker (Eds.), *Memory consolidation*. Hillsdale, N.J.: Erlbaum, 1984.

Kesner, R. P. Brain stimulation: Effects on memory. *Behavioral and Neural Biology*, 1982, *36*, 315–367.

Liang, K. C., & McGaugh, J. L. Lesions of the stria terminalis attenuate the amnestic effect of amygdaloid stimulation on avoidance responses. *Brain Research*, 1983a, *274*, 309–318.

Liang, K. C., & McGaugh, J. L. Lesions of the stria terminalis attenuate the enhancing effect of post-training epinephrine on retention of an inhibitory avoidance response. *Behavioural Brain Research*, 1983b, *9*, 49–58.

Liang, K. C., McGaugh, J. L., & Bennett, C. *Peripheral epinephrine modulates the effect of post-training amygdala stimulation on memory*. Manuscript submitted for publication, 1984.

Liang, K. C., McGaugh, J. L., Martinez, J. L., Jr., Jensen, R. A., Vasquez, B. J., & Messing, R. B. Posttraining amygdaloid lesions impair retention of an inhibitory avoidance response. *Behavioural Brain Research*, 1982, *4*, 237–249.

Liang, K. C., Messing, R. B., & McGaugh, J. L. Naloxone attenuates amnesia caused by amygdaloid stimulation: The involvement of a central opioid system. *Brain Research*, 1983, *271*, 41–49.

Martinez, J. L., Jr., Jensen, R. A., Messing, R. B., Vasquez, B. J., Soumireu-Mourat, B., Geddes, D., Liang, K. C., & McGaugh, J. L. Central and peripheral actions of amphetamine on memory storage. *Brain Research*, 1980, *182*, 157–166.

Martinez, J. L., Jr., Vasquez, B. J., Rigter, H., Messing, R. B., Jensen, R. A., Liang, K. C., & McGaugh, J. L. Attenuation of amphetamine-induced enhancement of learning by adrenal demedullation. *Brain Research*, 1980, *195*, 433–443.

McCarty, R., & Gold, P. E. Plasma catecholamines: Effects of footshock level and hormonal modulators of memory storage. *Hormones and Behavior*, 1981, *15*, 168–182.

McDougall, W. *Experimentelle Beitrage zur Lehre vom Gedachtniss*, by G. E. Mueller & A. Pilzecker. *Mind*, 1901, *10*, 388–394.

McGaugh, J. L. Facilitation and impairment of memory storage processes. In D. P. Kimble (Ed.), *The anatomy of memory*. Palo Alto, Calif.: Science & Behavior Books, 1965.

McGaugh, J. L. A multi-trace view of memory storage. In D. Bovet, F. Bovet-Nitti, & A. Oliverio (Eds.), *Recent advances in learning and retention*. Rome: Academia Nazionale Dei Lincei, 1968.

McGaugh, J. L. Drug facilitation of learning and memory. *Annual Review of Pharmacology*, 1973, *13*, 229–241.

McGaugh, J. L. Hormonal influences on memory. *Annual Review of Psychology*, 1983a, *34*, 297–323.

McGaugh, J. L. Preserving the presence of the past: Hormonal influences on memory storage. *American Psychologist*, 1983b, *38*, 161–174.

McGaugh, J. L., & Dawson, R. G. Modification of memory storage processes. In W. K. Honig & P. H. R. James (Eds.), *Animal memory*. New York: Academic Press, 1971. (Also revised for *Behavioral Sciences*, 1971, *16*, 45–63.)

McGaugh, J. L., & Gold, P. E. Conceptual and neurobiological issues in studies of treatments affecting memory storage. In G. H. Bower (Ed.), *The psychology of learning and motivation* (Vol. 8). New York: Academic Press, 1974.

McGaugh, J. L., & Gold, P. E. Modulation of memory by electrical stimulation of the brain. In M. R. Rosenzweig & E. L. Bennett (Eds.), *Neural mechanisms of learning and memory*. Cambridge, Mass.: MIT Press, 1976.

McGaugh, J. L., & Herz, M. J. *Memory consolidation*. San Francisco: Albion, 1972.

McGaugh, J. L., Martinez, J. L., Jr., Jensen, R. A., Hannan, T. J., Vasquez, B. J., Messing, R. B.,

Liang, K. C., Brewton, C. B., & Spiehler, V. R. Modulation of memory storage by treatments affecting peripheral catecholamines. In C. Ajmone Marsan & H. Matthies (Eds.), *Neuronal plasticity and memory formation.* New York: Raven Press, 1982.

McIntyre, D. C. Adrenalectomy: Protection from kindled convulsion induced amnesia in rats. *Physiology and Behavior*, 1976, *17*, 789–795.

Meligeni, J. A., Ledergerber, S. A., & McGaugh, J. L. Norepinephrine attenuation of amnesia produced by diethyldithiocarbamate. *Brain Research*, 1978, *149*, 155–164.

Messing, R. B., Jensen, R. A., Martinez, J. L., Jr., Spiehler, V. R., Vasquez, B. J., Soumireu-Mourat, B., Liang, K. C., & McGaugh, J. L. Naloxone enhancement of memory. *Behavioral and Neural Biology*, 1979, *27*, 266–275.

Mishkin, M. A. A memory system in the monkey. In *Philosophical Transactions of the Royal Society of London.* London: The Royal Society, 1982.

Mueller, G. E., & Pilzecker, A. Experimentelle Beitrage zur Lehre vom Gedachtniss. *Zeitschrift fuer Psychologie*, 1900, *1*, 1–288.

Ogren, S. O., Archer, T., & Ross, S. B. Evidence for a role of the locus coeruleus noradrenaline system in learning. *Neuroscience Letters*, 1980, *20*, 351–356.

Rapp, P. R., & Gallagher, M. Naloxone enhancement of memory processes: Dependence upon intact norepinephrine function. *Neuroscience Abstracts*, 1983, *9*, 828.

Russell, W. R., & Nathan, P. W. Traumatic amnesia. *Brain*, 1946, *69*, 280–300.

Squire, L. R., Cohen, N. J., & Nadel, L. The medial temporal region and memory consolidation: A new hypothesis. In H. Weingartner & E. Parker (Eds.), *Memory consolidation.* Hillsdale, N.J.: Erlbaum, 1984.

Squire, L. R., & Zola-Morgan, S. The neurology of memory: The case for correspondence between the findings of man and non-human primate. In J. A. Deutsch (Ed.), *The physiological basis of memory* (2nd ed.). New York: Academic Press, 1983.

Stein, L., Belluzzi, J. D., & Wise, C. D. Memory enhancement by central administration of norepinephrine. *Brain Research*, 1975, *84*, 329–335.

Sternberg, D. B., & Gold, P. E. Retrograde amnesia produced by electrical stimulation of the amygdala: Attenuation with adrenergic antagonists. *Brain Research*, 1981, *211*, 59–65.

Sternberg, D. B., Gold, P. E., & McGaugh, J. L. Memory facilitation and impairment with supraseizure electrical brain stimulation: Attenuation with pretrial propranolol injections. *Behavioral and Neural Biology*, 1983, *38*, 261–268.

Uhl, G. R., Kuhar, M. J., & Snyder, S. H. Enkephalin-containing pathway: Amygdaloid efferents in the stria terminalis. *Brain Research*, 1978, *149*, 223–228.

U'Prichard, D. C., Reisine, T. D., Mason, S. T., Fibiger, H. C., & Yamamura, H. I. Modulation of rat α- and β-adrenergic receptor populations by lesions of the dorsal adrenergic bundle. *Brain Research*, 1980, *187*, 143–154.

Weinberger, N. M., Gold, P. E., & Sternberg, D. B. Epinephrine enables Pavlovian fear conditioning under anesthesia. *Science*, 1984, *223*, 605–607.

Zornetzer, S. F., Abraham, W. C., & Appleton, R. The locus coeruleus and labile memory. *Pharmacology Biochemistry and Behavior*, 1978, *9*, 227–234.

CHAPTER TWENTY

Endogenous State Dependency: Memory Depends on the Relation between the Neurohumoral and Hormonal States Present after Training and at the Time of Testing

IVAN IZQUIERDO

Figure 20-1 is a simplified account of the events during and after behavioral training and during retention testing. Training triggers two parallel sets of events that may interact. One includes learning, which is followed by consolidation, which is followed by storage of what is salvaged from the labile consolidation process; stored information may or may not become available for retrieval, and thus in test sessions it may or may not be recalled; testing usually involves, in addition to retrieval, some degree of relearning (McGaugh & Herz, 1972; Gold & McGaugh, 1975; Izquierdo, 1980). Simultaneously with learning there are neurohumoral and hormonal changes that persist into the posttraining period and may influence learning, consolidation, storage, or availability for retrieval. Some of these neurohumoral and hormonal changes have actually been measured (peripheral catecholamine hypersecretion, central catecholamine, and β-endorphin release; see the following section) and others have been inferred (pituitary ACTH release, other neurotransmitter or hormonal changes) (Gold & McGaugh, 1975; Zornetzer, 1978; Gold & Delanoy, 1981; Bohus, Conti, Kovács, & Versteeg, 1982). The changes that occur in test sessions have been less studied and are believed to be smaller (see section on Relation between Posttraining and Pretesting Effects . . .). They may influence the learning process at the level of retrieval or relearning, or at the level of availability for retrieval. Exogenous treatments that affect learning or retrieval (or the phases that mediate between learning and retrieval) may do so through influences on the endogenous neurochemical changes (Gold & McGaugh, 1975; Zornetzer, 1978). The neurohumoral and hormonal changes that occur during

Ivan Izquierdo. Department of Biochemistry, Institute of Biosciences, UFRGS (Central), Pôrto Alegre, RS, Brazil.

or after training and during testing configure two different but related endogenous states.

This chapter deals primarily with data from this laboratory that suggest that learning and memory depend on the relationship between the endogenous state that develops after training and the one that develops during retention testing; or, in other words, that there is endogenous state dependency.

The origin of this idea is difficult to trace. Kety (1967, 1970, 1976) suggested that biogenic amines and hormones released in the peculiar "affective states" that accompany learning "might modulate trophic processes occurring at recently activated synapses in order to promote the persistence of those circuits that have led to reward or to the relief of discomfort." Implicit in that suggestion is the notion that a repetition of the neurochemical change(s) caused by the substances released will repeat the conditions appropriate for a facilitated operation of the circuits involved in the emission or omission of a given response. Spear (1973, 1978) and later Riccio and Concannon (1981) considered that "interoceptive cues experienced in a given drug (or hormonal) state might serve as contextual cues for retrieval" and that drug (or hormone)-induced memory reactivation might "depend on the reinstatement of a sufficient number (or kind) of retrieval attributes that were present at, or immediately following, original learning."

The first formal and explicit statement of the endogenous state dependency hypothesis was made by Zornetzer (1978):

> In normal memory formation the specific pattern of arousal present in the brain at the time of training may become an integral component of the stored information. The neural representation of this specific pattern of arousal might depend on the pattern of

Figure 20-1. Parallel sets of events triggered by behavioral training and testing: Events related to learning and memory, and neurohumoral and hormonal changes that may modulate the former at the points indicated by arrows.

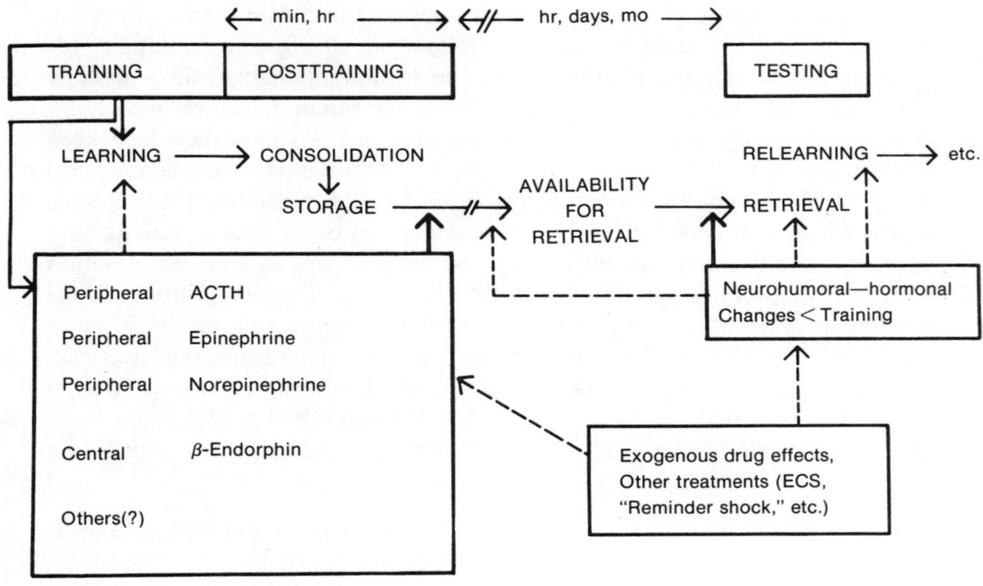

activity generated by brainstem acetylcholine, catecholamine and serotonin systems. It is this idiosyncratic and unique patterned brain state, present at the time of memory formation, that might need to be reproduced, or at least approximated, at the time of retrieval in order for the stored information to be elaborated. (p. 646)

Izquierdo (1980) added β-endorphin to the list of neurotransmitters proposed by Zornetzer (1978), and Riccio and Concannon (1981) suggested that the hormone ACTH, when present during testing, would increase "the similarity of the retrieval context to the original encoding episode."

This chapter reviews evidence that generally supports, but also amends and extends, the hypothesis as formulated by Zornetzer (1978) or Izquierdo (1980), and at the same time detracts from the notion that the neurohumoral or hormonal changes may be very specific from an informational point of view.

POSTTRAINING NEUROHUMORAL AND HORMONAL REGULATION OF MEMORY

The best-studied posttraining neurohumoral and hormonal changes are the following: (1) the hypersecretion of peripheral epinephrine and norepinephrine that occurs after inhibitory avoidance training (Gold & McCarty, 1981; Gold & Delanoy, 1981; Gold, McCarty, & Sternberg, 1982); (2) the apparent release of brain dopamine and norepinephrine (Gold & van Buskirk, 1978; Schütz, Schütz, Orsingher, & Izquierdo, 1979; Gold & Delanoy, 1981) and β-endorphin (Izquierdo *et al.*, 1980; Izquierdo, Dias, Perry, Souza, Elisabetsky, & Carrasco, 1982) that occurs following a variety of training procedures; and (3) the possible discharge of pituitary ACTH that presumably occurs in aversive situations (Dunn, 1980; Gold & Delanoy, 1981). A wealth of recent evidence suggests that these changes may modulate memory formation after training (Gold & McGaugh, 1975; Gold *et al.*, 1982; McGaugh *et al.*, 1982; Izquierdo *et al.*, 1982).

In the case of ACTH and of the central and peripheral catecholamines there appears to be an optimum level of posttraining secretion for memory formation; if the level is too low or too high memory is deficient. This has been inferred from experiments in which a presumably small or large endogenous release (e.g., by the use of low- and high-intensity training footshock, respectively) is coupled with different doses of injected ACTH, epinephrine, or norepinephrine; treatments that lead to a moderate posttraining increase of circulating catecholamines and possibly ACTH levels, or to a moderate depletion of brain norepinephrine, are followed by good performance in a retention test carried out one or more days later (Gold & van Buskirk, 1975, 1976, 1978; Gold & Delanoy, 1981).

In the case of brain β-endorphin, its release seems to be rather independent of the number or even of the presence of footshock stimulation during training (Izquierdo *et al.*, 1980, 1981, 1982), and the intraperitoneal (Izquierdo *et al.*, 1980, 1981, 1982; Izquierdo, 1982) or intracerebroventricular (Lucion, Rosito, Sapper, Palmini, & Izquierdo, 1982) administration of very small doses of this substance, compatible with the amounts that are endogenously released during training, causes a naloxone-reversible (Izquierdo, 1982) disruption of retention in many tasks. Naloxone gives alone causes memory facilitation also in many tasks (Izquierdo, 1979; Messing *et al.*, 1979), which led to the hypothesis that there is an endogenous mechanism mediated by β-endorphin that promotes forgetting (Izquierdo *et al.*, 1980, 1981, 1982; Izquierdo, 1982).

We have recently observed that this amnestic mechanism interacts with those mediated by ACTH and the sympathoadrenal system. In situations in which the posttraining administration of ACTH, epinephrine, or tyramine—a peripheral releaser of norepinephrine—cause retrograde amnesia (step-down inhibitory avoidance using a large platform and a high-intensity training footshock), the concomitant posttraining administration of naloxone antagonizes, and that of β-endorphin potentiates, the amnesia (Izquierdo & Dias, 1982a, 1982b). In situations that presumably entail a small release of endogenous ACTH and peripheral catecholamines, and therefore those in which their posttraining administration may help the animals to attain the optimum level of these substances for memory formation (Gold & Delanoy, 1981; Gold *et al.*, 1982) (i.e., step-down inhibitory avoidance using a small platform and a low-intensity training footshock), ACTH, epinephrine, and tyramine cause retrograde memory facilitation that is antagonized by β-endorphin and potentiated by naloxone (Izquierdo & Dias, 1982a, 1982b). It was recently shown that ACTH, epinephrine, and other substances release brain β-endorphin (Carrasco, Dias, Perry, Wofchuk, Souza, & Izquierdo, 1982). Therefore, it might be possible to explain the effects of ACTH and peripheral catecholamines according to the schema of Figure 20-2. These substances appear to have a dual influence on memory at the posttraining period, one facilitatory and the other inhibitory. The latter may be mediated at least in part by brain β-endorphin release. Depending on the dose and/or the circulating levels of ACTH and catecholamines, one or the other effect will predominate. At moderate doses and/or levels the facilitatory effect would be prevalent; as the dose or level increases, the inhibitory influence would predominate.

Since systemically administered ACTH and epinephrine affect brain stem norepinephrine levels, through a mechanism as yet unknown (Gold & van Buskirk, 1978; Gold & Delanoy, 1981), and opioids influence norepinephrine release at various central synapses (see Snyder & Childers, 1979, for references), it is possible that these various memory-modulating substances may interact at the level of central catecholamine systems (Figure 20-3), either by tending to "push" them to a low (β-endorphin) or to a high (ACTH, epinephrine) level of

Figure 20-2. Dual effect of peripheral ACTH and catecholamines on posttraining events involved in memory modulation; brain β-endorphin may mediate an inhibitory effect.

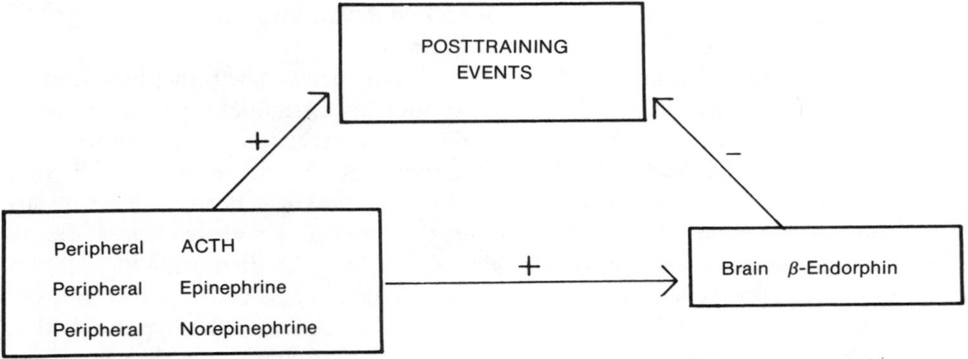

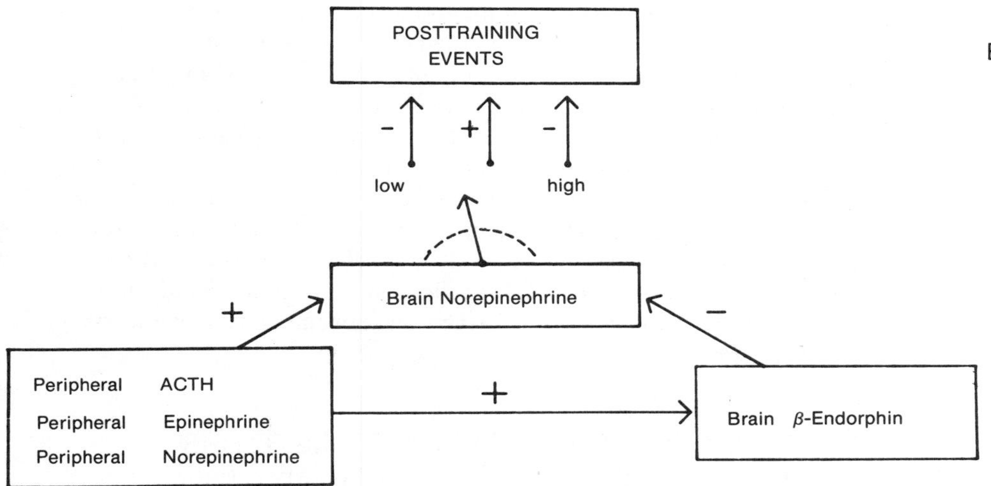

Figure 20-3. Possible participation of brain norepinephrine in the influences of posttraining ACTH, peripheral catecholamines, and brain β-endorphin on memory modulation.

activity. These interactions may coexist with others, and possibly the overall modulation of memory at the posttraining stage might result from a complex interplay among various neurotransmitter and hormone systems that may differ from task to task (Zornetzer, 1978; Squire & Davis, 1981).

NEUROHUMORAL AND HORMONAL REGULATION OF MEMORY DURING TESTING

By far, the largest concentration of efforts in studies on the regulation of memory by endogenous factors has been on the posttraining period (McGaugh & Herz, 1972; Gold & McGaugh, 1975; Zornetzer, 1978; Gold & Delanoy, 1981; Izquierdo *et al.*, 1981, 1982; McGaugh *et al.*, 1982; Gold *et al.*, 1982). The previous section is a much abridged account of those factors that have been best studied and/or that are relevant to the ensuing sections.

The neurohumoral and hormonal changes that occur during test sessions have been much less studied, but there are reasons to believe that they are smaller than those that follow after training. Brain β-endorphin is indeed released to a much lesser, if any, extent in test sessions of a variety of tasks (Izquierdo *et al.*, 1980, 1981, 1982). There are obvious reasons to think that test sessions of inhibitory avoidance in which no footshocks are given (i.e., Gold & van Buskirk, 1975, 1976, 1978; Gold & Delanoy, 1981; Gold *et al.*, 1982; Izquierdo & Dias, 1982a, 1982b) are accompanied by a much smaller discharge of ACTH or peripheral catecholamines than that of training sessions, particularly since these changes seem to depend on the stress or aversiveness associated with the task.

The administration of ACTH (Riccio & Concannon, 1981), neuroactive ACTH fragments (Rigter, Elbertse, & van Riezen, 1975; de Wied, Bohus, van Ree, & Urban, 1978), β-endorphin (de Wied *et al.*, 1978; Izquierdo, 1980), other endorphins (de Wied *et al.*, 1978), or enkephalins (Rigter, 1978) prior to testing enhances retrieval of previously learned aversive and nonaversive behaviors.

This enhancement may be manifested as an increased performance of avoidance responses (Izquierdo, 1980), as a retarded extinction (de Wied *et al.*, 1978), as a decreased performance of orienting responses in a habituation task (Izquierdo, 1980), or as a recovery from amnesia induced by various posttraining treatments (Rigter *et al.*, 1975; Rigter, 1978; Riccio & Concannon, 1981), in which case the effect is called antiamnestic. Noncontingent footshocks delivered prior to testing may also be antiamnestic (Schneider, 1979); that treatment would presumably release ACTH and/or peripheral catecholamines (Gold & McCarty, 1981; Gold & Delanoy, 1981). It has been postulated that the "reminder" or antiamnestic effect of ACTH (Riccio & Concannon, 1981) or of the enkephalins (Rigter, 1978) may be due to the release of endogenous β-endorphin (Carrasco, Dias, Perry, Wofchuk, Souza, & Izquierdo, 1982).

RELATION BETWEEN POSTTRAINING AND PRETESTING EFFECTS OF ACTH, β-ENDORPHIN, EPINEPHRINE, AND TYRAMINE: A CASE FOR ENDOGENOUS STATE DEPENDENCY

In the experiments commented on in this and following sections, adult female Wistar-derived rats from our own breeding stock (age 43 to 60 days) were used; the exception is the experiment of Figure 20-8, in which males of the same age were used. Animals were trained in a step-down inhibitory-avoidance task described elsewhere in detail (Izquierdo & Dias, 1982a, 1982b), in which a 5-cm-high, 25 × 25 cm wood platform and a .5 to 1.0 mA, 60-Hz footshock were used. Animals were tested 24 hours after the training trial.

As shown in Figure 20-4, the immediate posttraining administration of $ACTH_{1-24}$ (.2 μg/kg), epinephrine HCl (5.0 μg/kg), or human β-endorphin (1.0 μg/kg) causes retrograde amnesia in animals that receive 1.0 ml/kg of saline prior to testing. The amnesia is counteracted by the administration of any of the drug treatments prior to testing instead of saline; in each case, the antiamnestic effect is more pronounced when the treatment given on the test session is the same that was given after training. Therefore, all drugs are amnestic and all are antiamnestic; however, the animals are able to "recognize" to some extent the drug that had rendered them amnestic.

The extent of this recognition for ACTH and epinephrine is shown in Figures 20-5 and 20-6. Pretesting administration of each of these two substances, at a dose that is 60% of the one that was amnestic for at least 80% of the animals, when given after training fully reverses the effect of the latter. If the other drug is given, a full reversal of amnesia is obtained only with twice the amnestic dose. Therefore, rats are capable of discriminating between the antiamnestic effects of ACTH and epinephrine by a factor of 3.5 to 1, depending on which one was given after training.

Figure 20-7 offers an explanation of these results. As shown in Figure 20-4, the amnestic effects of ACTH, β-endorphin, and epinephrine on this task are interchangeable, so we may call them A, B, and C regardless of their chemical nature. A, B, and C are released from endogenous stores probably to a larger extent in training than in test sessions (see preceding section), so in normal animals (cf. the saline–saline groups) there is a difference between the posttraining and the test-session neurohumoral and hormonal states. When this difference is enlarged by the posttraining administration of any of the three

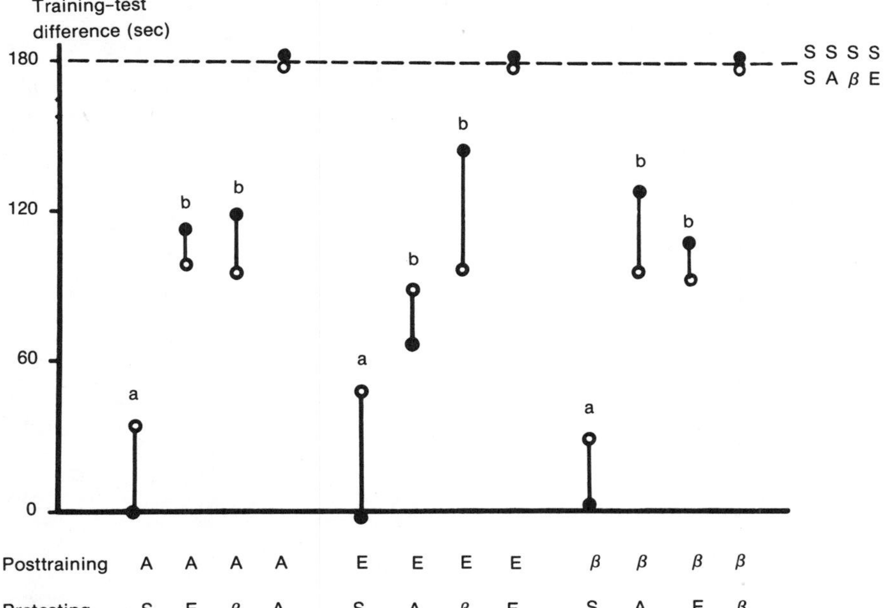

Figure 20-4. Retention (training–test step-down latency difference, in seconds) in rats that received a posttraining and/or a pretesting intraperitoneal injection of saline (S) (1.0 ml/kg), $ACTH_{1-24}$ (A) (.2 μg/kg), epinephrine HCl (E) (5.0 μg/kg), or human β-endorphin (β) (1.0 μg/kg); data expressed as medians (●) and means (○). The horizontal dashed line indicates the median and mean of the groups that received saline after training and one of the three drugs prior to testing; 10 or 15 animals per group. a, significant difference from the dashed line at $p < .001$ level; b, significant difference from a and from the dashed line at $p < .01$ or .001 level (Mann-Whitney *U*-tests, two-tailed). Note the amnestic effect of the posttraining injection of the three drugs, its reversal by their administration prior to testing, and the more pronounced antiamnestic effect of the drugs when the treatment given prior to testing was the same that was given after training.

substances, memory becomes poor. When this amplified difference is reduced by the pretesting injection of the same drug that was given after training, 60% of the amnestic dose will recover retention to normal levels. When the drug given on the test session is not the one for which levels were artificially enhanced at the posttraining period, twice the amnestic dose is needed.

Figure 20-8 shows the result of another experiment that emphasizes the nonspecificity (as to cue value) of the antiamnestic effect of ACTH, epinephrine, and β-endorphin. In this experiment, animals received a combination of $ACTH_{1-24}$ (.2 μg/kg), epinephrine HCl (5.0 μg/kg), and human β-endorphin (1.0 μg/kg) after training. Retention is poor in animals who receive this combination after training and saline prior to testing. Administration of any one of the drugs prior to testing results in a partial recovery from amnesia. Administration of any two of the drugs, or of the three, results in a full recovery.

The experiments summarized in this section present a strong case for endogenous state dependency and therefore agree with the hypothesis previously advanced by Zornetzer (1978), Izquierdo (1980), or Izquierdo *et al.* (1981, 1982), as well as with the suggestion of Spear (1973, 1978) or Riccio and Concannon

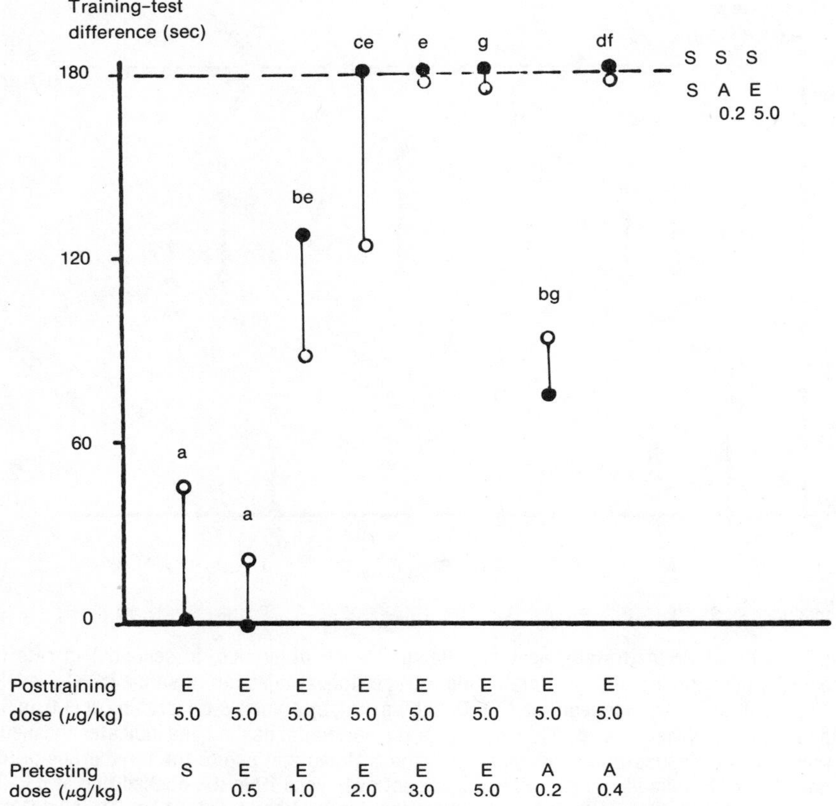

Figure 20-5. Median (●) and mean (○) retention scores of rats that received a posttraining intraperitoneal injection of 5.0 μg/kg of epinephrine (E) and a pretesting injection of saline (S) or various doses of epinephrine (.5 to 5.0 μg/kg) or of ACTH (A) (.2 or .4 μg/kg). The horizontal dashed line corresponds to the median and mean retention score of animals treated with saline after training and with saline, epinephrine (5.0 μg/kg), or ACTH (.2 μg/kg) prior to testing; 15 animals per group. a, significant difference from the dashed line, $p < .001$; b, same, $p <$.,01; c, same, $p < .05$; d, significant difference from its immediately preceding group, $p <$.,025; e, same, $p < .05$; f, significant difference the E-S group, $p <$.,01; g, same, $p < .001$ (Mann-Whitney *U*-tests, two-tailed). Note the dose-response curves for the antiamnestic effect of epinephrine against itself (full antiamnestic effect at 60% of the posttraining amnestic dose), and of ACTH against epinephrine (full antiamnestic effect only with twice the amnestic dose of ACTH; see Figure 20-6).

(1981) that drugs or hormones may serve a role as contextual cues. However, the present data introduce some important amendments and extensions to the hypothesis and to the suggestion. The major determinant of good retrieval would seem to be the establishment of a *difference* between the posttraining and the test session neurohumoral and hormonal states, rather than a matching between both. Each component of those states appears to have some cue value, but this is rather limited, and one may substitute for the other provided it is present in an adequate amount during testing.

In addition, a *reduction* of the normal difference between the two states does not seem to affect memory to an appreciable extent: Retention was as good in the animals who received saline after training and during testing as it was in those who received saline after training and one of the drugs prior to testing (Figures 20-4 to 20-8).

EXPLANATION OF THE POSTTRAINING AND PRETESTING DRUG EFFECTS THROUGH INFLUENCES ON AVAILABILITY FOR RETRIEVAL

As shown in Figure 20-1, endogenous substances or drugs that alter memory when acting on the posttraining period may do so through an influence on consolidation, storage, or availability for retrieval, and those acting on the test session may influence retrieval, relearning, or availability for retrieval.

Figure 20-6. Median (●) and mean (○) retention scores of rats that received a posttraining intraperitoneal injection of ACTH (A) (.2 μg/kg) and a pretesting injection of saline (S) or various doses of ACTH (.02 to .2 μg/kg) or of epinephrine (E) (5.0 or 10.0 μg/kg). The horizontal dashed line is the same in Figure 20-5; 15 animals per group. a,b,c,d,e, as in Figure 20-5; f, significant difference from the A-S group, $p < .01$; g, same, $p < .001$ (Mann–Whitney *U*-tests, two-tailed). Note the dose–response curves for the antiamnestic effect of ACTH against itself (full antiamnestic effect at 60% of the posttraining dose), and of epinephrine against ACTH (full antiamnestic effect only with twice the amnestic dose of epinephrine; see Figure 20-5).

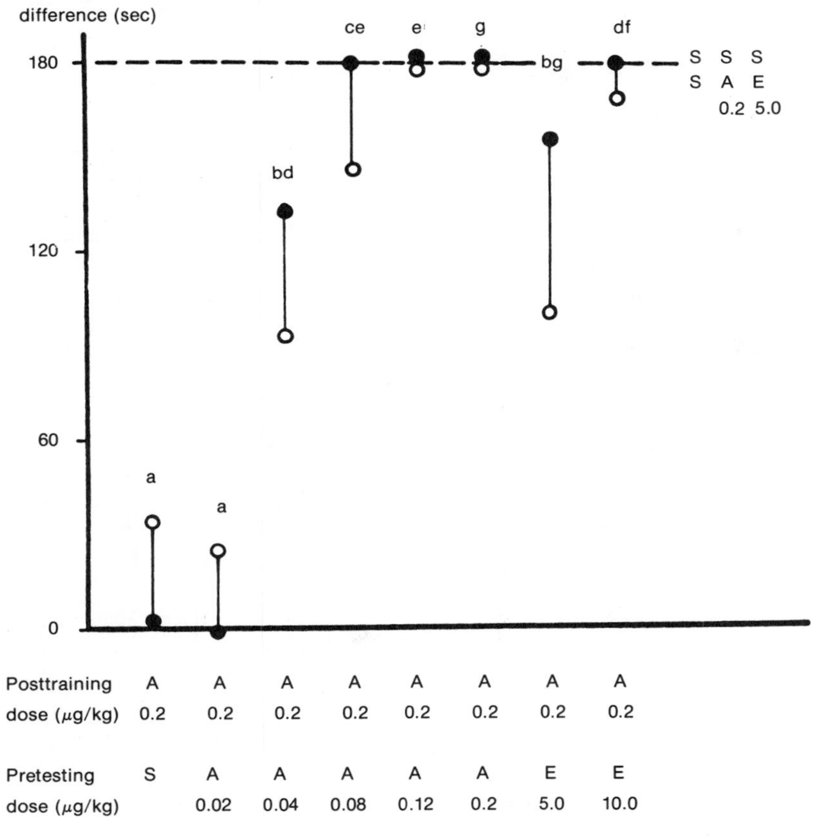

It is obvious that ACTH, β-endorphin, epinephrine, and tyramine given after training do not affect consolidation or storage, since animals thus treated may retrieve the learned information perfectly well provided they are submitted to an appropriate neurohumoral and hormonal state in the test session. It is also obvious that the pretesting effect of these substances consists of making available for retrieval information that had been consolidated and was stored but was not readily available. Therefore, the "site" of action of ACTH,

Figure 20-7. Explanation of the data of Figures 20-5 and 20-6. Since the effects of ACTH, epinephrine, and β-endorphin are quite interchangeable (see preceding figures), they may be called A, B, and C interchangeably and regardless of their chemical nature. A, B, and C represent their endogenous release at the training session, and a, b, and c represent their release at the test session, which should be smaller than that in the training session. The actual numerical values of A, B, C, a, b, and c are not important for this discussion, and a, b, and c may be equal to zero. In normal animals there is a difference between A + B + C and a + b +c (Δ) that correlates with good retention. When any of these drugs is given by injection after training, it adds to the amount of it that is endogenously released; the difference between the training and the test neurohumoral and/or hormonal states is enlarged (Δ') and memory becomes poor. When this enlarged difference is attenuated by administration of the same drug on the test session (Δ"), memory recovers to normal levels with only 60% of the dose of that drug that had been amnestic for at least 80% of the animals (AD_{80}). When the drug given on the test session is different from the one that was given after training (Δ'''), twice its AD_{80} is needed in order to recover memory to its normal level (i.e., for a full antiamnestic effect).

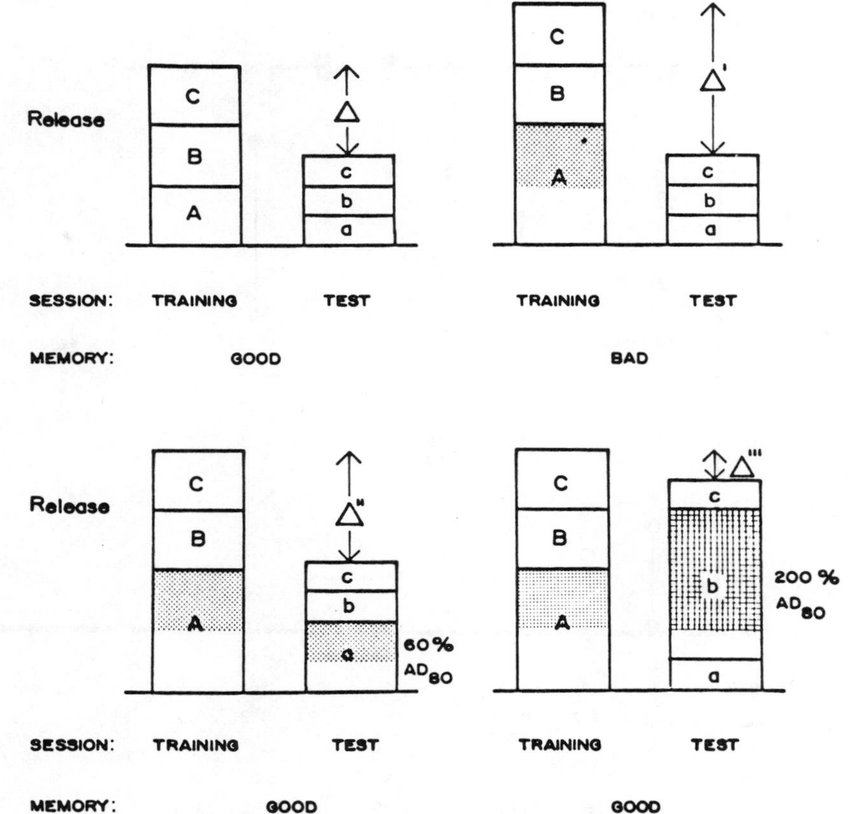

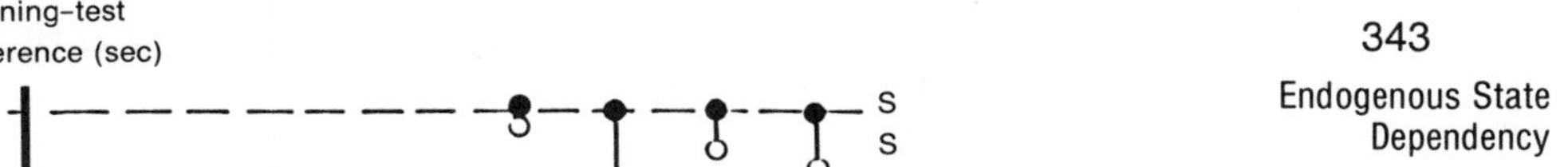

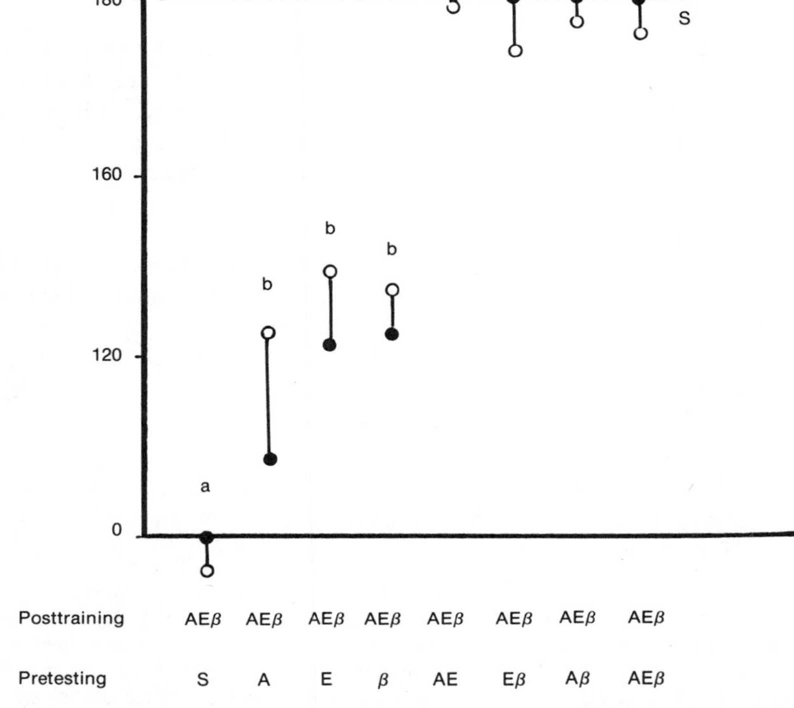

Figure 20-8. Symbols and abbreviations as in Figure 20-4. Note the amnestic effect of the combined posttraining injection of ACTH (.2 μg/kg), epinephrine (5.0 μg/kg), and β-endorphin (1.0 μg/kg) (AEβ) (a, significant difference from the dashed line or S-S group at $p < .001$ level), the partial antiamnestic effect of each of the three drugs given separately prior to testing (b, significant difference from a and from the dashed line at $p < .01$ to $< .001$ level), and the fully antiamnestic effect of administration of any two of the drugs, or of the three, prior to testing (Mann-Whitney *U*-tests, two-tailed). Male rats used in this experiment; 12 in the S-S group and 10 in all the others.

β-endorphin, and peripheral catecholamines would be primarily at the level of the (hitherto unknown) mechanisms that make stored information available for retrieval, and these mechanisms would be the ones that are actually state dependent.

It is possible that other posttraining amnestic treatments may also act on these mechanisms in addition to, or instead of, on consolidation or storage, among them, electroconvulsive shock or CO_2 inhalation, whose amnestic effects may be reversed by hormones or other treatments given prior to testing (Rigter *et al.*, 1975; Rigter, 1978; Schneider, 1979; Riccio & Concannon, 1981). However, these observations do not deny the existence of a process of consolidation or the influence of treatments thereon (see also Izquierdo, 1980, 1982; Izquierdo *et al.*, 1981, 1982). Consolidation exists, drugs may affect it, and in addition obviously availability for retrieval exists and some drugs do affect it, particularly certain hormones and neurotransmitters.

ADRENERGIC RECEPTORS INVOLVED IN THE POSTTRAINING AND PRETESTING EFFECT OF DRUGS ON RETENTION

In previous papers on the role of β-endorphin in endogenous state dependency (Izquierdo, 1980; Izquierdo *et al.*, 1981, 1982) we suggested that it might act on the same substrates when given after training and prior to testing. Although we have no way of knowing whether this is really so for ACTH or β-endorphin (see below), experiments with epinephrine and the peripheral norepinephrine releaser, tyramine, suggest that the posttraining and pretesting substrates of their action may be biochemically different, at least in part.

As shown in Figure 20-9, the concomitant intraperitoneal injection of the α_2-adrenergic receptor blocker, yohimbine HCl (2.0 mg/kg), antagonized the amnestic effect of posttraining epinephrine HCl (5.0 μg/kg) or tyramine HCl (1.0 mg/kg). The same dose of the α_1-blocker, prazosin HCl, or of the β_1–β_2-blocker, propranolol HCl, was ineffective.

Figure 20-9. This experiment and those of Figures 20-10 and 20-11 were run together, and for the sake of clarity, some of the groups are repeated in the three figures. Median (●) and mean (○) retention in animals that received yohimbine HCl (Y) (2.0 mg/kg), prazosin HCl (Z) (2.0 mg/kg), propranolol HCl (P) (2.0 mg/kg), epinephrine HCl (5.0 μg/kg), tyramine HCl (1.0 mg/kg), or a combination of one of the two latter with one of the three former, immediately after training, and saline (S) (1.0 ml/kg) prior to testing. The horizontal dashed line corresponds to the median and mean retention score of a group treated with saline after training and prior to testing. This group had 20 rats; all the others had 15. a, significant difference from any group whose median is 180 seconds at $p < .001$ level (Mann–Whitney *U*-tests, two-tailed). The amnestic effect of epinephrine and tyramine given after training was antagonized by the concomitant administration of yohimbine but not by that of prazosin or propranolol.

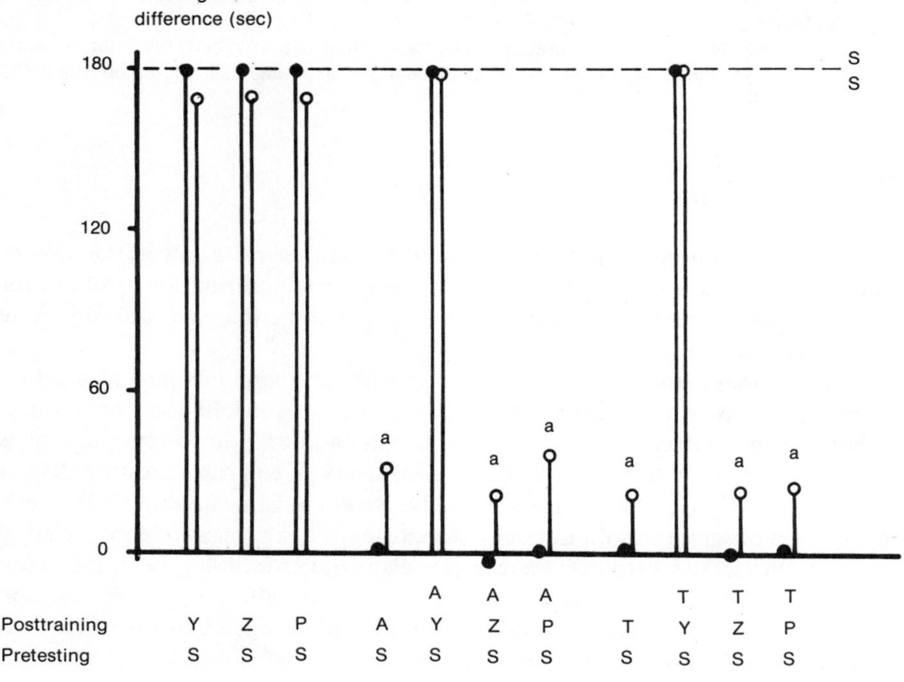

The antiamnestic action of tyramine or epinephrine against themselves (Figure 20-10) or their partial antiamnestic effect against each other (Figure 20-11) were antagonized by either prazosin or yohimbine, but not by propranolol.

Therefore, α_2-adrenergic receptors appear to be involved in the posttraining effect of the sympathomimetics epinephrine and tyramine, and both α_1- and α_2-receptors appear to be involved in their pretesting antiamnestic effect. There are pre- and postsynaptic α_2-receptors; the former inhibit norepinephrine release and the latter mediate some of the postsynaptic actions of epinephrine and norepinephrine (Langer, 1980). Clearly, the antagonism by yohimbine of the effects of epinephrine and tyramine can be explained only by a preferential influence on postsynaptic α_2-receptors; if it were only upon presynaptic ones, yohimbine would have actually facilitated the effects of tyramine instead of blocking them.

Thus, despite some possible overlap concerning the α_2-receptor population, there is a difference between the receptor populations involved in the posttraining and pretesting effects of epinephrine and tyramine: The latter involve α_1- in addition to α_2-receptors. This difference suggests that the neural substrates of the two sets of effects are not identical.

As shown in Figure 20-12, both the posttraining amnestic and the pretesting antiamnestic effects of ACTH and β-endorphin are antagonized by yohimbine but not by prazosin. This suggests that the former effect may be similar to,

Figure 20-10. Symbols and abbreviations as in Figure 20-9. Administration of any of the drugs prior to testing had no effect on retention in animals that received posttraining saline. The amnestic effect of posttraining epinephrine (A) was antagonized by administration of the same drug prior to testing, and that of tyramine (T) was also antagonized by tyramine given prior to testing. The antiamnestic effect of the two drugs was blocked by the concomitant pretesting injection of either yohimbine or prazosin, but not by that of propranolol. a, as in Figure 20-9; b, significant difference from a at $p < .001$ level (Mann–Whitney *U*-tests, two-tailed). Twenty animals in the S-S group, 15 in all others.

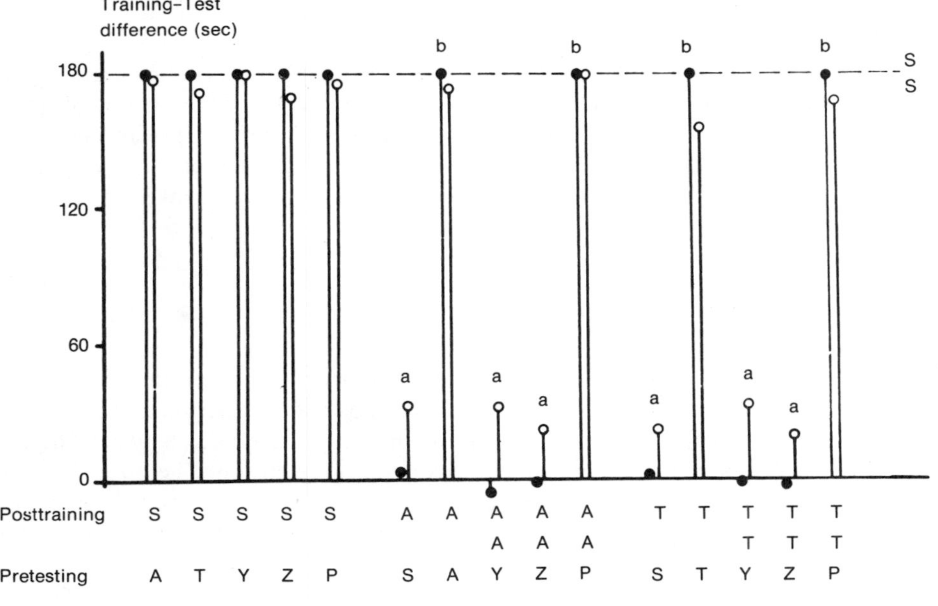

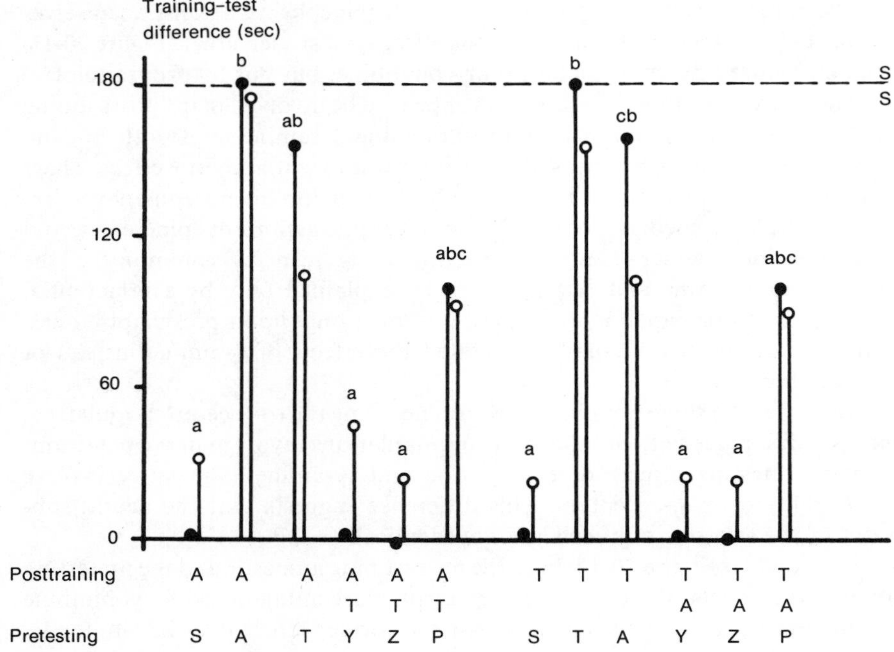

Figure 20-11. Symbols and abbreviations as in the two preceding figures. a,b, as in Figure 20-10; c, significant difference from both a and the dashed line at $p < .01$ lkevel (Mann–Whitney *U*-tests, two-tailed). Note that pretesting tyramine and epinephrine reverse the amnestic effect of each other's posttraining administration only partially; the antiamnestic effect of both drugs is antagonized by either yohimbine or prazosin given concomitantly prior to testing, but not by propranolol. Twenty animals in the S-S, T-A, A-T, T-AP, and A-TP groups; 15 in each of the others.

but the latter is at least partly different from, those of epinephrine and tyramine. ACTH does not release peripheral catecholamines (Gold *et al.*, 1982). β-Endorphin appears not to have been investigated in this respect, but the amnestic effect of another opioid, methionine-enkephalin, is not mediated by the adrenal medullae but requires the presence of enough peripheral epinephrine in order to become manifest (Izquierdo *et al.*, 1983). Therefore, it seems likely that the posttraining and pretesting effects of ACTH and β-endorphin may require the concomitant presence of an intact α_2-adrenergic receptor mechanism in order to occur.

CONCLUSIONS

The present data support the notion that memory depends on states induced by endogenous transmitters or hormones in the posttraining period and at the time of testing. A certain qualitative and quantitative difference between the two states appears necessary in order to ensure good retention. The hormones and transmitters have some limited cue value, but at least some of them may substitute for others, provided they are present in sufficient amounts at the time of testing.

These findings bypass the "memory molecule" approach to the neurochemistry of memory and suggest a return to Kety's (1967, 1970) concept that transmitter- or hormone-mediated changes, possibly at the synaptic level, may "promote the persistence of those circuits that have led to reward or to the relief of discomfort," and to the obvious consequence of that concept, that a reiteration of those neurochemical changes will again promote an enhanced operation of those circuits. Among the neurochemical changes that may be caused by hormones and transmitters and that may play a role in heightened synaptic function, synaptosomal membrane protein phosphorylation stands out as a potential candidate (Tielen, Lopes da Silva, Bär, & Gispen, 1982). Thus, the influence of posttraining or pretesting hormones and transmitters on memory might be viewed as being not very different from that of aspirin in pain relief or of vasodilators in angina pectoris: The drugs may act all over the body, but their action will be more deeply felt in the affected area. Hormones and neurotransmitters may biochemically affect many synapses, but their influence

Figure 20-12. Median (blocks) and mean (vertical bars) retention scores of animals that received yohimbine (Y), prazosin (Z), ACTH (A), epinephrine (E), β-endorphin (β), or combinations of the two former with the latter three, after training or prior to testing. Doses as in Figures 20-4 and 20-9 to 20-11. The horizontal dashed line indicates median and mean of groups treated with saline (S) after training and ACTH, epinephrine, or β-endorphin prior to testing. a, significant difference from dashed line at $p < .001$ level; b, significant difference from a at $p < .01$ or .001 level (Mann–Whitney U-tests, two-tailed); 15 animals per group. The amnestic effect of posttraining, ACTH, epinephine, or β-endorphin was antagonized by the simultaneous administration of yohimbine, but not by that of prazosin. The antiamnestic effect of ACTH, epinephrine, or β-endorphin against themselves was antagonized by yohimbine; and that of epinephrine, but not those of ACTH or β-endorphin, was in addition also antagonized by the simultaneous pretesting administrazion of prazosin.

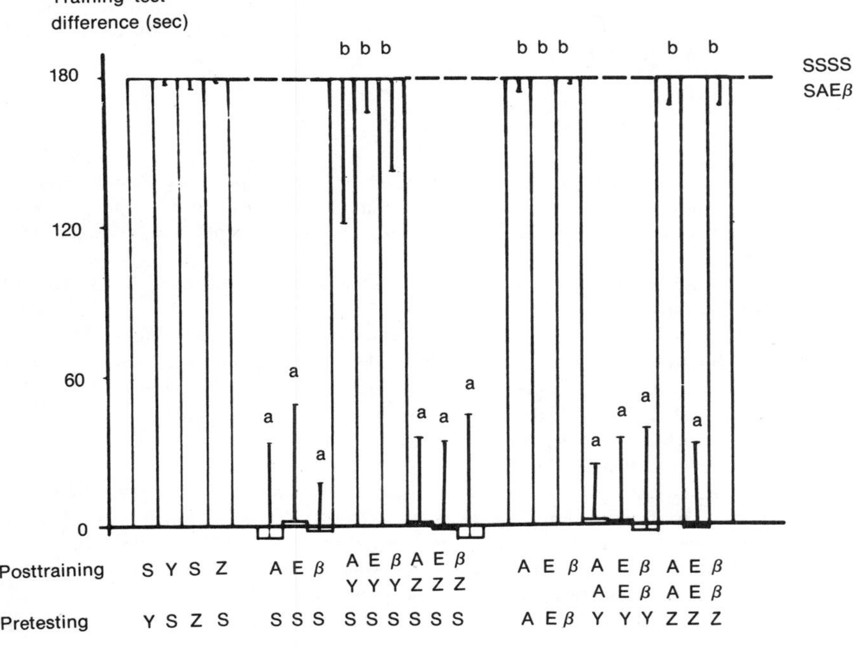

at those that are being particularly activated at a given time (and maybe in a given sequence or relation) may mark their influence on memory mechanisms. Whether this influence works in series or in parallel with macromolecular changes related to storage (Dunn, 1980), or whether the macromolecular changes are involved at all in storage processes, are problems beyond the scope of this chapter.

A question arises as to how peripherally acting substances, such as ACTH or circulating catecholamines, may affect such a definitely central process as availability for retrieval. There are several possibilities (Izquierdo & Thaddeu, 1975; Gold & Delanoy, 1981): by reflex influences on brain activity initiated at the periphery; through regional changes in cerebral blood flow; or through actual penetration into the brain at peculiarly permeable sites, such as the area postrema or the median eminence. β-Endorphin does penetrate through the blood–brain barrier to some extent (Houghten, Swann, & Li, 1980), and its influences on learning and memory are believed to be central (Izquierdo *et al.*, 1980, 1981, 1982; Lucion *et al.*, 1982; Izquierdo, 1982).

Finally, as to drug-induced state dependency (Spear, 1973, 1978), it seems likely that exogenous drugs may cause state-dependent learning, or affect consolidation or other parameters of the learning process, through influences on endogenous transmitter or hormone systems. A variety of drugs known to affect behavior release brain β-endorphin (Carrasco *et al.*, 1982), and others may affect ACTH or peripheral catecholamine activity (Gold & Delanoy, 1981; McGaugh *et al.*, 1982). Thus, the primary responsibility for drug-induced state dependency may lie with endogenous substances, and drug-induced state dependencies would be just special cases of modifications of the internal states that modulate the learning process (Figure 20-1).

ACKNOWLEDGMENTS

All experiments reported here were done in collaboration with Dr. Renato D. Dias. Work was supported by FINEP, FAPERGS, and PROPESP-UFRGS and by a senior research fellowship to the author from CNPq, Brasil.

REFERENCES

Bohus, B., Conti, L., Kovács, G. L., & Versteeg, D. H. G. Modulation of memory processes by neuropeptides: Interaction with neurotransmitter systems. In C. Ajmone-Marsan & H. Matthies (Eds.), *Neuronal plasticity and memory formation*. New York: Raven Press, 1982.

Carrasco, M. A., Dias, R. D., Perry, M. L. S., Wofchuk, S. T., Souza, D. O., & Izquierdo, I. Effect of morphine, ACTH, epinephrine, Met-, Leu- and des-Tyr-Met-enkephalin on β-endorphin-like immunoreactivity of rat brain. *Psychoneuroendocrinology*, 1982, *7*,

de Wied, D., Bohus, B., van Ree, J. M., & Urban, I. Behavioral and electrophysiological effects of peptides related to lipotropin (β-LPH). *Journal of Pharmacology and Experimental Therapeutics*, 1978, *204*, 570–580.

Dunn, A. J. Neurochemistry of learning and memory: An evaluation of recent data. *Annual Review of Psychology*, 1980, *31*, 343–390.

Gold, P. E., & Delanoy, R. L. ACTH modulation of memory storage processing. In J. L. Martinez, Jr., R. A. Jensen, R. B. Messing, H. Rigter, & J. L. McGaugh (Eds.), *Endogenous peptides and learning and memory processes*. New York: Academic, 1981.

Gold, P. E., & McCarty, R. Plasma catecholamines: Changes after footshock and seizure-producing frontal cortex stimulation. *Behavioral and Neural Biology*, 1981, *31*, 247–260.

Gold, P. E., McCarty, R., & Sternberg, D. B. Peripheral catecholamines and memory modulation.

In C. Ajmone-Marsan & H. Matthies (Eds.), *Neuronal plasticity and memory formation.* New York: Raven Press, 1982.

Gold, P. E., & McGaugh, J. L. A single-trace, two-process view of memory storage processes. In D. Deutsch & J. A. Deutsch (Eds.), *Short-term memory.* New York: Academic Press, 1975.

Gold, P. E., & van Buskirk, R. B. Facilitation of time-dependent memory processes with posttrial epinephrine injections. *Behavioral Biology*, 1975, *13*, 145–153.

Gold, P. E., & van Buskirk, R. B. Enhancement and impairment of memory processes with posttrial injections of adrenocorticotrophic hormone. *Behavioral Biology*, 1976, *16*, 387–400.

Gold, P. E., & van Buskirk, R. B. Posttraining brain norepinephrine concentrations: Correlation with retention performance of avoidance training and with peripheral epinephrine modulation of memory processing. *Behavioral Biology*, 1978, *23*, 509–520.

Houghten, R. A., Swann, R. W., & Li, C. H. β-Endorphin: Stability, clearance behavior, and entry into the central nervous system after intravenous injection of the tritiated peptide in rats and rabbits. *Proceedings of the National Academy of Sciences, USA*, 1980, *77*, 4588–4591.

Izquierdo, I. Effect of naloxone and morphine on various forms of memory in the rat: Possible role of endogenous opiate mechanisms in memory consolidation. *Psychopharmacology*, 1979, *66*, 199–203.

Izquierdo, I. Effect of beta-endorphin and naloxone on acquisition, memory and retrieval of shuttle avoidance and habituation learning in rats. *Psychopharmacology*, 1980, *69*, 111–115.

Izquierdo, I. β-Endorphin and forgetting. *Trends in Pharmacological Sciences*, 1982, *3*,

Izquierdo, I., & Dias, R. D. Effect of ACTH, epinephrine, β-endorphin, naloxone, and of the combination of naloxone or β-endorphin with ACTH or epinephrine on memory consolidation. *Psychoneuroendocrinology*, 1982a, *7*,

Izquierdo, I., Dias, R. D. Memory modulation by tyramine and guanethidine and their interaction with α-methyl-*p*-tyrosine, β-endorphin and naloxone. *Behavioral and Neural Biology*, 1982b.

Izquierdo, I., Dias, R. D., Carrasco, M. A., Perry, M. L., Souza, D. O., Netto, C. A., & Wofchuk, S. T. Effects of beta-endorphin, Met-, Leu- and des-Tyr-Met-enkephalin on learned behaviors: One or more effects? In S. Saito & J. L. McGaugh (Eds.), *Pharmacology of learning and memory.* Amsterdam: Excerpta Medica, 1983.

Izquierdo, I., Dias, R. D., Perry, M. L., Souza, D. O., Elisabetsky, E., & Carrasco, M. A. A physiological amnesic mechanism mediated by endogenous opioid peptides and its possible role in learning. In C. Ajmone-Marsan & H. Matthies (Eds.), *Neuronal plasticity and memory formation.* New York: Raven Press, 1982.

Izquierdo, I., Perry, M. L., Dias, R. D., Souza, D. O., Elisabetsky, E., Carrasco, M. A., Orsingher, O. A., & Netto, C. A. Endogenous opioids, memory modulation and state dependency. In J. L. Martinez, Jr., R. A. Jensen, R. B. Messing, H. Rigter, & J. L. McGaugh (Eds.), *Endogenous peptides and learning and memory processes.* New York: Academic Press, 1981.

Izquierdo, I., Souza, D. O., Carrasco, M. A., Dias, R. D., Perry, M. L., Eisinger, S., Elisabetsky, E., & Vendite, D. A. Beta-endorphin causes retrograde amnesia and is released from the rat brain by various forms of training and stimulation. *Psychopharmacology*, 1980, *70*, 173–177.

Izquierdo, I., & Thaddeu, R. C. The effect of adrenaline, tyramine and guanethidine on two-way avoidance conditioning and on pseudoconditioning. *Psychopharmacologia*, 1975, *43*, 85–87.

Kety, S. S. Intelligence, biology and social responsibility. In J. Zubin (Ed.), *Psychopathology of mental development.* New York: Grune & Stratton, 1975.

Kety, S. S. The biogenic amines in the central nervous system: Their possible roles in arousal, emotion and learning. In F. O. Schmitt (Ed.), *The neurosciences: Second study program.* New York: Rockefeller University Press, 1970.

Kety, S. S. Biological concomitants of affective states and their possible role in memory processes. In M. Rosenzweig & E. L. Bennett (Eds.), *Neural mechanisms of learning and memory.* Cambridge, Mass.: MIT Press, 1976.

Langer, S. Z. Presynaptic receptors and modulation of neurotransmission: Pharmacological implications and therapeutic relevance. *Trends in Neuroscience*, 1980, *3*, 110–112.

Lucion, A. B., Rosito, G., Sapper, D. B., Palmini, A. L., & Izquierdo, I. Intracerebroventricular administration of nanogram amounts of β-endorphin and Met-enkephalin causes retrograde amnesia in rats. *Behavioral Brain Research*, 1982, *4*, 111–115.

McGaugh, J. L., & Herz, M. J. *Memory consolidation.* San Francisco: Albion, 1972.

McGaugh, J. L., Martinez, J. L., Jr., Jensen, R. A., Hannan, T. J., Vasquez, B. J., Messing, R. B., Liang, K. C., Brewton, C. B., & Spiehler, V. Modulation of memory storage by treatments affecting peripheral catecholamines. In C. Ajmone-Marsan & H. Matthies (Eds.), *Neuronal plasticity and memory formation.* New York: Raven Press, 1982.

Messing, R. B., Jensen, R. A., Martinez, J. L., Jr., Spiehler, V., Vasquez, B. J., Soumireu-Mourat, B., Liang, K. C., & McGaugh, J. L. Naloxone enhancement of memory. *Behavioral and Neural Biology*, 1979, *27*, 266–275.

Riccio, D. C., & Concannon, J. T. ACTH and the reminder phenomena. In J. L. Martinez, Jr., R. A. Jensen, R. B. Messing, H. Rigter, & J. L. McGaugh (Eds.), *Endogenous peptides and learning processes.* New York: Academic Press, 1981.

Rigter, H. Attenuation of amnesia in rats by systemically administered enkephalins. *Science*, 1978, 200, 83–85.

Rigter, H., Elbertse, R., & van Riezen, H. Time-dependent anti-amnestic effect of $ACTH_{4-10}$ and desglycinamide-lysine vasopressin. In W. H. Gispen, Tj. B. van Wimersma Greidanus, B. Bohus, & D. de Wied (Eds.), *Progress in brain research: Hormones, homeostasis and the brain.* Amsterdam: Elsevier, 1975.

Schneider, A. M. Recovery from retrograde amnesia: A behavioral analysis. In M. A. B. Brazier (Ed.), *Brain mechanisms in memory and learning: From the single neuron to man.* New York: Raven Press, 1979.

Schütz, R. A., Schütz, M. T. B., Orsingher, O. A., & Izquierdo, I. Brain dopamine and noradrenaline levels in rats submitted to four different aversive behavioral tests. *Psychopharmacology*, 1979, *63*, 289–292.

Snyder, S. H., & Childers, S. R. Opiate receptors and opioid peptides. *Annual Review of Neuroscience*, 1979, *2*, 35–64.

Spear, N. E. Retrieval of memory in animals. *Psychological Review*, 1973, *80*, 163–194.

Spear, N. E. *The processing of memories, forgetting and retention.* Hillsdale, N.J.: Erlbaum, 1978.

Squire, L. R., & Davis, H. P. The pharmacology of memory: A neurobiological perspective. *Annual Review of Pharmacology and Toxicology*, 1981, *21*, 323–356.

Tielen, A. M., Lopes da Silva, F. H., Bär, P. R., & Gispen, W. H. Long-lasting posttetanic potentiation in the dentate area of rat hippocampal slices and correlated changes in synaptic membrane phosphorylation. In C. Ajmone-Marsan & H. Matthies (Eds.), *Neuronal plasticity and memory formation.* New York: Raven Press, 1982.

Zornetzer, S. F. Neurotransmitter modulation and memory: A new neuropharmacological phrenology? In M. A. Lipton, A. Di Mascio, & K. F. Killam (Eds.), *Psychopharmacology: A generation of progress.* New York: Raven Press, 1978.

Critical Commentaries

CHAPTER TWENTY-ONE

Current Biochemical Approaches to Memory Formation

BERNARD W. AGRANOFF

The chapters in this volume are characterized by a diversity of experimental approaches—ample evidence of the multidisciplinary nature that has characterized contemporary memory research. The diversity might alternatively be interpreted to mean that to some extent we are grasping at straws in our attempts to unravel the brain's secrets. I believe there is some truth in each of these interpretations. My own latent interests in the biochemical basis of behavior was stimulated by my acquaintance with Ralph Gerard, a pioneer in the neurosciences, who was influential in bringing me to the University of Michigan a number of years ago. (He subsequently became Dean of the Graduate Division at the University of California at Irvine, at a time when its Department of Psychobiology was in its infancy.) Before I initiated studies on the effects of inhibitors of protein synthesis on behavior, a topic to which I shall return, I read the available literature on DNA and RNA content in the brains of various species. I was puzzled about why the human DNA complement was not much greater than that of creatures with less complicated brains, since this organ would seem to represent a good fraction of the body's complexity. We now know that the brain indeed contains more unique sequence RNA than does other organs (Brown & Church, 1971) and further, that its expression can be modified behaviorally (Grouse, Schrier, Bennett, Rosenzweig, & Nelson, 1978). At any rate, it seemed useful at the time to examine the DNA and RNA content of Tryon maze-"bright" and maze-"dull" rats. We first developed a method for measuring brain RNA and DNA accurately (Santen & Agranoff, 1963) and then contacted Mark Rosenzweig, who had access to populations of the two kinds of rats (see Bennett, Diamond, Krech, & Rosenzweig, 1964). He kindly sent them to us, and when they arrived in Ann Arbor, we recognized our first problem. The breeding out of maze-"bright" and maze-"dull" strains had segregated many genes. The two varieties did not look alike and had different body weights and brain sizes. Having progressed this far, we nevertheless pursued the experiment. A finding of interest (which we did not report) was that in decapitating the rats, the maze-"dull" rats strongly resisted putting their heads into the guillotine, while the maze-"bright" rats were most obliging! It is now 20 years since this initiation into the world of behavior, but I have

Bernard W. Agranoff. Neuroscience Laboratory, University of Michigan, Ann Arbor, Michigan.

remained cautious in referring to an animal as "smart" or "stupid," particularly without reference to a given task. As is the case for humans, there seems to be more than one kind of intelligence test for laboratory animals.

Figure 21-1 summarizes a number of paradigms that use blockers of macromolecular synthesis in a variety of species. The studies served to establish that inhibition of brain protein synthesis can separate memory that is associated with a learning session (short-term memory, STM) from that which is maintained between training session days (long-term memory, LTM). The distinction lies in their relative susceptibilities to disruption. STM formation is generally unaffected, even though the experimental subject may be synthesizing brain protein at only a fraction of its normal rate. In contrast, LTM formation is blocked. The effectiveness of the agents depends on how early or late they are given in relation to the training session, a finding that has led to the conclusion that LTM is formed or is consolidated shortly after the training session. Much has been written regarding the pros and cons of such pharmacological approaches to complex behavior (Agranoff, 1981; Dunn, 1980; Rose, 1981). The results of many experiments with blockers of protein synthesis and of a smaller number with blockers of RNA synthesis generally agree that these agents consistently distinguish between STM and LTM formation in various paradigms (usually aversive) in a number of species. Nevertheless, a few laboratories have continued behavioral studies with this interventive approach. The latter studies have been primarily directed at the possible localization of brain sites susceptible to the agents by means of microinjection, and studies on the depth

Figure 21-1. Diagrammatic representation of various training tasks used in connection with interventive and correlative approaches to the study of memory. (1) A headless arthropod preparation used to condition a position habit; (2) restoration of posture in the goldfish after a float is fixed to the lower jaw; (3) one-trial taste avoidance in the chick; (4) an automated shuttle-box task used to condition shock avoidance in the goldfish; (5) and (6) a jump-up active-avoidance task and a Y-maze discrimination task, respectively, used in mice. (From Agranoff, 1981.)

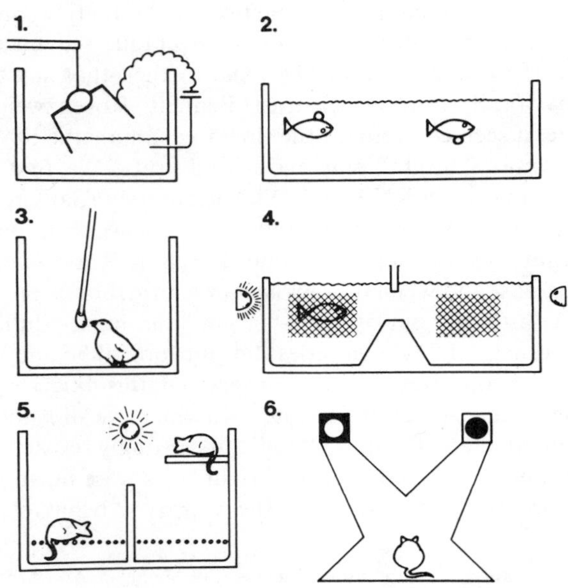

and duration of inhibition required to block LTM formation (Dunn, 1980; Rosenzweig & Bennett, Chapter 17, this volume).

A perhaps more cogent question raised by the interventive studies is regarding the nature of the critical protein-synthetic steps that might mediate LTM. Although experiments to answer this question have been attempted—for example, by means of double-labeling experiments with control and experimental animals—the needle has proved too small and the haystack too large. Unfortunately, we cannot yet distinguish whether the relevant disrupted steps in protein synthesis are related to the formation of specific "engrams" or are part of a general fixation signal or process. Some constraints on the possibilities can, however, be derived by inference. The known rates of *de novo* protein synthesis seem to be compatible with the temporal requirements for a process that mediates LTM formation (minutes to hours). Acquisition (STM formation) can, of course, occur much more rapidly, and it is therefore reasonable that this process be mediated by rapid posttranslational changes in preformed proteins in the region of the synapse, rather than by *de novo* syntheses of protein in the cell body. This has, in fact, been proposed (Agranoff, 1980) and demonstrated—for example, in protein phosphorylation in the mollusk (Hawkins & Kandel, Chapter 26, this volume), long-term potentiation in hippocampal slices (Baudry & Lynch, Chapter 28, this volume), and in whole rats undergoing training (Routtenberg, Chapter 33, this volume).

Although psychologists used the concepts of "short"- and "long"-term memory in human studies many years before they attempted to disrupt or enhance memory in animals, the terms deserve comment in relation to their use in studies on sensitization of the gill withdrawal response in *Aplysia*. Sensitization to a single exposure lasts for a few minutes or hours, whereas multiple exposures give rise to a long-lasting sensitization that may last for days or weeks (Pinsker, Hening, Carew, & Kandel, 1973). Note that in the interventive studies in a variety of species mentioned earlier, STM and LTM formation are conceived as two processes arising from the same training experience, whereas in the molluscan sensitization paradigm, "short"- and "long"-term memory describe the strength of a habit—what we might otherwise call partial learning, overtraining, and so forth. Presynaptic neurotransmitter release, second messenger activation, and protein phosphorylation have been correlated with this response in *Aplysia* (Hawkins & Kandel, Chapter 26, this volume). Mechanisms that explain the long-term behavioral effects are not yet apparent, since all of the biochemical changes observed thus far, even after multiple trials, appear to be of short duration (Eppler, Palazzolo, & Schwartz, 1982). Whether or not the habituation of long duration in *Aplysia* requires normally ongoing protein synthesis is an interesting question. It remains uncertain then whether the gill withdrawal habituation is a multiphasic process possessing STM and LTM components as defined in a number of other species, as discussed above.

Our laboratory has examined a model of neuronal growth in the goldfish that we hope will ultimately shed light on the nature of the biochemical basis of long-term behavioral change. The fish is well known for its ability to regenerate the axotomized optic nerve with great specificity and recovery of function. For biochemists, it provides the opportunity of examining changes that occur in CNS neurons that have been stimulated to elongate their processes and to re-form synaptic relationships. Of particular interest is the recent demonstration of growth-associated proteins (GAPs), which are axonally transported during regeneration in the toad (Skene & Willard, 1981b), and the goldfish visual system (Benowitz, Shashoua, & Yoon, 1981; Heacock & Agranoff, 1982; see Figure 21-2), as well as the rabbit hypoglossal nerve (Skene & Willard, 1981a). Might we anticipate the appearance of such proteins in relation to behavioral change, that is, in LTM formation? Although one could imagine that changing synaptic relationships indeed underlie behavioral change and that the cell body may well exert its control via transported proteins, there is little likelihood, even if we directed our search to identified GAPs, that we have reduced the size of the haystack significantly. It seems reasonable, however, to anticipate detection of such proteins under behavioral conditions known to affect brain structure, such as those of enriched compared with impoverished environmental conditions, an experimental paradigm pioneered by Krech, Rosenzweig, and Bennett (1962) in the rodent. Morphological alterations resulting from environmental manipulation have also been observed in the monkey (Floeter & Greenough, 1979), as well as in fish (Coss & Globus, 1978).

Although behavioral scientists have been studying a great variety of experimental species for many years, there has never been much question that their goal and that of the agencies that support their research has been to understand the functioning of the human brain. I would like to note the impressive progress that has been made in the detection of regional brain metabolism by the use of positron-labeled fluorodeoxyglucose visualized with a tomographic scanner. Positron emission tomography (PET) will certainly usher in a new era in the

Figure 21-2. Induction of increased axonal transport and of growth-associated proteins in the optic nerve of the goldfish following optic nerve crush. (A) Ten days after crush of the right optic nerve, increased rapid axonal transport can be detected in the left optic tectum. The regenerated nerve (postcrush, PC) transported much more labeled protein than the control (normal, N) side. (B) PAGE electrophoresis of the N and PC rapidly transported proteins. Markers (top to bottom) are M_r 68 K, 45 K, and 14 K. Note the prominent GAP at 43–45 K. Labeled tubulin and other proteins are transported in highly increased amounts by slow axonal flow (not shown). (From Heacock & Agranoff, 1982.)

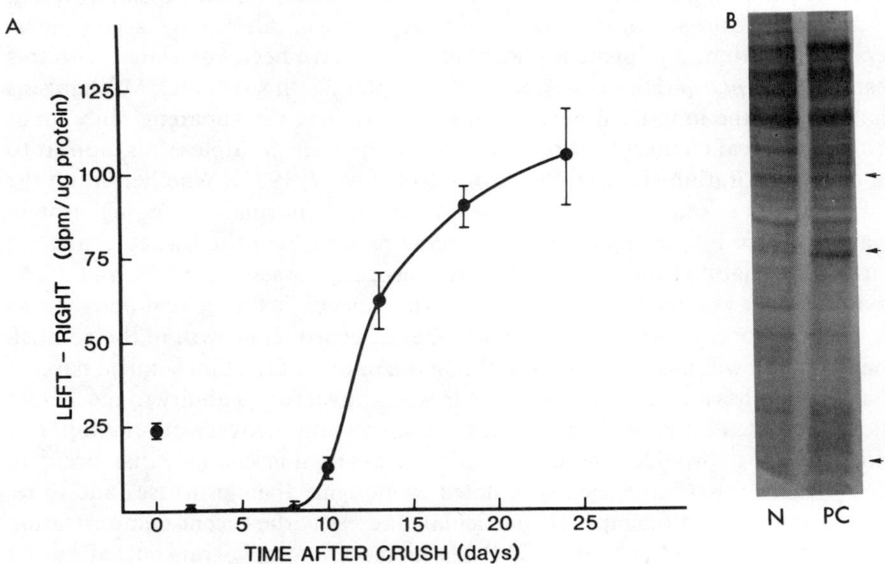

study of human behavior, extending the pioneering work of Kety, Sokoloff, Ingvar, Lassen, and others. We have seen but the tip of the iceberg. It will soon be possible to examine details of regional protein metabolism and neurotransmitter function under varying behavioral conditions (Phelps, Mazziotta, & Huang, 1982). In addition to refinements in PET scanning, great strides are also being made in other noninvasive modalities, for example, in nuclear magnetic resonance (NMR) imaging. This technique has no presently known damaging effects on the subject and can image the brain tomographically at high resolution comparable to that seen in the familiar X-ray CT scan. The drawback to NMR imaging is that the pictures that we have seen thus far demonstrate structure (the distribution of water and its physical state) in tissue rather than function. Technological progress has been rapid, however, and it may yet be possible to use NMR in a mode that images more interesting biomolecules, for example, ATP and phosphocreatine, via ^{31}P chemical shift data (Brownell, Budinger, Lauterber, & McGeer, 1982).

All in all, the next decade can be expected to be an exciting one in which neuropsychology forms a continuum with psychobiology, psychobiology with neuroscience, and neuroscience with biochemistry. We may even anticipate that neurological and psychiatric research may become less distinguishable than they are today.

REFERENCES

Agranoff, B. W. Biochemical events mediating the formation of short-term and long-term memory. In Y. Tsukada & B. W. Agranoff (Eds.), *Neurobiological basis of learning and memory*. New York: Wiley, 1980.

Agranoff, B. W. Learning and memory: Biochemical approaches. In G. J. Siegel, R. W. Albers, B. W. Agranoff, & R. Katzman (Eds.), *Basic neurochemistry* (3rd ed.). Boston: Little, Brown, 1981.

Bennett, E. L., Diamond, M. C., Krech, D., & Rosenzweig, M. R. Chemical and anatomical plasticity of brain. *Science*, 1964, *146*, 610–619.

Benowitz, L. I., Shashoua, V. E., & Yoon, M. G. Specific changes in rapidly transported proteins during regeneration of the goldfish optic nerve. *Journal of Neuroscience*, 1981, *1*, 300–307.

Brown, I. R., & Church, R. B. RNA transcription from nonrepetitive DNA in the mouse. *Biochemical and Biophysical Research Communications*, 1971, *42*, 850–856.

Brownell, G. L., Budinger, T. F., Lauterber, P. C., & McGeer, P. L. Positron tomography and nuclear resonance imaging. *Science*, 1982, *215*, 619–626.

Coss, R. G., & Globus, A. Spine stems on tectal interneurons in Jewel fish are shortened by social stimulation. *Science*, 1978, *200*, 787–790.

Dunn, A. J. Neurochemistry of learning and memory: An evaluation of relevant data. *Annual Review of Psychology*, 1980, *31*, 343–390.

Eppler, C. M., Palazzolo, M. J., & Schwartz, J. H. Characterization and localization of adenosine 3′:5′-monophosphate-binding proteins in the nervous system of *Aplysia*. *Journal of Neuroscience*, 1982, *2*, 1692–1704.

Floeter, M. K., & Greenough, W. T. Cerebellar plasticity: Modification of Purkinje cell structure by differential rearing in monkeys. *Science*, 1979, *206*, 227–229.

Grouse, L. D., Schrier, B. K., Bennett, E. L., Rosenzweig, M. R., & Nelson, P. G. Sequence diversity studies of rat brain RNA: Effects of environmental complexity on rat brain RNA diversity. *Journal of Neurochemistry*, 1978, *30*, 191–203.

Heacock, A. M., & Agranoff, B. W. Protein synthesis and transport in the regenerating goldfish visual system. *Neurochemical Research*, 1982, *7*, 771–788.

Krech, D., Rosenzweig, M. R., & Bennett, E. L. Relations between brain chemistry and problem-solving during rats raised in enriched and impoverished environments. *Journal of Comparative and Physiological Psychology*, 1962, *55*, 801–807.

Phelps, M. E., Mazziotta, J. C., & Huang, S.-C. Study of cerebral function with positron computed tomography. *Journal of Cerebral Blood Flow and Metabolism*, 1982, *2*, 113–162.

Pinsker, H. M., Hening, W. A., Carew, T. J., & Kandel, E. R. Long-term sensitization of a defensive withdrawal reflex in *Aplysia*. *Science*, 1973, *182*, 1039–1042.

Rose, S. P. R. What should a biochemistry of memory and learning be about? *Neuroscience*, 1981, *6*, 811–821.

Santen, R. J., & Agranoff, B. W. Studies on the estimation of deoxyribonucleic acid and ribonucleic acid in rat brain. *Biochimica et Biophysica Acta*, 1963, *72*, 251–262.

Skene, J. H. P., & Willard, M. Axonally transported proteins associated with axon growth in rabbit central and peripheral nervous systems. *Journal of Cell Biology*, 1981a, *89*, 96–103.

Skene, J. H. P., & Willard, M. Characteristics of growth-associated polypeptides in regenerating toad retinal ganglion cell axons. *Journal of Neuroscience*, 1981b, *1*, 419–426.

CHAPTER TWENTY-TWO

Whatever Happened to the Engram?

ADRIAN J. DUNN

Time was when the goal of many research projects was to determine the nature of the engram, the physical "substrate" of memory. The idea that specific molecules encoded specific memories never found favor with most neurobiologists, but most did believe that to make a permanent memory, synthesis of new macromolecules (e.g., new structural proteins) would be required. These would underlie any permanent changes in synaptic connectivity or axonal or dendritic morphology (e.g., see the work of Greenough, Chapter 32, this volume). The question was whether this new synthesis (not different macromolecules) could be detected among the high ongoing rate of macromolecular synthesis in the brain, that is, the needle in the haystack problem (Agranoff, Burrell, Dokas, & Springer, 1978; Dunn, 1976).

Now that the dust has settled on many of the putative molecular correlates of learning of the past, I perceive two separate biochemistries of memory. In one, now confined almost exclusively to studies in simple systems, the goal is to detect molecular changes correlated with plasticity, normally electrophysiological changes that can easily be translated into behavioral ones. In the other, predominant in higher organisms, the focus is on the factors that modulate memory.

Should we go to *Aplysia* for the engram? The work of Hawkins and Kandel (Chapter 26, this volume) in the abdominal ganglion is an elegant example of how changes in synaptic function can result in changes in behavior, and hence result in certain forms of memory. One can argue, as many have, whether the forms of behavioral adaptation demonstrated by Kandel and his colleagues are analogous to learning in higher organisms, but the importance of the work is that at least certain forms of behavioral adaptation can be explained in terms of synaptic physiology. Whether similar mechanisms underlie learning in higher organisms remains to be seen, but an important tool will be the analysis of the molecular correlates of the adaptation in *Aplysia.* When these have been fully worked out, and they appear to be within experimental reach, the same or related molecules can be studied in other systems. What then is the engram in Kandel's model? Is it the altered synapse, or the altered release of neurotransmitter? Is it the altered content of cyclic AMP or the activation of a protein kinase? Or is it the presumed phosphoprotein? In a sense, all of the

Adrian J. Dunn. Department of Neuroscience, University of Florida, Gainesville, Florida.

above possibilities (and more) are correct. However, from an experimental point of view, the most useful will be the phosphoprotein.

Could the engram be a phosphoprotein? It is intriguing that the work on hippocampal long-term potentiation (LTP) described by Baudry and Lynch (Chapter 28, this volume) has also linked a phosphoprotein to the electrophysiological change. The same protein (α-subunit of pyruvate dehydrogenase, PDH) seems to be behaviorally responsive, according to the work of Routtenberg (Chapter 33, this volume). However, a number of problems confound the simple interpretation. It is not clear why LTP at selected synapses, or behavioral treatments, should affect such a high proportion of hippocampal PDH, which is an essential glycolytic enzyme in both neurons and glia. Also, whereas the phosphoprotein described by Hawkins and Kandel (Chapter 26, this volume) seems likely to be part of the plasma membrane, PDH is a soluble mitochondrial enzyme. Moreover, other work with the hippocampal slice has identified a different phosphoprotein altered during LTP (Lopes da Silva, Bär, Tielen, & Gispen, 1982). Fortunately, all these problems are ultimately answerable with current techniques.

Turning to the second biochemistry of memory, what do we really mean by *modulation* of memory? It arises because performance of an acquired task can be affected by so many endogenous and exogenous factors (see Dunn, 1980, and Gold, Chapter 25, this volume; McGaugh, Liang, Bennett, & Sternberg, Chapter 19, this volume; and Izquierdo, Chapter 20, this volume). Experimentally, memory is not absolute, but its strength seems to be variable on a continuous scale. Reversal of amnestic treatments is commonplace and has been reported for all established amnestic treatments (see Dunn, 1980) so that we cannot be sure when an animal ever totally loses a memory.

Modulation refers to altering the *retrievability* of a memory. Retrievability is clearly affected by both the storage and retrieval processes. To what do we attribute increased strength or retrievability of memory? Is it the laying down of multiple traces (engrams) so that it is easier to find one of them? Or is it more readily retrievable because it is better connected? Does rehearsal increase the number of engrams, or merely the connections? These questions are currently unanswered. But we do know much about the factors that influence effective retrieval. The work of de Wied (Chapter 18, this volume), Gold (Chapter 25, this volume), and McGaugh and colleagues (Chapter 19, this volume) has clearly indicated that hormones known to be released during the stress of the experience (such as epinephrine, norepinephrine, ACTH, and perhaps vasopressin) can alter subsequent retention performance. A case has been made that the endogenous hormones may act in this way. Surprising perhaps is the inverted-U function seen in dose–response curves with the exogenous, or exogenous plus endogenous, hormones. It is tempting to invoke state dependence. Indeed, the results of Izquierdo (Chapter 20, this volume) amount to a sophisticated state-dependence model, but the extent to which the correct balance of circulating hormones can influence retrieval exhibited in this work is astounding. The problem is that whatever process accounts for the down leg of the curve, it must be distinct from that of the up phase.

The mechanism of none of these effects is known. Because of the constraints of the blood–brain barrier, none of the hormones will penetrate the brain in quantity, although small and possibly significant amounts will get through (Dunn, 1978). The alternatives are (1) that the hormones may act on the several regions of the brain that lack such a barrier; these include (in addition to the pineal and the pituitary, which are not technically "brain") the hypothalamic median eminence, the area postrema, the organum vasculosum laminae terminalis, and a variety of other midline circumventricular structures; (2) that the hormones alter cerebral bloodflow or vascular permeability—for which there is evidence (see Dunn, 1984); (3) that the primary site of action of the hormones is peripheral and that secondary neural or endocrine factors act on the CNS. ACTH has a variety of effects on brain chemistry, including protein synthesis, catecholamine metabolism, and a variety of other neurochemicals, some of which may be related to the effects on memory (Dunn, 1984). It may be significant that the catecholamines and ACTH are all part of the stress response. Because this response seems likely to have an important role in adaptation, it is not at all surprising that these hormones should modulate memory (see Dunn & Kramarcy, 1984).

Although perhaps not fundamental, the work on modulation may be of great importance for clinical aspects of memory. Because it is doubtful if nervous systems lacking the basic capacity to memorize could survive, most human problems with memory probably concern modulation.

Can we reconcile these two biochemistries of memory? I think not. It appears most likely that the modulatory effects occur during the storage process, but what do they affect? Is norepinephrine (or another endogenous hormone) a factor essential or facilitatory for neuroplasticity as suggested by the work of Kasamatsu, Pettigrew, and Ary (1981)? If so, does it affect the phosphoprotein engram? Or does it alter the transition between temporary (short-term) phosphoprotein memories and more stable (long-term) forms? We cannot disregard the wealth of evidence that retrograde actions on memory (at least as determined by performance) are time-locked to the experience, even though the time scale is subject to modulation (see Gold, Chapter 25, this volume). Thus, something must change, but current phosphoprotein models do not speak to this. Although hippocampal LTP has been shown to persist for weeks or more, whether the phosphoprotein changes have a similar duration is not known. Investigation of this phenomenon may provide important clues.

This essay has raised many questions and no answers. However, I have tried to put in perspective the important issues of the chemistry of memory. The engram is not dead yet!

REFERENCES

Agranoff, B. W., Burrell, H. R., Dokas, L. A., & Springer, A. D. Progress in biochemical approaches to learning and memory. In M. A. Lipton, A. DiMascio, & K. F. Killman (Eds.), *Psychopharmacology: A generation of progress*. New York: Raven Press, 1978.

Dunn, A. J. The chemistry of learning and the formation of memory. In W. H. Gispen (Ed.), *Molecular and functional neurobiology*. Amsterdam: Elsevier, 1976.

Dunn, A. J. (Commentary) Peptides and behavior: A critical analysis of research strategies. *Neurosciences Research Program Bulletin*, 1978, *16*, 490–635.

Dunn, A. J. Neurochemistry of learning and memory: An evaluation of recent data. *Annual Review of Psychology*, 1980, *31*, 343–390.

Dunn, A. J. Effects of ACTH, β-lipotropin, and related peptides on the central nervous system. In C. B. Nemeroff & A. J. Dunn (Eds.), *Peptides, hormones and behavior: Molecular and behavioral neuroendocrinology*. New York: Spectrum, 1984.

Dunn, A. J., & Kramarcy, N. R. Neurochemical responses in stress: Relationships between the hypothalamic–pituitary–adrenal and catecholamine systems. In L. L. Iversen, S. D. Iversen,

& S. H. Snyder (Eds.), *Handbook of psychopharmacology* (Vol. 18). New York: Plenum Press, 1984.

Kasamatsu, T., Pettigrew, J. D., & Ary, M. Cortical recovery from effects of monocular deprivation: Acceleration with norepinephrine and suppression with 6-hydroxydopamine. *Journal of Neurophysiology*, 1981, *45*, 254–266.

Lopes da Silva, F. H., Bär, P. R., Tielen, A. M., & Gispen, W. H. Changes in membrane phosphorylation correlated with long-lasting potentiation in rat hippocampal slices. In W. H. Gispen & A. Routtenberg (Eds.), *Progress in brain research* (Vol. 56). Amsterdam: Elsevier, 1982.

CHAPTER TWENTY-THREE

Human Learning and Memory Dysfunction: Neurochemical Changes in Senile Dementia

LESLIE L. IVERSEN / MARTIN N. ROSSOR

THE EFFECTS OF VASOPRESSIN ON LEARNING AND MEMORY AND ITS DISTRIBUTION IN HUMAN BRAIN

Professor de Wied and his colleagues have pioneered studies of the effects of peptides on animal behavior. Their extensive work on the effects of vasopressin in maintaining learned avoidance behavior and in memory consolidation (reviewed in Chapter 18) has been particularly important. However, controversy has arisen concerning the interpretation of the significance of these experimental findings. Does the ability of vasopressin to affect the retention of a learned task necessarily imply an action on the memory process itself, or might it result secondarily from some other primary site of action? Must the effects of a systemically administered peptide necessarily be attributed to a central action, or might the peptide act indirectly via some peripheral target? The latter seems a real possibility, as Le Moal and colleagues (1981) found that the effects of subcutaneously injected vasopressin in prolonging the extinction of avoidance behavior in rats could be blocked by peripherally acting vasopressin antagonists. Furthermore, the behavioral effects occurred at doses of vasopressin large enough to trigger vasopressor responses, suggesting that signals from peripheral visceral sources might have an important role in triggering the subsequent behavioral changes. Discussion also focused on the question of why, if vasopressin acts on a fundamental component of learning and memory mechanisms, its effects are only seen when learning occurs in response to punishment rather than to positive reinforcers? Might it have to do with the induction of a state of fear or anxiety, associated with heightened arousal, in the animal subject?

Most of these questions cannot yet be answered. Vasopressin does seem to exist in neurons and nerve terminals in many regions of the central nervous system outside the hypothalamus (Sofroniew & Weindl, 1978) and undoubtedly will prove to play some role other than a neuroendocrine one in these locations. We have measured vasopressin-like immunoreactivity in human postmortem brain samples (Rossor, Iversen, Hawthorn, Ang, & Jenkins, 1981). The levels were too low to be reliably measured in most of the 42 different brain regions examined, but the peptide could be detected in substantial concentrations in the

Leslie L. Iversen. Neuroscience Research Centre, Merck Sharpe & Dohme Ltd., Herts, England. Martin N. Rossor. MRC Neurochemical Pharmacology Unit, Medical Research Council Centre, Medical School, Cambridge, England. Present address: Department of Neurology, Kings College Hospital, London SE5, England.

locus ceruleus, substantia nigra, periaqueductal gray, and the lateral segment of globus pallidus (Table 23-1). The presence of substantial concentrations of vasopressin in the catecholamine nuclei of brain stem is particularly interesting and suggests a possible role of vasopressin in regulating the activity of central adrenergic neurons. When a series of brain samples from patients dying with senile dementia of Alzheimer type (SDAT) was examined, no significant differences in vasopressin content were found between the dementia and control groups, except in globus pallidus (Table 23-1). The impairment of learning and memory functions in such patients thus does not seem likely to be related to an abnormality of brain vasopressin.

THE CHOLINERGIC HYPOTHESIS OF DEMENTIA

There is an urgent need to obtain a better understanding of the nature of the pathological changes that underlie the loss of learning and memory function in the elderly. SDAT is the commonest form of senile dementia, and until recently little was known of the neurochemical changes that accompany it. In the last 5 years, however, this has changed as several groups have consistently observed abnormalities in cholinergic systems in postmortem brain, using the stable biosynthetic enzyme choline acetyltransferase (ChAT) as a marker for cholinergic neurons. The original observations of reduced ChAT activity in cortex and hippocampus (Bowen, Smith, White, & Davison, 1976; Davies & Maloney, 1976; Perry, Tomlinson, Blessed, Bergmann, Gibson, & Perry, 1978) have been confirmed by our own studies on a large series of control and SDAT cases in the Cambridge dementia project (Rossor, Garrett, Johnson, Mountjoy, Roth, & Iversen, 1982). We have also been able to confirm the important observation, first reported by Perry *et al.* (1978), that the extent of the cholinergic deficit, as measured by ChAT loss, correlates with severity of illness, as measured by the density of senile plaques present in cortex and hippocampus, or by premortem clinical ratings.

In our studies, involving about 50 SDAT cases and an equal number of age-matched controls, we find that ChAT activity is reduced by 40–60% in all regions of cerebral cortex and in hippocampus but is relatively unaffected in

Table 23-1. Arginine vasopression (AVP) content of control and SDAT postmortem human brain

	AVP content (pmol/g tissue)	
Brain region	Control	SDAT
Hypothalamus	37.73 ± 6.83	26.44 ± 6.05
Locus ceruleus	9.82 ± 1.44	7.24 ± 1.76
Substantia nigra–pars compacta	3.08 ± 0.43	2.30 ± 0.42
Substantia nigra–pars reticulata	2.04 ± 0.42	1.58 ± 0.38
Periaqueductal gray	0.54 ± 0.15	0.70 ± 0.24
Globus pallidus (lateral)	0.67 ± 0.14	0.27 ± 0.07[a]

Note. Values obtained by radioimmunoassay in acid extracts of frozen brain tissue (Rossor, Iversen, Hawthorn, Ang, & Jenkins, 1981) are means ± *SEM* for 10–17 brains. SDAT, senile dementia of Alzheimer type. Data from Rossor, Iversen, Mountjoy, Roth, Hawthorn, Ang, and Jenkins (1980).

[a] $p < .05$ when compared with control.

Table 23-2. Cerebral cortical choline acetyltransferase (ChAT) activities in Alzheimer disease in relation to age

Brodmann area	Percentage reductions from control values		
	Age < 79 years	Age > 79 years	
Frontal cortex			
4	62	(22)	
6	66	(17)	
8	73	(19)	
9	65	(31)	
10	63	(13)	NS
11	61	(31)	
24	59	(30)	
25	53	(17)	
32	61	(20)	
Temporal cortex			
20	66	49	
21	71	48	
22	73	45	
28	67	46	
38	71	44	

Note. Reductions in ChAT activity significant ($p < .01$) except for those for frontal cortical areas in the older age group, shown in parentheses. NS, not significant. Data from Rossor, Iversen, Johnson, Mountjoy, and Roth (1981).

most subcortical areas of brain. There is a striking and paradoxical relationship between the severity of the cholinergic deficit and age, with the youngest SDAT cases exhibiting the most widespread and severe abnormalities (Rossor, Iversen, Johnson, Mountjoy, & Roth, 1981; Rossor *et al.*, 1982). Indeed, in older patients (>79 years at death) in our series, large areas of cerebral cortex, including the entire frontal pole, show no significant loss of ChAT (Table 23-2). This is unrelated to the normal pattern of change in ChAT activity with age in human brain—we have observed surprisingly little change in ChAT in normal aging, the only cortical areas to show a significant decline with age being frontal cortex (Brodmann areas 8 and 10). In some cortical regions in the SDAT group there was even a paradoxical *increase* in ChAT activity with increasing age (Rossor, Iversen, Johnson, Mountjoy, & Roth, 1981; Rossor *et al.*, 1982).

The cholinergic deficit in SDAT may represent the selective loss or damage of part of the ascending projection to cortex that arises from a sheet of cholinergic cells deep in the forebrain, in the nucleus basalis of Meynert (Coyle, Price, & DeLong, 1983). Whitehouse and co-workers (1982) described a severe loss of cells from this nucleus in a small number of young SDAT cases (Whitehouse, Price, Struble, Clark, Coyle, & DeLong, 1982), but Perry *et al.* (1983) were unable to confirm this observation. In view of the age-dependency of the cholinergic changes, one might expect considerable variability in cell loss from the nucleus basalis, and further studies are clearly needed.

OTHER NEUROCHEMICAL ABNORMALITIES IN ALZHEIMER DISEASE

The cholinergic deficit is not the only neurochemical change in Alzheimer disease. Other afferent projections to cerebral cortex, including the noradrenergic fibers that arise from locus ceruleus (Bondareff, Mountjoy, & Roth,

1981) and the serotonin-containing fibers from raphe nuclei (Benton *et al.*, 1982) may also be damaged. There are variable changes in markers of intrinsic cortical interneurons. Thus, gamma-aminobutyric acid (GABA) and somatostatin concentrations are reduced in some areas of cerebral cortex, but two other intrinsic cortical neuropeptides, vasoactive intestinal polypeptide and cholecystokinin, are present in normal concentrations (Rossor, 1982; Rossor *et al.*, 1982; Coyle *et al.*, 1983). Our most recent analyses suggest that these other neurochemical abnormalities, like the cholinergic deficit, are most widespread and severe in the younger SDAT patients. Senile dementia of old age (>80 years at death) appears to represent a relatively "pure" cholinergic lesion, with little significant change in GABA or noradrenaline. This suggests that the now common convention of considering Alzheimer disease as part of a continuum with senile dementia of old age may be misleading. Neuropathological studies (Hubbard & Anderson, 1981) have also pointed to marked differences between these two groups: The cortical neuropathological changes were most widespread and severe in SDAT patients who died below the age of 80, whereas in the over-80 group there was little evidence for widespread loss of cortical tissue, and neuropathological changes tended to be confined to the temporal lobe.

SIGNIFICANCE OF THE NEUROCHEMICAL FINDINGS ON SDAT

The study of postmortem brains from patients dying with SDAT has begun to throw new light on the nature of the changes that occur in the brain in this condition. The evidence for loss or damage to ascending monoaminergic inputs to cerebral cortex is particularly intriguing. Although the function of these pathways is far from clear, there is circumstantial evidence linking both the cholinergic and noradrenergic projections with learning and memory functions (Rossor, 1982; Coyle *et al.*, 1983). It is known that cholinergic blocking drugs can cause a syndrome of short-term memory impairment similar to that seen in dementia, and there have already been attempts to test "cholinergic replacement therapy" in SDAT, so far without any notable success (Bartus, Dean, Beer, & Lippa, 1982). The complex pattern of other neurochemical changes in young SDAT patients suggests that this approach may be more likely to hold promise for the senile dementia of old age.

REFERENCES

Bartus, R. T., Dean, R. L., Beer, B., & Lippa, A. S. The cholinergic hypothesis of geriatric memory dysfunction. *Science*, 1982, *217*, 408–417.

Benton, J. S., Bowen, D. M., Allen, S. J., Haan, E. A., Davison, A. N., Neary, D., Murphy, R. P., & Snowden, J. S. Alzheimer's disease as a disorder of isodendritic core. *Lancet*, 1982, *1*, 456.

Bondareff, W., Mountjoy, C. Q., & Roth, M. Selective loss of neurones of origin of adrenergic projection to cerebral cortex (nucleus locus coeruleus) in senile dementia. *Lancet*, 1981, *1*, 783–784.

Bowen, D. M., Smith, C. B., White, P., & Davison, A. N. Neurotransmitter-related enzymes and indices of hypoxia in senile dementia and other abiotrophies. *Brain*, 1976, *99*, 459–466.

Coyle, J. T., Price, D. L., & DeLong, M. R. Alzheimer's disease: A disorder of cortical cholinergic innervation. *Science*, 1983, *219*, 1184–1190.

Davies, P., & Maloney, A. J. Selective loss of central cholinergic neurones in Alzheimer's disease. *Lancet*, 1976, *2*, 1403.

Hubbard, B. M., & Anderson, J. M. A quantitative study of cerebral atrophy in old age and senile dementia. *Journal of the Neurological Sciences*, 1981, *50*, 135–145.

Le Moal, M., Koob, G. F., Koda, L. Y., Bloom, F. E., Manning, M., Sawyer, W. H., & Rivier, J. Vasopressor receptor antagonist prevents behavioural effects of vasopressin. *Nature*, 1981, *291*, 491–493.

Perry, R. H., Candy, J. M., Perry, E. K., Irving, D., Blessed, G., Fairbairn, A. F., & Tomlinson, B. E. Extensive loss of choline acetyltransferase activity is not reflected by neuronal loss in the nucleus of Meynert in Alzheimer's disease. *Neuroscience Letters*, 1983, *29*, 311–315.

Perry, E. K., Tomlinson, B. E., Blessed, G., Bergmann, K., Gibson, P. H., & Perry, R. H. Correlation of cholinergic abnormalities with senile plaques and mental test scores in senile dementia. *British Medical Journal*, 1978, *2*, 1457–1459.

Rossor, M. N. Neurotransmitters and CNS disease: Dementia. *Lancet*, 1982, *2*, 1200–1204.

Rossor, M. N., Garrett, N. J., Johnson, A. L., Mountjoy, C. Q., Roth, M., & Iversen, L. L. A post-mortem study of the cholinergic and GABA systems in senile dementia. *Brain*, 1982, *105*, 313–330.

Rossor, M. N., Iversen, L. L., Hawthorn, J., Ang, V. Y., & Jenkins, J. S. Extrahypothalamic vasopressin in human brain. *Brain Research*, 1981, *214*, 349–355.

Rossor, M. N., Iversen, L. L., Johnson, A. J., Mountjoy, C. Q., & Roth, M. Cholinergic deficit in frontal cerebral cortex in Alzheimer's disease is age dependent. *Lancet*, 1981, *2*, 1422.

Rossor, M. N., Iversen, L. L., Mountjoy, C. Q., Roth, M., Hawthorn, J., Ang, V. Y., & Jenkins, J. S. Arginine vasopressin and choline acetyltransferase in brains of patients with Alzheimer type senile dementia. *Lancet*, 1980, *2*, 1367–1368.

Sofroniew, M. V., & Weindl, A. Projections from the parvocellular vasopressin and neurophysin-containing neurons of the suprachiasmatic nucleus. *American Journal of Anatomy*, 1978, *153*, 391–430.

Whitehouse, P. J., Price, D. L., Struble, R. G., Clark, A. W., Coyle, J. T., & DeLong, M. R. Alzheimer's disease and senile dementia: Loss of neurons in the basal forebrain. *Science*, 1982, *215*, 1237–1239.

CHAPTER TWENTY-FOUR

Current Perspectives on Memory Systems and Their Modulation

MICHELA GALLAGHER

In neurobiological research on memory the concept of modulation has gained increasing recognition. It is the purpose of this brief discussion to sketch the evolution of this concept and to outline some suggestions for future work that may lead to a clearer delineation of the biological events that are now viewed as modulatory in function.

As evidenced by the research discussed in this volume, the concept of memory modulation has grown primarily out of work designed to investigate memory consolidation. In many studies modeled after clinical descriptions of retrograde amnesia, it was demonstrated that a variety of posttraining treatments can alter retention of recent learning in laboratory animals. Originally, this research was directed toward determining the specific sites and mechanisms that preserve information in the brain. The concept of modulation appears to have emerged to denote that in addition to the neural systems within which the content of memory is preserved, other systems may be involved in memory processes by serving a more trophic function (Gold & McGaugh, 1975, 1978; Kety, 1970, 1976; McGaugh & Gold, 1976). In other words, a system that modulates memory is not one that contains specific information about an experience, and does not itself undergo any persistent long-term change in function. Rather, a modulating system may, in some way, regulate the extent to which changes will occur in neural circuits that are capable of preserving information for the life of a memory. Within this theoretical framework, modification of memory by posttraining treatments may not necessarily reveal the identity of systems that contain information in memory. Alternatively, such treatments may identify systems that serve to activate, amplify, or suppress change at still unspecified sites.

The validity of the concept of memory modulation is at present supported mainly by findings that indicate a dissociation between some sites where manipulations can modify memory and systems that could provide a plausible substrate for the content of memory. For example, many investigations have now reported that the functional state of hormonal systems outside the central nervous system can profoundly affect time-dependent memory processes (for a

Michela Gallagher. Department of Psychology, University of North Carolina, Chapel Hill, North Carolina.

recent review see McGaugh, 1983). Peripherally administered hormones and pharmacological agents that act peripherally have been found to alter retention across a variety of species and tasks. These results may indicate that the neurobiological events underlying memory storage are influenced by the functional state of widespread systems. At least these results would seem to illustrate that the specific sites where memory content is preserved may not necessarily be revealed by locating systems that are capable of modifying retention.

The concept of modulation also appears to be compatible with the recognized features of temporal lobe amnesia in man (Scoville & Milner, 1957). In such clinical cases established memories persist in the presence of a marked impairment in the ability to preserve new information encountered after temporal lobe damage. The fact that memories established prior to temporal lobe damage remain intact may be taken to suggest that the content of memory is not normally preserved within these structures. However, it appears that the preservation of certain information in other brain systems may depend on intact function in the temporal lobe. This description is consistent with the general idea that memory processes require not only a neural substrate that is capable of preserving the content of memory but may also include systems that regulate the capacity for change. Within the framework of memory modulation, the brain of the temporal lobe amnesic may be lacking functionally intact systems that normally regulate the capacity for change at extratemporal lobe sites that preserve information.

Although modulation provides a framework for interpreting findings such as those outlined so far in this discussion, ultimately the validity of the concept of memory modulation depends on a more direct demonstration. It remains to be established whether mechanisms that store information in memory are regulated by the functional state of systems that are now considered to be candidate modulators. This is a difficult question to address, since the relevant sites and mechanisms underlying memory for the kinds of training experiences typically used in research on memory consolidation are not known. Indeed, at present it may be fruitful to consider other approaches to research on modulation of neural changes in the nervous system that could be utilized in memory processes.

Specific examples of modulation of neural change can now be cited from research using invertebrate systems. In his paper, Krasne (1978) assembled evidence from work on invertebrates that provides strong support for the notion that the capacity for change in simple neural circuits is regulated. Based on these findings Krasne (1978) proposed that mechanisms that control the plastic properties of inherently malleable neurons may be a general feature of neural systems. Since sites of change underlying simple forms of learning are being elucidated in a number of invertebrate species, work in such systems may lead to further advances in our understanding of how changes that specifically preserve learning are regulated.

At the same time, as reflected in many chapters in this volume, progress is being made in research that has taken a model systems approach in mammals. Some of this work is currently focused on the use of intact animals that learn simple conditioned responses. Other research has concentrated on forms of neural change such as long-term potentiation that may be likely candidate mechanisms for preserving information. To these may be added research in developing animals that exhibit experience-dependent changes in neural organization and function during critical periods. All of these lines of investigation have in common an interst in localizing specific sites of persisting change in the mammalian nervous system. It seems likely that these model systems may, as such sites and mechanisms become better defined, prove extremely useful for the study of modulating influences. In fact a shift in this direction is already apparent. For example, the influence of one candidate modulating system in the brain, the norepinephrine (NE) system, has recently been investigated on the developmentally linked plastic properties of neurons in visual cortex (Pettigrew & Kasamatsu, 1978) as well as on the development and retention of long-term potentiation (Chepkova & Skrebitsy, 1982; Goddard, Bliss, Robertson, & Sutherland, 1980). Norepinephrine has also been found to enhance neural responses in hippocampus that are evoked by a stimulus paired with food reward (Segal & Bloom, 1976). Although the concept of memory modulation largely grew out of one particular approach to the study of memory, establishing the validity of this concept and determining the specific mechanisms involved may benefit from the adoption of other approaches.

A second direction for future research may be suggested that could be accomplished by using prevailing methods for studying memory modulation. At present, there is extensive evidence that treatments that affect a wide variety of systems in both the periphery and central nervous system are capable of modifying memory processes (for recent reviews see Dunn, 1980; McGaugh, 1983; Squire & Davis, 1981). It is not known to what extent various systems that appear to participate in memory processes do so independently of one another or to what extent some may be functionally related. However, interest in this question has recently emerged. In the final section of this discussion one substrate that may functionally link a number of modulating systems will be discussed. This substrate is provided by the brain NE system.

The assertion that brain NE function is involved in memory processes is not without controversy. The relevant issues have been discussed in several recent reviews and will not be detailed here (Dunn, 1980; McGaugh, 1983; Squire & Davis, 1981). However, as indicated in these reviews, it is clear that a variety of posttraining treatments that alter NE function affect retention of recent learning. There is also evidence that changes in the activity of this neurochemical system are evoked by training procedures. For the purpose of this discussion, an additional interesting finding is that manipulations of brain NE systems have recently been found to alter the effects of other treatments on memory processes. At present, there is some evidence indicating that the effects on memory processes of treatments aimed at altering either vasopressin or opioid peptide activity are dependent on brain NE function.

Vasopressin has received considerable interest as a potential modulator of memory processes (see de Wied & Bohus, 1979; de Wied, Chapter 18, this volume). A number of investigations have indicated that enhancement of retention produced by post-training vasopressin administration is abolished by interference with NE activity (see Bohus, Conti, Kovács, & Versteeg, 1982, and Kovács, Bohus, & Versteeg, 1979, for an overview of this research). Either administration of pharmacological agents that decrease NE or destruction of ascending NE projections to the forebrain produced by 6-hydroxydopamine (6-OHDA) lesions of the dorsal noradrenergic bundle have been found to block the effects of vasopressin in rats. In other studies it has been reported that vasopressin administration alters NE activity, as reflected in an increase in turnover in several brain regions (Tanaka, de Kloet, de Wied, & Versteeg, 1977). Other recent studies are providing additional anatomical and electrophysiological data that may provide a basis for significant interactions between these systems in brain (Olpe & Baltzer, 1981; Sofroniew, 1980; Sawchenko & Swanson, 1981).

Evidence for interactions between opioid peptides and NE-containing neurons in brain is already quite substantial. Opioid-peptide-containing neurons synapse directly onto NE cells in the locus ceruleus (LC) and A2 regions (Pickel, Segal, & Bloom, 1979). Electrophysiological studies indicate that opiate receptors on NE cells serve an inhibitory function (Bird & Kuhar, 1977; Pepper & Henderson, 1980). In addition, in brain regions innervated by NE terminals, opiate receptor mechanisms inhibit the evoked release of NE (for review see Starke, 1979), and the loss of opiate receptors in such regions following NE denervation has suggested the presence of presynaptic opiate receptors on NE terminals (Llorens, Martres, Baudry, & Schwartz, 1978).

Numerous studies have now reported that posttraining opiate manipulations alter time-dependent memory processes (for reviews see Gallagher & Kapp, 1981; Squire & Davis, 1981). An interesting finding that has emerged in this research is that either impairment or enhancement of retention can be obtained with low doses of opiate agonists and antagonists, respectively. Given the briefly summarized evidence linking opioid peptide and NE systems in brain, the possibility may be raised that the effects of opiate manipulations on memory are due to the regulation of NE activity by opiate receptor mechanisms. Some initial support for this suggestion was provided by Izquierdo and Graudenz (1980), who found that enhancement of retention produced by administration of an opiate antagonist was prevented by concurrent treatment with a norepinephrine antagonist, *dl*-propranolol. These investigators concluded that opiate antagonist administration may normally enhance retention by releasing NE neurons from inhibition by opioid peptides. Extending this original finding, we have recently demonstrated that 6-OHDA lesions of the dorsal noradrenergic bundle likewise prevent the effect of opiate antagonist administration on time-dependent memory processes (Rapp & Gallagher, 1983).

At present it is not clear whether specific components of the brain NE system may be differentially involved in modulating functions. Lesions of the dorsal noradrenergic bundle are assumed to primarily disrupt LC projections to forebrain. However, non-LC projections are also affected by such lesions. That this is the case is due to the fact that the ascending projections of the LC and lateral tegmental NE cell groups are not strictly segregated into different pathways (Jones & Moore, 1978), and given the proximity of the different NE ascending pathways throughout their ascending course, it is difficult to isolate the effects of 6-OHDA to one pathway. Although interest in the possible role of NE in memory has focused mainly on the LC projection system, lateral tegmental projections may also warrant further consideration. In this regard it is interesting to note that the more limited projection field of this system to forebrain nonetheless includes structures that have been prominently implicated in the modulation of memory—that is, the amygdala complex and septal region (Moore & Bloom, 1979). Since amygdala lesions have been found to prevent the effects of several treatments on memory processes, including peripheral administration of the hormone epinephrine (see McGaugh, 1983, for a recent discussion), components of the NE system that are sensitive to visceroceptive input may provide a link between the functional state of some peripheral systems and the central nervous system. As recently suggested by McGaugh (1983), it would be of considerable interest to determine whether other treatments that affect memory processes, such as epinephrine administration, are also dependent on intact brain NE function.

It is probable that the regulation of memory processes as embodied in the concept of modulation is not dependent on a single integrating system. Nonetheless, continuing attempts to elucidate interrelationships among the functions of modulating systems may reveal a degree of underlying circuitry for the regulation of neural change in the nervous system. This line of investigation may in itself be significant, even though an interface between modulators and the systems that provide a substrate for the content of memory remains more elusive.

REFERENCES

Bird, S. J., & Kuhar, M. J. Iontophoretic application of opiates to the locus coeruleus. *Brain Research*, 1977, *122*, 523–533.

Bohus, B., Conti, L., Kovács, G. L., & Versteeg, D. H. G. Modulation of memory processes by neuropeptides: Interaction with neurotransmitter systems. In C. Ajmone Marsan & H. Matthies (Eds.), *Neuronal plasticity and memory formation*. New York: Raven Press, 1982.

Chepkova, A. N., & Skrebitsky, V. G. Effects of some adrenergic drugs and neuropeptides on long-term potentiation in hippocampal slices. In C. Ajmone Marsan & H. Matthies (Eds.), *Neuronal plasticity and memory formation*. New York: Raven Press, 1982.

de Wied, D., & Bohus, B. Modulation of memory processes by neuropeptides of hypothalamic–neurohypophyseal origin. In M. A. B. Brazier (Ed.), *Brain mechanisms in memory and learning: From the single neuron to man*. New York: Raven Press, 1979.

Dunn, A. J. Neurochemistry of learning and memory: An evaluation of recent data. *Annual Review of Psychology*, 1980, *31*, 343–390.

Gallagher, M., & Kapp, B. S. Influence of amygdala opiate-sensitive mechanisms, fear-motivated responses, and memory processes for aversive experiences. In J. L. Martinez, Jr., R. A. Jensen, R. B. Messing, H. Rigter, & J. L. McGaugh (Eds.), *Endogenous peptides and learning and memory processes*. New York: Academic Press, 1981.

Goddard, G. V., Bliss, T. V. P., Robertson, A., II, & Sutherland, R. S. Noradrenaline levels affect long-term potentiation in the hippocampus. *Society for Neuroscience Abstracts*, 1980, *6*, 89.

Gold, P. E., & McGaugh, J. L. A single-trace, two-process view of memory storage processes. In D. Deutsch & J. A. Deutsch (Eds.), *Short term memory*. New York: Academic Press, 1975.

Gold, P., & McGaugh, J. L. Neurobiology and memory: Modulators, correlates and assumptions. In T. Teyler (Ed.), *Brain and learning*. Stamford, Ct.: Greylock, 1978.

Izquierdo, I., & Graudenz, M. Memory facilitation by naloxone is due to release of dopaminergic and beta-adrenergic systems from tonic inhibition. *Psychopharmacology*, 1980, *67*, 265–268.

Jones, B. E., & Moore, R. Y. Ascending projections of the locus coeruleus in the cat: Autoradiographic study. *Brain Research*, 1978, *127*, 23–53.

Kety, S. The biogenic amines in the central nervous system: Their possible roles in arousal, emotion and learning. In F. O. Schmitt (Ed.), *The neurosciences: Second study program*. Cambridge, Mass.: MIT Press, 1970.

Kety, S. Biological concomitants of affective states and their possible role in memory processes. In M. R. Rosenzweig & E. L. Bennett (Eds.), *Neural mechanisms of learning and memory*. Cambridge, Mass.: MIT Press, 1976.

Kovács, G. L., Bohus, B., & Versteeg, D. H. G. The effects of vasopressin on memory processes: The role of noradrenergic transmission. *Neuroscience*, 1979, *4*, 1529–1537.

Krasne, F. B. Extrinsic control of intrinsic neuronal plasticity: An hypothesis from work on simple systems. *Brain Research*, 1978, *140*, 197–216.

Llorens, C., Martres, M. P., Baudry, M., & Schwartz, J. C. Hypersensitivity to noradrenaline in cortex after chronic morphine: Relevance to tolerance and dependence. *Nature*, 1978, *274*, 603–605.

McGaugh, J. L. Hormonal influences on memory. *Annual Review of Psychology*, 1983, *34*, 297–323.

McGaugh, J. L., & Gold, P. E. Modulation of memory by electrical stimulation of the brain. In M. R. Rosenzweig & E. L. Bennett (Eds.), *Neural mechanisms of learning and memory*. Cambridge, Mass.: MIT Press, 1976.

Moore, R. Y., & Bloom, F. E. Central catecholamine neuron systems: Anatomy and physiology of the norepinephrine and epinephrine systems. In W. M. Cowan, Z. W. Hall, & E. R. Kandel (Eds.), *Annual review of neuroscience* (Vol. 2). Palo Alto, Calif.: Annual Reviews, 1979.

Olpe, H. R., & Baltzer, V. Vasopressin activates noradrenergic neurons in the rat locus coeruleus: A microiontophoretic investigation. *European Journal of Pharmacology*, 1981, *73*, 377–378.

Pepper, C. M., & Henderson, G. Opiates and opioid peptides hyperpolarize locus coeruleus neurons *in vitro*. *Science*, 1980, *209*, 394–396.

Pettigrew, J. D., & Kasamatsu, T. Local perfusion of noradrenaline maintains visual cortex plasticity. *Nature*, 1978, *271*, 761–763.

Pickel, V. M., Segal, M., & Bloom, F. E. A radioautographic study of the efferent pathways of the nucleus locus coeruleus. *Journal of Comparative Neurology*, 1979, *155*, 15–42.

Rapp, P. R., & Gallagher, M. Naloxone enhancement of memory processes: Dependence upon intact norepinephrine function. *Society for Neuroscience Abstracts*, 1983, *9*, 828.

Sawchenko, P. E., & Swanson, L. W. Central noradrenergic pathways for the integration of hypothalamic neuroendocrine and autonomic responses. *Science*, 1981, *214*, 685–687.

Scoville, W. B., & Milner, B. Loss of recent memory after bilateral hippocampal lesions. *Journal of Neurology, Neurosurgery, and Psychiatry*, 1957, *20*, 11–21.

Segal, M., & Bloom, F. The action of norepinephrine in the rat hippocampus: IV. The effects of locus coeruleus stimulation on evoked hippocampal unit activity. *Brain Research*, 1976, *107*, 513–525.

Sofroniew, M. V. Projections from vasopressin, oxytocin, and neurophysin neurons to neural targets in the rat and human. *Journal of Histochemistry and Cytochemistry*, 1980, *28*, 475–478.

Squire, L. R., & Davis, H. P. The pharmacology of memory: A neurobiological perspective. *Annual Review of Pharmacology and Toxicology*, 1981, *21*, 323–356.

Starke, K. Presynaptic regulation of release in the central nervous system. In D. Paton (Ed.), *The release of catecholamine from adrenergic neurons*. New York: Pergamon Press, 1979.

Tanaka, M., de Kloet, E., de Wied, D., & Versteeg, D. Arginine-vasopressin affects catecholamine metabolism in specific brain nuclei. *Life Sciences*, 1977, *20*, 1799–1808.

CHAPTER TWENTY-FIVE

Memory Modulation: Neurobiological Contexts

PAUL E. GOLD

INTRODUCTION

Over the last decade, there has been a significant conceptual change in the rationale for using posttraining treatments to modify memory. Instead of interpreting the results of such studies in terms of underlying constructs (e.g., short- or long-term memory), most contemporary studies discuss the results in terms of the neurobiological effects of those treatments that can modulate later retention performance. This transition in goals fosters more empirical statements about the findings, a change I believe is most useful.

In particular, the newer formulations of the research questions have led to increased attention being given to the roles of hormonal and neurotransmitter systems in regulating memory storage. The shift in emphasis provides an important basis for examining not only the effects on memory of many treatments but also for studying the relationships between the neuroendocrine responses to training and the storage of training-related information. One implication is that a full understanding of the neurobiology of learning and memory will require attention at an organismic level. Although memory storage must involve long-lasting modifications in neural networks, these intrinsic mechanisms are apparently regulated by many trophic systems. A major goal of memory modulation research, then, is to identify the systems that control the establishment of long-lasting changes in neural networks after experience as well as to understand the mechanisms by which the systems act. This statement of the problem is akin to identification in developmental neurobiology of not only the ontogenetic changes in connectivity but also the processes that initiate, terminate, and regulate these developmental changes. Viewed in this way, memory modulation offers the possibility of studying a fuller complement of cell biological processes responsible for memory storage.

The purpose of this chapter is to discuss memory modulation within a somewhat broader context than was included in earlier presentations, in the

Paul E. Gold. Department of Psychology, University of Virginia, Charlottesville, Virginia.

hope of bridging some of the information from the earlier chapters on neuropsychology and neurophysiology of memory to the subsequent chapters dealing with biochemical mechanisms underlying memory storage.

COMMENTARY

Before turning to this general theme, I want to address some of the specific results described in the earlier chapters on memory modulation. As reviewed earlier (Rosenzweig & Bennett, Chapter 17, this volume), the evidence overwhelmingly supports the view that treatments that substantially interfere with protein synthesis can produce retrograde amnesia. However, it is not clear that these experiments provide an appropriate test of the proposition that because antibiotics produce amnesia, protein synthesis is necessary for memory storage. This is an interpretation that is very difficult to reconcile with a variety of other pharmacological evidence indicating that many diverse drugs (e.g., amphetamine, metaraminol, vasopressin, adrenal steroids, *l*-tryptophan, picrotoxin) can attenuate memory impairments produced by antibiotics (cf. Dunn, 1980). This list of attenuating treatments is undoubtedly incomplete. The point is that these various treatments can permit memory storage to occur even in the presence of severe protein synthesis inhibition.

In fact, there is evidence suggesting that the effects of the inhibitors on memory may be mediated by mechanisms that may be common for many classes of amnestic agents. Specifically, recent findings suggest that most memory modulation treatments are ineffective in the presence of peripherally administered adrenergic receptor antagonists (Gold & Sternberg, 1978; Sternberg & Gold, 1980). The amnestic treatments that can be attenuated in this manner include not only antibiotics but also convulsant agents and subseizure amygdala stimulation. When viewed in conjunction with findings presented earlier by McGaugh and Izquierdo (McGaugh, Liang, Bennett, & Sternberg, Chapter 19, this volume; Izquierdo, Chapter 20, this volume)—that peripheral stress-related adrenomedullary hormones can produce amnesia—the findings suggest that a variety of amnestic agents, including the antibiotics, may act by eliciting a supraphysiological stress response. Thus, a great deal of caution is necessary before we can interpret amnesias produced by protein-synthesis inhibitors as direct evidence of a special role for protein synthesis in memory formation.

Leaving this issue, I would next like to address a series of experiments described by McGaugh and associates (Chapter 19, this volume) regarding the mechanism by which amygdala stimulation produces amnesia. The results suggest that amygdala stimulation may act on memory by eliciting, or by interacting with, a set of peripheral adrenergic responses. At the very least such findings emphasize the need to consider whole organism responses when dealing with the mechanisms underlying memory modulation, even if the manipulation involves very specific brain areas. In addition, it is important to remember that each manipulation we use—such as brain lesions, electrode implantations, electrical brain stimulation, drug injections—may result in a brain that is, in several respects, unlike the brain with which the animal began. In this regard, it becomes apparent that it is necessary to measure some of the central and peripheral consequences of the manipulations. Some of our recent research relating brain noradrenergic activity to memory storage provides an example relevant to this issue. Previously, we found that posttraining changes in central noradrenergic concentrations provide an excellent predictor of later retention performance. This relationship is consistent following a variety of training and treatment combinations (cf. Gold, McCarty, & Sternberg, 1982). On the basis of these earlier findings we examined brain noradrenergic activity following training and amygdala stimulation (Welsh & Gold, 1984a). The results were not at all what we expected. On assessing the norepinephrine content of eight brain regions in amygdala-implanted control animals, we found that nearly every area exhibited significantly decreased levels of norepinephrine. Furthermore, noradrenergic responses in implanted animals to training and stimulation were not consistent with the general pattern of results we had seen in earlier studies. Apparently, the pharmacological "rules" were modified in those animals that had electrodes in the amygdala. Thus, such findings indicate that amygdala-implanted animals have chronically altered brain noradrenergic systems. Certainly, the functions of other neurotransmitters and neuroendocrine systems may be chronically modified as well. It may therefore be difficult to use the findings obtained when studying amygdala stimulation effects on memory to direct us to an understanding of memory modulation in intact animals. More generally, if electrode implantation can result in pervasive changes in the nervous system, we must be alert to comparable modifications following brain lesions or pharmacological manipulations that may result in altered behaviors.

MODULATION OF NEURONAL PLASTICITY

The fact that the editors of this volume placed "memory modulation" between neurophysiological and biochemical studies of learning and memory implies that the topic offers a potential means of integrating these other areas of research. The principal modulation chapters focus on manipulations that modify behaviorally assessed memory. However, in addition to studies that examine memory by behavioral tests, there is a rapidly growing compilation of long-lasting neurobiological changes that might represent substrates of memory. Many examples are included in this volume, including anatomical, biochemical, and physiological modifications that outlast the initiating manipulations. With the increase in information about relatively durable physiological and biochemical changes in the brain, it may now be possible to establish more concrete biological approaches to the relationship between memory modulation and the processes that mediate specific types of brain modifications. This will be a necessary route if we are to avoid the trap described by Woodward, Moises, and Waterhouse (1979): "'Modulation' has become most useful as a linguistic junk bag into which we put processes we don't understand." Although this quotation was intended by its authors to apply to the new-found varieties of chemical communication between neurons, it may, if we are not careful, be equally applicable to modulation of memory processes. I believe we need to address two areas that may give more biological specificity to the definition of memory modulation. First, might pharmacological studies of neurohumoral modulation offer insights into the biological processes that underlie memory modulation? Second, can memory modulation treatments modify directly some forms of neuronal plasticity?

Regarding the first point, it may be possible to use some of the information derived from neuropharmacological investigations of chemical transmission to specify biological actions that may mediate the effects of neuroendocrine systems on memory. For example, there is considerable evidence supporting an important role for central noradrenergic activity in memory modulation (cf. Gold & Delanoy, 1981; Gold & Zornetzer, 1983). How then might noradrenergic release regulate the substrates of memory storage? Recent work from several laboratories suggests that norepinephrine (NE) may enhance the impact of neuronal communications in which the primary information is carried by other transmitters. For example, Waterhouse, Moises, and Woodward (1980) have found that when NE is applied iontophoretically to a neuron, the responses of that cell to other inputs, whether excitatory or inhibitory, are often enhanced (Waterhouse, *et al.*, 1980; Woodward, Moises, Waterhouse, Hoffer, & Freedman, 1979). Similarly, Rogawski and Aghajanian (1980) reported that the probability of lateral geniculate cells firing in response to electrical stimulation of the optic nerve is greatly enhanced by application of NE to the recording site. Thus, NE can apparently bias the sensitivity of some neurons to inputs from other transmitters. In the context of memory experiments, such results suggest that NE may exaggerate the impact of current (or immediately preceding) experiences by increasing the strength of relevant communications. In this way, NE could well modulate memory storage by enhancing the probability that these strengthened communications would have an enduring consequence. Such a view fits well with many of the neurophysiology and memory studies presented earlier (e.g., by Woody, Chapter 11, this volume; Weinberger, Diamond, & McKenna, Chapter 12, this volume) and is easily melded with the candidate cellular mechanisms of learning and memory in the ensuing chapters (e.g., Baudry & Lynch, Chapter 28; Hawkins & Kandel, Chapter 26).

Thus, one way in which memory modulation may gain significance in understanding the biological bases of memory is by identifying systems that regulate the neurophysiological and biochemical changes produced by experience. This possibility leads to a second issue: Can we forge more direct lines of evidence relating the phenomenon of memory modulation and some of the analogues of memory? In an attempt to address this question, we recently began to examine the possibility that neuroendocrine systems might be able to modulate long-term potentiation (LTP). The initial results are very encouraging. Peripheral injections of several adrenergic agonists can enhance the formation of LTP. For example, a subcutaneous injection of amphetamine or epinephrine enhances LTP in an inverted-U manner, characteristic of the analogous memory experiments, and at optimal doses consistent with those observed in behavioral studies (Delanoy, Gold, & Tucci, 1983; Gold, Delanoy, & Merrin, in press) (see Figure 25-1). Currently, the effects on LTP appear to be mediated by peripheral α_2-receptors. These pharmacological agents do not themselves appear to alter the evoked response. Instead, it seems likely that the conditions necessary to establish LTP (e.g., the intensity, frequency, or number of high-frequency trains) are reduced in the presence of adrenergic agonists; that is, there is a shift in the threshold parameters necessary for LTP. If correct, this view suggests that neurohumoral interactions, such as those described above, may regulate the probability that neuronal communication will establish durable neurobiological changes that underlie functional connectivity.

Although preliminary, such results give credence to both memory modula-

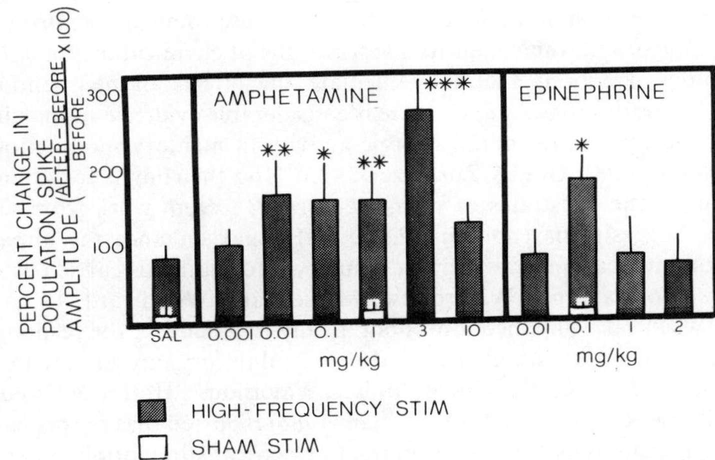

Figure 25-1. Percent changes (means ± *SEM*) in population spike amplitude (dentate granule cells) as measured on 10 test pulses (1 every 30 sec) collected 15–20 min after high-frequency stimulation of the perforant path in anesthetized rats. Note that peripheral injections of either amphetamine or epinephrine administered 15 min prior to the high-frequency stimulation enhanced the degree of LTP in a inverted-U dose–response manner. The small internal black bars (saline, 1.0 mg/kg amphetamine, 0.1 mg/kg epinephrine) illustrate the stability of the evoked response in animals that did not receive high-frequency stimulation (vs. saline group: $^{*}p < .05$; $^{**}p < .01$; $^{***}p < .01$; two tailed t-tests).

tion and LTP as systems relevant to understanding memory-storage processing. The findings that peripheral catecholamines can modulate LTP, particularly given the similarities between the drugs and dose–response characteristics with those of behavioral experiments, support the view that peripheral catecholamines act on memory by regulating the changes in the underlying neurobiological processes. Conversely, because LTP is susceptible to the same treatments as is behaviorally assessed memory, the analogue gains strength as a model system with which to study the biological bases of memory storage.

BRAIN STORAGE OF A MEMORY MODULATION "INCIDENT"

Izquierdo (Chapter 20, this volume) presented data suggesting that hormonal responses to training may produce an internal state that becomes an element of the experiential context. The extent to which this state is or is not reconstructed at the time of testing may, in part, control retention performance. Recently, we obtained results that indicated, to our surprise, that a single epinephrine injection can alter brain function for a considerable time thereafter (Welsh & Gold, 1984b). The experiments involved animals that underwent kindled seizure procedures (cf. Goddard, McIntyre, & Leech, 1969; Racine, 1978). The animals received a single stimulation train (60 Hz, 1 sec) each day at an intensity (250 μA) initially sufficient to elicit a brief afterdischarge. With repeated trials, the afterdischarge durations grew longer and the animals developed behavioral convulsions. Under these conditions, the progressive development of the seizure pattern was quite regular and reached asymptotic levels in about 10 days.

In this experiment, the animals received a single injection of saline or epinephrine (2.0 mg/kg) 30 min or 24 hr prior to stimulation (see Figure 25-2). During the subsequent daily stimulation trials, the epinephrine-treated animals exhibited significant retardation of the rate of kindling. The effect was evident in measurements of both afterdischarge durations and behavioral convulsion stages. Thus, a single epinephrine injection can proactively alter the rate of kindling for several days. Such findings have, I believe, some obvious and important implications for epileptogenesis. But in addition, the results suggest that an episode of high circulating epinephrine levels can itself produce a long-lasting change in neuronal function. One interpretation of these findings is that a single injection of epinephrine results in a long-lasting change in brain function—that is, the brain may store the information that high epinephrine levels occurred. The findings suggest that some hormonal responses may not only regulate neuronal changes responsible for memory storage but may also themselves initiate long-lasting alterations in neuronal function.

CONCLUSIONS

Considerable evidence in this chapter and others is consistent with the view that neuroendocrine activity following training may control the extent or nature of the alterations in central neurobiological systems. It will be important in the near future to try to specify the nature of the interactions between the neurohumoral responses and neural plasticity. How, for example, do peripheral adrenergic systems or pituitary peptides promote or regulate these brain modifications? Although epinephrine does not readily enter the central nervous system, the hormone has large effects on memory (McGaugh *et al.*, Chapter 19, this volume) and on such brain functions as electroencephalographic arousal (Baust, Niemczyk, & Vieth, 1963), cerebral oxygen consumption and blood flow (Dahlgren, Rosen, Sakabe, & Siesjo, 1980), central release of NE (cf. Gold *et al.*, 1982), and the electrophysiological phenomena described earlier in this chapter. Whether these effects are mediated directly by the restricted access of the amine to the central nervous system or by feedback from peripheral actions remains to be determined. Most demonstrations of memory modulation have employed avoidance procedures as the means for behavioral assay of brain plasticity. Therefore, it is unknown whether some hormones and neurotransmitters modulate plasticities for memory of a wide variety of motivational classes of training while other neurohumors modulate memory in more limited settings. Are there hormones that have gained specific functions as regulators of many neural changes? Or are there sets of hormones that each have independent, motivationally specific effects on neural plasticity? These possibilities are not mutually exclusive; some hormones may act on many forms of memory—epinephrine appears to enhance memory of appetitive learned responses as well as memory of avoidance responses—and others may act on more restricted sets of learned responses. Similarly, some neuroendocrine systems may prove effective in modulating several forms of neuronal plasticity, whereas others are more specific. These are empirical questions that can be addressed readily and will have importance for determining the biological nature of the interactions between neuroendocrine events, neural plasticity, and memory.

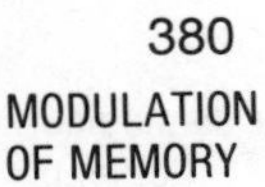

A

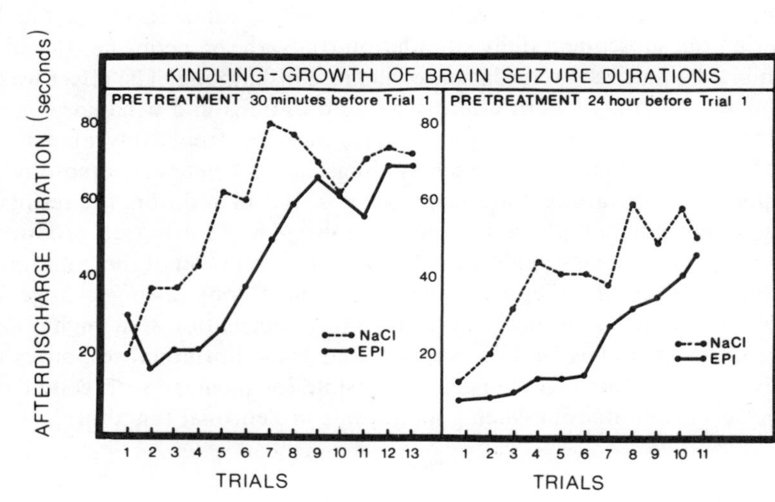

B

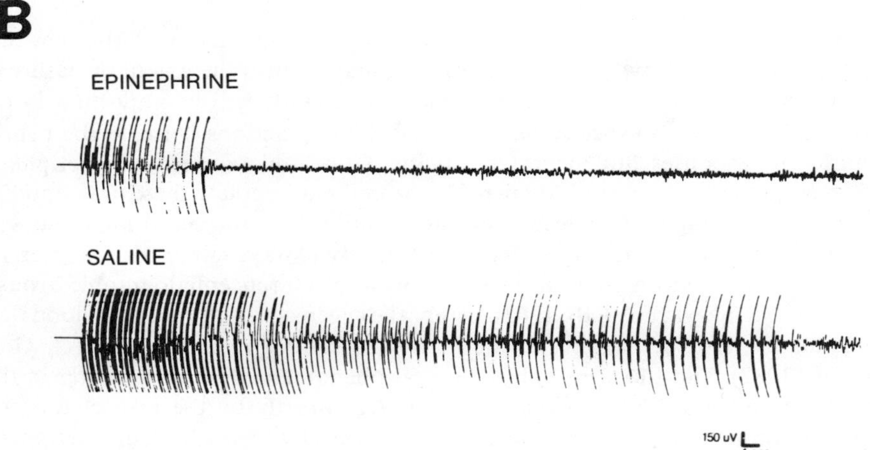

Figure 25-2. (A) Afterdischarge durations on successive days (1 stimulation per day) in animals receiving saline or a single epinephrine injection (2 mg/kg, i.p.) either 30 min (left) or 24 hr (right) prior to the first kindling trial (250 μA, 60 Hz, 1 sec). In both instances, the epinephrine pretreatment had no effect on the afterdischarge durations on Trial 1. However, beginning on Day 2, animals previously treated with epinephrine had afterdischarge durations shorter than those of saline-treated controls. This attenuation was still evident up to 10 days later, indicating that a single epinephrine injection administered as long as 24 hr before the first kindling trial can delay the progression of subsequent seizure activity. (B) Sample EEG recordings illustrating the typical pattern of afterdischarge activity observed in epinephrine-pretreated and saline-injected control animals on the second kindling trial.

In part because other chapters deal with behavioral tests of memory modulation, I have emphasized data that demonstrate peripheral catecholamine effects on long-lasting neurophysiological changes. At the present time, behavioral procedures remain as the surest means of generating brain modifications that are likely to underlie memory storage. Whether or not we later identify correctly the brain changes mediating memory, training an animal initiates the neurobiological substrates and modulators of memory, and retention tests provide behavioral assays for the neuronal changes. By combining these behavioral assay procedures with posttraining manipulations and measures of neurohormonal systems, we can hope to develop fairly clear ideas of the organismic responses to training that may regulate the cell biological events mediating long-lasting neuronal change. Nonetheless, although the behavioral measurements of memory are useful and often essential, the behavioral procedures may be too generous in a sense because the large amount of contextual information stored along with the specific stimuli selected by the experimenter suggests that substantial widespread brain alterations may well occur in even the simplest training procedures. The evidence that epinephrine—and therefore perhaps other neuroendocrine responses—can produce enduring changes in brain function extends still further the potential varieties of neurobiological "memories" of a training experience. In moving toward analyses of hormonal regulation of the cellular substrates of memory, it may therefore be useful to focus attention on some of the already identified forms of neuronal change. It is to be hoped that the results presented here—demonstrating some remarkable similarities between the effects of peripheral catecholamines on long-term potentiation and on behaviorally assessed memory—may lead to preparations in which it will be possible to specify the biological mechanisms by which neuroendocrine systems regulate neural plasticity.

ACKNOWLEDGMENTS

This work was supported by grants from the National Institute of Mental Health (MH 31141), the National Institute on Aging (AG 01643), and the University of Virginia Biomedical Research Support Council, and by an award from the James McKeen Cattell Foundation.

REFERENCES

Baust, W., Niemczyk, H., & Vieth, K. The action of blood pressure on the ascending reticular activating system with special reference to adrenalin-induced EEG arousal. *Electroencephalography and Clinical Neurophysiology*, 1963, *15*, 63–72.

Dahlgren, N., Rosen, I., Sakabe, T., & Siesjo, B. K. Cerebral functional, metabolic and circulatory effects of intravenous infusion of adrenaline in the rat. *Brain Research*, 1980, *184*, 143–152.

Delanoy, R. L., Gold, P. E., & Tucci, D. L. Amphetamine effects on long term potentiation of dentate granule cells. *Pharmacology, Biochemistry and Behavior*, 1983.

Dunn, A. J. Neurochemistry of learning and memory: An evaluation of recent data. *Annual Review of Psychology*, 1980, *31*, 343–390.

Goddard, G. V., McIntyre, D. C., & Leech, C. K. A permanent change in brain function resulting from daily electrical stimulation. *Experimental Neurology*, 1969, *25*, 295–330.

Gold, P. E., & Delanoy, R. L. ACTH modulation of memory storage processing. In J. Martinez (Ed.), *Endogenous peptides and memory*. New York: Academic Press, 1981.

Gold, P. E., Delanoy, R. L., & Merrin, J. Adrenergic modulation of long-term potentiation. *Brain Research*, in press.

Gold, P. E., McCarty, R., & Sternberg, D. B. Peripheral catecholamines and memory modulation. In C. Ajmone Marsan & H. Matthies (Eds.), *Neuronal plasticity and memory formation*. New York: Raven Press, 1982.

Gold, P. E., & Sternberg, D. B. Retrograde amnesia produced by several treatments. Evidence for a common neurobiological mechanism. *Science*, 1978, *20*, 367–369.

Gold, P. E., & Zornetzer, S. F. The mnemon and its juices: Neuromodulation of memory processes. *Behavior and Neural Biology*, 1983, *38*, 151–189.

Racine, R. J. Kindling: The first decade. *Neurosurgery*, 1978, *3*, 234–252.

Rogawski, M. A., & Aghajanian, C. K. Modulation of lateral geniculate neurone excitability by noradrenaline microiontophoresis or locus coeruleus stimulation. *Nature*, 1980, *287*, 731–734.

Sternberg, D. B., & Gold, P. E. Effects of α- and β-adrenergic receptor antagonists on retrograde amnesia produced by frontal cortex stimulation. *Behavior and Neural Biology*, 1980, *29*, 289–302.

Waterhouse, B. D., Moises, H. C., & Woodward, D. J. Noradrenergic modulation of somatosensory cortical neuronal responses to iontophoretically applied putative neurotransmitters. *Experimental Neurology*, 1980, *69*, 30–49.

Welsh, K. A., & Gold, P. E. *Brain catecholamine responses to footshock and amygdala stimulation*. Manuscript submitted for publication, 1984a.

Welsh, K. A., & Gold, P. E. Attenuation of epileptogenesis: Proactive effect of a single epinephrine injection of amygdaloid kindling. *Behavioral and Neural Biology*, 1984b, *40*, 179–185.

Woodward, D. J., Moises, H. C., & Waterhouse, B. D. Response to R. K. Dismukes, New concepts of molecular communication among neurons. *Behavioral and Brain Sciences*, 1979, *2*, 450.

Woodward, D. J., Moises, H. C., Waterhouse, B. D., Hoffer, B. J., & Freedman, R. Modulatory actions of norepinephrine in the central nervous system. *Federation Proceedings*, 1979, *38*, 2109–2116.

SECTION FOUR

Models and Cellular Mechanisms of Learning and Memory

CHAPTER TWENTY-SIX

Steps toward a Cell-Biological Alphabet for Elementary Forms of Learning

ROBERT D. HAWKINS / ERIC R. KANDEL

INTRODUCTION

Until recently, cellular neurobiologists interested in learning were primarily concerned with the question, What functional changes must take place in nerve cells for learning and memory to occur? During the past two decades there has been substantial progress in answering this question. Work on vertebrate systems such as the isolated spinal cord and on higher invertebrates such as *Aplysia*, *Drosophila*, *Hermissenda*, locust, and crayfish has led to the identification of cellular mechanisms for habituation, sensitization, and more recently, conditioning (Spencer, Thompson, & Nielson, 1966; Castellucci, Pinsker, Kupfermann, & Kandel, 1970; Kandel & Schwartz, 1982; Hawkins, Abrams, Carew, & Kandel, 1983; Byers, Davis, & Kiger, 1981; Duerr & Quinn, 1982; Alkon, 1979; Crow & Alkon, 1980; Hoyle, 1979; Krasne, 1969; Zucker, 1972). Based on these studies, one can begin to specify several features that the mechanisms of these different forms of learning have in common. These general features can be summarized as follows:

1. Elementary aspects of learning are not diffusely distributed in the brain but can be localized to the activity of specific nerve cells.
2. Learning produces alterations in the membrane properties and synaptic connections of those cells.
3. The changes in synaptic connections so far encountered have not involved formation of new synaptic contacts. On the contrary, memory storage lasting days and weeks has been shown to result from changes in the strength of already existing contacts.
4. These profound and prolonged changes in synaptic strength can be achieved by modulating the amount of chemical transmitter released by presynaptic terminals of neurons.

Robert D. Hawkins and Eric R. Kandel. Center for Neurobiology and Behavior, College of Physicians and Surgeons, Columbia University, and The New York State Psychiatric Institute, New York, New York.

5. In several instances the molecular mechanisms of learning involve cyclic nucleotide second messengers and modulation of specific ion channels.

The finding that unifying cell-biological principles may underlie several forms of learning raises another question: Do the mechanisms so far encountered form the beginning of an elementary cellular alphabet of learning? That is, can these units be combined to yield progressively more complex learning processes? We would like to suggest on theoretical grounds that such an alphabet exists and that certain higher-order forms of learning generally associated with cognition can be explained in cellular-connectionistic terms by combinations of a few relatively simple types of neuronal processes.

A particularly interesting focus for exploring a possible cellular alphabet for learning comes from the analysis of higher-order features of classical conditioning. These features are interesting for two reasons: (1) They have been extensively explored; and (2) they provide an important bridge between the experimental study of conditioning, which has been largely carried out in animals, and cognitive psychology, which until recently has been primarily concerned with human mentation. Furthermore, some of these higher-order features (second-order conditioning, blocking, and an unconditioned stimulus [UCS] preexposure effect) have been shown to occur in conditioning of a terrestrial mollusc, *Limax maximus* (Sahley, Rudy, & Gelperin, 1981), and preliminary experiments suggest that another (the effect of contingency) occurs in *Aplysia* (Hawkins, Carew, & Kandel, 1983). It therefore may be possible to analyze these features of conditioning on the cellular level in invertebrates.

Our purpose in this brief theoretical review is to illustrate that several higher-order features of classical conditioning can be derived from our current understanding of the cellular mechanisms of classical conditioning, sensitization, and habituation. Studies by Kamin, Rescorla, Wagner, Mackintosh, and others have shown that these higher-order features of conditioning appear to involve cognition in the sense that the animals' behavior depends on a comparison of current sensory input with an internal representation of the world (Kamin, 1969; Rescorla, 1978; Wagner, 1978; Dickinson & Mackintosh, 1978). Our goal is thus to suggest how cognitive psychology may converge with neurobiology so as to yield a new perspective in the study of learning. This perspective is similar in some ways to that of Hull (1943), who attempted over 40 years ago to explain a variety of complex forms of learning in terms of principles derived from simpler forms of learning. Our perspective differs from that of Hull, however, in that his system was based on postulates that were inferred from behavior, whereas our approach is based on directly observable cellular processes. We believe that a cell-biological approach to the rules of learning is likely to be more fruitful, since it attempts to explain higher level phenomena (behavior) in terms of more basic phenomena (cell biology) and thus avoids some of the circularity inherent in a purely behavioral approach.

To illustrate these points, we shall divide this chapter into two parts: First, we shall describe cellular mechanisms of three forms of learning in *Aplysia* and suggest how these mechanisms form the outline of a cellular alphabet of learning. Second, we will try to use this alphabet to account for several higher-order features of learning. For a more extensive summary of these arguments the reader is referred to our recent review (Hawkins & Kandel, in press).

THREE FORMS OF LEARNING IN *APLYSIA* HAVE COMMON CELLULAR FEATURES

Studies of learning in *Aplysia* have focused on the defensive withdrawal reflexes of the external organs of the mantle cavity. In *Aplysia* and in other molluscs, the mantle cavity, a respiratory chamber housing the gill, is covered by a protective sheet, the mantle shelf, which terminates in a fleshy spout, the siphon. When the siphon or mantle shelf is stimulated by light touch, the siphon, mantle shelf, and gill all contract vigorously and withdraw into the mantle cavity. This reflex is analogous to vertebrate defensive escape and withdrawal responses, which can be modified by experience. Unlike vertebrate withdrawal reflexes, however, the *Aplysia* withdrawal reflex is partly monosynaptic—siphon sensory neurons synapse directly on gill and siphon motor neurons (Figure 26-1). Nonetheless, this simple reflex can be modified by two forms of nonassociative learning, sensitization and habituation, as well as by associative learning, classical conditioning.

Habituation, perhaps the most simple form of learning, is a process whereby an animal learns through repeated presentation to ignore a weak stimulus, the consequences of which are neither noxious nor rewarding. Thus, an animal will initially respond to a weak tactile stimulus to the siphon by briskly withdrawing its gill and siphon. But if the tactile stimulus to the siphon is repeatedly presented, the animal will learn to ignore the stimulus, and will exhibit reflex responses that are reduced to a fraction of their initial value (Pinsker, Kupfermann, Castellucci, & Kandel, 1970).

At the cellular level, habituation involves a depression of transmitter release at the synapses that the siphon sensory neurons make on gill and siphon motor neurons and interneurons (Castellucci *et al.*, 1970; Castellucci & Kandel, 1974). This depression involves, at least in part, a decrease in the amount of Ca^{++} that flows into the terminals of the sensory neurons with each action potential (Figure 26-2A). Since Ca^{++} influx determines how much transmitter is

Figure 26-1. Partial neuronal circuit for the *Aplysia* gill and siphon withdrawal reflex and its modification by tail stimulation. Mechanosensory neurons (S.N.) from the siphon make direct excitatory synaptic connections onto gill and siphon motor neurons. Tail sensory neurons excite facilitator interneurons, which produce presynaptic facilitation of the siphon sensory neurons. Tail stimulation also produces excitation of gill and siphon motor neurons through pathways not shown in this figure.

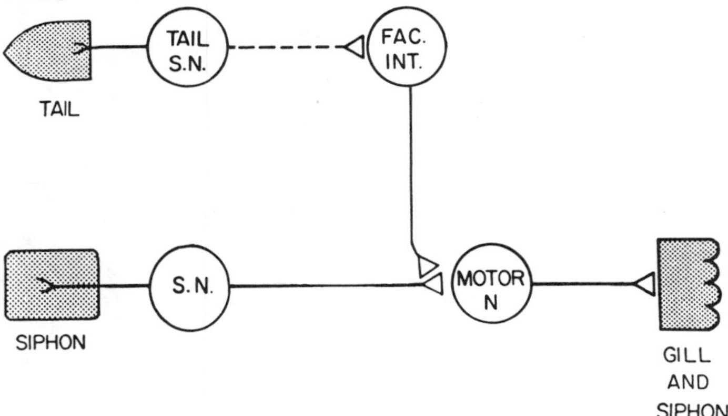

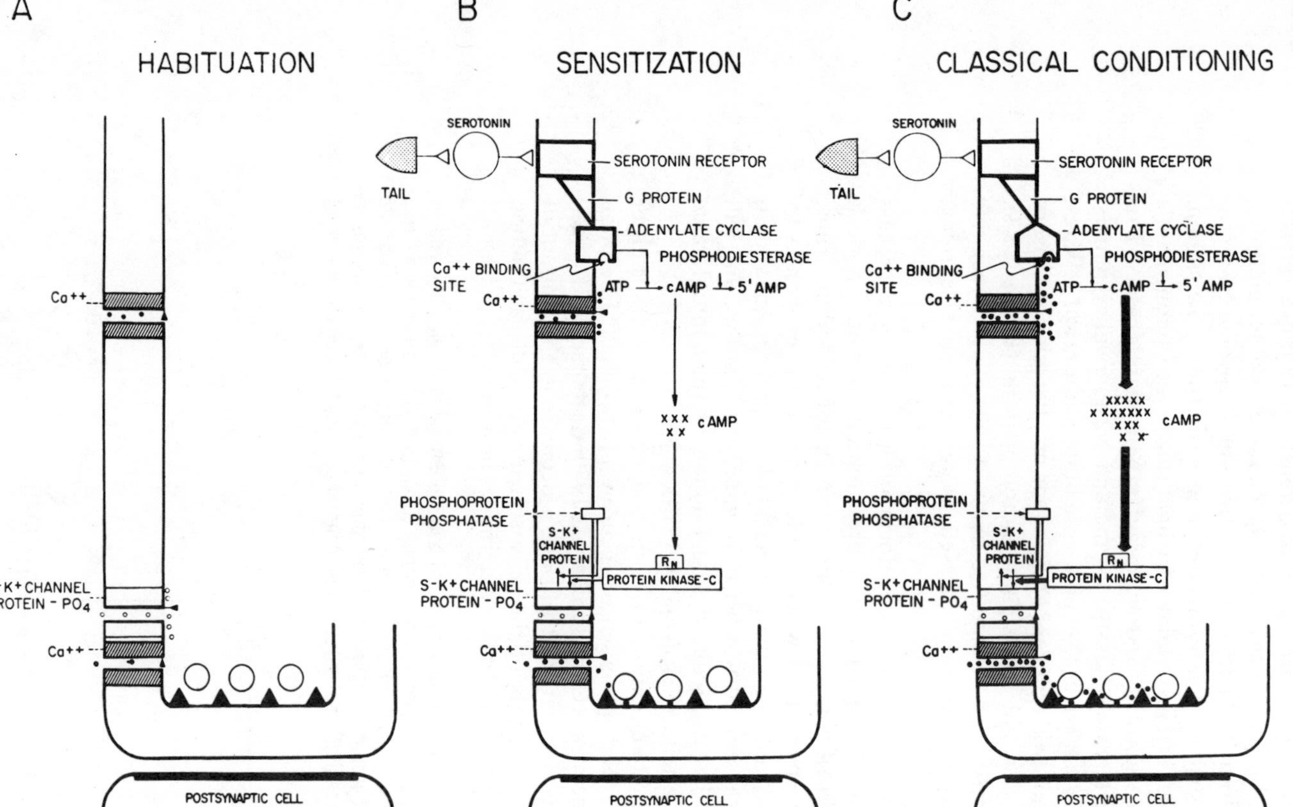

Figure 26-2. Cellular mechanisms of habituation, sensitization, and classical conditioning of the *Aplysia* gill and siphon withdrawal reflex. (A) Habituation: Repeated stimulation of a siphon sensory neuron (the presynaptic cell in the figure) produces prolonged inactivation of Ca^{++} channels in that neuron (represented by the closed gates), leading to a decrease in Ca^{++} influx during each action potential and decreased transmitter release. (B) Sensitization: Stimulation of the tail produces prolonged inactivation of K^+ channels in the siphon sensory neuron through a sequence of steps involving cAMP and protein phosphorylation (see the text for details). Closing these K^+ channels produces broadening of subsequent action potentials, which in turn produces an increase in Ca^{++} influx and increased transmitter release. (C) Classical conditioning: Tail stimulation produces amplified facilitation of transmitter release from the siphon sensory neuron if the tail stimulation is preceded by action potentials in the sensory neuron. This effect may be due to "priming" of the adenyl cyclase by Ca^{++} that enters the sensory neuron during the action potentials, so that the cyclase produces more cAMP when it is activated by the tail stimulation.

released, a decrease in Ca^{++} influx results in decreased release (Klein, Shapiro, & Kandel, 1980).

Sensitization is a somewhat more complex form of nonassociative learning in which an animal learns to strengthen its defensive reflexes and to respond vigorously to a variety of previously weak or neutral stimuli after it has been exposed to a potentially threatening or noxious stimulus. Thus, if a noxious sensitizing stimulus is presented to the neck or tail, the siphon and gill reflexes in response to siphon stimulation will be enhanced, as will inking, walking, and other defensive behavior (Pinsker *et al.*, 1970; Hawkins, Castellucci, & Kandel, unpublished observations; Walters, Carew, & Kandel, 1981). This enhancement persists for minutes to hours depending on the intensity of the sensitizing stimulus. Sensitization will not only enhance normal (naive) reflex responses, but it will enhance previously habituated reflex responses. Dishabituation, the restoration of a previously habituated response by a noxious stimulus, has been shown, on the cellular level, to be a special case of sensitization (Spencer *et al.*, 1966; Carew, Castellucci, & Kandel, 1971).

Sensitization involves the same cellular locus as habituation, the synapses that the sensory neurons make on their central target cells, and again the learning process involves an alteration in transmitter release; in this case an enhancement in the amount released (Castellucci *et al.*, 1970; Castellucci & Kandel, 1976). But sensitization involves more complex molecular machinery. This machinery has at least five steps (Figures 26-1 and 26-2B): (1) Stimulation of the tail activates a group of facilitator neurons that synapse on the terminals of the sensory neurons and act there to enhance transmitter release. This process is called *presynaptic facilitation.* (2) The facilitator cells are thought to utilize several different transmitters including serotonin, which activates an adenylate cyclase in the terminals of the sensory neurons. This enzyme increases the level of free cyclic AMP (cAMP) in those terminals. (3) Elevation of free cAMP, in turn, activates a second enzyme, the cAMP-dependent protein kinase. (4) The kinase acts by means of protein phosphorylation to close a particular type of K^+ channel and thereby decreases the total number of K^+ channels that are open during the action potential. (5) A decrease in K^+ current leads to broadening of subsequent action potentials, which in turn leads to an increase in Ca^{++} influx into the terminal and enhanced transmitter release (Kandel & Schwartz, 1982; Klein & Kandel, 1980; Siegelbaum, Camardo, & Kandel, 1982; Castellucci, Nairn, Greengard, Schwartz, & Kandel, 1982; Bernier, Castellucci, Kandel, & Schwartz, 1982; Hawkins, 1981a, 1981b; Hawkins, Castellucci, & Kandel, 1981b).

Classical conditioning resembles sensitization in that the response to a stimulus to one pathway is enhanced by activity in another. However, whereas sensitization leads to the indiscriminate enhancement of defensive responses to a variety of stimuli, classical conditioning leads to the selective enhancement of responses to stimuli that are temporally paired with the UCS.[1] In conditioning

1. We do not distinguish between the appearance of new responses and the strengthening of preexisting responses, since we think this difference is not fundamental. Rather, we believe that the neural connections for all possible stimulus–response associations are prewired, and training merely alters the strengths of those connections, in some cases bringing the response from below threshold to above threshold. Support for this view comes from experiments in which neural activity is recorded in various regions of the brain during conditioning. For example, at the

of the *Aplysia* withdrawal response, the UCS is a strong shock to the tail that produces a powerful set of defensive responses; the conditioned stimulus (CS) is a weak stimulus to the siphon that produces a very feeble response. After repeated pairing of the CS and UCS in a specified sequence (the CS must precede the UCS by approximately .5 seconds), the CS becomes much more effective and elicits a powerful gill and siphon withdrawal reflex. Enhancement of this reflex extinguishes with repeated presentation of the CS alone, and recovers with rest (Carew, Walters, & Kandel, 1981). The specificity of this reflex enhancement is revealed by differential conditioning experiments. In these experiments a weak CS to one site (either the siphon or the mantle shelf) is paired with a strong shock to the tail, whereas a stimulus to the other site is given unpaired with tail shock. The siphon and mantle shelf are innervated by different populations of sensory neurons (the LE cluster innervates the siphon skin and the RE cluster innervates the mantle shelf). Each pathway is capable of eliciting siphon and gill withdrawal. But when one of these pathways is paired with tail stimulation and the other is not, the response to the paired pathway is greatly enhanced compared to that of the unpaired pathway (Carew, Hawkins, & Kandel, 1983).

Classical conditioning uses presynaptic facilitation as the basic mechanism for strengthening synaptic connections much as does sensitization. However, the optimal enhancement that occurs with classical conditioning requires that the CS and UCS be temporally paired. Temporal specificity, the additional step involved in associative learning, is achieved by a convergence of the activity of the CS and the activity of the UCS at a specified locus within the neural circuit: the terminals of the sensory neurons. During each paired trial, action potentials in sensory neurons that are excited by the CS immediately precede activity in facilitator cells that are excited by the UCS. The action potentials in a sensory neuron somehow enhance the response of that sensory neuron to the transmitter (presumably serotonin) released by the facilitator neurons. As a result, the duration of subsequent action potentials in the sensory neuron is more enhanced, and more transmitter is released, than when action potentials in the sensory neuron are not paired with the UCS. Thus, at least some aspects of the mechanism for the temporal specificity of classical conditioning occur within the sensory neuron itself (Hawkins, Abrams, Carew, & Kandel, 1983; see also Walters & Byrne, 1983).

These experiments indicate that the mechanism of classical conditioning of the withdrawal reflex is simply an elaboration of the mechanism of sensitization of the reflex: presynaptic facilitation caused by an increase in action potential duration and Ca^{++} influx in the sensory neurons. The pairing specificity characteristic of classical conditioning results from the presynaptic facilitation being augmented or amplified by temporally paired spike activity in the sensory neurons. It is not yet known which aspect of the action potential in a sensory neuron interacts with the process of presynaptic facilitation to amplify it, nor which step in the biochemical cascade leading to presynaptic facilitation is sensitive to the action potential. As a working hypothesis Hawkins, Abrams,

---

beginning of an eye-blink conditioning experiment there is usually no overt response to the conditioned stimulus, but there is a detectable response in the motor nucleus controlling eye blink (e.g., Cegavske, Patterson, & Thompson, 1979). Training strengthens this preexisting neural response until it is above threshold for producing an observable behavioral response.

Carew, and Kandel (1983) proposed that the influx of Ca^{++} with each action potential provides the signal for activity, and that it interacts with the serotonin-sensitive adenylate cyclase in the terminals of the sensory neuron so that the cyclase produces more cAMP in response to serotonin (Figure 26-2C).

These findings suggest two interrelated hypotheses about how different forms of learning may be related. These hypotheses assume that learning is not a unitary process but a family of related processes that range from habituation to insight learning, with conditioning occupying an intermediate position. First, we propose that higher forms of learning may utilize the mechanisms of lower forms of learning as a general rule; and second, we speculate that this may occur because higher forms of learning have evolved from lower forms of learning. It is easy to imagine how the cellular mechanism of conditioning in *Aplysia* might have evolved from the mechanism of sensitization. For example, a small change in the adenyl cyclase might have made it sensitive to Ca^{++} that enters the cell during an action potential, thus giving rise to the activity dependence of facilitation. This example suggests that the mechanisms of yet higher forms of learning may similarly have evolved from the mechanism of conditioning. Higher forms of learning may also utilize the mechanisms of lower forms of learning within an individual animal. Thus, whereas individual neurons may possess only a few fundamental types of plasticity that are utilized in all forms of learning, combining the neurons in large numbers with specific synaptic connections (as occurs, e.g., in mammalian cortex) may produce the much more subtle and varied processes required for more advanced types of learning.

We will illustrate this idea by showing how some of the higher-order features of classical conditioning might be generated by small systems of neurons utilizing known types of synaptic plasticity. For the most part, our proposals are simply attempts to translate into neuronal terms ideas that have been proposed at an abstract level by experimental psychologists, with a particular debt to the theories of conditioning of Rescorla and Wagner. We have arbitrarily restricted ourselves to the use of physiological processes and neuronal connections that are known to occur in the neural circuit underlying the *Aplysia* gill and siphon withdrawal reflex. We should emphasize, however, that some of the higher-order behavioral phenomena discussed have not yet been tested for conditioning of that reflex. Our arguments on these points are therefore entirely speculative, and are simply meant to illustrate our general approach.

SEVERAL HIGHER-ORDER FEATURES OF CLASSICAL CONDITIONING CAN BE DERIVED FROM THE CELLULAR MECHANISMS OF SIMPLER FORMS OF LEARNING

Classical conditioning has two attractive features that account for its central role in the analysis of learning. The first is that in acquiring a conditioned response, an animal learns a fundamental relationship about the environment—that the CS predicts and may appear to cause the UCS. Second, classical conditioning is accompanied by several higher-order effects. Some of these were first described by Pavlov (1927) and the early students of associative learning; others have more recently been described by Kamin, Rescorla, Wagner, and others who have been interested in the cognitive or information-processing aspects of learning. According to this view, the animal builds up an image of the external world, compares the image of the world with reality—with the view of the world as validated by current sensory information—then modifies its behavior accordingly.

In view of the evidence for a cellular relationship between habituation, sensitization, and classical conditioning, it becomes interesting to examine the possibility that a general cellular alphabet exists for a wide variety of learning processes. Can one combine the elementary mechanisms involved in habituation, sensitization, and conditioning and thereby account for additional higher-order aspects of associative learning without requiring additional cellular mechanisms? Here we will consider several higher-order features: (1) stimulus specificity and generalization; (2) extinction, disinhibition, and spontaneous recovery; (3) second-order conditioning; (4) blocking; (5) degeneration of learning by intermittent presentation of the UCS alone or UCS preexposure. Our suggested explanations of these phenomena are not meant to be exclusive. We wish only to indicate how simple cellular processes such as synaptic depression and facilitation could be used in different combinatorial ways to contribute to these higher-order features of behavior.

Stimulus Specificity and Generalization

Animals learn to respond to the CS and not to other irrelevant stimuli. Activity-dependent enhancement of presynaptic facilitation readily confers this stimulus specificity (Figure 26-3): Only those sensory neurons that are active preceding the UCS undergo the amplified form of presynaptic facilitation, and thus only the response to the paired CS is selectively enhanced (see also Carew *et al.*, 1983; Hawkins, Abrams, Carew, & Kandel, 1983).

Stimulus specificity is not generally complete, however. Following conditioning, animals will respond to stimuli other than the CS, with the strength of responding depending on the degree of similarity between the test stimulus and the CS. We suggest two cellular explanations for this stimulus generalization. The first is sensitization: An aversive UCS will produce some enhancement of defensive responses to *all* stimuli, whether they are paired with it or not. This enhancement will simply be greater for the paired stimuli. The second explanation, which is basically similar to those proposed by Bush and Mosteller (1951) and Atkinson and Estes (1963), is that there will be some overlap in the sensory neurons and interneurons excited by different stimuli. Thus, conditioning of one stimulus will produce amplified presynaptic facilitation of some (but not all) of the neurons that are excited by a second stimulus and will therefore produce partial enhancement of the response to the second stimulus. The greater the similarity between the stimuli, the more overlap there will be in the neurons they excite, and the more generalization there will be. This mechanism can explain a wider range of generalization if activity-dependent amplification of presynaptic facilitation occurs not only at sensory neurons but also at interneurons. We believe this is likely to be true, since we do not feel there is anything unique about the sensory neurons.

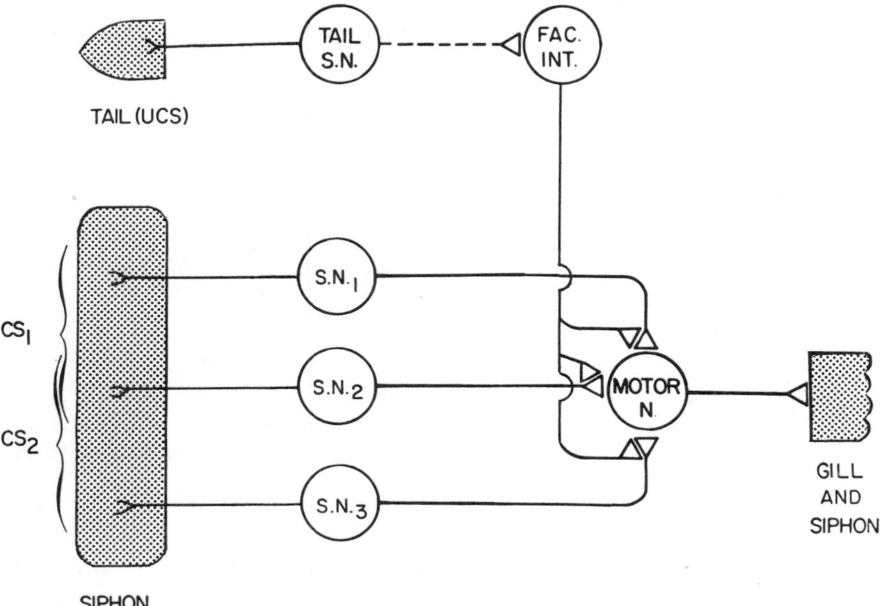

Figure 26-3. Proposed cellular mechanisms of stimulus specificity and generalization. CS_1 excites siphon sensory neurons 1 and 2, and CS_2 excites neurons 2 and 3. Only those sensory neurons that are active preceding the UCS will undergo the amplified form of presynaptic facilitation. Thus, conditioning of CS_1 will produce partial (but not complete) generalization to CS_2.

Extinction, Disinhibition, and Spontaneous Recovery

Conditioned responses can be eliminated by *extinction*—if the CS is presented repeatedly without reinforcement by the UCS, the response to the CS will gradually diminish and eventually disappear. Extinction, however, does not return an animal to its naive state. A number of experimental procedures can restore or reinstate responding to the CS. For example, if the CS is not presented for some time following extinction, the animal will show a partial to complete recovery of responding to the CS, thereby revealing that the animal remembers the original training.

We suggest that extinction and spontaneous recovery represent an interaction between habituation and classical conditioning: After the CS pathway has been classically conditioned, it can still undergo habituation. Repeated presentation of the CS leads to habituation due to synaptic depression of the input from the CS to the motor neuron, resulting in extinction of the learned response. Since habituation has a different neuronal mechanism than classical conditioning, its time course can be dramatically different. Thus, if the CS is presented only a few times during extinction, the consequent habituation can wear off rapidly. As a result, after habituation (extinction) wears off, learning will again be manifest (spontaneous recovery) in the response of the CS pathway (Figure 26-4).

Another procedure that reverses the effects of extinction is the presentation of a strong extraneous stimulus. Pavlov (1927) referred to this as disinhibition,

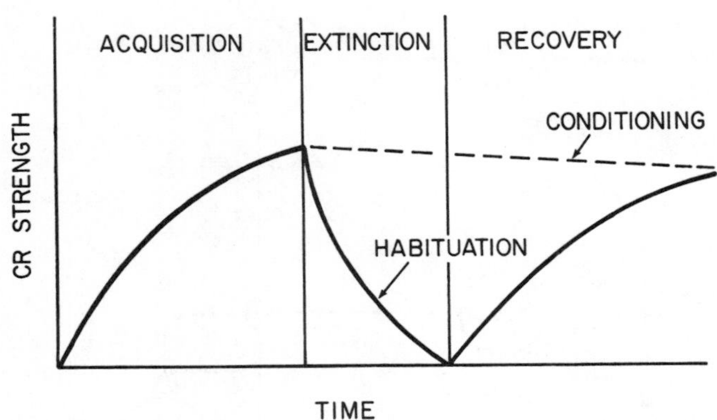

Figure 26-4. Proposed cellular mechanisms of extinction and spontaneous recovery. Repeated presentation of the CS during extinction produces habituation of the response to that CS, and the response recovers with rest. These processes are superimposed on the memory for the conditioning (the dashed line).

since he thought that extinction was due to inhibition that the extraneous stimulus removed. Since the characteristics of disinhibiting stimuli are similar to those of sensitizing stimuli, however, we would argue that disinhibition is simply due to sensitization, as has been shown for dishabituation (Spencer *et al.*, 1966; Groves & Thompson, 1970; Carew *et al.*, 1971).

There are several other parallels between extinction and habituation. For example, both processes generally occur faster with a shorter intertrial interval, and both occur more rapidly if they are repeated after a period of rest (Thompson & Spencer, 1966; Pavlov, 1927). These similarities support the idea that extinction has the same neuronal mechanism as habituation: synaptic depression.

Second-Order Conditioning

Second-order conditioning is the process whereby events that formerly did not reinforce behavior can become reinforcing. In the first stage of a second-order conditioning experiment an effective UCS is used to reinforce and thereby to strengthen the response to an initially ineffective CS_1 by pairing the two stimuli (CS_1-UCS). After such pairing, CS_1 can now itself serve as a reinforcing stimulus to strengthen the response to a new conditioned stimulus, CS_2, if those two stimuli are paired (CS_2-CS_1). Second-order conditioning is thought to be ubiquitous in everyday life and to bridge the gap between laboratory experiments and complex natural behavior, which often does not have obvious reinforcers. Second-order conditioning also illustrates the interchangeability of the CS and UCS, since the same stimulus can serve as either a CS or a UCS in a conditioning experiment.

Before considering a possible cellular mechanism of second-order conditioning we need to introduce three additional features of the neural circuitry of *Aplysia* that we believe may be general and that are important for the arguments that follow (Figure 26-5). First, in addition to the UCS, many CS inputs excite the facilitator neurons. Thus, these neurons may be thought of as a local arousal system (for earlier discussion of this point see Hawkins & Advocat, 1977; Kandel, 1978). Second, the facilitator neurons produce facilitation not only at the synapses from the sensory neurons to the motor neurons but also at the synapses from the sensory neurons to many interneurons, *including the facilitator neurons* themselves. This fact has the interesting consequence that the sensory neuron–facilitator neuron synapses (unlike the sensory neuron–motor neuron synapses) should act like Hebb synapses. That is, firing a sensory neuron just before firing of the facilitator neuron should produce selective strengthening of the synapse from that sensory neuron to the facilitator (compared to other inputs onto the facilitator) because of activity-dependent enhancement of the facilitation. Third, the facilitator neurons also produce excitation of gill and siphon motor neurons, either directly or indirectly (Hawkins, Castellucci, & Kandel, 1981a).

Figure 26-5A illustrates how our model of conditioning predicts second-order effects. Once a particular pathway—for example, the siphon—is paired

Figure 26-5. More complete neuronal circuit for the gill and siphon withdrawal reflex and its modification by tail stimulation. (A) Circuit for differential conditioning of responses to stimulation of the siphon and mantle shelf. (B) Simplified version of A, illustrating possible neural representations of S-R and S-S learning (see the text).

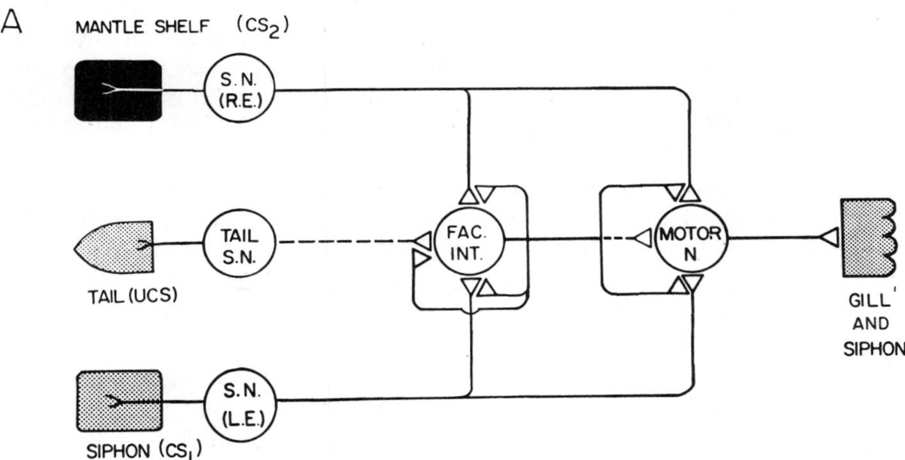

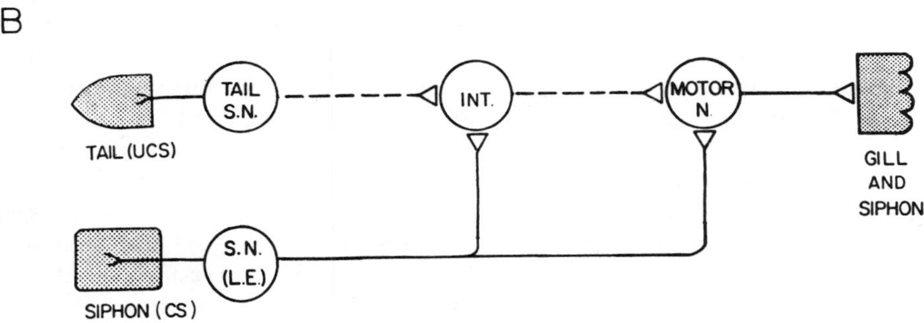

repeatedly with a UCS (to the tail), the CS pathway from the siphon becomes effective in producing a much stronger gill contraction to siphon stimulation. Moreover, activity-dependent enhancement of presynaptic facilitation occurs not only at the sensory neuron–motor neuron synapse but also at the sensory neuron–facilitator neuron synapse. As a result, the CS pathway now, in effect, becomes a potential UCS pathway, and CS_1 from the siphon might be able to serve as a UCS for conditioning of responses to other CSs such as the mantle.

Second-order conditioning thus demonstrates that learning does not simply change the ability of a stimulus to produce a motor response but also changes the ability of the stimulus to access some of the internal processing machinery over which the UCS previously had predominant control. This aspect of our model also suggests a possible reconciliation of two competing theories of learning. On the one hand, Guthrie (1935), Hull (1943), and others have proposed that an association is formed between the CS and the response (S-R) in classical conditioning. On the other hand, theorists like Tolman (1932) have proposed that associations are formed between the experimental stimuli (S-S). This S-S viewpoint seems closer to Pavlov's (1927) idea that the CS comes to substitute for the UCS, and thereby produces a response similar to the unconditioned response. Figure 26-5B, which is a simplified version of Figure 26-5A, shows that our model incorporates extremely simple neural representations of each of these theories. Thus, changes at the sensory neuron–motor neuron synapses in Figure 26-5 are obviously consistent with S-R theories, while changes at the sensory neuron–interneuron synapses are consistent with S-S theories, since those changes can be thought of as the process by which one stimulus (the CS) comes to substitute for another (the UCS) in the animal's internal processing machinery. This arrangement may seem more plausible if the interneuron in Figure 26-5B is considered as a sensory interneuron, so that the CS comes to produce perceptions in some sense similar to those produced by the UCS. Our model therefore suggests that any instance of learning will produce both S-R and S-S types of neuronal changes, with the type that is expressed perhaps depending on the experimental circumstances.

Blocking

The circuitry shown in Figure 26-5 might also explain a class of learning phenomena having to do with the predictability of the stimuli, which include blocking, overshadowing, and the effect of contingency. We will illustrate this point using blocking as an example. In the first stage of a blocking experiment, CS_1 is conditioned as usual. In the second stage, a second CS (CS_2) is added to CS_1, and the compound stimulus CS_1CS_2 is paired with the UCS. Generally, there is little conditioning of CS_2, whereas controls show that good conditioning of CS_2 is obtained if CS_1 is omitted or if CS_1 was not previously conditioned. A cognitive explanation that has been proposed is that an animal forms expectations about the world, compares current input with those expectations, and learns only when something unpredicted happens (Kamin, 1969). Because CS_1 comes to predict the UCS in the first stage of training, in the second stage the compound CS_1CS_2 is not followed by anything unexpected, and therefore little conditioning occurs. Rescorla and Wagner (1972) have formalized this explanation by suggesting that the strength of conditioning is proportional to the difference between the strength of the CS and that of the UCS. They expressed this relation in the following equation: $\Delta V_i = K(\lambda - \Sigma V_i)$, where V_i is the associative strength of element *i*, ΔV_i is the change in that strength on a given trial, *K* is a constant, and λ is the maximum strength attainable with the UCS being used. At the beginning of the first stage of training, the strength of CS_1 (V_1) will be small, $\lambda - V_1$ will be large, and the increment in the strength of CS_1 (ΔV_1) on each trial will be large. As training progresses, V_1 will become larger, ΔV_1 will become smaller, and V_1 will gradually approach λ. When the second stage of training starts, the strength of CS_2 (V_2) will be small, but the sum of V_1 and V_2 (ΣV_i) will nearly equal λ, so there will be little further change in the strengths of either CS_1 or CS_2.

A possible cellular embodiment of this proposal requires an additional piece of information, which is that the output of the facilitator neurons decreases during continued stimulation of those neurons. This mechanism is similar to one that has recently been proposed at the abstract level by Wagner (1981), who suggests that activity in the UCS "node" in a memory network puts that node in a refractory state for a transient period. In *Aplysia* this is true for two reasons: The facilitator neurons undergo accommodation and receive recurrent inhibition, both of which tend to make the facilitators fire only at the onset of a sustained stimulus (Hawkins *et al.*, 1981a, and unpublished observations). Thus, as the synapses from CS_1 to the facilitator neurons get progressively strengthened during the first stage of training, the facilitator neurons will fire more during CS_1 and consequently less during the UCS (due to the accommodation and recurrent inhibition caused by the firing during CS_1; see Figure 26-6). This process will asymptote when the firing during CS_1 is strong enough to prevent firing during the UCS.[2] Thus, when training with the compound stimulus CS_1CS_2 starts in the second stage of training, CS_2 will not be followed by firing in the facilitator neurons, and therefore CS_2 will not become conditioned. Firing of the facilitator neurons at the *onset* of CS_2 will not produce amplified facilitation, since that process requires a delay between CS onset and the onset of facilitation.

As Rescorla and Wagner (1972) point out, a similar explanation would apply if the same two types of trials (CS_1-UCS and CS_1CS_2-UCS) were alternated or intermixed, instead of being presented in two stages of training. According to the model we have described, early in training both CS_1 and CS_2 would gain in associative strength, but CS_1 would gain faster because it is paired with the UCS more frequently. This process would continue until the combined strength of CS_1 and CS_2 equaled the strength of the UCS. At that point the compound stimulus CS_1CS_2 would cause enough accommodation and recurrent inhibition in the facilitator neurons to prevent firing during the UCS, and no further conditioning would occur on the compound (CS_1CS_2-UCS) trials. In fact, CS_2 would then tend to undergo extinction, and the response to CS_2 would decline to some low level. CS_1 would also undergo extinction on the compound trials, but it would continue to be conditioned on the CS_1-UCS trials and would gain in strength until its strength equaled that of the UCS.

2. This is a simplification. As discussed below, each acquisition trial produces two competing processes at the sensory neuron synapses: facilitation caused by firing of the facilitator neurons and depression caused by firing of the sensory neurons. Thus, the asymptote of conditioning will actually be reached at a slightly lower level, when there is still just enough firing of the facilitators during the UCS to offset the synaptic depression which occurs on each trial.

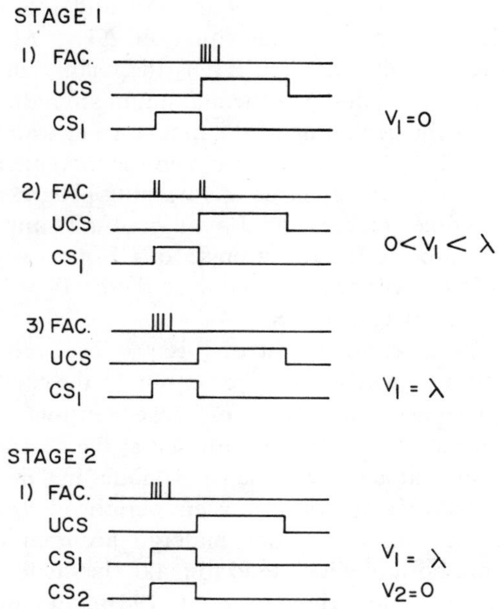

Figure 26-6. Proposed cellular mechanism of blocking. As conditioning of CS_1 proceeds (Stage 1, trials 1, 2, and 3), the facilitator neurons fire more during the CS period. This firing produces accommodation and recurrent inhibition, which reduce firing during the UCS period. When compound conditioning starts (Stage 2), CS_2 is not followed by firing of the facilitator neurons and therefore does not become conditioned.

These examples illustrate that our model incorporates in very rudimentary forms the notions of predictability and internal representation. The predicted effect of CS_1 is represented internally as the strength of the synapses from CS_1 to the facilitator neurons. The actual consequences of CS_1 are compared to this prediction through the operations of accommodation and recurrent inhibition, which in effect subtract the strength of CS_1 from the strength of the UCS that follows it. When these two strengths become equal, CS_1 can be said to fully predict the UCS, which thus loses its reinforcing power, and no further learning occurs. This subtraction process has the additional benefit of setting an upper limit on a positive-feedback circuit, thus circumventing a number of theoretical problems that have plagued Hebb-type models.

Degeneration of Learning by Intermittent Presentations of the UCS Alone or UCS Preexposure

In classical conditioning, animals learn not simply that the CS precedes the UCS (contiguity), but they also learn the contingency or correlation between the CS and UCS; that is, they learn how well one event predicts another. Thus, if unannounced UCSs occur between pairing trials, the ability of the CS to predict the UCS is reduced, and learning degenerates. In the limit, if the probability of unannounced UCSs is the same as the probability of announced (paired) UCSs, so that there is zero contingency, animals do not learn to associate the CS and UCS despite the fact that they are paired many times (Rescorla, 1968).

Rescorla and Wagner (1972) proposed that this effect could be explained by an extension of the argument they advanced for blocking, simply by including the stimuli that are always present in the experimental situation (the background stimuli) in the analysis. Thus, a zero contingency experiment can be considered as a blocking experiment in which CS background-UCS trials are intermixed with background-UCS trials. By the same argument outlined above, this would prevent conditioning to the experimental CS. Our cellular version of this argument requires that the conditioned background stimuli be capable of causing continuous excitation of the facilitator neurons, making them unresponsive to the UCS. Such continuous excitation of the facilitator neurons might be the neural representation of a state of conditioned anxiety.

Our neuronal explanation for blocking involves a rather short-term decrease in the output of the facilitator neurons during and following excitation of those neurons. The idea that the CS and UCS are interchangeable suggests a second explanation of the effect of contingency, which involves a long-term decrease in the input to the facilitator neurons. Thus, just as the CS pathway habituates with repeated presentations during extinction, so also can the US pathway undergo habituation with repeated presentations of the UCS. In a zero-contingency experiment, the unannounced UCS presentations will cause habituation of the UCS input, which will have the effect of making the UCS less effective on the CS-UCS trials. If this effect is strong enough, it will more than compensate for the extra sensitization of the CS pathway caused by the unannounced UCS presentations. Figure 26-7 illustrates how this might work in an experiment in which animals receive either five paired (CS-UCS) trials, five paired trials plus five unannounced UCS presentations, five unpaired trials, or five unpaired trials plus five unannounced UCS presentations. In this hypothetical example the addition of unannounced UCS presentations would cause not only a decrease in the difference between the paired and unpaired conditions, but also a decrease in the absolute strength of the paired CS. Results similar to those shown in Figure 26-7B have recently been obtained in an experiment with this design in *Aplysia* (Hawkins, Carew, & Kandel, 1983).

We have suggested two alternative explanations for degeneration of conditioning by presentation of unannounced UCSs: conditioning of background stimuli (based on our neuronal version of the Rescorla–Wagner model) and habituation of the UCS input. It may be possible to test these alternatives by performing an experiment in which the additional UCSs are signaled by a second CS (i.e., alternating CS_1-UCS and CS_2-UCS trials). The Rescorla–Wagner model predicts that conditioning of CS_1 in this case should be nearly the same as that produced by simple CS_1-UCS training, whereas the UCS habituation model predicts that conditioning of CS_1 should be reduced (unless pairing with a CS somehow prevents habituation of the UCS).

Learning can be impaired by unannounced presentations of the UCS *before* paired training begins as well as by unannounced UCSs during training. This treatment, which is called UCS preexposure, is thought to reduce the surprising or novel properties of the UCS and thus to reduce its effectiveness as a reinforcer. The neuronal mechanism of UCS preexposure could be the same as either (or both) of the mechanisms proposed above for degeneration of

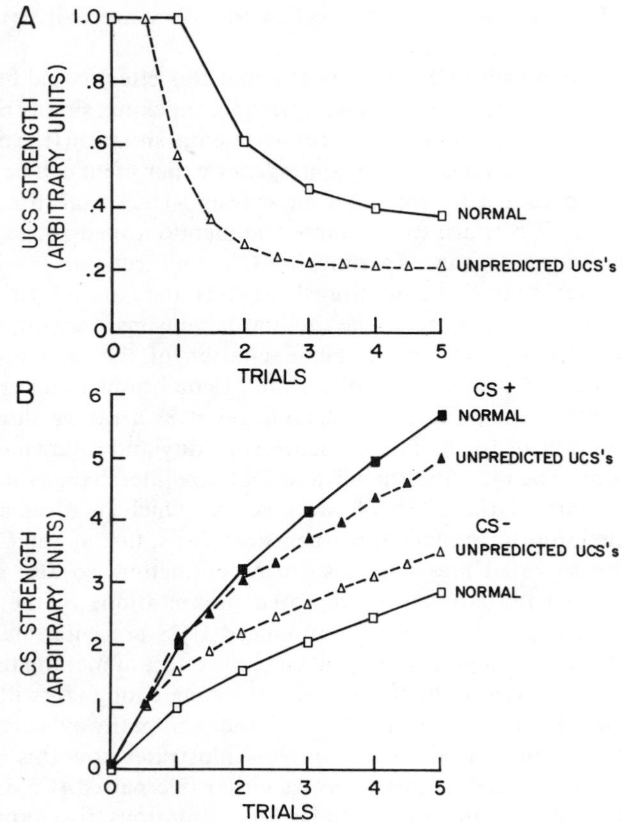

Figure 26-7. Proposed cellular mechanism of degeneration of learning by intermittent presentation of the UCS. (A) UCS strength on each trial in a hypothetical experiment described in the text. The UCS strength is assumed to decrease by 50% with each UCS presentation and to recover with a time constant of 20 minutes. (B) CS strength on each trial in the same hypothetical experiment. The CS is assumed to increase in strength by an amount proportional to the UCS strength when the UCS is presented alone and by twice that amount when the UCS is paired with the CS.

learning by unannounced presentations of the UCS during training, that is, either conditioning of background stimuli or habituation of the UCS input. The example of UCS habituation shown in Figure 26-7 includes one UCS preexposure, which contributes significantly to the net effect of the unannounced UCS presentations in that example.

CONCLUSION

The approach we have presented here attempts to explain a number of higher-order features of learning using combinations of the cellular mechanisms used in simple forms of learning. In particular, we have tried to provide neuronal versions of the Rescorla and Wagner models of conditioning so as to explain some of the phenomena those models address, including blocking and the effect of contingency. A basic feature of the Rescorla and Wagner models is that learning depends on the degree to which the UCS is surprising or unpredicted. In our neuronal model we propose that the concepts of predictability and surprise can be related to the more elementary concepts of habituation and sensitization, since the neuronal mechanism for predictability may be the same as that for habituation (synaptic depression or accommodation), and the neuronal mechanism for surprise may be the same as that for sensitization (conventional or activity-dependent presynaptic facilitation). Combinations of these mechanisms might also explain other learning phenomena we have not discussed here, including overshadowing, latent inhibition, and the effects of partial reinforcement, intertrial interval, CS strength, and UCS strength.

The model we describe differs from the Rescorla and Wagner models in an important way: It does not provide for negative learning in a way that is symmetrical with positive learning. Rather, our model depends on synaptic depression for negative learning. Thus, it is basically a two-process model, with the two processes being facilitation and depression. In this respect it is similar to the model of habituation of Groves and Thompson (1970), who proposed that presentation of any stimulus will tend to elicit two competing processes: facilitation of that stimulus pathway via excitation of facilitator neurons, and depression of that stimulus pathway through a homosynaptic mechanism. The net result will depend on the balance of the two processes, but in general, depression will predominate with repeated stimulation. We have attempted to extend this type of model to classical conditioning. For example, we propose that on trials early in training, facilitation of the CS pathway caused by firing of the facilitator neurons is greater than depression of the CS pathway caused by firing of the sensory neurons, and therefore the reflex is strengthened. With continued training, the facilitation becomes progressively weaker (see the preceding sections), and the asymptote of acquisition is reached when the facilitation and depression are equal. During extinction, the facilitator neurons fire even less on each trial (since they are excited only by the CS, whereas during acquisition they are excited by both the CS and the UCS), and therefore depression predominates until a new equilibrium is reached. We believe that this mechanism can adequately account for negative learning, although we realize that in many cases the predictions of a competing process model like ours are not obvious and that quantitative simulation will be necessary.

Our model cannot, however, account for learned inhibition—the actual reversal of sign of the effect of the CS—since the lowest depression can go is zero. Thus, our model provides no insight into conditioned inhibition and related learning phenomena. This is not because we have any quarrel with those phenomena but rather because we have restricted ourselves to the *Aplysia* circuitry shown in Figure 26-5, which does not include any inhibitory neurons. We do not yet know whether conditioned inhibition occurs in conditioning of the *Aplysia* withdrawal reflex, but if it does occur, we assume it could be modeled by the addition of inhibitory elements to the circuit shown in Figure 26-5.[3] Like the Rescorla–Wagner model, our model also has little to say

3. Figure 26-5 shows the minimal neuronal circuit necessary to account for differential conditioning of the gill and siphon withdrawal reflex and is not complete. Several known interneurons, including one inhibitory interneuron, have been omitted, and many other interneurons have probably not yet been discovered. For a more complete description of the known neuronal circuit, see Hawkins *et al.* (1981a).

about the exact nature of the conditioned response, since it is basically a stimulus–stimulus model.

In conclusion, we would emphasize the speculative nature of these proposals. First, although we have used cellular processes and patterns of neuronal connections known to occur in *Aplysia*, not all of the behavioral phenomena we have discussed have yet been demonstrated in *Aplysia*. Conditioning of the gill and siphon withdrawal reflex of *Aplysia* shows stimulus specificity, extinction, and recovery, and preliminary experiments suggest that it also shows the effect of contingency. Second-order conditioning, blocking, and UCS preexposure have not been tested in *Aplysia* (although they have been demonstrated in another mollusc, *Limax maximus*). Thus, there is no compelling reason to think that cellular processes that have been observed in *Aplysia* are relevant to all of these behavioral phenomena. Second, we do not provide any data suggesting that higher-order features of conditioning must necessarily emerge from the basic cellular mechanisms of more elementary forms of learning. Nor would we argue that participation of the cellular mechanisms that we have outlined here in higher-order features of conditioning would provide evidence for their role in yet more sophisticated types of learning. We would only argue that available evidence on the cellular mechanisms of elementary forms of learning suggests that it may be possible to develop a cellular alphabet of learning and that surprisingly complex forms of learning may be generated from combinations of this alphabet of simple cellular mechanisms. Most important, however, the hypotheses we have described should be testable on the neuronal level in several invertebrates. These tests should in turn indicate the degree to which the notions we have outlined here are useful.

REFERENCES

Alkon, D. L. Voltage-dependent calcium and potassium ion conductances: A contingency mechanism for an associative learning model. *Science*, 1979, *205*, 810–816.

Atkinson, R. C., & Estes, W. K. Stimulus sampling theory. In R. D. Luce, R. R. Bush, & E. Galanter (Eds.), *Handbook of mathematical psychology* (Vol. 2). New York: Wiley, 1963.

Bernier, L., Castellucci, V. F., Kandel, E. R., & Schwartz, J. H. Facilitatory transmitter causes a selective and prolonged increase in adenosine 3′:5′-monophosphate in sensory neurons mediating the gill and siphon withdrawal reflex in *Aplysia*. *Journal of Neuroscience*, 1982, *2*, 1682–1691.

Bush, R. R., & Mosteller, F. A model for stimulus generalization and discrimination. *Psychological Review*, 1951, *58*, 413–423.

Byers, D., Davis, R. L., Kiger, J. A. Defect in cyclic AMP phosphodiesterase due to the dunce mutation of learning in *Drosophila melanogaster*. *Nature*, 1981, *289*, 79–81.

Carew, T. J., Castellucci, V. F., & Kandel, E. R. An analysis of dishabituation and sensitization of the gill-withdrawal reflex in *Aplysia*. *International Journal of Neuroscience*, 1971, *2*, 79–98.

Carew, T. J., Hawkins, R. D., & Kandel, E. R. Differential classical conditioning of a defensive withdrawal reflex in *Aplysia californica*. *Science*, 1983, *219*, 397–400.

Carew, T. J., Walters, E. T., & Kandel, E. R. Classical conditioning in a simple withdrawal reflex in *Aplysia californica*. *Journal of Neuroscience*, 1981, *1*, 1426–1437.

Castellucci, V. F., & Kandel, E. R. A quantal analysis of the synaptic depression underlying habituation of the gill-withdrawal reflex in *Aplysia*. *Proceedings of the National Academy of Sciences, USA*, 1974, *71*, 5004–5008.

Castellucci, V., & Kandel, E. R. Presynaptic facilitation as a mechanism for behavioral sensitization in *Aplysia*. *Science*, 1976, *194*, 1176–1178.

Castellucci, V. F., Nairn, A., Greengard, P., Schwartz, J. H., & Kandel, E. R. Inhibitor of adenosine 3′:5′-monophosphate-dependent protein kinase blocks presynaptic facilitation in *Aplysia*. *Journal of Neuroscience*, 1982, *2*, 1673–1681.

Castellucci, V., Pinsker, H., Kupfermann, I., & Kandel, E. R. Neuronal mechanisms of habituation and dishabituation of the gill-withdrawal reflex in *Aplysia*. *Science*, 1970, *167*, 1745–1748.

Cegavske, C. F., Patterson, M. M., & Thompson, R. F. Neuronal unit activity in the abducens nucleus during classical conditioning of the nictitating membrane response in the rabbit (*Oryctolagus cuniculus*). *Journal of Comparative and Physiological Psychology*, 1979, *93*, 595–609.

Crow, T. J., & Alkon, D. L. Associative behavioral modification in *Hermissenda*: Cellular correlates. *Science*, 1980, *209*, 412–414.

Dickinson, A., & Mackintosh, N. J. Classical conditioning in animals. *Annual Review of Psychology*, 1978, *29*, 587–612.

Duerr, J. S., & Quinn, W. G. Three *Drosophila* mutants that block associative learning also affect habituation and sensitization. *Proceedings of the National Academy of Sciences, USA*, 1982, *79*, 3646–3650.

Groves, P. M., & Thompson, R. F. Habituation: A dual-process theory. *Psychological Review*, 1970, *77*, 419–450.

Guthrie, E. R. *The psychology of learning*. New York: Harper, 1935.

Hawkins, R. D. Identified facilitating neurons are excited by cutaneous stimuli used in sensitization and classical conditioning of *Aplysia*. *Society for Neuroscience Abstracts*, 1981a, *7*, 354.

Hawkins, R. D. Interneurons involved in mediation and modulation of gill-withdrawal reflex in *Aplysia*: III. Identified facilitating neurons increase Ca^{2+} current in sensory neurons. *Journal of Neurophysiology*, 1981b, *45*, 327–339.

Hawkins, R. D., Abrams, T. W., Carew, T. J., & Kandel, E. R. A cellular mechanism of classical conditioning in *Aplysia*: Activity-dependent amplification of presynaptic facilitation. *Science*, 1983, *219*, 400–405.

Hawkins, R. D., & Advocat, C. Effects of behavioral state on the gill-withdrawal reflex in *Aplysia californica*. *Neuroscience Symposia*, 1977, *3*, 16–32.

Hawkins, R. D., Carew, T. J., & Kandel, E. R. Effects of interstimulus interval and contingency on classical conditioning in *Aplysia*. *Society for Neuroscience Abstracts*, 1983, *9*, 168.

Hawkins, R. D., Castellucci, V. F., & Kandel, E. R. Interneurons involved in mediation and modulation of gill-withdrawal reflex in *Aplysia*: I. Identification and characterization. *Journal of Neurophysiology*, 1981a, *45*, 304–314.

Hawkins, R. D., Castellucci, V. F., & Kandel, E. R. Interneurons involved in mediation and modulation of gill-withdrawal reflex in *Aplysia*: II. Identified neurons produce heterosynaptic facilitation contributing to behavioral sensitization. *Journal of Neurophysiology*, 1981b, *45*, 315–326.

Hawkins, R. D., & Kandel, E. R. Is there a cell-biological alphabet for simple forms of learning? *Psychological Review*, in press.

Hoyle, G. Instrumental conditioning of the leg lift in the locust. *Neuroscience Research Program Bulletin*, 1979, *17*, 577–586.

Hull, C. L. *Principles of behavior*. New York: Appleton-Century-Crofts, 1943.

Kamin, L. J. Predictability, surprise, attention and conditioning. In B. A. Campbell & R. M. Church (Eds.), *Punishment and aversive behavior*. New York: Appleton-Century-Crofts, 1969.

Kandel, E. R. *A cell-biological approach to learning*. Bethesda, Md.: Society for Neuroscience, 1978.

Kandel, E. R., & Schwartz, J. H. Molecular biology of learning: Modulation of transmitter release. *Science*, 1982, *218*, 433–443.

Klein, M., & Kandel, E. R. Mechanism of calcium current modulation underlying presynaptic facilitation and behavioral sensitization in *Aplysia*. *Proceedings of the National Academy of Sciences, USA*, 1980, *77*, 6912–6916.

Klein, M., Shapiro, E., & Kandel, E. R. Synaptic plasticity and the modulation of the Ca^{++} current. *Journal of Experimental Biology*, 1980, *89*, 117–157.

Krasne, F. B. Excitation and habituation of the crayfish escape reflex: The depolarization response in lateral giant fibers of the isolated abdomen. *Journal of Experimental Biology*, 1969, *50*, 29–46.

Pavlov, I. P. *Conditioned reflexes* (G. V. Anrep, Trans.). London: Oxford University Press, 1927.

Pinsker, H. M., Kupfermann, I., Castellucci, V., & Kandel, E. R. Habituation and dishabituation of the gill-withdrawal reflex in *Aplysia*. *Science*, 1970, *167*, 1740–1742.

Rescorla, R. A. Probability of shock in the presence and absence of CS in fear conditioning. *Journal of Comparative and Physiological Psychology*, 1968, *66*, 1–5.

Rescorla, R. A. Some implications of a cognitive perspective on Pavlovian conditioning. In S. H.

Hulse, H. Fowler, & W. Honig (Eds.), *Cognitive processes in animal behavior*. Hillsdale, N.J.: Erlbaum, 1978.

Rescorla, R. A., & Wagner, A. R. A theory of Pavlovian conditioning: Variations in the effectiveness of reinforcement and nonreinforcement. In A. H. Black & W. F. Prokasy (Eds.), *Classical conditioning II: Current research and theory*. New York: Appleton-Century-Crofts, 1972.

Sahley, C., Rudy, J. W., & Gelperin, A. An analysis of associative learning in a terrestrial mollusc. I. Higher-order conditioning, blocking, and a transient US pre-exposure effect. *Journal of Comparative Physiology*, 1981, *144*, 1–8.

Siegelbaum, S. A., Camardo, J. S., & Kandel, E. R. Serotonin and cyclic AMP close single K^+ channels in *Aplysia* sensory neurons. *Nature*, 1982, *299*, 413–417.

Spencer, W. A., Thompson, R. F., & Nielson, D. R., Jr. Decrement of ventral root electrotonus and intracellularly recorded PSPs produced by iterated cutaneous afferent volleys. *Journal of Neurophysiology*, 1966, *29*, 253–273.

Thompson, R. F., & Spencer, W. A. Habituation: A model phenomenon for the study of neuronal substrates of behavior. *Psychological Review*, 1966, *173*, 16–43.

Tolman, E. C. *Purposive behavior in animals and men*. New York: Century, 1932.

Wagner, A. R. Expectancies and the priming of STM. In S. H. Hulse, H. Fowler, & W. Honig [*Eds.*], *Cognitive processes in animal behavior*. Hillsdale, N.J.: Erlbaum, 1978.

Walters, E. T., & Byrne, J. H. Associative conditioning of single neurons suggests a cellular mechanism for learning. *Science*, 1983, *219*, 405–408,

Walters, E. T., Carew, T. J., & Kandel, E. R. Associative learning in *Aplysia*: Evidence for conditioned fear in an invertebrate. *Science*, 1981, *211*, 504–506.

Zucker, R. S. Crayfish escape behavior and central synapses: II. Physiological mechanisms underlying behavioral habituation. *Journal of Neurophysiology*, 1972, *35*, 621–637.

CHAPTER TWENTY-SEVEN

Heterosynaptic Interaction at a Sympathetic Neuron as a Model for Induction and Storage of a Postsynaptic Memory Trace

BENJAMIN LIBET

Models for processes of learning and memory at the single neuron level continue to be based on two premises. These are (1) that learning involves a modification of synaptic efficacy; and (2) that the formation of an enduring appropriate molecular change in a neuron is responsible for the altered synaptic efficacy and constitutes a memory trace at the level of the single cell. These premises were already expressed in the pioneering hypotheses and experimental work of Hebb (1949, 1966) and Gerard (1949, 1955), among others. The discovery and analysis in sympathetic ganglia of novel, slow postsynaptic responses induced by synaptic inputs (see Libet, 1970, 1979c) presented characteristics that appear to meet some of the important requirements implicit in the premises for a neuronal model. I shall (1) first describe the relevant synaptic actions in mammalian sympathetic neurons, and (2) then discuss how they may be applicable to the present purposes. The latter would include the extent to which these synaptic actions may satisfy the needs of a synaptic model for learning–memory and special suggestions they uniquely offer in relation to the kinds of processes that could be operative in a model.

SLOW SYNAPTIC ACTIONS IN SYMPATHETIC GANGLIA

Two classes of slow postsynaptic responses are found in mammalian sympathetic neurons, each class being relevant to shorter- and longer-term retention, respectively. The first includes various slow *postsynaptic potential* (PSP) responding to neural inputs arriving in normal, orthodromic pathways. These change the excitability level of the cell, that is, its ability to achieve threshold for firing in response to a subsequent input. The changes last for some seconds to minutes after a "conditioning" input. The other class is represented by a much longer-lasting "*contingent synaptic action*," which forms the basis of a model relevant to forma-

Benjamin Libet. Department of Physiology, School of Medicine, University of California, San Francisco, California.

tion and durability of a memory trace. In this action there is no direct change in electrical excitability of the cell such as occurs during PSPs. Instead, one synaptic transmitter induces a long-term enhancement (LTE) of the postsynaptic potential elicited by another transmitter. It may therefore be termed a "contingent synaptic action." The modulatory or conditioning transmitter is dopamine (DA), and the response whose enhancement is contingent on the DA action is the slow (s)-EPSP elicited by a muscarinic action of acetylcholine (ACh). It will be emphasized that both classes of synaptic changes are induced in the *postsynaptic* element of the synapse, and in both there is or can be interaction between the effects of different sources of synaptic inputs onto the postsynaptic neuron—that is, they provide for *heterosynaptic* interactions.

Slow PSPs in Mammalian Sympathetic Ganglia

Orthodromic, preganglionic nerve impulses can elicit three kinds of slow PSPs in the principal neuron of mammalian sympathetic ganglia (reviewed in Libet, 1970, 1979c; Nishi, 1974; Kuba & Koketsu, 1978; Ashe & Libet, 1981b). These are in addition to the previously known fast (f)-EPSP which resembles the f-EPSP at the neuromuscular junction, spinal motoneurons, and many other central nervous system (CNS) sites. The f-EPSP in sympathetic neurons has a synaptic delay of < 1 msec and a duration on the order of 50–100 msec. The remarkably long synaptic delays and durations of the slow PSPs are summarized in Table 27-1.

A schema of the pathways, transmitters, and receptors for the *f-EPSP* and two of the slow PSPs (*s-IPSP* and *s-EPSP*; Figure 27-1) is shown in Figure 27-2. These all include a cholinergic step. ACh, released by the terminals of preganglionic axons, is the direct transmitter for the f- and s-EPSPs, but the postsynaptic receptors differ. The f-EPSP is mediated by a nicotinic receptor, blocked by curariform drugs and hexamethonium. The s-EPSP is mediated by a muscarinic receptor, blocked by atropinic drugs (quinuclidinyl benzilate hydrochloride [QNB] is effective at about $1\text{–}5 \times 10^{-8}$ M).

ACh appears to elicit the s-IPSP indirectly. In mammalian ganglia at least, there are strong and rather complete lines of evidence for a disynaptic pathway, as indicated in Figure 27-2 (Libet, 1970, 1979c; Ashe & Libet, 1982). In this, ACh acts at muscarinic receptors on a small type of DA-containing interneuron (known as small, intensely fluorescent [SIF] cells); DA released by SIF cells then acts as the direct transmitter for the s-IPSP in the principal neuron ("ganglion cell"). The SIF cells show remarkable resemblances to those in the

Table 27-1. PSPs and DA modulation in mammalian sympathetic neurons

	Synaptic delay (msec)	Duration (sec)	Transmitter	Postsynaptic receptor	Blocked by
f-EPSP	<1	.05–.1	ACh	Nicotinic	Curare, etc.
s-IPSP	25	1–10 ±	DA (NE)	α_2	Yohimbine
s-EPSP	100–300	5–100	ACh	Muscarinic	Atropine, QNB
ss-EPSP ("late" s-EPSP)	1000	100–2000	Peptide (?)	Peptidergic (?)	(?)
DA modulation of s-EPSP	(30 *sec* ±)	1–4 *hr* +	DA	D-1 (adenyl cyclase)	Neuroleptics (flupenthixol)

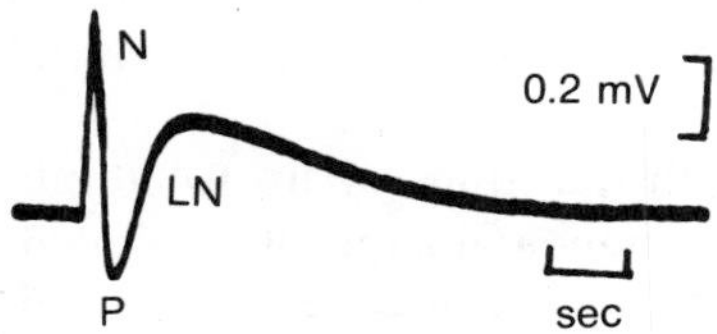

Figure 27-1. Postsynaptic potentials, recorded from surface of rabbit's superior cervical ganglion, partially curarized to depress fast (f)-EPSPs and prevent their firing the ganglion cells. Response to one train of preganglionic stimuli, 40 pps for .25 sec. Surface-negative potential "N" is seen during stimulation; N represents the summated fast EPSPs, with their peaks sloping in the downward direction because of the developing surface-positive (P) or hyperpolarizing component. The P phase outlasts and reaches its peak after the stimulus train; this is the s-IPSP. The "late-negative" (LN) depolarizing phase is the s-EPSP, which has a synaptic delay 200 to 300 msec longer than that for the s-IPSP. The form of this entire surface-recorded response is very similar to that obtained by an intracellular recording from a single principal neuron (see Libet & Tosaka, 1969). Polarity of active electrode is negative upward, in all surface (extracellular) recordings. (From Libet, 1980.)

Figure 27-2. Schema of intraganglionic synaptic connections, for mediation of fast and slow PSPs (except for the noncholinergic ss-EPSP). All of these preganglionic axons release ACh. Nicotinic ACh action for f-EPSP is blocked by curare; muscarinic actions for s-EPSP and on the SIF cell (DA-containing interneuron) are blocked by atropine (or QNB). DA action on s-IPSP receptor is blocked by α_2-antagonists (such as yohimbine). On the receptor modulating LTE for the s-EPSP, DA is blocked by D-1 antagonists (e.g., butaclamol, flupenthixol). (From Libet, 1977, as modified from Libet, 1970.)

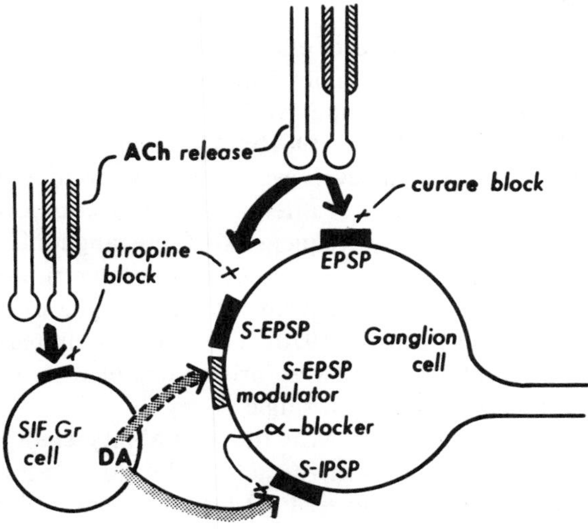

monoaminergic nuclei of the brain, for example, the locus ceruleus and substantia nigra (e.g., Moore, 1977; Descarries, Watkins, & Lapierre, 1977). They are relatively small in number, but each gives rise to a profuse network of beaded fibers that surrounds virtually all the principal neurons (Libet & Owman, 1974; Libet, 1980). In addition, the synaptic arrangement appears to be of a "loose" type; that is, transmitter released by the DA terminals would diffuse across variable distances greater than the 200 Å in classical chemical junctions for fast PSPs.

The "late-" or "double-slow" *ss-EPSP*, with durations of up to 30 min rather than seconds, is neither cholinergically nor monoaminergically mediated. In frog sympathetic ganglia, where this PSP was first discovered (Nishi & Koketsu, 1968), the transmitter appears to be a peptide closely related to the luteinizing hormone-releasing hormone (LH-RH) factor released by hypothalamic neurons for action on pituitary cells (Jan & Jan, 1982; Jan Jan, & Kuffler, 1980). The transmitter is not as well defined in mammalian ganglia. Another peptide, substance P, has been proposed for at least the inferior mesenteric ganglion (Konishi, Tsunoo, Yanaihara, & Otsuka, 1980; Jiang, Dun, & Karczmar, 1982), but it remains possible that different peptides may mediate similar ss-EPSP-type responses in the same or in different sympathetic ganglia of the same animal.

The ss-EPSP is readily visible in intact superior cervical ganglia of rabbits and rats even after complete blockade of the s-IPSP and s-EPSP by the powerful muscarinic antagonist QNB, as in Figure 27-3, or by any other strong atropinic drug. The ss-EPSP can be at least as large as the muscarinic s-EPSP. Its peak amplitudes can reach 25 to 50% of the action potential exhibited by the same group of ganglion cells; such magnitudes would make it clearly able to markedly affect cell excitability and even to initiate discharge of impulses postsynaptically. With a synaptic delay on the order of 1 *sec* and durations of up to 20 to 30 *min* after a relatively modest preganglionic neural input, these extraordinarily slow ss-EPSPs clearly introduce an enormously expanded time during which a monosynaptic response can alter the postsynaptic excitability level with which subsequent other inputs can interact.

Additional Features of All These Slow PSPs

1. The *neural inputs* required to elicit all of the slow PSPs are clearly in the physiological range of the normally functioning nervous system. All three slow PSPs require repetition of input volleys to achieve maximal responses (Libet, 1970, 1979c; Ashe & Libet, 1981b). However, both the s-EPSP and ss-EPSP can develop to maximal levels even with very low input frequencies, as low as 1/sec, providing the train of afferent impulses lasts long enough (see Figure 27-4 for ss-EPSP). Low frequencies of preganglionic impulses that continue for lengthy periods (seconds, minutes, and longer) have in fact been found to characterize the discharge from CNS to ganglia during autonomic functions *in vivo* (Jänig & Schmidt, 1970). The s-IPSP requires inputs at 20 to 40/sec for maximal amplitudes, but very brief trains of these (.25 sec) suffice. Lesser s-IPSPs are elicited even by a single volley.

2. Heterosynaptic interaction with the excitability changes induced by PSPs to other inputs also characterize each of the slow PSPs as well as the f-EPSP. The f-EPSP, s-IPSP, and s-EPSP responses have all been shown by

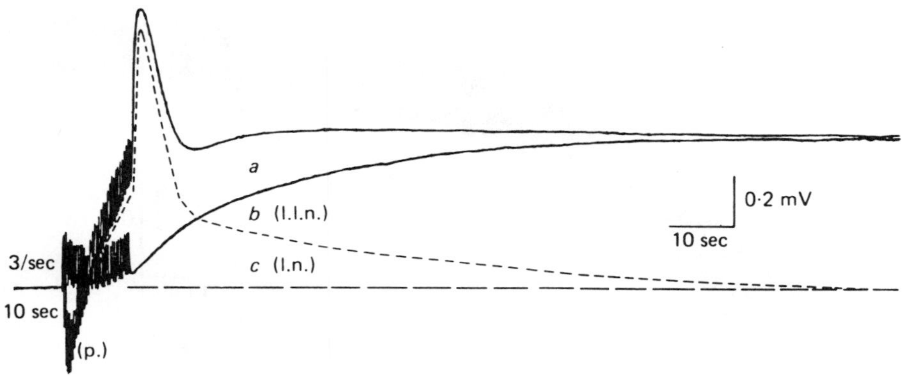

Figure 27-3. All postsynaptic potentials, including ss-EPSP, as seen in slow-speed tracing. Ganglionic potentials elicited by supramaximal stimulation of cervical sympathetic nerve; 10-sec train of 3 pps; D-tubocurarine present. Trace a, before, and trace b, after addition of QNB (.05 μM). Dashed curve c, subtraction of b from a. In trace a are exhibited in overlapping fashion: fast EPSPs depressed by D-tubocurarine (visible on this slow time base as brief, spike-like, surface-negative deflections during the stimulus train); s-IPSP (surface-positive, p.); s-EPSP ("late negative," l.n.); and ss-EPSP, an even slower depolarizing component ("late-late negative," l.l.n.). In trace b, the s-IPSP and s-EPSP components, each of which involves a muscarinic synaptic step, have been eliminated by QNB, leaving the fast EPSPs and the non-cholinergic ss-EPSP (l.l.n.) responses. Trace c shows the presumed combined contribution of the s-IPSP and s-EPSP components to the total response in a. A declining tail of the s-EPSP (l.n. component) persists for almost 2 min (see c). But the ss-EPSP (l.l.n. component) is just reaching its peak amplitude after about 2 min (see b); it continued for some minutes beyond the portion of the recording shown here. (From Ashe & Libet, 1981b.)

direct intracellular recordings to be elicited in a given single mammalian neuron (Libet & Tosaka, 1969). Indirect evidence indicates that the ss-EPSP also develops in the same cell as the other PSPs (Ashe & Libet, 1981b). In other words, the inputs that can elicit each and all of the PSPs can converge on the same cell.

An unequivocal direct demonstration of heterosynaptic interaction between excitability levels induced by the f- and s-EPSPs was made utilizing the stellate ganglion of the cat (Libet, 1964). With this structure, neural inputs from anatomically separate ventral roots, emanating from thoracic spinal cord, converge on the same pool of ganglionic neurons. Further, this ganglion displays a substantial s-EPSP but little or no s-IPSP response to an input train. A brief conditioning train of preganglionic nerve impulses in some of these input lines was delivered by stimulating the sympathetic chain. A testing volley, to indicate any heterosynaptic interaction with excitability changes that follow the conditioning train, was delivered in a separate root entering the input lines to the ganglion at a point where it could not be stimulated by the conditioning stimulus. Changes in excitability level of the ganglionic neurons would alter the ability of the test volley to fire those cells; this is reflected in the changes in amplitude of the compound population action potential elicited by a single test volley set at a supramaximal strength. The recovery curve of such test volleys during the postconditioning period indicates a raised excitability level lasting up to 30 sec (see Figure 27-5). The specific contribution of the s-EPSP to this change could be evaluated by selectively eliminating the s-EPSP with atropine.

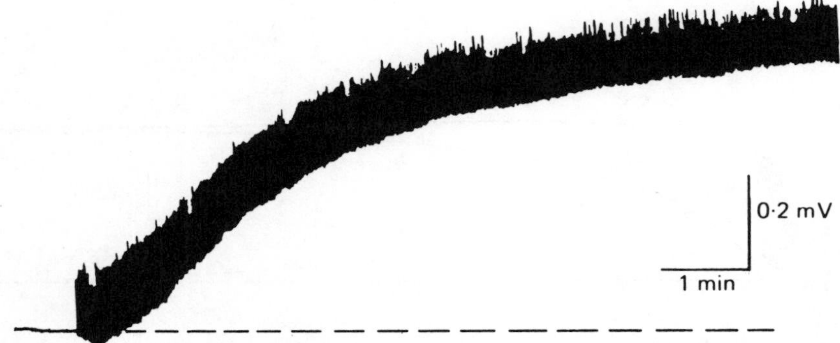

Figure 27-4. Noncholinergic ss-EPSP response to 1/sec input. Continuous stimulation of preganglionic nerve at 1/sec. The surface-negative ss-EPSP develops gradually over some minutes to its maximal level. Tubocurarine present to depress f-EPSPs; these are superimposed on the ss-EPSP, crowded together in the very slow tracing so as to produce the irregular thickening of the ss-EPSP tracing. QNB also is present to eliminate any s-IPSP and s-EPSP contributions. (From Ashe & Libet, 1981b.)

Recovery curves for the test spike then showed depression, not enhancement. Thus, the s-EPSPs elicited by the conditioning input enabled the f-EPSPs, elicited by each single test volley arriving in a completely separate input line, to fire more neurons than they otherwise could.

3. *Electrogenic mechanisms* for the slow PSPs differ in principle from those for all chemically mediated fast PSPs. The slow PSPs do not exhibit increases in ionic conductance, such as those that form the basis of all known fast EPSPs and IPSPs. In the case of mammalian sympathetic ganglia, the s-IPSP and s-EPSP are associated with no detectable change in membrane conductance at all (Libet, 1970, 1979c; Kobayashi & Libet, 1968, 1970). (In the case of the s-EPSP, an actual decrease in conductance can be observed during the response but only when the cell is depolarized to levels of membrane potential that are less negative than −60 mV. This appears to be due to an ability of ACh to close a special K^+ conductance channel that is open only in this depolarized range, both in frog ganglia [Brown & Adams, 1980] and in mammalian ganglia [Hashiguchi, Kobayashi, Tosaka, & Libet, 1982]. Muscarinic ACh closure of such voltage-sensitive K^+ channels [the "M" channels] can contribute a depolarizing component to the s-EPSP but only in a cell that is rather strongly depolarized to less than −60 mV. In the mammalian ganglion cell, the "physiological" s-EPSP is elicited with a large amplitude at all resting potentials, including those more negative than −60 mV, and this predominant component develops with no change in conductance [Hashiguchi, Ushiyama, Kobayashi, & Libet, 1978; Hashiguchi *et al.*, 1982].) At present our best speculation about the electrogenesis of the s-IPSP and s-EPSP in mammalian ganglia is that electrogenic ion pumps may be activated and provide the voltage change, with no change in membrane conductance. The electrogenic mechanism for the ss-EPSP is still not clear; in frog sympathetic ganglia it appears to be associated with a decrease in conductance, but its nature in mammalian ganglion cells is yet to be more adequately established.

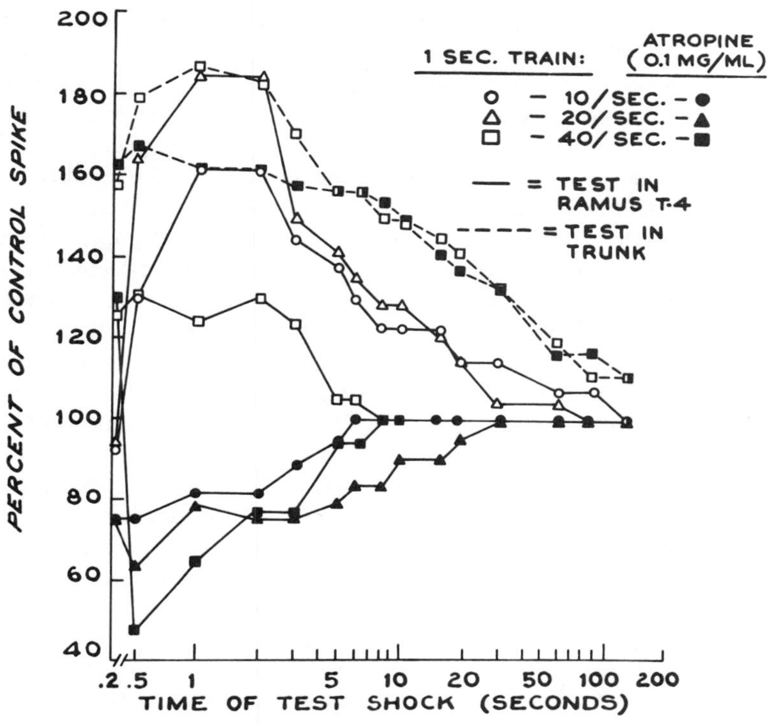

Figure 27-5. Heterosynaptic interaction between excitatory effects of fast and slow EPSPs. Stellate ganglion of cat, *in vitro*. Conditioning trains of preganglionic volleys each had a duration of 1 sec at the frequency indicated, and were applied to thoracic sympathetic chain below the entry of the ramus from thoracic (T)-4. Heterosynaptic test responses were each elicited by a single, supramaximal stimulus pulse to ramus T-4; the changes in the ganglionic discharge (compound spike height) produced by each test volley, relative to the control value before the conditioning input, are plotted against time after the conditioning input. These recovery curves were repeated later, after adding atropine to eliminate the s-EPSP component in the responses elicited by the conditioning input (see filled symbols). Homosynaptic test responses, to stimuli applied at the same point as the conditioning stimuli, are shown by the dashed lines; the large facilitation remaining after atropine in this case is presumed to be due to "posttetanic potentiation" (PTP) in the presynaptic terminals that were excited during the conditioning train that arrived in the same input line. (From Libet, 1964).

Cyclic GMP appears to be an intracellular mediator of the s-EPSP in mammalian ganglion cells. Muscarinic agonists stimulate guanylate cyclase to produce more cyclic GMP in these ganglia (Kebabian, Steiner, & Greengard, 1975). Cyclic GMP can itself elicit a slow depolarizing response (McAfee & Greengard, 1972), which has been shown to fulfill the requirement that it be developed with the same absence of an increase in membrane conductance as is found for the predominant component of the s-EPSP itself (Hashiguchi *et al.*, 1978, 1982). Mediation of the s-EPSP intracellularly by cylic GMP turns out to be of additional special interest in relation to the long-lasting contingent synaptic action by DA on the s-EPSP responses (see below).

Induction of Long-Term Enhancement (LTE) of s-EPSP by DA: A "Contingent Synaptic Action"

DA, shown to be synaptically releasable from monoaminergic interneurons, the SIF cells (Libet & Owman, 1974), was found to have two separate and independent postsynaptic actions (Libet & Tosaka, 1970). One of these, already discussed above, is to act as a direct transmitter for the hyperpolarizing s-IPSP response. The second action of DA was discovered unexpectedly during an experimental analysis of the first role. In this second role, DA induced a long-term enhancement (LTE) of the muscarinically mediated s-EPSP responses to another transmitter, ACh. This novel type of synaptic action, in which postsynaptic potentials elicited by one transmitter (ACh) are affected by a prior action of another transmitter (DA), may be referred to as a "contingent synaptic action." It should be emphasized that the induced change is in the s-EPSP response that is directly elicited by ACh, *not* one of altered membrane excitatory level that affects the ability of an s-EPSP to fire the neuron.

The contingent synaptic action by DA was initially established experimentally in relation to the direct slow depolarizing responses to a muscarinic agonist, such as acetyl-β-methacholine (MCh) or to ACh itself (with ACh-nicotinic action suitably blocked). The agonist was applied in a superfusion chamber with a sucrose-gap type of recording at about 20° C; test depolarizing responses to a constant-dose exposure to MCh could then be followed quantitatively before and at intervals after a brief exposure to DA. Following a brief exposure to exogenous DA, the test responses to MCh were increased in both amplitude and duration by about 50–100% (see Figure 27-6). When the test responses are repeated periodically without any further application of DA, they are found to remain enhanced for up to 3–4 hr at least; part of the gradual decline in the enhancement is probably due to deterioration of the preparation *in vitro*, but part of it is probably due to an actual gradual loss of the modulatory change. The other catecholamines, norepinephrine and epinephrine, are relatively ineffective for producing such an LTE of the muscarinic depolarizing response; this is in contrast to their ability to produce direct hyperpolarizing responses that are equivalent to the s-IPSP, for which they are considerably more effective than DA. (See "Discussion" in Ashe & Libet, 1982.)

The s-EPSP itself, as elicited synaptically by suitable preganglionic neural input, can also be shown to undergo a similar LTE after a temporary exposure to DA. However, to achieve this it was found necessary to block the enzyme catechol-*O*-methyltransferase (COMT) with an antagonist drug 3′,4′-dihydroxy-2-methylpropriophenone (U-0521); see Figure 27-7 (Ashe & Libet, 1981a). COMT is one of the two major enzymes that inactivate catecholamines at an early step in their degradation. Apparently, COMT can act as a potent barrier that limits the ability of DA to reach the appropriate postsynaptic receptors that mediate the LTE change. (This becomes more of a problem when studying s-EPSP test responses, which are contributed by ganglion cells throughout the thickness of the ganglion; in the case of direct MCh test responses, one is studying depolarizing responses primarily of ganglion cells near the surface, which can be reached by the briefly superfusing MCh.) Incidentally, this newly found physiological importance for COMT, in being able to limit at least this kind of synaptic action, could have considerable significance for the functions of catecholamines in the brain, where such a potential role is still to be

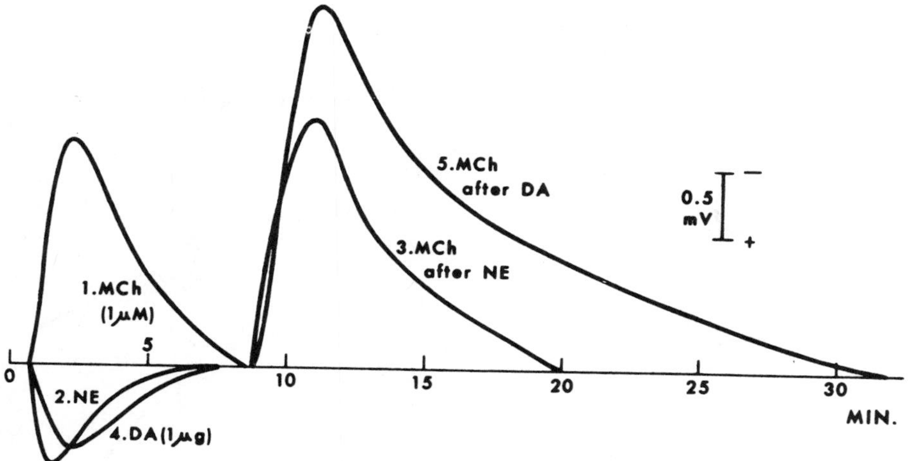

Figure 27-6. Modulatory enhancement of slow muscarinic depolarizations by DA. Surface-recorded responses of rabbit SCG (22°C) in a sucrose-gap chamber. The ganglion was pretreated with the potent muscarinic agonist bethanechol (BCh) to deplete intraganglionic DA; this procedure eliminates the initial hyperpolarizing component normally seen in the responses to methacholine (MCh) (see Libet & Owman, 1974). The first test shown is the response to a single-bolus injection of 1 μ mol MCh (approximately 200 μg) into the ganglionic superfusate. Test 2 is the response to 1 μg NE. Test 3 is a repeat of MCh, as in test 1, done shortly after the hyperpolarizing response to NE finished. Test 4 shows the response to 1 μg DA injected after the conclusion of MCh response 3. Test 5 is a repeat of MCh, as in test 1, shortly after the hyperpolarizing response to DA finished. The substantial increase in amplitude and duration of the MCh response seen in test 5 after DA, but not in test 3 after NE, can be exhibited by succeeding tests with MCh, repeated for some hours, even though no further DA is applied. (From Libet, 1979c, based on experiments reported in Libet & Tosaka, 1970.)

evaluated. In this role, COMT may be regarded as analogous to acetylcholinesterase in the case of synaptic actions by ACh, although with some important differences; in contrast to the more ubiquitous acetylcholinesterase actions, the COMT synaptic barrier appears to be largely effective only for the postsynaptic receptors in the sympathetic ganglia, apparently having little effectiveness for catecholamine actions at presynaptic terminals (see Ashe & Libet, 1981a).

An LTE of s-EPSP responses can also be induced by a conditioning train of preganglionic neural input, without the need for any application of exogenous DA (Mochida & Libet, 1983). This LTE, induced by a purely physiological synaptic input and acting on a physiological s-EPSP response, appears in fact to be mediated by an intraganglionic release of DA. The induction of the LTE is selectively blocked by drugs antagonistic to the D-1 type of DA receptor (see below); the action is not blocked by either α- or β-adrenergic antagonists. The same drugs were shown to block the LTE induced by exogenous DA (Ashe & Libet, 1981a). However, the LTE induced by the conditioning input train of impulses can be demonstrated fully without any COMT blocker. Presumably, the delivery of higher concentrations of dopamine by synaptic release sites that are closer to the postsynaptic receptor sites can get sufficient DA through the COMT barriers.

Clearly, an LTE can be generated completely endogenously in the ganglion, so that synaptically induced s-EPSP responses to preganglionic ACh are being

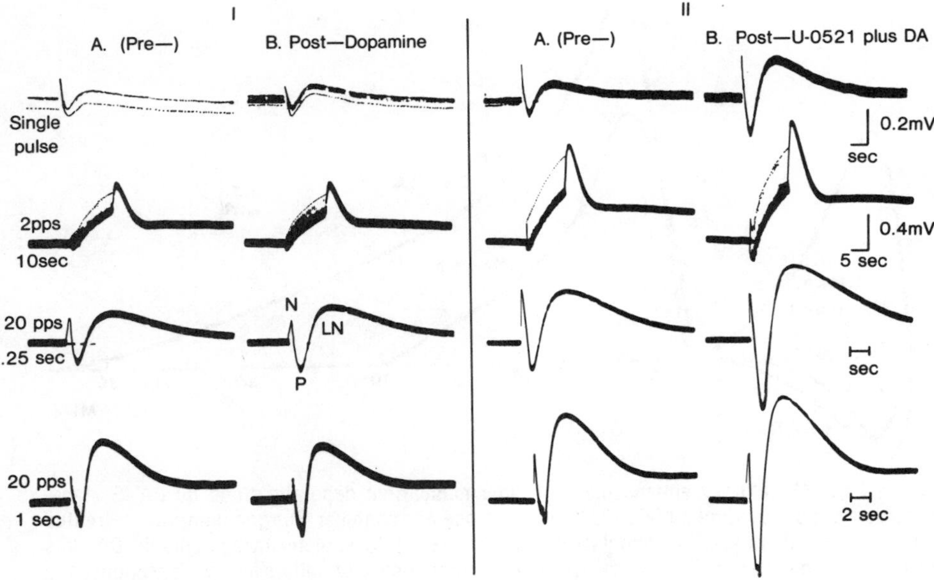

Figure 27-7. Changes in PSPs after exposure to DA, in the absence versus in the presence of a COMT inhibitor (U-0521). Pair (I and II) of superior cervical ganglia from same rabbit, both curarized (D-tubocurarine, 50 μM) to abolish firing of ganglion cells by f-EPSP. (Dihydroergotamine, 45 μM, was also present in both ganglia to antagonize α-adrenergic actions by DA.) Responses were recorded with surface electrodes, one on ganglion and other on postganglionic nerve. Preganglionic nerve was stimulated supramaximally, with pulse frequency and train duration indicated at left for each horizontal row. As in Figure 27-1, components labeled N (surface-negative), P (positive), and LN (late-negative) indicate net recordable f-EPSPs, s-IPSP, and s-EPSP, respectively. In response to the 2/sec, 10-sec trains of stimulus pulses, recorded at the slow speed indicated, the f-EPSPs appear spike-like (or with only tips visible) and are superimposed during the train on a combined s-IPSP and slower developing s-EPSP. After the 10-sec stimulus train, the longer lasting s-EPSP reaches its maximal amplitude but continues with a longer depolarizing tail (the end of which is cut off in this figure) that goes on for about 1 min (see tracing c in Figure 27-3). For each ganglion, column A gives test responses before and column B test responses approximately 45 min after a 30-min exposure to and then wash-out of DA (50 μM). For ganglion II, U-0521 (.3mM) was added to bathing medium 30 min before the addition of DA; after an additional 30 min with both agents they were both washed out. Voltage calibration in II horizontal row 2, applies to rows 2–4. (Note that both the s-IPSP and s-EPSP are enhanced after DA plus U-0521 in ganglion II. LTE of the s-IPSP is viewed as an indirect effect of a DA-modulatory action on the muscarinic ACh responses of the DA-interneurons or SIF cells so that the latter release more DA, not one on the direct hyperpolarizing action of the DA at the α_2-receptors for the s-IPSP; evidence for this is presented in our original paper.) (From Ashe & Libet, 1981a.)

enhanced following a temporary neural input that can release intraganglionic DA. This LTE has some important differences, however, from the long-term potentiation (LTP) that has been studied extensively in the hippocampus. First, LTE in the sympathetic ganglion can be achieved with very low frequencies of neural inputs. A conditioning train of 10 pps for 2 min induces a maximal LTE effect; even 3 pps for 6 min have also usually induced almost maximal changes. By contrast, LTP in the hippocampus reportedly requires conditioning trains with frequencies greater than 100 pps, even though train durations can be brief

(Dolphin, Errington, & Bliss, 1982). Second, ganglionic LTE represents a heterosynaptic interaction between two different neural transmitter inputs (DA and ACh) to the same cell. By contrast, LTP in the hippocampus is reportedly effective only when the test response is elicited by stimulating the same neural input line that was stimulated by the conditioning train. There may be some debate in this latter case as to whether precisely the same presynaptic terminals must be activated by both the conditioning and test nerve impulses. But in any case, there appears to be little room for an interaction among neural inputs from completely different sources in this LTP process.

Modulatory DA Receptor, for Inducing LTE

The postsynaptic receptor that mediates the contingent synaptic action of DA is uniquely different from classical receptors that mediate PSPs. This modulatory DA receptor produces no PSP or change in membrane excitability of its own; as already indicated, it leads only to a persisting change in PSPs elicited by another transmitter (ACh) (Libet & Tosaka, 1970; Kobayashi, Hashiguchi, & Ushiyama, 1978). Second, the modulatory DA receptor is specifically activated by DA or by certain specific DA agonists such as apomorphine (Libet, Kobayashi, & Tanaka, 1975) or 2-amino-6,7-dihydroxy-1,2,3,4-tetrahydro-naphalene (ADTN) (Mochida, 1982). DA and these specific agonists can elicit LTE at applied concentrations far below those required to produce any hyperpolarizing response such as in the s-IPSP. This, of course, contrasts with the s-IPSP receptor; although this receptor is normally activated by DA in the rabbit superior cervical ganglion, it can also be activated by other catecholamines and has in fact turned out to be an α_2-adrenergic type of receptor (e.g., Ashe & Libet, 1982).

The modulatory DA receptor in fact appears closely related to so-called D-1 type, as designated for those DA receptors in brain tissue that are coupled to the activation of adenylate cyclase (Kebabian & Calne, 1979). The ability of DA to stimulate adenyl cyclase in sympathetic ganglia was first demonstrated by the Greengard group utilizing slices of bovine superior cervical ganglion (Kebabian & Greengard, 1971). DA applied to intact ganglia of rabbit and rat has been reported by some to be ineffective (Lindl & Cramer, 1975), although not by others (Wamsley, Black, West, & Williams, 1980; Kalix, McAfee, Schorderet, & Greengard, 1974, found increases of only about 15%). However, blockade of COMT by the drug U-0521 has been found to enable exogenous DA to produce consistent increases in cyclic AMP concentrations of 50–100% in intact rabbit superior cervical ganglia (Mochida, Kobayashi, Tosaka, Ito, & Libet, 1981; Mochida, 1982), just as it had enabled exogenous DA to become effective in producing LTE of the s-EPSP response (Ashe & Libet, 1981a).

Cyclic AMP itself, applied exogenously, can completely mimic the DA modulatory action. Temporary exposure to cyclic AMP extracellularly can elicit a full LTE of the slow depolarizing test responses to MCh (Libet *et al.*, 1975); see Figure 27-8. Cyclic AMP injected intracellularly could also induce an LTE of the s-EPSP responses of the cell (Kobayashi *et al.*, 1978). When a treatment with cyclic AMP has induced its own LTE, exposure to DA does not produce any further increase in the enhancement of the muscarinic depolarizing test responses; this indicates that both actions are converging on the same mechanism.

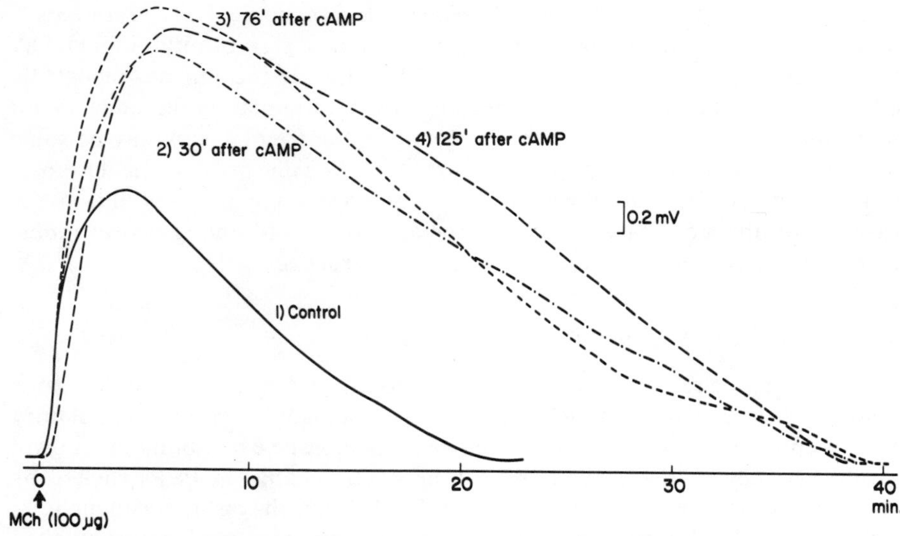

Figure 27-8. Modulation of slow muscarinic depolarizations by cyclic AMP. Experimental conditions similar to those in Figure 27-6. After "control" depolarizing response (1), to a test dose of MCh, the ganglion was superfused for 8 min with Ringer containing dibutyryl cyclic AMP (1 m*M*) (instead of being briefly exposed to DA or NE, as in Figure 27-6). Subsequent test responses to MCh were made at 30, 76, and 125 min after ending the exposure to cyclic AMP (shown in tracings 2–4, respectively). (From data reported in Libet, Kobayashi, & Tanaka, 1975.)

The D-1 antagonist drugs specifically block both actions by the D-1 agonists of DA, that is, they block the adenyl cyclase stimulation and the LTE of s-EPSPs in the sympathetic ganglia. Those drugs shown to be effective are butaclamol, spiroperidol, and flupenthixol, the latter being one of the most selective antagonists for D-1 as opposed to other DA receptors (Seeman, 1980). On the other hand, adrenergic antagonists, whether for the alpha actions (e.g., dihydroergotamine) or for the beta actions (propranolol and sotalol), as well as the D-2 antagonist sulpiride, have been found to be ineffective against LTE. The specificity of D-1 antagonists has been demonstrated for all three methods of inducing LTE in the ganglia: these are LTE induction (1) by exogenous DA for either the s-EPSP (Ashe & Libet, 1981a) or (2) the direct slow depolarizing responses to applied MCh (Mochida *et al.*, 1981; Mochida, 1982; see Figure 27-9), as well as (3) the induction of LTE for s-EPSP responses by a conditioning train of neural input (Mochida & Libet, 1983).

The effects on DA stimulation of cyclic AMP synthesis are a bit more complicated, but they are fully in accord with the conclusion that the LTE action by DA is specifically mediated by a D-1 receptor. DA induces a greater increase in cyclic AMP than does the specific agonist ADTN, even though both elicit the same maximal amount of LTE. However, the additional or "extra" production of cyclic AMP by DA can only be blocked by a β-adrenergic antagonist and not by a D-1 antagonist. It appears therefore that DA can activate adenyl cyclase in the sympathetic ganglion through two different receptors, a D-1 and a β-adrenergic type; its entire action on adenyl cyclase can only be blocked by the simultaneous application of both a D-1 antagonist like butaclamol plus the β-antagonist propranolol (Mochida *et al.*, 1981; Mochida,

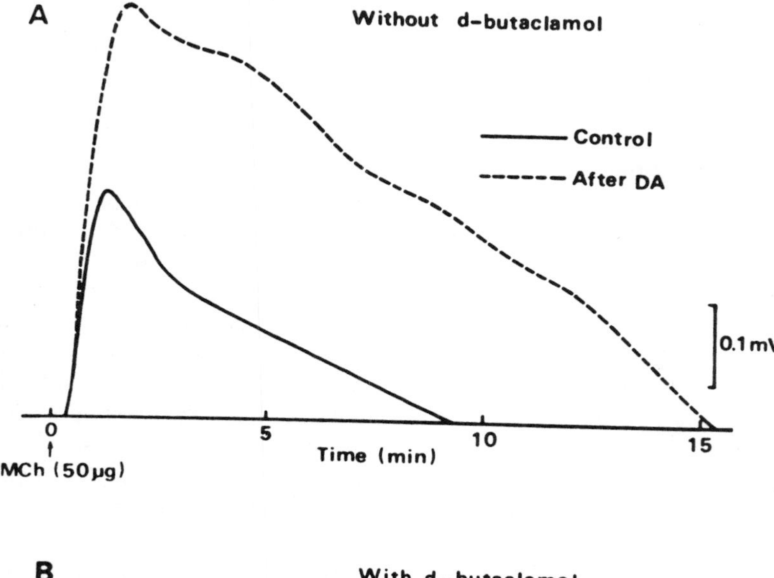

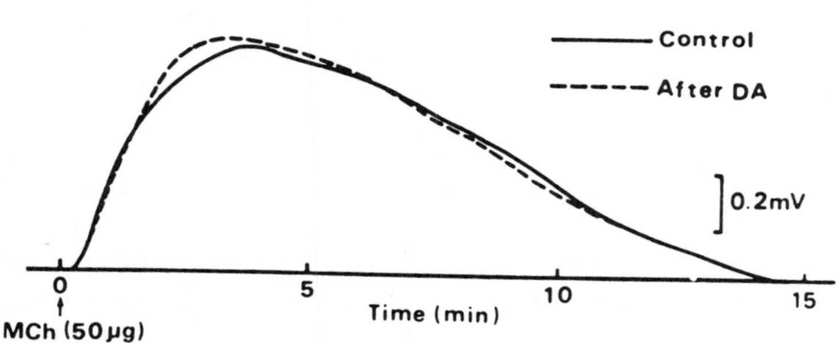

Figure 27-9. D-1 antagonist blocks DA induction of the LTE (of muscarinic depolarizing responses). Slow depolarizing test responses to each injection of MCh (50 μg) into superfusing fluid; recorded in a sucrose-gap chamber at room temperature. Paired superior cervical ganglia from same rabbit. (A) Ganglion shows usual LTE of the MCh test response, following brief single exposure to DA. (B) Ganglion shows no LTE after DA; a D-1 antagonist, *d*-butaclamol (7 μM), was present from the start throughout its tests. (From Mochida, 1982, as reported by Mochida, Kobayashi, Tosaka, Ito, & Libet, 1981.)

1982). It appears that only the cyclic AMP generated by activating D-1 receptors is capable of inducing the LTE change in the muscarinic s-EPSPs; in accord with this, the β-agonist isoproterenol does elicit a substantial increase in cyclic AMP synthesis, but this agonist is relatively ineffective for inducing any LTE. Perhaps the β-receptors coupled to adenyl cyclase are located in non-neuronal elements of the ganglia (e.g., Kebabian, Bloom, Steiner, & Greengard, 1975). In any case, if one counts only the D-1 actions, there is, in fact, good correlation between the ability to stimulate adenyl cyclase production of cyclic AMP and the ability to induce LTE, whether by DA or its specific agonists for the D-1 receptor.

Induction, Storage, and Retention of LTE

The ability to distinguish among these three aspects of the LTE process appeared largely as a result of a fortuitous finding that cyclic GMP, the putative intracellular mediator of the s-EPSP, can selectively interfere with the storage phase. This ability and its time-dependent characteristics greatly raised the potential relevance of the LTE process to the issues of learning and formation of a memory trace (Libet *et al.*, 1975). In brief, it appears that the initial induction of the LTE *change* (change in the slow depolarizing s-EPSP response to ACh) begins probably after roughly 30 sec following the arrival of DA at the postsynaptic sites. However, the retention of this change, so that the altered responses persist for hours thereafter, appears to require a storage, or if you will, a "consolidation" process; the storage process appears to begin only after about 4 to 5 min following the exposure to DA (or at least it is completely reversible up until that time), and it appears to be completed within an additional 5 to 10 min, that is, after a total of 10 to 15 min following the initial induction by DA. The storage process appears to lead to the formation of a relatively durable form of the change in the neuron that is responsible for the alteration of the s-EPSP responses to ACh. This alteration at some point in the molecular mechanisms that mediate the s-EPSP then gradually reverses over a period of at least several hours, when the mechanisms have then reverted to their preinduction state. The evidence for this series of effects is given briefly in the following.

Initial induction of the change in the muscarinic depolarizing test responses can be easily detected to appear within less than 5 min following temporary exposure to DA when studied in the sucrose-gap superfusion chamber (Libet & Tosaka, 1970; Libet *et al.*, 1975). (It is not possible to study this timing aspect when using a conditioning train of preganglionic neural input rather than exogenous DA, unless one elicits the test responses heterosynaptically by stimulating a separate neural input from that used in the conditioning. In the homosynaptic or the conditioning line itself, well-known alterations in presynaptic function generally will continue for some 10 min to as much as 30 min, and thereby impose an additional alteration on the test responses delivered in the same line.) In order to catch the enhancement of the MCh depolarization at the moment of occurrence, the DA was applied to the ganglion during an ongoing low-level depolarization produced by a continuous superfusion with low concentration of MCh, instead of the usual DA application before an MCh test. A relatively sudden upturn in the amplitude of the continuous MCh depolarization was observed at about 30 sec ± following the arrival of the DA at the postsynaptic elements (Tanaka & Libet, unpublished observations). The arrival of DA was signaled by the beginning of a small superimposed hyperpolarizing response to the concentration of DA employed. When a similar level of depolarization was sustained by superfusing with raised K^+ (10 m*M*) instead of with MCh, the superimposed response to the same brief application of DA showed a hyperpolarizing response similar in form to that seen with normal Ringer (4 mM K^+); that is, *no* depolarizing inflection appeared at about 30 sec.

Evidence for the storage process and its temporal characteristics was based on the time-dependent ability of cyclic GMP to antagonize the retention of the LTE change (Figure 27-10). If superfusion with cyclic GMP at a low concentration (25–50 μM) was begun at any time up to about 5 min following the exposure to DA, then no later enhancement of the MCh depolarizing tests was observable. If onset of cyclic GMP application occurred between the period of 5 to 15 min after DA, later tests with MCh could show some partial degree of enhancement. But if cyclic GMP was begun later than 15 min following DA, the usual full enhancement of later MCh tests was observable in the same way as found for the control ganglion with no treatment by cyclic GMP. The precise timing of this time-dependent ability of cyclic GMP to antagonize or disrupt the storage–retention process is somewhat uncertain, although the range in minutes is clear enough. The superfusion with cyclic GMP must itself be applied for 5 min or more in order to allow sufficient time for penetration into even the surface neurons of the ganglion; this factor would tend to make the actual timings later than those judged from the onset of cyclic GMP treatment. On the other hand, the sucrose-gap experiments must be conducted at room temperature, about 20–22° C; at more normal body temperature of about 37° C, the speed of the changes induced by DA and their ability to be disrupted may both be faster. It is additionally important to note that these cyclic GMP actions on LTE were fully repeated in all respects when the induction was produced by a superfusion with cyclic AMP instead of DA.

Second, the antagonistic effect of the cyclic GMP was specific for the enhancement itself. That is, the later MCh test responses remained at their pretreatment levels (as judged with respect to a paired control ganglion in the same time period); they were simply not enhanced. Third, the cyclic GMP treatment disrupted only that LTE induced by an exposure to DA or to cyclic AMP that preceded a given cyclic GMP treatment. A later second exposure to either DA or cyclic AMP, one that was *not* followed by treatment with cyclic GMP, could still induce an LTE of subsequent MCh responses. In other words, there was no permanent destruction of the storage mechanisms involved, only a specific reversible antagonism of them during the presence of cyclic GMP.

The more durable alteration in the s-EPSP responsiveness that persisted for hours was not affected by cyclic GMP when the latter was applied after the initial roughly 15 min (following the exposure to DA), as already indicated above. This clearly distinguishes between the action of cyclic GMP on the storage or consolidation process involved in producing the more durable change and the nature of the durable change itself.

The nature of the molecular changes in the postsynaptic neuron responsible for both the initial and long-term enhancement of s-EPSP responses is currently under investigation, as partly described above. The question can be divided into two aspects: (1) Where is the site of the change in the postsynaptic neuron? and (2) What is the nature of the biochemical or conformational change at such a site? On the first question one may initially distinguish between possible sites on the cell membrane and those located intracellularly. Membrane sites of change could involve the muscarinic receptors that are activated by ACh to elicit the s-EPSP. Intracellular sites could lie somewhere in the series of reactions initiated by the cyclic GMP, produced by the receptor-coupled guanylate cyclase,

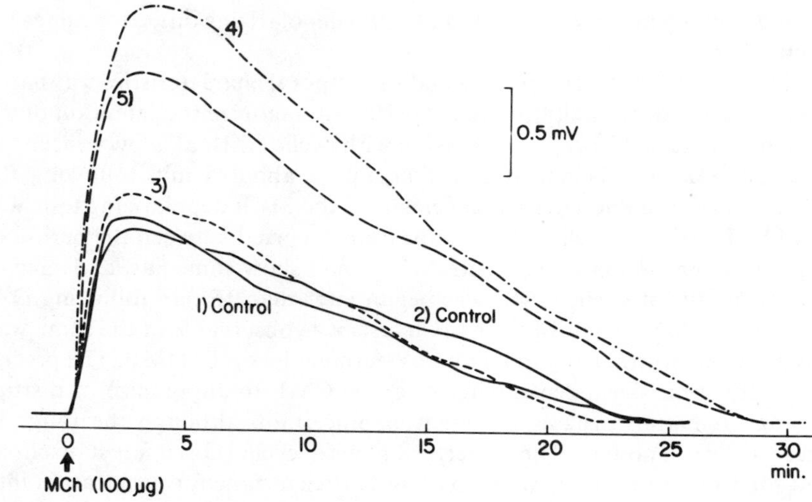

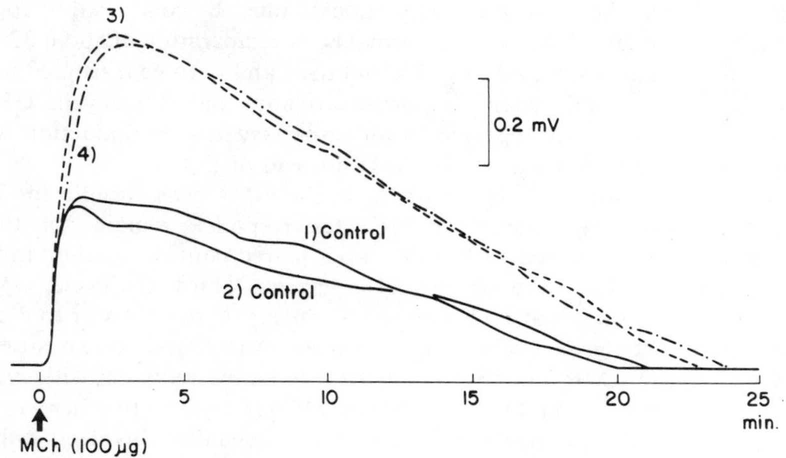

Figure 27-10. Time-dependent effect of cyclic GMP, in antagonizing LTE induced by DA. Experimental conditions similar to those in Figure 27-6. After initial two control responses to MCh (1 and 2), each of the paired ganglia was exposed to a single dose of DA injected into the superfusing fluid. In the upper ganglion, superfusion with dibutyryl cyclic GMP (50 μM) was begun 4 min after DA and maintained for 8 min (i.e., until 12 min after DA). Test 3, with MCh, applied 35 min after DA (23 min after end of cyclic GMP), shows no enhancement. A second exposure to DA followed test 3, but no cyclic GMP was applied after this DA. MCh tests 4 and 5 followed the second DA by 35 and 85 min, respectively, and do show LTE; this demonstrates (a) that this ganglion was in fact capable of developing the LTE response to DA and (b) that cyclic GMP antagonized only that LTE induced by a preceding DA action. In the lower ganglion, similar superfusion with cyclic GMP was delayed until 30 min after the first dose of DA. MCh test 3, applied 60 min after the DA (22 min after the end of cyclic GMP), shows the usual good enhancement. A second exposure to DA followed test 3. MCh test 4, applied 60 min after the second DA, shows no further change; this demonstrates that the first DA had already elicited a maximal LTE in spite of its being followed by the cyclic GMP that started 30 min after the DA. (From Libet, Kobayashi, & Tanaka, 1975.)

that lead electrogenically to the final change in membrane potential that constitutes the s-EPSP (see Figure 27-11). Irrespective of which of the foregoing sites may be the place at which change occurs, production of the change is presumably tied to cyclic AMP as the intracellular mediator. But since cyclic AMP can mediate a wide variety of chemical changes, whether by phosphorylative or nonphosphorylative routes, there will need to be some way of narrowing down the possibilities. One of these has already been investigated by us (Ashe & Libet, 1984), namely, that of a new synthesis of protein such as has been postulated by others for the production of enduring memory traces generally. Two inhibitors of protein synthesis, anisomycin and cyclohexamide, were found to be unable to prevent either the induction or the retention of the LTE change initiated by DA. The ability of these inhibitors actually to block protein synthesis in our specific preparations of sympathetic ganglia was tested by their effects on the incorporation of tritiated leucine into total protein; both inhibitors, in the concentrations found ineffective against LTE, did inhibit incorporation of [^{3}H]leucine by more than about 95%.

Figure 27-11. Schema summarizing slow postsynaptic responses to ACh and DA, in the principal neuron ("ganglion cell") of rabbit superior cervical ganglion. ACh released by preganglionic axons acts at nicotinic receptors (n) to elicit f-EPSP (by increasing ionic conductance for Na^+ and K^+); at muscarinic receptor (m), to stimulate guanylate cyclase and lead to an s-EPSP (with no change in membrane conductance); at muscarinic receptor (m) on the SIF cell, which then releases DA. DA acts at α_2-receptors to elicit an s-IPSP (with no detectable change in membrane conductance, but not mediated by cyclic AMP; see Libet, 1979d). DA also acts at D-1 type receptors, separate and distinct from the α_2-receptors, to stimulate adenylate cyclase; the resultant cyclic AMP induces LTE of the s-EPSP response to ACh (as shown by the dashed s-EPSP tracing). Cyclic GMP can antagonize ("disrupt") the storage process for producing the more enduring form of the modulatory change responsible for the LTE. Possible alternative sites at which the modulatory change is operative are indicated by the dashed arrows to points in the sequence that leads to the s-EPSP response. (Modified from Libet, Kobayashi, & Tanaka, 1975.)

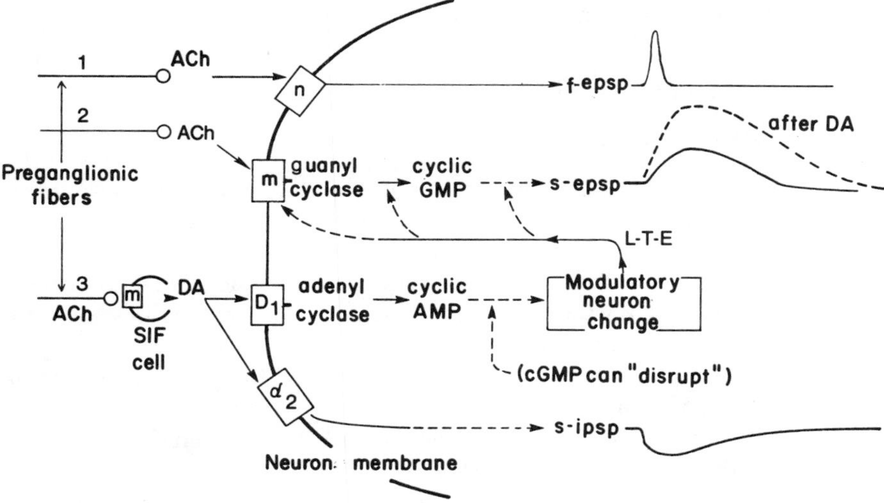

Summary Schema

A schema that summarizes the roles of the synaptic transmitters and the cyclic nucleotides in mediating both the slow postsynaptic potential responses and the contingent action of DA on the s-EPSP is presented in Figure 27-11. The schema is self-explanatory and is directly related to the foregoing text. However, it seems worthwhile to elaborate further on the interactions between the two cyclic nucleotides, cyclic AMP and cyclic GMP. With cyclic GMP as the intracellular mediator of the s-EPSP, and cyclic AMP as the mediator of the DA-induced LTE of the s-EPSP, we have in effect cyclic AMP acting to enhance or potentiate a cyclic-GMP-mediated cellular PSP action. Both synaptic actions, s-EPSP and its LTE modulation by DA, may thus be termed "metabotropic" (see McGeer, Eccles, & McGeer, 1978) in contrast to fast PSPs in which transmitters simply open ionic conductance channels in the membrane. But in addition, cyclic GMP can antagonize production of the cyclic-AMP-mediated LTE, in the time-dependent fashion described above. This raises the possibility that the cyclic GMP generated in association with the s-EPSP could antagonize its own enhancement by the DA-activated D-1 receptor system. Clearly, this would have to be limited in scope, since it would otherwise not be possible ever to see any LTE of s-EPSP or of MCh depolarizing responses. Indirect evidence suggests that such a negative feedback mechanism can operate but only in association with very large and prolonged muscarinic depolarizing actions. For example, preliminary evidence (Tanaka & Libet, unpublished observations) indicated that when the very potent muscarinic agonist bethanechol was applied to the ganglion, an LTE change by DA could be produced only if the exposure to DA was delayed for about an hour after the bethanechol response. Bethanechol induces a much larger and longer-lasting depolarization than does an equimolar application of MCh and might be expected to generate much more intracellular cyclic GMP.

RELATION OF SYMPATHETIC NEURON TO MODELING OF ALTERED SYNAPTIC EFFICACY IN LEARNING AND MEMORY

Neural Induction of Synaptic Changes during Learning

Associative Learning and Heterosynaptic Interaction

Associative learning presumably involves the modification of the response to one neural input as a function of associated activity in another input. To accommodate such a mechanism, it would appear that a synaptic model would have to include a provision for heterosynaptic interaction between different neural inputs ending on the same neural element. The interactions should be possible for inputs of differing sources and transmitter actions at the postsynaptic site; simple integrative effects elicited by different synaptic endings that are delivered from the same afferent source would not meet the essential requirements. One of the strengths of the sympathetic ganglion for such modeling is that both general classes of its slow synaptic actions meet this fundamental requirement. The slow PSPs (the s-IPSP, s-EPSP, and ss-EPSP) all induce changes in the excitability level of the cell that can interact with any other neural input that may arrive during the course of a slow PSP; the integration of the two separate effects on excitability would affect the tendency to fire out efferent impulses from the postsynaptic unit. The contingent synaptic action of DA appears to be a more selective one, in which the postsynaptic potential generated by another input is rather specifically altered for some time. However, it provides an example in principle for the possibility that other such contingent synaptic actions among different inputs may also exist. Indeed, some such type of mechanism has been shown for the ability of norepinephrine to alter the responses of Purkinje cells to other neural transmitter inputs (e.g., Woodward, Moises, Waterhouse, Hoffer, & Freedman, 1979), although thus far such alterations have been only short-lived following the removal of the modulating norepinephrine agent. A longer-lasting change of about 30 min has been shown for postsynaptic responses in the caudate nucleus after a brief superfusion with DA in a preparation of a slice of brain under controlled conditions (Yamamoto, 1973). More recently, it has been reported that epinephrine can induce an enhancement lasting many hours in the ss-EPSPs of the frog sympathetic ganglion (Nishi & Katayama, 1981); in this case, the monoamine has induced a change in the postsynaptic responses to a peptide transmitter, probably closely related to LH-RH, rather than in the PSP responses to the muscarinic action of ACh.

A postsynaptic locus for the heterosynaptic interactions, as in the present slow synaptic actions in sympathetic ganglia, would also appear to offer much more scope than interactions at presynaptic terminals or sites, although the latter have certainly been found to be functionally possible (e.g., Hawkins, Abrams, Carew, & Kandel, 1983). In general the variety and number of presynaptic terminals converging on a postsynaptic soma-dendritic element are far greater than on presynaptic terminals. The continuity of relatively large dendritic and somatic regions of the postsynaptic element also increases the potentialities for integration among even widely distributed inputs. And the postsynaptic dendro-somatic element presumably has much greater metabolic resources, which could be employed in achieving the molecular changes needed for a neuronal memory trace.

Homosynaptic models would obviously be deficient in respect to this general issue, even though they may provide important examples of processes that could mediate long-lasting changes in synaptic plasticity. The homosynaptic models that have been offered in connection with alterations in synaptic efficacy have included simple presynaptic posttetanic potentiation (PTP), following a conditioning train of rather high-frequency impulses arriving at such endings (e.g., McGeer *et al.*, 1978, p. 502). More recently, there has, of course, been the LTP studied particularly extensively in the hippocampus. Homosynaptic models would also include those in which morphological changes (number, size, shape) are induced in presynaptic terminals by use or disuse and by regeneration following denervative degenerations and the like.

Temporal Contiguity among Inputs

Associative learning situations may require a defined temporal association of two different inputs within some limited range of time intervals. Presumably to satisfy this requirement, Hebb (1949) postulated that an increase in synaptic strength would only occur when a given input is active at the same time as other inputs or when a particular input coincided with the cell's activation and firing. In the sympathetic ganglion model, interactions with slow PSPs may satisfy such temporal requirements when the time intervals are in seconds to minutes, as they commonly are. However, the induction of the longer-lasting contingent synaptic change by DA inputs does not appear to require close temporal coupling with the preganglionic ACh input whose responses are being modified. The conditioning DA input, whether via exogenous DA application or via a conditioning train of preganglionic impulses, can be effective in inducing LTE of s-EPSPs even when it is delivered at variable times that occur either before or after those inputs that elicit an s-EPSP; these time differentials can be on the order of at least many minutes. However, the quantitative possibilities for a temporal linkage have not been investigated in sympathetic ganglia and, of course, not at all yet in the brain, where such a feature might be more developed. On the other hand, very long intervals for associative learning are clearly possible and important, as for example in the work of John Garcia on appetitive changes. Finally, as has been pointed out for the case of associative conditioning via a cellular mechanism in *Aplysia* (Walters & Byrne, 1983), a cellular model that is not strictly dependent on concurrent activation of different inputs at a given postsynaptic site offers a mechanism that could potentially be used in a flexible way, for different associative effects in differing functional conditions and for different neuronal systems.

The *extraordinary synaptic delays* before the onsets of the s-EPSP and ss-EPSP (about 250 msec and 1000 msec, respectively) as well as the slow rates of rise (a few seconds to a few minutes to reach peak amplitudes, respectively) impose further interesting and potentially significant limitations on the temporal interactions between two different inputs at this postsynaptic site. Arrival of a second input during the synaptic delay and early rise of a slow EPSP would have little or nothing to interact with, unless it also happened to elicit a slow type of PSP with durations lasting into seconds. Even more striking is the apparent delay of about 30 sec that appears to be required between the time that DA arrives at the postsynaptic site and the appearance of the modulatory change that DA induces in the s-EPSP response to ACh (see above). This variety of initial delays after a conditioning type of input, before meaningful interaction with another input becomes possible, adds a potentially significant feature to the neuronal model that may be relevant to learning phenomena at the behavioral level.

Physiological Parameters of Conditioning Inputs

The conditioning inputs that can produce both the variety of slow PSPs and the DA-contingent synaptic action are all obtainable with impulse frequencies and train durations that have been found commonly to exist in the normal course of physiological events *in vivo*, both in the preganglionic autonomic nerve fibers and in firing rates of various intracerebral structures. As was indicated above, frequencies of preganglionic nerve impulses as low as 1 to 3/sec can be effective for each of these, although the train durations required to achieve the maximal amplitudes of the synaptic action run into the range of minutes in the case of the ss-EPSP and the DA-modulatory action.

Shorter-Term Changes

Short-term retention (i.e., during some seconds to minutes after a conditioning trial) can be accommodated by the slow PSPs in the sympathetic neuron. As already indicated, durations of excitability changes associated with these responses can last from some seconds (s-IPSP and s-EPSP) up to 30 min (for ss-EPSP) within a single postsynaptic element. The long synaptic delays and slow rise times for s-EPSP and ss-EPSP add further dimensions to the modes of interaction with succeeding inputs, as discussed above.

Reverberating circuits in which neuronal networks are continuously active had been postulated to provide altered neuronal responses during short-term retention of a learned change (e.g., Gerard, 1949, 1955; Hebb, 1949, 1966). Such a dynamic view of repetitive neural actions, which could maintain altered responsiveness for periods of seconds to minutes, was based on the necessity to incorporate the relatively brief neuronal actions known at the time; these brief actions were the action potentials or fast PSPs, with durations in milliseconds and tens of milliseconds. Although such a postulate is not excluded, it is at present made unnecessary by the availability of the slow PSPs. The latter make it possible for sufficiently long postsynaptic interactions to occur at a level of a single or monosynaptic junction, with no continual reverberation of inputs being required.

Longer-Term Changes

Longer-term retentions have importantly different characteristics from those of short-term retentions, as is well known. Longer-term retentions can be interfered with most easily during an initial period of some minutes after learning has occurred. The time-dependent sensitivity is assumed to reflect a distinction between storage or consolidation processes and the final appearance of a more stable form of a memory trace (e.g., Gerard, 1955; McGaugh, 1966; McGaugh & Herz, 1972). The longer-lasting, more stable form of alteration, once it is "laid down" or consolidated, appears to depend on some molecular change in the neuron that does not require continued operation of active neuronal inputs and the like for its retention; this last point could be demonstrated in direct experimental tests with deep anesthesia or deep cold following a learning experience (Ransmeier & Gerard, 1954). Both of these characteristics—initial disruptability during a storage or consolidation phase and the appearance of a more stable form of the alteration in synaptic efficacy—are in fact features of the contingent synaptic action by DA in the sympathetic neuron. Additionally, the relative specificity of the DA modulatory action, in enhancing the s-EPSP response to ACh input, would provide a degree of selectivity for those neural inputs that are interacting on this longer-term basis. The "disruptability" of the longer-term retention during an initial period of some minutes provides a particularly striking resemblance to the behavior of this process in actual learning; the achievement of this effect by a physiological agent such as cyclic GMP lends further credence to the potential significance of the present mechanism. The role of cyclic AMP as intracellular mediator of the storage–consolidation process suggests possible metabolic routes in the production of the more enduring molecular change (e.g., Nestler & Greengard, 1982). On the other hand, the apparent noninvolvement of protein synthesis in the present model of the storage process (1) suggests that the storage process for the kind of intermediate-term retention in the present mechanism may be different from that involved in consolidating the production or formation of much longer-term memory traces; or (2) could suggest a reconsideration of the view that protein synthesis plays a specific rather than an indirect supporting role in the storage mechanisms for all retentions.

Other Similarities and Relevance of Sympathetic Neuron to Brain Processes in Learning and Memory

Many of the specific ingredients of the present mechanisms in the sympathetic neuron appear, in fact, to exist, both specifically and in principle, in various cerebral systems.

1. Postsynaptic actions of ACh in the brain are mostly muscarinic in nature, as they are for the s-EPSP and on the DA-containing interneuron (SIF) cell. They have been shown at least in some specific cases to elicit a slow depolarizing response that resembles the s-EPSP of the sympathetic neuron (Krnjević, Pumain, & Renaud, 1971). Muscarinic agonists do stimulate the production of cyclic GMP in certain brain structures as in sympathetic ganglia (e.g., Kebabian *et al.*, 1975). And atropinic drugs that antagonize the muscarinic actions are well known to have potent behavioral effects. Implication of cerebral cholinergic systems in the learning and memory process has long received experimental support, particularly in the work of Deutsch (1973). Finally, a deficiency in the cholinergic system has thus far been shown to be the single most striking change in Alzheimer disease (Terry & Davies, 1980; Davies, 1979), a disease in which the loss of the ability to form or consolidate a memory trace is the most prominent feature.

2. Peptidergic systems of considerable variety have been established histochemically in recent years (Hökfelt, Johansson, Ljungdahl, Lundberg, & Schultzberg, 1980). The nature of the actual and specific functions that such potential transmitters may have synaptically in the brain is still to be established adequately. But at least the neural substrates are present that could provide the kind of very slow ss-EPSP found to be mediated by a peptide in sympathetic ganglia (Jan *et al.*, 1980, for the frog sympathetic ganglion).

3. Monoaminergic systems. The monoaminergic projections from nuclei in the brainstem to much of the forebrain as well as other parts of the brain and spinal cord are now well known. There are some striking similarities between the morphological features of the dopaminergic interneurons, the SIF cells within sympathetic ganglia and those of the cerebral monoaminergic projections (Libet & Owman, 1974; Libet, 1978, 1980). In both cases, relatively small numbers of cells send axonal terminations to very large numbers of widely distributed neurons. In addition, most of the presynaptic sites for release of these monoaminergic transmitters appear to be not in close apposition or contact with the the postsynaptic sites containing their putative receptors (for the case of ganglia, see Libet, 1979c, 1980; for the case of brain, see Descarries *et al.*, 1977). This arrangement has been referred to by me as one of "loose synapses" (Libet, 1965, 1979a, 1979b, 1980) or as "nonsynaptic" by some others (e.g., Dismukes, 1979). In any case, it is in accord with the more diffuse and slower time characteristics of the functions presumed to be carried out by such transmitter systems. It is in sharp contrast to the classical electron-microscopic morphology assigned to chemical transmitter synapses for the fast types of PSPs; in these, there is the well-known highly organized apposition of the pre- and postsynaptic membranes with a synaptic cleft of approximately 200 Å.

The specific synaptic mechanisms or functions for the monoamine transmitters in the brain have not yet been adequately analyzed and defined. The functions are likely to prove to encompass a variety of synaptic actions, including direct excitatory and inhibitory ones. But more subtle modulatory actions will probably have to be sought in order to account for what appear to be their roles in a variety of important behavioral functions. This is not the place to review the latter in detail, but only to recall them in a general way so as to indicate the suggestive possibilities by which the DA system in the sympathetic ganglion might be functioning in relation to the learning–memory issue under discussion. Both norepinephrine and dopamine cerebral systems have been implicated by the evidence for some type of functional role in the learning and memory process. The monoamines appear to have important roles in the motivational aspect of behavior; this includes the evidence for their probable mediation of self-stimulating activity in the Olds phenomenon. They are also implicated in the setting of attentive levels; there is, for example, the clinical evidence in the use of drugs that heighten release of DA in the brain for improving the attentive and therefore the learning capabilities of so-called hyperkinetic children (Everett, 1977). In connection with the pharmacological agents that antagonize the specific DA receptors in the brain, it should be noted that most of the neuroleptic drugs appear to have a stronger antagonistic action against the so-called D-2 receptor than against the D-1 type, the one related to the DA receptor that mediates the contingent synaptic action in the ganglia. It appears to be antagonism for D-2 receptors that probably underlies the useful actions of the neuroleptic drugs in schizophrenia. One of the phenothiazines, flupenthixol, is much more selectively potent against the D-1 type of receptor than are the other phenothiazines (Seeman, 1980). It might prove to be of great interest therefore to test the more specific D-1 antagonist flupenthixol for effects on behavioral learning and memory functions.

The diffuseness of monoamine action in both ganglia and brain, and the kinds of general behavioral functions attributed to the monoamine systems in the brain, argues against a view that the DA-contingent synaptic action is mediating specific associational learned responses. Rather, one might speculate that this DA type of synaptic mechanism might be employed as a kind of "permissive mechanism" in fostering the ability of the neuronal systems to engage their storage or consolidation mechanism in a given learning and memory situation; that is, it might provide the kind of "glue" that Thompson and his associates have referred to (Chapter 9, this volume). The involvement of this "glue" factor might depend on the engagement or activity in the motivational and attentive systems at the time of the learning process.

ACKNOWLEDGMENTS

Some as yet unpublished data described in this chapter are from experiments done in collaboration with Drs. John H. Ashe, Haruo Kobayashi, Sumiko Mochida, and Tetsuro Tanaka. All investigations on which the chapter is based were supported by U.S. Public Health Service Grant NS-00884.

REFERENCES

Ashe, J. H., & Libet, B. Modulation of slow postsynaptic potentials by dopamine in rabbit sympathetic ganglion. *Brain Research*, 1981a, *217*, 93–106.

Ashe, J. H., & Libet, B. Orthodromic production of non-cholinergic slow depolarizing response in the superior cervical ganglion of the rabbit. *Journal of Physiology*, 1981b, *320*, 333–346.

Ashe, J. H., & Libet, B. Pharmacological properties and monoaminergic mediation of the slow IPSP, in mammalian sympathetic ganglion. *Brain Research*, 1982, *242*, 345–349.

Ashe, J. H., & Libet, B. Effect of inhibitors of protein synthesis on dopamine modulation of the slow-EPSP in rabbit superior cervical ganglion. *Brain Research*, 1984, *290*, 170–173.

Brown, D. A., & Adams, P. R. Muscarinic suppression of a novel voltage-sensitive K^+ current in a vertebrate neurone. *Nature*, 1980, *283*, 673–676.

Davies, P. Neurotransmitter-related enzymes in senile dementia of the Alzheimer type. *Brain Research*, 1979, *171*, 319–327.

Descarries, L., Watkins, K. C., & Lapierre, Y. Noradrenergic axon terminals in the cerebral cortex of rat: III. Topometric ultrastructural analysis. *Brain Research*, 1977, *133*, 197–222.

Deutsch, J. A. The cholinergic synapse and the site of memory. In J. A. Deutsch (Ed.), *The physiological basis of memory*. New York & London: Academic Press, 1973.

Dismukes, R. K. New concepts of molecular communication among neurons. *Behavioral and Brain Sciences*, 1979, *2*, 409–448.

Dolphin, A. C., Errington, M. L., & Bliss, T. V. P. Long-term potentiation of the perforant path *in vivo* is associated with increased glutamic release. *Nature*, 1982, *297*, 496–498.

Everett, G. M. Dopamine and the hyperkinetic child. In E. Costa & G. L. Gessa (Eds.), *Advances in biochemical psychopharmacology* (Vol. 16: *Nonstriatal dopaminergic neurons*). New York: Raven Press, 1977.

Gerard, R. W. Physiology and psychiatry. *American Journal of Psychiatry*, 1949, *106*, 161–173.

Gerard, R. W. The academic lecture: The biological roots of psychiatry. *American Journal of Psychiatry*, 1955, *112*, 81–90.

Hashiguchi, T., Kobayashi, H., Tosaka, T., & Libet, B. Two muscarinic depolarizing mechanisms in mammalian sympathetic neurons. *Brain Research*, 1982, *242*, 378–383.

Hashiguchi, T., Ushiyama, N., Kobayashi, H., & Libet, B. Does cyclic GMP mediate the slow excitatory postsynaptic potential: Comparison of changes in membrane potential and conductance. *Nature*, 1978, *271*, 267–268.

Hawkins, R. D., Abrams, T. W., Carew, T. J., & Kandel, E. R. A cellular mechanism of classical conditioning in *Aplysia*: Activity-dependent amplification of presynaptic facilitation. *Science*, 1983, *219*, 400–405.

Hebb, D. O. *The organization of behavior: A neuropsychological theory*. New York & London: Wiley, 1949.

Hebb, D. O. *Textbook of psychology*. Philadelphia: Saunders, 1966.

Hökfelt, T., Johansson, O., Ljungdahl, A., Lundberg, J. M., & Schultzberg, M. Peptidergic neurones. *Nature*, 1980, *284*, 515–521.

Jan, L. Y., & Jan, Y. N. Peptidergic transmission in sympathetic ganglia of the frog. *Journal of Physiology*, 1982, *327*, 219–246.

Jan, Y. N., Jan, L. Y., & Kuffler, S. W. Further evidence for peptidergic transmission in sympathetic ganglia. *Proceedings of the National Academy of Sciences, USA*, 1980, *77*, 5008–5012.

Jänig, W., & Schmidt, R. F. Single unit responses in the cervical sympathetic trunk upon somatic stimulation. *Pflügers Archiv*, 1970, *314*, 199–216.

Jiang, Z.-G., Dun, N. J., & Karczmar, A. G. Substance P: A putative sensory transmitter in mammalian autonomic ganglia. *Science*, 1982, *217*, 739–741.

Kalix, P., McAfee, D. A., Schorderet, M., & Greengard, P. Pharmacological analysis of synaptically-mediated increase in cyclic adenosine monophosphate in rabbit superior cervical ganglion. *Journal of Pharmacology and Experimental Therapeutics*, 1974, *188*, 676–687.

Kebabian, J. W., Bloom, F. E., Steiner, A. L., & Greengard, P. Neurotransmitters increase cyclic nucleotides in postganglionic neurons: Immunocytochemical demonstration. *Science*, 1975, *190*, 157–159.

Kebabian, J. W., & Calne, D. B. Multiple receptors for dopamine. *Nature*, 1979, *277*, 93–96.

Kebabian, J. W., & Greengard, P. Dopamine-sensitive adenyl cyclase: Possible role in synaptic transmission. *Science*, 1971, *174*, 1346–1349.

Kebabian, J. W., Steiner, A. L., & Greengard, P. Muscarinic cholinergic regulation of cyclic guanosine 3′,5′-monophosphate in autonomic ganglia: Possible role in synaptic transmission. *Journal of Pharmacology and Experimental Therapeutics*, 1975, *193*, 474–488.

Kobayashi, H., Hashiguchi, T., & Ushiyama, N. Postsynaptic modulation by cyclic AMP, intra- or extra-cellularly applied, or by stimulation of preganglionic nerve, in mammalian sympathetic ganglion cells. *Nature*, 1978, *271*, 268–270.

Kobayashi, H., & Libet, B. Generation of slow postsynaptic potentials without increases in ionic conductance. *Proceedings of the National Academy of Sciences, USA*, 1968, *60*, 1304–1311.

Kobayashi, H., & Libet, B. Actions of noradrenaline and acetylcholine on sympathetic ganglion cells. *Journal of Physiology* (London), 1970, *208*, 353–372.

Konishi, S., Tsunoo, A., Yanaihara, N., & Otsuka, M. Peptidergic excitatory and inhibitory synapses in mammalian sympathetic ganglia; roles of substance P and enkephalin. *Biomedical Research*, 1980, *1*, 528–536.

Krnjević, K., Pumain, R., & Renaud, L. The mechanism of excitation by acetylcholine in the cerebral cortex. *Journal of Physiology* (London), 1971, *215*, 247–268.

Kuba, K., & Koketsu, K. Synaptic events in sympathetic ganglia. *Progress in Neurobiology*, 1978, *11*, 77–169.

Libet, B. Slow synaptic responses and excitatory changes in sympathetic ganglia. *Journal of Physiology* (London), 1964, *174*, 1–25.

Libet, B. Slow synaptic responses in autonomic ganglia. In D. R. Curtis & A. K. McIntyre (Eds.), *Studies in physiology*. Berlin: Springer, 1965.

Libet, B. Generation of slow inhibitory and excitatory postsynaptic potentials. *Federation Proceedings*, 1970, *29*, 1945–1956.

Libet, B. The role SIF cells play in ganglionic transmission. In E. Costa & G. L. Gessa (Eds.), *Advances in biochemical psychopharmacology* (Vol. 16: *Nonstriatal dopaminergic neurons*). New York: Raven Press, 1977.

Libet, B. Slow postsynaptic responses in sympathetic ganglion cells, as models for the slow potential changes in the brain. In D. Otto (Ed.), *Multidisciplinary perspectives in event-related brain potential research*. Washington, D.C.: U.S. Government Printing Office, 1978.

Libet, B. Dopaminergic synaptic processes in the superior cervical ganglion: Models for synaptic actions. In A. Horn, J. Korf, & B. H. C. Westerink (Eds.), *The neurobiology of dopamine*. London: Academic Press, 1979a.

Libet, B. Neuronal communication and synaptic modulation: experimental evidence vs. conceptual categories (Commentary to R. K. Dismukes: New concepts of molecular communication among neurons). *Behavioral and Brain Sciences*, 1979b, *2*, 409–448.

Libet, B. Slow synaptic actions in ganglionic functions. In C. McC. Brooks, K. Koizumi, & A. Sato (Eds.), *Integrative functions of the autonomic nervous system*. Tokyo: Tokyo University Press; Amsterdam: Elsevier/North-Holland Biomedical Press, 1979c.

Libet, B. Which postsynaptic action of dopamine is mediated by cyclic AMP? *Life Sciences*, 1979d, *24*, 1043–1058.

Libet, B. Functional roles of SIF cells in slow synaptic actions. In O. Eränkö, S. Soinila, & H. Päivärinta (Eds.), *Advances in biochemical psychopharmacology* (Vol. 25: *Histochemistry and cell biology of autonomic neurons, SIF cells, and paraneurons*). New York: Raven Press, 1980.

Libet, B., Kobayashi, H., & Tanaka, T. Synaptic coupling into the production and storage of a neuronal memory trace. *Nature*, 1975, *258*, 155–157.

Libet, B., & Owman, C. Concomitant changes in formaldehyde-induced fluorescence of dopamine interneurones and in slow inhibitory postsynaptic potentials of rabbit superior cervical ganglion, induced by stimulation of preganglionic nerve or by a muscarinic agent. *Journal of Physiology* (London), 1974, *237*, 635–662.

Libet, B., & Tosaka, T. Slow inhibitory and excitatory postsynaptic responses in single cells of mammalian sympathetic ganglia. *Journal of Neurophysiology*, 1969, *32*, 43–50.

Libet, B., & Tosaka, T. Dopamine as a synaptic transmitter and modulator in sympathetic ganglia; a different mode of synaptic action. *Proceedings of the National Academy of Sciences, USA*, 1970, *67*, 667–673.

Lindl, T., & Cramer, H. Evidence against dopamine as a mediator of the rise of cyclic AMP in the superior cervical ganglion of the rat. *Biochemical and Biophysical Research Communications*, 1975, *65*, 731–739.

McAfee, D. A., & Greengard, P. Adenosine 3′,5′-monophosphate: Electrophysiological evidence for a role in synaptic transmission. *Science*, 1972, *178*, 310–312.

McGaugh, J. L. Time-dependent processes in memory storage. *Science*, 1966, *153*, 1351–1358.

McGaugh, J. L., & Herz, M. J. (Eds.). *Memory consolidation*. San Francisco: Albion, 1972.

McGeer, P. L., Eccles, J. C., & McGeer, E. G. *Molecular neurobiology of the mammalian brain*. New York & London: Plenum Press, 1978.

Mochida, S. Physiological characterization of two dopamine receptors in the superior cervical ganglion of rabbits. *Journal of Tokyo Medical College*, 1982, *40*, 201–213.

Mochida, S., Kobayashi, H., Tosaka, T., Ito, J., & Libet, B. Specific dopamine receptor mediates the production of cyclic AMP in the rabbit sympathetic ganglia and thereby modulates the muscarinic postsynaptic responses. *Advances in Cyclic Nucleotide Research*, 1981, *14*, 685.

Mochida, S., & Libet, B. Long-term-enhancement (LTE) of slow(s-) EPSP induced by physiological preganglionic conditioning train, either homo- or heterosynaptically. *Society for Neuroscience Abstracts*, 1983, *9*, 1212.

Moore, R. Y. Catecholamine pathways in the brain. *Neurosciences Research Program Bulletin*. 1977, *15*, 160–169.

Nestler, E. J., & Greengard, P. Nerve impulses increase the phosphorylation state of protein I in rabbit superior cervical ganglion. *Nature*, 1982, *296*, 452–454.

Nishi, S. Ganglionic transmission. In J. H. Hubbard (Ed.), *The peripheral nervous system*. New York: Plenum, 1974.

Nishi, S., & Katayama, Y. The noncholinergic excitatory transmission in sympathetic ganglia. In J. Salánki (Ed.), *Advances in physiological sciences* (Vol. 4: *Proceedings of the 28th International Congress of Physiological Sciences, 1980: Physiology of excitable membranes*). Budapest: Pergamon Press–Akadémiai Kiadó, 1981.

Nishi, S., & Koketsu, K. Early and late after-discharges of amphibian sympathetic ganglion cells. *Journal of Neurophysiology*, 1968, *313*, 109–130.

Ransmeier, R. E., & Gerard, R. W. Effects of temperature, convulsion and metabolic factors on rodent memory and EEG. *American Journal of Physiology*, 1954, *179*, 663–664.

Seeman, P. Brain dopamine receptors. *Pharmacological Review*, 1980, *32*, 229–313.

Terry, R. D., & Davies, P. Dementia of the Alzheimer type. *Annual Review of Neuroscience*, 1980, *3*, 77–95.

Walters, E. T., & Byrne, J. H. Associative conditioning of single sensory neurons suggests a cellular mechanism for learning. *Science*, 1983, *219*, 405–408.

Wamsley, J. K., Black, A. C., Jr., West, J. R., & Williams, T. H. Cyclic AMP synthesis in guinea pig superior cervical ganglia: Response to pharamcological and preganglionic physiological stimulation. *Brain Research*, 1980, *182*, 415–421.

Woodward, D. J., Moises, H. C., Waterhouse, B. D., Hoffer, B. J., & Freedman, R. Modulatory action of norepinephrine in the central nervous system. *Federation Proceedings*, 1979, *38*, 2109–2116.

Yamamoto, C. Neurotransmitter actions studied in brain slices. *Progress in Brain Research*, 1973, *17*, 64–70. (In Japanese)

CHAPTER TWENTY-EIGHT

Glutamate Receptor Regulation and the Substrates of Memory

MICHEL BAUDRY / GARY LYNCH

INTRODUCTION

Over the past 30 years two strategies have evolved to investigate the biochemical basis of learning and memory. The first is a correlational approach, consisting in determining the various biochemical events that accompany a learning experience, with the hope of successfully identifying those that are necessary, sufficient, and exclusive, as proposed by S. Rose (1981). The second consists in identifying biochemical processes with properties that satisfy the requirements imposed by the behavioral phenomenon of memory. A difficulty that has plagued the hypotheses arising from this second approach has been in demonstrating that inhibition of the postulated biochemical event produces a selective anterograde amnesia. Memory formation requires the coordinated activities of routine physiological and psychological events that themselves are not necessarily part of memory (e.g., perception, homeostasis, activity). If the candidate memory chemistry participates in these "lower-order" events, then inhibitors could produce disruption of learning without necessarily touching the actual memory mechanism.

This chapter will describe our own efforts over the past several years to identify chemical processes that make plausible candidates for a memory mechanism. Because of the widespread evidence that it participates in certain types of memory formation, the hippocampus has been the brain structure chosen for the investigation; in addition our search was guided by the Ariane thread of synaptic plasticity so prevalent in this region. In particular, the long-term potentiation of synaptic transmission that follows high-frequency stimulation delivered to various extrinsic and intrinsic hippocampal pathways (Bliss & Lømo, 1973; Bliss & Gardner-Medwyn, 1973) was used to define biochemical end points that could exhibit the appropriate properties of a memory mechanism.

After reviewing the evidence in favor of a transmitter role for glutamate in several excitatory neurons in the hippocampus, we will describe studies concerning the identification of the postsynaptic glutamate receptors. We will then

Michel Baudry and Gary Lynch. Center for the Neurobiology of Learning and Memory, University of California, Irvine, California.

discuss the existence of a biochemical mechanism that participates in the regulation of these receptors. The elucidation of this mechanism revealed a complex interaction between the cell surface receptor and the cell cytoskeleton that provided the basis for a specific hypothesis concerning the way information is stored in central synapses. Preliminary testing of the hypothesis at the behavioral level on complex maze learning will then be presented. Finally, we will attempt to demonstrate that this biochemical process matches the properties expected of a memory mechanism.

GLUTAMATE AS A TRANSMITTER IN HIPPOCAMPUS

At the beginning of our investigation into the chemical basis of plasticity at hippocampal synapses, we were guided by the increasingly strong evidence that glutamate or a closely related compound was the excitatory transmitter in various extrinsic as well as intrinsic pathways in this structure. This subject has been covered by recent reviews (Roberts, Storm-Mathisen, & Johnston, 1980; DiChiara & Gessa, 1981), and here we will only summarize the pertinent evidence.

Unlike other transmitters, glutamate is involved in multiple metabolite pathways, and its presence in neurons as well as reduction in its level following lesions of various pathways must be viewed as necessary but not sufficient evidence for a transmitter role. However, a strong case has been made that high-affinity uptake can be used as a marker for glutamate neurons, especially in the hippocampal formation (Storm-Mathisen, 1977). Following incubation of slices with [^{3}H]L-glutamate or [^{3}H]D-aspartate or following intraventricular administration of [^{3}H]D-glutamate, autoradiographic localization of these amino acids exhibited a clear lamina pattern, with intense labeling in the terminal zones of the perforant path, the mossy fibers, and the pyramidal cell axons. The labeling was markedly reduced following axotomy of these pathways. Comparable results were obtained biochemically by measuring the transport of labeled amino acids in synaptosomes prepared from microdissected samples from slices (Storm-Mathisen & Iversen, 1979).

Depolarization has been shown by a large number of laboratories to induce a calcium-dependent release of endogenous as well as exogenously loaded glutamate (Nadler, Vala, White, Lynch, & Cotman, 1976; Malthe-Sorenssen, Skrede, & Fonnum, 1979). Moreover, electrical stimulation of an identified pathway (i.e., Schaffer-commissural system) causes a Ca-dependent release of exogenously loaded [^{3}H]glutamate (Wieraszko & Lynch, 1978). The Ca-dependent release of glutamate was also abolished by axotomy of hippocampal pathways.

Glutamate and other acidic amino acids have powerful excitatory effects on the firing of neurons in the central nervous system (Curtis & Johnston, 1974). However, it appears that a multiplicity of acidic amino acid receptors exists (McLennan, 1981; Watkins & Evans, 1981), and in the absence of specific agonists and antagonists it has proved difficult to demonstrate that antagonists of glutamate receptors block synaptic transmission in specific pathways. Nonetheless, two groups have shown that drugs that block excitatory effects of glutamate or aspartate selectively block one of two inputs to the dentate gyrus granule cells (Wheal & Miller, 1980; Koerner & Cotman, 1981).

Moreover, experiments with perfused slices indicate that aminophosphonobutyric acid (APB) and D-α-aminoadipic acid (α-AA) cause a rapid and reversible inhibition of synaptic potentials in field CA1 and dentate gyrus (Dunwiddie, Madison, & Lynch, 1978; Fagni, Baudry, & Lynch, 1983a).

Thus, glutamate is transported into nerve terminals with a high-affinity system, is released in a Ca-dependent manner following electrical stimulation of specific pathways, and exerts potent depolarizing effects mimicking the effect of the natural transmitter; and glutamate antagonists block synaptic transmission. However, it cannot yet be excluded that another compound very similar to glutamate could be in fact the transmitter used in the hippocampal formation, and such a role has been recently attributed to a dipeptide acetyl-aspartyl glutamate (Zaczek, Koller, Cotter, Heller, & Coyle, 1983).

IDENTIFICATION OF A SYNAPTIC RECEPTOR FOR GLUTAMATE

Synapses *a priori* can change their efficiency by either of two mechanisms: modifying the amount of transmitter released by each nerve impulse or increasing or decreasing the responses of the target cells to the same amount of transmitter. In view of the generality of the phenomenon of receptor regulation (Schwartz, Costentin, Martres, Protais, & Baudry, 1978; Reisine, 1981; Creese & Sibley, 1981), we decided to investigate the possibility that plasticity at hippocampal synapses could be due to a plasticity of the glutamate receptor. When we initiated this study, little was known of the characteristics of glutamate receptors in the hippocampus. A few binding studies using radiolabeled glutamate as a ligand had suggested the existence of a high-affinity binding site in synaptic membranes, but with a very different pharmacological profile from the receptor evidenced by electrophysiological studies (Roberts, 1974; Michaelis, Michaelis, & Boyarsky, 1974; Foster & Roberts, 1978; Biziere, Thompson, & Coyle, 1980; De Barry, Vincendon, & Gombos, 1980). This led us to investigate in detail the properties of glutamate receptors in the hippocampus using a combination of binding studies and physiological techniques.

Binding Studies using [^{3}H]L-Glutamate as a Ligand for the Glutamate Receptor

In the absence of well-established and selective agonists, or antagonists, [^{3}H]glutamate has been generally used to study the glutamate receptor in membrane preparations. We indeed found that crude synaptic membranes from hippocampus possess two high-affinity binding sites for [^{3}H]glutamate: an Na-independent binding site and an Na-dependent one (Baudry & Lynch, 1981a). The binding to both sites is saturable and reversible, and kinetic studies both at equilibrium and during association and dissociation provided an estimate of the apparent dissociation constant (K_d) of .5 μM and 2.5 μM respectively. For both sites, Scatchard analyses of the binding revealed homogeneous populations with Hill coefficients not significantly different from unity, suggesting the absence of cooperativity of the binding. The pharmacological profiles of the binding to both sites were markedly different and indicated that the Na-dependent binding was almost certainly related to a high-affinity uptake site for glutamate. On the other hand, the Na-independent binding was inhibited by several excitatory amino acids including quisqualic, ibotenic, D,L-homocysteic, and L-aspartic acids but not by *N*-methyl aspartic acid or kainic acid. The binding was also inhibited by two glutamate antagonists, α-AA and APB, but not by glutamate diethyl ester (GDEE). An interesting property of the Na-independent [^{3}H]glutamate binding is that it is markedly inhibited by low concentrations of sodium ions (Baudry & Lynch, 1979). The concentration of sodium eliciting half-maximal inhibition was found to be .75 m*M*, whereas the maximal inhibition (representing an 80% inhibition) was reached at a concentration of 2.5 m*M*. Sodium was 10 times more potent than lithium and 100 times more potent than potassium in reducing binding. This inhibition of the binding by sodium explains why in the presence of high concentrations of sodium required to fully observe the Na-dependent binding site (100 m*M* of sodium) only one site is detected and not a combination of two sites. By analogy with other neurotransmitter receptors (e.g., gamma-aminobutyric acid [GABA] and glycine with chloride; Young & Snyder, 1974; Mohler & Okada, 1978), it is possible that the sodium-induced decrease in binding is due to the existence of interactions between the recognition site for glutamate and an associated sodium channel (see below).

Although the number of the Na-independent binding sites exhibits relatively small variations across brain areas, there is a clear tendency toward lower levels of binding in telencephalic regions as compared to mesencephalic and metencephalic regions, whereas the opposite is true for the Na-dependent binding sites. During development, the amount of binding sites (expressed in pmol/hippocampus) increased 40 times between the postnatal Day 4 and adult (Baudry, Arst, Oliver, & Lynch, 1981). In fact, the time course of the postnatal increase in binding sites is quite similar to that of synapse addition in the hippocampus. If we consider the binding in terms of density of sites (expressed in pmol/mg protein) this density increases threefold between postnatal Day 4 and Day 9, when it reaches a maximum, and then slowly decreases to reach the adult value at postnatal Day 22. This suggests that the binding sites are not associated with glial cells or myelin that undergo extensive development after the second postnatal week. Subcellular localization of the binding sites provides evidence for a synaptic localization, since the sites are highly enriched in synaptic fractions and synaptic junctions, whereas only small amounts of binding are found in myelin and mitochondrial fractions (Foster, Mena, Fagg, & Cotman, 1981). Finally, the number of binding sites is not modified following lesion of one of the main afferent connections of the hippocampus, namely, the commissural pathway (Baudry, Kramer, & Lynch, 1983a).

Thus, in terms of localization and developmental pattern, the binding sites are clearly associated with postsynaptic neuronal structures in the hippocampus. The ionic interaction suggests a linkage with a sodium channel while the pharmacological profile is compatible with an association with an excitatory amino acid synaptic receptor.

Physiological Studies of Glutamate Receptors in Hippocampal Slices

Most of the physiological studies of glutamate receptors in mammalian central nervous system (CNS) have been performed using iontophoretic application of agonists and antagonists. They have provided evidence for the existence of multiple receptors for excitatory amino acids, mainly based on the differential effects of antagonists on responses to various agonists (Watkins & Evans, 1981). From these studies, Watkins and coworkers, have proposed the classification of these receptors into three types: an NMA receptor selectively stimulated by *N*-methyl-D-aspartic acid, a kainate receptor, and a quisqualate receptor. None of these types corresponds to the glutamate binding site found in membranes from hippocampus or other brain regions. We used two physiological responses to excitatory amino acids in the hippocampal slice preparation to try to resolve these discrepancies. First, we quantified the depolarization induced by bath-applied amino acids by measuring the decrease in the field potentials elicited by antidromic or orthodromic stimulation of the CA1 pyramidal cells. Second, we assayed the amino-acid-induced stimulation of Na efflux in hippocampal slices previously loaded with ^{22}Na using a technique described by Luini, Goldberg, and Teichberg (1981) in striatal slices.

Perfusion with glutamate depolarized the slices, but this disappeared (desensitized) on successive applications (Fagni, Baudry, & Lynch, 1983b). Remarkably enough, this desensitization was not accompanied by any change in the field potential elicited by either antidromic or orthodromic stimulation of the CA1 pyramidal cells, suggesting that bath-applied L-glutamate was acting on a receptor different from the receptor activated by the endogenous transmitter. Moreover, α-AA and APB at concentrations that blocked synaptic transmission were without effect on the depolarizing action of L-glutamate (Fagni *et al.*, 1983a). Following this observation, we found a similar desensitization to the depolarizing effect of D-glutamate, L-aspartate, *N*-methylaspartate but not to D,L-homocysteate or kainate. Thus, a first subdivision of excitatory amino acids was made between those exhibiting the desensitization phenomenon and those that did not. The two antagonists α-AA and APB were then found to affect differentially the depolarizing actions of various excitatory amino acids. That is, α-AA blocked the responses to *N*-methylaspartate and D,L-homocysteate but not to kainate, whereas APB blocked the responses to D,L-homocysteate but not to *N*-methylaspartate or kainate. A second subdivision of the receptors could therefore be obtained using this differential blockade. A minimal set of four receptor types was necessary to account for these results (Figure 28-1):

1. a synaptic receptor (tentatively defined as a G_1 receptor), nondesensitizing, stimulated by D,L-homocysteate, blocked by α-AA and APB.
2. an NMA receptor stimulated by *N*-methylaspartate, desensitizing, blocked by α-AA.
3. a glutamate receptor (tentatively defined as a G_2 receptor), desensitizing, stimulated by L-glutamate, not blocked by α-AA or APB.
4. a kainate receptor, nondesensitizing, not blocked by α-AA or APB.

A very similar pattern of data was obtained using the stimulation of the ^{22}Na efflux in hippocampal slices (Baudry, Kramer, Fagni, Recasens, & Lynch, 1983). Moreover, we found a good correlation between the order of potency of various agonists to depolarize CA1 pyramidal cells and to stimulate ^{22}Na efflux rate. In addition we could provide evidence for a presynaptic localization for some of the kainate and NMA receptors. The G_2 receptor was also found to exhibit supersensitivity following denervation or during the postnatal period,

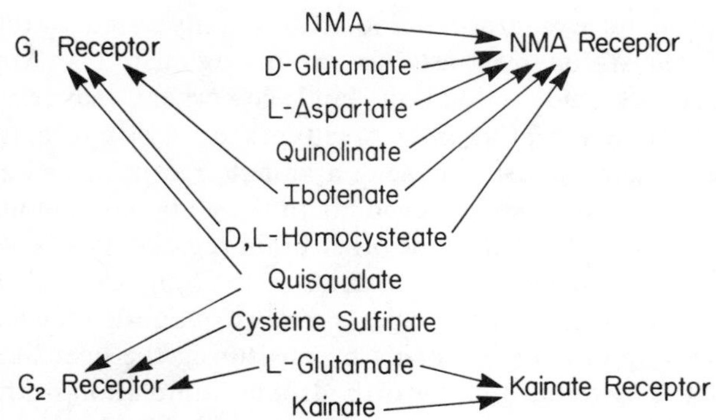

Figure 28-1. Classification of glutamate receptors in the hippocampus. Biochemical and physiological studies led us to propose the existence of at least four classes of glutamate receptors in the hippocampus, differentially activated by various acidic amino acids: (1) a synaptic receptor (G_1 receptor) stimulated by homocysteic acid, (2) a glutamate receptor (G_2 receptor) stimulated by L-glutamate, (3) an NMA receptor, and (4) a kainate receptor.

results in agreement with an extrasynaptic localization (Baudry, Kramer, & Lynch, 1983a). If this classification is correct, can we now equate the glutamate binding site to the G_1 synaptic receptor (it is clearly not related to the NMA or the kainate receptor; Table 28-1)? Both α-AA and APB inhibit the binding site and they block the G_1 site. D,L-Homocysteate and quisqualate stimulate the G_1 site and inhibit the binding site. There is evidence that the synaptic receptor is associated with a sodium channel, and our data suggest that the binding site is associated with a sodium channel. A paradox lies in the observation that bath-applied L-glutamate does not activate the G_1 synaptic receptor, whereas L-glutamate binds with high affinity to a site exhibiting most of the properties of the G_1 site. However, it should be stressed that in the presence of high concentrations of sodium (the situation normally occurring in the slices) no binding can be detected, suggesting that the presence of sodium shifts the receptor toward a configuration with a lower affinity for L-glutamate. This, together with the existence of very efficient uptake systems for L-glutamate, is the likely explanation for why exogenously applied L-glutamate does not stimulate the G_1 receptor.

Table 28-1. Comparison of various properties of the Na-independent "glutamate" binding site, the homocysteate "receptor," and the transmitter receptor in hippocampus

	Na-independent "glutamate" binding site	Homocysteate "receptor" (effects on physiology and sodium flux)	Transmitter receptor
Agonists	Inhibited by L-glutamate, homocysteate, quisqualate Not inhibited by *N*-methyl-D-aspartate, L-aspartate, D-glutamate, kainate		
Antagonists	α-Aminoadipate	α-Aminoadipate	α-Aminoadipate
Localization	Synaptic Postsynaptic	Postsynaptic	Postsynaptic
Effects of ions	Interacts with sodium	Opens sodium channel	Opens sodium channel
Desensitization		Does not desensitize	Does not desensitize

Thus, there is fairly strong evidence that the Na-independent glutamate binding site present in hippocampal membranes is indeed associated with a postsynaptic glutamate receptor in hippocampus, and it becomes of considerable interest to study regulatory mechanisms that could be implicated in synaptic plasticity.

GLUTAMATE RECEPTOR REGULATION

Having established that the glutamate binding site represents a postsynaptic glutamate receptor, we sought to determine if its properties could be altered by conditions known to affect synaptic efficiency. Our initial efforts followed from the observation that long-term potentiation of synaptic transmission was dependent on the concentration of extracellular calcium ions (Dunwiddie & Lynch, 1979). We therefore studied the properties of glutamate binding following manipulation of calcium levels both in membrane preparations and in hippocampal slices.

Manipulation of Calcium Levels in Membrane Preparations

Whereas monovalent cations inhibited glutamate binding, calcium ions were found to markedly stimulate it (Baudry & Lynch, 1979). The concentration of calcium eliciting half-maximal stimulation was about 30 μM, and the maximal stimulation was reached at a concentration of 100–200 μM. The effect of calcium exhibited a strong positive cooperativity with a Hill coefficient of about 2. The increase in binding was due to a change in the number of binding sites without changes in their apparent affinity for glutamate. In addition, the binding measured in the presence of calcium ions had the same pharmacological profile as in its absence, suggesting that the cation induces the unmasking of receptors normally present in the membranes but inaccessible to the ligand. Two methods were used to determine whether the effect of calcium on glutamate receptor binding was reversible. First, membranes were preincubated with calcium, then the free calcium was removed by washing and centrifugation, and the number of receptors was determined in the absence of calcium. We found that the effect of calcium was largely irreversible under these conditions. In the second method, membranes were preincubated with calcium, and then calcium was chelated with the calcium chelator EGTA and the binding immediately measured. Again, we found that the effect was totally irreversible (Baudry, Kramer, & Lynch, 1983b). This second method allowed us to determine the time course of the stimulation by calcium of glutamate binding, by adding the EGTA at various time intervals after the addition of calcium to membranes. The calcium-induced increase in binding was very rapid, being half-maximal at about 1 minute and maximal at 5 minutes. This was very exciting, since it could provide the basis for rapid changes in synaptic efficacy such as seen after brief bursts of electrical stimulation. Trying to find the underlying mechanisms, we were fortunate to test for the effect of proteinase inhibitors on the calcium-induced increase in glutamate binding, and in particular for the actions of leupeptin, a relatively specific inhibitor of calcium-activated thiol-proteinase (Toyo-Oka, Shimizu, & Masaki, 1978). Leupeptin had no effect on basal glutamate binding but totally inhibited the calcium-induced increase in glutamate binding (Vargas, Greenbaum, & Costa, 1980; Baudry, Bundman, Smith, & Lynch, 1981). The concentration of leupeptin providing half-maximal inhibition was about 20 μM, and the maximal inhibition obtained at about 80 μM. As previously with EGTA, leupeptin was added at various time intervals following the addition of calcium to membranes, providing a second estimate of the time course for the stimulation by calcium of glutamate binding. Half-maximal stimulation was obtained at 2 minutes and maximal stimulation at about 10 minutes. These results suggested that calcium increased the number of glutamate binding sites by stimulating a membrane-bound Ca-dependent proteinase. To confirm this hypothesis we determined the effects of exogenous proteinases on the number of glutamate binding sites in hippocampal membranes. Among various proteinases, trypsin and chymotrypsin were found to significantly increase the number of glutamate binding sites (Baudry & Lynch, 1980). Several other data suggest that the calcium-induced increase in glutamate receptor binding is due to a reorganization of the membranes; in particular the effect of calcium is absent at or below 20° C and is suppressed by treatments of membranes with detergents or with phospholipase D (Baudry, Smith, & Lynch, 1981).

Manipulation of Calcium Levels in the Slice Preparation

Because it was possible that the above-described regulatory mechanism was produced artifactually as a result of tissue homogenization and subcellular fractionation, it was important to verify that, in a relatively intact preparation containing the main features of the cellular organization, calcium ions were still able to regulate the properties of glutamate receptor binding. Again, two different approaches were used to modify the levels of calcium. The first consisted of varying the concentration of calcium in the slice incubation medium, whereas in the second, brief bursts of high-frequency electrical stimulation were administered to the Schaffer-commissural pathways. Increasing the concentration of calcium from 0 to 2.5 mM in the slice incubation medium resulted in a twofold increase in the number of glutamate receptor binding sites measured in membranes isolated from the slices (Baudry, Siman, Smith, & Lynch, 1983). Interestingly, the binding to membranes measured in the presence of a concentration of calcium providing the maximal stimulation (250 μM) was not changed, suggesting that the same mechanism is responsible for the stimulation by calcium of glutamate binding both in the membrane preparation or in incubated slices. This was further confirmed by showing that leupeptin totally prevented the increase in binding elicited by increased calcium concentration in the slice incubation medium (Figure 28-2). In agreement with previous reports, we also found that increasing calcium concentrations under these conditions resulted in an increase in proteolytic activity in the slices, which was markedly inhibited by the thiol-proteinase inhibitor leupeptin.

Electrical stimulation in the hippocampus has been shown to considerably decrease the extracellular concentration of calcium (at least in the cell body layer), and it has been shown that hippocampal dendrites are able to generate calcium spikes (Wong, Prince, & Basbaum, 1979; Hotson, Prince, & Schwartzkroin, 1979). It is thus a reasonable assumption that following stimulation (especially at high frequency) intracellular calcium levels can rise (at least

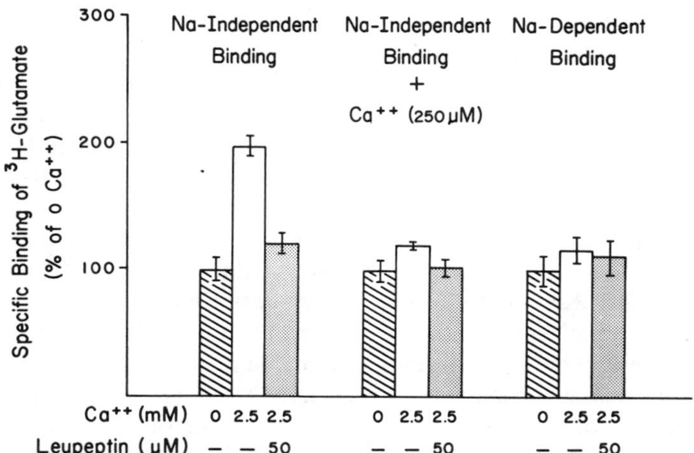

Figure 28-2. Effects of leupeptin on the calcium-induced increase in [^{3}H]glutamate binding in hippocampal slices. Hippocampal slices were incubated with the indicated calcium concentrations in the absence or presence of leupeptin (50 μM). Synaptic membranes from 6–8 slices were prepared and immediately assayed for [^{3}H]glutamate binding at a [^{3}H]L-glutamate concentration of 100 n*M*, in the absence or presence of 250 μM calcium chloride or in the presence of 100 m*M* sodium chloride (Na-dependent binding). Results are expressed as percentage of the respective control values obtained in membranes from slices incubated in the absence of calcium and are means $\pm$ *SEM* of 6–8 experiments. (Data from Baudry, Siman, Smith, & Lynch, 1983.)

temporarily). Following high-frequency stimulation of the Schaffer-commissural system, we found that the maximal number of glutamate binding sites was increased without change in their apparent affinity for glutamate (Baudry, Oliver, Creager, Wieraszko, & Lynch, 1980). The effect was not observed when the experiment was performed in calcium-free incubation medium, or when the slices were stimulated at low frequency (Lynch, Halpain, & Baudry, 1982). The increase in binding was detected as soon as 5 minutes after the electrical train (the shortest time interval tested) and still present with the same amplitude after 45 minutes. In addition, the increase in binding correlated well with the increase in synaptic efficacy elicited by the high-frequency train of stimulation. Slices showing large potentiation of their synaptic responses exhibited the highest increase in binding, whereas slices showing poor potentiation exhibited no significant increase in binding.

It appears then that both in membrane preparation and in slices calcium ions exert a potent and relatively selective regulatory influence on glutamate receptor binding (the effect of calcium is mimicked, although to a lesser degree, by manganese and strontium) (Baudry & Lynch, 1981b). This effect is irreversible, sensitive to a variety of treatments altering protein–protein or protein–lipid interactions and, most important, is totally blocked by inhibitors of calcium-activated proteinases.

CALCIUM-ACTIVATED PROTEINASE AND CYTOSKELETON INTERACTION

The results discussed above pointed to an important role of calcium-activated proteinase in the regulation of glutamate receptor binding. However, although the existence in neurons of such enzymes had been reported by a number of laboratories (see Ishiura, 1981, for a review), two main aspects of our hypothesis did not agree well with what was known of these enzymes; the enzymes were found mainly in the soluble fraction, suggesting a cytoplasmic localization, whereas our hypothesis required a membrane localization (or at least an association with membranes); they were half-maximally stimulated by calcium concentrations in the range .5–1.0 m*M*, whereas calcium stimulated glutamate binding with an EC_{50} of 25–30 μM. In recent years it was found in a large variety of tissues, including brain, that two forms of these enzymes exist, with a low (5–50 μM) and a high (100–500 μM) threshold for calcium (Mellgren, 1980; De Martino, 1981; Kishimoto, Kajikawa, Tabuchi, Shiota, & Nishizuka, 1981; Zimmerman & Schlaepfer, 1982). Murachi proposed the generic name of "calpain" to designate these enzymes, with calpain I corresponding to the low threshold for calcium and calpain II to the high threshold for calcium. Although it was initially thought that calpain I was the result of an autodigestion of calpain II, it seems now clearly demonstrated that these two enzymes are different peptidic chains (however, it is also evident that autodigestion of calpain II results in the appearance of Ca-dependent proteinase with a low threshold for calcium). Recently we were able to detect the presence of these enzymes in cortical and hippocampal membranes by extraction in low ionic conditions (Siman, Baudry, & Lynch, 1983). The enzymes were partially purified and their properties studied using a casein substrate. Two forms of calcium-activated proteinases were extracted and in view of their calcium dependencies, inhibitor sensitivities, and molecular weight were found identical to calpain I and calpain II, thus indicating that these enzymes are indeed associated with such synaptic membranes.

What are the substrates of these calcium-activated proteases? The first substrates identified in the soluble fraction of neurons were the neurofilament proteins (Pant & Gainer, 1980). Since then several other substrates have been identified. Interestingly, most of these are members of the cytoskeleton-associated proteins, such as microtubule-associated proteins (MAPs), neurofilament proteins, or even tubulin (Sandoval & Weber, 1978; Pant & Gainer, 1980; Malik, Meyers, Iqbal, Sheikh, Scotto, & Wisniewski, 1981). In addition, we were able to provide evidence for the existence of an additional substrate of calpain I (Baudry, Bundman, Smith, & Lynch, 1981). When synaptic membranes were incubated in the presence of calcium and the proteins subsequently separated on SDS-polyacrylamide gels, we found that a high-molecular-weight doublet protein with a molecular weight of about 220 to 230,000 was partly degraded. This effect exhibited an EC_{50} for calcium of about 30 μM and was totally blocked by the proteinase inhibitor leupeptin. The effect was absent below 20°C and mimicked by strontium and manganese but not by a variety of other divalent cations. The migration profile on the gel of this high-molecular-weight peptide was very similar to that of a protein named "fodrin" by Levine and Willard (1981); part of the slowly transported proteins, fodrin was shown to be localized in a variety of cells in the inner part of the plasma membranes, forming a network resembling the spectrin network in the erythrocytes. The similarities between fodrin and spectrin have been now extensively described; both proteins consist of two polypeptide chains, α and β, with a molecular weight of 230,000 to 235,000, and are organized as a tetramer $(\alpha\beta)_2$ with a high percentage of α-helicity; in addition, the α-subunits of both proteins are very closely related, since antibodies to α-spectrin recognize α-fodrin, and peptide maps of the α-subunit are very similar. Spectrin and fodrin bind actin and calmodulin and induce the gelation of F-actin (Glenney, Glenney, & Weber, 1982; Carlin, Bartelt, & Siekevitz, 1983). Finally, both proteins are involved in the capping of cell surface receptors in a variety of cell types (Levine & Willard, 1983; Nelson, Colaco, & Lazarides, 1983).

We purified fodrin from rat brain as described by Levine and Willard (1981) and found that it comigrated with the high-molecular-weight doublet protein that is degraded by incubation with calcium. Moreoever, purified calpain I from erythrocytes was found to degrade purified fodrin as well as the fodrin situated in synaptic membranes (Siman, Baudry, & Lynch, in press); in addition, the affinity of fodrin for calpain was about 50 n*M*, in the same range as that of other substrates for calpain. These data clearly indicate that fodrin is a relatively specific substrate of calpain I.

These results can be integrated into a model of the organization of synaptic membranes and their interaction with the underlying cytoskeleton. Since the best-understood membrane organization is that of the erythrocyte, our model is derived from that described for this system (Branton, Cohen, & Tyler, 1981; Figure 28-3).

We propose thus that glutamate receptors are present in synaptic membranes under two configurations, one accessible to the ligand under normal conditions, a stable receptor, and another not accessible to the ligand (or exhibiting a very low affinity for it) that we designate as labile. Following the calcium-induced degradation of fodrin, the labile receptors are transformed into stable receptors. This transition from labile to stable is regulated by constraints imposed on the movement of cell surface receptors by their interaction with the cytoskeleton through the fodrin network. MAPs have been found to have some immunological similarities with ankyrin (Bennett & Davis, 1981) and would thus be the link between microtubules and plasma membranes.

Figure 28-3. Schematic model of the relationship between cytoskeletal elements and glutamate receptors in telencephalic membranes.

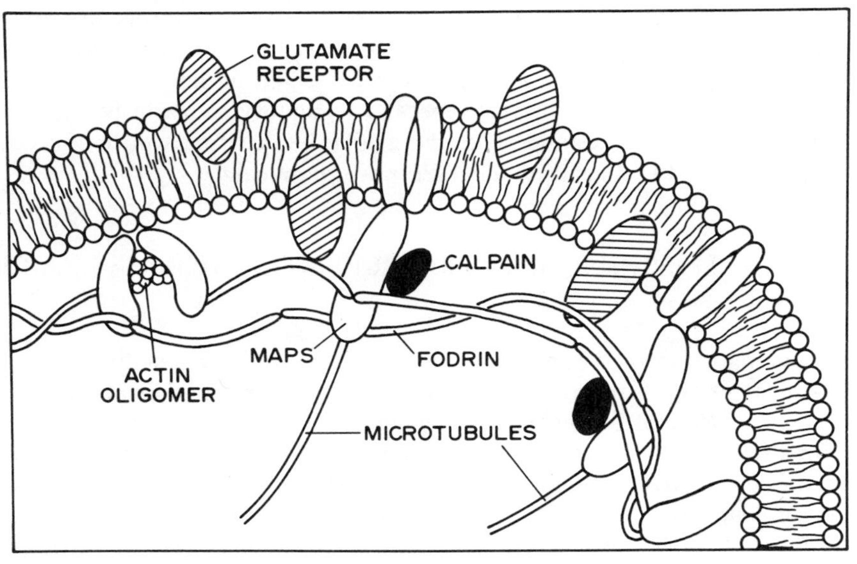

In addition, on the basis of immunological studies, the existence of an ankyrin-like molecule has been suggested in the brain (Bennett, 1978). Fodrin tetramers form a filamentatous network underlying the plasma membranes, attached to the membranes via interaction with the ankyrin-like protein (and possibly the MAPs) and with actin oligomers. It is interesting that brain fodrin has been shown to bind with high affinity to erythrocyte ankyrin (Burridge, Kelly, & Mangeat, 1982). By its association with actin, fodrin might thus be dually linked with the neurofilaments, whereas its postulated interaction with the MAPs could also confer to this protein a link with the microtubules. Fodrin would thus be the ideal molecule to mediate the interaction between cell surface receptors and the cytoskeletal elements. Somewhere in this network of structural proteins we have to assume the presence of calpain I present in an inactive form as long as calcium levels remain low. When calcium levels rise (as a result of high-frequency stimulation), calpain I is activated and rapidly degrades fodrin, thereby modifying the interaction between cell surface receptors and cytoskeleton, allowing the transition of labile to stable glutamate receptors. In addition, considering the role of cytoskeleton in the regulation of cell shape (Ralston, 1978; Marchesi, 1979) in a variety of cell types, it is possible that this same process is used to modify the shape of the postsynaptic dendritic spine. Changes in shape of dendritic spines have been found in hippocampus after high-frequency electrical stimulation (Lee, Schottler, Oliver, & Lynch, 1980; Lee, Oliver, Schottler, & Lynch, 1981; Greenough, Chapter 32, this volume).

Thus, the model provides a relatively precise description of the sequence of events leading from a brief burst of electrical activity to a permanent change in structure and receptor number. Does a change in receptor number result in an increased efficacy of synaptic transmission? It would if for each nerve impulse the amount of transmitter release totally saturates the available receptors. There is now some electrophysiological evidence that this is the situation found at various synapses in the central nervous system (Jack, Redman, & Wong, 1981). In this regard, we mentioned earlier that the telencephalic studies of the brain exhibit lower levels of receptors than the mesencephalic and cerebrocephalic structures. Further studies are now in progress to address the issue of relative release of neurotransmitter versus number of available receptors in various brain structures. It is indeed conceivable that two categories of synapses exist, one in which the release of the neurotransmitter is the limiting factor, the receptors being in excess; for this type, the regulatory step will be localized presynaptically. In the second type, the available receptors will be the rate-limiting step and the regulation localized postsynaptically.

BEHAVIORAL EFFECTS OF THE CALCIUM-ACTIVATED PROTEINASE INHIBITOR LEUPEPTIN

Another prediction of the model is that inhibition of calpain should result in impairment of the learning of tasks requiring the participation of this post-synaptically localized biochemical machinery.

In a first series of experiments leupeptin was injected peripherally, and rats were trained to find a hidden platform in a large water maze. No significant effect of leupeptin was obtained during the acquisition period, but in the retention tests, the rats injected with leupeptin searched the platform in a different way and relatively less often in the correct place (Morris & Baker, 1984). This experiment, although not conclusive, encouraged us to pursue the investigation of the effect of leupeptin on learning. In experiments currently performed, leupeptin is perfused at a slow rate (.5 μl/hour) directly in the lateral ventricle by the use of an osmotic pump, and the rats are tested for their performance in an eight-arm radial maze in which they have to adopt an optimal strategy for food reward. The task is rendered more complicated by the introduction of a delay between the fourth and the fifth choice, during which the rat is returned to its home cage for periods ranging from 15 to 60 minutes. Control rats injected with saline have no problem in performing this task with a mean number of errors of about one per trial and per day. On the other hand, the rats injected with leupeptin performed very poorly, averaging more than three errors per trial and per day (Staubli, Baudry, & Lynch, 1984).

Thus, these preliminary experiments strongly suggest that another prediction of the model, namely, that an impairment of memory would be produced by inhibition of Ca-dependent proteinase, has been verified.

CALPAIN, GLUTAMATE RECEPTOR REGULATION, AND MEMORY

The above-described calpain–glutamate receptor interaction has a number of features that make it an attractive candidate for a memory-producing process (Lynch & Baudry, 1984). It is triggered by an event—elevation of intracellular calcium concentrations into the low micromolar range—that can be expected to occur occasionally but is almost certainly not part of the moment-to-moment operation of neurons. This should allow testing of the linkage between the biochemical mechanism and memory, since it should be possible to block activation of the proteinase without interfering with routine physiological operation. The results produced by calpain are irreversible and likely to have important effects on the efficiency of neuronal circuits. The mechanism thus provides a straightforward cellular explanation for the extreme duration of memory.

Calpain-induced receptor uncovering occurs in synaptic membranes and appears to be much more pronounced in the telencephalon, and while not required of a memory mechanism, these features are nonetheless desirable. With regard to synapses, theorists have long argued that the substrates of memory will be found in synapses. The regional localization of the process we are proposing leads to the strong prediction that it will be involved in some types of memory and not in others; moreover, it should be possible to use data from the neuropsychological literature to define these two categories.

Testing of the hypothesis has been started, and the first findings are encouraging. Learning does produce increases in hippocampal glutamate receptors (Mamounas, Thompson, Lynch, & Baudry, 1984), and an inhibitor of calpain blocks some but not all forms of learning. While many more experiments of these types are now under way, progress will probably be dependent on the development of an adequate pharmacology for regulating calpain activity. Recent discoveries of endogenous inhibitors and activators of the enzyme (Murachi, Tanaka, Hatanaka, & Murakami, 1981; Murachi, Hatanaka, Yasumoto, Nayakama, & Tanaka, 1981; De Martino & Blumenthal, 1982) encourage the belief that this will be possible.

ACKNOWLEDGMENTS

This work was supported by Grant Nos. NSF 81-12156 (to M. B.), NSF BNS 76-17370 (to G. L.), and AFOSR 82-0116 (to G. L.).

REFERENCES

Baudry, M., Arst, D., Oliver, M., & Lynch, G. Development of glutamate binding sites and their regulation by calcium in rat hippocampus. *Developmental Brain Research*, 1981, *1*, 37–48.

Baudry, M., Bundman, M., Smith, E., & Lynch, G. Micromolar levels of calcium stimulate proteolytic activity and glutamate receptor binding in rat brain synaptic membranes. *Science*, 1981, *212*, 937–938.

Baudry, M., Kramer, K., Fagni, L., Recasens, M., & Lynch, G. Classification and properties of excitatory amino acid receptors in hippocampus: II. Biochemical studies using the sodium efflux assay. *Molecular Pharmacology*, 1983, *24*, 222–228.

Baudry, M., Kramer, K., & Lynch, G. Classification and properties of acidic amino acid receptors in hippocampus: III. Supersensitivity during the post-natal period and following denervation. *Molecular Pharmacology*, 1983a, *24*, 229–234.

Baudry, M., Kramer, K., & Lynch, G. Irreversibility and time-course of the calcium-stimulation of ^{3}H-glutamate binding to rat hippocampal membranes. *Brain Research*, 1983b, *270*, 142–145.

Baudry, M., & Lynch, G. Regulation of glutamate receptors by cations. *Nature*, 1979, *282*, 748–750.

Baudry, M., & Lynch, G. Regulation of hippocampal glutamate receptors: Evidence for the involvement of a calcium-activated protease. *Proceedings of the National Academy of Sciences, USA*, 1980, *77*, 2298–2302.

Baudry, M., & Lynch, G. Characterization of two ^{3}H-glutamate binding sites in rat hippocampal membranes. *Journal of Neurochemistry*, 1981a, *36*, 811–820.

Baudry, M., & Lynch, G. Hippocampal glutamate receptors. *Molecular and Cellular Biochemistry*, 1981b, *38*, 5–18.

Baudry, M., Oliver, M., Creager, R., Wieraszko, A., & Lynch, G. Increase in glutamate receptors following repetitive electrical stimulation in hippocampal slices. *Life Sciences*, 1980, *27*, 325–330.

Baudry, M., Siman, R., Smith, E. K., & Lynch, G. Regulation by calcium ions of glutamate receptor binding in hippocampal slices. *European Journal of Pharmacology*, 1983, *90*, 161–168.

Baudry, M., Smith, E., & Lynch, G. Influences of temperature, detergents and enzymes on glutamate receptor binding and its regulation by calcium in rat hippocampal membranes. *Molecular Pharmacology*, 1981, *20*, 280–286.

Bennett, V. Immunoreactive forms of human erythrocyte ankyrin are present in diverse cells and tissues. *Nature*, 1978, *281*, 597–599.

Bennett, V., & Davis, J. Erythrocyte ankyrin: Immunoreactive analogues are associated with mitotic structures in cultured cells and with microtubules in brain. *Proceedings of the National Academy of Sciences, USA*, 1981, *78*, 7550–7554.

Biziere, K., Thompson, H., & Coyle, J. T. Characterization of specific, high-affinity binding sites for L-^{3}H-glutamic acid in rat brain membranes. *Brain Research*, 1980, *183*, 421–433.

Bliss, T. V. P., & Gardner-Medwin, A. R. Long-lasting potentiation of synaptic transmission in the dentate area of the unanesthetized rabbit following stimulation of the perforant path. *Journal of Physiology* (London), 1973, *232*, 357–374.

Bliss, T. V. P., & Lømo, T. Long-lasting potentiation of synaptic transmission in the dentate area of the anaesthetized rabbit following stimulation of the perforant path. *Journal of Physiology* (London), 1973, *232*, 331–356.

Branton, D., Cohen, C. M., & Tyler, J. Interaction of cytoskeletal proteins on the human erythrocyte membrane. *Cell*, 1981, *24*, 24–32.

Burridge, K., Kelly, T., & Mangeat, P. Non-erythrocyte spectrins: Actin-membrane attachment proteins occurring in many cell types. *Journal of Cell Biology*, 1982, *95*, 478–486.

Carlin, R. K., Bartelt, D. C., & Siekevitz, P. Identification of fodrin as a major calmodulin-binding protein in postsynaptic density preparations. *Journal of Cell Biology*, 1983, *96*, 443–448.

Creese, I., & Sibley, D. R. Receptor adaptations to centrally acting drugs. *Annual Review of Pharmacology and Toxicology*, 1981, *21*, 357–391.

Curtis, D. R., & Johnston, G. A. R. Amino acid transmitters in the mammalian central nervous system. *Reviews of Physiology*, 1974, *69*, 97–188.

De Barry, J., Vincendon, G., & Gombos, G. High affinity glutamate binding during postnatal development of rat cerebellum. *FEBS Letters*, 1980, *109*, 175–179.

De Martino, G. N. Calcium-dependent proteolytic activity in rat liver: Identification of two proteases with different calcium requirements. *Archives of Biochemistry and Biophysics*, 1981, *211*, 253–257.

De Martino, G. N., & Blumenthal, D. K. Identification and partial purification of a factor that stimulates calcium-dependent proteases. *Biochemistry Journal*, 1982, *21*, 4303–4310.

DiChiara, G., & Gessa, G. L. (Eds.). *Advances in biochemical psychopharmacology* (Vol. 27: *Glutamate as a neurotransmitter*). New York: Raven Press, 1981.

Dunwiddie, T. V., & Lynch. G. The relationship between extracellular calcium concentrations and the induction of hippocampal long-term-potentiation. *Brain Research*, 1979, *169*, 103–110.

Dunwiddie, T. V., Madison, D., & Lynch, G. S. Synaptic transmission is required for initiation of long-term potentiation. *Brain Research*, 1978, *150*, 413–417.

Fagni, L., Baudry, M., & Lynch, G. Classification and properties of excitatory amino acid receptors in hippocampus: I. Electrophysiological studies of an apparent desensitization and interactions with drugs which block transmission. *Journal of Neuroscience*, 1983a, *3*, 1538–1546.

Fagni, L., Baudry, M., & Lynch, G. Desensitization to glutamate does not affect synaptic transmission in rat hippocampal slices. *Brain Research*, 1983b, *261*, 167–171.

Foster, A., Mena, E., Fagg, G., & Cotman, C. Glutamate and aspartate binding sites are enriched in synaptic junctions isolated from rat brain. *Journal of Neuroscience*, 1981, *1*, 620–626.

Foster, A. C., & Roberts, P. J. High-affinity L-^{3}H-glutamate binding to postsynaptic receptor sites on rat cerebellar membranes. *Journal of Neurochemistry*, 1978, *31*, 1467–1477.

Glenney, J. R., Glenney, P., & Weber, K. Erythroid spectrin, brain fodrin, and intestinal brush border proteins (TW-260/240) are related molecules containing a common calmodulin-binding subunit bound to a variant cell-type specific subunit. *Proceedings of the National Academy of Sciences, USA*, 1982, *79*, 4002–4005.

Hotson, J. R., Prince, D. A., & Schwartzkroin, P. D. Anomalous inward rectification in hippocampal neurons. *Journal of Neurophysiology*, 1979, *42*, 889–895.

Ishiura, S. Calcium-dependent proteolysis in living cells. *Life Sciences*, 1981, *29*, 1079–1087.

Jack, J. J. B., Redman, S. J., & Wong, K. The components of synaptic potentials evoked in cat spinal motoneurones by impulses in single group Ia afferents. *Journal of Physiology* (London), 1981, *321*, 65–96.

Kishimoto, A., Kajikawa, N., Tabuchi, H., Shiota, M., & Nishizuka, Y. Calcium-dependent neutral proteases, widespread occurrence of a species of protease active at lower concentrations of calcium. *Journal of Biochemistry*, 1981, *90*, 889–892.

Koerner, J. F., & Cotman, C. W. Micromolar L-2-amino-4-phosphobutyric acid selectively inhibits perforant path synapses from lateral entorhinal cortex. *Brain Research*, 1981, *216*, 192–198.

Lee, K., Oliver, M., Schottler, F., & Lynch, G. Electron microscopic studies of brain slices: The effects of high frequency stimulation on dendritic ultrastructure. In G. Kerkut (Ed.), *Electrical activity in isolated mammalian CNS preparations*. New York: Academic Press, 1981.

Lee, K., Schottler, F., Oliver, M., & Lynch, G. Brief bursts of high-frequency stimulation produce two types of structural change in rat hippocampus. *Journal of Neurophysiology*, 1980, *44*, 247–258.

Levine, J., & Willard, M. Fodrin: Axonally transported polypeptides associated with the internal periphery of many cells. *Journal of Cell Biology*, 1981, *90*, 631–643.

Levine, J., & Willard, M. Redistribution of fodrin (a component of the cortical cytoplasm) accompanying capping of cell surface molecules. *Proceedings of the National Academy of Sciences, USA*, 1983, *80*, 191–195.

Luini, A., Goldberg, D., & Teichberg, V. Distinct pharmacological properties of excitatory amino acid receptors in the rat striatum: Study by the Na^{+} efflux assay. *Proceedings of the National Academy of Sciences, USA*, 1981, *78*, 3250–3254.

Lynch, G., & Baudry, M. The biochemistry of memory: A new and specific hypothesis. *Science*, 1984, *224*, 1057–1063.

Lynch, G., Halpain, S., & Baudry, M. Effects of high-frequency synaptic stimulation on glutamate receptor binding studied with a modified *in vitro* hippocampal slice preparation. *Brain Research*, 1982, *244*, 101–111.

Malik, M. N., Meyers, L. A., Iqbal, K., Sheikh, A. M., Scotto, L., & Wisniewski, H. M. Calcium-activated proteolysis of fibrous proteins in central nervous system. *Life Sciences*, 1981, *29*, 795–802.

Malthe-Sorenssen, D., Skrede, K. K., & Fonnum, F. Calcium-dependent release of D-^{3}H-aspartate evoked by selective electrical stimulation of excitatory afferent fibers to hippocampal pyramidal cells. *Neuroscience*, 1979, *4*, 1255–1263.

Mamounas, L., Thompson, R. F., Lynch, G., & Baudry, M. Classical conditioning of the rabbit eyelid response increases glutamate receptor binding in hippocampal synaptic membranes. *Proceedings of the National Academy of Sciences, USA*, 1984, *81*, 2478–2482.

Marchesi, V. T. Spectrin: Present status of a putative cyto-skeletal protein of the red cell membrane. *Journal of Membrane Biology*, 1979, *51*, 101–131.

McLennan, H. On the nature of receptors for various excitatory amino acids in the mammalian central nervous system. In G. DiChiara & G. L. Gessa (Eds.), *Advances in biochemical psychopharmacology* (Vol. 27: *Glutamate as a Neurotransmitter*). New York: Raven Press, 1981.

Mellgren, R. L. Canine cardiac calcium-dependent proteases: Resolution of two forms with different requirements for calcium. *FEBS Letters*, 1980, *109*, 129–133.

Michaelis, E. K., Michaelis, M. L., & Boyarsky, L. L. High-affinity glutamic acid binding to brain synaptic membranes. *Biochimica Biophysica Acta*, 1974, *367*, 338–348.

Mohler, H., & Okada, T. Properties of γ-aminobutyric acid receptor binding with (+)-^{3}H-bicuculline methiodide in rat cerebellum. *Molecular Pharmacology*, 1978, *14*, 256–265.

Morris, R., & Baker, M. Does long-term potentiation/synaptic enhancement have anything to do with learning or memory? In N. Butters & L. Squire (Eds.), *Neuropsychology of memory*. New York: Guilford Press, 1984.

Murachi, T., Hatanaka, M., Yasumoto, Y., Nakayama, N., & Tanaka, K. A quantitative distribution study on calpain and calpastatin in rat tissues and cells. *Biochemistry International*, 1981, *2*, 651–656.

Murachi, T., Tanaka, K., Hatanaka, M., & Murakami, T. Intracellular Ca^{2+}-dependent protease (calpain) and its high-molecular weight endogenous inhibitor (calpastatin). *Advances in Enzyme Regulation*, 1981, *19*, 407–424.

Nadler, J. V., Vala, K. V., White, W. F., Lynch, G. S., & Cotman, C. W. Aspartate and glutamate as possible transmitters of excitatory hippocampal afferents. *Nature*, 1976, *260*, 538–540.

Nelson, W. J., Colaco, A. L. S., & Lazarides, E. Involvement of spectrin in cell-surface receptor capping in lymphocytes. *Proceedings of the National Academy of Sciences, USA*, 1983, *80*, 1626–1630.

Pant, H. C., & Gainer, H. Properties of a calcium-activated protease in squid axoplasm which selectively degrades neurofilament proteins. *Journal of Neurobiology*, 1980, *11*, 1–12.

Ralston, G. B. The structure of spectrin and the shape of the red blood cell. *Trends in Biochemical Sciences*, 1978, *3*, 195–198.

Reisine, T. Adaptive changes in catecholamine receptors in the central nervous system. *Neurosciences*, 1981, *6*, 1471–1502.

Roberts, P. J. Glutamate receptors in rat central nervous system. *Nature*, 1974, *252*, 399–401.

Roberts, P. J., Storm-Mathisen, J., & Johnston, G. (Eds.). *Glutamate as a transmitter*. New York: Wiley, 1980.

Rose, S. P. R. What should a biochemistry of learning and memory be about. *Neuroscience*, 1981, *6*, 811–821.

Sandoval, I. V., & Weber, K. Calcium-induced inactivation of microtubule formation in brain extracts. *European Journal of Biochemistry*, 1978, *92*, 463–470.

Schwartz, J. C., Costentin, J., Martres, M. P., Protais, P., & Baudry, M. Modulation of receptor mechanisms in the CNS: Hyper- and hyposensitivity to catecholamines. *Neuropharmacology*, 1978, *17*, 665–680.

Siman, R., Baudry, M., & Lynch, G. Purification from synaptosomal plasma membranes of calpain I, a thiol-protease activated by micromolar calcium concentrations. *Journal of Neurochemistry*, 1983, *41*, 950–956.

Siman, R., Baudry, M., & Lynch, G. Brain fodrin: Substrate for the endogenous calcium-activated protease calapin I. *Proceedings of the National Academy of Sciences, USA*, in press.

Staubli, U., Baudry, M., & Lynch, G. Leupeptin, a thiol-proteinase inhibitor, causes a selective impairment of spatial maze performance in rats. *Behavioral and Neural Biology*, 1984, *40*, 58–69.

Storm-Mathisen, J. Localization of transmitter candidates in the brain: The hippocampal formation as a model. *Progress in Neurobiology*, 1977, *8*, 119–181.

Storm-Mathisen, J., & Iversen, L. L. Uptake of ^{3}H-glutamic acid in excitatory nerve endings: Light and electron microscopic observations in the hippocampal formation of the rat. *Neuroscience*, 1979, *4*, 1237–1253.

Toyo-Oka, T., Shimizu, T., & Masaki, T. Inhibition of proteolytic activity of a calcium-activated neutral protease by leupeptin and antipain. *Biochemical and Biophysical Research Communications*, 1978, *82*, 484–491.

Vargas, F., Greenbaum, L., & Costa, E. Participation of cystein proteinase in the high-affinity Ca^{++}-dependent binding of glutamate to hippocampal synaptic membranes. *Neuropharmacology*, 1980, *19*, 791–794.

Watkins, J. C., & Evans, R. H. Excitatory amino acid transmitters. *American Review of Pharmacology and Toxicology*, 1981, *21*, 165–204.

Wheal, H. V., & Miller, J. J. Pharmacological identification of acetylcholine and glutamate excitatory systems in the dentate gyrus of the rat. *Brain Research*, 1980, *182*, 145–155.

Wieraszko, A., & Lynch, G. Stimulation-dependent release of possible transmitter substances from hippocampal slices studied with localized perfusion. *Brain Research*, 1978, *160*, 372–376.

Wong, R. K. S., Prince, D. A., & Basbaum, A. I. Intradendritic recordings from hippocampal neurons. *Proceedings of the National Academy of Sciences, USA*, 1979, *76*, 986–990.

Young, A. B., & Snyder, S. H. The glycine synaptic receptor: Evidence that strychnine binding is associated with the ionic conductance mechanism. *Proceedings of the National Academy of Sciences, USA*, 1974, *71*, 4002–4005.

Zaczek, R., Koller, K., Cotter, R., Heller, D., & Coyle, J. T. *N*-Acetyl-aspartylglutamate: An endogenous peptide with high affinity for a brain "glutamate" receptor. *Proceedings of the National Academy of Sciences, USA*, 1983, *80*, 1116–1119.

Zimmerman, V. J. P., & Schlaepfer, W. W. Characterization of a brain calcium-activated protease that degrades neurofilament proteins. *Biochemistry*, 1982, *21*, 3977–3983.

Critical Commentaries

CHAPTER TWENTY-NINE

Where Is the Locus of Long-Term Potentiation?

T. V. P. BLISS / A. C. DOLPHIN

INTRODUCTION

A question central to neuroscience is whether enduring changes in synaptic plasticity provide the physiological basis for learning and memory. In the simple nervous system of a marine invertebrate, *Aplysia californica*, presynaptic depression and facilitation can account for habituation, sensitization, and classical conditioning (Hawkins & Kandel, Chapter 26, this volume). As yet there are no similar demonstrations linking synaptic plasticity to simple or associative memory in vertebrates. There are, however, several reports that long-lasting changes in the efficiency of synaptic transmission can occur in identified neural systems in vertebrates. One example is the superior cervical ganglion, where the long-term increase in the amplitude of the slow EPSP produced by a brief exposure to dopamine is postsynaptically mediated (see Libet, Chapter 27, this volume). Another example, and one of particular interest because it occurs in a structure that has been associated with disorders of memory, is long-term potentiation (LTP) in the hippocampus. Brief trains of high-frequency stimulation delivered to any one of a number of excitatory hippocampal pathways will induce a potentiation of synaptic transmission lasting for several hours or days (Bliss & Lømo, 1973; see Bliss, 1979, for review). The question of whether LTP is pre- or postsynaptically mediated remains unresolved (Bliss & Dolphin, 1982). Our purpose here is to review recent findings and to assess to what extent they provide support for one or other locus of action.

First, we note that LTP of the population spike appears to consist of two distinct components (Wilson, Levy, & Steward, 1981; Bliss, Goddard, & Riives, 1983): a component that is accounted for by potentiation of the population EPSP, and an additional component that is probably due to an increased excitability of the postsynaptic cell population, which we shall not discuss further here.

Next, we need some definitions. By a presynaptic mechanism we mean one that results in an afferent fiber releasing more transmitter per action potential,

T. V. P. Bliss. Division of Neurophysiology and Neuropharmacology, National Institute for Medical Research, London NW7, England.

A. C. Dolphin. Department of Pharmacology, St. George's Hospital Medical School, London SW17, England.

irrespective of the means by which this is accomplished. By a postsynaptic mechanism we mean one in which the release of the same amount of transmitter produces a greater synaptic effect. We should emphasize that these definitions are concerned only with the final expression of the processes underlying LTP; a mechanism whose end result was the release of more transmitter would be classified as presynaptic even if the locus of control, in the useful phrase introduced by Douglas, Goddard, and Riives (1982), were postsynaptic, involving, say, the release of a trophic factor from postsynaptic cells. These definitions are empirical and allow for the classification of possible synaptic processes that do not fall obviously into a pre- or postsynaptic category; for example, if high-frequency stimulation resulted in the presynaptic release of a cotransmitter that affected the coupling of the postsynaptic receptor to its associated ion channels and thus modulated the efficacy of the primary transmitter, the release of which was unchanged, then this would be classified as a postsynaptic mechanism.

TESTS FOR THE SYNAPTIC LOCUS OF LTP

There are three well-established and relatively direct ways of showing whether a change in synaptic efficacy is pre- or postsynaptically mediated: (1) quantal analysis, (2) measurement of the physiological response to a fixed amount of transmitter, (3) measurement of transmitter release. As yet, there are no published reports of a quantal analysis of LTP, although miniature EPSPs have been recorded in CA3 pyramidal cells (Brown, Wong, & Prince, 1979). This is a serious gap in the LTP literature. However, in the present context, the diagnostic value of a quantal study will depend on the result. An increase in quantal size would not in itself distinguish between pre- and postsynaptic mechanisms. An increase in quantal content without change in quantal size would provide powerful evidence against a postsynaptic mechanism.

Measurements of the response of single CA1 cells to glutamate before and after the induction of LTP have revealed either no change (Turner, Baimbridge, & Miller, 1982), or a decrease in responsiveness (Lynch, Gribkoff, & Deadwyler, 1977). Before these results can be regarded as definitive evidence against a postsynaptic locus, it has to be established that glutamate is in fact the transmitter. This assumption has recently been brought into question by Fagni, Baudry, and Lynch (1983), who suggest that homocysteic acid rather than glutamate may be the ligand for the synaptic receptor in this pathway and that glutamate acts on extrasynaptic receptors, which readily desensitize.

A sustained increase in the release of a transmitter analogue, D-aspartate, following high-frequency stimulation has been reported by Skrede and Malthe-Sørenssen (1981) for the Schaffer-collateral afferents to CA1. Using an *in vivo* technique to perfuse perforant path terminals with radiolabeled glutamine, the immediate precursor for glutamate, we have found that LTP is accompanied by a prolonged increase in the release of newly synthesized glutamate (Dolphin, Errington, & Bliss, 1982a). Our results are summarized in Figure 29-1. We have confirmed this finding in other experiments in which radiolabeled glutamine was continually perfused (Dolphin, Errington, & Bliss, 1982b). The release of [^{3}H]glutamate is at least partially stimulus dependent, but we have no firm evidence that the elevated level is associated with an increase in the amount of transmitter released per action potential, rather than, for instance, an increase

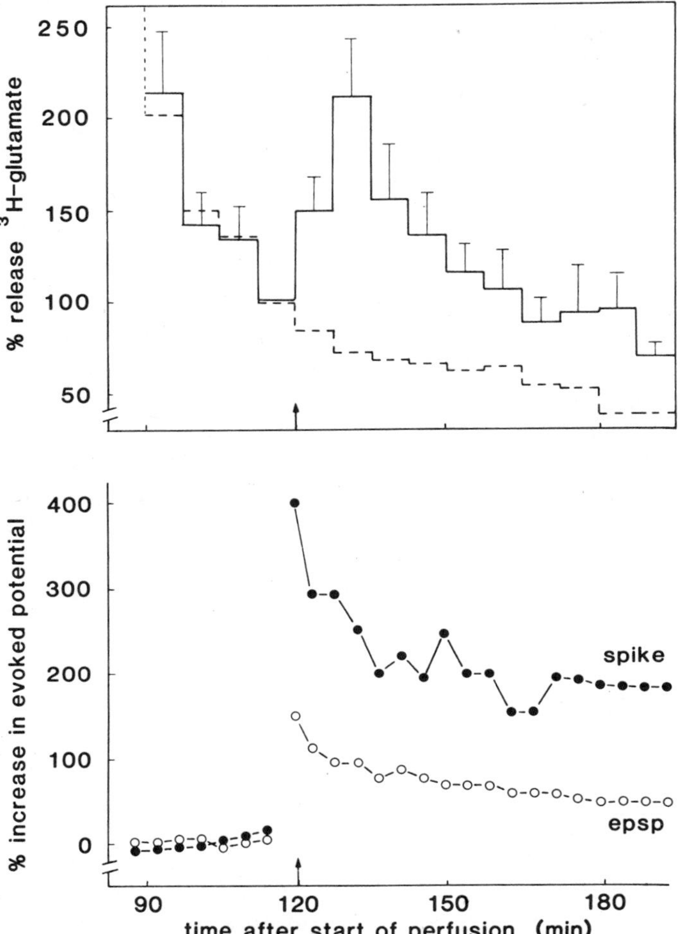

Figure 29-1. LTP and [^{3}H]glutamate release in urethane-anesthetized rats with implanted push–pull cannula. [^{3}H]Glutamine was infused into the dentate gyrus in 3 μl of Krebs buffer, 1 hr before the start of perfusion at 10 μl/min. Fractions of perfusate of 7.5-min duration were collected, and the [^{3}H]glutamate present was estimated as previously described (Dolphin, Errington, & Bliss, 1982a). Histogram: [^{3}H]Glutamate release in sequential fractions of perfusate from 11 animals, calculated as percentages of the fraction ending at 120 min. The perforant path was stimulated throughout the experiment at 0–1 Hz, and a high-frequency train (250 Hz, 500 msec) was given at 120 min. Control results from seven animals not given the high-frequency train are shown by the dotted line. Graph: The mean percentage change in the amplitude of the population spike and population EPSP, monitored by a recording electrode attached to the push–pull cannula and positioned in the granule cell body layer, are shown for the 11 animals that were given the high-frequency train. (Adapted, with additional data, from Dolphin, Errington, & Bliss, 1982a.)

in the spontaneous firing rate of cells in the entorhinal cortex that give rise to perforant path fibers. It is also possible that there is an increase in spillover of glutamate unconnected with synaptic transmission, either from perforant path terminals or from depolarized glial cells. Another type of objection arises from the use of radiolabeled compounds; for example, newly synthesized glutamate might be preferentially formed in, or released from, potentiated terminals. However, we have recently found that the level of endogeneously released glutamate is also increased following the induction of LTP (Lynch, Errington, & Bliss, in press).

The release studies are strongly suggestive, but further work is required before the conclusion that LTP has a presynaptic component can confidently be drawn. On the other hand, iontophoretic experiments have not so far produced evidence consistent with a postsynaptic locus.

Numerous other experiments have addressed, if less directly than those discussed so far, the question of the synaptic locus of LTP. In several cases, as we shall see, the data suggest a postsynaptic involvement in LTP.

Morphological Studies

Changes in the morphology of synaptic spines have been observed following high-frequency stimulation of the perforant path (Fifkova & van Harreveld, 1977). An increase in the small number of synapses terminating on dendritic shafts of pyramidal cells in CA1 has also been noted (Lee, Schottler, Oliver, & Lynch, 1980); in our terminology this represents a combination of a pre- and postsynaptic mechanism. These results are of considerable interest, since changes of this sort could in principle embody both a mechanism and a locus for LTP. But as yet there is no evidence to indicate whether the observed changes can explain all or even a significant part of the physiological potentiation.

Biochemical Studies

Apart from measurements of transmitter release, biochemical studies of events associated with LTP have concentrated on two areas: changes in protein phosphorylation and changes in glutamate binding.

Both cyclic nucleotides and Ca^{++} have been implicated in various forms of synaptic plasticity (see Hawkins & Kandel, Chapter 26, and Libet, Chapter 27, this volume). These two classes of second messenger are known to activate protein kinases, which phosphorylate substrate proteins in neural tissue as elsewhere. It has been postulated that phosphorylation of receptor proteins (Smilowitz, Hadjian, Dwyer, & Feinstein, 1981) and ion channels (Hawkins & Kandel, Chapter 26, this volume) may modulate their activity. For this reason several groups have investigated the relation between LTP and protein phosphorylation. The first study was by Browning, Dunwiddie, Bennett, Gispen, and Lynch (1979), who found that in synaptosomes prepared from slices in which the Schaffer and commissural afferents to CA1 pyramidal cells had been tetanized, the endogenous phosphorylation of a 40 kD protein—later identified as the α-subunit of the mitochondrial enzyme pyruvate dehydrogenase (PDH)—was substantially increased. The increased phosphorylation of this enzyme is associated with a decrease in its activity. Since PDH supports pyruvate-dependent calcium uptake into mitochondria, a reduction in its activity would markedly reduce the ability of the enzyme to buffer Ca^{++}, and cytoplasmic Ca^{++} levels would remain elevated for a longer period following influx into the cell, thus providing a potential mechanism for LTP. Several important questions remain unanswered by these studies. First, are the mitochondria that show changes in phosphorylation post- as well as presynaptically located? Since mitochondria are highly concentrated in presynaptic terminals and are absent from dendritic spines, a change in the calcium buffering capacity of mitochondria is more likely to affect presynaptic terminals rather than individual dendritic spines. Second, the precise trigger for the change in the phosphorylation of pyruvate dehydrogenase is also a matter for speculation, as is the time course of the change. Lastly, Hoch, Dingledine, and Wilson (1984) have suggested that PDH-kinase rather than PDH may be the enzyme affected, calling into question the interpretation put on their results by Browning *et al.* (1979).

Similar studies have been carried out by Bär, Schotman, Gispen, Tielen, and Lopes da Silva (1980), who examined protein phosphorylation in hippocampal slices 15 minutes after a tetanus to the perforant path. Changes were found in the phosphorylation of a number of proteins, and it may be significant that one of these, the neuronal protein B-50, is highly concentrated in presynaptic terminals (Sorensen, Kleine, & Mahler, 1981).

Baudry and Lynch (1980) have proposed a mechanism for LTP based on an increase in the number of postsynaptic receptors. In agreement with this model, Baudry, Oliver, Creager, Wieraszko, and Lynch (1980) found an increased binding of glutamate in CA1 following high-frequency stimulation of Schaffer-commissural fibers. Sastry and Goh (1984), however, have failed to replicate this finding. The reason for the discrepancy is unclear, but in any case it remains to be shown whether the increased binding reported by Baudry *et al.* (1980) is to physiologically active receptors; as mentioned previously, there have been no reports of increased responsiveness to applied glutamate after high-frequency trains.

Physiological and Pharmacological Studies

Calcium, over and above its essential role in synaptic transmission, plays an important, though poorly understood, role in the genesis of LTP. Low external Ca^{++} prevents LTP (Dunwiddie, Madison, & Lynch, 1978; Wigstrøm, Swann, & Andersen, 1979), and high Ca^{++} can produce LTP even in the absence of a high-frequency train (Turner *et al.*, 1982; Bliss, Dolphin, & Feasey, 1984). However, the site of action of Ca^{++} in these experiments is unknown. Two recent intracellular studies of LTP in CA1 pyramidal cells have given a conflicting picture of the possible postsynaptic role of Ca^{++} in the genesis of LTP. Lynch, Larson, Kelso, Barrionuevo, and Schottler (1983) injected the Ca^{++}-chelating agent EGTA into CA1 cells and found that this procedure prevented the development of LTP in the injected cell, as predicted by the Baudry–Lynch model. On the other hand, Wigstrøm, McNaughton, and Barnes (1982) were able to impose a hyperpolarizing voltage on individual CA1 cells without affecting their ability to develop LTP. Even allowing for electrotonic decrement of the imposed hyperpolarization, it seems likely that voltage-dependent calcium channels would have been affected by this maneuver, and entry of Ca^{++} into the cells correspondingly reduced. If this apparent discrepancy can be resolved, these experiments will have significant consequences for theories of the mechanism of LTP.

The use of pharmacological blockers offers a promising approach, since if LTP were to fail in the presence of specific transmitter antagonists, this would be powerful evidence for, at the least, a postsynaptic locus of control. The problem is that no completely effective high-affinity antagonists for any of the presumed amino acid transmitters exists, nor is it clear that the actions of any of the drugs that have been used for this purpose are entirely postsynaptic. Nevertheless, using hippocampal slices, Dunwiddie *et al.* (1978) found that LTP in the Schaffer-commissural input to CA1 is blocked by aminophosphonobutyrate, and Collingridge, Kehl, and McLennan (1983) reported a similar result with aminphosphonovalerate and D-γ-glutamylglycine. We have done similar experiments using a push–pull cannula *in vivo*, and found that while D-γ-glutamylglycine completely blocks the onset of LTP in the perforant path as long as the drug is present in the perfusate, potentiation develops without further high-frequency trains when it is removed (Dolphin, 1983). These studies must therefore be regarded as inconclusive. In other experiments, a modulatory action of monoamines on LTP has been revealed; LTP is depressed in animals depleted of norepinephrine or serotonin (Bliss *et al.*, 1983) and enhanced *in vitro* in the presence of added norepinephrine (Hopkins & Johnston, 1982). The nature and locus of this effect has not yet been examined.

Indirect evidence in favor of a presynaptic locus has been provided by Sastry (1982), who found that the excitability of perforant path terminals was reduced after a high-frequency train, with a time course similar to that of LTP. Changes in the membrane potential of afferent terminals, which this finding presumably reflects, could provide a mechanism for increased transmitter release.

A necessary condition for the induction of LTP, at least in the perforant path, is that the stimulus train be of sufficient strength (McNaughton, Douglas, & Goddard, 1978). This implies a cooperativity among concurrently active afferents, which could be mediated via extracellular space, glial cells, or through postsynaptic neurons. A brief tetanus delivered to the inhibitory commissural pathway to granule cells immediately before a perforant path train can prevent the induction of LTP (Douglas, 1982). Wigstrøm and Gustafsson (1983) have shown that LTP can be produced at lower stimulus strengths in CA1 if GABA-ergic inhibitory inputs are blocked with pictrotoxin. These results suggest that the threshold for LTP may be a dynamic parameter whose level is set by inhibitory tone. Whether or not this is the case, it is difficult to avoid the conclusion, in the absence of any anatomical evidence for axo-axonic contacts in the hippocampus, that postsynaptic cells are involved in the control of LTP. On the other hand, recent results from our laboratory indicate that the increased release of endogenous glutamate associated with LTP of the perforant path does not occur when the induction of LTP is suppressed by commissural stimulation (Bliss, Douglas, Errington, & Lynch, unpublished observations). It cannot be concluded, therefore, that the observations discussed in this paragraph compel a postsynaptic mechanism as we have defined it; it is possible, for instance, that a dendritically released factor (see Duffy, Teyler, & Shashoua, 1981) influences the mechanisms responsible for release.

CONCLUSIONS

There is no compelling evidence in favor of either an exclusively presynaptic or an exclusively postsynaptic locus for LTP. The increase in transmitter release associated with LTP points firmly toward a presynaptic locus; the case will be strengthened if it can be confirmed that manipulations that affect LTP also affect the increase in transmitter release in the same way. The available evidence does not exclude the possibility that there is both a pre- and postsynaptic locus. Confirmation of the latter will require the demonstration, so far lacking, that the response of the postsynaptic membrane to applied transmitter is enhanced during LTP. Nevertheless, there is considerable circumstantial evidence that postsynaptic cells are involved in the genesis of LTP, whether or not the final expression of the effect is presynaptic.

REFERENCES

Bär, P. R., Schotman, P., Gispen, W. H., Tielen, A. M., & Lopes da Silva, F. H. Changes in synaptic membrane phosphorylation after tetanic stimulation in the dentate area of the rat hippocampal slice. *Brain Research*, 1980, *198*, 478–484.

Baudry, M., & Lynch, G. Hypothesis regarding the cellular mechanisms responsible for long-term potentiation in the hippocampus. *Experimental Neurology*, 1980, *68*, 202–204.

Baudry, M., Oliver, M., Creager, R., Wieraszko, A., & Lynch, G. Increase in glutamate receptors following repetitive electrical stimulation in hippocampal slices. *Life Sciences*, 1980, *27*, 325–330.

Bliss, T. V. P. Synaptic plasticity in the hippocampus. *Trends in Neurosciences*, 1979, *2*, 42–45.

Bliss, T. V. P., & Dolphin, A. C. What is the mechanism of long-term potentiation in the hippocampus. *Trends in Neurosciences*, 1982, *5*, 289–290.

Bliss, T. V. P., Dolphin, A. C., & Feasey, K. J. Elevated calcium induces a long-lasting potentiation of commissural responses in hippocampal CA3 cells of the rat *in vivo*. *Journal of Physiology*, 1984, *350*, 65P.

Bliss, T. V. P., Goddard, G. V., Riives, M. Reduction in long-term potentiation in the dentate gyrus of the rat following selective depletion of monoamines. *Journal of Physiology*, 1983, *334*, 475–491.

Bliss, T. V. P., & Lømo, T. Long-lasting potentiation of synaptic transmission in the dentate area of the anaesthetized rabbit following stimulation of the perforant path. *Journal of Physiology*, 1973, *232*, 331–356.

Brown, T. H., Wong, R. K. S., & Prince, D. A. Spontaneous miniature synaptic potentials in hippocampal neurons. *Brain Research*, 1979, *177*, 194–199.

Browning, M., Dunwiddie, T., Bennett, W., Gispen, W., & Lynch, G. Synaptic phosphoproteins: Specific changes after repetitive stimulation of the hippocampal slice. *Science*, 1979, *203*, 60–62.

Collingridge, G. L., Kehl, S. J., & McLennan, H. Excitatory amino acids in synaptic transmission in the Schaffer collateral–commissural pathway of the rat hippocampus. *Journal of Physiology*, 1983, *334*, 33–46.

Dolphin, A. C. The excitatory amino acid D-glutamylglycine masks rather than prevents long-term potentiation of the perforant path. *Neuroscience*, 1983, *10*, 377–383.

Dolphin, A. C., Errington, M. L., & Bliss, T. V. P. Long-term potentiation of the perforant path *in vitro* is associated with increased glutamate release. *Nature*, 1982a, *297*, 496–498.

Dolphin, A. C., Errington, M. L., & Bliss, T. V. P. Sustained increase in glutamate release associated with long-term potentiation of perforant path *in vitro*. *Society for Neuroscience Abstracts*, 1982b, *8*, 740.

Douglas, R. M., Goddard, G. V., & Riives, M. Inhibitory modulation of long-term potentiation: Evidence for a post-synaptic locus of control. *Brain Research*, 1982, *240*, 259–272.

Duffy, C., Teyler, T. J., & Shashoua, V. E. Long-term potentiation in the hippocampal slice: Evidence for stimulated secretion of newly synthesized proteins. *Science*, 1981, *212*, 1148–1151.

Dunwiddie, T., Madison, D., & Lynch, G. Synaptic transmission is required for initiation of long-term potentiation. *Brain Research*, 1978, *150*, 413–417.

Fagni, L., Baudry, M., & Lynch, G. Desensitisation to glutamate does not affect synaptic transmission in rat hippocampal slices. *Brain Research*, 1983, *261*, 167–177.

Fifkova, E., & van Harreveld, A. Long-lasting morphological changes in dendritic spines of dentate granule cells following stimualtion of the entorhinal area. *Journal of Neurocytology*, 1977, *6*, 211–230.

Hoch, D. B., Dingledine, R. J., & Wilson, J. E. Long-term potentiation in the hippocampal slice: Possible involvement of pyruvate dehydrogenase. *Brain Research*, 1984, *302*, 125–134.

Hopkins, W. F., & Johnston, D. Noradrenergic modulation of long-term potentiation in the hippocampus. *Society for Neuroscience Abstracts*, 1982, *8*, 740.

Lee, K. S., Schottler, F., Oliver, M., & Lynch, G. Brief burst of high-frequency stimulation produce two types of structural change in rat hippocampus. *Journal of Neurophysiology*, 1980, *44*, 247–258.

Lynch, M., Errington, M. L., & Bliss, T. V. P. Sustained increase in release of endogenous glutamate associated with long-term potentiation of the perforant path in the anaesthetized rat. *Neuroscience Letters*, in press.

Lynch, G., Gribkoff, V., & Deadwyler, S. A. Long-term potentiation is accompanied by a reduction in dendritic responsiveness to glutamic acid. *Nature*, 1977, *266*, 737–739.

Lynch, G., Larson, J., Kelso, S., Barrionuevo, G., & Schottler, F. Intracellular injections of EGTA block induction of hippocampal long-term potentiation. *Nature*, 1983, *305*, 719–721.

McNaughton, D. L., Douglas, R. M., & Goddard, G. V. Synaptic enhancement in fascia dentata; cooperativity among coactive afferents. *Brain Research*, 1978, *157*, 277–293.

Sastry, B. R. Presynaptic change associated with long-term potentiation in hippocampus. *Life Sciences*, 1982, *30*, 2003–2008.

Sastry, B. R., & Goh, J. W. Long-lasting potentiation in hippocampus is not due to an increase in glutamate receptors. *Life Sciences*, 1984, *34*, 1497–1501.

Skrede, K. K., & Malthe-Sørenssen, D. Increased resting and evoked release of transmitter following repetitive electrical tetanization in hippocampus: A biochemical correlate to long-lasting synaptic potentiation. *Brain Research*, 1981, *208*, 436–441.

Smilowitz, H., Hadjian, R. A., Dwyer, J., & Feinstein, M. B. Regulation of acetylcholine receptor phosphorylation by calcium and calmodulin. *Proceedings of the National Academy of Sciences, USA*, 1981, *78*, 4708–4712.

Sorensen, R. G., Kleine, L. P., & Mahler, H. R. Presynaptic localization of phosphoprotein B-50. *Brain Research Bulletin*, 1981, *7*, 57–61.

Turner, R. W., Baimbridge, K. G., & Miller, J. J. Calcium-induced long-term potentiation in the hippocampus. *Neuroscience*, 1982, *7*, 1411–1416.

Wigstrøm, H., & Gustafsson, B. Facilitated induction of hippocampal long-lasting potentiation during blockade of inhibition. *Nature*, 1983, *301*, 603–604.

Wigstrøm, H., McNaughton, B. L., & Barnes, C. A. Long-term synaptic enhancement in hippocampus is not regulated by postsynaptic membrane potential. *Brain Research*, 1982, *233*, 195–199.

Wigstrøm, H., Swann, J. W., & Andersen, P. Calcium dependency of synaptic long-lasting potentiation in the hippocampal slice. *Acta Physiologica Scandinavica*, 1979, *105*, 126–128.

Wilson, R. C., Levy, W. B., & Steward, O. Changes of translation of synaptic excitation to dentate granule cell discharge accompanying long-term potentiation: II. An evaluation of mechanisms utilizing dentate gyrus dually innervated by surviving ipsilateral and sprouted crossed tempero-dentate inputs. *Journal of Neurophysiology*, 1981, *46*, 339–355.

CHAPTER THIRTY

Functions of Afferent Coactivity in Long-Term Potentiation

W. C. ABRAHAM / G. V. GODDARD

In order to discuss the neurobiology of learning and memory, it is first necessary to realize that both "learning" and "memory" are inferences. The inferences may be drawn from an observed change in behavior, or they may be drawn from introspection. In most instances the neurobiologist would prefer inferences drawn from observed behavior, although introspection may serve as a source of hypotheses. Since it is readily accepted by neurobiologists that behavior is largely a product of nervous system activity, it is a straightforward matter to assert that changes in behavior are reflections of changes in the nervous system. Instead of studying minutely the changes in behavior that might reasonably infer learning or memory, therefore, many neurobiologists prefer to study minutely any change in nervous system connectivity that might reasonably be expected to result in the alteration of behavior. It is usual, but by no means universal, to concentrate on changes that bear formal resemblance to the inferred processes of learning or memory such as those (1) resulting from neural activity, (2) resulting in the increased probability of a particular output, and (3) lasting for a reasonably long period of time.

One of the most promising of such changes is the phenomenon (or phenomena) of long-term potentiation (LTP) as observed originally by Bliss and Lømo (1973). In this model, field potentials are recorded from the hilus of the dentate gyrus (DG) with relatively gross electrodes that measure the average dendritic depolarizations (population EPSP) and near-synchronous action potentials (population spike, PS) of a large number of granule cells as they respond to monosynaptic input from perforant path fibers activated by test shocks through an electrode located in the angular bundle. Bliss and Lømo (1973) showed in the rabbit that both the population EPSP and PS responses to standard test shocks are increased in amplitude following high-frequency stimulation of the perforant path fibers and remain increased for many hours. Bliss and Gardner-Medwin (1973), using chronically implanted electrodes, showed that such perforant path LTP may last for days or even weeks, and this has since been confirmed in rats and monkeys (Douglas & Goddard, 1975; Goddard & Douglas, 1976). Thus, LTP exhibits those basic attributes listed

W. C. Abraham and G. V. Goddard. Department of Psychology, University of Otago, Dunedin, New Zealand.

above that are inferred to belong to neural events underlying the learning process.

These findings alone are not sufficient to permit speculation about the participation of LTP in any but the simplest kinds of learning. LTP would take on much greater significance if it displayed properties similar to those inferred to subserve more complex behaviors such as associative conditioning. In particular we are interested in mechanisms that can explain how the spatiotemporal contiguity of two stimuli can strengthen the response to one or the other when separately presented. Here we will review evidence that LTP has associative-like properties and thus may provide a useful model for characterizing neural events underlying these higher forms of learning. Most of this work has been done in the DG of anesthetized or awake rats, and in general we will confine our review to studies using these preparations. Observations of LTP in other areas of hippocampus, both *in vivo* and *in vitro*, are reported elsewhere in this volume (cf. Baudry & Lynch, Chapter 28).

COOPERATIVITY

A fundamental aspect of associative learning is that more than one stimulus is required for response alteration to occur. Thus, in simplistic neural terms, we would expect activity in a single afferent fiber to be insufficient to alter either its synaptic strength or more generally the postsynaptic cell's probability of firing; that is, more than one fiber will need to be contiguously active in order for changes to occur. In fact, of course, a given stimulus will activate a population of neurons, and thus the association of two stimuli may require the interaction of a large number of cells. It is interesting to note, then, that the production of LTP also requires coactivity of some minimal number of fibers.

McNaughton, Douglas, and Goddard (1978) first demonstrated that the coactivity of a number of perforant path (PP) fibers afferent to the DG is required to produce LTP. They termed this feature of LTP "cooperativity." Their demonstration involved three separate tests of cooperativity. The first finding was that for a single stimulating electrode to elicit LTP, the stimulation intensity had to be great enough to activate a large number of surrounding fibers. The response in the DG to such threshold stimulation was well above EPSP threshold, typically very close to PS threshold. Increases in stimulus strength, activating more fibers, generated additional LTP in the original subset of test fibers until some asymptotic level was reached for that electrode placement. A threshold stimulus intensity for LTP has also been observed in areas CA1 and CA3 of the hippocampus (Yamamoto & Sawada, 1981; Lee, 1982). These data indicate that LTP is not a property of single synapses or fibers but requires coactivity of a large population of afferents.

The two remaining demonstrations of cooperativity by McNaughton *et al.* (1978) involved placing stimulating electrodes separately in the medial (MPP) and lateral (LPP) components of the PP. In the first experiment, an apparently saturated level of LTP was generated for each electrode placement individually. When trains were then delivered to both pathways nearly simultaneously (staggered by .5 msec), additional LTP was observed in both pathways when individually tested. In the other test the MPP and LPP stimulation strengths were kept just subthreshold for LTP when tetani were given to each pathway alone. However, when the two pathways were driven nearly simultaneously at these same stimulation strengths, LTP was generated in each pathway. If the tetanic stimulation of the two pathways were separated by a few hundred milliseconds, cooperativity was not observed (McNaughton, unpublished observations).

The importance of the two pathway experiments is that the MPP and LPP are known to terminate on separate but adjacent areas of the granule cell dendritic arbor (middle third and distal third, respectively) (Hjorth-Simonsen & Jeune, 1972; Steward, 1976; McNaughton & Barnes, 1977). Thus, cooperativity between these two pathways may not reflect local dendritic or local extracellular environment alterations. Their interaction involves communication over a measurable distance. Importantly, this interaction is activity dependent, since tetanizing one pathway alone in fact depresses synaptic transmission in the untetanized pathway (Abraham & Goddard, 1983).

The cooperative interaction of pathways terminating at different dendritic loci has gained further support by recent demonstrations of cooperativity between septal and PP afferents to the DG (Fantie, 1982; Robinson & Racine, 1982). Fantie, using within-animal comparisons, reported that pairing of septal and PP trains in one hemisphere produced significantly greater PP EPSP potentiation than in the hemisphere receiving septal and PP trains staggered every 20 minutes. In this study no septal evoked potentials were observed in the DG either before or after potentiation. The ability of single-pulse activation of the septum to facilitate granule cell discharge during PP input was observed to become more powerful following the cotetanization. Robinson and Racine (1982), having produced an asymptotic level of PP LTP, were able to generate additional increases in the PS but not the EPSP through subsequent pairings of septal and PP trains. The septal evoked potential recorded in this study was not altered by these treatments. Together, these studies show that cooperativity can be exhibited between afferents arising from very different regions of brain. Since the septal terminals are thought to be largely restricted to the proximal 20–30 μm of the granule cell dendritic tree, 70–80 μm from the nearest PP terminals (Mosko, Lynch, & Cotman, 1973; Crutcher, Madison, & Davis, 1981), these data give strength to the idea that cooperativity can work at a distance. What is still not known is the degree of synaptic specificity of cooperativity, that is, whether synapses terminating on sections of dendrite between those cooperating in LTP are affected or not. Experiments are currently being performed in our laboratory in collaboration with David Bilkey to test whether MPP synaptic strength is altered after concurrent tetanization of septal and LPP afferents.

REVERSIBILITY OF LONG-TERM POTENTIATION

Levy and Steward (1979) have described a unique form of cooperative interaction between the ipsilateral PP and the crossed PP whose terminals spread to a similar extent over the outer two-thirds of the granule cell dendrites. In normal animals the crossed PP does not exhibit LTP, presumably because its terminal density is too low to reach LTP threshold. However, conjunctive tetanization of the crossed and ipsilateral fibers produced LTP of the EPSP evoked by test stimulation of either pathway alone. The interesting aspect of this study is that the maintenance of LTP in the crossed pathway was dependent on the subsequent nature of activity in the much larger ipsilateral pathway.

When additional trains were delivered to the ipsilateral path alone, the previously established LTP in the crossed system was eliminated. The pattern of potentiation–depotentiation was repeatable several times in a single animal. This is the only study to date demonstrating the reversibility of LTP. Except for passive decay over time, all other studies by us and others have found LTP to be a one-way, increase-only phenomenon. The importance of Levy and Steward's finding is such that careful testing of this phenomenon in other systems is warranted.

BLOCKADE OF LONG-TERM POTENTIATION

Since LTP results from the cooperative activity of a population of afferents, it is also of interest to know whether there exist afferents to the DG whose activity, when concurrent with PP activity, will prevent the development of LTP. Douglas, Goddard, and Riives (1982) have demonstrated that the fibers arising from one dentate hilus and innervating the contralateral DG serve such a role. Single conditioning shocks delivered to this pathway inhibit the granule cells from firing in response to a subsequent single PP stimulus, probably via a disynaptic GABA-mediated feed-forward inhibitory mechanism (Buzsaki & Eidelberg, 1982; Douglas, McNaughton, & Goddard, 1983). Such single-pulse stimulation was not sufficient to affect the production of PP LTP. On the other hand, tetanization of the commissural pathway was effective in preventing LTP from occurring in response to PP tetanization. Partial blockade of LTP was produced by a commissural–PP train for intervals as long as 50 msec. It is not known why high-frequency commissural activity can alter LTP production, whereas single-pulse stimulation is ineffective, but this stimulus dependence of LTP blockade mirrors well the stimulus dependence of LTP production in the PP, which also requires high-frequency stimulation, a finding that also remains unexplained.

A recent study in CA1 of *in vitro* hippocampal slices also provides evidence of inhibitory neuronal control of LTP (Wigstrøm & Gustafsson, 1983). Drugs such as picrotoxin and bicuculline, which block transmission across GABA-ergic inhibitory synapses, were shown to lower the threshold for LTP of Schaffer-collateral inputs onto pyramidal cells. The drugs were effective with regard to LTP without altering the pretetanus synaptic response to test stimulation of the Schaffer collaterals. Such findings in CA1 raise the likelihood that commissural blockade of LTP in the DG also works via inhibitory interneurons. We do not yet know the synaptic specificity of this effect, that is, whether commissural activity will inhibit LTP for all granule cell afferents capable of displaying it or just for PP afferents. Nonetheless, the inhibitory control of LTP represents another example of afferent interactions at a distance since the inhibitory synapses cluster around the granule cell bodies whereas the PP terminals are located more distally on the dendrites 100–300 μm away.

MONOAMINERGIC MODULATION OF LONG-TERM POTENTIATION

There is a relatively large hippocampal projection of serotonergic and noradrenergic fibers arising from midbrain raphe nuclei and the locus ceruleus (LC), respectively. Although there exists a sparse monoaminergic innervation of the

DG molecular layer, the primary terminal fields for these afferents are in the hilus subadjacent to the granule cell layer (Azmitia & Segal, 1978; Loy, Koziell, Lindsey, & Moore, 1980). Thus, monoaminergic fibers appear to innervate granule cells only weakly but display a dense innervation of hilar interneurons. If hilar interneurons play a role in modulating LTP, as suggested above by studies of the commissural system, then monoaminergic modulation of interneuron activity may lead to modulation of PP LTP as well. This possibility was recently tested by Bliss, Goddard, and Riives (1983) using a variety of pharmacological manipulations to interrupt monoaminergic synaptic transmission. They showed that the depletion of hippocampal norepinephrine reduced to some extent the capacity for LTP of the PP EPSP. Serotonin depletions more profoundly affected LTP by raising the threshold, reducing the asymptotic level, and hastening the decay. These effects were apparent for both potentiation of the EPSP and the increased probability of granule cell discharge. These data suggest that particularly the raphe nuclei normally exert a tonic modulatory control of PP LTP, perhaps involving suppression of the activity of hilar inhibitory interneurons. Interruption of monoaminergic transmission would thus disrupt LTP through disinhibition of hilar neurons. In CA1 of *in vitro* hippocampal slices, on the other hand, depletions of hippocampal monoamines have not been observed to affect LTP (Dunwiddie, Roberson, & Worth, 1982). The reason for this discrepancy is not clear, but perhaps severing the monoaminergic inputs during slicing of the tissue causes enough disruption of these pathways to obscure any effects of the drug manipulations. Alternatively, the findings of Bliss *et al.* (1983) may depend on some alteration of the hippocampal system that is secondary to chronic monoamine depletion.

In a manner similar to that found for the septal pathway, short high-frequency conditioning trains delivered to the LC facilitate granule cell discharge to a PP test pulse delivered 30–40 msec later (Bliss & Wendlandt, 1977; Assaf, Mason, & Miller, 1979; Abraham & Goddard, 1982; Harley, Lacaille, & Milway, 1982; but see Winson, 1980). Recently we have attempted to test whether such LC stimulation can also modify PP LTP (Abraham & Goddard, 1982). Two different pairings of LC and PP trains were used. Either the pathways were concurrently tetanized in a cooperativity-style experiment or the LC trains followed the PP trains by 200 msec in a reinforcement-style experiment. In neither paradigm were the LC trains able to alter PP LTP of either the EPSP or the PS. The capacity for short-term LC facilitation of granule cell excitability remained unaltered as well.

In contrast to our LC-stimulation findings, there are two recent reports of catecholamine-mediated facilitation of granule cell excitability in response to PP input. Amphetamine, which enhances both norepinephrine and dopamine neurotransmission, was shown to improve LTP of the PP-evoked PS under certain stimulus conditions (Delanoy, Tucci, & Gold, 1983). Howwever, since the amphetamine probably was not fully metabolized by the end of the experiment (10 minutes posttetanus), it is uncertain whether the PS facilitation outlasts the presence of the drug in the system. The other report indicated that either repeated pairing of single stimuli to the LC and the PP or long periods of low-frequency LC stimulation alone will produce long-lasting enhancement of granule cell discharge in response to PP synaptic transmission (Harley *et al.*, 1982). Since there was no change in the PP EPSP, the latter data suggest a chronic change in the tonic noradrenergic input to the DG and require further experiments to identify its reliability and mechanism of action.

Given the weakness of the effect of norepinephrine depletion and the mixed effects of LC stimulation on LTP, it appears that norepinephrine does not play a major modulatory role in the production of PP LTP. On the other hand the serotonin depletion data of Bliss *et al.* (1983), taken together with the evidence that serotonin plays a role in certain synaptic modifications in *Aplysia* (Hawkins & Kandel, Chapter 26, this volume), suggest that in fact the serotonergic system may be more effective in facilitating PP LTP.

SUMMARY

We have posed the question of whether LTP of the PP input to the DG has associative-like properties. The experiments most relevant to this issue have examined whether a separate set of afferents, coactive with the tetanized PP fibers but arising from different regions of brain and terminating on different dendritic loci of a common set of granule cells, can modulate the production of LTP in the PP. Most of the afferents tested so far have in fact been capable of influencing PP LTP. Stimulation of the medial septum concurrently with PP tetani enhances the level of LTP observed in the PP and perhaps in the septal–granule cell connection as well. LTP is also under a tonic modulatory control, probably exerted by the inhibitory hilar interneurons. Coactivity of these interneurons with PP fibers disrupts the production of LTP, and it appears likely, although more data are needed on this point, that the suppression of activity of these neurons will facilitate LTP. Apparent sources of control of the hilar modulation of LTP include the contralateral dentate hilar neurons, the serotonergic input from midbrain raphe nuclei and, to a lesser extent, the noradrenergic input from the LC. Finally, it is quite clear that even within the PP itself the production of LTP requires cooperative action in a large number of coactive fibers. Together these data indicate that PP LTP is not a property of single afferent fibers but is produced and shaped by the associative interaction among a number of afferent inputs. Thus LTP fulfills the essential requirements prescribed for neural models of associative learning. As such, it plays an important role in bridging the chasm between neuropsychological theory and neurobiology.

REFERENCES

Abraham, W. C., & Goddard, G. V. Asymmetric relations between homosynaptic long-term potentiation and heterosynaptic long-term depression. *Nature*, 1983, *305*, 717–719.

Abraham, W. C., & Goddard, G. V. Modulation of synaptic transmission and LTP in rat dentate gyrus by stimulation in and near the locus coeruleus. *Society for Neuroscience Abstracts*, 1982, *8*, 131.

Assaf, S. Y., Mason, S. T., & Miller, J. J. Noradrenergic modulation of neuronal transmission between the entorhinal cortex and the dentate gyrus of the rat. *Journal of Physiology*, 1979, *292*, 52P.

Azmitia, E. C., & Segal, M. An autoradiographic analysis of the differential ascending projections of the dorsal and median raphe nuclei in the rat. *Journal of Comparative Neurology*, 1978, *179*, 641–668.

Bliss, T. V. P., & Gardner-Medwin, A. R. Long-lasting potentiation of synaptic transmission in the dentate area of the unanesthetized rabbit following stimulation of the perforant path. *Journal of Physiology*, 1973, *232*, 357–374.

Bliss, T. V. P., Goddard, G. V., & Riives, M. Reduction of long-term potentiation in the dentate gyrus of the rat following selective depletion of monoamines. *Journal of Physiology*, 1983, *334*, 475–491.

Bliss, T. V. P., & Lømo, T. Long-lasting potentiation of synaptic transmission in the dentate area of the anesthetized rabbit following stimulation of the perforant path. *Journal of Physiology*, 1973, *232*, 331–356.

Bliss, T. V. P., & Wendlandt, S. Effects of stimulation of locus coeruleus on synaptic transmission in the hippocampus. *Proceedings of the International Union of Physiological Sciences*, 1977, *13*, 81.

Buzsaki, G., & Eidelberg, E. Direct afferent excitation and long-term potentiation of hippocampal interneurons. *Journal of Neurophysiology*, 1982, *48*, 597–607.

Crutcher, K. A., Madison, R., & Davis, J. N. A study of the rat septohippocampal pathway using anterograde transport of horseradish peroxidase. *Neuroscience*, 1981, *6*, 1973–1981.

Delanoy, R. L., Tucci, D. L., & Gold, P. E. Amphetamine effects on long-term potentiation in dentate granule cells. *Pharmacology, Biochemistry and Behavior*, 1983, *18*, 137–139.

Douglas, R. M., & Goddard, G. V. Long-term potentiation of the perforant path-granule cell synapse in the rat hippocampus. *Brain Research*, 1975, *86*, 205–215.

Douglas, R. M., Goddard, G. V., & Riives, M. Inhibitory modulation of long-term potentiation: Evidence for a postsynaptic locus of control. *Brain Research*, 1982, *240*, 259–272.

Douglas, R. M., McNaughton, B. L., & Goddard, G. V. Commissural inhibition and facilitation of granule cell discharge in fascia dentata. *Journal of Comparative Neurology*, 1983, *219*, 285–294.

Dunwiddie, T. V., Roberson, N. L., & Worth, T. Modulation of long-term potentiation: Effects of adrenergic and neuroleptic drugs. *Pharmacology, Biochemistry and Behavior*, 1982, *17*, 1257–1264.

Fantie, B. D. Augmentation of dentate granule cell population spikes after high frequency trains delivered to the septum and the perforant path. *Society for Neuroscience Abstracts*, 1982, *8*, 86.

Goddard, G. V., & Douglas, R. M. Does the engram of kindling model the engram of normal long term memory? In J. A. Wada (Ed.), *Kindling*. New York: Raven Press, 1976.

Harley, C. W., Lacaille, J.-C., & Milway, S. Potentiation of the perforant path evoked potential in the dentate gyrus by locus coeruleus stimulation. *Society for Neuroscience Abstracts*, 1982, *8*, 131.

Hjorth-Simonsen, A., & Jeune, S. Origin and termination of the hippocampal perforant path in the rat studied by silver impregnation. *Journal of Comparative Neurology*, 1972, *144*, 215–232.

Lee, K. S. Cooperation amongst afferents to the stratum radiatum of CA1 for long-term potentiation of evoked responses. *Society for Neuroscience Abstracts*, 1982, *8*, 215.

Levy, W. B., & Steward, O. Synapses as associative memory elements in the hippocampal formation. *Brain Research*, 1979, *175*, 233–245.

Loy, R., Koziell, D. A., Lindsey, J. D., & Moore, R. Y. Noradrenergic innervation of the adult rat hippocampal formation. *Journal of Comparative Neurology*, 1980, *159*, 699–710.

McNaughton, B. L., & Barnes, C. A. Physiological identification and analysis of dentate granule cell responses to stimulation of the medial and lateral perforant pathways in the rat. *Journal of Comparative Neurology*, 1977, *175*, 439–454.

McNaughton, B. L., Douglas, R. M., & Goddard, G. V. Synaptic enhancement in fascia dentata: Cooperativity among coactive afferents. *Brain Research*, 1978, *157*, 277–293.

Mosko, S., Lynch, G., & Cotman, C. W. The distribution of septal projections to the hippocampus of the rat. *Journal of Comparative Neurology*, 1973, *52*, 163–174.

Robinson, G., & Racine, R. J. Long-term potentiation in the dentate gyrus: Cooperativity between septal and entorhinal afferents. *Society for Neuroscience Abstracts*, 1982, *8*, 215.

Steward, O. Topographic organization of the projections from the entorhinal area to the hippocampal formation of the rat. *Journal of Comparative Neurology*, 1976, *167*, 285–314.

Wigstrøm, H., & Gustafsson, B. Facilitated induction of hippocampal long-lasting potentiation during blockade of inhibition. *Nature*, 1983, *301*, 603–604.

Winson, J. Raphe influences on neuronal transmission from perforant pathway through dentate gyrus. *Journal of Neurophysiology*, 1980, *44*, 937–950.

Yamamoto, C., & Sawada, S. Important factors in induction of long-term potentiation in thin hippocampal sections. *Experimental Neurology*, 1981, *14*, 122–130.

CHAPTER THIRTY-ONE

Presynaptic versus Postsynaptic Control over Long-Term Synaptic Enhancement

BRUCE L. MCNAUGHTON / CAROL A. BARNES / G. RAO

This volume presents important new fuel for the controversy as to whether the ultimate control over the generation of long-term synaptic enhancement (LTE) in the hippocampal formation depends on postsynaptic integration or whether presynaptic activation at high frequency is a sufficient condition. Since the resolution of this issue is crucial to an understanding of how this process might be used as an information storage device, we would like to take this opportunity to selectively review the evidence that has accumulated on both sides of the synaptic fence and to discuss the new evidence in this perspective.

At the outset, however, it must be emphasized that the important issue is not necessarily whether the persistent physiological change responsible for the increased synaptic strength is pre- or postsynaptic. The primary question concerns the logic of the control mechanism. Does LTE have the logical properties required to represent in memory the association of neural events in such a way that an event might be recalled in its entirety following the presentation of a subset of the event as a key? Although rigorous proof is lacking that a mechanism determined solely by the temporal pattern of activity of individual neurons (e.g., posttetanic potentiation) could not accomplish this, in the three decades since Hebb presented his postsynaptic integration model no viable presynaptic alternative has been suggested.[1] Indeed, Eccles (1977) has made the point that purely presynaptic mechanisms would be unworkable since most central neurons regularly exhibit firing frequencies well in excess of those necessary to induce LTE. If such activity alone caused long-lasting changes in the neuron's terminals, the system would very soon become saturated.

1. The heterosynaptic facilitation model for associative conditioning in invertebrates is the exception that proves the rule in this case. In one sense this is actually a special case of postsynaptic integration requiring conjunction of activity on a presynaptic (serotonin) fiber and a postsynaptic sensory nerve terminal. In addition, the requirement for specific terminal-to-terminal hard wiring makes it suitable for the association of predetermined events only. The capacity to associate a random set from a large number of possible inputs (as in mammalian associative learning) would appear to be lacking with this mechanism.

Bruce L. McNaughton, Carol A. Barnes, and G. Rao. Department of Psychology, University of Colorado, Boulder, Colorado.

The first evidence that LTE might require postsynaptic integration was provided by the demonstration that a substantial number of perforant path fibers must be coactive at high frequency in order for LTE to occur (McNaughton, Douglas, & Goddard, 1978). This observation alone was enough to distinguish LTE from posttetanic potentiation, a phenomenon seen at most central and peripheral synapses (including those of the perforant path), and was the primary basis for the adoption of the term "enhancement." Further support for the conclusion that LTE was not long-term "potentiation" came from the demonstration that potentiation of perforant path synapses involved an increase in the probability of transmitter release, whereas LTE did not (McNaughton, 1982). Thus, LTE and potentiation must act through different mechanisms. Neither of these observations, however, preclude the possibility that LTE could be an intrinsicially presynaptic phenomenon. McNaughton *et al.* (1978) explicitly stated that the demonstration of cooperativity among coactive afferents did not rule out a presynaptic mechanism since a requirement for actual postsynaptic convergence was not demonstrated. It remained possible (although perhaps unlikely) that interactions among adjacent coactive presynaptic terminals might occur regardless of which postsynaptic elements were contacted. Similarly, the fact that LTE does not involve an increase in the parameter p in the quantal release equation ($m = n \times p$) does not rule out a presynaptic mechanism involving the parameter n. It was pointed out (McNaughton, 1982) that an increase in n might come about by increasing the number of quanta available for release, by increasing the number of sites for release, or by the formation of new synaptic contacts.

In an attempt to demonstrate a postsynaptic locus of control over LTE, Wigstrom, McNaughton, and Barnes (1982) recorded both intracellularly and extracellularly from CA1 neurons *in vitro*. The generation of LTE in single neurons was compared in the presence and absence of large hyperpolarizing currents that both blocked postsynaptic discharge and caused a significant shift in the average membrane potential at the postsynaptic membrane sites activated during the high-frequency stimulation. The logic of these experiments was that if a postsynaptic treatment could be found that altered LTE in the single cell recorded from without altering the LTE seen in the extracellular field potential, then LTE must be regulated by postsynaptic factors. No effect of membrane hyperpolarization was observed, however, and it was concluded that if postsynaptic integration was involved in the control mechanism it must be integration of chemical rather than electrical signals.

Lynch, Larson, Kelso, Barrionuevo, and Schottler (1983) have now made use of the same logic to suggest that LTE must involve postsynaptic integration. They report that intracellular injections of the calcium chelator EGTA block LTE in the single cell without affecting either LTE recorded extracellularly from the population as a whole, or potentiation recorded intracellularly. This suggests that postsynaptic factors were altered by the EGTA, whereas the presynaptic terminals were unaffected. Due to the importance of this conclusion, one would hope that Lynch *et al.* will provide quantitative data on the magnitudes and time constants of potentiation measured both intra- and extracellularly to confirm that there has really been no effect of the EGTA on the presynaptic terminals connected to the cell recorded from.

Although the results of Lynch *et al.* provide rather compelling evidence that the control of LTE resides with the postsynaptic cell, this does not rule out that this might be due to a postsynaptic influence on the amount of transmitter released presynaptically. Evidence for such an increase has now been presented by Dolphin, Errington, and Bliss (1982; see Bliss & Dolphin, Chapter 29, this volume). Using the push–pull cannula technique in the anesthetized *in vivo* preparation they found a large increase in the rate of release of labeled glutamate from the vicinity of the molecular layer that paralleled the time course of LTE. There is an important objection, however, to the conclusion from these results that the primary mechanism of LTE is increased transmitter release. It appears to be equally plausible that the increased release is a secondary consequence of LTE. Such increased release, for example, would be expected if local hippocampal neurons increased either their spontaneous or their evoked release of glutamate as a result of the increased perforant path synaptic efficacy. At the very least it must be shown that the increased release in the experiments of Dolphin *et al.* is coming from perforant path terminals.

To investigate the possibility that LTE might result in increased spontaneous activity of local neurons, we have measured the multiple-unit activity recorded from both the granule cell layer and the CA1 pyramidal cell layer during the induction of LTE in perforant path terminals. The multiple-unit activity density was recorded as described in McNaughton (1980), using rats anesthetized with an initial dose of Nembutal and maintained on urethane. One recording electrode was located in the hilus fascia dentata to record the field EPSP. A second recording electrode was located in the same lamellar axis as the first, either in the pyramidal layer of CA1 or in the granular layer. We could find no consistent evidence for any increase in either granule cell or CA1 pyramidal cell activity following the induction of substantial amounts of LTE (see Figure 31-1). These results are somewhat surprising since one might expect that increasing the synaptic gain of the major input pathway would increase the spontaneous postsynaptic discharge. The failure to observe this suggests that either the spontaneous rate of the perforant path fibers themselves is extremely low or that the inhibitory circuitry of the fascia dentata provides sufficient negative feedback to keep the output constant. The latter explanation might well account for the apparent discrepancy between these results and the earlier report of Deadwyler, Gribkoff, and Lynch (1976) suggesting that some single units in the fascia dentata do show increased rates following perforant path stimulation. It is possible that the single units recorded from in these studies were in fact inhibitory interneurons (basket cells). These would have to increase their rate if the output of the granule cell population were to be kept constant following LTE.

Although one might argue that the Dolphin *et al.* results could be explained by increased spontaneous rate of the perforant path fibers themselves, this seems very unlikely, since this should alter both the presynaptic fiber potential and the probability of evoked transmitter release following perforant path stimulation. Neither of these is associated with the induction of LTE.

In summary, if one is to accept both the evidence of postsynaptic control (Lynch *et al.*, 1983) and of increased presynaptic release (Dolphin *et al.*, 1982) the only conclusion remaining would appear to be that integration of inputs to the postsynaptic neuron plays a regulatory role in the subsequent release of transmitter from the presynaptic terminals. This must be due to an increase in n, possibly by the formation of new sites for release or new synapses. Such a mechanism is remarkably similar in detail to the specific postulate made by Hebb (1949) more than 30 years ago.

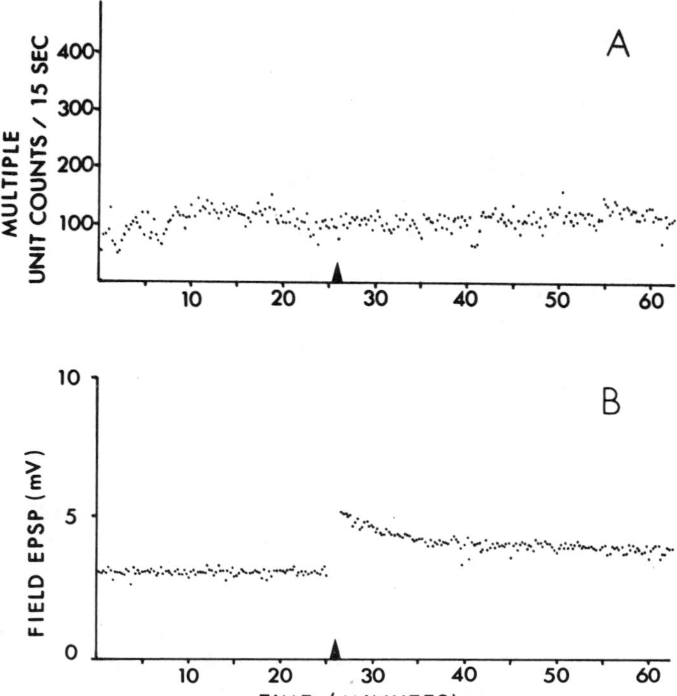

Figure 31-1. Effect of LTE on multiple-unit activity recorded from the granule cell layer of the hippocampal formation of a rat under urethane anesthesia. The multiple-unit record (A) represents spike counts over consecutive 15-second intervals. The amplitude of the field EPSP recorded simultaneously (once every 15 seconds) is shown in B. The arrow indicates the time of delivery of five bursts of high-frequency stimulation (10 pulses at 400 Hz per burst). Significant LTE was observed in the EPSP, whereas no change was observed in the multiple-unit counts.

REFERENCES

Deadwyler, S. A., Gribkoff, V., & Lynch, G. Long-lasting changes in the spontaneous activity of hippocampal neurons following stimulation of the entorhinal cortex. *Brain Research Bulletin*, 1976, *1*, 1–17.

Dolphin, A. C., Errington, M. L., & Bliss, T. V. P. Long-term potentiation of the perforant path *in vivo* is associated with increased glutamate release. *Nature*, 1982, *297*, 496–498.

Eccles, J. C. An instruction-selection theory of learning in the cerebellar cortex. *Brain Research*, 1977, *127*, 327–352.

Hebb, D. O. *The organization of behavior*. New York: Wiley, 1949.

Lynch, G., Larson, J., Kelso, S., Barrionuevo, G., & Schottler, F. Intracellular injections of EGTA block induction of hippocampal long-term potentiation. *Nature*, 1983, *305*, 719–721.

McNaughton, B. L. Evidence for two physiologically distinct perforant pathways to the fascia dentata. *Brain Research*, 1980, *199*, 1–19.

McNaughton, B. L. Long-term synaptic enhancement and short-term potentiation in rat fascia dentata act through different mechanisms. *Journal of Physiology* (London), 1982, *324*, 249–262.

McNaughton, B. L., Douglas, R. M., & Goddard, G. V. Synaptic enhancement in fascia dentata: Co-operativity among coactive afferents. *Brain Research*, 1978, *157*, 277–293.

Wigstrom, H., McNaughton, B. L., & Barnes, C. A. Long-term, synaptic enhancement in hippocampus is not regulated by postsynaptic membrane potential. *Brain Research*, 1982, *233*, 195–199.

CHAPTER THIRTY-TWO

Possible Structural Substrates of Plastic Neural Phenomena

WILLIAM T. GREENOUGH

In the final section of this volume, the subject of structural substrates of plasticity has been mentioned, albeit briefly, in two of the chapters. Both Kandel (Hawkins & Kandel, Chapter 26, this volume) and Lynch (Baudry & Lynch, Chapter 28, this volume) presented data indicating that modification of synapse morphology and synapse numbers may accompany physiologically demonstrated plastic change in the systems they study. These two types of change exemplify the dominant categories of both morphological and functional change proposed to underlie memory for the last several decades: (1) those that alter the efficacy of previously existing synapses, and (2) those that alter the number of synapses through selective formation and/or loss. Both sorts of change are presumed to store memory in terms of altered functional circuitry. I wish to (1) expand on some of the morphological evidence bearing on these two categories of structural change, remaining mindful that one type of change may easily be mistaken for another; (2) suggest that *in vivo* mammalian studies of learning and conceptually related developmental phenomena have provided evidence for both types of change; (3) point out that evidence for alterations in the numbers or pattern of occurrences of synapses is stronger than that for changes in the properties of individual synapses in adult learning situations; and (4) present data indicating that this is also true for the *in vitro* plasticity phenomenon discussed by Lynch (Baudry & Lynch, Chapter 28, this volume).

A preliminary comment relates to the *measurement methodologies* employed in quantitative morphological studies of developmental and other plastic phenomena. Although the use of methodologies adequate to discriminate between potentially confounded measures, such as changes in size versus density of synapses, is increasingly frequent (e.g., Vrensen & DeGroot, 1975), use of modern stereological or similarly adequate quantitative methods is far from ubiquitous (e.g., Dyson & Jones, 1980). Such methods will probably be routine in the future, and we will need to consider which results of prior research can be taken at face value and which must be reevaluated in proper quantitative terms. A second problem, which may be more troubling, has not yet been addressed

William T. Greenough. Departments of Psychology and Anatomical Sciences, and Neural and Behavioral Biology Program, University of Illinois, Urbana–Champaign, Champaign, Illinois.

adequately and may defy simply quantitative compensation. This is the problem of ascribing shifts in the relative frequency of various synaptic properties to changes in the properties of continuously existing synapses versus changes in the numbers of synapses with or without those properties, due to formation or loss of synapses. Knowledge of baseline values, especially of synapse densities prior to and following any experimental manipulation, are essential even in studies oriented only toward qualitative change in existing synapses. But such information may at best merely warn of possible misinterpretation. I know of no way in which, using discrete pre- and postmanipulation samples (other than samples from simple, isogenetic species), changes within existing synapses and synapse formation and loss can be strictly discriminated.

My next point has to do with the evidence from developmental studies that *synapses form and/or are lost differentially as a result of differential experience.* Although any single study in this area is subject to criticism, two conclusions seem firmly justified from the overall body of work. The first is that sensory restriction during early development is often associated with a reduction in the number of synapses per nerve cell in the deprived sensory system. The second is that this sort of change is not unique to early development. Light-microscopic evidence for these points has come primarily from quantitative Golgi studies (Valverde, 1971; Rothblat & Schwartz, 1979; Coleman & Riesen, 1968), but indirect light-microscopic evidence has also been presented (e.g., Gyllensten, Malmfors, & Norrlin, 1965). The most convincing evidence that early sensory deprivation can have such effects is Cragg's (1975) study of dark-rearing effects in kitten visual cortex. Here, stereological methods were used to correct light-microscopic neuronal and electron-microscopic synapse density estimates for size differences, such that accurate estimates of synapse frequency per neuron could be calculated. The results showed a clear reduction in the deprived kittens. (I should add that the size of the effects reported was considerably greater than might be expected from the quantitative Golgi data that we and others have collected, and I have no immediate explanation for this.) This sort of finding has not been universal in either electron-microscopic (e.g., Fifkova, 1970) or light-microscopic (e.g., Globus & Scheibel, 1967) studies, and the extent to which the differences stem from differences in species, quantitative methods, and other methodological aspects is unclear. (Indeed, whether the relationship between experience and synapse frequency per neuron is linear, or even positive, or the circumstances under which it is, remain to be determined.) That sensory manipulations affect the pattern of connections in predictable ways is perhaps best indicated by the work of Hubel, Wiesel, and their collaborators (e.g., LeVay, Wiesel, & Hubel, 1980), in which monocular deprivation reduces morphological and functional connectivity between the deprived eye's afferents and their visual cortex target neurons.

Consistent evidence at the light-microscopic level for effects of experience upon connectivity has also come from studies in which the complexity of the housing environment is manipulated. Following initial reports of greater cortical weight and thickness in rats reared in complex environments (EC) compared with their socially housed (SC) or isolation-housed (IC) counterparts (Rosenzweig, Bennett, & Diamond, 1972), our quantitative Golgi studies indicated more extensive dendritic fields in EC than in SC or IC rat visual cortex (Greenough & Volkmar, 1973). From the perspective of memory, the most interesting outcome from this paradigm is that both the effects on cortical weight and those on dendritic fields also occurred in adults (Juraska, Greenough, Elliott, Mack, & Berkowitz, 1980; Rosenzweig *et al.*, 1972; Green, Greenough, & Schlumpf, 1983; Uylings, Kuypers, Diamond, & Veltman, 1978). Such results, shown in Figure 32-1, increase the likelihood that changes of this sort could underlie memory.

To test the association of these effects with experiences involving more traditional memory tasks, we studied effects of extensive maze training on visual cortex (Greenough, Juraska, & Volkmar, 1979). Compared with handled controls, maze-trained rats had significantly greater branching in the upper region (beyond 250 μm from the soma) of Layer IV and V pyramidal neurons in visual cortex. We also performed a second experiment using split-brain rats and opaque contact occluders to direct visual aspects of maze training either to one hemisphere or, alternately across training days, to both hemispheres (Chang & Greenough, 1982). Untrained split-brain controls indicated that occluder insertion alone had no effect on quantitative Golgi measures. As Figure 32-2 shows, in bilaterally trained rats, upper apical dendritic branching of Layer V visual cortex pyramidal cells was greater than in controls, as in the prior study. In the unilaterally trained rats, branching of the same cell type in the hemisphere opposite the nonoccluded eye exceeded that opposite the occluded eye (Figure 32-2). These results largely rule out possible hormonal and metabolic causation of the structural effects of training. They appear to involve specifically visual aspects of the training experience.

In a related experiment still in progress, we have observed that this altered dendritic branching generalizes to another type of training (Larson & Greenough, 1981). Rats were trained to reach into a tube for food, using either the preferred or the nonpreferred forepaw or both, following the procedure of Hyden and

Figure 32-1. Mean total length of all dendrites per neuron for three visual cortex cell populations in rats housed in environmental complexity (EC) or individual cages (IC) from 145 to 230 days of age. Animals were reared socially in laboratory cages prior to 145 days. Dendritic length is significantly greater in Layer III pyramidal neurons and Layer IV stellate neurons. (From Juraska, Greenough, Elliott, Mack, & Berkowitz, 1980. Copyright 1980, Academic Press. Reprinted by permission.)

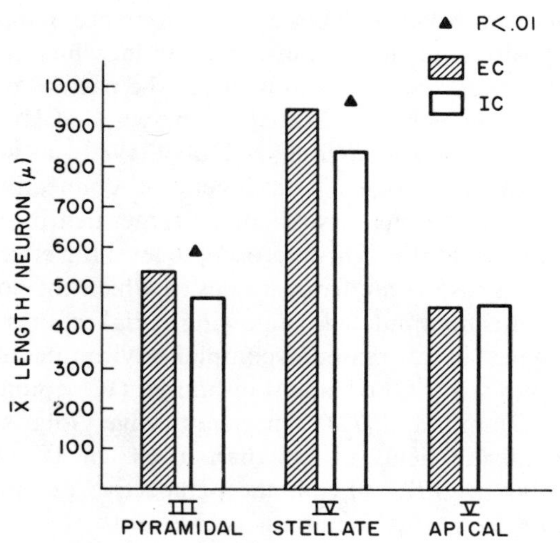

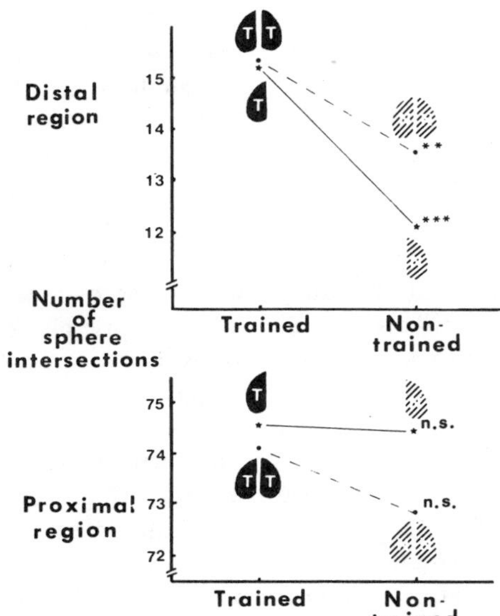

Figure 32-2. Effects of 25 days' maze training (on novel daily problems) on apical dendrites of adult rats' visual cortical Layer V pyramidal neurons. Concentric sphere intersections with dendrite provide an estimate of total dendritic length. TT, trained with alternating eye occlusion on alternate days; NN, nontrained, handled control; N, hemisphere opposite eye occluded during training; T, hemisphere opposite nonoccluded eye. $^{**}p < .025$; $^{***}p < .01$. (From Chang & Greenough, 1982. Copyright 1982, Elsevier Biomedical Press. Reprinted by permission.)

Egyhazi (1964). We examined Layer V pyramidal neurons in the frontolateral cortex region from which we were able to elicit forepaw extension at lowest threshold with electrical stimulation through the dura mater. As in the maze-training studies, the upper apical dendritic region was more extensive in hemispheres opposite trained than untrained forepaws. This region was also more highly branched in the hemisphere opposite the forepaw preferred for reaching in nontrained controls. This "preference effect" in naive animals complicates interpretation of differences in animals trained with preferred or nonpreferred forepaws. There are differences favoring the trained hemispheres in both groups, but the effects of preference-reversal training would be larger and the effects of practice on the preferred paw smaller if we consider the ratio between hemispheres in controls as the pretraining baseline. Regardless of the details of the effects of these two procedures, the overall results clearly indicate that the reach-training experience leads to altered dendritic branching, again in a within-animal design that largely eliminates hormonal, metabolic, or other nonspecific interpretations. Moreover, the same basic type of change, an alteration in dendritic field size and/or pattern, occurs after three different situations, all of which are likely to involve learning, in adult animals.

Although we have yet to confirm it electron-microscopically, the most likely interpretation of these results appears to be that training, as well as the other experience manipulations discussed above, alters the number and/or pattern of synaptic connections in these brain areas. We cannot, of course, jump from this finding to the conclusion that synapse formation (or some related selective maintenance phenomenon) underlies—or is even involved in—memory for aspects of the training. However, the association between events involving memory and altered dendritic structure is quite strong, and this certainly remains a plausible hypothesis.

Considerable evidence also indicates that a variety of structural changes in existing synapses may occur as a result of differential experience. Changes in the size and shape of processes, vesicle density, cleft width and curvature, paramembrane densities, and other measures have been reported as a function of age and differential developmental experience (e.g., Greenough, West, & DeVoogd, 1978; Vrensen & Cardozo, 1981; Vrensen & DeGroot, 1975; Wesa, Chang, & Greenough, 1982; see Greenough & Chang, in press, for review).

There is only one electron-microscopic study of adult mammalian central nervous system (CNS) response to experience manipulations of which I am aware. Vrensen and Cardozo (1981) compared visual cortex synapses in rabbits that had received extensive visual discrimination training with those of non-discrimination-trained controls. Trained animals had narrower synaptic clefts and an increased frequency of perforations or interruptions in the postsynaptic density. Postsynaptic density perforations in rat visual cortex have previously been found to increase with age and following rearing in complex versus isolated environments (Greenough *et al.*, 1978), as well as during reactive synaptogenesis in the hippocampal formation (Nieto-Sampedro, Hoff, & Cotman, 1982). Vrensen and Cardozo (1981) reported no significant effect of training on synaptic density. However, neuronal density was not examined, and a small increase in synapse numbers per neuron could have been obscured both by an increase in tissue volume and by normal variation in the large number of existing synapses.

Thus light-microscopic evidence is relatively consistent in indicating probable increases in the number of synapses per neuron with differential experience and training in both young and adult subjects. Electron-microscopic analyses of synapses per neuron have indicated effects of visual deprivation during development (Cragg, 1975). For adults, proper stereological quantification of synapses per neuron remains to be done.

Finally, a recent finding bears on the data that Lynch presented with regard to structural changes following long-term potentiation (LTP) treatments in the Schaffer-collateral system. We (Chang & Greenough, 1984) have recently studied the extent to which LTP treatment-induced structural changes persist in hippocampal slices maintained *in vitro*. LTP was induced by three 100-Hz, 1-sec (or 200-Hz, .5-sec) stimulus trains at two sites surrounding the CA1 sample area, which yielded spike potentiation averaging 300% to a series of five test pulses at 10–15 min after stimulation, declining to about 150% at 8-hr delay. Control slices that received the same number of pulses at 1 Hz or continuous high-frequency stimulation (40 or 100 Hz for 10 min) showed no LTP. Tissue was fixed at 10–15 min, 2 hr, and 8 hr after LTP treatment for electron-microscopic quantification. We measured the numbers of spine and shaft synapses, classifying spines into those with heads and the stubby, headless "sessile" type as shown in Figure 32-3A, and also measured the perimeter and area of synaptic processes. At the 10–15 min interval, our data were in very good agreement with those of Lee, Oliver, Schottler, and Lynch (1981). Relative to low-frequency stimulation controls there was an increase in the number of shaft synapses per unit area, an increase in the number of sessile spine synapses, and no increase in the number of the more frequent headed spine synapses in LTP treated slices. There was also a reduction of the perimeter to area ratio of spine heads, indicating, as concluded by Lee *et al.* (1981) from reduced variation in spine measures, that spine heads had become rounder. None of these effects occurred in the high-frequency control group. The potentiation-associated increase in shaft and sessile spine synapses, and physiologically demonstrable

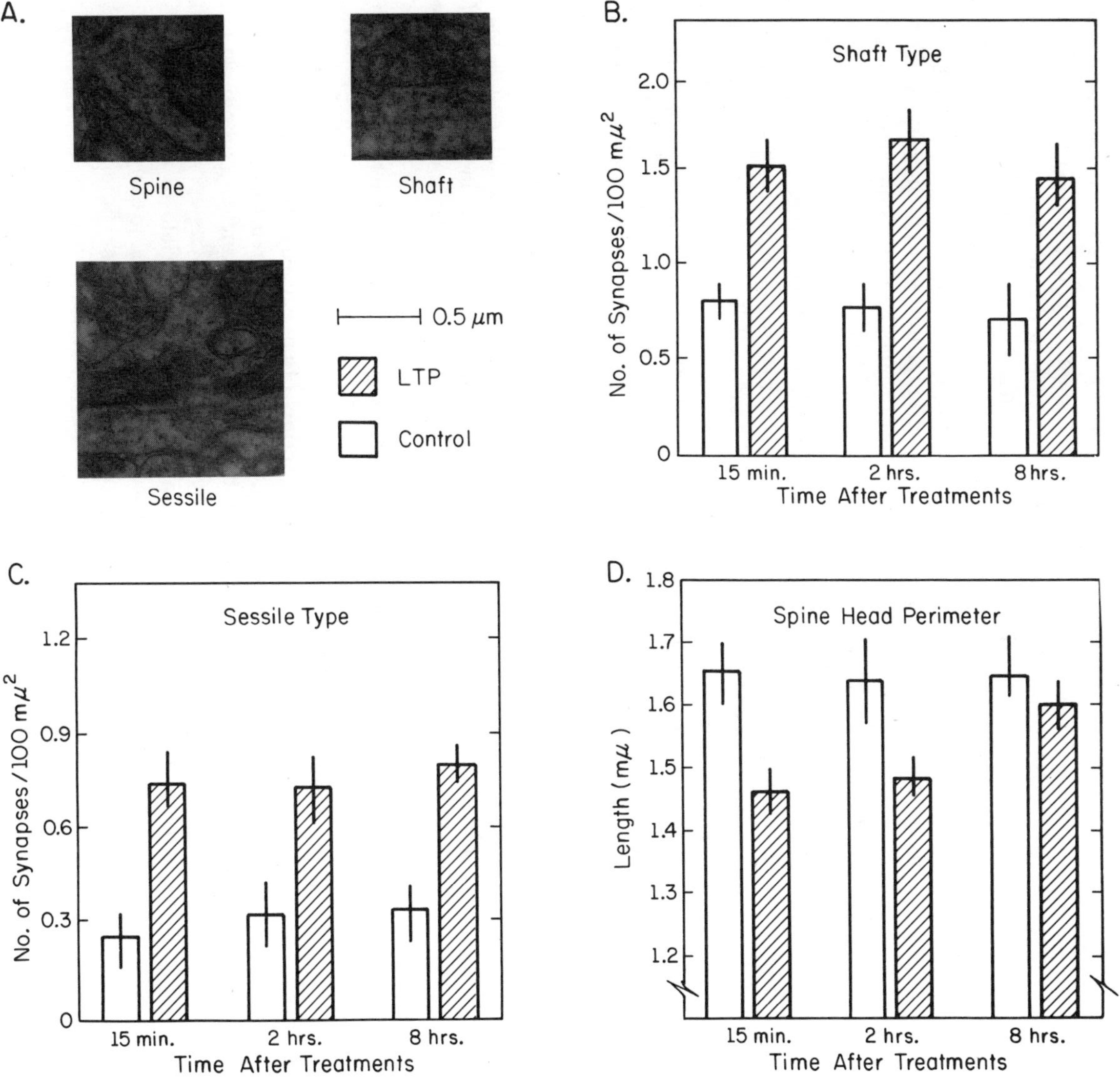

Figure 32-3. (A) Synapse types; (B) persistence of LTP effects on frequency of shaft synapses; (C) persistence of LTP effects on frequency of sessile synapses; (D) significant decrease in spine head perimeter is present at 10–15 min and 2 hr but absent at 8 hr after LTP treatment. LTP treatment had no significant effect on frequency of spine synapses. (From Chang & Greenough, in press).

LTP, persisted over a further 8 hr of *in vitro* incubation, whereas the effect on spine head shape disappeared after 2 hr (Figure 32-3). This result (1) confirms the Lee *et al.* (1981) report that potentiating stimulation increases the frequency of synapses and alters the shape of spine heads within as little as 10–15 min; (2) indicates that changes in spine head shape are not essential to the maintenance of LTP; and (3) indicates that equal or greater amounts of stimulation in patterns that do not produce LTP do not produce similar structural changes.

In addition, the shaft and sessile spine synapse increase appeared to have two components. Shaft synapses were more frequent both on dendrites larger than 2 μm in diameter and on smaller dendrites. The sessile spine increase was associated only with smaller dendrites. The larger dendrites may be those of inhibitory interneurons and the smaller dendrites those of the CA1 pyramidal cells (see Anderson, Gross, Lϕmo, & Sveen, 1969). Most physiological studies of LTP have concentrated on the effects on pyramidal cells, but potentiation of inhibitory interneurons has also been demonstrated (Buzsaki & Eidelberg, 1982). Our findings suggest that an increase in the number of axo-dendritic shaft synapses may be associated with potentiation of both cell populations. Moreover, the fact that the sessile synapse increase was confined to smaller dendrites may indicate a gradual transformation of newly formed synapses on pyramidal cells to the headed spine configuration, or that spine synapses on these neurons are transformed into sessile and/or shaft synapses, following LTP treatment. Wilson, Groves, Kitai, and Linder (1983) have recently proposed that spine shape may be continuously modulated by a microfilament network. In any case, the simplest interpretation of the lasting structural effects in this model of neural plasticity is an increase in the number of synapses.

Thus, taken together, the results of experiments involving developmental experience manipulations, adult experience manipulations, and adult training, as well as an *in vitro* model of neural plasticity, all point to changes in the number of synapses as a possible memory substrate. I should emphasize that this is unlikely to be the only type of plastic change exhibited by the nervous system. Qualitative changes in synapses have been demonstrated in similar paradigms, and it seems quite plausible that different types of structurally detectable plastic change might act in concert in the same storage process or separately in different types of information storage, or that individuals may differ depending on their own histories and characteristics in the pattern of changes associated with the storage of information even from a seemingly identical experience.

A final point I wish to mention concerns the manner in which changes in the numbers of synapses may arise. Developmental studies (e.g., Boothe, Greenough, Lund, & Wrege, 1979; Cragg, 1975; LeVay *et al.*, 1980) have indicated that CNS synapse production often exceeds the "final" level of synapses in the mature organism. It has been suggested (e.g., Changeux & Danchin, 1976; Greenough, 1978) that selective maintenance of a subpopulation of those synapses produced in development, perhaps as a result of neural activity, yields a functional "wiring diagram" appropriate to the organism's developmental history. Such a process need not be limited to early development. It seems quite plausible that the generation of transient or "potential" synapses, perhaps influenced by overall neural activity levels or activity of a particular system (such as the noradrenergic system, which has been proposed to modulate plasticity), continues into adulthood and that selective maintenance of synapses from this population allows the nervous system to continually adjust its organization to the informational demands of the organism's environment.

ACKNOWLEDGMENTS

Research described here and not otherwise reported was supported by NSF BNS 77-23660, NSF BNS 82-16916, and the Retirement Research Foundation. I thank E. J. Green and J. L. Fuchs for helpful comments.

REFERENCES

Anderson, P., Gross, G. N., Lømo, T., & Sveen, O. Participation of inhibitory and excitatory interneurons in the control of hippocampal cortical output. In M. A. B. Brazier (Ed.), *The interneuron.* Los Angeles: University of California Press, 1969.

Boothe, R. G., Greenough, W. T., Lund, J. S., & Wrege, K. A quantitative investigation of spine and dendritic development of neurons in visual cortex (area 17) of *Macaca nemestrina* monkeys. *Journal of Comparative Neurology*, 1979, *186*, 473–490.

Buzsaki, G., & Eidelberg, E. Direct afferent excitation and long-term potentiation of hippocampal interneurons. *Journal of Neurophysiology*, 1982, *48*, 597–607.

Chang, F.-L. F., & Greenough, W. T. Lateralized effects of monocular training on dendritic branching in adult split-brain rats. *Brain Research*, 1982, *232*, 283–292.

Chang, F.-L. F., & Greenough, W. T. Transient and enduring morphorlogical correlates of synaptic activity and efficacy change in the rat hippocampal slice. *Brain Research*, in press.

Changeux, J.-P., & Danchin, A. Selective stabilisation of developing synapses as a mechanism for the specification of neuronal networks. *Nature*, 1976, *264*, 705–712.

Coleman, P. D., & Riesen, A. H. Environmental effects on cortical dendritic fields: I. Rearing in the dark. *Journal of Anatomy*, 1968, *102*, 363–374.

Cragg, B. G. The development of synapses in kitten visual cortex during visual deprivation. *Experimental Neurology*, 1975, *46*, 445–451.

Dyson, S. E., & Jones, D. G. Quantitation of terminal parameters and their interrelationships in maturing central synapses: A perspective for experimental studies. *Brain Research*, 1980, *183*, 43–59.

Fifkova, E. The effect of monocular deprivation on the synaptic contacts of the visual cortex. *Journal of Neurobiology*, 1970, *1*, 285–294.

Globus, A., & Scheibel, A. B. The effect of visual deprivation on cortical neurons: A Golgi study. *Experimental Neurology*, 1967, *19*, 331–345.

Green, E. J., Greenough, W. T., & Schlumpf, B. E. The effects of complex or isolated environments on cortical dendrites of middle-aged rats. *Brain Research*, 1983, *264*, 233–240.

Greenough, W. T. Development and memory: The synaptic connection. In T. Teyler (Ed.), *Brain and learning*. Stamford, Conn.: Greylock, 1978.

Greenough, W. T., & Chang, F.-L. F. Anatomically-detectable correlates of information storage in the nervous systems of mammals. In C. W. Cotman (Ed.), *Neuronal plasticity*. New York: Guilford Press, in press.

Greenough, W. T., Juraska, J. M., & Volkmar, F. R. Maze training effects on dendritic branching in occipital cortex of adult rats. *Behavioral and Neural Biology*, 1979, *26*, 287–297.

Greenough, W. T., & Volkmar, F. R. Pattern of dendritic branching in occipital cortex of rats reared in complex environments. *Experimental Neurology*, 1973, *40*, 491–504.

Greenough, W. T., West, R. W., & DeVoogd, T. J. Subsynaptic plate perforations: changes with age and experience in the rat. *Science*, 1978, *202*, 1096–1098.

Gyllensten, L., Malmfors, T., & Norrlin, M. Effect of visual deprivation on the optic centers of growing and adult mice. *Journal of Comparative Neurology*, 1965, *124*, 149–160.

Hyden, H., & Egyhazi, E. Changes in RNA content and base composition in cortical neurons of rats in a learning experiment involving transfer of handedness. *Proceedings of the National Academy of Sciences, USA*, 1964, *52*, 1030–1035.

Juraska, J. M., Greenough, W. T., Elliott, C., Mack, K., & Berkowitz, R. Plasticity in adult rat visual cortex: An examination of several cell populations after differential rearing. *Behavioral and Neural Biology*, 1980, *29*, 157–167.

Larson, J. R., & Greenough, W. T. Effects of handedness training on dendritic branching of neurons in forelimb area of rat motor cortex. *Society for Neuroscience Abstracts*, 1981, *7*, 65.

Lee, K., Oliver, M., Schottler, F., & Lynch, G. Electron microscopic studies of brain slices: The effects of high-frequency stimulation on dendritic ultrastructure. In G. A. Kerkut & H. V. Wheal (Eds.), *Electrophysiology of isolated mammalian CNS preparations*. New York: Academic Press, 1981.

LeVay, S., Wiesel, T. N., & Hubel, D. H. The development of ocular dominance columns in normal and visually deprived monkeys. *Journal of Comparative Neurology*, 1980, *191*, 1–51.

Nieto-Sampedro, M., Hoff, S. F., & Cotman, C. W. Perforated postsynaptic densities: Probable intermediates in synapse turnover. *Proceedings of the National Academy of Sciences, USA*, 1982, *79*, 5718–5722.

Rosenzweig, M. R., Bennett, E. L., & Diamond, M. C. Chemical and anatomical plasticity of brain: Replications and extensions. In J. Gaito (Ed.), *Macromolecules and behavior* (2nd ed.). New York: Appleton-Century-Crofts, 1972.

Rothblat, L. A., & Schwartz, M. The effect of monocular deprivation on dendritic spines in visual cortex of young and adult albino rats: Evidence for a sensitive period. *Brain Research*, 1979, *161*, 156–161.

Uylings, H. B. M., Kuypers, K., Diamond, M. C., & Veltman, W. A. M. Effects of differential environments on plasticity of dendrites of cortical pyramidal neurons in adult rats. *Experimental Neurology*, 1978, *62*, 658–677.

Valverde, F. Rate and extent of recovery from dark rearing in the mouse. *Brain Research*, 1971, *33*, 1–11.

Vrensen, G., & Cardozo, J. N. Changes in size and shape of synaptic connections after visual training: An ultrastructural approach of synaptic plasticity. *Brain Research*, 1981, *218*, 79–97.

Vrensen, G., & De Groot, D. The effect of monocular deprivation on synaptic terminals in the visual cortex of rabbits: A quantitative electron microscopic study. *Brain Research*, 1975, *93*, 15–24.

Wesa, J. M., Chang, F.-L. F., Greenough, W. T., & West, R. W. Synaptic contact curvature: effects of differential rearing on rat occipital cortex. *Developmental Brain Research*, 1982, *4*, 253–257.

Wilson, C. W., Groves, P. M., Kitai, S. T., & Linder, J. C. Three-dimensional structure of dendritic spines in the rat neostriatum. *Journal of Neuroscience*, 1983, *3*, 383–398.

CHAPTER THIRTY-THREE

Brain Phosphoproteins Kinase C and Protein F1: Protagonists of Plasticity in Particular Pathways

ARYEH ROUTTENBERG

It is evident that phosphorylation of brain proteins now occupies a central role in the development, modulation, and plasticity of synapses (see Libet, Chapter 27, Baudry & Lynch, Chapter 28, and Hawkins & Kandel, Chapter 26, this volume). This is gratifying to the present author, who suggested the hypothesis more than a decade ago that posttranslational modification of particular brain proteins is a necessary step in altering synaptic relationships (see, e.g., Routtenberg, Holian, & Brunngraber, 1971, and reviews by Routtenberg, 1979, 1982b). The growing body of information on the function and characterization of brain phosphoproteins (Gispen & Routtenberg, 1982) provides a selection of protein substrates that may serve the plastic process.

There is little uniformity of opinion, however, as to the particular proteins that promote synaptic plasticity when one considers recent proposals concerning plasticity and phosphoprotein metabolism (e.g., Baudry & Lynch, 1980; Kandel & Schwartz, 1982). In our recent work (Routtenberg, Lovinger, Cain, Akers, & Steward, 1983) we have discovered that a phosphoprotein substrate with molecular weight of 47 kD and isoelectric point of 4.5, completely different from other substrates yet discussed, is directly related to the expression of plasticity. Some bases for this discrepancy in the substrate proteins involved in plasticity will be considered later in the present chapter.

The only interlaboratory validation surrounds the alpha subunit of pyruvate dehydrogenase. This phosphoprotein was first identified in brain by Morgan and Routtenberg (1980). It was then shown to be altered by behavioral training by Morgan and Routtenberg (1981) and confirmed by Lynn-Cook and Wilson (1983). Although initial results indicated that electrical stimulation of hippocampus decreased pyruvate dehydrogenase phosphorylation (Browning, Baudry, & Lynch, 1982), recent studies in our laboratory confirm the report by Bar, Tielen, Lopes da Silva, Zwiers, and Gispen (1982) of a lack of significant

Aryeh Routtenberg. Departments of Psychology and Neurobiology/Physiology, Northwestern University, Evanston, Illinois.

or persistent change in this phosphoprotein substrate following electrical activation.

There is, for the most part then, a lack of agreement on the phosphoprotein substrates involved in promoting plasticity when one considers synaptic plasticity in either hippocampal or invertebrate systems. Since one may expect a different distribution of protein substrates pre- and postsynaptically, it is not surprising that there is also substantial disagreement concerning the hypothesized synaptic location of protein substrate changed. Thus, Hawkins and Kandel (Chapter 26, this volume) propose a presynaptic locus for the change in phosphoprotein metabolism, whereas Baudry and Lynch (Chapter 28, this volume) propose a postsynaptic site for the molecular change related to synaptic plasticity.

In the present chapter I have chosen to discuss synaptic plasticity observed in *Aplysia* and in hippocampus to illustrate some of the problems in the identification of the phosphoprotein substrates that may participate in information storage. The remarks are critical, not in the negative sense, but in the analytic one, to focus discussion on issues that may lead to convergent identification, using selected systems, of the particular phosphoprotein substrates involved in synaptic plasticity.

PLASTICITY IN *APLYSIA*

The crucial relation in the development of synaptic plasticity in *Aplysia* involves serotonergic presynaptic modulation of the sensory neuron terminal (Hawkins & Kandel, Chapter 26, this volume). What is the anatomical evidence that a serotonin terminal in fact terminates on a sensory neuron terminal? In a double-labeling study, Bailey, Kandel, and Chen (1981) injected [^{3}H]serotonin into L29, defined as a serotonin-containing cell by Kandel and Schwartz (1982), and horseradish peroxidase (HRP) into sensory neurons. A total of nine double-labeled profiles were observed in direct contact; six of these were between vesicle-containing profiles.

It is obvious that morphological results are limited, since they provide little indication of functional synaptic relationships. Moreover, the direction of relation, if functional, cannot be specified. Finally, it is not shown that the sensory terminal component of these dual-labeled profiles in fact contacted the postsynaptic motor neuron, as specified in their model.

The resolution of these issues also requires information concerning the percentage of the total number of terminals of the facilitator interneuron, previously identified as a serotonin-containing cell (see below) that contact sensory neuron terminals.

Given that these dual-labeled profiles were not in abundance, inasmuch as few such images were observed, is it reasonable to focus on this possibly minor synaptic interaction as the centerpiece of plasticity in *Aplysia*? It may be important to consider the possibility that the understanding of the neuropil in *Aplysia* abdominal ganglion is, in fact, quite complex and not as well worked out as one would like.

This caveat also applies to its cellular histophysiology, where some serious doubts now exist (Kistler, Hawkins, Koester, Kandel, & Schwartz, 1983) concerning the prior specification of serotonin in L29 cells (Kandel & Schwartz,

1982). This recent report underscores the uncertainty in defining the synaptic relationships predicated to underlie *Aplysia* synaptic plasticity.

In determining whether this synaptic relation exists in sufficient abundance, one is addressing the broader issue of the biological significance of this presynaptic relationship to the behavioral plasticity of *Aplysia.* That is, whereas *electrophysiological plasticity* may be demonstrated with the connections specified in the model, *behavioral plasticity* in *Aplysia* may simply occur by the use of a different set of connections, conceivably involving these same neurons, in part, but with a different synaptic arrangement.

This issue is, of course, crucial to the evaluation of the role of phosphoproteins in synaptic plasticity. It was suggested by Kandel and Schwartz (1982) that plasticity in *Aplysia* requires a phosphorylation mechanism (see Figure 26-2C, Hawkins & Kandel, Chapter 26, this volume). The only evidence that has been provided, however, for a phosphorylation change associated with sensitization or conditioning involved one preliminary analysis of the entire abdominal ganglion (Paris, Castellucci, Kandel, & Schwartz, 1981). Note that the phosphoprotein specified was not the same as pointed to by Neary, Crow, and Alkon (1981) in their study of *Hermissenda.* This lack of agreement in studies of invertebrate plasticity suggests an incomplete understanding of the role of phosphoproteins in the expression of plasticity. Whether specific alterations can be demonstrated at all is a matter of some concern, since the *Aplysia* model, although ideal for certain aspects of neurophysiological analysis (but see below) may not be well suited for specifying particular phosphoprotein substrates. For example, since the ion-channel-related phosphoprotein proposed to be altered is likely to be present in every cell and terminal in *Aplysia*, the sensitization- or conditioning-induced change would influence only a small proportion of the total amount of that phosphoprotein harvested. One may well presume that any reliable change observed would involve an alteration that was quantitatively large, an unlikely occurrence in the proposed model of Hawkins and Kandel. In what follows, a solution to this problem is offered in our study of the intact hippocampus.

The role of phosphorylation in *Aplysia* plasticity has been ostensibly based on observation of the electrophysiological effects of injection of protein kinase or its inhibitor. These results are difficult to interpret in any specific manner since it may be expected that the catalytic subunit of a cyclic-nucleotide-dependent kinase will phosphorylate several different phosphoprotein substrates. It would be difficult to determine which of these substrates is responsible for the electrophysiological effects observed. In fact, the electrophysiological effects observed may arise as a secondary consequence of the initial action of the particular phosphoprotein substrate injected. Moreover, before the kinase or its inhibitor could influence the terminal substrate, it must be transported from the cell body to the terminal. This transport affords the opportunity for the kinase to phosphorylate nonterminal (cell body, axon) substrates that may influence, directly or indirectly, the electrophysiological results inferred at the presynaptic terminal. Given this uncertainty, it would seem premature to conclude that phosphoproteins in the sensory neuron terminal determine synaptic or behavioral plasticity in *Aplysia.*

There are biophysical issues concerning the inferences of events occurring in the presynaptic terminal from recordings in the distant cell body (see Farley & Alkon, 1983). There may be some difficulty, for example, in extrapolating the electrophysiological properties of presynaptic terminals based on intracellular recording and the injection of protein kinase or its inhibitors into the cell body.

PHOSPHOPROTEINS IN HIPPOCAMPAL PATHWAYS

Aplysia and the hippocampus share certain common features (Figure 33-1). Indeed, in the first two studies of brain phosphorylation and synaptic plasticity in the hippocampus using long-term potentiation (LTP; see Gispen & Routtenberg, 1982, for reviews) an essentially similar paradigm was used. That is, specific pathways were activated and the effects of electrical stimulation were related to modification of synaptic phosphoproteins.

An essential problem with these initial studies (see Browning, Dunwiddie, Bennett, Gispen, & Lynch, 1979; Browning *et al.*, 1982; Bar *et al.*, 1982; Lopes da Silva, Bar, Tielen, & Gispen, 1982) is the use of the hippocampal slice preparation first developed by Yamamoto (1972) and Skrede and Westgaard (1971). Although such preparations may be suitable for certain electrophysiological studies, there is an inherent difficulty in studying a 400-μm slice that is estimated to have 60–100 μm of dead tissue on each cut surface (Teyler, 1980). At the outset then, one will be studying, from the neurochemical point of view, a proteolytic factory containing 30–50% dead tissue.

This issue is crucial, since as presently conducted, *the site of recording, where the tissue is healthier, will invariably underrepresent what is studied neurochemically.* Moreover, the amount of dead tissue in the slice used for chemical analysis can be expected to vary. As in invertebrate associative conditioning discussed earlier, the suggested phosphoprotein substrate altered following hippocampal electrical stimulation was different in the two studies using the *in vitro* hippocampal slice system. Perhaps such lack of agreement may be ascribed to variability in the viability of the slice, the ratio of live to dead tissue,

Figure 33-1. *Aplysia* and dissected hippocampus (after Blackstad, Brink, Hem, & Jeune, 1970), not drawn to scale.

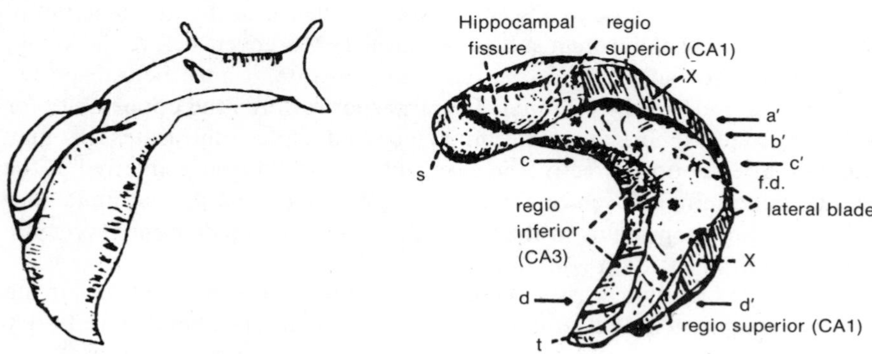

and other related factors (e.g., amount of recurrent inhibition) since no universally accepted criteria or standard exists for specifying the health of the preparation.

After consideration of these (and several other) difficulties involved in using the slice preparation we concluded that *it was essential to study the problem in an intact preparation with blood supply uninterrupted, afferent and efferent connections intact*, therefore to minimize the dead tissue contaminating the neurochemical analysis.

This decision led us to study *in situ* synaptic plasticity of LTP in the intact hippocampal formation. In retrospect, this decision may have been most crucial in studying the relation of synaptic plasticity and brain phosphoprotein metabolism. Because the hippocampal formation possesses a rigid topographic and laminar arrangement (e.g., Ruth, Collier, & Routtenberg, 1983), the neuropil seemed more tractable to analysis than the invertebrate systems studied. Moreover, there would be a considerable advantage provided if activation of a signigificant proportion of the hippocampal formation could be achieved. Following the lead provided by Lømo (1971), we sought the "bottleneck" of the perforant path, the region of fiber confluence, which then fans out to innervate a considerable portion of the dorsal hippocampus (see Figure 33-2).

Our next concern was to preserve the tissue so that its *in vitro* analysis would reflect alterations in phosphoprotein metabolism engendered by synaptic activation. In this regard we introduced the back-phosphorylation or "*post hoc*" procedure several years ago (Routtenberg, Ehrlich, & Rabjohns, 1975). Issues related to this method have been discussed in detail elsewhere (Routtenberg, 1982a).

Finally, in contrast to the two prior studies using the hippocampal slice preparation, we monitored the potentiation electrophysiologically. Thus, in contrast to prior hippocampal studies and, in fact, invertebrate studies to date, we felt it absolutely essential to relate alterations in phosphoprotein metabolism quantitated densitometrically to alterations in synaptic plasticity monitored electrophysiologically.

We have found that LTP produces a selective alteration in phosphoprotein metabolism. Specifically the phosphoprotein, designated protein F1, of 47 kD molecular weight and isoelectric point of 4.5, is significantly increased in its phosphorylation by long-term synaptic potentiation (see Figure 33-3). Of importance to understanding the significance of this result is the absence of a change (1) in the metabolism of other major brain phosphoproteins following LTP and (2) in protein F1 when low-frequency stimulation of the perforant path in which no alteration of synaptic relationships is observed. Thus, mere synaptic activation does not change protein F1 phosphorylation.

If protein F1 were to play an important role in LTP, one would predict that the extent of change in synaptic plasticity would be directly related to the change in phosphoprotein metabolism. In our first study we discovered a statistically significant direct relationship (Routtenberg *et al.*, 1983) using a 2-min *in vitro* reaction initiated by gamma-labeled (^{32}P) ATP.

Because it is difficult to be certain whether this reflects an increase in protein kinase activity or an increase in the phosphorylation of available sites, we have studied this problem using a 10-sec reaction that would primarily assay protein kinase activity. We have found in a recent study that LTP significantly increased protein F1 phosphorylation and that there was a direct relation

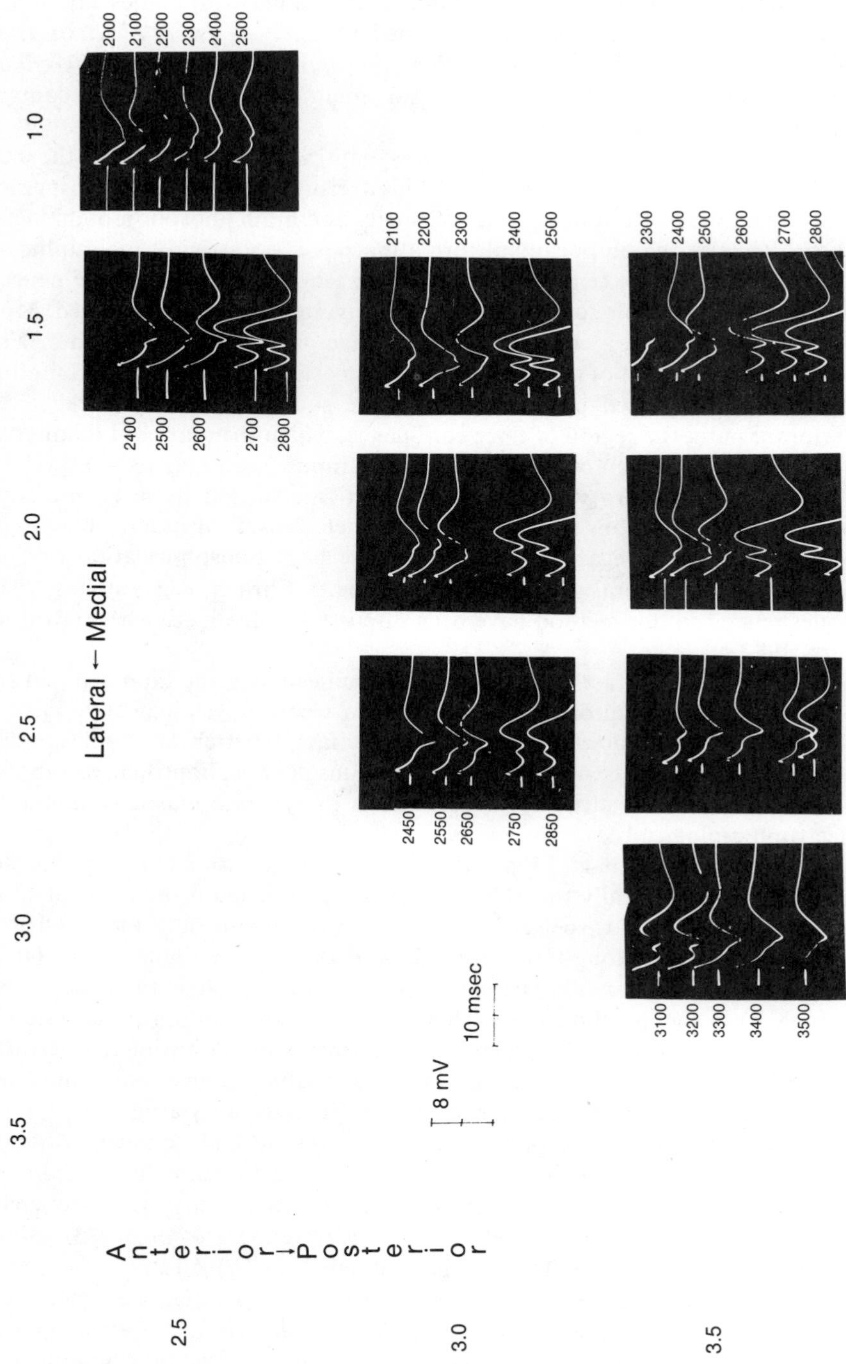

Lateral ← Medial
1.0
1.5
2.0
2.5
3.0
3.5
Anterior → Posterior
2.5
3.0
3.5
8 mV
10 msec
2000 2100 2200 2300 2400 2500
2400 2500 2600 2700 2800
2100 2200 2300 2400 2500
2450 2550 2650 2750 2850
2300 2400 2500 2600 2700 2800
3100 3200 3300 3400 3500

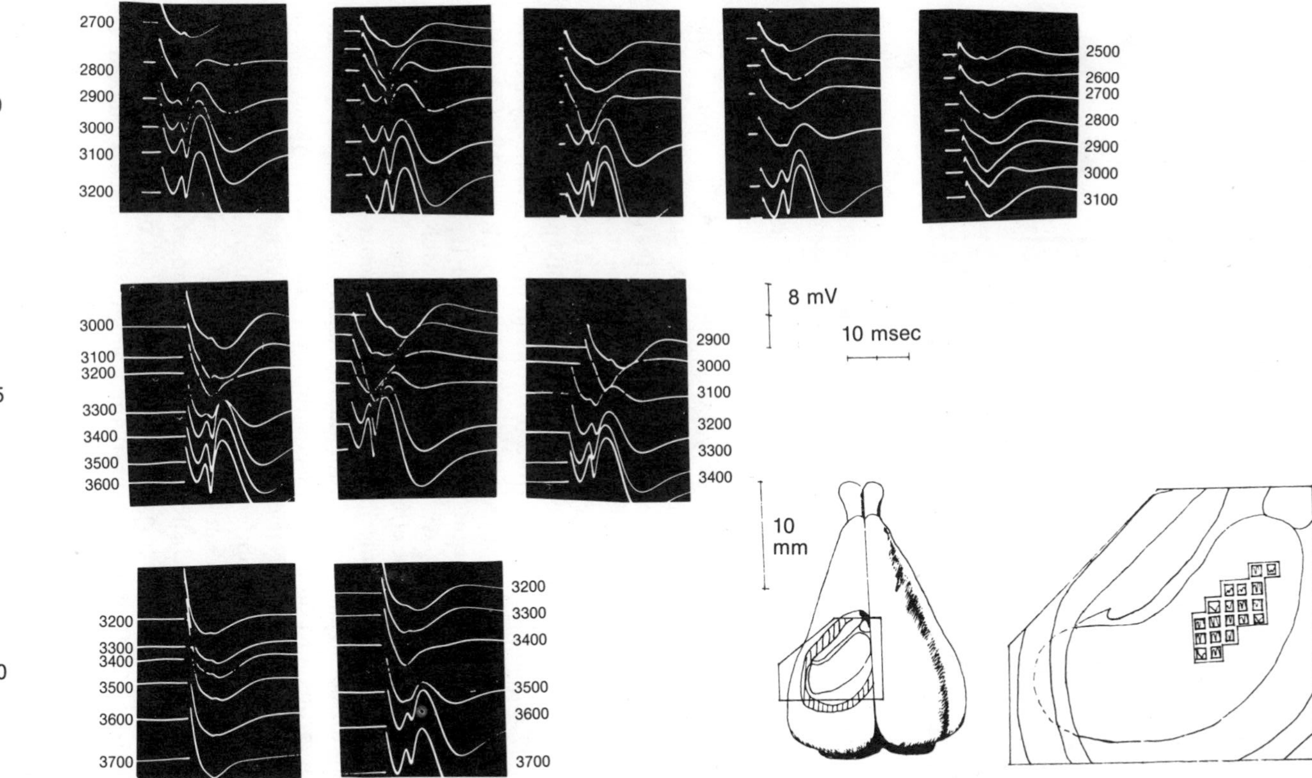

Figure 33-2. A map of dentate gyrus laminar profile following single pulses to angular bundle–perforant path. This illustrates septo-temporal extent of local invasion of dorsal hippocampus by stimulating the "bottleneck" of Lømo (1971). Region of dissection is region of potential reversal which, in this case, extends from 2.5 to 5.0 mm posterior to bregma. Note that at each level of the dentate gyrus, negative-going (down) population spike seen at the granule cell body layer (e.g., 2700 [refers to μm below the cortical surface] at 2.5 AP, 1.5 ML; 3000 at 4.0 AP, 3.5 ML) is reversed at the dendritic molecular layer (2400 at 2.5 AP, 1.5 ML; 2700 at 4.0 AP, 3.5 ML).

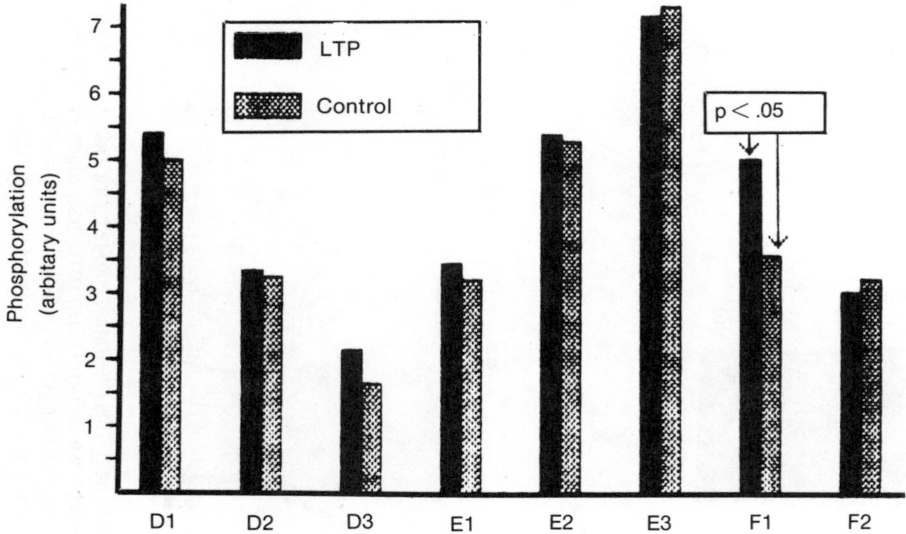

Figure 33-3. LTP selectively increases protein F1 phosphorylation. Note that no other phosphoprotein studies demonstrated an increase and that the increase is present 5 min after LTP; 2-min *in vitro* reaction.

(Figure 33-4) between synaptic plasticity extent and protein F1 phosphorylation (Routtenberg *et al.*, 1983; Routtenberg, Lovinger, & Steward, in press).

We have recently been intrigued by the question of the duration of change in protein F1 phosphorylation. This issue arises because of the demonstration of electrophysiological alterations extending to hours and days in the plasticity of LTP (e.g., Barnes & McNaughton, 1980). To study this problem, electrodes are chronically implanted in the perforant path and in the dentate gyrus. We have discovered that 3 days after the induction of LTP in these chronic preparations there is a significant increase in protein F1 phosphorylation in potentiated animals (Lovinger, Akers, Nelson, Barnes, McNaughton, & Routtenberg, in press). Because these effects are seen after 3 days, it will be important to determine the biochemical mechanism (e.g., kinase activation or increase in substrate?) for this surprisingly long-lasting change in phosphoprotein metabolism.

What is protein F1 and what is its function? Elsewhere (Akers, Cain, Gonzales-Mariscal, Lovinger, Nelson, & Routtenberg, 1983; Nelson, Friedman, O'Neill, Lewis, Mishkin, & Routtenberg, 1983; Routtenberg, in press) we have proposed that protein F1 is identical to protein B-50 (for review, see Zwiers, Jolles, Aloyo, Oestreicher, & Gispen, 1982), a 47 kD phosphoprotein. In addition to having a similar molecular weight and isoelectric point to B-50, it is peptide-sensitive (ACTH, opioid, insulin) and Ca^{2+}-phospholipid-dependent. It is also cyclic-nucleotide-independent. This agrees with the proposal of Aloyo, Zwiers, and Gispen (1982) that B-50 is a substrate protein for the novel phospholipid-dependent kinase, protein kinase C, described by Nishizuka and coworkers (see Takai, Kishimoto, Inoue, & Nishizuka, 1977; Takai *et al.*, 1982; and Nishizuka, 1983, for review).

We have proposed the hypothesis that *an essential step in the development of synaptic plasticity is the activation of protein kinase C leading to the phosphorylation of protein F1*. This hypothesis, which is currently under test, has been gathering support from several different lines of evidence recently obtained in our laboratory. At this writing there has been little to discourage our view that activation of protein kinase C and phosphorylation of protein F1 are essential steps in the expression of synaptic plasticity.

PROTEASES: ROLE IN PLASTICITY

It has been proposed by Baudry and Lynch (Chapter 28, this volume) that synaptic plasticity emerges following a sequence of events involving an increase in intracellular calcium, activation of a neutral thiol proteinase (calpain), which then uncovers cryptic glutamate receptors. Use of calpain inhibitors such as leupeptin is critical in demonstrating support for this hypothesis.

There are several neutral thiol proteinase substrates not necessarily related to glutamate receptor function that could conceivably be equally well blocked in their proteolytic cleavage by leupeptin. One particularly interesting example is protein kinase C (Kikkawa, Takai, Minakuchi, Inohara, & Nishizuka, 1982), which may require the action of a neutral thiol proteinase both for its conversion from an inactive proenzyme to an active kinase and for releasing the catalytic subunit of the kinase (Kishimoto, Kajikawa, Shiota, & Nishizuka, 1983). Thus, the effects of leupeptin may be directed at protein kinase C, which would thus lend support to our hypothesis on the role of kinase C in synaptic plasticity. It is conceivable, therefore, that LTP involves the neutral thiol proteinases, but their action may be directed at kinase C and

Figure 33-4. Extent of LTP is directly related to F1 phosphorylation. No other phosphoprotein demonstrated a significant correlation; 10-sec reaction.

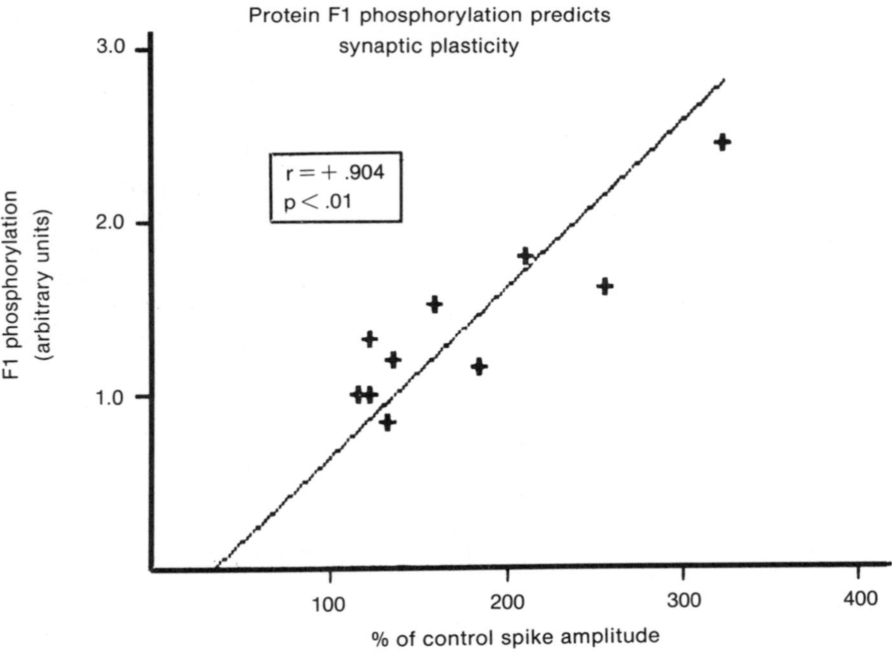

protein F1 rather than glutamate receptors. In general, neutral thiol proteinase inhibitors may be acting on other proteinases that are unrelated to the glutamate receptor.

The proteinase inhibitor leupeptin is also not specific for neutral thiols but will also inhibit serine proteinases. One would need to evaluate the possibility that the observed effects of leupeptin were, in fact, not directed at another class of proteinase inhibitors.

CODA

This review has been critical of claims made purporting to describe the physicochemical basis of plasticity in *Aplysia* and in the hippocampus. The fact that the resulting models are entirely different as to synaptic locus (pre- vs. postsynaptic) and as to the protein substrate regulated by the phosphorylation reaction testifies to our incomplete understanding of the problem.

If we are to understand plasticity of synapses as a general mechanism present in vertebrates and invertebrates alike, then one would hope that phosphoprotein substrates common to the process would be found. The present discussion is an attempt to guide and accelerate the search for such a general mechanism. It is essential to realize, however, that there is at present no crucial evidence to support such a hope. Indeed the argument for discontinuity needs to be given detailed consideration. It is conceivable, for example, that there are two alphabets, such as are found in Western and Eastern cultures, each with its own set of rules, using symbols with totally unrelated shapes. (This distinctiveness has been exploited in the treatment of dyslexia; Rozin, Portitsky, & Sotsky, 1971). The parallel is obvious if one supposes that both the molecular machinery and the rules and logic of the system producing plasticity are distinct in vertebrates and invertebrates, even though the need to communicate is present in both cases. Thus, perhaps the alphabet used by invertebrates and that used by higher vertebrates have distinctive and nonoverlapping mechanisms.

It may be worth noting that a phospholipid-dependent kinase with the properties of kinase C has recently been reported in the *Aplysia* nervous system (De Riemer, Albert, Kaczmarek, & Greengard, 1983). Since I have pointed out that the work on protease inhibitors in the hippocampal slice preparation may act on this enzyme, the possibility exists that our hypothesis indicating a crucial role for kinase C in synaptic plasticity could conceivably apply to three different systems evaluating plasticity, *Aplysia*, LTP in hippocampal slice, and LTP in intact hippocampus. This final thought allows for conceiving of convergence of different approaches onto a specific biochemical mechanism of synaptic plasticity.

REFERENCES

Akers, R. F., Cain, S. T., Gonzales-Mariscal, G., Lovinger, D. M., Nelson, R. B., & Routtenberg, A. Hypothesis: A 47 kD phosphoprotein (F1) serves as molecular trigger for synaptic plasticity. *Neuroscience Abstracts*, 1983, *9*, 1030.

Aloyo, V. J., Zwiers, H., & Gispen, H. B-50 protein kinase and kinase C in rat brain. In W. H. Gispen & A. Routtenberg (Eds.), *Progress in brain research* (Vol. 56: *Brain phosphoproteins: Characterization and function*). Amsterdam: Elsevier/North-Holland, 1982.

Bailey, C. H., Kandel, P., & Chen, M. Active zone at *Aplysia* synapses: Organization of presynaptic dense projections. *Journal of Neurophysiology*, 1981, *46*, 356–368.

Bar, P. R., Tielen, A. M., Lopes da Silva, F. H., Zwiers, H., & Gispen, W. H. Membrane phosphoproteins of rat hippocampus: Sensitivity to tetantic stimulation and enkephalin. *Brain Research*, 1982, *245*, 69–79.

Barnes, C. A., & McNaughton, B. L. Spatial memory and hippocampal synaptic plasticity in senescent and middle-aged rats. In D. Stein (Ed.), *The psychobiology of aging: Problems and perspectives*. Amsterdam: Elsevier/North-Holland, 1980.

Baudry, M., & Lynch, G. Regulation of hippocampal glutamate receptors: Evidence for the involvement of a calcium-activated protease. *Proceedings of the National Academy of Sciences, USA*, 1980, *77*, 2298–2302.

Blackstad, T. W., Brink, K., Hem, J., & Jeune, B. Distribution of hippocampal mossy fibers in the rat: An experimental study with silver impregnation methods. *Journal of Comparative Neurology*, 1970, *138*, 433–450.

Browning, M., Baudry, M., & Lynch, G. Evidence that high frequency stimulation influences the phosphorylation of pyruvate dehydrogenase and that the activity of this enzyme is linked to mitochondrial calcium sequestration. In W. H. Gispen & A. Routtenberg (Eds.), *Progress in brain research* (Vol. 56: *Brain phosphoproteins: Characterization and function*). Amsterdam: Elsevier/North-Holland, 1982.

Browning, M., Dunwiddie, T., Bennett, W., Gispen, W., & Lynch, G. Synaptic phosphoproteins: Specific changes after repetitive stimulation of the hippocampal slice. *Science*, 1979, *203*, 60–62.

De Riemer, S. A., Albert, K. A., Kaczmarek, A. K., & Greengard, P. Calcium/phospholid-dependent protein phosphorylation in *Aplysia* neurons. *Neuroscience Abstracts*, 1983, *9*, 217.

Farley, J., & Alkon, D. L. Cellular analysis of gastropod learning. In A. H. Greenberg (Ed.), *Invertebrate receptors*. New York: Marcel Dekker, 1983.

Gispen, W. H., & Routtenberg, A. (Eds.), *Progress in brain research* (Vol. 56: *Brain phosphoproteins: Characterization and function*). Amsterdam: Elsevier North-Holland, 1982.

Kandel, E. R., & Schwartz, J. H. Molecular biology of learning: Modulation of transmitter release. *Science*, 1982, *218*, 433–443.

Kikkawa, U., Takai, Y., Minakuchi, R., Inohara, S., & Nishizuka, Y. Calcium-activated, phospholipid-dependent protein kinase from rat brain. *Journal of Biological Chemistry*, 1982, *257*, 13341–13348.

Kishimoto, A., Kajikawa, N., Shiota, M., & Nishizuka, Y. Proteolytic activation of calcium-activated, phospholipid-dependent protein kinase by calcium-dependent neutral protease. *Journal of Biological Chemistry*, 1983, *258*, 1156–1164.

Kistler, H. B., Jr., Hawkins, R. D., Koester, J., Kandel, E. R., & Schwartz, J. H. Immunocytochemical studies of neurons producing presynaptic facilitation in the abdominal ganglion of *Aplysia californica*. *Neuroscience Abstracts*, 1983, *9*, 917.

Lømo, T. Patterns of activation in a monosynaptic cortical pathway: The perforant path input to the dentate area of the hippocampal formation. *Experimental Brain Research*, 1971, *12*, 18–45.

Lopes da Silva, F. H., Bar, P. R., Tielen, A. M., & Gispen, W. H. Changes in membrane phosphorylation correlates with long-lasting potentiation in rat hippocampal slices. In W. H. Gispen & A. Routtenberg (Eds.), *Progress in brain research* (Vol. 56: *Brain phosphoproteins: Characterization and function*). Amsterdam: Elsevier/North-Holland, 1982.

Lovinger, D. M., Akers, R. F., Nelson, R. B., Barnes, C. A., McNaughton, B. L., & Routtenberg, A. Protein F1 (47 kD, 4.5 pI) *in vitro* phosphorylation increased by and directly related to three day growth of long term synaptic enhancement. *Neuroscience Abstracts*, in press.

Lynn-Cook, B. D., & Wilson, J. E. Effects of experiences on synaptic protein phosphorylation *in vitro*. *Pharmacology Biochemistry and Behavior*, 1983, *18*, 949–952.

Morgan, D. G., & Routtenberg, A. Evidence that a 41,000 dalton brain phosphoprotein is pyruvate dehydrogenase. *Biochemical and Biophysical Research Communications*, 1980, *95*, 569–576.

Morgan, D. G., & Routtenberg, A. Brain pyruvate dehydrogenase: Phosphorylation and enzyme activity altered by a training experience. *Science*, 1981, *214*, 470–471.

Neary, J. T., Crow, T., & Alkon, D. L. Change in a specific phosphoprotein band following associative learning in *Hermissenda*. *Nature*, 1981, *293*, 658–660.

Nelson, R., Friedman, D., O'Neill, J. B., Lewis, M., Mishkin, M., & Routtenberg, A. Protein phosphorylation and opioid receptor gradients in monkey cerebral cortex: Phosphorylation state of a 47 kD phosphoprotein. *Neuroscience Abstracts*, 1983, *9*, 585.

Nishizuka, Y. Phospholipid degradation and signal translation for protein phosphorylation. *Trends in Biochemical Sciences*, 1983, *8*, 13–16.

Paris, C. G., Castellucci, V. F., Kandel, E. R., & Schwartz, J. H. Protein phosphorylation, presynaptic facilitation, and behavioral sensitization in *Aplysia. Cold Spring Harbor Conferences on Cell Proliferation*, 1981, *8*, 1361–1375.

Routtenberg, A. Anatomical localization of phosphoprotein and glycoprotein substrates of memory. *Progress in Neurobiology*, 1979, *12*, 85–113.

Routtenberg, A. Identification and back-titration of brain pyruvate dehydrogenase: Functional significance for behavior. In W. H. Gispen & A. Routtenberg (Eds.), *Progress in brain research* (Vol. 56: *Brain phosphoproteins: Characterization and function*). Amsterdam: Elsevier/North-Holland, 1982a.

Routtenberg, A. Memory formation as a post-translational modification of brain proteins. In C. A. Ajmone Marsden & H. Matthies (Eds.), *Mechanisms and models of neural plasticity*. New York: Raven Press, 1982b.

Routtenberg, A. Phosphoprotein regulation of memory formation: Enhancement and control of synaptic plasticity by protein kinase C and protein F1. *Proceedings of the New York Academy of Sciences*, in press.

Routtenberg, A., Ehrlich, Y. H., & Rabjohns, R. Effect of a training experience on phosphorylation of a specific protein in neocortical and subcortical membrane preparations. *Federation Proceedings*, 1975, *34*, 293.

Routtenberg, A., Holian, O., & Brunngraber, E. Memory consolidation and glucosamine-1-C^{14} incorporation into glycoproteins. *Transactions of the American Society for Neurochemistry*, 1971, *2*, 103.

Routtenberg, A., Lovinger, D., Cain, S., Akers, R., & Steward, O. Effects of long-term potentiation of perforant path synapses in the intact hippocampus on in vitro phosphorylation of a 47 kD protein (F-1). *Federation Proceedings*, 1983, *42*, 755.

Routtenberg, A., Lovinger, D. M., & Steward, O. Selective increase in phosphorylation state of a 47 kD protein (F1) directly related to long-term potentiation. *Behavioral and Neural Biology*, in press.

Rozin, P., Portitsky, S., & Sotsky, R. American children with reading problems can easily learn to read English represented by Chinese characters. *Science*, 1971, *171*, 1264–1267.

Ruth, R. E., Collier, T. J., & Routtenberg, A. Topography between entorhinal cortex and the dentate septotemporal axis in rats: I. Medial and intermediate entorhinal projecting cells. *Journal of Comparative Neurology*, 1982, *209*, 69–78.

Skrede, K. K., & Westgaard, R. H. The transverse hippocampal slice: A well-defined cortical structure maintained in vitro. *Brain Research*, 1971, *35*, 589–593.

Takai, Y., Kishimoto, A., Inoue, M., & Nishizuka, Y. Studies on a cyclic nucleotide-independent protein kinase and its proenzyme in mammalian tissues. *Journal of Biological Chemistry*, 1977, *252*, 7603–7609.

Takai, Y., Minakuchi, R., Kikkawa, U., Sano, K., Kaibuchi, K., Yu, B., Natsubara, T., & Nishizuka, Y. Membrane phospholipid turnover, receptor function and protein phosphorylation. In W. H. Gispen & A. Routtenberg (Eds.), *Progress in brain research* (Vol. 56: *Brain phosphoproteins: Characterization and function*). Amsterdam: Elsevier/North-Holland, 1982.

Teyler, T. J. Brain slice preparation: Hippocampus. *Brain Research Bulletin*, 1980, *5*, 391–403.

Yamamoto, C. Activation of hippocampal neurons by mossy fiber stimulation in thin brain sections *in vitro*. *Experimental Brain Research*, 1972, *14*, 423–435.

Zwiers, H., Jolles, J., Aloyo, V. J., Oestreicher, A. B., & Gispen, W. H. ACTH and synaptic membrane phosphorylation in rat brain. In W. H. Gispen & A. Routtenberg (Eds.), *Progress in brain research* (Vol. 56: *Brain phosphoproteins: Characterization and function*). Amsterdam: Elsevier/North-Holland, 1982.

CHAPTER THIRTY-FOUR

Postsynaptic Mechanisms in Long-Lasting Potentiation of Synaptic Transmission

FORREST F. WEIGHT

The cellular mechanisms involved in learning and memory are difficult to elucidate in the mammalian central nervous system (CNS) due to its complex structure and organization. One of the mechanisms underlying learning and memory is generally believed to be a lasting alteration in the efficacy of transmission at synapses. Some understanding of the mechanisms involved in the regulation of synaptic efficacy may be gained by studying model systems where synaptic mechanisms can be investigated in detail. Such studies on the sympathetic ganglia of bullfrog have revealed that certain neurotransmitters can produce long-lasting effects on neuronal membrane properties and that these actions can result in a long-lasting potentiation in the efficacy of synaptic transmission. This chapter reviews those studies on the postsynaptic potentiation of synaptic transmission and the underlying membrane mechanisms.

LONG-LASTING POTENTIATON OF SYNAPTIC TRANSMISSION

One cellular hypothesis for learning proposes that the use of one synaptic pathway may produce postsynaptic changes that result in a lasting enhancement in the efficacy of transmission in a second synaptic pathway (see Eccles, 1953). In view of this possibility, it seemed important to determine experimentally whether the stimulation of one synaptic pathway can result in postsynaptic changes that will produce a long-lasting alteration in the effectiveness of transmission in another synaptic pathway. Because of the complexity of neural connections in the CNS, we felt that this problem could be investigated in detail in a simple system in which the synaptic organization and the synaptic mechanisms are known. We investigated this problem in the sympathetic ganglion of the bullfrog, which satisfies these criteria particularly well. In this preparation, it is possible to selectively stimulate presynaptic pathways that elicit several

Forrest F. Weight. Laboratory of Preclinical Studies, National Institute on Alcohol Abuse and Alcoholism, Rockville, Maryland.

different types of synaptic responses that are physiologically and pharmacologically well characterized (for review, see Weight, 1983).

In sympathetic ganglia, a single electrical stimulus to preganglionic nerve fibers elicits an excitatory postsynaptic potential (EPSP) that frequently initiates the generation of an action potential in the ganglion cell. In cells uncomplicated by action-potential generation, the EPSP has a rapid time course, rising to a peak in 3–4 msec and decaying exponentially with a duration of 30–50 msec (Figure 34-1A, left). This synaptic response is designated a fast EPSP because of its rapid time course in comparison with other types of long-duration postsynaptic potentials in sympathetic ganglia. The neurotransmitter mediating the fast EPSP has been identified as acetylcholine (ACh); the postsynaptic response results from the action of ACh on nicotinic postsynaptic receptors. In addition to this fast synaptic response, repetitive stimulation of the preganglionic cholinergic fibers results in generation of a long-lasting depolarization, the slow EPSP. This synaptic response has a time course that is on the order of a thousand times longer than that of the fast EPSP, rising to a peak in several seconds and having a duration of 30–60 sec. The transmitter mediating the slow EPSP has been identified as ACh, and the postsynaptic response results from its action on muscarinic postsynaptic receptors. The slow EPSP can be mimicked by the iontophoretic administration of the muscarinic agonist methacholine (MCh) (Figure 34-1C).

In order to test whether the postsynaptic mechanisms involved in the generation of the slow EPSP can affect the fast EPSP, we activated muscarinic postsynaptic receptors by the iontophoretic application of MCh (Schulman & Weight, 1976). Iontophoresis was used because both the fast and the slow EPSP are elicited by stimulation of the same preganglionic fibers. Consequently, if the preganglionic fibers are stimulated repetitively to elicit a slow EPSP, that stimulation will result in posttetanic changes in transmitter release that will affect the amplitude of subsequent fast EPSPs. Figure 34-1 illustrates the effect of the muscarinic postsynaptic response on fast EPSP generation. In Figure 34-1A, superimposed fast EPSPs are shown before (left) and during (right) the MCh response. As can be seen, both the amplitude and the duration of the fast EPSP are greatly increased during the muscarinic response. The change in amplitude and shape of the fast EPSP can be seen particularly well in Figure 34-1B in the superimposed tracings of the fast EPSPs before and during the MCh response. The average peak amplitude of the fast EPSP changed from 5.6 ± 1.3 mV ($\pm SD$) in the control to 7.7 ± 2.7 mV during the MCh response ($n = 20$; $p < .005$), and the half-width increased from an average of 21.8 ± 1.6 msec in the control to 28.3 ± 3.7 msec during the response ($n = 20$; $p < .001$). This enhancement of fast EPSP amplitude was not a consequence of the depolarization produced by MCh for two reasons. First, membrane depolarization decreases the amplitude of the fast EPSP (Nishi & Koketsu, 1960; Weitsen & Weight, 1977). Second, the amplitude of the fast EPSP was increased when membrane potential was held at resting level during the MCh response (Figure 34-1D). In the experiment illustrated in Figure 34-1D, in the absence of membrane potential change during the MCh response, the average fast EPSP amplitude increased from 2.7 mV in the control to 3.3 mV during the MCh response ($n = 20$; $p < .025$). Note also the increase in the number of larger amplitude fast EPSPs during the MCh response; for example, the number of fast EPSPs with an amplitude greater than 3.25 mV increased from 3 in the

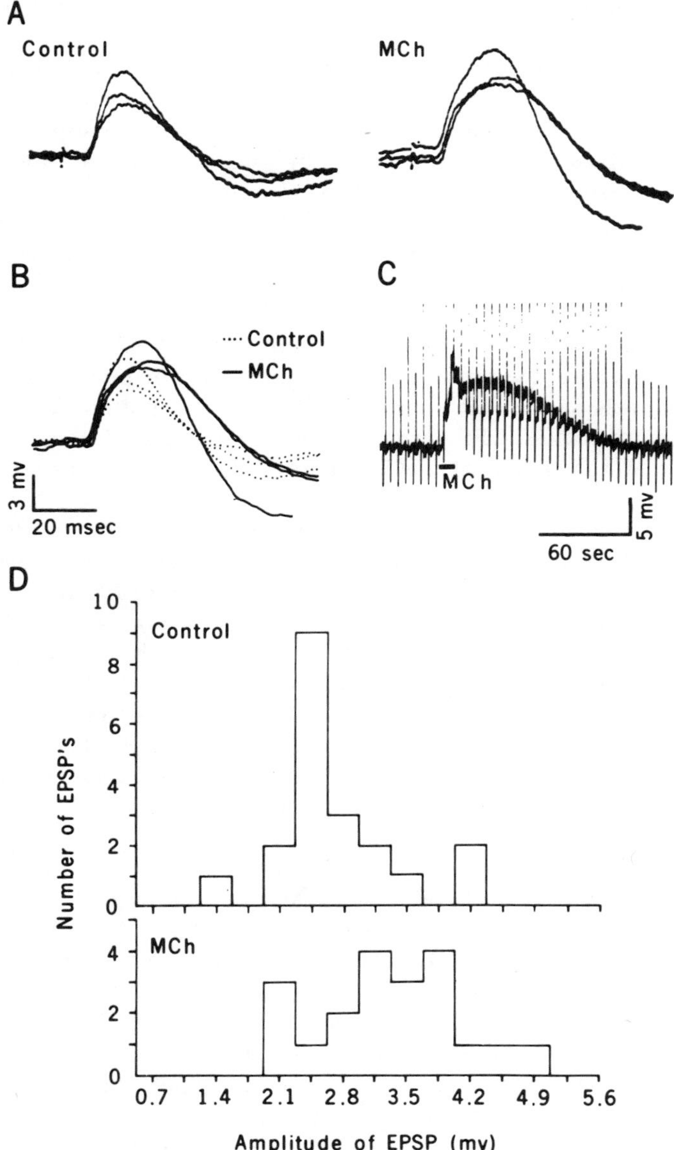

Figure 34-1. Effect of methacholine (MCh) on fast EPSP. (A) Monosynaptic fast EPSPs before (left) and during (right) MCh response. Intracellular recording from a B cell. (B) Comparison of fast EPSPs before and during MCh responses. Superimposed tracings of control (dotted lines) and potentiated (solid lines) EPSPs from A. (C) Response of B cell to MCh administered by iontophoresis. Time of administration indicated by bar labeled MCh. Changes in membrane resistance tested by hyperpolarizing constant-current pulse, with bridge balanced before stimulation. (D) Histograms of effect of MCh on fast EPSP amplitude. Top: amplitude distribution of fast EPSPs for 25 sec prior to administration of MCh. Bottom: amplitude distribution of fast EPSP during MCh response with membrane potential held at resting level. (From Schulman & Weight, 1976.)

control to 10 during the MCh response. Since fast EPSPs greater than a certain amplitude trigger action potentials, such an increase in the number of large, fast EPSPs can have a significant effect on the transmission of impulses at synapses.

Having shown that the iontophoretic administration of MCh can increase fast EPSP amplitude, we asked whether such a postsynaptic potentiation of synaptic potentials can also be produced by stimulation of a synaptic pathway (Schulman & Weight, 1976). To test this, we utilized a separate preganglionic pathway that elicits another long-lasting postsynaptic potential. Repetitive stimulation of the VIIIth spinal nerve produces in postganglionic neurons a depolarization lasting many minutes, the late-slow EPSP (Figure 34-2A). This synaptic response is mediated by a peptide neurotransmitter resembling luteinizing hormone-releasing factor (LH-RF) (Jan & Jan, 1982). As with the MCh response, we tested the effect of this long-lasting synaptic response on the generation of the fast EPSP. Figure 34-2B shows that both the amplitude and the duration of the fast EPSP were also greatly increased during the late-slow EPSP. In addition, as can be seen in Figure 34-2B, the larger fast EPSPs often initiated the generation of action potentials.

To test the effect of fast EPSP augmentation on the transmission of impulses at the synapse, the following experiment was performed (Schulman & Weight, 1976). A fast EPSP was elicited every 5 sec before and after stimulation of the VIIIth spinal nerve, and the number of action potentials elicited by the fast EPSPs were tabulated. Figure 34-2C illustrates a histogram constructed from such an experiment; the histogram indicates the number of action potentials (spikes) occurring in each 30-sec time interval, that is, the number of spikes elicited by six fast EPSPs. Prior to stimulation (S), the fast EPSPs were subthreshold for spike generation; after stimulation, however, the fast EPSPs generated spikes for a time period of 2.5 min. At the peak of the response, five out of six fast EPSPs elicited the generation of action potentials. This clearly demonstrates that stimulation of one synaptic pathway can produce a long-lasting potentiation of synaptic transmission in another pathway. In central neurons, fast EPSPs can converge and summate for a time period on the order of 10–15 msec to generate action potentials in the postsynaptic neuron; the summation of such EPSPs is, however, algebraic or less (Burke, 1967). On the other hand, the membrane mechanisms involved in the generation of the slow EPSP and the late-slow EPSP result in an augmentation of fast EPSP amplitude that facilitates the generation of postsynaptic action potentials. In addition, the potentiation of synaptic transmission observed in the above experiment occurred over a time period of 2.5 min (15×10^4 msec). Synaptic transmission was thus potentiated by this postsynaptic mechanism for a time period on the order of 10,000 times longer than spike generation by the convergent summation of fast EPSPs.

In addition to the potentiation of fast EPSP amplitude, membrane excitability is also increased by the postsynaptic mechanisms underlying both the slow EPSP and the late-slow EPSP (Schulman & Weight, 1976; Adams & Brown, 1980; Jan, Jan, & Kuffler, 1980). This increased membrane excitability is manifested in several ways. First, there is a marked increase in the spontaneous firing of action potentials during the response to either the synaptic or the pharmacological activation of muscarinic or LH-RF receptors. This increased firing is not due simply to depolarization, since it cannot be elicited by a similar depolarization of the membrane by current. Second, when the mem-

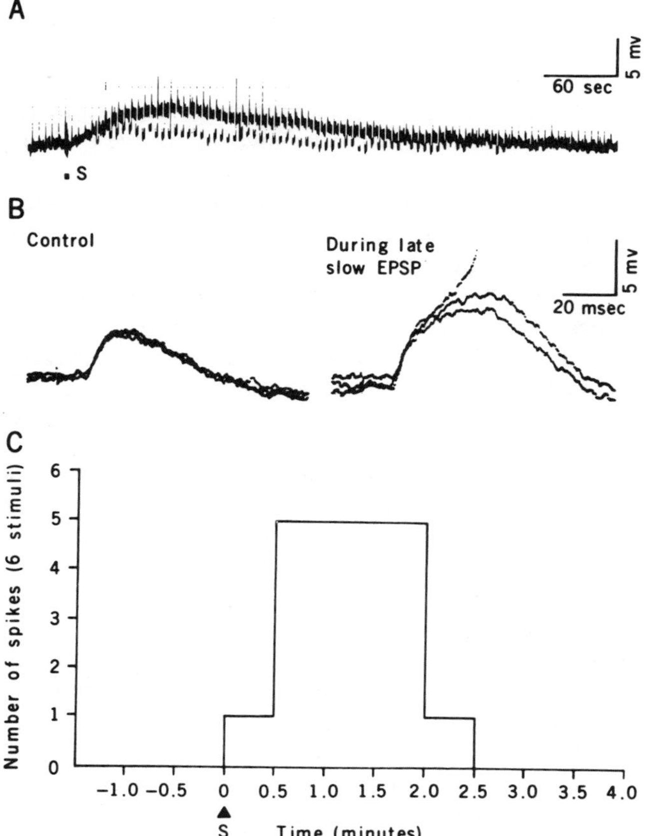

Figure 34-2. Effect of late-slow EPSP on fast EPSP. (A) Late-slow EPSP with conductance decrease. The period of stimulation of VIIIth nerve is indicated by bar labeled S. Intracellular recording in a B cell. Membrane resistance increased by 19.5 megohms during the late-slow EPSP. (B) Monosynaptic fast EPSPs elicited by stimulation of sympathetic chain. Left: records of fast EPSPs prior to the late-slow EPSP. Right: records of fast EPSPs during late-slow EPSP. (C) Effect of late-slow EPSP on spike generation by fast EPSPs. Same experiment as in B. The graph divides the experimental period into 30-sec segments. During each segment, six fast EPSPs were elicited. During the 4.5-min control period, no fast EPSPs fired spikes. After stimulation of the VIIIth nerve (labeled S), enlarged fast EPSPs began to fire spikes. Spike generation ceased after about 2.5 min, although fast EPSPs remained enlarged for the duration of the late-slow EPSP. (From Schulman & Weight, 1976.)

brane is depolarized by current pulses, there is a marked facilitation in both the frequency and the duration of repetitive spike discharges during both the muscarinic and the peptide responses. Third, there is a lowering of the threshold for action-potential initiation and an activation of spike discharges at the termination of hyperpolarizing current pulses ("anodal break" response) during both responses. The long-lasting potentiation of synaptic transmission associated with both the muscarinic and the peptide responses apparently results from the combination of both increased fast EPSP amplitude and increased membrane excitability.

The membrane mechanisms responsible for generating the slow EPSP and the late-slow EPSP have been investigated by several laboratories (for review, see Weight, 1983). The primary mechanism involved in the electrogenesis of the slow EPSP has been proposed to be a decrease in potassium (K^+) conductance (Weight & Votava, 1970). That hypothesis was based on the following observations: (1) Membrane conductance is usually decreased (resistance increased) during the response (Figure 34-1C); (2) membrane depolarization increases the amplitude of the response; (3) progressive membrane hyperpolarization usually decreases and can reverse the slow EPSP; (4) the reversal potential for the slow EPSP is near the K^+ equilibrium potential; (5) altering extracellular K^+ shifts the reversal potential in a manner consistent with a K^+ conductance; (6) removal of extracellular chloride (Cl^-) has no significant effect on the slow EPSP or its reversal potential.

The proposal that the slow EPSP involves a decreased K^+ conductance has received strong support from recent voltage-clamp experiments (Adams, Brown, & Constanti, 1982; Weight & MacDermott, 1982). Voltage-clamp analysis of the ionic mechanisms involved in slow EPSP generation necessitates the characterization of the membrane currents in order to determine the current or currents that are altered during the slow EPSP. Voltage-clamp analysis suggests that there are at least three major K^+ currents in the membrane of these neurons (Adams *et al.*, 1982; Weight & MacDermott, 1982). Figure 34-3 illustrates these current schematically. One type of K^+ current is a voltage-activated or delayed rectifier current (Figure 34-3,I); this current is activated by membrane depolarization and is blocked by tetraethylammonium (TEA). The second type is a calcium (Ca^{2+})-activated K^+ current (Figure 34-3,II); this current is dependent on depolarization-induced Ca^{2+} influx and is blocked by divalent cation Ca^{2+} antagonists such as cobalt (Co^{2+}). Recent data indicate that there is both a fast and a slow Ca^{2+}-activated K^+ current in these neurons (MacDermott & Weight, 1982). The third type of K^+ current is a slow voltage-dependent K^+ current that is reduced or blocked by muscarinic receptor activation and consequently has been designated the "M" current (Figure 34-3,III). Inhibition of this voltage-dependent K^+ current by muscarinic receptor activation appears to be the primary ionic mechanism underlying the generation of the slow EPSP. In addition to the muscarinicially mediated decrease in a voltage-dependent K^+ conductance, which is observed at membrane potentials between -30 and -70 mV, recent voltage-clamp experiments indicate that the response to muscarinic receptor activation also frequently involves a voltage-dependent increase in membrane conductance at membrane potentials negative to -70 mV (McCort, Nash, & Weight, 1982). The latter response would presumably not contribute to the generation of the slow EPSP at resting membrane potentials positive to -70 mV.

The primary membrane mechanism involved in the generation of the late-slow EPSP appears to be identical to the mechanism involved in the slow EPSP, namely, a decrease in a voltage-dependent K^+ conductance (Schulman & Weight, 1976; Adams & Brown, 1980; Jan *et al.*, 1980; Sejnowski, 1982; Jan & Jan, 1982; Katayama & Nishi, 1982). Although this peptide response appears to be identical to the effect of muscarinic receptor activation, it is not due to the release of ACh because it persists in the presence of atropine (Adams & Brown,

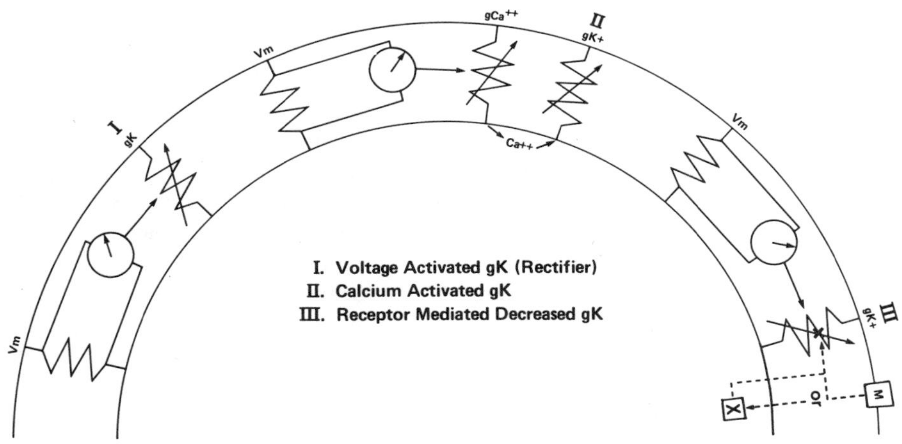

Figure 34-3. Schematic illustration of three types of potassium (K^+) channels that have been identified in the membrane of bullfrog sympathetic neurons. I: a voltage-activated or delayed-rectifier K^+ channel. II: a calcium (Ca^{2+})-activated K^+ channel; III: a voltage-dependent K^+ channel that is inhibited by muscarinic receptor activation, the "M" channel. (From Weight & MacDermott, 1982.)

1980). As with the muscarinic response, the peptide response also frequently involves a voltage-dependent increase in membrane conductance at hyperpolarized membrane potentials (Jan *et al.*, 1980; Sejnowski, 1982; Jan & Jan, 1982; Katayama & Nishi, 1982).

The molecular basis of the membrane permeability changes that generate both slow EPSPs is poorly understood. It had been proposed that cyclic nucleotides are intracellular second messengers mediating the generation of these responses. That hypothesis, however, has not been supported by several recent investigations (for review, see Weight, 1983). On the other hand, recent data indicate that calcium ions can function as an intracellular mediator for one type of membrane permeability change, the Ca^{2+}-activated K^+ conductance (Meech, 1978). Using the Ca^{2+}-sensitive dye arsenazo III, a direct correlation between intracellular Ca^{2+} transients and activation of the Ca^{2+}-activated K^+ conductance has been demonstrated in bullfrog sympathetic neurons (Smith, MacDermott, & Weight, 1983). The possibility that alterations of intracellular Ca^{2+} are associated with the slow EPSPs has not been studied in detail. Recent biochemical investigations suggest that changes in membrane protein phosphorylation are associated with changes in intracellular Ca^{2+} (Pant & Weight, 1980; Weight, Pant, & McCort, 1981). Further investigation is needed, however, to establish whether the molecular basis of the Ca^{2+}-activated membrane permeability change involves the phosphorylation of membrane proteins.

SUMMARY AND CONCLUSIONS

This chapter has reviewed studies on a long-lasting potentiation in the efficacy of transmission at synapses in the sympathetic ganglion of bullfrog, and the postsynaptic mechanisms underlying that potentiation. Synaptic activation of muscarinic cholinergic receptors on these sympathetic neurons results in the generation of a slow EPSP. Fast EPSPs are increased in amplitude and duration during the muscarinic postsynaptic response. A similar potentiation of fast EPSPs is observed during the late-slow EPSP, which is a peptide-mediated response elicited by a separate synaptic pathway. The enhancement of fast EPSP amplitude increases the probablity of postsynaptic action potential generation, and thus increases the efficacy of impulse transmission at the synapses. Stimulation of one synaptic pathway is therefore capable of increasing the efficacy of synaptic transmission in a second synaptic pathway by a postsynaptic mechanism. Furthermore, this enhancement of synaptic efficacy is long-lasting by virtue of the long duration of the slow EPSPs. The primary membrane mechanism underlying this long-lasting synaptic potentiation is a decrease in a voltage-dependent K^+ conductance for both the muscarinic and the peptide-mediated responses. The molecular basis of this membrane permeability change is poorly understood but will be an important topic for future investigation.

REFERENCES

Adams, P. R., & Brown, D. A. Luteinizing hormone-releasing factor and muscarinic agonists act on the same voltage-sensitive K^+-current in bullfrog sympathetic neurones. *British Journal of Pharmacology*, 1980, *68*, 353–355.

Adams, P. R., Brown, D. A., & Constanti, A. Pharmacological inhibition of the M-current. *Journal of Physiology*, 1982, *332*, 223–262.

Burke, R. E. Composite nature of the monosynaptic excitatory postsynaptic potential. *Journal of Neurophysiology*, 1967, *30*, 1114–1137.

Eccles, J. C. *The neurophysiological basis of mind: The principles of neurophysiology*. Oxford: Clarendon Press, 1953.

Jan, L. Y., & Jan, Y. N. Peptidergic transmission in sympathetic ganglia of the frog. *Journal of Physiology*, 1982, *327*, 219–246.

Jan, Y. N., Jan, L. Y., & Kuffler, S. W. Further evidence for peptidergic transmission in sympathetic ganglia. *Proceedings of the National Academy of Sciences, USA*, 1980, *77*, 5008–5012.

Katayama, Y., & Nishi, S. Voltage-clamp analysis of peptidergic slow depolarizations in bullfrog sympathetic ganglion cells. *Journal of Physiology*, 1982, *333*, 305–313.

MacDermott, A. B., & Weight, F. F. Action potential repolarization may involve a transient, Ca^{2+}-sensitive outward current in a vertebrate neurone. *Nature*, 1982, *300*, 185–188.

McCort, S. M., Nash, J. W., & Weight, F. F. Voltage clamp analysis of slow muscarinic excitation in sympathetic neurons of bullfrog. *Neuroscience Abstracts*, 1982, *8*, 501.

Meech, R. W. Calcium-dependent potassium activation in nervous tissue. *Annual Review of Biophysics and Bioengineering*, 1978, *7*, 1–8.

Nishi, S., & Koketsu, K. Electrical properties and activities of single sympathetic neurons in frog. *Journal of Cellular and Comparative Physiology*, 1960, *55*, 15–30.

Pant, H. C., & Weight, F. F. Effect of calcium and cyclic nucleotides on protein phosphorylation in bullfrog sympathetic ganglia. *Federation Proceedings*, 1980, *39*, 1626.

Schulman, J. A., & Weight, F. F. Synaptic transmission: Long-lasting potentiation by a postsynaptic mechanism. *Science*, 1976, *194*, 1437–1439.

Sejnowski, T. J. Peptidergic synaptic transmission in sympathetic ganglia. *Federation Proceedings*, 1982, 41, 2923–2928.

Smith, S. J., MacDermott, A. B., & Weight, F. F. Detection of intracellular Ca^{2+} transients in sympathetic neurons using arsenazo III. *Nature*, 1983, *304*, 350–352.

Weight, F. F. Synaptic mechanisms in amphibian sympathetic ganglia. In L.-G. Elfvin (Ed.), *Autonomic ganglia*. Chichester, England: Wiley, 1983.

Weight, F. F., & MacDermott, A. B. Membrane ion channels and nerve cell excitability. In M. R. Klee *et al.* (Eds.), *Physiology and pharmacology of epileptogenic phenomena*. New York: Raven Press, 1982.

Weight, F. F., Pant, H. C., & McCort, S. M. Protein phosphorylation and membrane permeability change correlated with intracellular calcium in nervous tissue. *Proceedings of the Eighth International Congress of Pharmacology*, 1981, 317.

Weight, F. F., & Votava, J. Slow synaptic excitation in sympathetic ganglion cells: Evidence for synaptic inactivation of potassium conductance. *Science*, 1970, *170*, 755–757.

Weight, F. F., & Votava, J. Inactivation of potassium conductance in slow postsynaptic excitation. *Science*, 1971, *172*, 504.

Weitsen, H. A., & Weight, F. F. Synaptic innervation of sympathetic ganglion cells in the bullfrog. *Brain Research*, 1977, *128*, 197–211.

Author Index

Page numbers in italics denote material in figures and tables.

Subject Index

Page numbers in italics denote material in figures and tables.